Hymns and Psalms

With all my love.
Daddy. September
1989

Hymns and Psalms was prepared
by representatives of the British
Methodist Conference and by
members of the Baptist Union,
Churches of Christ, Church of
England, Congregational Federation,
Methodist Church in Ireland,
United Reformed Church, and the
Wesleyan Reform Union.

Hymns and Psalms

Methodist Publishing House
London

© 1983 Methodist Publishing House

First Published 1983
Reprinted 1984
This impression (incorporating
corrections) 1986

ISBN 0 946550 06 9

The Methodist Conference meeting in
Plymouth, 1982 authorised this hymn
book for use in all Methodist churches in
the Connexion, and in succession to the
1933 Methodist Hymn Book

Music origination by
Halstan & Co. Ltd
Amersham, Buckinghamshire

Printed and bound in Great Britain
at The Bath Press, Avon

CONTENTS

PREFACE

HYMNS and Psalms have been in the past, and still are today, distinctive features of Christian worship. They unite the intellect, the emotions, the will, and the voice, in the human response to God's grace; and they also point beyond our human faculties and abilities, for God addresses us in them, and through them applies the good news of Jesus Christ to our lives. Their combination of music and poetry provides a medium for God's Word, and a way in which our hearts and minds may become open to that Word. Hymns and Psalms, in as much as they are based on what God 'has done, is doing, and has promised to do' (to quote James Wallis's 1841 Preface to his *Psalms and Hymns*), can provide a focus for worship, because they proclaim God's creating and redeeming love, and because they express our response to that love. They assist in making possible a worship which is God's approach to us, and our approach to God; George Herbert might have described hymns, as he did prayer, as 'God's breath in man returning to its birth'. And as we sing hymns together, they form part of a worship which is a growth in Christian understanding and fellowship.

The choice of the title *Hymns and Psalms* reflects a concern with this growth in understanding and fellowship. It also expresses the belief that this occurs most naturally within the long and honoured tradition of Christian worship, going back to the earliest times of the church. The title is itself a biblical phrase, recalling our debt both to the early church and to Ancient Israel. As a hymn book title it recalls distinguished predecessors, such as the 1841 *Psalms and Hymns* quoted above, and also John Wesley's *Psalms and Hymns* for the use of all christians (1737), which it resembles both in name and in intention. It affirms our thankfulness for the classic traditions of spirituality which we have inherited.

The publication of *Hymns and Psalms* owes its origin to a decision of the British Methodist Conference of 1979, which resolved that a new hymn book should be prepared, to embody the best traditions of Methodist hymnody and to be a contribution to the life and worship of the universal church. The same Conference empowered its Faith and Order Committee to encourage as wide a participation of other churches in the project as should prove practicable. The present committee has been greatly heartened by the degree of participation by many denominations in its work; and it has become increasingly aware of the potential of this book to build from accepted denominational traditions towards a richer sharing of our diverse interests and our common heritage. The Methodist Conference has been able to scrutinise the various drafts of this book to ensure that the Methodist emphases are present within it, and has authorised it as a successor to the *Methodist Hymn Book* of 1933; agreeing also to its full title, *Hymns and Psalms, A Methodist and Ecumenical Hymn Book.*

The 1933 Preface declared that 'the claims of poetry have always been in mind, but those of religion have been paramount, and not a few hymns have been selected chiefly because they are dear to the people of God.' The same principle has been followed in this book. *Hymns and Psalms* is unusual among hymn books in the very great debt owed by its compilers to the public correspondence which has guided and informed their work: careful note has been taken throughout of the public response to preliminary drafts of its contents. There is no doubt that one result of this public participation has been to give *Hymns and Psalms* a breadth of appeal and sympathy which should greatly assist its avowed intention of assisting the growing together of the people of God.

This intention will be evident also in the methods of editing used. Since the purpose of the book is to provide an ordered and authoritative collection of material commonly available and used in the various denominations, the editing of this material has taken account of present practice as well as of historical research. Textual alterations have been made only where these could be pastorally as well as editorially sanctioned. Even this degree of editing may mean that initially some congregations will find differences in words and in musical setting from the texts and tunes with which they are familiar. These changes have been kept to a minimum: but without such alterations the present publication would not have enhanced significantly the hymn-singing in fellowship of those who come from different traditions. As far as possible (in material open to copyright changes, and insofar as metrical and poetical considerations permit) the compilers have endeavoured to offer hymnody which takes equal account of the place of both women and men in the life of the church, so that no one may be inhibited by insensitive editing from making a full offering of herself or himself in God's service.

In other respects the compilers have sought to recognise that many changes have taken place, both inside and outside the Christian church, since the publication of the great 1933 hymn book. The great and terrifying events which have occurred since then have revolutionised our thinking about the world in which we live and the condition of human kind. The second world war, for instance, put an end to the idea that the 1914–18 war had been a war to end all wars, and the discovery of the concentration camps revealed a systematic and dreadful inhumanity which uncovered hitherto unimagined possibilities of evil in men and women. 'After Auschwitz', said Theodor Adorno, 'no poetry.'

The war ended with the dropping of the atomic bombs on Hiroshima and Nagasaki, and since then the possibility of the destruction of whole portions of the world by nuclear weapons has become more frightening year by year. At the same time there have been other revolutions of amazing potential for good and for evil: in communications, in information storage and retrieval, in genetic engineering, in the development of materials for germ warfare. Fifty years after 1933, we live in a global village, linked instantaneously to our brothers and sisters in other countries, and concerned inevitably with their hopes and fears, their triumphs and disasters. In compiling this hymn book, the committee has sought to respond to our changing times, and to produce a book which articulates the needs, the joys, and the fears of the contemporary world. Such an editorial policy has an honourable history. Isaac Watts wrote in the Preface to *Hymns and Spiritual Songs:* ''The most frequent tempers and changes of our spirit, and conditions of our life, are here copied, and the breathings of our piety expressed according to the variety of our passions, our love, our fear, our hope, our desire, our sorrow, our wonder, and our joy, as they are refined into devotion, and act under the influence and conduct of the blessed Spirit; all conversing with God the Father *by the new and living way* of access to the throne, even the person and mediation of our Lord Jesus Christ.''

This policy has been implemented in two ways. First, by including a considerable number of hymns written during the last twenty or thirty years, many of which are attempting to give a new expression to the everlasting truth of the Gospel. It is a matter of rejoicing to the committee that it has been able to engage in its work at a time when modern hymnody has flourished more vigorously than at any previous time in this century. Secondly, the structure of the book has been designed to allow a strong second section on **God's World**. This is concerned with the natural world and human use of creation, with the social order, and with the human condition. In this section will be found hymns which give expression to the needs of the world and the Christian response to those needs.

The section on **God's World** is preceded by the first section on **God's Nature**, in which the hymns explore and celebrate the nature of the Eternal Father, the life of the Eternal Word, and the work of the Eternal Spirit. The third section, **God's People**, is concerned with Christian living and with the function and purpose of the church. The structure of the book has therefore been carefully designed, and it has been modified during the

committee's deliberations in the light of debate and criticism. As a
result, the compilers can echo the words of John Wesley's
magnificent Preface to the 1780 *Collection of Hymns for the use of the
People called Methodists*, and can appropriate them with confidence
for the present book:

> It is not so large as to be either cumbersome, or expensive: and it is
> large enough to contain such a variety of hymns as will not soon be
> worn threadbare. It is large enough to contain all the important truths of
> our most holy religion, whether speculative or practical; yea, to
> illustrate them all, and to prove them both by Scripture and reason: and
> this is done in a regular order. The hymns are not carelessly jumbled
> together, but carefully ranged under proper heads, according to the
> experience of real Christians. So that this book is, in effect, a little body
> of experimental and practical divinity.

To the surprise of the committee responsible for *Hymns and
Psalms* the public reaction regarding the place of the Psalms in this
book was vigorous and widespread, arguing strongly and consis-
tently for their inclusion. There is no doubt that the reading and
singing of the Psalms has become an established feature of the
worship of many churches. A careful selection of Psalms suited to
various lectionary systems in current use has therefore been added
to the hymns, with a sequential numeration which will simplify
reference to them. Indications for responsive reading have been
given, and settings for congregational singing have been included.
   The compilers of this book would also recommend to its users
the advice of John Wesley: 'Sing ALL!' Its potential for good
depends principally on the whole-hearted vocal participation of all
who are present at worship. For this reason, congregational
singing, in town and in country, has been an over-riding concern
in the selection of the music; very few items have been included
specifically for festival use, or for occasions when choirs are an
essential feature. 'Sing ALL!' should also encourage the development of a generous repertoire, as the book becomes progressively
better known: only by the use of material from the broad spectrum
of hymnody which is offered will Christians of different traditions
be enabled to grow together in understanding and fellowship.
   As the music of this book has been selected to encourage
congregational singing, so too the words of the hymns have been
chosen because they are representative of the best of ancient and
modern hymn writing. All of them, in Wesley's words, 'talk
common sense'; the greatest of them demonstrate, as he finely put
it, 'the purity, the strength, and the elegance of the English
language; and, at the same time, the utmost simplicity and
plainness, suited to every capacity.' Wesley desired his readers to

judge 'whether there be not in some of the following hymns the true Spirit of Poetry, such as cannot be acquired by art or labour, but must be the gift of nature'; but he considered that the needs of the religious life were of paramount importance. His last words in the Preface should ring in the hearts of all compilers of hymn books, and all users of them:

> That which is of infinitely more moment than the Spirit of Poetry, is the spirit of piety. And I trust, all persons of real judgement will find *this* breathing through the whole Collection. It is in this view chiefly, that I would recommend it to every truly pious Reader, as a means of raising or quickening the spirit of devotion; of confirming his faith; of enlivening his hope; and of kindling and increasing his love to God and man. When Poetry thus keeps its place, as the handmaid of Piety, it shall attain, not a poor perishable wreath, but a crown that fadeth not away.

Over two hundred years later, throughout the world, men and women are seeking a deeper awareness of God and a fuller commitment to God's service. The compilers of this book believe that these aims can be greatly furthered by a hymn book which is rooted firmly in denominational traditions, and which makes available to all Christians the riches of classical, evangelical, catholic, and charismatic hymnody of the past and the present. By approaching God through them, and attending to God's word in them, may we all grow nearer to God, and in so doing grow nearer to one another in faith and fellowship.

RICHARD G. JONES *(Chairman)*
IVOR H. JONES *(Convener)*

London, December 1983

I

GOD'S NATURE—God's Being and Majesty   1– 20

THE ETERNAL FATHER

THE ETERNAL WORD

THE ETERNAL SPIRIT

1

OLD 100th   L.M.

Melody from the *Genevan Psalter* (1551)
(English rhythmic form of last line)

For this tune in a lower key see No. 61

ALTERNATIVE HARMONISATION
(with Melody in the Tenor)

As set by John Dowland (1563–1626) in
T. Ravenscroft's *Psalmes* (1621)

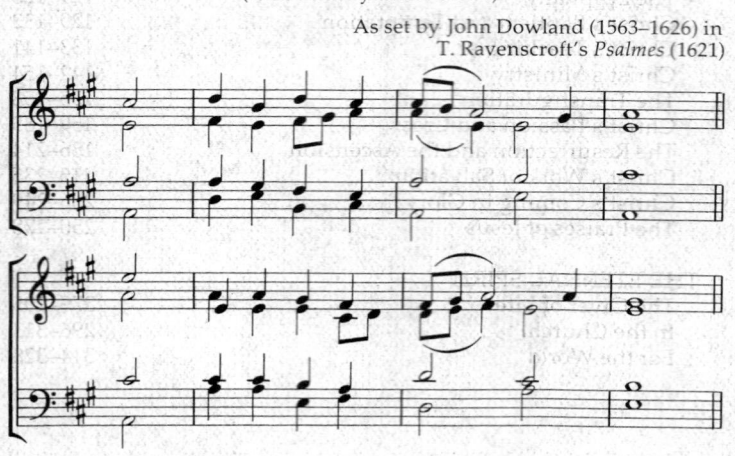

GOD'S NATURE—*God's Being and Majesty*

Psalm 100

1 ALL people that on earth do dwell,
  Sing to the Lord with cheerful voice:
  Him serve with mirth, his praise forth tell;
  Come ye before him and rejoice.

2 The Lord, ye know, is God indeed;
  Without our aid he did us make:
  We are his folk, he doth us feed;
  And for his sheep he doth us take.

3 O enter then his gates with praise;
  Approach with joy his courts unto;
  Praise, laud, and bless his name always,
  For it is seemly so to do.

4 For why, the Lord our God is good;
  His mercy is for ever sure;
  His truth at all times firmly stood,
  And shall from age to age endure.

William Kethe (d. 1594)

GOD'S NATURE—*God's Being and Majesty*

Melody and bass (slightly altered)
probably by Jeremiah Clarke (c. 1673–1707)

For this tune in a lower key see No. 209

1 BEGIN, my tongue, some heavenly theme;
   Awake, my voice, and sing
The mighty works, or mightier name,
   Of our eternal King.

2 Tell of his wondrous faithfulness,
   And sound his power abroad;
Sing the sweet promise of his grace,
   The quickening word of God.

3 Engraved as in eternal brass,
   The mighty promise shines;
Nor can the powers of darkness rase
   Those everlasting lines.

4 His every word of grace is strong
   As that which built the skies;
The voice that rolls the stars along
   Speaks all the promises.

5 Now shall my leaping heart rejoice
   To know thy favour sure:
I trust the all-creating voice,
   And faith desires no more.

Isaac Watts (1674–1748)

GOD'S NATURE—*God's Being and Majesty*

3

HALAD   55.55.55.54.

Philippino 'folk' melody by Elena G. Maquiso (1961)
Harmonised by Peter Fletcher (1934–   )

1. FATHER in heaven,
   Grant to your children
     Mercy and blessing,
     Songs never ceasing,
   Love to unite us,
   Grace to redeem us—
     Father in heaven,
     Father our God.

2. Jesus, Redeemer,
   May we remember
     Your gracious passion,
     Your resurrection.
   Worship we bring you,
   Praise we shall sing you—
     Jesus, Redeemer,
     Jesus our Lord.

3. Spirit descending,
   Whose is the blessing,
     Strength for the weary,
     Help for the needy,
   Sealed in our sonship
   Yours be our worship—
     Spirit descending,
     Spirit adored.

   Daniel T. Niles (1908–70)

4
RIDGE D.S.M.

Samuel Wesley (1766–1837)
from *Original Hymn Tunes* (1828)

GOD'S NATURE—*God's Being and Majesty*

1 FATHER, in whom we live,
       In whom we are, and move,
   Glory and power and praise receive
       Of thy creating love.
   Let all the angel throng
       Give thanks to God on high;
   While earth repeats the joyful song,
       And echoes to the sky.

2 Incarnate Deity,
       Let all the ransomed race
   Render in thanks their lives to thee,
       For thy redeeming grace.
   The grace to sinners showed
       Ye heavenly choirs proclaim,
   And cry: 'Salvation to our God,
       Salvation to the Lamb!'

3 Spirit of holiness,
       Let all thy saints adore
   Thy sacred energy, and bless
       Thy heart-renewing power.
   Not angel tongues can tell
       Thy love's ecstatic height,
   The glorious joy unspeakable,
       The beatific sight.

4 Eternal, triune Lord!
       Let all the hosts above,
   Let all the sons of men, record
       And dwell upon thy love.
   When heaven and earth are fled
       Before thy glorious face,
   Sing all the saints thy love has made
       Thine everlasting praise.

Charles Wesley (1707–88)

Melody from the
Chartres Antiphoner (1784)
Harmonised by John Wilson

GOD'S NATURE—*God's Being and Majesty*

1 FATHER most holy, merciful and loving,
   Jesus, Redeemer, ever to be worshipped,
   Life-giving Spirit, Comforter most gracious,
       God everlasting;

2 Three in a wondrous unity unbroken,
   One perfect Godhead, love that never faileth,
   Light of the angels, succour of the needy,
       Hope of all living;

3 All thy creation serveth its creator;
   Thee every creature praiseth without ceasing;
   We too would sing thee psalms of true devotion;
       Hear, we beseech thee.

4 Lord God Almighty, unto thee be glory,
   One in Three Persons, over all exalted;
   Thine, as is meet, be honour, praise, and blessing,
       Now and for ever.

c. 10th Century; tr. *Alfred Edward Alston* (1862–1927)

1 HAIL! Holy, holy, holy Lord!
   Whom One in Three we know;
   By all thy heavenly host adored,
   By all thy church below.

2 One undivided Trinity
   With triumph we proclaim;
   Thy universe is full of thee,
   And speaks thy glorious name.

3 Thee, holy Father, we confess,
   Thee, holy Son, adore,
   Thee, Spir't of truth and holiness,
   We worship evermore.

4 Three Persons equally divine
   We magnify and love;
   And both the choirs ere long shall join
   To sing thy praise above:

5 Hail! Holy, holy, holy Lord,
   Our heavenly song shall be,
   Supreme, essential One, adored
   In co-eternal Three.

Charles Wesley (1707–88)

GOD'S NATURE—*God's Being and Majesty*

7

NICAEA   11 12.12 10.

J. B. Dykes (1823–76)

1 HOLY, holy, holy, Lord God Almighty!
    Early in the morning our song shall rise to thee:
  Holy, holy, holy, merciful and mighty,
    God in Three Persons, blessèd Trinity!

2 Holy, holy, holy! All the saints adore thee,
    Casting down their golden crowns around the glassy sea;
  Cherubim and seraphim falling down before thee,
    Who wert, and art, and evermore shalt be.

3 Holy, holy, holy! Though the darkness hide thee,
    Though the eye of sinful man thy glory may not see,
  Only thou art holy; there is none beside thee,
    Perfect in power, in love, and purity.

4 Holy, holy, holy, Lord God Almighty!
    All thy works shall praise thy name in earth and sky and sea;
  Holy, holy, holy, merciful and mighty,
    God in Three Persons, blessèd Trinity!

Reginald Heber (1783–1826)
based on Revelation 4:8–11

GOD'S NATURE—*God's Being and Majesty*

GOD'S NATURE—*God's Being and Majesty*

1 HOW shall I sing that majesty
   Which angels do admire?
Let dust in dust and silence lie;
   Sing, sing, ye heavenly choir.
Thousands of thousands stand around
   Thy throne, O God most high;
Ten thousand times ten thousand sound
   Thy praise; but who am I?

2 Thy brightness unto them appears,
   Whilst I thy footsteps trace;
A sound of God comes to my ears,
   But they behold thy face.
They sing because thou art their Sun;
   Lord, send a beam on me;
For where heav'n is but once begun
   There alleluias be.

3 How great a being, Lord, is thine,
   Which doth all beings keep!
Thy knowledge is the only line
   To sound so vast a deep.
Thou art a sea without a shore,
   A sun without a sphere;
Thy time is now and evermore,
   Thy place is everywhere.

John Mason (c. 1645–94)

9

ST DENIO (JOANNA) 11 11.11 11.

Welsh Hymn Melody (1839)
(Founded on a folk-tune)

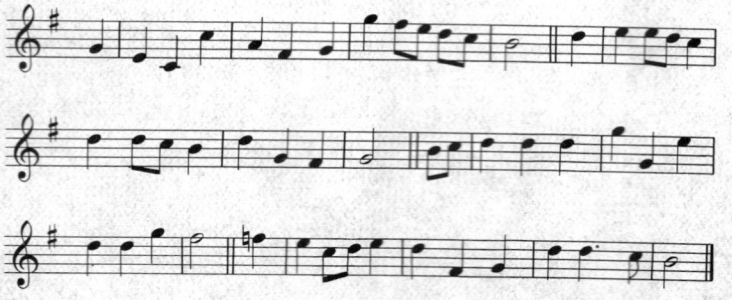

DESCANT

C. S. Lang (1891–1971)

GOD'S NATURE—*God's Being and Majesty*

1 IMMORTAL, invisible, God only wise,
   In light inaccessible hid from our eyes,
   Most blessèd, most glorious, the Ancient of Days,
   Almighty, victorious, thy great name we praise.

2 Unresting, unhasting, and silent as light,
   Nor wanting, nor wasting, thou rulest in might—
   Thy justice like mountains high soaring above
   Thy clouds which are fountains of goodness and love.

3 To all life thou givest, to both great and small;
   In all life thou livest, the true life of all;
   We blossom and flourish as leaves on the tree,
   And wither and perish; but naught changeth thee.

4 Great Father of glory, pure Father of light,
   Thine angels adore thee, all veiling their sight;
   All laud we would render: O help us to see
   'Tis only the splendour of light hideth thee.

5 Immortal, invisible, God only wise,
   In light inaccessible hid from our eyes,
   Most blessèd, most glorious, the Ancient of Days,
   Almighty, victorious, thy great name we praise.

W. Chalmers Smith (1824–1908)

10(i)
LUCKINGTON 10 4.66.66. 10 4.   Basil Harwood (1859–1949)

GOD'S NATURE—*God's Being and Majesty*

1 LET all the world in every corner sing:
      My God and King!
    The heavens are not too high,
    His praise may thither fly;
    The earth is not too low,
    His praises there may grow.
  Let all the world in every corner sing:
      My God and King!

2 Let all the world in every corner sing:
      My God and King!
    The church with psalms must shout,
    No door can keep them out;
    But above all, the heart
    Must bear the longest part.
  Let all the world in every corner sing:
      My God and King!

George Herbert (1593–1633)

10(ii)

AUGUSTINE

Erik Routley (1917–82)

Unison

LET all the world in ev-'ry cor-ner sing: My God and King!

Harmony

The heavens are not too high, His

The heavens are not too high, His

GOD'S NATURE—*God's Being and Majesty*

sing: My God and King!

Harmony

The church with psalms must shout, No

The church with psalms must shout, No

door can keep them out; But a - bove all, the

door can keep them out; But a - bove all, the

GOD'S NATURE—*God's Being and Majesty*

George Herbert (1593–1633)

GOD'S NATURE—*God's Being and Majesty*

11(i)

MARYTON L.M.

H. P. Smith (1825–98)

11(ii)

OMBERSLEY L.M.

W. H. Gladstone (1840–91)

GOD'S NATURE—*God's Being and Majesty*

1 LORD of all being, throned afar,
   Thy glory flames from sun and star;
      Centre and soul of every sphere,
      Yet to each loving heart how near.

2 Sun of our life, thy quickening ray
   Sheds on our path the glow of day;
      Star of our hope, thy softened light
      Cheers the long watches of the night.

3 Our midnight is thy smile withdrawn,
   Our noontide is thy gracious dawn,
      Our rainbow arch thy mercy's sign;
      All, save the clouds of sin, are thine.

4 Lord of all life, below, above,
   Whose light is truth, whose warmth is love,
      Before thy ever-blazing throne
      We ask no lustre of our own.

5 Grant us thy truth to make us free,
   And kindling hearts that burn for thee,
      Till all thy living altars claim
      One holy light, one heavenly flame.

Oliver Wendell Holmes (1809–94)

12
ST BARTHOLOMEW L.M.

Henry Duncalf (d. 1762)
(from W. Riley's *Parochial Harmony*
(London 1762))

1 MY God, my King, thy various praise
Shall fill the remnant of my days;
Thy grace employ my humble tongue,
Till death and glory raise the song.

2 The wings of every hour shall bear
Some thankful tribute to thine ear,
And every setting sun shall see
New works of duty done for thee.

3 Thy truth and justice I'll proclaim;
Thy bounty flows, an endless stream;
Thy mercy swift; thine anger slow,
But dreadful to the stubborn foe.

4 Let distant times and nations raise
The long succession of thy praise;
And unborn ages make my song
The joy and labour of their tongue.

5 But who can speak thy wondrous deeds?
Thy greatness all our thoughts exceeds;
Vast and unsearchable thy ways,
Vast and immortal be thy praise.

Isaac Watts (1674–1748)

GOD'S NATURE—*God's Being and Majesty*

Arranged by John Wilson

Sopranos. (Other voices sing unison melody).

5 But who can speak thy won-drous deeds? Thy great-ness all our thoughts ex-ceeds; Vast, un-search-a-ble thy ways, Vast, im-mor-tal be thy praise.

GOD'S NATURE—*God's Being and Majesty*

13(i)

PRAISE, MY SOUL 87.87.87.

John Goss (1800–80)

Unison

1 PRAISE, my soul, the King of hea - ven; To his feet thy tri-bute bring. Ran-somed, healed, re - stored, for - gi - ven, Who like thee his praise should sing? Praise him! Praise him!

GOD'S NATURE—*God's Being and Majesty*

Praise him! Praise him! Praise the ev-er-last-ing King!

2 Praise him for his grace and fa - vour To our fa-thers in dis-tress; Praise him, still the same for ev - er Slow to chide, and swift to bless. Praise him! Praise him!

Harmony

GOD'S NATURE—*God's Being and Majesty*

Praise him! Praise him! Glo-rious in his faith-ful-ness.

Unison (upper voices only, ad lib.)

3 Fa-ther-like, he tends and spares us; Well our fee-ble

frame he knows; In his hands he gent-ly bears us,

Res-cues us from all our foes. Praise him! Praise him!

GOD'S NATURE—*God's Being and Majesty*

Praise him! Praise him! Wide-ly as his mer-cy flows.

Descant

Descant by Leonard Blake (1907—   )

4 An-gels in the height, a-dore__ him; Ye be-hold him

All other voices

4 An-gels in the height, a-dore him; Ye be-hold him

face to face; Sun and moon, bow down be-fore him,

face to face; Sun and moon, bow down be-fore him,

GOD'S NATURE—*God's Being and Majesty*

13(i)(cont.)

13(ii)

REGENT SQUARE 87.87.87.

Henry Smart (1813–79)

GOD'S NATURE—*God's Being and Majesty*

For this tune in a higher key see No. 80

1 PRAISE, my soul, the King of heaven;
　　To his feet thy tribute bring.
　Ransomed, healed, restored, forgiven,
　　Who like thee his praise should sing?
　　　Praise him! Praise him!
　　Praise the everlasting King!

2 Praise him for his grace and favour
　　To our fathers in distress;
　Praise him, still the same for ever,
　　Slow to chide, and swift to bless.
　　　Praise him! Praise him!
　　Glorious in his faithfulness.

3 Father-like, he tends and spares us;
　　Well our feeble frame he knows;
　In his hands he gently bears us,
　　Rescues us from all our foes.
　　　Praise him! Praise him!
　　Widely as his mercy flows.

4 Angels in the height, adore him;
　　Ye behold him face to face;
　Sun and moon, bow down before him,
　　Dwellers all in time and space.
　　　Praise him! Praise him!
　　Praise with us the God of grace!

Henry Francis Lyte (1793–1847)
based on Psalm 103

GOD'S NATURE—*God's Being and Majesty*

14

Melody probably by
R. Williams (c. 1781–1821)

Unison

GOD'S NATURE—*God's Being and Majesty*

1 PRAISE the Lord, his glories show,
   Alleluia!
   Saints within his courts below,
   Angels round his throne above,
   All that see and share his love.

2 Earth to heaven, and heaven to earth,
   Tell his wonders, sing his worth;
   Age to age and shore to shore,
   Praise him, praise him evermore!

3 Praise the Lord, his mercies trace;
   Praise his providence and grace,
   All that he for us has done,
   All he sends us through his Son.

4 Strings and voices, hands and hearts,
   In the concert play your parts;
   All that breathe, your Lord adore,
   Praise him, praise him evermore!

Henry Francis Lyte (1793–1847)

15(i)

AUSTRIA 8.7.8.7.D. Franz Joseph Haydn (1732–1809)

15(ii)

LAUS DEO (REDHEAD 46) 8.7.8.7. Richard Redhead (1820–1901)

GOD'S NATURE—*God's Being and Majesty*

For this tune in a higher key see No. 445

DESCANT

Alan Gray (1855–1935)
(slightly altered)

VERSE 2 (2nd part)

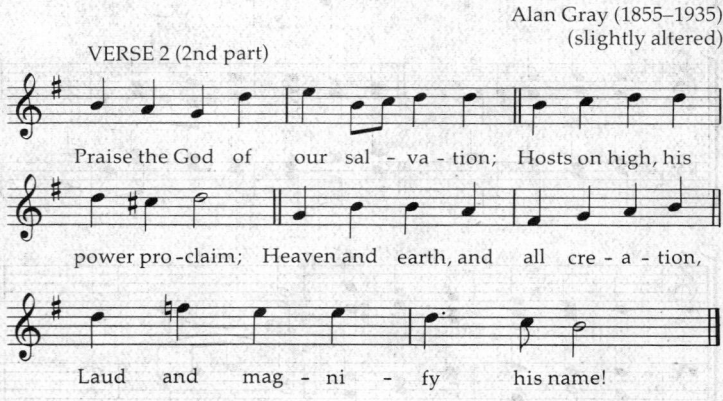

Praise the God of our sal - va - tion; Hosts on high, his

power pro-claim; Heaven and earth, and all cre - a - tion,

Laud and mag - ni - fy his name!

1 PRAISE the Lord! Ye heavens, adore him;
   Praise him, angels in the height;
   Sun and moon, rejoice before him;
   Praise him, all ye stars and light:

Praise the Lord, for he hath spoken;
   Worlds his mighty voice obeyed;
   Laws that never shall be broken
   For their guidance he hath made.

2 Praise the Lord, for he is glorious!
   Never shall his promise fail;
   God hath made his saints victorious;
   Sin and death shall not prevail.

Praise the God of our salvation;
   Hosts on high, his power proclaim;
   Heaven and earth, and all creation,
   Laud and magnify his name!

Foundling Hospital Collection (c. 1796)
based on Psalm 148

GOD'S NATURE—*God's Being and Majesty*

16
LOBE DEN HERREN 14.14.4 7.8.

Melody from *Praxis Pietatis Melica*
(1668 edition) as set in
The Chorale Book for England (1863)

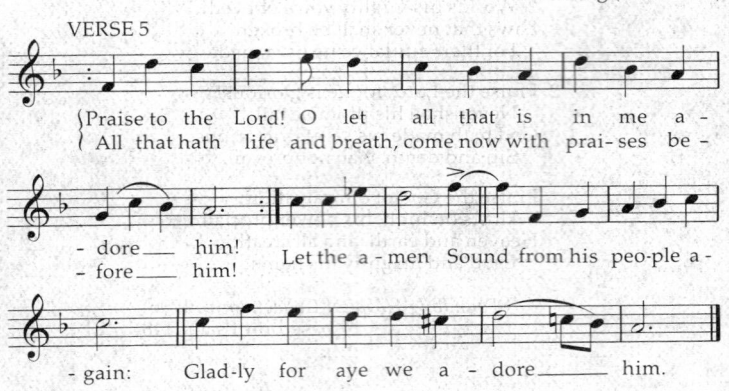

DESCANT

C. S. Lang (1891–1971)

VERSE 5

Praise to the Lord! O let all that is in me a-
All that hath life and breath, come now with prai-ses be-

-dore___ him! Let the a-men Sound from his peo-ple a-
-fore___ him!

-gain: Glad-ly for aye we a-dore___ him.

GOD'S NATURE—*God's Being and Majesty*

1 PRAISE to the Lord, the Almighty, the King of creation!
O my soul, praise him, for he is thy health and salvation!
   All ye who hear,
   Brothers and sisters, draw near,
Praise him in glad adoration.

2 Praise to the Lord, who doth prosper thy work and defend thee;
Surely his goodness and mercy here daily attend thee:
   Ponder anew
   What the Almighty can do,
Who with his love doth befriend thee.

3 Praise to the Lord, who doth nourish thy life and restore thee,
Fitting thee well for the tasks that are ever before thee,
   Then to thy need
   He like a mother doth speed,
Spreading the wings of grace o'er thee.

4 Praise to the Lord, who, when darkness of sin is abounding,
Who, when the godless do triumph, all virtue confounding,
   Sheddeth his light,
   Chaseth the horrors of night,
Saints with his mercy surrounding.

5 Praise to the Lord! O let all that is in me adore him!
All that hath life and breath, come now with praises before him!
   Let the amen
   Sound from his people again:
Gladly for aye we adore him.

Joachim Neander (1650–80)
tr. *Catherine Winkworth* (1827–78)
and *Rupert E. Davies* (1909–) v. 3

17(i)

GONFALON ROYAL L.M.

P. C. Buck (1871–1947)

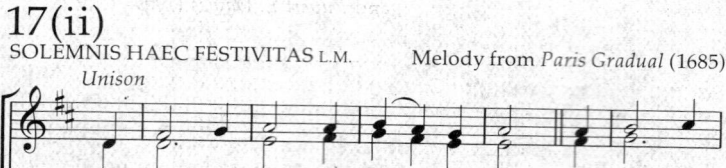

Unison

A – – – men.

17(ii)

SOLEMNIS HAEC FESTIVITAS L.M.

Melody from *Paris Gradual* (1685)

Unison

GOD'S NATURE—*God's Being and Majesty*

1 SING to the Lord a joyful song,
   Lift up your hearts, your voices raise;
To us his gracious gifts belong,
   To him our songs of love and praise;

2 For life and love, for rest and food,
   For daily help and nightly care,
Sing to the Lord, for he is good,
   And praise his name, for it is fair;

3 For strength to those who on him wait
   His truth to prove, his will to do,
Praise ye our God, for he is great,
   Trust in his name, for it is true.

4 For joys untold, that from above
   Cheer those who love his sweet employ,
Sing to our God, for he is love,
   Exalt his name, for it is joy.

5 For he is Lord of heaven and earth,
   Whom angels serve and saints adore,
The Father, Son, and Holy Ghost,
   To whom be praise for evermore.
                                    (Amen)

John Samuel Bewley Monsell (1811–75)

(See after facing page for an alternative version of verse 4)

GOD'S NATURE—*God's Being and Majesty*

1   WE give immortal praise
        To God the Father's love,
    For all our comforts here,
        And better hopes above.
    He sent his own eternal Son
    To die for sins that man had done.

2   To God the Son belongs
        Immortal glory too,
    Who bought us with his blood
        From everlasting woe:
    And now he lives, and now he reigns,
    And sees the fruit of all his pains.

3   To God the Spirit's name
        Immortal worship give,
    Whose new-creating power
        Makes the dead sinner live:
    His work completes the great design,
    And fills the soul with joy divine.

4   Almighty God, to thee
        Be endless honours done,
    The undivided Three,
        And the mysterious One:
    Where reason fails with all her powers,
    There faith prevails, and love adores.

Isaac Watts (1674–1748)

18 (cont.)

ALTERNATIVE VERSION FOR VERSE 4
(with Melody in the Tenor)

Arranged by John Wilson

Organ
and
Voices

4 Al – migh-ty God, to thee Be
end – less hon-ours done, The un-di – vi-ded
Three, And the mys-te – rious One:
Where rea-son fails with all her powers,

GOD'S NATURE—*God's Being and Majesty*

19

DATCHET 11 11. 11 11.

George J. Elvey (1816–93)

GOD'S NATURE—*God's Being and Majesty*

1 WITH gladness we worship, rejoice as we sing,
  Free hearts and free voices how blessèd to bring;
  The old, thankful story shall scale thine abode,
  Thou King of all glory, most bountiful God.

2 Thy right would we give thee—true homage thy due,
  And honour eternal, the universe through,
  With all thy creation, earth, heaven and sea,
  In one acclamation we celebrate thee.

3 Renewed by thy Spirit, redeemed by thy Son,
  Thy children revere thee for all thou hast done.
  O Father! Returning to love and to light,
  Thy children are yearning to praise thee aright.

4 We join with the angels, and so there is given
  From earth Alleluia, in answer to heaven.
  Amen! Be thou glorious below and above,
  Redeeming, victorious, and infinite Love!

George Rawson (1807–89)

20
DARWALL'S 148th   6.6.6.6.44.44.

Melody by John Darwall (1731–89)

DESCANT

Leonard Blake (1907–   )

VERSE 4

Tri - umph in God a - bove, And with a
well-tuned heart _____ Sing _____ thou the songs of
love. (Let all) Let all thy days Till life shall
end, ___ What - e'er he send, Be filled with praise.

1 YE holy angels bright,
      Who wait at God's right hand,
   Or through the realms of light
      Fly at your Lord's command,
         Assist our song,
            Or else the theme
            Too high doth seem
         For mortal tongue.

2 Ye blessèd souls at rest,
      Who ran this earthly race,
   And now, from sin released,
      Behold the Saviour's face,
         His praises sound,
            As in his light
            With sweet delight
         Ye do abound.

3 Ye saints who toil below,
      Adore your heavenly King,
   And onward as ye go
      Some joyful anthem sing;
         Take what he gives,
            And praise him still
            Through good and ill,
         Who ever lives.

4 My soul, bear thou thy part,
      Triumph in God above,
   And with a well-tuned heart
      Sing thou the songs of love.
         Let all thy days
            Till life shall end,
            Whate'er he send,
         Be filled with praise.

Richard Baxter (1615–91) and others

21

EISENACH L.M.

Melody by J. H. Schein (1628)
Harmony adapted from J. S. Bach (1685–1750)

For this tune in a higher key see No. 49

DESCANT

John Wilson

VERSE 7

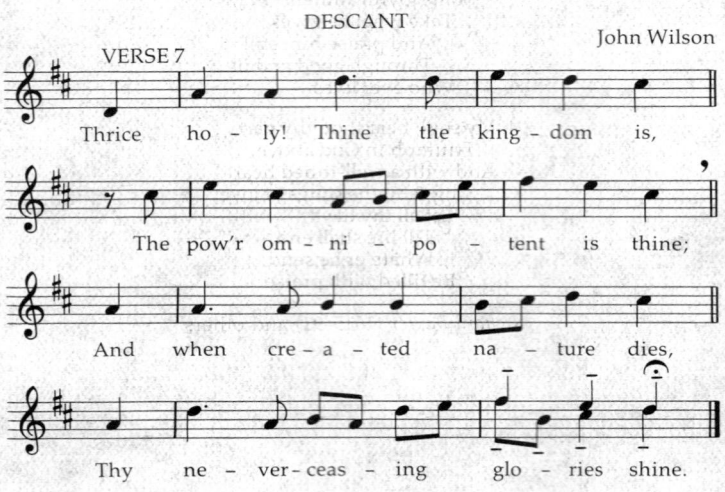

Thrice ho - ly! Thine the king - dom is,

The pow'r om - ni - po - tent is thine;

And when cre - a - ted na - ture dies,

Thy ne - ver - ceas - ing glo - ries shine.

THE ETERNAL FATHER

The Lord's Prayer

1 FATHER of all, whose powerful voice
    Called forth this universal frame,
Whose mercies over all rejoice,
    Through endless ages still the same:

2 Inflame our hearts with perfect love,
    In us the work of faith fulfil;
So not heaven's host shall swifter move
    Than we on earth, to do thy will.

3 On thee we cast our care; we live
    Through thee, who know'st our every need;
O feed us with thy grace, and give
    Our souls this day the living bread.

4 Eternal, spotless Lamb of God,
    Before the world's foundation slain,
Sprinkle us ever with thy blood,
    O cleanse, and keep us ever clean!

5 Giver and Lord of life, whose power
    And guardian care for all are free,
To thee, in fierce temptation's hour,
    From sin and Satan let us flee.

6 Thine, Lord, we are, and ours thou art;
    In us be all thy goodness showed.
Renew, enlarge, and fill our heart
    With peace, and joy, and heaven, and God.

7 Thrice holy! Thine the kingdom is,
    The power omnipotent is thine;
And, when created nature dies,
    Thy never-ceasing glories shine.

John Wesley (1703–91)

God's Creating and Sustaining Power

22(i)
WARRINGTON L.M.

R. Harrison (1748–1810)
(original harmony, except in last 2 bars)

For this tune in a lower key see No. 188

22(ii)
TRURO L.M.

Melody from T. Williams's *Psalmodia Evangelica* (1789)

THE ETERNAL FATHER

For a descant to this tune, see No. 433(i)

1 GIVE to our God immortal praise,
   Mercy and truth are all his ways:
      Wonders of grace to God belong,
      Repeat his mercies in your song.

2 Give to the Lord of lords renown;
   The King of kings with glory crown:
      His mercies ever shall endure,
      When lords and kings are known no more.

3 He built the earth, he spread the sky,
   And fixed the starry lights on high:
      Wonders of grace to God belong,
      Repeat his mercies in your song.

4 He fills the sun with morning light,
   He bids the moon direct the night:
      His mercies ever shall endure,
      When suns and moons shall shine no more.

5 He sent his Son with power to save
   From guilt and darkness and the grave:
      Wonders of grace to God belong,
      Repeat his mercies in your song.

6 Through this vain world he guides our feet,
   And leads us to his heavenly seat:
      His mercies ever shall endure,
      When this vain world shall be no more.

Isaac Watts (1674–1748)
based on Psalm 136

May also be sung to No. 26, DUKE STREET

God's Creating and Sustaining Power

23

ES SIND DOCH SELIG ALLE 88.7.88.7.D.

Original form of melody
by M. Greiter (c. 1500–50)
Harmonised by John Wilson

Unison or harmony

1 GOD speaks, and all things come to be;
God speaks, and Sa - tan's le - gions flee,
Scat - tered by love's brave splen - dour;
God speaks, and our for - give - ness seals;

2 Grant this to me, Lord, let me live
And, liv - ing, keep your word, and give
My life to gain its trea - sure.
Here but a stran - ger, let me trace

3 Bless'd are they all who hun - ger sore
To see your righ - teous ness once more
En - throned in hearts and na - tions.
Bless'd are the pure in heart, who seek

THE ETERNAL FATHER

God speaks, and gen-'rous grace re - veals
My path to ward a rest - ing place
To hear what God the Lord will speak

In pre - cepts wise and ten - der.
Where I shall find pure plea - sure.
In bliss - ful con - tem - pla - tions.

Though all I see must have an end,
Much kind - ness you have shown to me,
Bless'd be our God, who gives us light;

God's sta - tutes past all time ex - tend,
Pro - mise and pledge of joy to be;
Bless'd be the mer - cy and the might

(continued on following page)

God's Creating and Sustaining Power

By breadth and length un - boun - ded.
Con - tin - ue thus your bless - ing!
Which all the day at - tend us.

Though we are crea - tures of a day,
Wis - dom that mould - ed all my life,
Bless'd be the pro - mi - ses of grace,

Though heaven and earth may pass a - way,
Guide me, in days so full of strife,
Bless'd be the laws that still em - brace,

God's word is deep - er found - ed.
Gen - tly my heart pos - ses - sing.
En - ligh - ten, and de - fend us.

THE ETERNAL FATHER

1 GOD speaks, and all things come to be;
  God speaks, and Satan's legions flee,
    Scattered by love's brave splendour;
  God speaks, and our forgiveness seals;
  God speaks, and generous grace reveals
    In precepts wise and tender.
  Though all I see must have an end,
  God's statutes past all time extend,
    By breadth and length unbounded.
  Though we are creatures of a day,
  Though heaven and earth may pass away,
    God's word is deeper founded.

2 Grant this to me, Lord, let me live
  And, living, keep your word, and give
    My life to gain its treasure.
  Here but a stranger, let me trace
  My path toward a resting place
    Where I shall find pure pleasure.
  Much kindness you have shown to me,
  Promise and pledge of joy to be;
    Continue thus your blessing!
  Wisdom that moulded all my life,
  Guide me, in days so full of strife,
    Gently my heart possessing.

3 Bless'd are they all who hunger sore
  To see your righteousness once more
    Enthroned in hearts and nations.
  Bless'd are the pure in heart, who seek
  To hear what God the Lord will speak
    In blissful contemplations.
  Bless'd be our God, who gives us light;
  Bless'd be the mercy and the might
    Which all the day attend us.
  Bless'd be the promises of grace,
  Bless'd be the laws that still embrace,
    Enlighten, and defend us.

Erik Routley (1917–82)
based on Psalm 119

God's Creating and Sustaining Power

For this tune in a higher key see No. 425

THE ETERNAL FATHER

1 GOD is a name my soul adores,
    The almighty Three, the eternal One;
Nature and grace with all their powers
    Confess the Infinite unknown.

2 Thy voice produced the sea and spheres,
    Bade the waves roar, the planets shine;
But nothing like thyself appears
    Through all these spacious works of thine.

3 Still restless nature dies and grows;
    From change to change the creatures run:
Thy being no succession knows,
    And all thy vast designs are one.

4 A glance of thine runs through the globe,
    Rules the bright worlds and moves their frame;
Of light thou form'st thy dazzling robe,
    Thy ministers are living flame.

5 How shall polluted mortals dare
    To sing thy glory or thy grace?
Beneath thy feet we lie afar,
    And see but shadows of thy face.

6 Who can behold the blazing light?
    Who can approach consuming flame?
None but thy wisdom knows thy might,
    None but thy word can speak thy name.

Isaac Watts (1674–1748)

May also be sung to No. 488, BROCKHAM

God's Creating and Sustaining Power

25

HE'S GOT THE WHOLE WORLD   Irreg.

Traditional. Arranged by
Peter Fletcher (1935–   )

1 HE'S got the whole world in his hand.
He's got the whole world in his hand.
He's got the whole wide world in his hand.
He's got the whole world in his hand.

2 He's got you and me, brother, in his hand.
He's got you and me, brother, in his hand.
He's got you and me, brother, in his hand.
He's got the whole world in his hand.

3 He's got you and me, sister, in his hand.
He's got you and me, sister, in his hand.
He's got you and me, sister, in his hand.
He's got the whole world in his hand.

4 He's got the whole world in his hand.
He's got the whole world in his hand.
He's got the whole wide world in his hand.
He's got the whole world in his hand.

Traditional

THE ETERNAL FATHER

Melody, and most of the bass, from H. Boyd's
Psalm and Hymn tunes (1793)
Later attributed to J. Hatton (d. 1793)

For this tune in a lower key see No. 710(i)

1 HIGH in the heavens, eternal God,
    Thy goodness in full glory shines;
  Thy truth shall break through every cloud
    That veils and darkens thy designs.

2 For ever firm thy justice stands,
    As mountains their foundations keep;
  Wise are the wonders of thy hands;
    Thy judgements are a mighty deep.

3 Thy providence is kind and large,
    Both man and beast thy bounty share;
  The whole creation is thy charge,
    But saints are thy peculiar care.

4 My God, how excellent thy grace,
    Whence all our hope and comfort springs!
  The race of Adam in distress
    Flies to the shadow of thy wings.

5 Life, like a fountain rich and free,
    Springs from the presence of the Lord;
  And in thy light our souls shall see
    The glories promised in thy word.

                    Isaac Watts (1674–1748)
                    based on Psalm 36:5–9

God's Creating and Sustaining Power

27(i)

MONKLAND   77. Refrain

Arranged by J. Wilkes (1861)
from a tune composed or adapted
by John Antes (1740–1811)

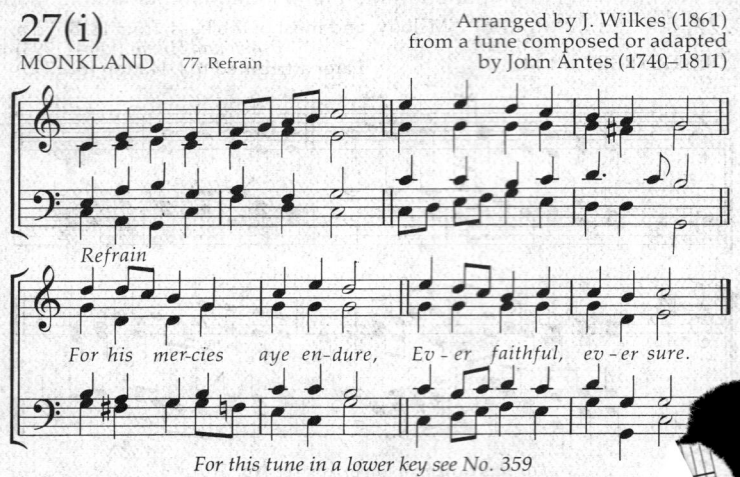

Refrain

For his mer-cies   aye en-dure,   Ev – er faithful, ev – er sure.

For this tune in a lower key see No. 359

ALTERNATIVE VERSION FOR VERSE 8

Arranged by John Wilson

Descant

Let us praise the Lord, ___   Al –   – le – lu – ia!

Organ (and voices in unison)

For his ___ mer-cies aye en-dure, Al –   le – lu – ia!

THE ETERNAL FATHER

1 O WORSHIP the King, all-glorious above;
  O gratefully sing his power and his love:
    Our Shield and Defender, the Ancient of Days,
    Pavilioned in splendour, and girded with praise.

2 O tell of his might, O sing of his grace,
  Whose robe is the light, whose canopy space;
    His chariots of wrath the deep thunder-clouds form,
    And dark is his path on the wings of the storm.

3 The earth with its store of wonders untold,
  Almighty, thy power hath founded of old;
    Hath stablished it fast by a changeless decree,
    And round it hath cast, like a mantle, the sea.

4 Thy bountiful care what tongue can recite?
  It breathes in the air, it shines in the light;
    It streams from the hills, it descends to the plain,
    And sweetly distils in the dew and the rain.

5 Frail children of dust, and feeble as frail,
  In thee do we trust, nor find thee to fail;
    Thy mercies how tender, how firm to the end,
    Our Maker, Defender, Redeemer, and Friend.

6 O measureless Might, ineffable Love,
  While angels delight to hymn thee above,
    Thy humbler creation, though feeble their lays,
    With true adoration shall sing to thy praise.

Robert Grant (1779–1838)
based on Psalm 104

God's Creating and Sustaining Power

29

MOSCOW 66.4.666.4

Melody by Felice de Giardini (1716–96)

THE ETERNAL FATHER

1 THOU whose almighty word
  Chaos and darkness heard,
    And took their flight,
  Hear us, we humbly pray,
  And where the gospel day
  Sheds not its glorious ray,
    Let there be light!

2 Thou who didst come to bring
  On thy redeeming wing
    Healing and sight,
  Health to the sick in mind,
  Sight to the inly blind,
  O now to all mankind
    Let there be light!

3 Spirit of truth and love,
  Life-giving, holy Dove,
    Speed forth thy flight;
  Move on the waters' face,
  Bearing the lamp of grace,
  And in earth's darkest place
    Let there be light!

4 Blessèd and holy Three,
  Glorious Trinity,
    Wisdom, Love, Might,
  Boundless as ocean's tide
  Rolling in fullest pride,
  Through the world far and wide
    Let there be light!

John Marriott (1780–1825)

God's Creating and Sustaining Power

30

BRIDEGROOM 8.7.8.7.6.   Peter Cutts (1937–   )

Unison

A and B may be sung by contrasted groups of voices.

ALTERNATIVE HARMONY VERSION

THE ETERNAL FATHER

So,_____ Lord, art thou_____ to me.

So, Lord,_____ art thou to_____ me.

Fine

vv. 2–5

1 AS the bridegroom to his chosen,
   As the king unto his realm,
   As the keep unto the castle,
   As the pilot to the helm,
     So, Lord, art thou to me.

2 As the fountain in the garden,
   As the candle in the dark,
   As the treasure in the coffer,
   As the manna in the ark,
     So, Lord, art thou to me.

3 As the music at the banquet,
   As the stamp unto the seal,
   As the med'cine to the fainting,
   As the wine-cup at the meal,
     So, Lord, art thou to me.

4 As the ruby in the setting,
   As the honey in the comb,
   As the light within the lantern,
   As the father in the home,
     So, Lord, art thou to me.

5 As the sunshine in the heavens,
   As the image in the glass,
   As the fruit unto the fig-tree,
   As the dew unto the grass,
     So, Lord, art thou to me.

Paraphrased from *John Tauler* (1300–61)
   by *Emma Frances Bevan* (1827–1909)

God's Revealing and Transforming Love

31

BETTER WORLD   8.3.8.3.8 8 8.3

Old English Air

God   is love,   God   is love!

God   is love,   God   is love!

God is love,   God is love!

THE ETERNAL FATHER

1 COME, let us all unite and sing—
    God is love!
While heaven and earth their praises bring—
    God is love!
Let every soul from sin awake,
Each in his heart sweet music make,
And sweetly sing for Jesus' sake—
    God is love!

2 O tell to earth's remotest bound—
    God is love!
In Christ is full redemption found—
    God is love!
His blood can cleanse our sins away;
His Spirit turns our night to day,
And leads our souls with joy to say—
    God is love!

3 How happy is our portion here—
    God is love!
His promises our spirits cheer—
    God is love!
He is our sun and shield by day,
By night he near our tents will stay,
He will be with us all the way—
    God is love!

4 In Zion we shall sing again—
    God is love!
Yes, this shall be our highest strain—
    God is love!
Whilst endless ages roll along,
In concert with the heavenly throng,
This shall be still our sweetest song—
    God is love!

Howard Kingsbury (c. 1850)

God's Revealing and Transforming Love

32

ES FLOG EIN KLEINS WALDVÖGELEIN 7.6.7.6.D.

German Traditional
Melody (17th
century or earlier)

THE ETERNAL FATHER

1 'ERE God had built the mountains,
    Or raised the fruitful hills;
 Before he filled the fountains
    That feed the running rills;
 In me, from everlasting,
    The wonderful I AM
 Found pleasures never wasting,
    And Wisdom is my name.

2 'When, like a tent to dwell in,
    He spread the skies abroad,
 And swathed about the swelling
    Of ocean's mighty flood,
 He wrought by weight and measure,
    And I was with him then;
 Myself the Father's pleasure,
    And mine, the sons of men.'

3 Thus Wisdom's words discover
    Thy glory and thy grace,
 Thou everlasting lover
    Of our unworthy race:
 Thy gracious eye surveyed us
    Ere stars were seen above;
 In wisdom thou hast made us,
    And died for us in love.

4 And couldst thou be delighted
    With creatures such as we,
 Who, when we saw thee, slighted
    And nailed thee to a tree?
 Unfathomable wonder,
    And mystery divine;
 The voice that speaks in thunder
    Says: 'Sinner, I am thine!'

William Cowper (1731–1800)

May also be sung to No. 132, PEARSALL

God's Revealing and Transforming Love

33

KILMARNOCK C.M.

Melody, and almost all the harmony, by Neil Dougall (1776–1862)

For this tune in a higher key see No. 758(ii)

1 COME, let us to the Lord our God
   With contrite hearts return;
   Our God is gracious, nor will leave
   The desolate to mourn.

2 His voice commands the tempest forth,
   And stills the stormy wave;
   And though his arm be strong to smite,
   'Tis also strong to save.

3 Long has the night of sorrow reigned;
   The dawn shall bring us light;
   God shall appear, and we shall rise
   With gladness in his sight.

4 Our hearts, if God we seek to know,
   Shall know him and rejoice;
   His coming like the morn shall be,
   Like morning songs his voice.

5 As dew upon the tender herb,
   Diffusing fragrance round;
   As showers that usher in the spring,
   And cheer the thirsty ground:

6 So shall his presence bless our souls,
   And shed a joyful light;
   That hallowed morn shall chase away
   The sorrows of the night.

John Morison (1750–98)
as in Scottish Paraphrases (1781)
based on Hosea 6:1–4

May also be sung to No. 698, BYZANTIUM

THE ETERNAL FATHER

34

INVITATION L.M.   Later form of a tune by J. F. Lampe (1703–51) mostly as in *The Temple Church Choral Service Book*, 1880

For this tune in a higher key see No. 395

1 ETERNAL depth of love divine,
   In Jesus, God with us, displayed;
 How bright thy beaming glories shine!
   How wide thy healing streams are spread!

2 With whom dost thou delight to dwell?
   Sinners, a vile and thankless race;
 O God, what tongue aright can tell
   How vast thy love, how great thy grace!

3 The dictates of thy sovereign will
   With joy our grateful hearts receive;
 All thy delight in us fulfil;
   Lo! All we are to thee we give.

4 To thy sure love, thy tender care,
   Our flesh, soul, spirit, we resign:
 O fix thy sacred presence there,
   And seal the abode for ever thine!

5 O King of Glory! Thy rich grace
   Our feeble thought surpasses far;
 Yea, even our sins, though numberless,
   Less numerous than thy mercies are.

6 Still, Lord, thy saving health display,
   And arm our souls with heavenly zeal;
 So fearless shall we urge our way
   Through all the powers of earth and hell.

Nicolaus Ludwig von Zinzendorf (1700–60)
tr. John Wesley (1703–91)

May also be sung to No. 394, ETON

God's Revealing and Transforming Love

35

BENIFOLD 8.33.6.D.

Francis Westbrook (1903–75)

THE ETERNAL FATHER

1 GLORY, love, and praise, and honour,
  For our food
  Now bestowed
  Render we the Donor.
Bounteous God, we now confess thee,
  God, who thus
  Blessest us,
  Meet it is to bless thee.

2 Knows the ox his master's stable,
  And shall we
  Not know thee,
  Nourished at thy table?
Yes, of all good gifts the Giver
  Thee we own,
  Thee alone
  Magnify for ever.

Part 2

3 Thankful for our every blessing,
  Let us sing
  Christ the Spring,
  Never, never ceasing.
Source of all our gifts and graces
  Christ we own,
  Christ alone
  Calls for all our praises.

4 He dispels our sin and sadness,
  Life imparts,
  Cheers our hearts,
  Fills with food and gladness.
Who himself for all has given,
  Us he feeds,
  Us he leads
  To a feast in heaven.

Charles Wesley (1707–88)

God's Revealing and Transforming Love

36

MEAD HOUSE 8.7.8.7.D.

Cyril V. Taylor (1907–   )

THE ETERNAL FATHER

1 GOD is Love: let heaven adore him;
    God is Love: let earth rejoice;
  Let creation sing before him,
    And exalt him with one voice.
  He who laid the earth's foundation,
    He who spread the heavens above,
  He who breathes through all creation,
    He is Love, eternal Love.

2 God is Love: and he enfoldeth
    All the world in one embrace;
  With unfailing grasp he holdeth
    Every child of every race.
  And when human hearts are breaking
    Under sorrow's iron rod,
  Then they find that selfsame aching
    Deep within the heart of God.

3 God is Love: and though with blindness
    Sin afflicts the souls of men,
  God's eternal loving-kindness
    Holds and guides them even then.
  Sin and death and hell shall never
    O'er us final triumph gain;
  God is Love, so Love for ever
    O'er the universe must reign.

Timothy Rees (1874–1939) alt.

May also be sung to No. 64, ARFON

God's Revealing and Transforming Love

37

ELEVATION 7.6.7.6.7.8.7.6.

R. Mellor (1816–89)

THE ETERNAL FATHER

1   GOOD thou art, and good thou dost,
      Thy mercies reach to all,
    Chiefly those who on thee trust,
      And for thy mercy call;
    New they every morning are;
  As parents when their children cry,
      Us thou dost in pity spare,
        And all our wants supply.

2   Mercy o'er thy works presides;
      Thy providence displayed
    Still preserves, and still provides
      For all thy hands have made;
    Keeps with most distinguished care
  The man who on thy love depends;
      Watches every numbered hair,
        And all his steps attends.

3   Who can sound the depths unknown
      Of thy redeeming grace,
    Grace that gave thine only Son
      To save a ruined race?
    Millions of transgressors poor
  Thou hast for Jesus' sake forgiven,
      Made them of thy favour sure,
        And snatched from hell to heaven.

4   Millions more thou ready art
      To save, and to forgive;
    Every soul and every heart
      Of man thou wouldst receive:
    Father, now accept of mine,
  Which now, through Christ, I offer thee;
      Tell me now, in love divine,
        That thou hast pardoned me.

Charles Wesley (1707–88)

God's Revealing and Transforming Love

38
SOVEREIGNTY   88.88.88   John Newton (1802–86)

Who is   a   pard-ning God   like

THE ETERNAL FATHER

thee? Or who has grace so rich and
free? Or who has grace so rich and free?

1 GREAT God of wonders! All thy ways
    Display the attributes divine;
But countless acts of pardoning grace
    Beyond thine other wonders shine:
Who is a pardoning God like thee?
    Or who has grace so rich and free?

2 In wonder lost, with trembling joy
    We take the pardon of our God—
Pardon for crimes of deepest dye,
    A pardon bought with Jesus' blood:

3 Pardon—from an offended God!
    Pardon—for sins of deepest dye!
Pardon—bestowed through Jesus' blood!
    Pardon—that brings the rebel nigh!

4 O may this strange, this matchless grace,
    This God-like miracle of love,
Fill the wide earth with grateful praise,
    As now it fills the choirs above!

Samuel Davies (1723–61)

May also be sung to No. 529, CAREY'S (SURREY)

God's Revealing and Transforming Love

39

GROSVENOR · 88.6.D.

Edward Harwood (1707–87)
(slightly adapted)

THE ETERNAL FATHER

1 LORD God, by whom all change is wrought,
By whom new things to birth are brought,
    In whom no change is known;
Whate'er thou dost, whate'er thou art,
Thy people still in thee have part;
    Still, still thou art our own.

2 Ancient of Days, we dwell in thee;
Out of thine own eternity
    Our peace and joy are wrought;
We rest in our eternal God,
And make secure and sweet abode
    With thee, who changest not.

3 Spirit, who makest all things new,
Thou leadest onward; we pursue
    The heavenly march sublime.
'Neath thy renewing fire we glow,
And still from strength to strength we go,
    From height to height we climb.

4 Darkness and dread we leave behind;
New light, new glory still we find,
    New realms divine possess;
New births of grace new raptures bring;
Triumphant, the new song we sing,
    The great Renewer bless.

5 To thee we rise, in thee we rest;
We stay at home, we go in quest,
    Still thou art our abode.
The rapture swells, the wonder grows,
As full on us new life still flows
    From our unchanging God.

Thomas Hornblower Gill (1819–1906)

God's Revealing and Transforming Love

40

CROSSINGS 8.9.8.9.D.

C. Armstrong Gibbs (1889–1960)

THE ETERNAL FATHER

1 THEE will I love, my God and King,
    Thee will I sing,
    My strength and tower;
For evermore thee will I trust,
    O God most just
    Of truth and power;
    Who all things hast
    In order placed,
Yea, for thy pleasure hast created;
    And on thy throne
    Unseen, unknown,
    Reignest alone
    In glory seated.

2 Set in my heart thy love I find;
    My wandering mind
    To thee thou leadest:
My trembling hope, my strong desire
    With heavenly fire
    Thou kindly feedest.
    Lo, all things fair
    Thy path prepare,
Thy beauty to my spirit calleth,
    Thine to remain
    In joy or pain,
    And count it gain
    Whate'er befalleth.

3 O more and more thy love extend,
    My life befriend
    With heavenly pleasure;
That I may win thy paradise,
    Thy pearl of price,
    Thy countless treasure;
    Since but in thee
    I can go free
From earthly care and vain oppression,
    This prayer I make
    For Jesus' sake,
    That thou me take
    In thy possession.

Robert Bridges (1844–1930)

God's Revealing and Transforming Love

41

DRESDEN (LUCERNE) 88.8.D.   Melody by J. Schmidlin (1722–72)

THE ETERNAL FATHER

1 THEE will I praise with all my heart,
And tell to all how good thou art,
  How marvellous thy works of grace;
Thy name I will in songs record,
And joy and glory in my Lord,
  Extolled above all thanks and praise.

2 The Lord will save his people here;
In times of need their help is near
  To all by sin and hell oppressed;
And they that know thy name will trust
In thee, who, to thy promise just,
  Hast never left a soul distressed.

3 The Lord is by his judgements known;
He helps his poor afflicted one,
  His sorrows all he bears in mind;
The mourner shall not always weep,
Who sows in tears in joy shall reap,
  With grief who seeks with joy shall find.

4 A helpless soul that looks to thee
Is sure at last thy face to see,
  And all thy goodness to partake;
The sinner who for thee doth grieve,
And longs, and labours to believe,
  Thou never, never wilt forsake.

Charles Wesley (1707–88)
based on Psalm 9

God's Revealing and Transforming Love

42

MARTHAM   L.M.

J. H. Maunder (1858–1920)

1 O LOVE of God, how strong and true,
 Eternal and yet ever new;
  Uncomprehended and unbought,
  Beyond all knowledge and all thought!

2 O heavenly love, how precious still,
 In days of weariness and ill,
  In nights of pain and helplessness,
  To heal, to comfort, and to bless.

3 O wide-embracing, wondrous love,
 We read thee in the sky above;
  We read thee in the earth below,
  In seas that swell and streams that flow.

4 We read thee best in him who came
 To bear for us the cross of shame,
  Sent by the Father from on high,
  Our life to live, our death to die.

5 We read thy power to bless and save
 E'en in the darkness of the grave;
  Still more in resurrection light
  We read the fullness of thy might.

6 O love of God, our shield and stay
 Through all the perils of our way;
  Eternal love, in thee we rest,
  For ever safe, for ever blest!

Horatius Bonar (1808–89)

May also be sung to No. 21, EISENACH

THE ETERNAL FATHER

Melody and most of the harmony from
John Randall's *Psalm and Hymn Tunes* (1794)
Probably by Charles Collignon (1725–85)

For this tune in a lower key see Nos. 48 and 744(iii)

Psalm 23

1 THE God of love my Shepherd is,
   And he that doth me feed;
   While he is mine, and I am his,
   What can I want or need?

2 He leads me to the tender grass,
   Where I both feed and rest;
   Then to the streams that gently pass:
   In both I have the best.

3 Or if I stray, he doth convert
   And bring my mind in frame:
   And all this not for my desert,
   But for his holy name.

4 Yea, in death's shady black abode
   Well may I walk, not fear;
   For thou art with me, and thy rod
   To guide, thy staff to bear.

5 Surely thy sweet and wondrous love
   Shall measure all my days;
   And, as it never shall remove,
   So neither shall my praise.

George Herbert (1593–1633)

May also be sung to No. 469(ii), ST COLUMBA

God's Revealing and Transforming Love

Joseph Gelineau (1920–   )

Verses 1–2
Unison

1 THE Lord is my Shepherd; There is
2 He guides me a - long the right path;___ He is

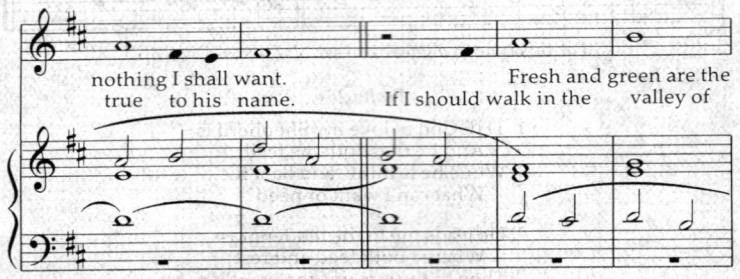

nothing I shall want. Fresh and green are the
true to his name. If I should walk in the valley of

pastures Where he gives me re - pose. Near
darkness, No evil would I fear. You are

THE ETERNAL FATHER

restful waters he leads me,   To re -
there with your crook and your staff;___   With

Verses 3–5
Unison

- vive my drooping spi - rit. 3 You have pre-pared a
these you give me com - fort. 4 Surely goodness and
           5 To the Father and

banquet for me ___ In the sight of my foes;
kindness shall follow me All the days of my life.
Son give glory, Give glory to the Spirit:

God's Revealing and Transforming Love

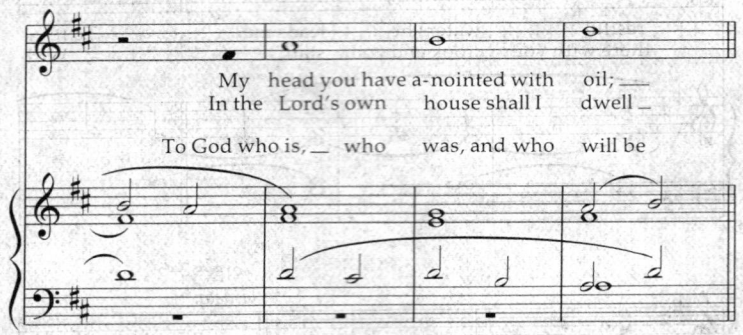

My head you have a-nointed with oil; ___
In the Lord's own house shall I dwell ___

To God who is, ___ who was, and who will be

My cup is o - ver flow - ing.
For ev - er and ev - er.
For ev - er and ev - er.

ANTIPHON I (♩ = 𝅝 of Psalm)   A. Gregory Murray (1905–   )

Unison His good-ness shall fol-low me always, To the end of my days.

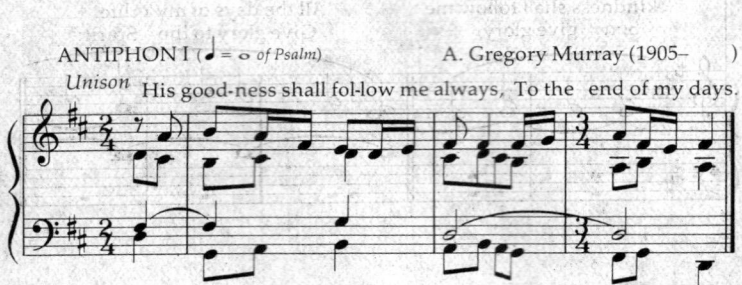

THE ETERNAL FATHER

ANTIPHON II (♩ = ○ of Psalm)
Unison

A. Gregory Murray

The Lord— is my Shep - herd, no-thing shall I want: He leads me by safe— paths, no - thing shall I fear.

God's Revealing and Transforming Love

45(i)

THAILAND 5.6.5.6. (Anapaestic)

Melody by Charoen Vijaya
Harmonised by Peter Fletcher (1935–   )

45(ii)

NORMANDY 5.6.5.6.D.

Unison

Basque Carol Melody,
collected and extended by
C. Edgar Pettman (1865–1943)
Harmonised and arranged
Guthrie Foote (1897–1972)

THE ETERNAL FATHER

1 THE great love of God
    Is revealed in the Son,
Who came to this earth
    To redeem everyone.

2 That love, like a stream
    Flowing clear to the sea,
Makes clean every heart
    That from sin would be free.

3 It binds the whole world,
    Every barrier it breaks,
The hills it lays low,
    And the mountains it shakes.

4 It's yours, it is ours,
    O how lavishly given!
The pearl of great price,
    And the treasure of heaven.

Daniel T. Niles (1908–70)

God's Revealing and Transforming Love

46(i)

ABRIDGE (ST STEPHEN) C.M.

Melody by Isaac Smith (1734–1805)
From *A Collection of Psalm Tunes* (c. 1780)

46(ii)

JERUSALEM C.M.

S. Grosvenor (1816–66)

THE ETERNAL FATHER

1 WHAT shall I do my God to love,
    My loving God to praise?
The length, and breadth, and height to prove,
    And depth of sovereign grace?

2 Thy sovereign grace to all extends,
    Immense and unconfined;
From age to age it never ends;
    It reaches all mankind.

3 Throughout the world its breadth is known,
    Wide as infinity;
So wide it never passed by one,
    Or it had passed by me.

4 My trespass was grown up to heaven;
    But, far above the skies,
In Christ abundantly forgiven,
    I see thy mercies rise.

5 The depth of all-redeeming love
    What angel tongue can tell?
O may I to the utmost prove
    The gift unspeakable!

6 Come quickly, gracious Lord, and take
    Possession of thine own;
My longing heart vouchsafe to make
    Thine everlasting throne.

Charles Wesley (1707–88)

God's Revealing and Transforming Love

Melody from H. F. Hemy's
Easy Hymn Tunes for Catholic Schools (1851)
Harmony by Eric Thiman (1900–75)

THE ETERNAL FATHER

1 WHAT shall I do my God to love,
   My Saviour, and the world's, to praise?
 Whose tenderest compassions move
   To me and all the fallen race,
 Whose mercy is divinely free
 For all the fallen race, and me!

2 I long to know, and to make known,
   The heights and depths of love divine,
 The kindness thou to me hast shown,
   Whose every sin was counted thine:
 My God for me resigned his breath;
 He died to save my soul from death.

3 How shall I thank thee for the grace
   On me and all mankind bestowed?
 O that my every breath were praise!
   O that my heart were filled with God!
 My heart would then with love o'erflow,
 And all my life thy glory show.

Charles Wesley (1707–88)

God's Revealing and Transforming Love

Melody and most of the harmony from
John Randall's *Psalm and Hymn Tunes* (1794)
Probably by Charles Collignon (1725–85)

For this tune in a higher key see No. 43

THE ETERNAL FATHER

1 THY ceaseless, unexhausted love,
    Unmerited and free,
  Delights our evil to remove,
    And help our misery.

2 Thou waitest to be gracious still;
    Thou dost with sinners bear,
  That, saved, we may thy goodness feel,
    And all thy grace declare.

3 Thy goodness and thy truth to me,
    To every soul, abound,
  A vast, unfathomable sea,
    Where all our thoughts are drowned.

4 Its streams the whole creation reach,
    So plenteous is the store,
  Enough for all, enough for each,
    Enough for evermore.

5 Faithful, O Lord, thy mercies are,
    A rock that cannot move;
  A thousand promises declare
    Thy constancy of love.

6 Throughout the universe it reigns,
    Unalterably sure;
  And while the truth of God remains
    The goodness must endure.

Charles Wesley (1707–88)

God's Revealing and Transforming Love

49

EISENACH L.M.

Melody by J. H. Schein (1628)
Harmony adapted from J. S. Bach (1685–1750)

For this tune in a lower key see No. 21

THE ETERNAL FATHER

1 ETERNAL Power, whose high abode
  Becomes the grandeur of a God;
    Infinite length beyond the bounds
    Where stars revolve their little rounds!

2 Thee while the first archangel sings,
  He hides his face beneath his wings,
    And throngs of shining thrones around
    Fall worshipping, and spread the ground.

3 Lord, what shall earth and ashes do?
  We would adore our Maker too;
    From sin and dust to thee we cry,
    The Great, the Holy, and the High!

4 Earth from afar has heard thy fame,
  And babes have learnt to lisp thy name;
    But O the glories of thy mind
    Leave all our soaring thoughts behind!

5 God is in heaven, we dwell below;
  Be short our tunes, our words be few;
    A sacred reverence checks our songs,
    And praise sits silent on our tongues.

Isaac Watts (1674–1748)
alt. *John Wesley* (1703–91)

Melody from T. Moore's
Psalm–Singer's Pocket Companion
(Glasgow *c.* 1756)

For this tune in a lower key see No. 328(i)

THE ETERNAL FATHER

1 BEHOLD, the mountain of the Lord
    In latter days shall rise
On mountain-tops, above the hills,
    And draw the wondering eyes.

2 To this the joyful nations round,
    All tribes and tongues, shall flow;
Up to the hill of God, they'll say,
    And to his house, we'll go.

3 The beam that shines from Zion's hill
    Shall lighten every land;
The King who reigns in Salem's towers
    Shall all the world command.

4 Among the nations he shall judge;
    His judgements truth shall guide;
His sceptre shall protect the just,
    And quell the sinner's pride.

5 No strife shall vex Messiah's reign
    Or mar the peaceful years;
To ploughshares men shall beat their swords,
    To pruning-hooks their spears.

6 No longer hosts, encountering hosts,
    Shall crowds of slain deplore;
They hang the trumpet in the hall,
    And study war no more.

7 Come then, O come from every land
    To worship at his shrine;
And, walking in the light of God,
    With holy beauties shine.

Scottish Paraphrases (1745 and 1781) alt.
based on Isaiah 2:2-5 and Micah 4:1-5

God's Justice and Perfection

51

WESTMINSTER (TURLE) C.M.

J. Turle (1802–82)

THE ETERNAL FATHER

1 MY God, how wonderful thou art,
   Thy majesty how bright,
   How beautiful thy mercy-seat,
   In depths of burning light!

2 How dread are thine eternal years,
   O everlasting Lord,
   By prostrate spirits day and night
   Incessantly adored!

3 How beautiful, how beautiful
   The sight of thee must be,
   Thine endless wisdom, boundless power,
   And awesome purity!

4 O how I fear thee, living God,
   With deepest, tenderest fears,
   And worship thee with trembling hope
   And penitential tears!

5 Yet I may love thee too, O Lord,
   Almighty as thou art,
   For thou hast stooped to ask of me
   The love of my poor heart.

6 No earthly father loves like thee;
   No mother, e'er so mild,
   Bears and forbears as thou hast done
   With me, thy sinful child.

7 Father of Jesus, love's reward,
   What rapture will it be
   Prostrate before thy throne to lie,
   And gaze, and gaze on thee.

Frederick William Faber (1814–63)

52(i)

LLANGLOFFAN   7.6.7.6.D.

Welsh hymn melody
Harmonised by David Evans (1874–1948)

THE ETERNAL FATHER

1 O GOD, thou art the Father
   Of all that have believed:
   From whom all hosts of angels
   Have life and power received.
   O God, thou art the Maker
   Of all created things,
   The righteous Judge of judges,
   The Almighty King of kings.

2 High in the heavenly Zion
   Thou reignest God adored;
   And in the coming glory
   Thou shalt be Sovereign Lord.
   Beyond our ken thou shinest,
   The everlasting Light;
   Ineffable in loving,
   Unthinkable in might.

3 Thou to the meek and lowly
   Thy secrets dost unfold;
   O God, thou doest all things,
   All things both new and old.
   I walk secure and blessèd
   In every clime or coast,
   In name of God the Father,
   And Son, and Holy Ghost.

Ascribed to *Columba* (521–97)
tr. *Duncan MacGregor* (1854–1923)

May also be sung to No. 125, CRÜGER (HERRNHUT)

God's Justice and Perfection

52(ii)

DURROW 7.6.7.6.D.

Traditional Irish melody
Harmonised by William France (1912–   )

THE ETERNAL FATHER

1 O GOD, thou art the Father
   Of all that have believed:
From whom all hosts of angels
   Have life and power received.
O God, thou art the Maker
   Of all created things,
The righteous Judge of judges,
   The Almighty King of kings.

2 High in the heavenly Zion
   Thou reignest God adored;
And in the coming glory
   Thou shalt be Sovereign Lord.
Beyond our ken thou shinest,
   The everlasting Light;
Ineffable in loving,
   Unthinkable in might.

3 Thou to the meek and lowly
   Thy secrets dost unfold;
O God, thou doest all things,
   All things both new and old.
I walk secure and blessèd
   In every clime or coast,
In name of God the Father,
   And Son, and Holy Ghost.

Ascribed to *Columba* (521–97)
tr. *Duncan MacGregor* (1854–1923)

May also be sung to No. 125, CRÜGER (HERRNHUT)

God's Justice and Perfection

53

CANNOCK L.M.

Walter K. Stanton (1891–1978)

1 GOD is the refuge of his saints,
    When storms of sharp distress invade;
Ere we can offer our complaints,
    Behold him present with his aid!

2 Let mountains from their seats be hurled
    Down to the deep, and buried there,
Convulsions shake the solid world,
    Our faith shall never yield to fear.

3 Loud may the troubled ocean roar;
    In sacred peace our souls abide;
While every nation, every shore,
    Trembles, and dreads the swelling tide.

4 There is a stream, whose gentle flow
    Makes glad the city of our God,
Life, love, and joy still gliding through,
    And watering our divine abode.

5 This sacred stream, thy vital word,
    Thus all our raging fear controls;
Sweet peace thy promises afford,
    And give new strength to fainting souls.

6 Zion enjoys her Monarch's love,
    Secure against the threatening hour;
Nor can her *firm foundation* move,
    Built on his faithfulness and power.

*May also be sung
to No. 562,
LASUS*

Isaac Watts (1674–1748)
based on Psalm 46

THE ETERNAL FATHER

54

Melody attributed to Martin Luther (1483–1546);
as in Schumann's *Geistliche Lieder* (1539).
Harmony mostly from
Michael Praetorius (1571–1621)

1 O GOD, thy being who can sound?
   Thee to perfection who can know?
O height immense! No words are found
   Thy countless attributes to show.

2 Unfathomable depths thou art!
   O plunge me in thy mercy's sea;
Void of true wisdom is my heart:
   With love embrace and cover me.

3 Eternity thy fountain was,
   Which, like thee, no beginning knew;
Thou wast ere time began his race,
   Ere glowed with stars the ethereal blue.

4 Unchangeable, all-perfect Lord,
   Essential life's unbounded sea,
What lives and moves lives by thy word;
   It lives, and moves, and is from thee.

5 Parent of good, thy bounteous hand
   Incessant blessings down distils,
And all in air, or sea, or land
   With plenteous food and gladness fills.

6 Greatness unspeakable is thine,
   Thou sun, whose undiminished ray,
When short-lived worlds are lost, shall shine
   When earth and heav'n are fled away.

Ernst Lange (1650–1727)
tr. *John Wesley (1703–91)*
alt. *Rupert E. Davies (1909–   )*

God's Justice and Perfection

55(i)

JOSIAH 7.6.7.6.7.7.7.6.

William Arnold (1768–1832)
(slightly adapted)

THE ETERNAL FATHER

1 PRAISE the Lord who reigns above
   And keeps his court below;
Praise the holy God of love,
   And all his greatness show;
Praise him for his noble deeds,
   Praise him for his matchless power:
Him from whom all good proceeds
   Let earth and heaven adore.

2 Celebrate the eternal God
   With harp and psaltery,
Timbrels soft and cymbals loud
   In his high praise agree:
Praise him every tuneful string;
   All the reach of heavenly art,
All the powers of music bring,
   The music of the heart.

3 Him, in whom they move and live,
   Let every creature sing,
Glory to their Maker give,
   And homage to their King:
Hallowed be his name beneath,
   As in heaven on earth adored;
Praise the Lord in every breath,
   Let all things praise the Lord.

Charles Wesley (1707–88)
based on Psalm 150

55(ii)

FLANDERS 7.6.7.6.7.7.7.6.

Donald Swann (1923–)

1 PRAISE the Lord who reigns a-bove And keeps his court be-low; Praise the ho-ly God of love, And all his greatness show;

THE ETERNAL FATHER

Praise him for his no-ble deeds, Praise him for his match-less power: Him from whom all good pro-ceeds Let earth and heaven a-dore.

2 Celebrate the eternal God
   With harp and psaltery,
Timbrels soft and cymbals loud
   In his high praise agree:
Praise him every tuneful string;
   All the reach of heavenly art,
All the powers of music bring,
   The music of the heart.

3 Him, in whom they move and live,
   Let every creature sing,
Glory to their Maker give,
   And homage to their King:
Hallowed be his name beneath,
   As in heaven on earth adored;
Praise the Lord in every breath,
   Let all things praise the Lord.

Charles Wesley (1707–88) based on Psalm 150

God's Justice and Perfection

THE ETERNAL FATHER

1 PRAISE to the living God!
    All praisèd be his name,
Who was, and is, and is to be,
    For aye the same!
The one eternal God
    Ere aught that now appears:
The First, the Last, beyond all thought
    His timeless years!

2 Formless, all lovely forms
    Declare his loveliness;
Holy, no holiness of earth
    Can his express.
Lo, he is Lord of all!
    Creation speaks his praise,
And everywhere, above, below,
    His will obeys.

3 His Spirit floweth free,
    High surging where it will:
In prophet's word he spake of old,
    He speaketh still.
Established is his law,
    And changeless it shall stand,
Deep writ upon the human heart,
    On sea, on land.

4 Eternal life hath he
    Implanted in the soul;
His love shall be our strength and stay,
    While ages roll.
Praise to the living God!
    All praisèd be his name,
Who was, and is, and is to be,
    For aye the same.

Medieval Jewish Doxology
tr. *Max Landsberg* (1845–1928) and
Newton Mann (1836–1926)

57(i)
BARNARDO 7.7.11.8. Alan Gulliver (1958–)

Unison

1 SING a new song to the Lord, _____ He to whom won-ders be – long! _____ Re – joice in his triumph and tell of his power O sing to the Lord a new song! _____

57(ii)
ONSLOW SQUARE 7.7.11.8. D. G. Wilson (1940–)

Unison

1 SING a new song to the Lord,__ He to whom won-ders be-

THE ETERNAL FATHER

long!___ Re - joice___ in his tri-umph_ and tell___ of his
power___ O sing___ to the Lord___ a new song!___
song!_____

2 Now to the ends of the earth
   See his salvation is shown;
   And still he remembers his mercy and truth,
   Unchanging in love to his own.

3 Sing a new song and rejoice,
   Publish his praises abroad!
   Let voices in chorus, with trumpet and horn,
   Resound for the joy of the Lord!

4 Join with the hills and the sea
   Thunders of praise to prolong!
   In judgement and justice he comes to the earth—
   O sing to the Lord a new song!

Timothy Dudley-Smith (1926–   )
based on Psalm 98

God's Justice and Perfection

58(i)

CHURCH TRIUMPHANT L.M.   James William Elliott (1833–1915)

For this tune in a higher key see No. 279

58(ii)

NIAGARA L.M.   Robert Jackson (1840–1914)

For this tune in a lower key see No. 619(i)

THE ETERNAL FATHER

1 THE Lord is King! Lift up thy voice,
   O earth, and all ye heavens, rejoice!
      From world to world the joy shall ring:
      'The Lord omnipotent is King!'

2 The Lord is King! Who then shall dare
   Resist his will, distrust his care,
      Or murmur at his wise decrees,
      Or doubt his royal promises?

3 The Lord is King! Child of the dust,
   The Judge of all the earth is just;
      Holy and true are all his ways;
      Let every creature speak his praise.

4 He reigns! Ye saints, exalt your strains;
   Your God is King, your Father reigns:
      And he is at the Father's side,
      The Man of love, the Crucified.

5 Alike pervaded by his eye
   All parts of his dominion lie,
      This world of ours and worlds unseen:
      How thin the boundary between!

6 One Lord, one empire, all secures:
   He reigns, and life and death are yours;
      Through earth and heaven one song shall ring:
      'The Lord omnipotent is King!'

Josiah Conder (1789–1855)

God's Justice and Perfection

From *The Parish Choir* (1851)
(with altered rhythms)

THE ETERNAL FATHER

1 THE Lord Jehovah reigns;
    His throne is built on high,
  The garments he assumes
    Are light and majesty:
His glories shine with beams so bright,
No mortal eye can bear the sight.

2   The thunders of his hand
    Keep the wide world in awe;
  His wrath and justice stand
    To guard his holy law;
And where his love resolves to bless,
His truth confirms and seals the grace.

3   Through all his mighty works
    Amazing wisdom shines,
  Confounds the powers of hell,
    And breaks their dark designs;
Strong is his arm, and shall fulfil
His great decrees and sovereign will.

4   And will this sovereign King
    Of Glory condescend?
  And will he write his name
    My Father and my Friend?
I love his name, I love his word—
Join all my powers to praise the Lord.

Isaac Watts (1674–1748)

God's Justice and Perfection

60(i)
TIMELESS LOVE 8.7.8.7.77.

Norman L. Warren (1934–   )

Unison

Who is like him? Praise the Lord!

60(ii)
ALL SAINTS 8.7.8.7.77.

Adapted by W. H. Monk (1823–89) from
a melody in *Geistreiches Gesangbuch*
(Darmstadt, 1698) (harmony slightly altered)

THE ETERNAL FATHER

1 TIMELESS love! We sing the story,
   Praise his wonders, tell his worth;
Love more fair than heaven's glory,
   Love more firm than ancient earth!
Tell his faithfulness abroad:
Who is like him? Praise the Lord!

2 By his faithfulness surrounded,
   North and south his hand proclaim;
Earth and heaven formed and founded,
   Skies and seas, declare his name!
Wind and storm obey his word:
Who is like him? Praise the Lord!

3 Truth and righteousness enthrone him,
   Just and equal are his ways;
More than happy, those who own him,
   More than joy, their songs of praise!
Sun and Shield and great Reward:
Who is like him? Praise the Lord!

Timothy Dudley-Smith (1926–   )
based on Psalm 89:1–18

God's Justice and Perfection

61

OLD 100th L.M.

Melody of Psalm 134 in *Genevan Psalter* (1551), with English (1563) form of rhythm in last line

For this tune in a higher key see No. 1

THE ETERNAL FATHER

1 SING to the Lord with joyful voice;
  Let every land his name adore;
The farthest isles shall send the noise
  Across the ocean to the shore.

2 Nations, attend before his throne
  With solemn fear, with sacred joy;
Know that the Lord is God alone;
  He can create, and he destroy.

3 His sovereign power, without our aid,
  Made us of clay, and formed us men;
And when like wandering sheep we strayed,
  He brought us to his fold again.

4 We are his people, we his care,
  Our souls and all our mortal frame;
What lasting honours shall we rear,
  Almighty Maker, to thy name?

5 We'll crowd thy gates with thankful songs,
  High as the heavens our voices raise;
And earth with her ten thousand tongues
  Shall fill thy courts with sounding praise.

6 Wide as the world is thy command,
  Vast as eternity thy love;
Firm as a rock thy truth must stand
  When rolling years shall cease to move.

Isaac Watts (1674–1748)
based on Psalm 100

John W. David (1837–1902)

THE ETERNAL FATHER

1 CAPTAIN of Israel's host, and Guide
   Of all who seek the land above,
   Beneath thy shadow we abide,
   The cloud of thy protecting love;
   Our strength, thy grace; our rule, thy word;
   Our end, the glory of the Lord.

2 By thine unerring Spirit led,
   We shall not in the desert stray;
   We shall not full direction need,
   Nor miss our providential way;
   As far from danger as from fear,
   While love, almighty love, is near.

Charles Wesley (1707–88)

May also be sung to No. 500, ABINGDON

God's Patience and Guidance

63(i)

MEINE HOFFNUNG 87.87.337.

Later form of a melody from J. Neander's
Alpha and Omega (1680). Harmony from
The Chorale Book for England (1863)

63(ii)

MICHAEL 87.87.337.
Unison

Herbert Howells (1892–1983)

THE ETERNAL FATHER

1 ALL my hope on God is founded;
    He doth still my trust renew.
  Me through change and chance he guideth,
    Only good and only true.
        God unknown,
        He alone
    Calls my heart to be his own.

2 Human pride and earthly glory,
    Sword and crown betray our trust;
  What with care and toil we fashion,
    Tower and temple, fall to dust.
        But God's power,
        Hour by hour,
    Is my temple and my tower.

3 God's great goodness aye endureth,
    Deep his wisdom passing thought;
  Splendour, light, and life attend him,
    Beauty springeth out of naught.
        Evermore
        From his store
    New-born worlds rise and adore.

4 Daily doth the almighty giver
    Bounteous gifts on us bestow;
  His desire our soul delighteth,
    Pleasure leads us where we go.
        Love doth stand
        At his hand;
    Joy doth wait on his command.

5 Still from man to God eternal
    Sacrifice of praise be done,
  High above all praises praising
    For the gift of Christ his Son.
        Christ doth call
        One and all;
    Ye who follow shall not fall.

Robert Bridges (1844–1930) alt.
based on *Joachim Neander* (1650–80)

63(iii)
GROESWEN 87.87.337.

John A. Lloyd (1815–74)

THE ETERNAL FATHER

1 ALL my hope on God is founded;
      He doth still my trust renew.
   Me through change and chance he guideth,
      Only good and only true.
         God unknown,
         He alone
      Calls my heart to be his own.

2 Human pride and earthly glory,
      Sword and crown betray our trust;
   What with care and toil we fashion,
      Tower and temple, fall to dust.
         But God's power,
         Hour by hour,
      Is my temple and my tower.

3 God's great goodness aye endureth,
      Deep his wisdom passing thought;
   Splendour, light, and life attend him,
      Beauty springeth out of naught.
         Evermore
         From his store
      New-born worlds rise and adore.

4 Daily doth the almighty giver
      Bounteous gifts on us bestow;
   His desire our soul delighteth,
      Pleasure leads us where we go.
         Love doth stand
         At his hand;
      Joy doth wait on his command.

5 Still from man to God eternal
      Sacrifice of praise be done,
   High above all praises praising
      For the gift of Christ his Son.
         Christ doth call
         One and all;
      Ye who follow shall not fall.

Robert Bridges (1844–1930) alt.
based on *Joachim Neander* (1650–80)

God's Patience and Guidance

64

ARFON 8.7.8.7.D.

Traditional melody, found
both in Wales and in France

THE ETERNAL FATHER

1 GOD has spoken—by his prophets,
   Spoken his unchanging word,
Each from age to age proclaiming
   God, the one, the righteous Lord.
'Mid the world's despair and turmoil
   One firm anchor holds us fast:
God is King, his throne eternal,
   God the first, and God the last.

2 God has spoken—by Christ Jesus,
   Christ, the everlasting Son,
Brightness of the Father's glory,
   With the Father ever one;
Spoken by the Word incarnate,
   God from God, ere time began,
Light from Light, to earth descending,
   Man, revealing God to man.

3 God is speaking—by his Spirit,
   Speaking to the hearts of men,
In the age-long word expounding
   God's own message, now as then,
Through the rise and fall of nations
   One sure faith yet standing fast;
God still speaks, his word unchanging,
   God the first, and God the last.

George Wallace Briggs (1875–1959) alt.

God's Patience and Guidance

65(i)
LONDON NEW C.M.

Melody from *Scottish Psalter* (1635)
as adapted in J. Playford's *Psalms
and Hymns in Solemn Musick* (1671)

65(ii)
IRISH C.M.

Melody from *Hymns and
Sacred Poems* (Dublin, 1749)

THE ETERNAL FATHER

1 GOD moves in a mysterious way
     His wonders to perform;
   He plants his footsteps in the sea,
     And rides upon the storm.

2 Deep in unfathomable mines
     Of never-failing skill
   He treasures up his bright designs,
     And works his sovereign will.

3 Ye fearful saints, fresh courage take,
     The clouds ye so much dread
   Are big with mercy, and shall break
     In blessings on your head.

4 Judge not the Lord by feeble sense,
     But trust him for his grace;
   Behind a frowning providence
     He hides a smiling face.

5 His purposes will ripen fast,
     Unfolding every hour;
   The bud may have a bitter taste,
     But sweet will be the flower.

6 Blind unbelief is sure to err,
     And scan his work in vain;
   God is his own interpreter,
     And he will make it plain.

          William Cowper (1731–1800)

God's Patience and Guidance

66
GREAT IS THY FAITHFULNESS

11.10.11.10.
and Refrain

W. M. Runyan (1870–1957)

Refrain

Great is thy faith-ful-ness! Great is thy faith-ful-ness!

Morn-ing by morn-ing new mer-cies I see;

THE ETERNAL FATHER

All I have need-ed thy hand has pro-vi-ded,

Great is thy faith-ful-ness, Lord, un-to me.

1 GREAT is thy faithfulness, O God my Father,
   There is no shadow of turning with thee;
Thou changest not, thy compassions, they fail not;
   As thou hast been thou for ever wilt be:
   Great is thy faithfulness! Great is thy faithfulness!
   Morning by morning new mercies I see;
   All I have needed thy hand has provided.
   Great is thy faithfulness, Lord, unto me.

2 Summer and winter, and springtime and harvest,
   Sun, moon and stars in their courses above,
Join with all nature in manifold witness
   To thy great faithfulness, mercy and love:

3 Pardon for sin and a peace that endureth,
   Thy own dear presence to cheer and to guide;
Strength for today and bright hope for tomorrow,
   Blessings all mine, with ten thousand beside!

Thomas O. Chisholm (1866–1960)

God's Patience and Guidance

67(i)

ALBERTA   10.4.10.4.10.10.   William H. Harris (1883–1973)

Unison

67(ii)

LUX BENIGNA   10.4.10.4.10.10.   J. B. Dykes (1823–76)

THE ETERNAL FATHER

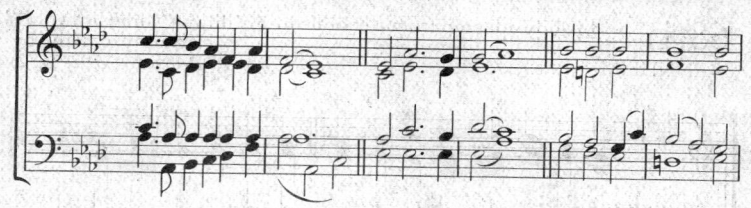

1 LEAD, kindly Light, amid the encircling gloom,
      Lead thou me on;
The night is dark, and I am far from home,
      Lead thou me on.
Keep thou my feet; I do not ask to see
The distant scene; one step enough for me.

2 I was not ever thus, nor prayed that thou
      Should'st lead me on;
I loved to choose and see my path; but now
      Lead thou me on.
I loved the garish day, and, spite of fears,
Pride ruled my will: remember not past years.

3 So long thy power hath blessed me, sure it still
      Will lead me on,
O'er moor and fen, o'er crag and torrent, till
      The night is gone;
And with the morn those angel faces smile,
Which I have loved long since, and lost awhile.

John Henry Newman (1801–90)

God's Patience and Guidance

68(i)
MANNHEIM 8.7.8.7.8.7.

Melody adapted from a chorale in F. Filitz's *Choralbuch* (1847)
Harmony chiefly by
Lowell Mason (1792–1872)

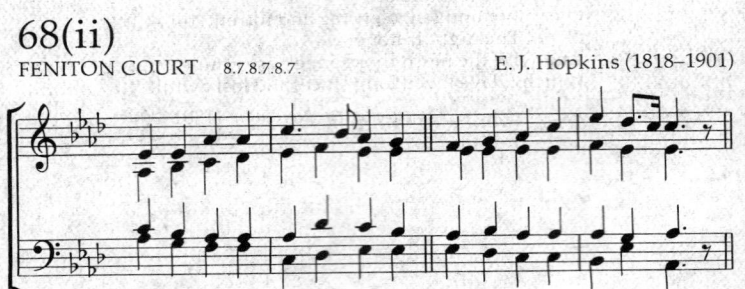

68(ii)
FENITON COURT 8.7.8.7.8.7.

E. J. Hopkins (1818–1901)

THE ETERNAL FATHER

1 LEAD us, heavenly Father, lead us
   O'er the world's tempestuous sea;
Guard us, guide us, keep us, feed us,
   For we have no help but thee,
Yet possessing every blessing
   If our God our Father be.

2 Saviour, breathe forgiveness o'er us;
   All our weakness thou dost know,
Thou didst tread this earth before us,
   Thou didst feel its keenest woe;
Tempted, taunted, yet undaunted,
   Through the desert thou didst go.

3 Spirit of our God, descending,
   Fill our hearts with heavenly joy,
Love with every passion blending,
   Pleasure that can never cloy;
Thus provided, pardoned, guided,
   Nothing can our peace destroy.

James Edmeston (1791–1867) alt.

God's Patience and Guidance

69(i)
DOMINUS REGIT ME 8.7.8.7 (Iambic) J. B. Dykes (1823–76)

69(ii)
CLIFF LANE 8.7.8.7 (Iambic) Brian R. Hoare (1935–   )

THE ETERNAL FATHER

1 THE King of love my Shepherd is,
   Whose goodness faileth never;
 I nothing lack if I am his
   And he is mine for ever.

2 Where streams of living water flow
   My ransomed soul he leadeth,
 And where the verdant pastures grow
   With food celestial feedeth.

3 Perverse and foolish oft I strayed,
   But yet in love he sought me,
 And on his shoulder gently laid,
   And home rejoicing brought me.

4 In death's dark vale I fear no ill
   With thee, dear Lord, beside me;
 Thy rod and staff my comfort still,
   Thy cross before to guide me.

5 Thou spread'st a table in my sight;
   Thy unction grace bestoweth;
 And O what transport of delight
   From thy pure chalice floweth!

6 And so through all the length of days
   Thy goodness faileth never:
 Good Shepherd, may I sing thy praise
   Within thy house for ever.

Henry Williams Baker (1821–77)
based on Psalm 23

God's Patience and Guidance

70

CRIMOND C.M.

Melody attributed to Jessie S. Irvine (1836–87)
Harmonised by William McKie (1901-84)

Psalm 23

1 THE Lord's my Shepherd, I'll not want;
    He makes me down to lie
In pastures green; he leadeth me
    The quiet waters by.

2 My soul he doth restore again,
    And me to walk doth make
Within the paths of righteousness,
    E'en for his own name's sake.

3 Yea, though I walk in death's dark vale,
    Yet will I fear no ill;
For thou art with me, and thy rod
    And staff me comfort still.

4 My table thou hast furnishèd
    In presence of my foes;
My head thou dost with oil anoint,
    And my cup overflows.

5 Goodness and mercy all my life
    Shall surely follow me,
And in God's house for evermore
    My dwelling-place shall be.

Scottish Psalter (1650)

May also be sung to No. 33, KILMARNOCK

THE ETERNAL FATHER

71

WINSCOTT L.M.

S. S. Wesley (1810–76)

1 LORD, you have searched and known my ways
   And understood my thought from far;
How can I rightly sound your praise
   Or tell how great your wonders are?

2 Besetting me, before, behind,
   Upon my life your hand is laid;
Caught in the compass of your mind
   Are all the creatures you have made.

3 Such knowledge is too wonderful,
   Too high for me to understand—
Enough that the Unsearchable
   Has searched my heart and held my hand.

Peter G. Jarvis (1925–)
based on Psalm 139:1–6

God's Patience and Guidance

72

1 IN all my vast concerns with thee,
    In vain my soul would try
To shun thy presence, Lord, or flee
    The notice of thine eye.

2 Thy all-surrounding sight surveys
    My rising and my rest,
My public walks, my private ways,
    The secrets of my breast.

3 My thoughts lie open to thee, Lord,
    Before they're formed within;
And, ere my lips pronounce the word,
    Thou know'st the sense I mean.

4 O wondrous knowledge, deep and high;
    Where can a creature hide?
Within thy circling arms I lie,
    Beset on every side.

5 So let thy grace surround me still,
    And like a bulwark prove,
To guard my soul from every ill,
    Secured by sovereign love.

Isaac Watts (1674–1748)
based on Psalm 139

THE ETERNAL FATHER

73

WILTSHIRE C.M.

George T. Smart (1776–1867)

1 THROUGH all the changing scenes of life,
    In trouble and in joy,
    The praises of my God shall still
      My heart and tongue employ.

2 Of his deliverance I will boast,
    Till all that are distressed
  From my example comfort take,
    And charm their griefs to rest.

3 O magnify the Lord with me,
    With me exalt his name;
  When in distress to him I called,
    He to my rescue came.

4 The hosts of God encamp around
    The dwellings of the just;
  Deliverance he affords to all
    Who on his succour trust.

5 O make but trial of his love;
    Experience will decide
  How blest are they, and only they,
    Who in his truth confide.

6 Fear him, ye saints, and you will then
    Have nothing else to fear;
  Make you his service your delight,
    Your wants shall be his care.

Nahum Tate (1652–1715) and
Nicholas Brady (1659–1726)
based on Psalm 34

God's Patience and Guidance

74(i)

EVELYNS 6.5.6.5.D.

W. H. Monk (1823–89)

THE ETERNAL WORD

1 AT the name of Jesus
      Every knee shall bow,
  Every tongue confess him
      King of Glory now.
  'Tis the Father's pleasure
      We should call him Lord,
  Who from the beginning
      Was the mighty Word.

2 Humbled for a season,
      To receive a name
  From the lips of sinners
      Unto whom he came,
  Faithfully he bore it
      Spotless to the last,
  Brought it back victorious
      When from death he passed:

3 Bore it up triumphant
      With its human light,
  Through all ranks of creatures
      To the central height,
  To the throne of Godhead,
      To the Father's breast;
  Filled it with the glory
      Of that perfect rest.

4 In your hearts enthrone him;
      There let him subdue
  All that is not holy,
      All that is not true;
  Crown him as your captain
      In temptation's hour:
  Let his will enfold you
      In its light and power.

5 For this same Lord Jesus
      Shall return again,
  With his Father's glory,
      With his angel train;
  All the wreaths of empire
      Meet upon his brow,
  And our hearts confess him
      King of Glory now.

Caroline Maria Noel (1817–77) alt.

The Eternal Glory of the Word

74(ii)

CAMBERWELL 6.5.6.5.D.

Michael Brierley (1932–   )

Unison (Marziale—moderately fast)

THE ETERNAL WORD

1 AT the name of Jesus
    Every knee shall bow,
Every tongue confess him
    King of Glory now.
'Tis the Father's pleasure
    We should call him Lord,
Who from the beginning
    Was the mighty Word.

2 Humbled for a season,
    To receive a name
From the lips of sinners
    Unto whom he came,
Faithfully he bore it
    Spotless to the last,
Brought it back victorious
    When from death he passed:

3 Bore it up triumphant
    With its human light,
Through all ranks of creatures
    To the central height,
To the throne of Godhead,
    To the Father's breast;
Filled it with the glory
    Of that perfect rest.

4 In your hearts enthrone him;
    There let him subdue
All that is not holy,
    All that is not true;
Crown him as your captain
    In temptation's hour:
Let his will enfold you
    In its light and power.

5 For this same Lord Jesus
    Shall return again,
With his Father's glory,
    With his angel train;
All the wreaths of empire
    Meet upon his brow,
And our hearts confess him
    King of Glory now.

Caroline Maria Noel (1817–77) alt.

The Eternal Glory of the Word

74(iii)

CUDDESDON 6.5.6.5.D.

W. H. Ferguson (1874–1950)

Unison

THE ETERNAL WORD

1 AT the name of Jesus
      Every knee shall bow,
  Every tongue confess him
      King of Glory now.
  'Tis the Father's pleasure
      We should call him Lord,
  Who from the beginning
      Was the mighty Word.

2 Humbled for a season,
      To receive a name
  From the lips of sinners
      Unto whom he came,
  Faithfully he bore it
      Spotless to the last,
  Brought it back victorious
      When from death he passed:

3 Bore it up triumphant
      With its human light,
  Through all ranks of creatures
      To the central height,
  To the throne of Godhead,
      To the Father's breast;
  Filled it with the glory
      Of that perfect rest.

4 In your hearts enthrone him;
      There let him subdue
  All that is not holy,
      All that is not true;
  Crown him as your captain
      In temptation's hour:
  Let his will enfold you
      In its light and power.

5 For this same Lord Jesus
      Shall return again,
  With his Father's glory,
      With his angel train;
  All the wreaths of empire
      Meet upon his brow,
  And our hearts confess him
      King of Glory now.

Caroline Maria Noel (1817–77) alt.

75

THE ETERNAL WORD

1 CHRIST, our King before creation,
  Life, before all life began,
Crowned in deep humiliation
  By your partners in God's plan,
Make us humble in believing,
  And, believing, bold to pray:
'Lord, forgive our self-deceiving,
  Come and reign in us today!'

2 Lord of time and Lord of history,
  Giving, when the world despairs,
Faith to wrestle with the mystery
  Of a God who loves and cares,
Make us humble in believing,
  And, believing, bold to pray:
'Lord, by grace beyond conceiving,
  Come and reign in us today!'

3 Word that ends our long debating,
  Life of God which sets us free,
Through your body recreating
  Life as life is meant to be,
Make us humble in believing,
  And, believing, bold to pray:
'Lord, in us your aim achieving,
  Come and reign in us today!'

Ivor H. Jones (1934–)

76
KILMARNOCK C.M.

Melody, and almost all the harmony,
by Neil Dougall (1776–1862)

For this tune in a higher key see No. 758(ii)

1 CAN we by searching find out God
    Or formulate his ways?
  Can numbers measure what he is
    Or words contain his praise?

2 Although his being is too bright
    For human eyes to scan,
  His meaning lights our shadowed world
    Through Christ, the Son of Man.

3 Our boastfulness is turned to shame,
    Our profit counts as loss,
  When earthly values stand beside
    The manger and the cross.

4 We there may recognise his light,
    May kindle in its rays,
  Find there the source of penitence,
    The starting-point for praise.

5 There God breaks in upon our search,
    Makes birth and death his own:
  He speaks to us in human terms
    To make his glory known.

Elizabeth Cosnett (1936–   )

May also be sung to No. 703, EPWORTH

THE ETERNAL WORD

77

ANTIOCH C.M. (Extended)

Mostly from
W. Holford's *Voce di Melodia* (*c*.1834)
(with echoes of Handel?)

Small notes organ only

(and heav'n and na - ture sing)

1 JOY to the world, the Lord is come!
  Let earth receive her King;
  Let every heart prepare him room,
    And heaven and nature sing,
      And heaven and nature sing,
        And heaven, and heaven and nature sing.

2 Joy to the world, the Saviour reigns!
  Let all their songs employ;
  While fields and floods, rocks, hills and plains
    Repeat the sounding joy,
      Repeat the sounding joy,
        Repeat, repeat the sounding joy.

3 He rules the world with truth and grace,
  And makes the nations prove
  The glories of his righteousness
    And wonders of his love,
      And wonders of his love,
        And wonders, wonders of his love.

Isaac Watts (1674–1748)
based on Psalm 98

The Eternal Glory of the Word

78

EASTVIEW 66.66.88

J. Vernon Lee (1892–1959)

THE ETERNAL WORD

The Offices of Christ

1 JOIN all the glorious names
    Of wisdom, love, and power,
  That ever mortals knew,
    That angels ever bore:
  All are too mean to speak his worth,
  Too mean to set my *Saviour* forth.

2 But O what gentle terms,
    What condescending ways
  Doth our *Redeemer* use
    To teach his heavenly grace!
  Mine eyes with joy and wonder see
  What forms of love he bears for me.

3 Great *Prophet* of my God,
    My tongue would bless thy name;
  By thee the joyful news
    Of our salvation came:
  The joyful news of sins forgiven,
  Of hell subdued and peace with heaven.

4 Jesus my great *High-Priest*
    Offered his blood and died;
  My guilty conscience seeks
    No sacrifice beside:
  His powerful blood did once atone,
  And now it pleads before the throne.

5 My dear almighty *Lord*,
    My *Conqueror* and my *King*,
  Thy sceptre and thy sword,
    Thy reign of grace, I sing;
  Thine is the power: behold I sit
  In willing bonds before thy feet.

6 Now let my soul arise,
    And tread the tempter down;
  My *Captain* leads me forth
    To conquest and a crown.
  A feeble saint shall win the day,
  Though death and hell obstruct the way.

7 Should all the hosts of death,
    And powers of hell unknown,
  Put their most dreadful forms
    Of rage and mischief on,
  I shall be safe, for *Christ* displays
  Superior power, and guardian grace.

Isaac Watts (1674–1748)

May also be sung to No. 59, ST JOHN (ADORATION)

The Eternal Glory of the Word

79

DIVINUM MYSTERIUM   8.7.8.7.8.7.7.   Late form of a Plainsong Melody, as given in *Piae Cantiones* (1582)

THE ETERNAL WORD

1 OF the Father's love begotten
  Ere the worlds began to be,
He is Alpha and Omega,
  He the source, the ending he,
Of the things that are, that have been,
  And that future years shall see,
    Evermore and evermore.

2 By his word was all created;
  He commanded and 'twas done;
Earth and sky and boundless ocean,
  Universe of three in one,
All that sees the moon's soft radiance,
  All that breathes beneath the sun,
    Evermore and evermore.

3 This is he whom seers in old time
  Chanted of with one accord,
Whom the voices of the prophets
  Promised in their faithful word;
Now he shines, the long-expected;
  Let creation praise its Lord,
    Evermore and evermore.

4 O ye heights of heaven, adore him;
  Angel hosts, his praises sing;
All dominions, bow before him,
  And extol our God and King;
Let no tongue on earth be silent,
  Every voice in concert sing,
    Evermore and evermore!

Prudentius (348–*c.* 410)
tr. *John Mason Neale* (1818–66) and
Henry Williams Baker (1821–77)

The Eternal Glory of the Word

80

REGENT SQUARE 8.7.8.7.8.7.

Henry Smart (1813–79)

For this tune in a lower key see No. 13(ii)

THE ETERNAL WORD

1 TO the Name of our salvation,
　　Laud and honour let us pay,
　Which for many a generation
　　Hid in God's foreknowledge lay,
　But with holy exultation
　　We may sing aloud today.

2 Jesus is the Name we treasure,
　　Name beyond what words can tell;
　Name of gladness, Name of pleasure,
　　Ear and heart delighting well;
　Name of sweetness passing measure,
　　Saving us from sin and hell.

3 'Tis the Name that whoso preacheth
　　Speaks like music to the ear;
　Who in prayer this Name beseecheth
　　Sweetest comfort findeth near;
　Who its perfect wisdom reacheth,
　　Heavenly joy possesseth here.

4 Jesus is the Name exalted
　　Over every other name;
　In this Name, whene'er assaulted,
　　We can put our foes to shame:
　Strength to them who else had halted,
　　Eyes to blind, and feet to lame.

5 Therefore we in love adoring,
　　This most blessèd Name revere,
　Holy Jesu, thee imploring
　　So to write it in us here
　That, hereafter heavenward soaring,
　　We may sing with angels there.

Anonymous (15th Century)
tr. *John Mason Neale* (1818–66) and others

May also be sung to No. 402, GRAFTON

The Eternal Glory of the Word

81(i)

STUTTGART 8.7.8.7.

Adapted from a melody in
C. F. Witt's *Harmonia Sacra* (Gotha, 1715)

For this tune in a higher key see No. 122

81(ii)

CROSS OF JESUS 8.7.8.7.

John Stainer (1840–1901)

For this tune in a lower key see Nos. 230 and 298(ii)

THE ETERNAL WORD

1 COME, thou long-expected Jesus,
   Born to set thy people free,
From our fears and sins release us,
   Let us find our rest in thee.

2 Israel's strength and consolation,
   Hope of all the earth thou art,
Dear desire of every nation,
   Joy of every longing heart.

3 Born thy people to deliver,
   Born a child and yet a king,
Born to reign in us for ever,
   Now thy gracious kingdom bring.

4 By thine own eternal Spirit
   Rule in all our hearts alone;
By thine all-sufficient merit
   Raise us to thy glorious throne.

Charles Wesley (1707–88)

The Promise of the Messiah

82

BRISTOL C.M.

Melody, and most of the harmony, from T. Ravenscroft's *Psalmes* (1621)

THE ETERNAL WORD

1 HARK the glad sound! The Saviour comes,
   The Saviour promised long;
 Let every heart prepare a throne,
   And every voice a song.

2 He comes the prisoners to release,
   In Satan's bondage held;
 The gates of brass before him burst,
   The iron fetters yield.

3 He comes the broken heart to bind,
   The bleeding soul to cure,
 And with the treasures of his grace
   To enrich the humble poor.

4 Our glad hosannas, Prince of Peace,
   Thy welcome shall proclaim;
 And heaven's eternal arches ring
   With thy belovèd name.

Philip Doddridge (1702–51)

May also be sung to No. 577, BROOMSGROVE

The Promise of the Messiah

THEODORIC 666.66. (Refrain)

Melody as in *Piae Cantiones* (1582)
Harmony by Gustav Holst (1874–1934)
(adapted by J.W.)

Moderato maestoso

Melody

Solo (optional)

1 Long a - go,
2 God in time,
3 Ma - ry, hail!
4 Jour - ney ends!

(v.3 *p*)

mf

S.A.T.B. ad lib.

Ped. (*small notes org. only*)

pro - phets knew   Christ would come,   born a Jew,
God in man,   This is God's   time - less plan:
Though a - fraid,   She be - lieved,   she o - beyed.
Where a - far   Beth - lem shines,   like a star,

Come to make   all things new;   Bear his Peo - ple's
He will come,   as a man,   Born him - self of
In her womb,   God is laid;   Till the time ex -
Sta - ble door   stands a - jar.   Un - born Son of

THE ETERNAL WORD

bur - den, Free - ly love and par - don:
wo - man, God di - vine - ly hu - man:
-pec - ted, Nur - tured and pro - tec - ted:
Ma - ry, Sa - viour, do not tar - ry!

↳ v.4 Refrain

REFRAIN
Voices (Vv. 1–3)

Ring, bells, ring, ring, ring! Sing, choirs, sing,

Ring, ring! Sing,

Organ
(Sw.)
(all verses)

L.H.
(Gt.)

sing, sing! When he comes,

sing!

vv. 1–3

The Promise of the Messiah

When he comes, Who will make him wel - come?

(Gt.)

REFRAIN of v.4
Congregation sing normal Refrain melody
Voice Parts

Ring,——

Ring, bells, ring, ring, ring!

Ring,———— bells,———— ring!

Sing,——

Sing, choirs, sing, sing, sing! Je - sus comes!

Sing,———— choirs,— sing!

We will make him wel - come!

Je - sus comes!
We make wel - come!
We will make him wel - come!

We make wel - come!

THE ETERNAL WORD

1 LONG ago, prophets knew
  Christ would come, born a Jew,
  Come to make all things new;
  Bear his People's burden,
    Freely love and pardon:
    Ring, bells, ring, ring, ring!
    Sing, choirs, sing, sing, sing!
    When he comes,
      When he comes,
    Who will make him welcome?

2 God in time, God in man,
  This is God's timeless plan:
  He will come, as a man,
  Born himself of woman,
  God divinely human:
    Ring, bells, ring, ring, ring! etc.

3 Mary, hail! Though afraid,
  She believed, she obeyed.
  In her womb, God is laid;
  Till the time expected,
  Nurtured and protected:
    Ring, bells, ring, ring, ring! etc.

4 Journey ends! Where afar
  Bethlem shines, like a star,
  Stable door stands ajar.
  Unborn Son of Mary,
  Saviour, do not tarry!
    Ring, bells, ring, ring, ring!
    Sing, choirs, sing, sing, sing!
      Jesus comes!
      Jesus comes!
    We will make him welcome!

F. Pratt Green (1903–)

Words reprinted by permission of
Stainer & Bell Ltd.
For permission to reproduce see p. xiii.

May also be sung to the version of THEODORIC at No. 220

The Promise of the Messiah

Melody adapted by W. H. Havergal (1793–1870)
from a chorale in the
Musikalisches Hand-Buch (Hamburg, 1690)

THE ETERNAL WORD

1 ON Jordan's bank the Baptist's cry
   Announces that the Lord is nigh;
      Awake and hearken, for he brings
      Glad tidings from the King of kings!

2 Then cleansed be every Christian breast,
   And furnished for so great a guest!
      Yea, let us each our heart prepare
      For Christ to come and enter there.

3 For thou art our salvation, Lord,
   Our refuge, and our great reward;
      Without thy grace we waste away
      Like flowers that wither and decay.

4 To heal the sick stretch out thy hand,
   And bid the fallen sinner stand;
      Shine forth, and let thy light restore
      Earth's own true loveliness once more.

5 All praise, eternal Son, to thee
   Whose advent sets thy people free,
      Whom, with the Father, we adore,
      And Holy Ghost, for evermore.

Charles Coffin (1676–1749)
tr. *John Chandler* (1806–76) and others

The Promise of the Messiah

85

VENI IMMANUEL 88.88.88.

Melody from *The Hymnal Noted* (Part II, 1856) Copied by
J. M. Neale (1818–66)
'from a French Missal'
(now known to be 15th Cent.)

Re - joice! Re - joice! Im - ma - - nu - el

Shall come to thee, O Is - - ra - el.

THE ETERNAL WORD

1 O COME, O come, Immanuel,
And ransom captive Israel,
That mourns in lonely exile here
Until the Son of God appear:
Rejoice! Rejoice! Immanuel
Shall come to thee, O Israel.

2 O come, O come, thou Lord of might,
Who to thy tribes, on Sinai's height,
In ancient times didst give the law
In cloud, and majesty, and awe:

3 O come, thou Rod of Jesse, free
Thine own from Satan's tyranny;
From depths of hell thy people save,
And give them vict'ry o'er the grave:

4 O come, thou Key of David, come,
And open wide our heav'nly home;
Make safe the way that leads on high,
And close the path to misery:

5 O come, thou Day-spring, come and cheer
Our spirits by thine advent here;
Disperse the gloomy clouds of night,
And death's dark shadows put to flight:

18th Century Latin
tr. *John Mason Neale* (1818–66) and others

The Promise of the Messiah

Walter Greatorex (1877–1949)
(Descant by John Wilson)

Descant for V. 4

4 Tell out, my soul, the glo-ries of his word! Firm____ is his pro-mise, and____ his mer-cy sure.____ Tell out the great - - ness of the

THE ETERNAL WORD

Lord To chil-dren's chil - dren for ev - - - er - more!

1 TELL out, my soul, the greatness of the Lord!
   Unnumbered blessings, give my spirit voice;
Tender to me the promise of his word;
   In God my Saviour shall my heart rejoice.

2 Tell out, my soul, the greatness of his name!
   Make known his might, the deeds his arm has done;
His mercy sure, from age to age the same;
   His holy name—the Lord, the Mighty One.

3 Tell out, my soul, the greatness of his might!
   Powers and dominions lay their glory by;
Proud hearts and stubborn wills are put to flight,
   The hungry fed, the humble lifted high.

4 Tell out, my soul, the glories of his word!
   Firm is his promise, and his mercy sure.
Tell out, my soul, the greatness of the Lord
   To children's children and for evermore!

Timothy Dudley-Smith (1926–)
based on Luke 1:46–55

The Promise of the Messiah

'Most high-ly fa-voured la - dy.' Glo — — ri - a!

*The word 'Gloria' may optionally be sung in unison.

THE ETERNAL WORD

1 THE Angel Gabriel from heaven came,
His wings as drifted snow, his eyes as flame;
'All hail', said he, 'thou lowly maiden Mary,
Most highly favoured lady.'
Gloria!

2 'For known a blessèd Mother thou shalt be,
All generations laud and honour thee,
Thy son shall be Immanuel, by seers foretold;
Most highly favoured lady.'
Gloria!

3 Then gentle Mary meekly bowed her head,
'To me be as it pleaseth God', she said,
'My soul shall laud and magnify his holy name':
Most highly favoured lady.
Gloria!

4 Of her, Immanuel, the Christ was born
In Bethlehem, all on a Christmas morn,
And Christian folk throughout the world will ever say
'Most highly favoured lady.'
Gloria!

Basque Carol paraphrased by
Sabine Baring-Gould (1834–1924)

The Promise of the Messiah

88

THE HOLLY AND THE IVY Irregular   English Traditional Carol

The hol-ly and the i-vy Are

danc-ing in a ring, Round the ber-ry-bright red

can-dles And the white and shin-ing King.

THE ETERNAL WORD

1 THE holly and the ivy
   Are dancing in a ring,
 Round the berry-bright red candles
   And the white and shining King.

2 Oh, one is for God's people
   In every age and day.
 We are watching for his coming.
   We believe and we obey.

3 And two is for the prophets
   And for the light they bring.
 They are candles in the darkness,
   All alight for Christ the King.

4 And three for John the Baptist.
   He calls on us to sing:
 'O prepare the way for Jesus Christ,
   He is coming, Christ the King.'

5 And four for Mother Mary.
   'I cannot see the way,
 But you promise me a baby.
   I believe you. I obey.'

6 And Christ is in the centre,
   For this is his birthday,
 With the shining lights of Christmas
   Singing: 'He has come today!'

Emily Chisholm (1910–   )

The order of verses follows the customary themes in Advent. An original, alternative order is to be found in Partners in Praise.

Words reprinted by permission of
Stainer & Bell Ltd.
For permission to reproduce see p. xiii.

The Promise of the Messiah

89
DUNDEE C.M.

Melody from *Scottish Psalter* (1615)
Harmony from T. Ravenscroft's *Psalmes* (1621)

SECOND VERSION
(with later form of rhythm)

DUNDEE C.M.

THE ETERNAL WORD

1 THE race that long in darkness pined
   Has seen a glorious light:
   The people dwell in day, who dwelt
   In death's surrounding night.

2 To hail thy rise, thou better Sun,
   The gathering nations come,
   Joyous as when the reapers bear
   The harvest treasures home.

3 To us a child of hope is born,
   To us a Son is given;
   Him shall the tribes of earth obey,
   Him all the hosts of heaven.

4 His name shall be the Prince of Peace,
   For evermore adored,
   The Wonderful, the Counsellor,
   The great and mighty Lord.

5 His power increasing still shall spread,
   His reign no end shall know;
   Justice shall guard his throne above,
   And peace abound below.

John Morison (1750–98)
as in *Scottish Paraphrases* (1781)
based on Isaiah 9:2–7

May also be sung to No. 6, DUNFERMLINE

The Promise of the Messiah

90

ES IST EIN' ROS' ENTSPRUNGEN

76.76.676.

German Carol Melody
Harmonised by
Michael Praetorius (1571–1621)

1. A GREAT and migh-ty won-der, A
   The Vir-gin bears the In-fant With

full and ho - ly cure!
vir - gin - hon - our pure:

Refrain

Re - peat the hymn a - gain! 'To God on high be

THE ETERNAL WORD

glo - ry, And peace on earth to men!'

(Alto) 'And peace___ on earth to men!'

1 A GREAT and mighty wonder,
      A full and holy cure!
   The Virgin bears the Infant
      With virgin-honour pure:
         Repeat the hymn again!
         'To God on high be glory,
      And peace on earth to men!'

2 The Word becomes incarnate
      And yet remains on high!
   And cherubim sing anthems
      To shepherds, from the sky:

3 While thus they sing your Monarch,
      Those bright angelic bands,
   Rejoice, ye vales and mountains,
      Ye oceans, clap your hands:

4 Since all he comes to ransom,
      By all be he adored,
   The Infant born in Bethlem,
      The Saviour and the Lord:

5 And idol forms shall perish,
      And error shall decay,
   And Christ shall wield his sceptre,
      Our Lord and God for aye:

> Germanus (*c.* 634–734)
> tr. *John Mason Neale* (1818–66)
> and others

Christ's Birth

BONN 8.33.6.D.   Melody and bass by J. G. Ebeling (1637–76)

THE ETERNAL WORD

1 ALL my heart this night rejoices,
        As I hear,
        Far and near,
    Sweetest angel voices:
  'Christ is born!' their choirs are singing,
        Till the air
        Everywhere
    Now with joy is ringing.

2 Hark, a voice from yonder manger,
        Soft and sweet,
        Doth entreat,
    'Flee from woe and danger;
  Come, O come; from all doth grieve you
        You are freed,
        All you need
    I will surely give you.'

3 Come then, let us hasten yonder;
        Here let all,
        Great and small,
    Kneel in awe and wonder;
  Love him who with love is yearning;
        Hail the star
        That from far
    Bright with hope is burning!

4 Thee, O Lord, with heed I'll cherish,
        Live to thee,
        And with thee
    Dying, shall not perish;
  But shall dwell with thee for ever,
        Far on high,
        In the joy
    That can alter never.

Paul Gerhardt (1607–76)
tr. *Catherine Winkworth* (1827–78)

Christ's Birth

92(i)

IRIS 87.87. (Refrain)

Flemish or French traditional melody
arranged Martin Shaw (1875–1958)

Refrain

Come _____ and

Come _____ and

(1st) wor - ship Christ, the new-born King. ——
(2nd) wor - ship, Wor-ship Christ, the new - born King.

THE ETERNAL WORD

92(ii)

FENITON COURT 87.87.87. E. J. Hopkins (1818–1901)

1 ANGELS, from the realms of glory,
   Wing your flight o'er all the earth;
Ye who sang creation's story,
   Now proclaim Messiah's birth:
      Come and worship,
      Worship Christ, the new-born King.

2 Shepherds in the field abiding,
      Watching o'er your flocks by night,
God with man is now residing,
      Yonder shines the infant Light:

3 Sages, leave your contemplations;
      Brighter visions beam afar;
Seek the great Desire of nations;
      Ye have seen his natal star:

4 Saints before the altar bending,
      Watching long in hope and fear,
Suddenly the Lord, descending,
      In his temple shall appear:

5 Though an infant now we view him,
      He shall fill his Father's throne,
Gather all the nations to him;
      Every knee shall then bow down:

James Montgomery (1771–1854)

Christ's Birth

A VIRGIN MOST PURE 11 11. 11 11. (Refrain)

Traditional. Arranged
Elizabeth Poston (1905–   )
in *The Cambridge Hymnal*

1 A _ VIR-GIN most pure, as the pro-phets do tell, _ Hath
brought forth a _ ba-by, as it hath be-fell, To
be _ our Re-deem-er from death, hell, and sin, Which

THE ETERNAL WORD

[continued ▶

A – dam's trans-gress-ion hath wrap-pèd us   in: *Aye and*

1 A VIRGIN most pure, as the prophets do tell,
   Hath brought forth a baby, as it hath befell,
   To be our Redeemer from death, hell, and sin,
   Which Adam's transgression hath wrappèd us in:
       Aye and therefore be merry, rejoice and be you merry,
       Set sorrows aside;
       Christ Jesus our Saviour was born on this tide.

2 At Bethlem in Jewry a city there was,
   Where Joseph and Mary together did pass,
   And there to be taxèd with many one mo',
   For Caesar commanded the same should be so:

3 But when they had entered the city so fair,
   A number of people so mighty was there,
   That Joseph and Mary, whose substance was small,
   Could find in the inn there no lodging at all:

4 Then they were constrained in a stable to lie,
   Where horses and asses they used for to tie;
   Their lodging so simple they took it no scorn,
   But against the next morning our Saviour was born:

5 The King of all kings to this world being brought,
   Small store of fine linen to wrap him was sought;
   And when she had swaddled her young son so sweet,
   Within an ox-manger she laid him to sleep:

6 Then God sent an angel from heaven so high,
   To certain poor shepherds in fields where they lie,
   And bade them no longer in sorrow to stay,
   Because that our Saviour was born on this day:

7 Then presently after the shepherds did spy
   A number of angels that stood in the sky;
   They joyfully talkèd, and sweetly did sing,
   To God be all glory, our heavenly King:

Traditional

Christ's Birth

there – fore— be— mer – ry, re – joice—— and be you mer – ry, Set sor – rows a – side; Christ Je – sus our Sav – iour was born— on this tide.

THE ETERNAL WORD

94

AWAY IN A MANGER   11 11.11 11.   W. J. Kirkpatrick (1838–1921)

1 AWAY in a manger, no crib for a bed,
   The little Lord Jesus laid down his sweet head;
   The stars in the bright sky looked down where he lay,
   The little Lord Jesus asleep on the hay.

2 The cattle are lowing, the baby awakes,
   But little Lord Jesus no crying he makes.
   I love thee, Lord Jesus! Look down from the sky,
   And stay by my bedside till morning is nigh.

3 Be near me, Lord Jesus; I ask thee to stay
   Close by me for ever, and love me, I pray.
   Bless all the dear children in thy tender care,
   And fit us for heaven, to live with thee there.

Anonymous

Christ's Birth

95

MARY'S CHILD   4.3.6.D.   Geoffrey Ainger (1925–   )
Unison. Medium pace.

1 Born in the night, Ma - ry's child, A long way from your home: Com - ing in need, Ma - ry's child, Born in a bor - rowed room.

THE ETERNAL WORD

1   BORN in the night,
          Mary's child,
    A long way from your home:
       Coming in need,
          Mary's child,
    Born in a borrowed room.

2   Clear shining Light,
          Mary's child,
    Your face lights up our way;
       Light of the world,
          Mary's child,
    Dawn on our darkened day.

3   Truth of our life,
          Mary's child,
    You tell us God is good;
       Prove it is true,
          Mary's child,
    Go to your cross of wood.

4   Hope of the world,
          Mary's child,
    You're coming soon to reign;
       King of the earth,
          Mary's child,
    Walk in our streets again.

Geoffrey Ainger (1925–   )

Words and music reprinted by permission of
Stainer & Bell Ltd.
For permission to reproduce see p. xiii

Christ's Birth

96

YORKSHIRE (STOCKPORT) 10 10.10 10.10 10. J. Wainwright (1723–68)

THE ETERNAL WORD

1 CHRISTIANS, awake, salute the happy morn
  Whereon the Saviour of the world was born;
  Rise to adore the mystery of love,
  Which hosts of angels chanted from above;
  With them the joyful tidings first begun
  Of God incarnate and the Virgin's Son.

2 Then to the watchful shepherds it was told,
  Who heard the angelic herald's voice, 'Behold,
  I bring good tidings of a Saviour's birth
  To you and all the nations upon earth;
  This day has God fulfilled his promised word,
  This day is born a Saviour, Christ the Lord.'

3 He spake; and straightway the celestial choir
  In hymns of joy, unknown before, conspire.
  The praises of redeeming love they sang,
  And heaven's whole orb with alleluias rang;
  God's highest glory was their anthem still,
  Peace upon earth, and unto men goodwill.

4 To Bethlem straight the enlightened shepherds ran,
  To see the wonder God had wrought for man:
  Then to their flocks, still praising God, return,
  And their glad hearts with holy rapture burn;
  Amazed, the wondrous tidings they proclaim,
  The first apostles of his infant fame.

5 Like Mary, let us ponder in our mind
  God's wondrous love in saving lost mankind;
  Trace we the Babe, who has retrieved our loss,
  From his poor manger to his bitter cross;
  Tread in his steps, assisted by his grace,
  Till our first heavenly state again takes place.

6 Then may we hope, the angelic hosts among,
  To sing, redeemed, a glad triumphal song;
  He that was born upon this joyful day
  Around us all his glory shall display;
  Saved by his love, incessant we shall sing
  Th' eternal praise of heaven's almighty King.

John Byrom (1692–1763) alt.

Christ's Birth

97

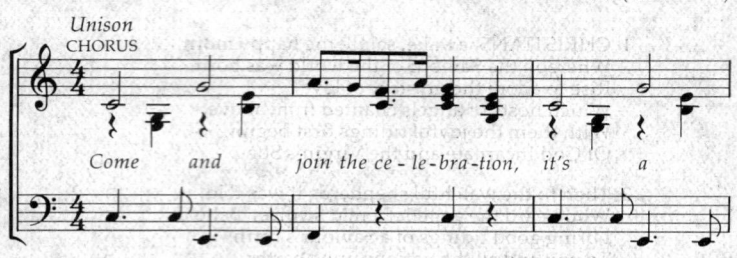

Unison
CHORUS

Come   and   join the ce - le - bra - tion, it's   a

ve - ry spe - cial day;   Come   and

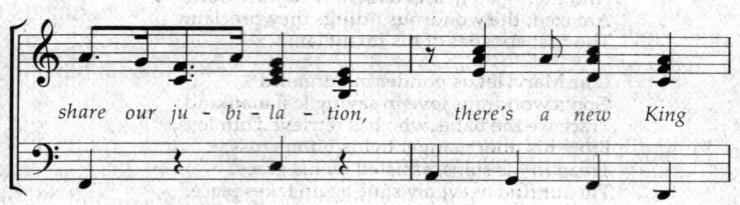

share   our ju - bi - la - tion,   there's   a   new King

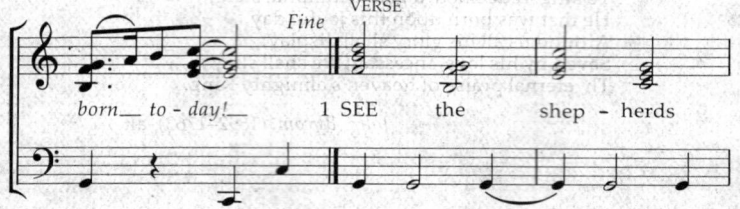

Fine   VERSE

born___ to - day!___   1 SEE   the   shep - herds

THE ETERNAL WORD

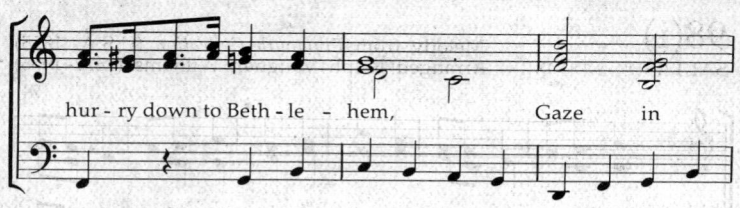

hur - ry down to Beth - le - hem, Gaze in

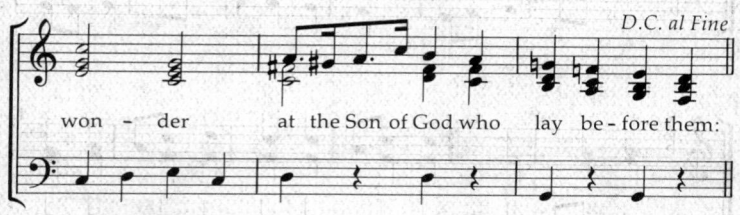

D.C. al Fine

won – der at the Son of God who lay be - fore them:

Come and join the celebration, it's a very special day;
Come and share our jubilation, there's a new King born today!

1 SEE the shepherds hurry down to Bethlehem,
   Gaze in wonder at the Son of God who lay before them:

2 Wise men journey, led to worship by a star,
   Kneel in homage, bringing precious gifts from lands afar, so,

3 'God is with us', round the world the message bring,
   He is with us, 'Welcome', all the bells on earth are pealing:

Valerie Collison (1933–)

Christ's Birth

THE ETERNAL WORD

1 CRADLED in a manger, meanly
   Laid the Son of Man his head;
Sleeping his first earthly slumber
   Where the oxen had been fed.
Happy were those shepherds listening
   To the holy angel's word;
Happy they within that stable,
   Worshipping their infant Lord.

2 Happy all who hear the message
   Of his coming from above;
Happier still who hail his coming,
   And with praises greet his love.
Blessèd Saviour, Christ most holy,
   In a manger thou didst rest;
Canst thou stoop again, yet lower,
   And abide within my breast?

3 Evil things are there before thee;
   In the heart, where they have fed,
Wilt thou pitifully enter,
   Son of Man, and lay thy head?
Enter, then, O Christ most holy;
   Make a Christmas in my heart;
Make a heaven of my manger:
   It is heaven where thou art.

4 And to those who never listened
   To the message of thy birth,
Who have winter, but no Christmas
   Bringing them thy peace on earth,
Send to these the joyful tidings;
   By all people, in each home,
Be there heard the Christmas anthem:
   Praise to God, the Christ has come!

George Stringer Rowe (1830–1913)

May also be sung to No. 559(ii), MANOR HOUSE

98(ii)

ST WINIFRED 8.7.8.7.D.

S. J. P. Dunman (1843–1913)

THE ETERNAL WORD

1 CRADLED in a manger, meanly
   Laid the Son of Man his head;
Sleeping his first earthly slumber
   Where the oxen had been fed.
Happy were those shepherds listening
   To the holy angel's word;
Happy they within that stable,
   Worshipping their infant Lord.

2 Happy all who hear the message
   Of his coming from above;
Happier still who hail his coming,
   And with praises greet his love.
Blessèd Saviour, Christ most holy,
   In a manger thou didst rest;
Canst thou stoop again, yet lower,
   And abide within my breast?

3 Evil things are there before thee;
   In the heart, where they have fed,
Wilt thou pitifully enter,
   Son of Man, and lay thy head?
Enter, then, O Christ most holy;
   Make a Christmas in my heart;
Make a heaven of my manger:
   It is heaven where thou art.

4 And to those who never listened
   To the message of thy birth,
Who have winter, but no Christmas
   Bringing them thy peace on earth,
Send to these the joyful tidings;
   By all people, in each home,
Be there heard the Christmas anthem:
   Praise to God, the Christ has come!

   George Stringer Rowe (1830–1913)

May also be sung to No. 559(ii), MANOR HOUSE

THIS ENDRIS NYGHT   C.M.

English Carol Melody, 15th Century
Harmonised by
Ralph Vaughan Williams (1872–1958)

THE ETERNAL WORD

1 FROM east to west, from shore to shore,
   Let earth awake and sing
The holy child whom Mary bore,
   The Christ, the Lord, the King!

2 For lo! The world's Creator wears
   The fashion of a slave:
Our human flesh the Godhead bears,
   His creature, man, to save.

3 He shrank not from the oxen's stall,
   Nor scorned the manger-bed;
And he, whose bounty feedeth all,
   At Mary's breast was fed.

4 To shepherds poor the Lord most high,
   Great Shepherd, was revealed;
While angel choirs sang joyously
   Above the midnight field.

5 All glory be to God above,
   And on the earth be peace
To all who long to taste his love,
   Till time itself shall cease.

Caelius Sedulius (c. 450)
tr. *John Ellerton* (1826–93)

VOM HIMMEL HOCH L.M.

Melody attributed to Martin Luther (1483–1546);
as in Schumann's *Geistliche Lieder* (1539)
Harmony mostly from
Michael Praetorius (1571–1621)

Verses 1–3 may be sung by a group or solo voice, with or without accompaniment.

OPTIONAL VERSION FOR LAST VERSE
Later form of same melody

Harmony from J. S. Bach's *Christmas Oratorio* (1734)

THE ETERNAL WORD

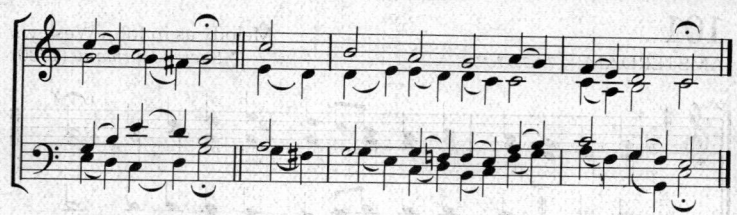

The angel's message:

1 FROM heaven above to earth I come,
  To bear good news to every one;
    Glad tidings of great joy I bring,
    Whereof I now will say and sing:

2 To you this night is born a child
  Of Mary, chosen mother mild;
    This new-born babe of lowly birth
    Shall be the joy of all the earth.

3 This is the Christ who far on high
  Has heard your sad and bitter cry;
    Himself will your salvation be;
    Himself from sin will make you free.

The children welcome Christ:

4 Welcome to earth, thou noble guest,
  Through whom this sinful world is blest!
    Thou com'st to share our misery;
    What can we render, Lord, to thee?

5 Were earth a thousand times as fair,
  Beset with gold and jewels rare,
    She yet were far too poor to be
    A narrow cradle, Lord, for thee.

The congregation's response:

6 Ah, dearest Jesus, holy child,
  Make thee a bed, soft, undefiled,
    Within my heart, that it may be
    A quiet chamber kept for thee.

7 My heart for very joy doth leap;
  My lips no more can silence keep;
    I too must sing with joyful tongue
    That sweetest ancient cradle song:

8 'Glory to God in highest heaven,
  Who unto man his Son has given!'
    While angels sing with pious mirth
    A glad new year to all the earth.

Martin Luther (1483–1546)
tr. *Catherine Winkworth* (1827–78) alt.

Christ's Birth

THE ETERNAL WORD

1 GLORY be to God on high,
    And peace on earth descend:
God comes down, he bows the sky,
    And shows himself our friend:
God the invisible appears:
    God, the blest, the great I AM,
Sojourns in this vale of tears,
    And Jesus is his name.

2 Him the angels all adored,
    Their Maker and their King;
Tidings of their humbled Lord
    They now to mortals bring.
Emptied of his majesty,
    Of his dazzling glories shorn,
Being's source begins to be,
    And God himself is born!

3 See the eternal Son of God
    A mortal son of man
Dwelling in an earthly clod
    Whom heaven cannot contain!
Stand amazed, ye heavens, at this!
    See the Lord of earth and skies;
Humbled to the dust he is,
    And in a manger lies.

4 We, earth's children, now rejoice,
    The Prince of Peace proclaim;
With heaven's host lift up our voice,
    And shout Immanuel's name:
Knees and hearts to him we bow;
    Of our flesh and of our bone,
Jesus is our brother now,
    And God is all our own.

Charles Wesley (1707–88) alt.

102

ST CECILIA   66.66.   L. G. Hayne (1836–83)

SECOND VERSION
(with original form of rhythm)

ST CECILIA   66.66.   L. G. Hayne (1836–83)

THE ETERNAL WORD

1 GOD from on high has heard;
    Let sighs and sorrows cease;
  The skies unfold, and lo!
    Descends the gift of peace.

2 Hark! On the midnight air
    Celestial voices swell;
  The hosts of heaven proclaim
    God comes on earth to dwell.

3 Haste with the shepherds; see
    The mystery of grace:
  A manger-bed, a child,
    Is all the eye can trace.

4 Is this the eternal Son,
    Who on the starry throne
  Before the worlds begun
    Was with the Father one?

5 Yes, faith can pierce the cloud
    Which shrouds his glory now,
  And hail him God and Lord,
    To whom all creatures bow.

6 O child! Thy silence speaks,
    And bids us not refuse
  To bear what flesh would shun,
    To spurn what flesh would choose.

7 Fill us with holy love,
    Heal thou our earthly pride;
  Born in each lowly heart,
    For ever there abide.

Charles Coffin (1676–1749)
tr. *James Russell Woodford* (1820–85)

103

GOD REST YOU MERRY   8.6.8.6.8.6 (Refrain).   English Traditional Melody

Refrain

O__ ti - dings of com - fort and joy,__ com-fort and

joy! O__ ti - dings of com - fort and joy!

THE ETERNAL WORD

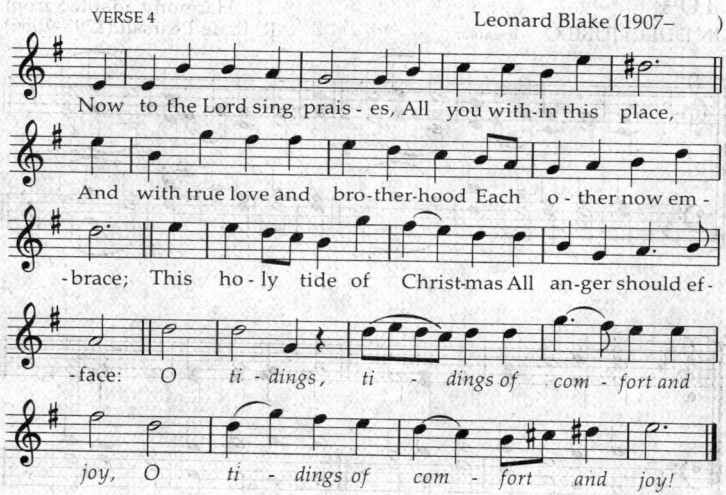

VERSE 4 — Leonard Blake (1907–)

Now to the Lord sing prais-es, All you with-in this place, And with true love and bro-ther-hood Each o-ther now em--brace; This ho-ly tide of Christ-mas All an-ger should ef--face: O ti-dings, ti-dings of com-fort and joy, O ti-dings of com-fort and joy!

1 GOD rest you merry, gentlemen,
   Let nothing you dismay,
   For Jesus Christ our Saviour
   Was born upon this day,
   To save us all from Satan's power
   When we were gone astray:
   O tidings of comfort and joy, comfort and joy!
   O tidings of comfort and joy!

2 From God our heavenly Father
   A blessèd angel came,
   And unto certain shepherds
   Brought tidings of the same,
   How that in Bethlehem was born
   The Son of God by name:

3 And when to Bethlehem they came,
   Whereat this infant lay,
   They found him in a manger,
   Where oxen feed on hay;
   His mother Mary kneeling
   Unto the Lord did pray:

4 Now to the Lord sing praises,
   All you within this place,
   And with true love and brotherhood
   Each other now embrace;
   This holy tide of Christmas
   All anger should efface:

Traditional

Christ's Birth

Christ is born to - day___ Christ is born to - day!___

THE ETERNAL WORD

1 GOOD Christians all, rejoice
  With heart and soul and voice!
    Give ye heed to what we say;
    Jesus Christ is born today!
  Ox and ass before him bow,
  And he is in the manger now.
    Christ is born today!
    Christ is born today!

2 Good Christians all, rejoice
  With heart and soul and voice!
    Now ye hear of endless bliss,
    Jesus Christ was born for this;
  He hath oped the heavenly door,
  And all are blest for evermore.
    Christ was born for this!
    Christ was born for this!

3 Good Christians all, rejoice
  With heart and soul and voice!
    Now ye need not fear the grave;
    Jesus Christ was born to save,
  Calls you one and calls you all,
  To gain his everlasting hall.
    Christ was born to save!
    Christ was born to save!

John Mason Neale (1818–66) alt.

105(i)

HERMITAGE 6.7.6.7.

R. O. Morris (1886–1948)

1 LOVE came down at Christmas,
 Love all lovely, Love divine;
 Love was born at Christmas,
 Star and angels gave the sign.

2 Worship we the Godhead,
 Love incarnate, Love divine;
 Worship we our Jesus:
 But wherewith for sacred sign?

3 Love shall be our token,
 Love be yours and love be mine,
 Love to God and all the world,
 Love for plea and gift and sign.

Christina Georgina Rossetti (1830–94)

With the second tune the words
Sing Nowell are added after each verse.

THE ETERNAL WORD

105(ii)

LOVE INCARNATE   6.7.6.7. and refrain   C. Edgar Pettman (1866–1943)

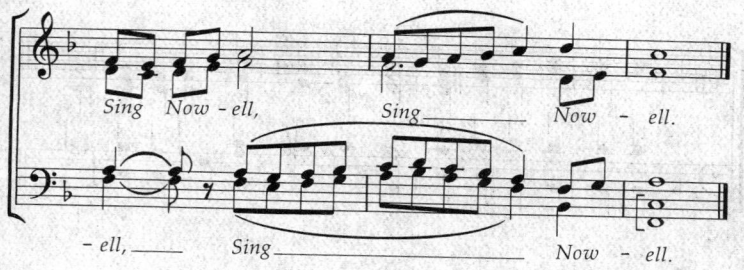

Christ's Birth

106

MENDELSSOHN 77.77.D. (Refrain)

From a chorus in Mendelssohn's *Festgesang* (1840), originally adapted by W. H. Cummings (1855)

THE ETERNAL WORD

Hark! The her-ald-an-gels sing Glo-ry __ to the new-born King.

1 HARK! The herald-angels sing
   Glory to the new-born King,
   Peace on earth, and mercy mild,
   God and sinners reconciled.
   Joyful, all ye nations, rise,
   Join the triumph of the skies;
   With the angelic host proclaim:
   'Christ is born in Bethlehem.'
      Hark! The herald-angels sing
      Glory to the new-born King.

2 Christ, by highest heaven adored,
   Christ, the everlasting Lord,
   Late in time behold him come,
   Offspring of a virgin's womb.
   Veiled in flesh the Godhead see!
   Hail, the incarnate Deity!
   Pleased as man with men to dwell,
   Jesus, our Immanuel:

3 Hail, the heaven-born Prince of Peace!
   Hail, the Sun of Righteousness!
   Light and life to all he brings,
   Risen with healing in his wings.
   Mild he lays his glory by,
   Born that man no more may die,
   Born to raise the sons of earth,
   Born to give them second birth:

Charles Wesley (1707–88)

Christ's Birth

107

CRANHAM   Irreg.

Gustav Holst (1874–1934)

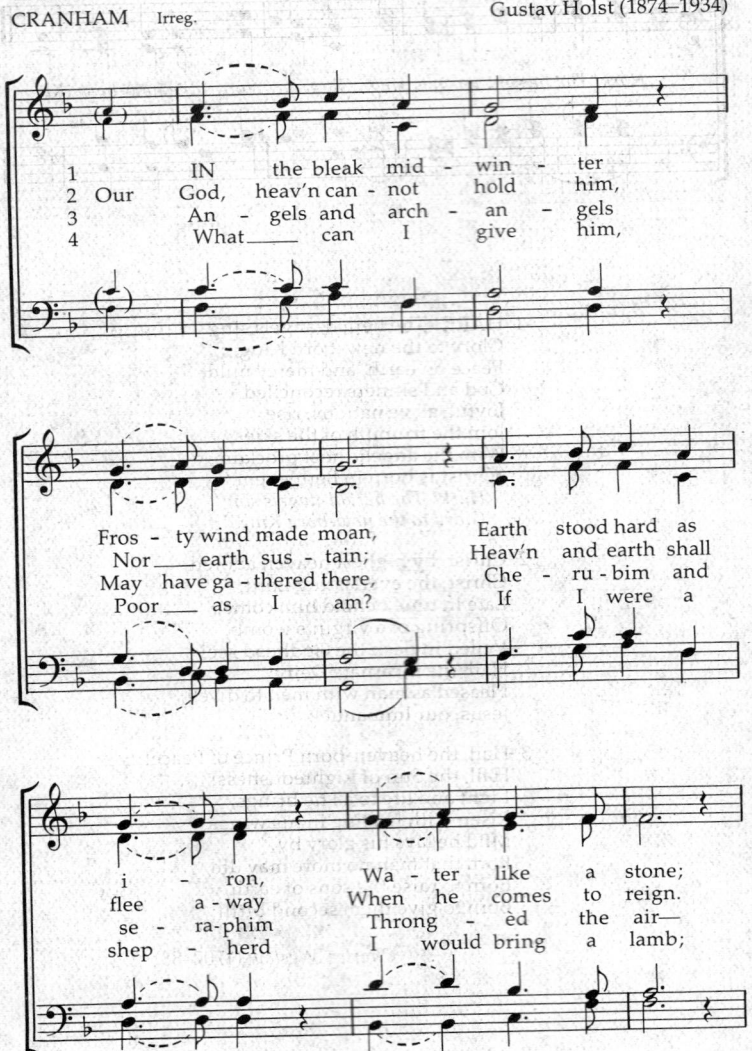

1   IN the bleak mid - win - ter
2 Our God, heav'n can - not hold him,
3   An - gels and arch - an - gels
4   What___ can I give him,

Fros - ty wind made moan,
Nor___ earth sus - tain;
May have ga - thered there,
Poor___ as I am?

Earth stood hard as
Heav'n and earth shall
Che - ru - bim and
If I were a

i - ron,
flee a - way
se - ra - phim
shep - herd

Wa - ter like a stone;
When he comes to reign.
Throng - èd the air—
I would bring a lamb;

THE ETERNAL WORD

Snow had fall - en, snow on snow,
In the bleak mid - win - ter A
But his mo - ther on - ly,
If I were a wise man

Snow on snow, In the bleak mid -
sta - ble-place suf - ficed The Lord God Al -
In her mai - den bliss, Wor - shipped the Be -
I would do my part; Yet what I can I

- win - ter, Long a - go.
- migh - ty, Je - sus Christ.
- lov - èd With a kiss.
give him With Give my heart.

Christina Georgina Rossetti (1830–94)

Christ's Birth

108

NOEL D.C.M.

English Traditional Melody,
adapted and extended
by Arthur Sullivan (1842–1900)

THE ETERNAL WORD

1 IT came upon the midnight clear,
   That glorious song of old,
From angels bending near the earth
   To touch their harps of gold:
'Peace on the earth, goodwill to men,
   From heaven's all-gracious King!'
The world in solemn stillness lay
   To hear the angels sing.

2 Still through the cloven skies they come,
   With peaceful wings unfurled;
And still their heavenly music floats
   O'er all the weary world;
Above its sad and lowly plains
   They bend on hovering wing;
And ever o'er its Babel sounds
   The blessèd angels sing.

3 Yet with the woes of sin and strife
   The world has suffered long;
Beneath the angel strain have rolled
   Two thousand years of wrong;
And man, at war with man, hears not
   The love-song which they bring.
O hush the noise, ye men of strife,
   And hear the angels sing!

4 For lo, the days are hastening on,
   To prophets shown of old,
When with the ever-circling years
   Shall come the time foretold,
When the new heaven and earth shall own
   The Prince of Peace their King,
And all the world repeat the song
   Which now the angels sing.

Edmund Hamilton Sears (1810–76) alt.

Christ's Birth

109

ST JOHN (ADORATION) 66.66.88.

From *The Parish Choir* (1851)
(with altered rhythms)

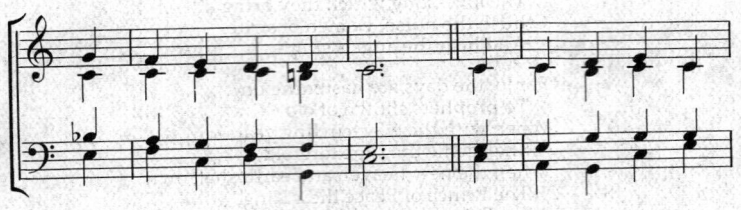

THE ETERNAL WORD

1   LET earth and heaven combine,
         Angels and men agree,
     To praise in songs divine
         The incarnate Deity,
     Our God contracted to a span,
     Incomprehensibly made man.

2   He laid his glory by,
         He wrapped him in our clay;
     Unmarked by human eye,
         The latent Godhead lay;
     Infant of days he here became,
     And bore the mild Immanuel's name.

3   Unsearchable the love
         That has the Saviour brought;
     The grace is far above
         Or men or angels' thought:
     Suffice for us that God, we know,
     Our God, is manifest below.

4   He deigns in flesh to appear,
         Widest extremes to join;
     To bring our vileness near,
         And make us all divine:
     And we the life of God shall know,
     For God is manifest below.

5   Made perfect first in love,
         And sanctified by grace,
     We shall from earth remove,
         And see his glorious face:
     His love shall then be fully showed,
     And man shall all be lost in God.

Charles Wesley (1707–88)

110
ADESTE FIDELES Irreg.
Eighteenth-century melody probably by J. F. Wade (1711–86)
Harmonised mainly by
W. H. Monk (1823–89)

THE ETERNAL WORD

1   O COME, all ye faithful,
     Joyful and triumphant,
  O come ye, O come ye to Bethlehem;
     Come and behold him,
     Born the King of angels:
  O come, let us adore him, Christ the Lord.

2   True God of true God,
     Light of Light eternal,
  Lo, he abhors not the virgin's womb;
     Son of the Father,
     Begotten, not created:

3   See how the shepherds,
     Summoned to his cradle,
  Leaving their flocks, draw nigh to gaze;
     We too will thither
     Bend our joyful footsteps:

4   Lo, star-led chieftains,
     Magi, Christ adoring,
  Offer him incense, gold, and myrrh;
     We to the Christ-child
     Bring our hearts' oblations:

5   Sing, choirs of angels,
     Sing in exultation,
  Sing, all ye citizens of heaven above:
     'Glory to God
     In the highest':

(*Christmas Day*)
6   Yea, Lord, we greet thee,
     Born this happy morning,
  Jesus, to thee be glory given:
     Word of the Father,
     Now in flesh appearing:

18th Century
tr. *Frederick Oakeley*
(1802–80) and others

111

O JESULEIN SÜSS   10.9.8 8.10.

1 O LITTLE one sweet, O little one mild,
Thy Father's purpose thou hast fulfilled;
Thou cam'st from heaven to mortal ken,
Equal to be with us poor men,
O little one sweet, O little one mild.

2 O little one sweet, O little one mild,
With joy thou hast the whole world filled;
Thou camest here from heaven's domain,
To bring men comfort in their pain,
O little one sweet, O little one mild.

3 O little one sweet, O little one mild,
In thee love's beauties are all distilled;
Then light in us thy love's bright flame,
That we may give thee back the same,
O little one sweet, O little one mild.

S. Scheidt (1650)
tr. *Percy Dearmer* (1867–1936)

THE ETERNAL WORD

112

STILLE NACHT   Irreg.

Melody by Franz Gruber (1787–1863)
Harmonised by
Arthur Hutchings (1906–   )

1 SILENT night, holy night:
   Sleeps the world; hid from sight,
   Mary and Joseph in stable bare
   Watch o'er the child belovèd and fair
     Sleeping in heavenly rest.

2 Silent night, holy night:
   Shepherds first saw the light,
   Heard resounding clear and long,
   Far and near, the angel-song:
     'Christ the Redeemer is here!'

3 Silent night, holy night:
   Son of God, O how bright
   Love is smiling from thy face!
   Strikes for us now the hour of grace,
     Saviour, since thou art born!

Joseph Mohr (1792–1848)
tr. *Stopford Augustus Brooke* (1832–1916)

Christ's Birth

113(i)

FOREST GREEN D.C.M. (Irregular)

English Traditional Melody
Harmonised by
Ralph Vaughan Williams (1872–1958)

THE ETERNAL WORD

1 O LITTLE town of Bethlehem,
    How still we see thee lie!
Above thy deep and dreamless sleep
    The silent stars go by.
Yet in thy dark street shineth
    The everlasting light;
The hopes and fears of all the years
    Are met in thee tonight.

2 O morning stars, together
    Proclaim the holy birth,
And praises sing to God the King,
    And peace to all the earth!
For Christ is born of Mary;
    And, gathered all above,
While mortals sleep, the angels keep
    Their watch of wondering love.

3 How silently, how silently,
    The wondrous gift is given!
So God imparts to human hearts
    The blessings of his heaven.
No ear may hear his coming;
    But in this world of sin,
Where meek souls will receive him still
    The dear Christ enters in.

4 O holy Child of Bethlehem,
    Descend to us, we pray;
Cast out our sin, and enter in;
    Be born in us today!
We hear the Christmas angels
    The great glad tidings tell;
O come to us, abide with us,
    Our Lord Immanuel!

Phillips Brooks (1835–93)

113(ii)

English Traditional Melody
Arranged by
Ralph Vaughan Williams (1872–1958)

KINGSFOLD D.C.M. (Irregular)

THE ETERNAL WORD

1 O LITTLE town of Bethlehem,
   How still we see thee lie!
 Above thy deep and dreamless sleep
   The silent stars go by.
 Yet in thy dark street shineth
   The everlasting light;
 The hopes and fears of all the years
   Are met in thee tonight.

2 O morning stars, together
   Proclaim the holy birth,
 And praises sing to God the King,
   And peace to all the earth!
 For Christ is born of Mary;
   And, gathered all above,
 While mortals sleep, the angels keep
   Their watch of wondering love.

3 How silently, how silently,
   The wondrous gift is given!
 So God imparts to human hearts
   The blessings of his heaven.
 No ear may hear his coming;
   But in this world of sin,
 Where meek souls will receive him still
   The dear Christ enters in.

4 O holy Child of Bethlehem,
   Descend to us, we pray;
 Cast out our sin, and enter in;
   Be born in us today!
 We hear the Christmas angels
   The great glad tidings tell;
 O come to us, abide with us,
   Our Lord Immanuel!

Phillips Brooks (1835–93)

Christ's Birth

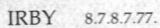

114

IRBY 8.7.8.7.77.

Henry J. Gauntlett (1805–76)

OPTIONAL VERSION
(FOR SELECTED VERSES)

Harmonised by A. H. Mann (1850–1929)

THE ETERNAL WORD

1 ONCE in royal David's city
   Stood a lowly cattle-shed,
 Where a mother laid her baby
   In a manger for his bed:
 Mary was that mother mild,
 Jesus Christ her little child.

2 He came down to earth from heaven
   Who is God and Lord of all,
 And his shelter was a stable,
   And his cradle was a stall;
 With the poor and mean and lowly
 Lived on earth our Saviour holy.

3 And through all his wondrous childhood
   He would honour and obey,
 Love, and watch the lowly maiden
   In whose gentle arms he lay.
 Christian children all must be
 Mild, obedient, good as he.

4 For he is our childhood's pattern,
   Day by day like us he grew,
 He was little, weak, and helpless,
   Tears and smiles like us he knew;
 And he feeleth for our sadness,
 And he shareth in our gladness.

5 And our eyes at last shall see him,
   Through his own redeeming love,
 For that child so dear and gentle
   Is our Lord in heaven above;
 And he leads his children on
 To the place where he is gone.

6 Not in that poor lowly stable,
   With the oxen standing by,
 We shall see him; but in heaven,
   Set at God's right hand on high;
 When like stars his children crowned
 All in white shall wait around.

Cecil Frances Alexander (1818–95)

Christ's Birth

115

SUSSEX CAROL 88.88.88.

English Traditional Melody
Harmonised by
Ralph Vaughan Williams (1872–1958)

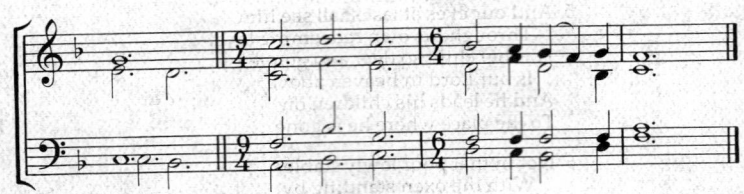

THE ETERNAL WORD

1 ON Christmas night all Christians sing
   To hear the news the angels bring:
   On Christmas night all Christians sing
   To hear the news the angels bring:
   News of great joy, news of great mirth,
   News of our merciful King's birth.

2 Then why should we on earth be so sad,
   Since our Redeemer made us glad,
   Then why should we on earth be so sad,
   Since our Redeemer made us glad,
   When from our sin he set us free,
   All for to gain our liberty?

3 When sin departs before his grace,
   Then life and health come in its place;
   When sin departs before his grace,
   Then life and health come in its place;
   Angels and men with joy may sing,
   All for to see the new-born King.

4 All out of darkness we have light,
   Which made the angels sing this night:
   All out of darkness we have light,
   Which made the angels sing this night:
   'Glory to God and peace to men,
   Now and for evermore. Amen.'

Traditional

*If desired the first two lines of each verse
may be sung by a soloist or choir.*

Christ's Birth

THE ETERNAL WORD

1 ON the eve of Christmas,
   In the fields at night-time,
      The shepherds watched their flocks near
      Bethlehem of Judah:
   Bright angels appearing,
      Bright angels appearing,
      Gave the joyful tidings.

2 'Born is now the baby,
   Christ, the world's Redeemer,
   Our God in flesh incarnate,
   Lying in a manger:
   To Bethlehem go now;
      To Bethlehem go now;
      There shall you behold him.'

3 'Mystery amazing!
   Let us go to seek him,
   To Bethlehem returning,
   As the angels told us.
   The Saviour, we seek him,
      The Saviour, we seek him:
      Mystery amazing!'

4 At the inn arriving,
   In the lowly stable
      They found him with the cattle,
      With Mary and with Joseph.
   The Saviour they worshipped,
      The Saviour they worshipped,
      Kneeling there before him.

5 On this happy morning,
   Come let us adore him,
   With heart and voice rejoicing,
   Worship our Redeemer,
   O come and adore him,
      O come and adore him
      Who came for us at Christmas!

Bemba Song
tr. *Arthur Morris Jones* (1899–)

1st and 5th line may be sung by a leader

Christ's Birth

117

HUMILITY (OXFORD) 77.77. (Refrain)

John Goss (1800–80)

Solo or Unison

Refrain   *Harmony*

THE ETERNAL WORD

1 SEE, amid the winter's snow,
Born for us on earth below,
See, the Lamb of God appears,
Promised from eternal years!
  Hail, thou ever-blessèd morn!
  Hail, redemption's happy dawn!
  Sing through all Jerusalem:
  Christ is born in Bethlehem!

2 Lo, within a manger lies
He who built the starry skies,
He who, throned in height sublime,
Sits amid the cherubim!

3 Say, you holy shepherds, say,
What your joyful news to-day;
Wherefore have you left your sheep
On the lonely mountain steep?

4 'As we watched at dead of night;
Lo, we saw a wondrous light;
Angels, singing "Peace on earth",
Told us of a Saviour's birth.'

5 Sacred Infant, all divine,
What a tender love was thine,
Thus to come from highest bliss
Down to such a world as this!

Edward Caswall (1814–78) alt.

Christ's Birth

118

CALYPSO CAROL Irregular

Michael A. Perry (1942–)
Arranged by Martin Ellis (1943–)

THE ETERNAL WORD

1 SEE him lying on a bed of straw;
   Draughty stable with an open door,
   Mary cradling the babe she bore;
      The Prince of Glory is his name:
      O now carry me to Bethlehem
      To see the Lord appear to men,
      Just as poor as was the stable then,
         The Prince of Glory when he came.

2 Star of silver, sweep across the skies,
   Show where Jesus in the manger lies;
   Shepherds, swiftly from your stupor rise
      To see the Saviour of the world:

3 Angels, sing again the song you sang,
   Bring God's glory to the heart of man;
   Sing that Bethlem's little baby can
      Be salvation to the soul:

4 Mine are riches from your poverty;
   From your innocence, eternity;
   Mine, forgiveness by your death for me;
      Child of sorrow for my joy:

Michael Perry (1942–   )

119

THE FIRST NOWELL   Irregular

English Traditional Melody
Arranged with Descant by
Leonard Blake (1907–   )

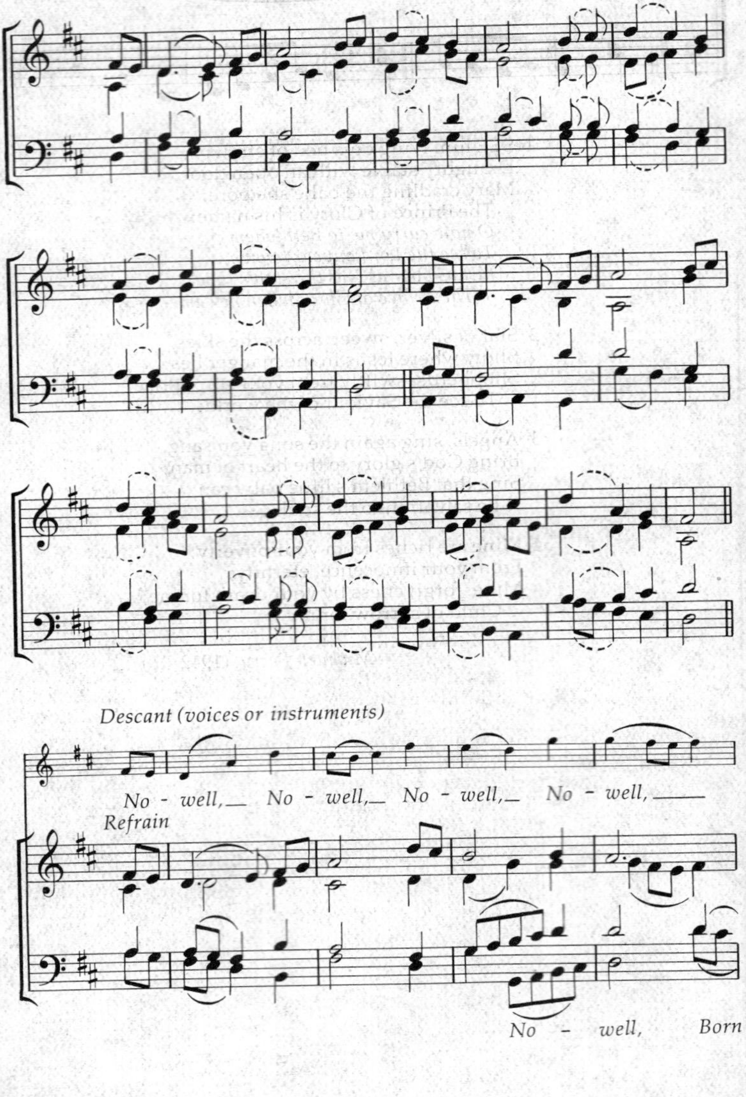
Descant (voices or instruments)
No - well, No - well, No - well, No - well,
Refrain
No - well, Born

Born is the King of Is - - ra - el.

1 THE first Nowell the angel did say
  Was to certain poor shepherds in fields as they lay:
  In fields where they lay a-keeping their sheep
  On a cold winter's night that was so deep:
      Nowell, Nowell, Nowell, Nowell,
      Born is the King of Israel.

2 They lookèd up and saw a star,
  Shining in the east, beyond them far,
  And to the earth it gave great light,
  And so it continued both day and night:

3 And by the light of that same star,
  Three wise men came from country far;
  To seek for a king was their intent,
  And to follow the star wherever it went:

4 This star drew nigh to the north-west,
  O'er Bethlehem it took its rest,
  And there it did both stop and stay
  Right over the place where Jesus lay:

5 Then entered in those wise men three,
  Full reverently upon their knee,
  And offered there in his presence
  Their gold and myrrh and frankincense:

6 Then let us all with one accord
  Sing praises to our heavenly Lord,
  That hath made heaven and earth of nought,
  And with his blood mankind hath bought:

                                        Anonymous

120(i)

WINCHESTER OLD C.M.

Melody from T. Est(e)'s *Psalmes* (1592)
Harmony adapted from Est(e) (1592)
and Ravenscroft (1621)

*If preferred, this tune may be sung in its original
rhythm, with a minim for the first and last note of
each line.*

DESCANT VERSION

*Descant with Organ
Other voices sing melody as above.*

Alan Gray (1855–1935)

The Descant Version may be used for verse 5 or verse 6.

THE ETERNAL WORD

1 WHILE shepherds watched their flocks by night,
  All seated on the ground,
The angel of the Lord came down,
  And glory shone around.

2 'Fear not,' said he (for mighty dread
  Had seized their troubled mind),
'Glad tidings of great joy I bring
  To you and all mankind.

3 'To you in David's town this day
  Is born of David's line
A Saviour, who is Christ the Lord;
  And this shall be the sign:

4 'The heavenly Babe you there shall find
  To human view displayed,
All meanly wrapped in swaddling bands,
  And in a manger laid.'

5 Thus spake the seraph; and forthwith
  Appeared a shining throng
Of angels praising God, and thus
  Addressed their joyful song:

6 'All glory be to God on high,
  And to the earth be peace;
Goodwill henceforth from heaven to men
  Begin and never cease.'

Nahum Tate (1652–1715)

Christ's Birth

120(ii)

LYNGHAM C.M. Ext.

T. Jarman (1776–1861)

THE ETERNAL WORD

1 WHILE shepherds watched their flocks by night,
    All seated on the ground,
The angel of the Lord came down,
    And glory shone around.

2 'Fear not,' said he (for mighty dread
    Had seized their troubled mind),
'Glad tidings of great joy I bring
    To you and all mankind.

3 'To you in David's town this day
    Is born of David's line
A Saviour, who is Christ the Lord;
    And this shall be the sign:

4 'The heavenly Babe you there shall find
    To human view displayed,
All meanly wrapped in swaddling bands,
    And in a manger laid.'

5 Thus spake the seraph; and forthwith
    Appeared a shining throng
Of angels praising God, and thus
    Addressed their joyful song:

6 'All glory be to God on high,
    And to the earth be peace;
Goodwill henceforth from heaven to men
    Begin and never cease.'

Nahum Tate (1652–1715)

Christ's Birth

121

C. Kocher (1786–1872)
Adapted by W. H. Monk (1823–89)

DIX 77.77.77.

DESCANT VERSION FOR LAST VERSE

Arranged by John Wilson

Sopranos (other voices sing unison melody)

Organ

5 In the heaven-ly coun – try bright Need they no cre –

– a – ted light; Thou its light, its joy, its crown,

THE ETERNAL WORD

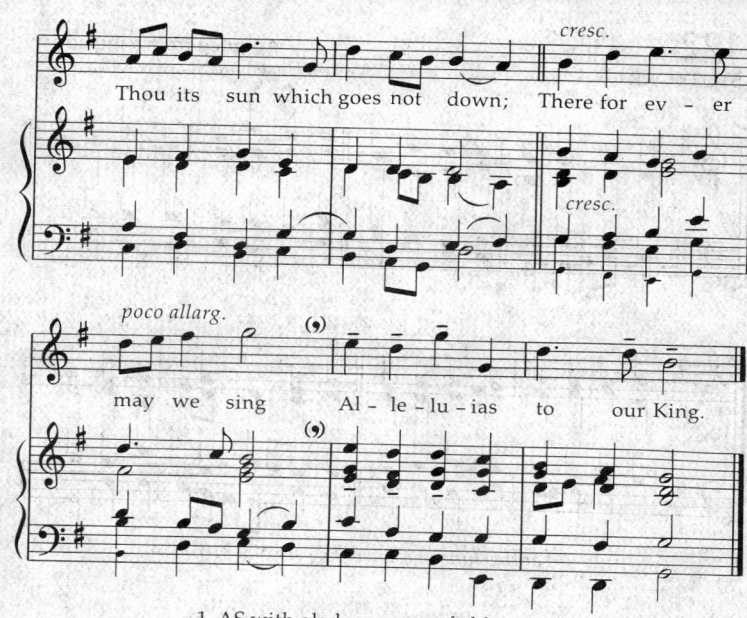

Thou its sun which goes not down; There for ev - er
may we sing Al - le - lu - ias to our King.

1 AS with gladness men of old
   Did the guiding star behold,
   As with joy they hailed its light,
   Leading onward, beaming bright,
   So, most gracious Lord, may we
   Evermore be led to thee.

2 As with joyful steps they sped,
   Saviour, to thy lowly bed,
   There to bend the knee before
   Thee, whom heaven and earth adore,
   So may we with willing feet
   Ever seek thy mercy-seat.

3 As they offered gifts most rare
   At thy cradle rude and bare,
   So may we with holy joy,
   Pure, and free from sin's alloy,
   All our costliest treasures bring,
   Christ, to thee, our heavenly King.

4 Holy Jesus, every day
   Keep us in the narrow way;
   And, when earthly things are past,
   Bring our ransomed souls at last
   Where they need no star to guide,
   Where no clouds thy glory hide.

5 In the heavenly country bright
   Need they no created light;
   Thou its light, its joy, its crown,
   Thou its sun which goes not down;
   There for ever may we sing
   Alleluias to our King.

William Chatterton Dix (1837–98)

The Epiphany

122

For this tune in a lower key see No. 81(i)

DESCANT FOR LAST VERSE

John Wilson

5 Ho - ly Je - sus, in thy bright - ness
To the Gen - tile world dis-played, With the Fa — ther
and the Spi - rit End - less praise to thee be paid.

THE ETERNAL WORD

1 BETHLEHEM, of noblest cities
    None can once with thee compare;
  Thou alone the Lord from heaven
    Didst for us incarnate bear.

2 Fairer than the sun at morning
    Was the star that told his birth,
  To the world its God announcing
    Seen in fleshly form on earth.

3 Eastern sages at his cradle
    Make oblations rich and rare;
  See them give, in deep devotion,
    Gold and frankincense and myrrh.

4 Sacred gifts of mystic meaning:
    Incense doth their God disclose,
  Gold the King of kings proclaimeth,
    Myrrh his sepulchre foreshows.

5 Holy Jesus, in thy brightness
    To the Gentile world displayed,
  With the Father and the Spirit
    Endless praise to thee be paid.

Prudentius (348–c. 410)
tr. *Edward Caswall* (1814–78) and others

123(i)

SPEAN 11.10.11.10. (Dactylic.)　　　　　John Frederick Bridge (1844–1924)

123(ii)

JESMIAN 11.10.11.10. (Dactylic.)　　　　　George Thalben-Ball (1896–   )

THE ETERNAL WORD

1 BRIGHTEST and best of the sons of the morning,
    Dawn on our darkness, and lend us thine aid;
Star of the east, the horizon adorning,
    Guide where our infant Redeemer is laid.

2 Cold on his cradle the dew-drops are shining;
    Low lies his head with the beasts of the stall;
Angels adore him in slumber reclining,
    Maker, and Monarch, and Saviour of all.

3 Say, shall we yield him, in costly devotion,
    Odours of Edom, and offerings divine,
Gems of the mountain and pearls of the ocean,
    Myrrh from the forest or gold from the mine?

4 Vainly we offer each ample oblation;
    Vainly with gifts would his favour secure;
Richer by far is the heart's adoration;
    Dearer to God are the prayers of the poor.

5 Brightest and best of the sons of the morning,
    Dawn on our darkness, and lend us thine aid;
Star of the east, the horizon adorning,
    Guide where our infant Redeemer is laid.

Reginald Heber (1783–1826)

May also be sung to No. 700(ii), EPIPHANY HYMN

The Epiphany

124(i)

MORWENSTOW 89.99.98.

Christopher Dearnley (1930–   )

124(ii)

FOYE 89.99.98.

Valerie Ruddle (1932–   )

THE ETERNAL WORD

1 CHILD of the stable's secret birth,
  The Lord by right of the lords of earth,
  Let angels sing of a King new-born—
  The world is weaving a crown of thorn:
      A crown of thorn for that infant head
      Cradled soft in the manger bed.

2 Eyes that shine in the lantern's ray;
  A face so small in its nest of hay—
  Face of a child who is born to scan
  The world of men through the eyes of man:
      And from that face in the final day
      Earth and heaven shall flee away.

3 Voice that rang through the courts on high
  Contracted now to a wordless cry,
  A voice to master the wind and wave,
  The human heart and the hungry grave:
      The voice of God through the cedar trees
      Rolling forth as the sound of seas.

4 Infant hands in a mother's hand,
  For none but Mary may understand
  Whose are the hands and the fingers curled
  But his who fashioned and made our world;
      And through these hands in the hour of death
      Nails shall strike to the wood beneath.

5 Child of the stable's secret birth,
  The Father's gift to a wayward earth,
  To drain the cup in a few short years
  Of all our sorrows, our sins and tears—
      Ours the prize for the road he trod:
      Risen with Christ; at peace with God.

Timothy Dudley-Smith (1926–   )

The Epiphany

CRÜGER (HERRNHUT) 7.6.7.6.D.

Adapted by W. H. Monk (1823–89)
from a melody in
J. Crüger's *Gesangbuch* (1640)

THE ETERNAL WORD

1 HAIL to the Lord's Anointed,
   Great David's greater Son!
Hail, in the time appointed,
   His reign on earth begun!
He comes to break oppression,
   To set the captive free,
To take away transgression,
   And rule in equity.

2 He comes, with succour speedy,
   To those who suffer wrong;
To help the poor and needy,
   And bid the weak be strong;
To give them songs for sighing,
   Their darkness turn to light,
Whose souls, condemned and dying,
   Were precious in his sight.

3 He shall come down like showers
   Upon the fruitful earth;
Love, joy, and hope, like flowers,
   Spring in his path to birth;
Before him, on the mountains,
   Shall peace the herald go;
And righteousness, in fountains,
   From hill to valley flow.

4 Kings shall fall down before him,
   And gold and incense bring;
All nations shall adore him,
   His praise all people sing;
To him shall prayer unceasing
   And daily vows ascend,
His kingdom still increasing,
   A kingdom without end.

5 O'er every foe victorious,
   He on his throne shall rest;
From age to age more glorious,
   All-blessing and all-blest.
The tide of time shall never
   His covenant remove;
His name shall stand for ever,
   His changeless name of Love.

James Montgomery (1771–1854)
based on Psalm 72

The Epiphany

126(i)
OLD 120th 6.6.6.6.6.6.

Melody from *Psalms* (1570)
Harmony from T. Ravenscroft's *Psalmes* (1621)

126(ii)
HAIL TO THE LORD 6.6.6.6.6.6.

Malcolm Williamson (1931–)

Unison. Rather quick

1 HAIL to the Lord who comes, Comes to his

THE ETERNAL WORD

tem - ple gate!   Not   with his an - gel host,

Not   in   his king - ly state: No shouts pro-claim him

nigh, No crowds his com - ing   wait;____

1 HAIL to the Lord who comes,
   Comes to his temple gate!
 Not with his angel host,
   Not in his kingly state:
 No shouts proclaim him nigh,
   No crowds his coming wait;

2 But borne upon the throne
   Of Mary's gentle breast,
 Watched by her duteous love,
   In her fond arms at rest;
 Thus to his Father's house
   He comes, the heavenly Guest.

3 There Joseph at her side
   In reverent wonder stands;
 And, filled with holy joy,
   Old Simeon in his hands
 Takes up the promised child,
   The glory of all lands.

4 O Light of all the earth,
   Thy children wait for thee:
 Come to thy temples here,
   That we, from sin set free,
 Before thy Father's face
   May all presented be.

John Ellerton (1826–93)

The Epiphany

Melody from *Piae Cantiones* (1582)
Arranged by Geoffrey Shaw (1879–1943)

All (Unison)

1 UN-TO us a boy is born! King of all cre - a - tion,

Came he to a world for-lorn, The Lord of ev-ery na - tion, The

Lord of ev-ery na - tion. 2 Cra-dled in a stall was he With

Senza Ped.

THE ETERNAL WORD

sleep-y cows and ass – es; But the ve-ry beasts could see That

he all men sur – pass – es, That he all men sur-pass – es.

All Tenors and Basses

3 He – rod then with fear was filled: 'A prince', he said, 'in

Ped.

Jew – ry!' All the lit – tle boys he killed At

The Epiphany

Beth-lem in his fu-ry, At Beth-lem in his fu-ry.

Trebles

4 Now may Ma-ry's son, who came So long a-go to love us, Lead us all with hearts a-flame Un-to the joys a-bove us, Un-to the joys a-bove us.

THE ETERNAL WORD

5 O - me-ga and Al-pha he! Let the or-gan thun - der,

While the choir with peals of glee Doth rend the air a -

-sun - der, Doth rend the air a - sun - der.

15th Century
tr. *Percy Dearmer* (1867–1936)

The Epiphany

128(i)

GLENFINLAS 6.5.6.5.

K. G. Finlay (1882–1974)

128(ii)

WORSHIP 6.5.6.5.

A. H. Mann (1850–1929)

THE ETERNAL WORD

1 WISE men, seeking Jesus,
   Travelled from afar,
Guided on their journey
   By a beauteous star.

2 But if we desire him,
   He is close at hand;
For our native country
   Is our Holy Land.

3 Prayerful souls may find him
   By our quiet lakes,
Meet him on our hillsides
   When the morning breaks.

4 In our fertile cornfields
   While the sheaves are bound,
In our busy markets,
   Jesus may be found.

5 Fishermen talk with him
   By the great North Sea,
As the first disciples
   Did in Galilee.

6 Every town and village
   In our land might be
Made by Jesus' presence
   Like sweet Bethany.

7 He is more than near us,
   If we love him well;
For he seeketh ever
   In our hearts to dwell.

James Thomas East (1860–1937)

129

CRUCIS VICTORIA C.M.

M. B. Foster (1851–1922)

DESCANT

From *Hymns for Church and School* (1964)

THE ETERNAL WORD

1 CHRIST, when for us you were baptized
     God's Spirit on you came,
  As peaceful as a dove, and yet
     As urgent as a flame.

2 God called you his belovèd Son,
     Called you his Servant too;
  His kingdom you were called to preach,
     His holy will to do.

3 Straightway and steadfast until death
     You then obeyed his call,
  Freely as Son of Man to serve,
     And give your life for all.

4 Baptize us with your Spirit, Lord,
     Your cross on us be signed,
  That likewise in God's service we
     May perfect freedom find.

F. Bland Tucker (1895-1984)

130(i)

HEINLEIN (AUS DER TIEFE)   7.7.7.7.

Melody from the *Nürnbergisches Gesangbuch* (1676–77), alt.
Attributed
to Martin Herbst (1654–81)

130(ii)

BUCKLAND   7.7.7.7.

L. G. Hayne (1836–83)

The tune Aus der Tiefe *may be used for verses 1–4, and*
Buckland *for verse 5.*

THE ETERNAL WORD

1 FORTY days and forty nights
    Thou wast fasting in the wild;
  Forty days and forty nights
    Tempted still, yet undefiled.

2 Sunbeams scorching day by day;
    Chilly dewdrops nightly shed;
  Prowling beasts about thy way;
    Stones thy pillow, earth thy bed.

3 Shall not we thy sorrows share,
    Learn thy discipline of will,
  And, like thee, by fast and prayer
    Wrestle with the powers of ill?

4 What if Satan, vexing sore,
    Flesh and spirit shall assail?
  Thou, his vanquisher before,
    Wilt not suffer us to fail.

5 Watching, praying, struggling thus,
    Vict'ry ours at last shall be;
  Angels minister to us
    As they ministered to thee.

George Smyttan (1822–70) and
Francis Pott (1832–1909) alt.

131(i)
GRAINGER C.M.

G. F. Brockless (1887–1957)

Melody from the
Scottish Psalter (1635)
(as harmonised in
The English Hymnal, 1906)

131(ii)
CAITHNESS C.M.

For this tune in a higher key see No. 218

THE ETERNAL WORD

1 LORD, who throughout these forty days
    For us didst fast and pray,
  Teach us with thee to mourn our sins,
    And close by thee to stay.

2 As thou with Satan didst contend,
    And didst the victory win,
  O give us strength in thee to fight,
    In thee to conquer sin.

3 As thirst and hunger thou didst bear,
    So teach us, gracious Lord,
  To die to self, and daily live
    By thy most holy word.

4 And through these days of penitence,
    And through thy Passiontide,
  Yea, evermore, in life and death,
    Jesus, with us abide.

Claudia F. Hernaman (1838–98)

132

PEARSALL   7.6.7.6.D.

R. L. de Pearsall (1795–1856)

THE ETERNAL WORD

1 WHEN Jesus came to Jordan
   To be baptized by John,
He did not come for pardon,
   But as his Father's Son.
He came to share repentance
   With all who mourn their sins,
To speak the vital sentence
   With which good news begins.

2 He came to share temptation,
   Our utmost woe and loss,
For us and our salvation
   To die upon the cross.
So when the Dove descended
   On him, the Son of Man,
The hidden years had ended,
   The age of grace began.

3 Come, Holy Spirit, aid us
   To keep the vows we make;
This very day invade us,
   And every bondage break.
Come, give our lives direction,
   The gift we covet most:
To share the resurrection
   That leads to Pentecost.

F. Pratt Green (1903–   )

Words reprinted by permission of
Stainer & Bell Ltd.
For permission to reproduce see p. xiii.

Christ's Baptism and Temptation

THE BEATITUDES

William Llewellyn (1925–   )

Note: *Each Bar, whether 2/4 or 3/4, is to have the same duration.*

ORGAN INTRODUCTION
Flowing easily

ANTIPHON (sung by all)

Show us your ways, O Lord, Teach us your paths. ___

Solo — All (or Full Choir)

Blest are the poor in spi-rit; For theirs is the king-dom of heaven.

Solo — All (or Full Choir)

Blest are they_ that mourn; For they shall

THE ETERNAL WORD

Christ's Teaching

133(cont.)

Solo

Blest are the mer-ci-ful;

All (or choir)

For they shall ob-tain mer-cy.

ANTIPHON *(sung by all)*

f Show us your ways, O Lord,

Teach us your paths.

Solo

Blest are the pure in heart;

All (or choir)

For they shall see God.

Solo

Blest are the

THE ETERNAL WORD

peace-ma-kers;   For they shall be called God's sons.

Solo

Blest are they which are per-se-cu-ted   for right-eous-ness'

All (or choir)

sake;   The king-dom of heaven is theirs.

ANTIPHON *(sung by all)*

Show us your   ways, O Lord,   Teach us   your   paths.

Psalm 25:4 and
Matthew 5:3–10

Christ's Teaching

134(i)

ST BERNARD C.M.

Melody, and most of the bass, from *Easy Hymn-Tunes for Catholic Schools* (1851) (based on an 18th-century German melody)

134(ii)

NIAMRYL C.M.

Geoffrey Laycock (1927–86)

THE ETERNAL WORD

1 'FORGIVE our sins as we forgive',
    You taught us, Lord, to pray,
  But you alone can grant us grace
    To live the words we say.

2 How can your pardon reach and bless
    The unforgiving heart
  That broods on wrongs, and will not let
    Old bitterness depart?

3 In blazing light your cross reveals
    The truth we dimly knew,
  How small the debts men owe to us,
    How great our debt to you!

4 Lord, cleanse the depths within our souls,
    And bid resentment cease;
  Then, reconciled to God and man,
    Our lives will spread your peace.

Rosamond E. Herklots (1905–   )

Christ's Teaching

135

GO TELL IT ON THE MOUNTAIN

7.6.7.6. (Refrain)

North American Spiritual
Arranged by Martin How (1931–   )

THE ETERNAL WORD

Go, tell it on the mountain,
Over the hills and everywhere;
Go, tell it on the mountain
That Jesus is his name.

1 HE possessed no riches, no home to lay his head;
   He fasted in the desert, he gave to others bread:

2 He reached out and touched them, the blind, the deaf,
      the lame;
   He spoke and listened gladly to anyone who came:

3 Some turned away in anger, with hatred in the eye;
   They tried him and condemned him, then led him out to
      die:

4 'Father, now forgive them', up on the cross he said;
   In three more days he was alive and risen from the
      dead:

5 He still comes to people, his life moves through the
      lands;
   He uses us for speaking, he touches with our hands:

Geoffrey Marshall-Taylor alt.

136

VOX DILECTI   D.C.M.

J. B. Dykes (1823–76)

(Vv. 2 & 3 only)

THE ETERNAL WORD

1 I HEARD the voice of Jesus say:
   'Come unto me and rest;
Lay down, thou weary one, lay down
   Thy head upon my breast.'
I came to Jesus as I was,
   Weary and worn and sad,
I found in him a resting-place,
   And he has made me glad.

2 I heard the voice of Jesus say:
   'Behold, I freely give
The living water; thirsty one,
   Stoop down and drink and live.'
I came to Jesus, and I drank
   Of that life-giving stream;
My thirst was quenched, my soul revived,
   And now I live in him.

3 I heard the voice of Jesus say:
   'I am this dark world's Light;
Look unto me, thy morn shall rise,
   And all thy day be bright.'
I looked to Jesus, and I found
   In him my star, my sun;
And in that light of life I'll walk,
   Till travelling days are done.

Horatius Bonar (1808–89)

Christ's Teaching

137

Urdu melody
Harmonised by Francis Westbrook (1903–75)

1 JE-SUS the Lord said: 'I am the Bread, The Bread of__ Life_for man-
Unison

-kind am I. The Bread of__ Life_ for man-kind am I, The

Bread of__ Life_ for man-kind am I'. Je - sus the Lord said:

THE ETERNAL WORD

'I am the Bread, The Bread of __ Life _ for man-kind am I'.

1 JESUS the Lord said: 'I am the Bread,
   The Bread of Life for mankind am I.
   The Bread of Life for mankind am I,
   The Bread of Life for mankind am I'.
   Jesus the Lord said: 'I am the Bread,
   The Bread of Life for mankind am I'.

2 Jesus the Lord said: 'I am the Door,
   The Way and the Door for the poor am I.
   The Way and the Door for the poor am I,
   The Way and the Door for the poor am I'.
   Jesus the Lord said: 'I am the Door,
   The Way and the Door for the poor am I'.

3 Jesus the Lord said: 'I am the Light,
   The one true Light of the world am I.
   The one true Light of the world am I,
   The one true Light of the world am I'.
   Jesus the Lord said: 'I am the Light,
   The one true Light of the world am I'.

4 Jesus the Lord said: 'I am the Shepherd,
   The one good Shepherd of the sheep am I.
   The one good Shepherd of the sheep am I,
   The one good Shepherd of the sheep am I'.
   Jesus the Lord said: 'I am the Shepherd,
   The one good Shepherd of the sheep am I'.

5 Jesus the Lord said: 'I am the Life,
   The Resurrection and the Life am I.
   The Resurrection and the Life am I,
   The Resurrection and the Life am I'.
   Jesus the Lord said: 'I am the Life,
   The Resurrection and the Life am I'.

Anonymous
tr. *Dermott Monahan* (1906-57)

138

SEEK YE FIRST Irreg.

Karen Lafferty
Arranged by Richard Bradshaw

Unison

1 SEEK ye first the king - dom of God,

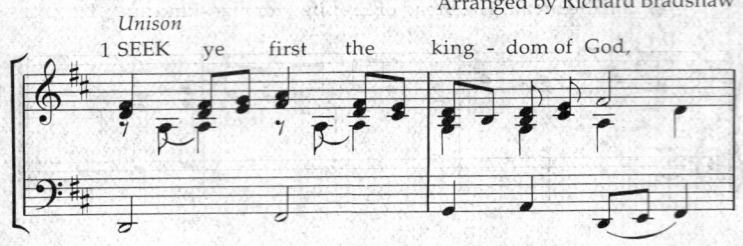

And his right - eous - ness,

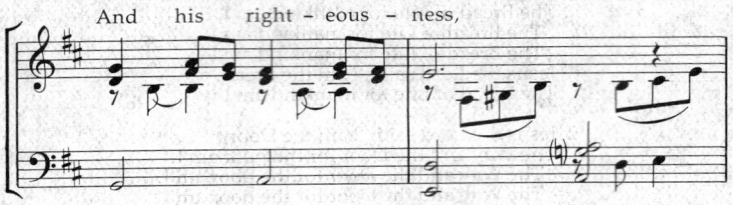

And all these things shall be add-ed un-to you;

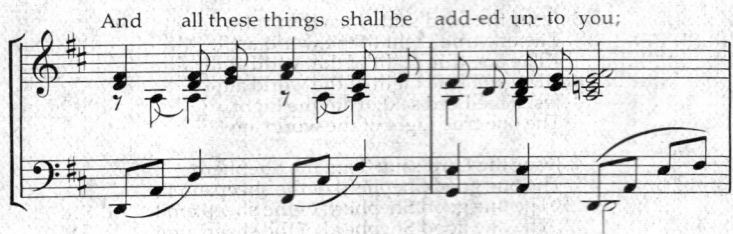

Al - le - lu-, Al - le - lu - - ia:

THE ETERNAL WORD

1 SEEK ye first the kingdom of God,
And his righteousness,
And all these things shall be added unto you;
Allelu-, Alleluia:
Alleluia, Alleluia, Alleluia,
Allelu-, Alleluia!

2 Ask, and it shall be given unto you;
Seek, and ye shall find;
Knock, and the door shall be opened unto you;
Allelu-, Alleluia:

3 Man shall not live by bread alone,
But by every word
That proceeds from the mouth of the Lord;
Allelu-, Alleluia:

Karen Lafferty
based on Matthew 6:33, 7:7,
and Deuteronomy 8:3

Christ's Teaching

139

TETHERDOWN   5.5.5.5.6.5.6.5.   Gerald L. Barnes (1935–)

1 THE kingdom of God
    Is justice and joy,
For Jesus restores
    What sin would destroy;
God's power and glory
    In Jesus we know,
And here and hereafter
    The kingdom shall grow.

2 The kingdom of God
    Is mercy and grace,
The lepers are cleansed,
    The sinners find place,
The outcast are welcomed
    God's banquet to share,
And hope is awakened
    In place of despair.

3 The kingdom of God
    Is challenge and choice,
Believe the good news,
    Repent and rejoice!
His love for us sinners
    Brought Christ to his cross,
Our crisis of judgement
    For gain or for loss.

4 God's kingdom is come,
    The gift and the goal,
In Jesus begun,
    In heaven made whole;
The heirs of the kingdom
    Shall answer his call,
And all things cry glory
    To God all in all!

Bryn Rees (1911–83)

May also be sung to No. 598, PADERBORN

THE ETERNAL WORD

140

Martin Shaw (1875–1958)

1 THE voice of God goes out to all the world;
His glory speaks across the universe.
The great King's herald cries from star to star:
With power, with justice, he will walk his way.

2 The Lord has said: 'Receive my messenger,
My promise to the world, my pledge made flesh,
A lamp to every nation, light from light':
With power, with justice, he will walk his way.

3 The broken reed he will not trample down,
Nor set his heel upon the dying flame.
He binds the wounds, and health is in his hand:
With power, with justice, he will walk his way.

4 Anointed with the Spirit and with power,
He comes to crown with comfort all the weak,
To show the face of justice to the poor:
With power, with justice, he will walk his way.

5 His touch will bless the eyes that darkness held,
The lame shall run, the halting tongue shall sing,
And prisoners laugh in light and liberty:
With power, with justice, he will walk his way.

Peter Icarus

Christ's Teaching

141(i)
ST CATHERINE 8.7.8.7.

S. Flood Jones (1826–95)

141(ii)
WRAYSBURY 8.7.8.7.

E. J. Hopkins (1818–1901)
(harmony slightly simplified)

THE ETERNAL WORD

1 JESUS calls us! O'er the tumult
      Of our life's wild restless sea,
   Day by day his clear voice soundeth,
      Saying: 'Christian, follow me';

2 As of old apostles heard it
      By the Galilean lake,
   Turned from home and toil and kindred,
      Leaving all for his dear sake.

3 Jesus calls us from the worship
      Of the vain world's golden store,
   From each idol that would keep us,
      Saying: 'Christian, love me more'.

4 In our joys and in our sorrows,
      Days of toil and hours of ease,
   Still he calls, in cares and pleasures:
      'Christian, love me more than these'.

5 Jesus calls us! By thy mercies,
      Saviour, may we hear thy call,
   Give our hearts to thine obedience,
      Serve and love thee best of all.

Cecil Frances Alexander (1818–95)

142

ANGELUS L.M.   Founded on a melody in *Heilige Seelenlust*

1 AT even, when the sun was set,
   The sick, O Lord, around thee lay;
   O in what divers pains they met!
   O with what joy they went away!

2 Once more 'tis eventide, and we,
   Oppressed with various ills, draw near;
   What if thy form we cannot see?
   We know and feel that thou art here.

3 O Saviour Christ, our woes dispel;
   For some are sick, and some are sad,
   And some have never loved thee well,
   And some have lost the love they had;

4 And none, O Lord, has perfect rest,
   For none is wholly free from sin;
   And they who fain would serve thee best
   Are conscious most of wrong within.

5 O Saviour Christ, thou too art man;
   Thou hast been troubled, tempted, tried;
   Thy kind but searching glance can scan
   The very wounds that shame would hide.

6 Thy touch has still its ancient power;
   No word from thee can fruitless fall:
   Hear, in this solemn evening hour,
   And in thy mercy heal us all.

Henry Twells (1823–1900)

THE ETERNAL WORD/Christ's Ministry

143

ST JOHN (CALKIN)   6.6.6.6.88.

J. B. Calkin (1827–1905)
(harmony slightly altered)

The original key of D flat may be preferred

1   BEHOLD a little child,
        Laid in a manger bed;
     The wintry blasts blow wild
        Around his infant head.
     But who is this, so lowly laid?
     'Tis he by whom the worlds were made.

2   The hands that all things made
        An earthly craft pursue;
     Where Joseph plies his trade,
        There Jesus labours too,
     That weary men in him may rest,
     And faithful toil through him be blest.

3   Christ, Master Carpenter,
        We come rough-hewn to thee;
     At last, through wood and nails,
        Thou mad'st us whole and free.
     In this thy world remake us, planned
     To truer beauty of thine hand.

            William Walsham How (1823–97)
            and *Donald McIlhagga* (1933–)

Christ's Ministry

THE ETERNAL WORD

1 FIERCE raged the tempest o'er the deep,
   Watch did thine anxious servants keep;
   But thou wast wrapped in guileless sleep,
                    Calm and still.

2 'Save, Lord, we perish!' was their cry,
   'O save us in our agony!'
   Thy word above the storm rose high:
                    'Peace! Be still.'

3 The wild winds hushed; the angry deep
   Sank, like a little child, to sleep;
   The sullen billows ceased to leap,
                    At thy will.

4 So, when our life is clouded o'er,
   And storm-winds drift us from the shore,
   Say, lest we sink to rise no more:
                    'Peace! Be still.'

Godfrey Thring (1823–1903)

145

CHEREPONI 7.7.9.(Refrain)

Melody from
harmonised by compil
New Church Praise (197

Unison
Refrain

Je - su,_____ Je - su, _____ Fill us with your love, Show

us how to serve The neigh-bours we have from

you._____   *Verses*
1 KNEELS at the feet of his

Fine

friends,_____ Si-lent-ly wash-es their feet,_____

THE ETERNAL WORD

Mas-ter who acts as a slave_____ .to them._____

Repeat Refrain

> *Jesu, Jesu,*
> *Fill us with your love,*
> *Show us how to serve*
> *The neighbours we have from you.*

1 KNEELS at the feet of his friends,
  Silently washes their feet,
  Master who acts as a slave to them.
    Jesu, Jesu. . . . .

2 Neighbours are rich folk and poor,
  Neighbours are black folk and white,
  Neighbours are nearby and far away.
    Jesu, Jesu. . . . .

3 These are the ones we should serve,
  These are the ones we should love.
  All these are neighbours to us and you.
    Jesu, Jesu. . . . .

4 Kneel at the feet of our friends,
  Silently washing their feet,
  This is the way we should live with you.
    Jesu, Jesu. . . . .

T. S. Colvin (1925–   )
based on a song from N. Ghana

Christ's Ministry

146(i)

WESTRIDGE 8.5.8.3.

Martin Shaw (1875–1958)

146(ii)

DERWENT 8.5.8.3.

C. L. Naylor (1869–1945)

THE ETERNAL WORD

1 JESUS, friend of little children,
    Be a friend to me;
  Take my hand, and ever keep me
    Close to thee.

2 Teach me how to grow in goodness
    Daily as I grow;
  Thou hast been a child, and surely
    Thou dost know.

3 Never leave me nor forsake me,
    Ever be my friend;
  For I need thee from life's dawning
    To its end.

Walter John Mathams (1853–1931)

Christ's Ministry

147

1 JESUS, my Lord, how rich thy grace,
    Thy bounties how complete!
  How shall I count the matchless sum?
    How pay the mighty debt?

2 High on a throne of radiant light
    Dost thou exalted shine;
  What can my poverty bestow
    When all the worlds are thine?

3 But thou hast brethren here below,
    The partners of thy grace,
  And wilt confess their humble names
    Before thy Father's face.

4 In them thou may'st be clothed and fed,
    And visited and cheered;
  And in their accents of distress
    My Saviour's voice is heard.

5 Thy face with reverence and with love
    I in thy poor would see;
  O let me rather beg my bread
    Than hold it back from thee.

Philip Doddridge (1702–51)

May also be sung to No. 265(i), METZLER'S REDHEAD

THE ETERNAL WORD

148

ANTWERP L.M.

William Smallwood (1831–97)

For this tune in a lower key see No. 225

1 JESUS, thy far-extended fame
    My drooping soul exults to hear;
  Thy name, thy all-restoring name,
    Is music in a sinner's ear.

2 Sinners of old thou didst receive
    With comfortable words and kind,
  Their sorrows cheer, their wants relieve,
    Heal the diseased, and cure the blind.

3 And art thou not the Saviour still,
    In every place and age the same?
  Hast thou forgot thy gracious skill,
    Or lost the virtue of thy name?

4 Faith in thy changeless name I have;
    The good, the kind physician, thou
  Art able now our souls to save,
    Art willing to restore them now.

5 Wouldst thou the body's health restore,
    And not regard the sin-sick soul?
  The soul thou lovest yet the more,
    And surely thou shalt make it whole.

6 My soul's disease, my every sin,
    To thee, O Jesus, I confess;
  In pardon, Lord, my cure begin,
    And perfect it in holiness.

Charles Wesley (1707–88) alt.

Christ's Ministry

149(i)

ALL SAINTS   8.7.8.7.77.

Adapted by W. H. Monk (1823–99)
from a melody in *Geistreiches Gesangbuch*
(Darmstadt, 1698) (harmony slightly altered)

149(ii)

ST LEONARD   8.7.8.7.7.7.

J. C. Bach (1642–1703)

THE ETERNAL WORD

1 ONE there is above all others
    Well deserves the name of friend;
His is love beyond a brother's,
    Costly, free, and knows no end;
They who once his kindness prove
Find it everlasting love.

2 Which of all our friends, to save us,
    Could or would have shed his blood?
But our Jesus died to have us
    Reconciled in him to God;
This was boundless love indeed;
Jesus is a friend in need.

3 When he lived on earth abasèd,
    Friend of sinners was his name;
Now, above all glory raisèd,
    He rejoices in the same;
Still he calls them brethren, friends,
And to all their wants attends.

4 O for grace our hearts to soften!
    Teach us, Lord, at length to love;
We, alas, forget too often
    What a friend we have above;
But when home our souls are brought
We shall love thee as we ought.

John Newton (1725–1807)

150
ST SEPULCHRE L.M.

G. Cooper (1820–76)

THE ETERNAL WORD

1 O THOU, whom once they flocked to hear,
    Thy words to hear, thy power to feel;
  Suffer the sinners to draw near,
    And graciously receive us still.

2 They that be whole, thyself hast said,
    No need of a physician have;
  But I am sick, and want thine aid,
    And ask thine utmost power to save.

3 Thy power, and truth, and love divine,
    The same from age to age endure;
  A word, a gracious word of thine,
    The most inveterate plague can cure.

4 Helpless howe'er my spirit lies,
    And long hath languished at the pool,
  A word of thine shall make me rise,
    Shall speak me in a moment whole.

5 Make this my Lord's accepted hour;
    Come, O my soul's physician thou!
  Display thy justifying power,
    And show me thy salvation now.

Charles Wesley (1707–88)
based on John 5:2–9

151

HEALER 11.6.11.5.

Peter D. Smith (1938–)

Unison

1 WHEN Je-sus the heal-er passed through Ga-li-lee, —— Heal us, heal us to-day! —— The deaf came to hear and the blind came to see. Heal us, Lord Je-sus! ——

G D G C
D Bmi Emi Ami D G
Bmi Emi Ami D
G Bmi Emi G D G

THE ETERNAL WORD

1 WHEN Jesus the healer passed through Galilee—
   Heal us, heal us today!—
The deaf came to hear and the blind came to see.
   Heal us, Lord Jesus!

2 A paralysed man was let down through a roof—
   Heal us, heal us today!—
His sins were forgiven; his walking the proof.
   Heal us, Lord Jesus!

3 The death of his daughter caused Jairus to weep—
   Heal us, heal us today!—
The Lord took her hand and he raised her from sleep.
   Heal us, Lord Jesus!

4 When blind Bartimaeus cried out to the Lord—
   Heal us, heal us today!—
His faith made him whole and his sight was restored.
   Heal us, Lord Jesus!

5 The twelve were commissioned and sent out by twos—
   Heal us, heal us today!—
To make the sick whole and to spread the good news.
   Heal us, Lord Jesus!

6 The lepers were healed and the demons cast out;
   Heal us, heal us today! —
Now lame leap for joy and the dumb laugh and shout;
   Heal us, Lord Jesus!

7 There's still so much sickness and suffering today;
   Heal us, heal us today!—
We gather together for healing, and pray:
   Heal us, Lord Jesus!

Peter Smith (1938–)

Words and music reprinted by permission of
Stainer & Bell Ltd and the Methodist Church
Division of Education and Youth. Additional
optional parts for instruments are printed in
Partners in Praise. For permission to reproduce
see p. xiii.

Christ's Ministry

152
LAWES' PSALM 47 6.6.6.6.88.

Melody and bass by
Henry Lawes (1596–1662)
(original rhythm)

THE ETERNAL WORD

1 SON of the Lord most high,
     Who gave the worlds their birth,
   He came to live and die
     The Son of Man on earth;
   In Bethlem's stable born was he,
   And humbly bred in Galilee.

2 Born in so low estate,
     Schooled in a workman's trade,
   Not with the high and great
     His home the Highest made;
   But, labouring by his brethren's side,
   Life's common lot he glorified.

3 Then, when his hour was come,
     He heard his Father's call;
   And, leaving friends and home,
     He gave himself for all,
   Glad news to bring, the lost to find,
   To heal the sick, the lame, the blind.

4 Toiling by night and day,
     Himself oft burdened sore,
   Where hearts in bondage lay,
     Himself their burden bore;
   Till, scorned by them he died to save,
   Himself in death, as life, he gave.

5 O lowly majesty,
     Lofty in lowliness!
   Blest Saviour, who am I
     To share thy blessedness?
   Yet thou hast called me, even me,
   Servant divine, to follow thee.

George Wallace Briggs (1875–1959)

Christ's Ministry

153(i)
STORIES OF JESUS   8.4.8.4.5.4.5.4.   F. A. Challinor (1866–1952)

153(ii)
KILGETTY   8.4.8.4.5.4.5.4.   Irish Folksong Melody
Arranged by
George Thalben-Ball (1896–)

THE ETERNAL WORD

1 TELL me the stories of Jesus
   I love to hear;
Things I would ask him to tell me
   If he were here;
   Scenes by the wayside,
   Tales of the sea,
   Stories of Jesus,
   Tell them to me.

2 First let me hear how the children
   Stood round his knee;
And I shall fancy his blessing
   Resting on me;
   Words full of kindness,
   Deeds full of grace,
   All in the love-light
   Of Jesus' face.

3 Tell me, in accents of wonder,
   How rolled the sea,
Tossing the boat in a tempest
   On Galilee;
   And how the Master,
   Ready and kind,
   Chided the billows,
   And hushed the wind.

4 Into the city I'd follow
   The children's band,
Waving a branch of the palm-tree
   High in my hand;
   One of his heralds,
   Yes, I would sing
   Loudest hosannas,
   Jesus is King!

5 Show me that scene in the garden,
   Of bitter pain;
And of the cross where my Saviour
   For me was slain;
   And, through the sadness,
   Help me to see
   How Jesus suffered
   For love of me.

6 Tell me with joy of his rising
   Up from the grave;
And how he still lives triumphant,
   Ready to save.
   Wonderful story,
   Jesus my friend,
   Living and loving
   Right to the end.

W. H. Parker (1845–1929) alt.
v. 6 *Ruth Fagg*

Christ's Ministry

154

MARGARET Irreg.

Timothy Matthews (1826–1910)

THE ETERNAL WORD

1 THOU didst leave thy throne
   And thy kingly crown
When thou camest to earth for me,
   But in Bethlehem's home
   Was there found no room
For thy holy nativity:
   O come to my heart, Lord Jesus!
There is room in my heart for thee.

2 Heaven's arches rang
   When the angels sang,
Proclaiming thy royal degree;
   But of lowly birth
   Cam'st thou, Lord, on earth,
And in great humility:
   O come to my heart, Lord Jesus!
There is room in my heart for thee.

3 The foxes found rest,
   And the bird its nest,
In the shade of the cedar tree;
   But thy couch was the sod,
   O thou Son of God,
In the deserts of Galilee:
   O come to my heart, Lord Jesus!
There is room in my heart for thee.

4 Thou camest, O Lord,
   With the living word
That should set thy people free;
   But, with mocking scorn,
   And with crown of thorn,
They bore thee to Calvary:
   O come to my heart, Lord Jesus!
Thy cross is my only plea.

5 When heaven's arches ring,
   And her choirs shall sing,
At thy coming to victory,
   Let thy voice call me home,
   Saying, 'Yet there is room,
There is room at my side for thee!'
   And my heart shall rejoice, Lord Jesus,
When thou comest and callest for me.

Emily Elizabeth Steele Elliott (1836–97)

Christ's Ministry

155

FENITON   7.8.7.8. Alleluias

Sydney H. Nicholson (1875–1947)

THE ETERNAL WORD

1 CHRIST upon the mountain-peak
   Stands alone in glory blazing;
 Let us, if we dare to speak,
   With the saints and angels praise him:
       Alleluia!

2 Trembling at his feet, we saw
   Moses and Elijah speaking;
 All the prophets and the law
   Shout through them their joyful greeting:
       Alleluia!

3 Swift the cloud of glory came,
   God proclaiming in its thunder
 Jesus as his Son, by name;
   Nations, cry aloud in wonder!
       Alleluia!

4 This is God's belovèd Son:
   Law and prophets fade before him;
 First and Last, and only One,
   Let creation now adore him:
       Alleluia!

Brian A. Wren (1936–)

The Transfiguration

156
VENICE S.M.

William Amps (1824–1910)

For this tune in a higher key see No. 449(i)

THE ETERNAL WORD

1 HOW good, Lord, to be here!
   Your glory fills the night;
   Your face and garments, like the sun,
   Shine with unborrowed light.

2 How good, Lord, to be here,
   Your beauty to behold,
   Where Moses and Elijah stand,
   Your messengers of old.

3 Fulfiller of the past,
   Promise of things to be:
   We hail your body glorified,
   And our redemption see.

4 Before we taste of death,
   We see your kingdom come;
   We still would hold the vision bright,
   And make this hill our home.

5 How good, Lord, to be here!
   Yet we may not remain;
   But since you bid us leave the mount
   Come with us to the plain.

Joseph Armitage Robinson (1858–1933) alt.

The Transfiguration

157

TRANSFIGURATION   6.6.8.5.6.6.8.4.   Christopher Dearnley (1930–   )

Flowing smoothly, unhurried

1   Once-on a moun-tain-top There stood three start-led men; They
2   Yet __ ma - ny lived and died Who found of him __ no trace. 'Thou
3   And minds that learn to scan Cre - a - tion like __ a book Know

Unison

watched the wheels of na - ture stop And hea-ven break in. Their
art   a God' (the pro - phet cried) 'Who hi-dest thy face.' The
no -thing lives out - side their plan, So ne - ver look. O

THE ETERNAL WORD

friend of ev-ery day, The face they knew for his, They__
earth lies all ex-plored, The heavens are ours__ to climb, And__
Lord of hid-den light, For - give us who __des-pise The__

saw, for one half-hour, the way He al - ways is.
still no man has seen his God At a - ny time.
things which lie be - yond our sight, And give__ us eyes.

Michael Hewlett (1916–)

The Transfiguration

158

UNDE ET MEMORES   10 10.10 10.10 10.   W. H. Monk (1823–89)

1 STAY, Master, stay upon this heavenly hill;
A little longer, let us linger still;
With all the mighty ones of old beside,
Near to the aweful Presence still abide;
Before the throne of light we trembling stand,
And catch a glimpse into the spirit-land.

2 Stay, Master, stay! We breathe a purer air;
This life is not the life that waits us there;
Thoughts, feelings, flashes, glimpses come and go;
We cannot speak them—nay, we do not know;
Wrapt in this cloud of light we seem to be
The thing we fain would grow—eternally.

3 No, saith the Lord, the hour is past, we go;
Our home, our life, our duties lie below.
While here we kneel upon the mount of prayer,
The plough lies waiting in the furrow there.
Here we sought God that we might know his will;
There we must do it, serve him, seek him still.

Samuel Greg (1804–76)

THE ETERNAL WORD / The Transfiguration

159

WINCHESTER NEW L.M.   Adapted from a melody in *Musicalisches Hand-Buch* (Hamburg, 1690)

1 RIDE on, ride on in majesty!
   Hark, all the tribes 'Hosanna!' cry;
      Thine humble beast pursues his road
      With palms and scattered garments strowed.

2 Ride on, ride on in majesty!
   In lowly pomp ride on to die:
      O Christ, thy triumphs now begin
      O'er captive death and conquered sin.

3 Ride on, ride on in majesty!
   The wingèd squadrons of the sky
      Look down with sad and wondering eyes
      To see the approaching sacrifice.

4 Ride on, ride on in majesty!
   Thy last and fiercest strife is nigh;
      The Father, on his sapphire throne,
      Expects his own anointed Son.

5 Ride on, ride on in majesty!
   In lowly pomp ride on to die;
      Bow thy meek head to mortal pain,
      Then take, O God, thy power, and reign.

Henry Hart Milman (1791–1868)

Christ's Passion and Cross

160

ST THEODULPH 7.6.7.6.D.

M. Teschner (1584–1635)
Arranged W. H. Monk (1823–89)

V. 4 ends here

1 ALL glory, laud, and honour
    To thee, Redeemer, King,
To whom the lips of children
    Made sweet hosannas ring!
Thou art the King of Israel,
    Thou David's royal Son,
Who in the Lord's name comest,
    The King and Blessèd One.

2 The company of angels
    Are praising thee on high,
And mortal men and all things
    Created make reply.
The people of the Hebrews
    With palms before thee went;
Our praise and prayer and anthems
    Before thee we present.

3 To thee before thy Passion
    They sang their hymns of praise;
To thee now high exalted
    Our melody we raise.
Thou didst accept their praises;
    Accept the prayers we bring,
Who in all good delightest,
    Thou good and gracious King.

4 All glory, laud, and honour
    To thee, Redeemer, King,
To whom the lips of children
    Made sweet hosannas ring!

Theodulph of Orleans (d. 821)
tr. *John Mason Neale* (1818–66)

THE ETERNAL WORD

161

KING'S LANGLEY C.M.

Traditional May-Day carol melody, collected by
Lucy Broadwood (1858–1929) and harmonised by
Ralph Vaughan Williams (1872–1958)

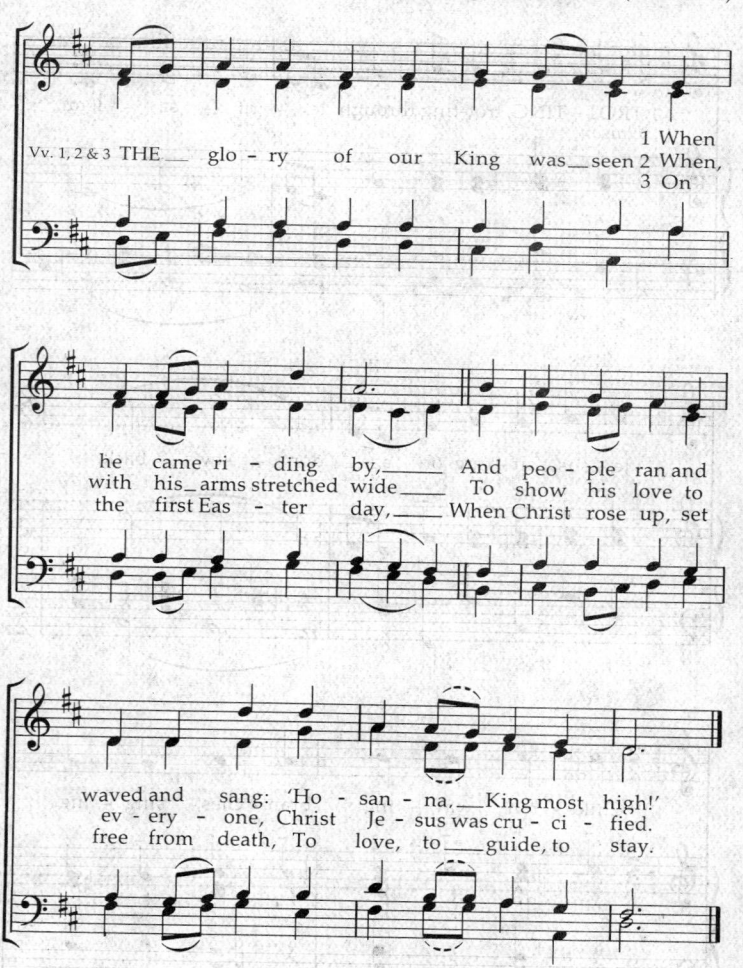

Vv. 1, 2 & 3 THE glo-ry of our King was seen
1 When he came ri-ding by, And peo-ple ran and waved and sang: 'Ho-san-na, King most high!'

2 When, with his arms stretched wide To show his love to ev-ery-one, Christ Je-sus was cru-ci-fied.

3 On the first Eas-ter day, When Christ rose up, set free from death, To love, to guide, to stay.

Margaret Cropper (1886–1980) alt.

Christ's Passion and Cross

162

TROTTING 9.9.8.12.

Eric Reid (1936–70)

1 TROT – TING, trot-ting through Je – ru – sa – lem,
Unison

Je – sus, sit-ting on a ___ don – key's back,

Child – ren wav – ing bran – ches, sing – ing:

*Pedal notes for an organ accompaniment are shown by downward stems.

THE ETERNAL WORD

'Hap-py is he that— comes in the name of the

Lord!'

1 TROTTING, trotting through Jerusalem,
   Jesus, sitting on a donkey's back,
   Children waving branches, singing:
   'Happy is he that comes in the name of the Lord!'

2 Many people in Jerusalem
   Thought he should have come on a mighty horse
   Leading all the Jews to battle:
   'Happy is he that comes in the name of the Lord!'

3 Many people in Jerusalem
   Were amazed to see such a quiet man
   Trotting, trotting on a donkey:
   'Happy is he that comes in the name of the Lord!'

4 Trotting, trotting through Jerusalem,
   Jesus, sitting on a donkey's back;
   Let us join the children singing:
   'Happy is he that comes in the name of the Lord!'

Eric Reid (1936–70)

Christ's Passion and Cross

163
CHILDREN'S PRAISE 7.7.7.7. (Refrain) Curwen's *Tune Book* (1842)

Hark! Hark! Hark! While children's voices sing,

Hark! Hark! Hark! While children's voices sing Loud ho - san - nas

THE ETERNAL WORD

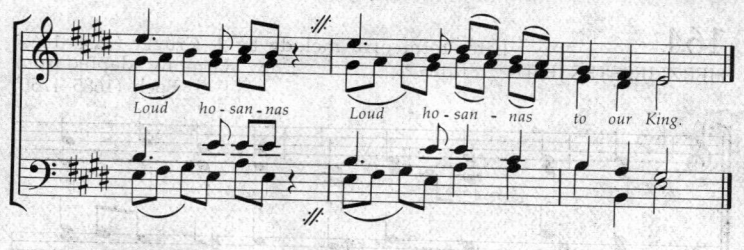

Loud ho-san-nas Loud ho-san-nas to our King.

1 CHILDREN of Jerusalem
   Sang the praise of Jesus' name;
   Children, too, of modern days,
   Join to sing the Saviour's praise:
   Hark! While children's voices sing
   Loud hosannas to our King.

2 We are taught to love the Lord,
   We are taught to read his word,
   We are taught the way to heaven;
   Praise for all to God be given:

3 Parents, teachers, old and young,
   All unite to swell the song;
   Higher and yet higher rise,
   Till hosannas reach the skies:

   John Henley (1800–42)

164
HERZLIEBSTER JESU 11 11.11 5.

Later form of a melody by J. Crüger (1598–1662)
Harmony adapted from
J. S. Bach (1685–1750)

THE ETERNAL WORD

1 AH, holy Jesus, how hast thou offended,
   That man to judge thee hath in hate pretended?
   By foes derided, by thine own rejected,
        O most afflicted.

2 Who was the guilty? Who brought this upon thee?
   Alas, my treason, Jesus, hath undone thee.
   'Twas I, Lord Jesus, I it was denied thee:
        I crucified thee.

3 Lo, the good Shepherd for the sheep is offered:
   The slave hath sinnèd, and the Son hath suffered:
   For man's atonement, while he nothing heedeth,
        God intercedeth.

4 For me, kind Jesus, was thy incarnation,
   Thy mortal sorrow, and thy life's oblation;
   Thy death of anguish and thy bitter passion,
        For my salvation.

5 Therefore, kind Jesus, since I cannot pay thee,
   I do adore thee, and will ever pray thee,
   Think on thy pity and thy love unswerving,
        Not my deserving.

Robert Bridges (1844–1930),
based on *Johann Heermann* (1585-1647)

Christ's Passion and Cross

165(i)

BENEATH THE CROSS OF JESUS. 7.6.8.6.8.6.8.6.   I. D. Sankey (1840–1908)

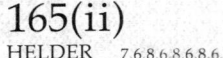

165(ii)

HELDER 7.6.8.6.8.6.8.6.

Melody by
Bartholomaeus Helder (1585–1635)
Gothaer Cantional (1648)

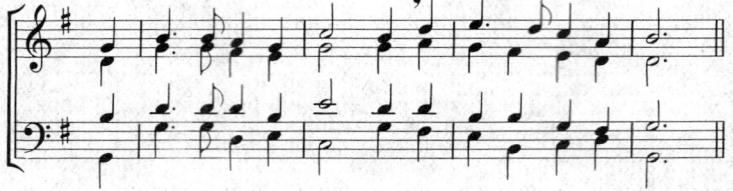

THE ETERNAL WORD

1 BENEATH the cross of Jesus
   I fain would take my stand—
The shadow of a mighty rock
   Within a weary land;
A home within a wilderness,
   A rest upon the way,
From the burning of the noontide heat
   And the burden of the day.

2 O safe and happy shelter,
   O refuge tried and sweet,
O trysting-place where heaven's love
   And heaven's justice meet!
As to the holy patriarch
   That wondrous dream was given,
So seems my Saviour's cross to me
   A ladder up to heaven.

3 I take, O cross, thy shadow,
   For my abiding-place!
I ask no other sunshine than
   The sunshine of his face;
Content to let the world go by,
   To know no gain nor loss—
My sinful self my only shame,
   My glory all—the cross.

Elizabeth Cecilia Clephane (1830–69)

Christ's Passion and Cross

Adapted from a tune by
Felice de Giardini (1716–96)

THE ETERNAL WORD

1 GOD of unexampled grace,
    Redeemer of mankind,
Matter of eternal praise
    We in thy passion find;
Still our choicest strains we bring,
    Still the joyful theme pursue,
Thee the friend of sinners sing,
    Whose love is ever new.

2 Endless scenes of wonder rise
    From that mysterious tree,
Crucified before our eyes
    Where we our Maker see;
Jesus, Lord, what hast thou done?
    Publish we the death divine,
Stop, and gaze, and fall, and own
    Was never love like thine!

3 Never love nor sorrow was
    Like that my Saviour showed;
See him stretched on yonder cross,
    And crushed beneath our load!
Now discern the Deity,
    Now his heavenly birth declare;
Faith cries out: 'Tis he, 'tis he,
    My God, that suffers there!

Charles Wesley (1707–88)

167
ADORATION (HUNT) 8.7.8.7.   J. Eric Hunt (1903–58)

1 IN the cross of Christ I glory:
   Towering o'er the wrecks of time,
All the light of sacred story
   Gathers round its head sublime.

2 When the woes of life o'ertake me,
   Hopes deceive and fears annoy,
Never shall the cross forsake me,
   Lo, it glows with peace and joy.

3 When the sun of bliss is beaming
   Light and love upon my way,
From the cross the radiance streaming
   Adds more lustre to the day.

4 Bane and blessing, pain and pleasure,
   By the cross are sanctified;
Peace is there that knows no measure,
   Joys that through all time abide.

5 In the cross of Christ I glory:
   Towering o'er the wrecks of time,
All the light of sacred story
   Gathers round its head sublime.

May also be sung
to No. 251,
ALL FOR JESUS

John Bowring (1792–1872)

THE ETERNAL WORD

168

ORIENTIS PARTIBUS 77.77.4.

Medieval French Melody
Arranged by Ralph Vaughan Williams (1872–1958)

1 JESUS comes with all his grace,
   Comes to save a fallen race:
   Object of our glorious hope,
   Jesus comes to lift us up.
        Alleluia!

2 Let the living stones cry out;
   Let the seed of Abram shout;
   Praise we all our lowly King,
   Give him thanks, rejoice, and sing.
        Alleluia!

3 He has our salvation wrought,
   He our captive souls has bought,
   He has reconciled to God,
   He has washed us in his blood.
        Alleluia!

4 We are now his lawful right,
   Walk as children of the light;
   We shall soon obtain the grace,
   Pure in heart, to see his face.
        Alleluia!

5 We shall gain our calling's prize;
   After God we all shall rise,
   Filled with joy, and love, and peace,
   Perfected in holiness.
        Alleluia!

Charles Wesley (1707–88)

Christ's Passion and Cross

Melody from J. Crüger (1598–1662)

*If desired, vv. 3, 4 & 5 may be sung in unison a fourth
lower in C minor: v. 5 may be sung as a contralto solo.*

THE ETERNAL WORD

1 JESUS in the olive grove,
  Waiting for a traitor's kiss,
  Rises free from bitterness.

2 As he wakes his comrades up,
  Torches flicker in the glen;
  Shadows turn to marching men.

3 In that dawn of blows and lies
  Church and State conspire to kill,
  Hang three rebels on a hill.

4 Innocent and guilty drown
  In a flood of blood and sweat.
  How much darker can it get?

5 How much darker must it be
  For a God to see and care
  That we perish in despair?

6 It is God himself who dies!
  God in man shall set us free:
  God as Man—and only he.

7 Let him claim us as his own;
  We will serve as best we can
  Such a God and such a Man!

F. Pratt Green (1903–)

Words reprinted by permission of
Stainer & Bell Ltd.
For permission to reproduce see p. xiii.

170

CRUCIFER 10.10 (Refrain)

Sydney H. Nicholson (1875–1947)

Refrain

Lift high the cross, the love of Christ pro - claim

Till all the world a - dore his sa - cred name.

Fine

Verses in Harmony

THE ETERNAL WORD

Lift high the cross, the love of Christ proclaim
Till all the world adore his sacred name.

1 FOLLOW the path on which our Captain trod,
   Our King victorious, Christ the Son of God:

2 Each new-born soldier of the Crucified
   Bears on his brow the seal of him who died:

3 Led on their way by this triumphant sign,
   The hosts of God in conquering ranks combine:

4 From farthest regions let them homage bring,
   And on his cross adore their Saviour King:

5 O Lord, once lifted on the glorious tree,
   As thou hast promised, draw men unto thee:

6 Set up thy throne, that earth's despair may cease
   Beneath the shadow of its healing peace:

M. R. Newbolt (1874–1956)
based on *G. W. Kitchin* (1827–1912)

Christ's Passion and Cross

171(i)
ST FRANCIS XAVIER C.M.

John Stainer (1840–1901)

Later form of melody from
E. Prys' *Llyfr y Psalmau* (1621)
Bass by
Orlando Gibbons (1583–1625)

171(ii)
SONG 67 (ST MATTHIAS) C.M.

THE ETERNAL WORD

1 MY God, I love thee—not because
    I hope for heaven thereby,
  Nor yet because who love thee not
    Are lost eternally.

2 Thou, O my Jesus, thou didst me
    Upon the cross embrace;
  For me didst bear the nails and spear,
    And manifold disgrace;

3 And griefs and torments numberless,
    And sweat of agony,
  Yea, death itself, and all for one
    Who was thine enemy.

4 Then why, O blessèd Jesus Christ,
    Should I not love thee well?
  Not for the sake of winning heaven,
    Nor of escaping hell;

5 Not with the hope of gaining aught,
    Not seeking a reward;
  But as thyself hast lovèd me,
    O ever-loving Lord!

6 E'en so I love thee, and will love,
    And in thy praise will sing;
  Solely because thou art my God,
    And my eternal King.

17th Century
tr. *Edward Caswall* (1814–78)

THE ETERNAL WORD

1 O DEAREST Lord, thy sacred head
　　With thorns was pierced for me;
　O pour thy blessing on my head,
　　That I may think for thee.

2 O dearest Lord, thy sacred hands
　　With nails were pierced for me;
　O shed thy blessing on my hands,
　　That they may work for thee.

3 O dearest Lord, thy sacred feet
　　With nails were pierced for me;
　O pour thy blessing on my feet,
　　That they may follow thee.

4 O dearest Lord, thy sacred heart
　　With spear was pierced for me;
　O pour thy spirit in my heart,
　　That I may live for thee.

Father Andrew (H. E. Hardy) (1869–1946)

May also be sung to No. 539(ii), AYRSHIRE

173

LOVE UNKNOWN 6.6.6.6.4.44.4.

John Ireland (1879–1962)

1 MY song is love unknown,
   My Saviour's love to me,
 Love to the loveless shown,
    That they might lovely be.
       O who am I,
          That for my sake
          My Lord should take
       Frail flesh and die?

2 He came from his blest throne,
    Salvation to bestow;
 But men made strange, and none
    The longed-for Christ would know.
       But O my Friend,
          My Friend indeed,
          Who at my need
       His life did spend!

THE ETERNAL WORD

3 Sometimes they strew his way,
   And his sweet praises sing;
Resounding all the day
   Hosannas to their King.
      Then 'Crucify!'
         Is all their breath,
         And for his death
      They thirst and cry.

4 Why, what hath my Lord done?
   What makes this rage and spite?
He made the lame to run,
   He gave the blind their sight.
      Sweet injuries!
         Yet they at these
         Themselves displease,
      And 'gainst him rise.

5 They rise, and needs will have
   My dear Lord made away;
A murderer they save,
   The Prince of Life they slay.
      Yet cheerful he
         To suffering goes,
         That he his foes
      From thence might free.

6 In life no house, no home,
   My Lord on earth might have;
In death no friendly tomb
   But what a stranger gave.
      What may I say?
         Heaven was his home;
         But mine the tomb
      Wherein he lay.

7 Here might I stay and sing,
   No story so divine:
Never was love, dear King,
   Never was grief like thine!
      This is my Friend,
         In whose sweet praise
         I all my days
      Could gladly spend.

        Samuel Crossman (1624–84)

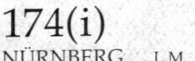

174(i)

NÜRNBERG L.M.

From an original
hymn-tune by J. S. Bach (1685–1750)
Adapted by John Wilson (1905–)

For this tune in a higher key see No. 547

174(ii)

ELTHAM L.M.

Nathaniel Gawthorn's
Harmonia Perfecta (London, 1730)
Harmonised by S. S. Wesley (1810–76)
Adapted by Eric Thiman (1900–75)

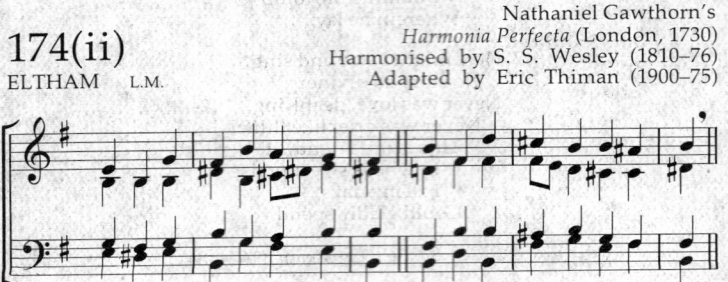

THE ETERNAL WORD

1 NATURE with open volume stands
   To spread her Maker's praise abroad,
And every labour of his hands
   Shows something worthy of a God.

2 But in the grace that rescued man
   His brightest form of glory shines;
Here on the cross 'tis fairest drawn
   In precious blood and crimson lines.

3 Here his whole name appears complete;
   Nor wit can guess, nor reason prove,
Which of the letters best is writ,
   The power, the wisdom, or the love.

4 O the sweet wonders of that cross
   Where God the Saviour loved and died!
Her noblest life my spirit draws
   From his dear wounds and bleeding side.

5 I would for ever speak his name
   In sounds to mortal ears unknown,
With angels join to praise the Lamb,
   And worship at his Father's throne.

Isaac Watts (1674–1748)

May also be sung to No. 519, RIVAULX

Christ's Passion and Cross

THE ETERNAL WORD

1 O LOVE divine, what hast thou done!
    The immortal God hath died for me!
The Father's co-eternal Son
    Bore all my sins upon the tree;
The immortal God for me hath died!
My Lord, my Love is crucified—

2 Is crucified for me and you,
    To bring us rebels back to God;
Believe, believe the record true,
    We all are bought with Jesu's blood,
Pardon for all flows from his side:
My Lord, my Love is crucified.

3 Then let us stand beneath the cross,
    And feel his love a healing stream,
All things for him account but loss,
    And give up all our hearts to him;
Of nothing think or speak beside:
My Lord, my Love is crucified.

Charles Wesley (1707–88) alt.

May also be sung to No. 275(ii), ST CHRYSOSTOM

176

PASSION CHORALE 7.6.7.6.D.

Melody by H. L. Hassler (1564–1612),
as set by J. S. Bach
in the *St. Matthew Passion* (1727)

ALTERNATIVE VERSION
(for a verse by the Choir alone)

Melody by H. L. Hassler (1565–1612),
as set by J. S. Bach
in the *St. Matthew Passion* (1727)

PASSION CHORALE 7.6.7.6.D.

THE ETERNAL WORD

1 O SACRED Head, sore wounded,
   With grief and pain weighed down,
How scornfully surrounded
   With thorns, thine only crown!
How pale art thou with anguish,
   With sore abuse and scorn!
How does that visage languish
   Which once was bright as morn!

2 O Lord of life and glory,
   What bliss till now was thine!
I read the wondrous story,
   I joy to call thee mine.
Thy grief and thy compassion
   Were all for sinners' gain;
Mine, mine was the transgression,
   But thine the deadly pain.

3 What language shall I borrow
   To praise thee, dearest friend,
For this thy dying sorrow,
   Thy pity without end?
Lord, make me thine for ever,
   Nor let me faithless prove;
O let me never, never
   Abuse such dying love!

4 Be near me, Lord, when dying;
   O show thy cross to me,
That I, for succour flying,
   My eyes may fix on thee;
And then, thy grace receiving,
   Let faith my fears dispel,
For whoso dies believing
   In thee, dear Lord, dies well.

Paul Gerhardt (1607–76)
tr. *James Waddell Alexander* (1804–59)
and *Rupert E. Davies* (1909–)

Christ's Passion and Cross

177

PANGE LINGUA   8.7.8.7.8.7.   Plainsong Melody (Sarum form), Mode iii

A - men.

THE ETERNAL WORD

1 SING, my tongue, the glorious bättle,
  Sing the ending of the fräy;
 Now above the cross, the trophy,
  Sound the loud triumphant läy:
 Tell how Christ, the world's Redeemer,
  As a victïm won the day.

2 Tell how, when at length the füllness
  Öf th' appointed time was cöme,
 He, the Word, was born of woman,
  Left for us his Father's höme,
 Showed us human life made perfect,
  Shone as light ämid the gloom.

3 Thus, with thirty years accömplished,
  Wënt he forth from Nazarëth,
 Destined, dedicate, and willing,
  Wrought his work, and met his dëath;
 Like a lamb he humbly yielded
  On the cross hïs dying breath.

4 Faithful cross, thou sign of trïumph,
  Nöw for man the noblest trëë,
 None in foliage, none in blossom,
  None in fruit thy peer may bë;
 Symbol of the world's redemption,
  For the weight thät hung on thee!

5 Unto God be praise and glöry:
  Tö the Father and the Sön,
 To th' eternal Spirit, honour
  Now and evermore be döne;
 Praise and glory in the highest,
  While the timelëss ages run.

                    (Ämën)

          Venantius Fortunatus (c.535-c.600)
            tr. *Percy Dearmer* (1867–1936) alt.

Dots over the words indicate
the number of plainsong notes
to each syllable.

          May also be sung to No. 266, PICARDY

178

HORSLEY C.M.

William Horsley (1774–1858)

THE ETERNAL WORD

1 THERE is a green hill far away,
   Outside a city wall,
   Where the dear Lord was crucified,
   Who died to save us all.

2 We may not know, we cannot tell,
   What pains he had to bear,
   But we believe it was for us
   He hung and suffered there.

3 He died that we might be forgiven,
   He died to make us good,
   That we might go at last to heaven,
   Saved by his precious blood.

4 There was no other good enough
   To pay the price of sin;
   He only could unlock the gate
   Of heaven, and let us in.

5 O dearly, dearly has he loved,
   And we must love him too,
   And trust in his redeeming blood,
   And try his works to do.

Cecil Frances Alexander (1818–95)

Christ's Passion and Cross

179

GONFALON ROYAL L.M.

P. C. Buck (1871–1947)

Unison. With movement.

THE ETERNAL WORD

1 THE royal banners forward go,
   The myst'ry of the cross to show,
      When he in flesh, all flesh who made,
      Is on the tree of death displayed.

2 For us he bore those pains severe,
   The cruel wounds, the soldier's spear;
      By blood and water from his side
      Our souls from sin are purified.

3 Fulfilled is now what David told
   In faithful prophet's song of old,
      Inviting all the world to see:
      Our God has suffered on the tree!

4 O tree, most beautiful, most glad,
   O tree in royal purple clad,
      Chosen from noble stock to bear
      The holy limbs that suffer there!

5 O tree, on whose blest arms is laid
   The price that has the balance swayed,
      Our souls from slav'ry to regain,
      And rescue us from hell's domain!

6 To thee, eternal Three in One,
   Let homage due by all be done;
      Whom by the cross thou dost restore,
      Preserve and govern evermore.

                                    Amen.

Venantius Fortunatus (c. 535–c. 600)
tr. *Rupert E. Davies* (1909–) and others

Christ's Passion and Cross

180
ROCKINGHAM L.M.

Adapted by Edward Miller (1731–1807)
from a melody *Tunbridge* in *A Second Supplement to
Psalmody in Miniature* (*c.* 1780)

THE ETERNAL WORD

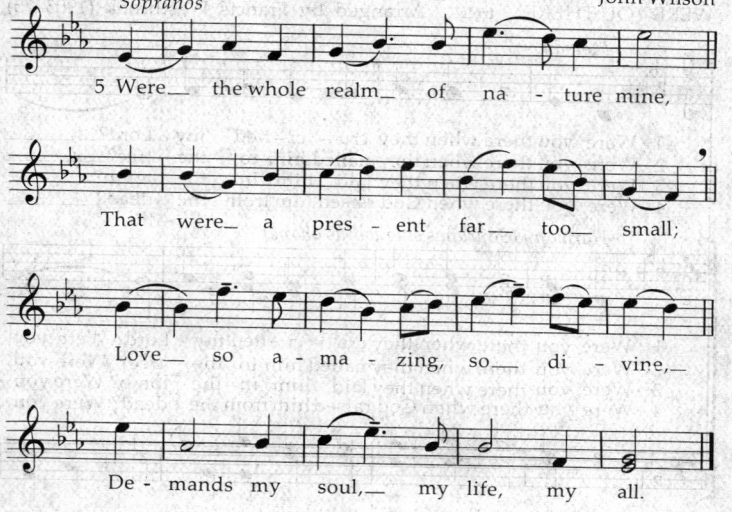

Sopranos
John Wilson

5 Were the whole realm of na-ture mine,

That were a pres-ent far too small;

Love so a-ma-zing, so di-vine,

De-mands my soul, my life, my all.

1 WHEN I survey the wondrous cross,
  On which the Prince of Glory died,
My richest gain I count but loss,
  And pour contempt on all my pride.

2 Forbid it, Lord, that I should boast
  Save in the death of Christ my God;
All the vain things that charm me most,
  I sacrifice them to his blood.

3 See from his head, his hands, his feet,
  Sorrow and love flow mingled down;
Did e'er such love and sorrow meet,
  Or thorns compose so rich a crown?

4 His dying crimson, like a robe,
  Spreads o'er his body on the tree;
Then am I dead to all the globe,
  And all the globe is dead to me.

5 Were the whole realm of nature mine,
  That were a present far too small;
Love so amazing, so divine,
  Demands my soul, my life, my all.

Isaac Watts (1674–1748)

Christ's Passion and Cross

WERE YOU THERE   Irreg.

American Folk Hymn Melody
Arranged by Francis Westbrook (1903–75)

Melody

1 Were you there when they cru – ci –fied my Lord?_____
2 Were you there when they nailed him to the tree?_____
3 Were you there when they laid him in the tomb?_____
4 Were you there when God raised him from the dead?_____

Harmony (Sopranos sing words above)

1 Were you there when they cru – ci –fied my Lord? Were you
2 Were you there when they nailed him to the tree? Were you
3 Were you there when they laid him in the tomb? Were you
4 Were you there when God raised him from the dead? Were you

Were you there when they cru – ci –fied my
Were you there when they nailed him to the
Were you there when they laid him in the
Were you there when God raised him from the

there? Were you there when they cru – ci – fied my
there? Were you there when they nailed him to the
there? Were you there when they laid him in the
there? Were you there when God raised him from the

THE ETERNAL WORD

Lord?_____
tree?_____
tomb?_____
dead?_____

Oh!

Lord? when they cru-ci-fied my Lord?
tree? when they nailed him to the tree?
tomb? when they laid him in the tomb?
dead? when God raised him from the dead?

Oh!_____

Some-times it caus-es me to trem-ble, trem-ble, trem-ble;

Some-times it caus-es me to trem-ble, trem-ble, trem-ble;

Were you there when they cru-ci-fied my Lord?
Were you there when they nailed him to the tree?
Were you there when they laid him in the tomb?
Were you there when God raised him from the dead?

Were you there when they cru-ci-fied my Lord?
Were you there when they nailed him to the tree?
Were you there when they laid him in the tomb?
Were you there when God raised him from the dead?

American Folk Hymn

Christ's Passion and Cross

182(i)
BOW BRICKHILL   L.M.   Sydney H. Nicholson (1875–1947)

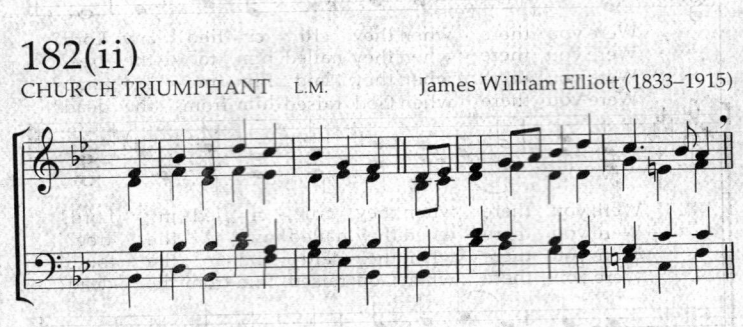

182(ii)
CHURCH TRIUMPHANT   L.M.   James William Elliott (1833–1915)

THE ETERNAL WORD

For this tune in a higher key see No. 279

1 WE sing the praise of him who died,
　Of him who died upon the cross;
The sinner's hope let men deride:
　For this we count the world but loss.

2 Inscribed upon the cross we see,
　In shining letters, 'God is love';
He bears our sins upon the tree;
　He brings us mercy from above.

3 The cross—it takes our guilt away;
　It holds the fainting spirit up;
It cheers with hope the gloomy day,
　And sweetens every bitter cup;

4 It makes the coward spirit brave,
　And nerves the feeble arm for fight;
It takes all terror from the grave,
　And gilds the bed of death with light;

5 The balm of life, the cure of woe,
　The measure and the pledge of love,
The sinner's refuge here below,
　The angels' theme in heaven above.

Thomas Kelly (1769–1855)

May also be sung to No. 425, BRESLAU

183

SONG 13   77.77.

Melody and bass by Orlando Gibbons (1583–1625)
(rhythm simplified)

For another version of this tune see No. 737

1 WHEN my love to Christ grows weak,
   When for deeper faith I seek,
   Then in thought I go to thee,
   Garden of Gethsemane.

2 There I walk amid the shades,
   While the lingering twilight fades,
   See that suffering, friendless One,
   Weeping, praying there alone.

3 When my love for man grows weak,
   When for stronger faith I seek,
   Hill of Calvary, I go
   To thy scenes of fear and woe;

4 There behold his agony,
   Suffered on the bitter tree;
   See his anguish, see his faith,
   Love triumphant still in death.

5 Then to life I turn again,
   Learning all the worth of pain,
   Learning all the might that lies
   In a full self-sacrifice.

6 And I praise with firmer faith
   Christ who vanquished pain and death;
   And to Christ enthroned above
   Raise my song of selfless love.

John Reynell Wreford (1800–81) alt.

THE ETERNAL WORD

184

ST GREGORY C.M.

Robert Wainwright (1748–82)
as in Webbe's *Psalm Tunes* (1808)

1 WITH glorious clouds encompassed round,
   Whom angels dimly see,
 Will the Unsearchable be found,
   Or God appear to me?

2 Will he forsake his throne above,
   Himself to me impart?
 Answer, thou Man of grief and love,
   And speak it to my heart!

3 In manifested love explain
   Thy wonderful design;
 What meant the suffering Son of Man,
   The streaming blood divine?

4 Didst thou not in our flesh appear,
   And live and die below,
 That I may now perceive thee near,
   And my Redeemer know?

5 Come then, and to my soul reveal
   The heights and depths of grace,
 The wounds which all my sorrows heal,
   That dear disfigured face.

6 I view the Lamb in his own light,
   Whom angels dimly see,
 And gaze, transported at the sight,
   Through all eternity.

May also be sung
to No. 297(i),
MANCHESTER

Charles Wesley (1707–88)

Christ's Passion and Cross

185(i)
RYBURN 88.88.88.

Norman Cocker (1889–1953)

185(ii)
DIDSBURY 88.88.88.

Cyril V. Taylor (1907–)

THE ETERNAL WORD

1 WOULD Jesus have the sinner die?
   Why hangs he then on yonder tree?
What means that strange expiring cry?
   Sinners, he prays for you and me:
Forgive them, Father, O forgive!
They know not that by me they live.

2 Thou loving, all-atoning Lamb,
   Thee—by thy painful agony,
Thy sweat of blood, thy grief and shame,
   Thy cross and passion on the tree,
Thy precious death and life—I pray:
Take all, take all my sins away!

3 O let me kiss thy bleeding feet,
   And bathe and wash them with my tears;
The story of thy love repeat
   In every drooping sinner's ears;
That all may hear the quickening sound,
Since I, even I, have mercy found.

4 O let thy love my heart control,
   Thy love for every sinner free,
That every fallen human soul
   May taste the grace that found out me;
That all mankind with me may prove
Thy sovereign, everlasting love!

Charles Wesley (1707–88)

May also be sung to No. 629(ii) EUPHONY

Christ's Passion and Cross

186

RIDGEWAY 5.5.5.4.

Brian R. Hoare (1935–)

1 AFTER darkness, light;
After winter, spring;
After dying, life:
Alleluia!

2 Take his body down;
Lay it in the tomb;
Love has overcome:
Alleluia!

3 Turn away in grief;
Turn away in faith;
Celebrate his death:
Alleluia!

4 Come whatever may,
God will have his way;
Welcome, Easter Day:
Alleluia! Alleluia!

F. Pratt Green (1903–)

THE ETERNAL WORD/ The Resurrection and the Ascension

187

Al - le - lu – ia!   Al - le - lu – ia!

1 AWAY with gloom, away with doubt!
   With all the morning stars we sing;
 With all the sons of God we shout
    The praises of a King,
      Alleluia! Alleluia!
    Of our returning King.

2 Away with death, and welcome life;
   In him we died and live again;
 And welcome peace, away with strife!
    For he returns to reign.
      Alleluia! Alleluia!
    The Crucified shall reign.

3 Then welcome beauty, he is fair;
   And welcome youth, for he is young;
 And welcome spring; and everywhere
    Let merry songs be sung!
      Alleluia! Alleluia!
    For such a King be sung!

Edward Shillito (1872–1948)

The Resurrection and the Ascension

For this tune in a higher key see No. 22(i)

THE ETERNAL WORD

1 ALL ye that seek the Lord who died,
  Your God for sinners crucified,
    Now, now let all your grief be o'er!
    Believe, and ye shall weep no more.

2 The Lord of life is risen indeed,
  To death delivered in your stead;
    His rise proclaims your sins forgiven,
    And shows the living way to heaven.

3 Haste then, ye souls that first believe,
  Who dare the gospel word receive,
    Your faith with joyful hearts confess,
    Be bold, be Jesus' witnesses.

4 Go, tell the followers of your Lord
  Their Jesus is to life restored;
    He lives, that they his life may find;
    He lives to quicken all mankind.

Charles Wesley (1707–88)

May also be sung to No. 12, ST BARTHOLOMEW

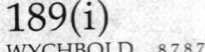

189(i)
WYCHBOLD 8.7.8.7.   W. G. Whinfield (1865–1919)

189(ii)
SICILIAN MARINERS 8.7.8.7.   18th-century Italian or Sicilian Melody

THE ETERNAL WORD

1 CHRIST, above all glory seated!
   King triumphant, strong to save!
Dying, thou hast death defeated;
   Buried, thou hast spoiled the grave.

2 Thou art gone where now is given,
   What no mortal might could gain,
On the eternal throne of heaven
   In thy Father's power to reign.

3 There thy kingdoms all adore thee,
   Heaven above and earth below;
While the depths of hell before thee
   Trembling and defeated bow.

4 We, O Lord, with hearts adoring,
   Follow thee above the sky;
Hear our prayers thy grace imploring,
   Lift our souls to thee on high.

5 So when thou again in glory
   On the clouds of heaven shalt shine,
We thy flock may stand before thee,
   Owned for evermore as thine.

6 Hail! All hail! In thee confiding,
   Jesus, thee shall all adore,
In thy Father's might abiding
   With one Spirit evermore!

c. 5th Century
tr. *James Russell Woodford* (1820–85)

190

TRURO L.M.

Melody from T. Williams's *Psalmodia Evangelica* (1789)

For a descant to this tune see No. 433(i)

THE ETERNAL WORD

1 CHRIST is alive! Let Christians sing;
  His cross stands empty to the sky:
  Let streets and homes with praises ring;
  His love in death shall never die.

2 Christ is alive! No longer bound
  To distant years in Palestine,
  He comes to claim the here and now,
  And conquer every place and time.

3 Not throned above, remotely high,
  Untouched, unmoved by human pains,
  But daily, in the midst of life,
  Our Saviour with the Father reigns.

4 In every insult, rift and war,
  Where colour, scorn or wealth divide,
  He suffers still, yet loves the more,
  And lives, though ever crucified.

5 Christ is alive! His Spirit burns
  Through this and every future age,
  Till all creation lives and learns
  His joy, his justice, love, and praise.

Brian A. Wren (1936–)

May also be sung to No. 53, CANNOCK

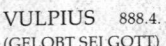

191

VULPIUS 888.4.
(GELOBT SEI GOTT)

Melody from M. Vulpius's *Gesangbuch* (1609)
Harmonised by Henry G. Ley (1887–1962)

Al - le - lu - ia, Al - le - lu - ia, Al - le - lu - ia!

❋*From this point the following Descant may start:*

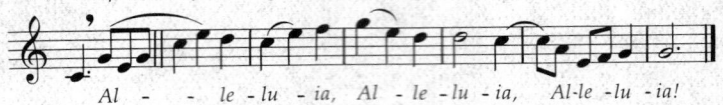

Al - - - le - lu - ia, Al - le - lu - ia, Al - le - lu - ia!

THE ETERNAL WORD

1 GOOD Christians all, rejoice and sing!
   Now is the triumph of our King!
   To all the world glad news we bring:
   > *Alleluia!*

2 The Lord of Life is risen for aye;
   Bring flowers of song to strew his way;
   Let all the world rejoice and say:
   > *Alleluia!*

3 Praise we in songs of victory
   That Love, that Life which cannot die,
   And sing with hearts uplifted high:
   > *Alleluia!*

4 Thy name we bless, O risen Lord,
   And sing today with one accord
   The life laid down, the Life restored:
   > *Alleluia!*

C. A. Alington (1872–1955)

192(i)

WÜRTEMBERG 77.77.4.

Melody from *Hundert Arien* (Dresden, 1694)
Harmonised by W. H. Monk (1823–89)

Al - le - lu - ia!

192(ii)

ORIENTIS PARTIBUS 77.77.4.

Medieval French Melody
Arranged by
Ralph Vaughan Williams (1872–1958)

Unison

THE ETERNAL WORD

Al - le - lu - ia!

1 CHRIST the Lord is risen again!
Christ has broken every chain!
Hark, the angels shout for joy,
Singing evermore on high:

Alleluia!

2 He who gave for us his life,
Who for us endured the strife,
Is our Paschal Lamb today;
We too sing for joy, and say:

Alleluia!

3 He who bore all pain and loss
Comfortless upon the cross,
Lives in glory now on high,
Pleads for us, and hears our cry:

Alleluia!

4 He who slumbered in the grave
Is exalted now to save;
Now through Christendom it rings
That the Lamb is King of kings:

Alleluia!

5 Now he bids us tell abroad
How the lost may be restored,
How the penitent forgiven,
How we too may enter heaven:

Alleluia!

M. Weisse (c. 1480–1534)
tr. *Catherine Winkworth (1827–78)*

Melody from *Lyra Davidica* (1708),
as altered in the mid-18th century

THE ETERNAL WORD

1 CHRIST the Lord is risen today;
   Alleluia!
   Sons of men and angels say:
   Raise your joys and triumphs high;
   Sing, ye heavens; thou earth, reply:

2 Love's redeeming work is done,
   Fought the fight, the battle won;
   Vain the stone, the watch, the seal;
   Christ hath burst the gates of hell:

3 Lives again our glorious King;
   Where, O death, is now thy sting?
   Once he died our souls to save;
   Where's thy victory, boasting grave?

4 Soar we now where Christ hath led,
   Following our exalted Head;
   Made like him, like him we rise;
   Ours the cross, the grave, the skies:

5 King of Glory! Soul of bliss!
   Everlasting life is this,
   Thee to know, thy power to prove,
   Thus to sing, and thus to love:

Charles Wesley (1707–88)

The Resurrection and the Ascension

194
AVE VIRGO VIRGINUM 7.6.7.6.D.

Melody from
J. Horn's *Gesangbuch* (1544)

THE ETERNAL WORD

1 COME, ye faithful, raise the strain
   Of triumphant gladness;
 God has brought his Israel
   Into joy from sadness,
 Loosed from Pharaoh's bitter yoke
   Jacob's sons and daughters,
 Led them with unmoistened foot
   Through the Red Sea waters.

2 'Tis the spring of souls today;
   Christ has burst his prison,
 And from three days' sleep in death
   As a sun has risen;
 All the winter of our sins,
   Long and dark, is flying
 From his light, to whom we give
   Laud and praise undying.

3 Now the queen of seasons, bright
   With the day of splendour,
 With the royal feast of feasts
   Comes its joy to render;
 Comes to glad Jerusalem,
   Who with true affection
 Welcomes in unwearied strains
   Jesus' resurrection.

4 Neither could the gates of death,
   Nor the grave's dark portal,
 Nor the watchers, nor the seal,
   Hold thee as a mortal;
 But today amidst thine own
   Thou didst stand, bestowing
 Thine own peace, which evermore
   Passes human knowing.

John of Damascus (−c. 750)
tr. *John Mason Neale* (1818–66) alt.

195

CHERRY TREE CAROL 7.6.7.6. (Irreg.)

Traditional Melody
Arranged by John Wilson

1 GOOD Joseph had a garden,
　Close by that sad green hill
Where Jesus died a bitter death
　To save mankind from ill.

2 One evening in that garden,
　Their faces dark with gloom,
They laid the Saviour's body
　Within good Joseph's tomb.

3 There came the holy women
　With spices and with tears;
The angels tried to comfort them,
　But could not calm their fears.

4 Came Mary to that garden
　And sobbed with heart forlorn;
She thought she heard the gardener ask:
　'Whom seekest thou this morn?'

5 She heard her own name spoken,
　And then she lost her care:
All in his strength and beauty
　The risen Lord stood fair!

6 Good Joseph had a garden;
　Amid its trees so tall
The Lord Christ rose on Easter Day:
　He lives to save us all.

7 And as he rose at Easter
　He is alive for aye,
The very same Lord Jesus Christ
　Who hears us sing today.

8 Go tell the Lord Christ's message,
　The Easter triumph sing,
Till all his waiting children know
　That Jesus is their King.

Alda M. Milner-Barry (1875–1940)

THE ETERNAL WORD

196

William Youens (1834–1911)
(harmony slightly altered)

1 I KNOW that my Redeemer lives—
What joy the blest assurance gives!
  He lives, he lives, who once was dead;
  He lives, my everlasting Head.

2 He lives, to bless me with his love;
He lives, to plead for me above;
  He lives, my hungry soul to feed;
  He lives, to help in time of need.

3 He lives, and grants me daily breath;
He lives, and I shall conquer death;
  He lives, my mansion to prepare;
  He lives, to lead me safely there.

4 He lives, all glory to his name;
He lives, my Saviour, still the same;
  What joy the blest assurance gives,
  I know that my Redeemer lives!

Samuel Medley (1738–99)

The Resurrection and the Ascension

THE ETERNAL WORD

1 HAIL the day that sees him rise,
                    Alleluia!
  Ravished from our wistful eyes!
  Christ, awhile to mortals given,
  Reascends his native heaven:

2 There the glorious triumph waits:
  Lift your heads, eternal gates;
  Wide unfold the radiant scene;
  Take the King of Glory in!

3 Him though highest heaven receives,
  Still he loves the earth he leaves;
  Though returning to his throne,
  Still he calls mankind his own:

4 See! He lifts his hands above;
  See! He shows the prints of love;
  Hark! His gracious lips bestow
  Blessings on his church below:

5 Master, parted from our sight,
  High above yon azure height,
  Grant our hearts may thither rise,
  Following thee beyond the skies:

6 There we shall with thee remain,
  Partners of thy endless reign;
  There thy face forever see,
  Find our heaven of heavens in thee!

Charles Wesley (1707–88)

The Resurrection and the Ascension

198

ST ALBINUS   7.8.7.8.4.

Henry J. Gauntlett (1805–1876)
(rhythm slightly altered)

THE ETERNAL WORD

1 JESUS lives! Thy terrors now
    Can, O death, no more appal us;
Jesus lives! By this we know
    Thou, O grave, canst not enthral us:
        Alleluia!

2 Jesus lives! Our hearts know well
    Nought from us his love shall sever;
Life, nor death, nor powers of hell,
    Part us now from Christ for ever:
        Alleluia!

3 Jesus lives! Henceforth is death
    Entrance-gate of life immortal;
This shall calm our trembling breath
    When we pass its gloomy portal:
        Alleluia!

4 Jesus lives! For us he died:
    Hence may we, to Jesus living,
Pure in heart and act abide,
    Praise to him and glory giving:
        Alleluia!

5 Jesus lives! To him the throne
    High o'er heaven and earth is given;
May we go where he is gone,
    Live and reign with him in heaven:
        Alleluia!

C. F. Gellert (1715–69)
tr. *Frances Elizabeth Cox* (1812–97) alt.

199

THE ETERNAL WORD

1 JESUS, Lord, Redeemer,
   Once for sinners slain,
Crucified in weakness,
   Raised in power, to reign,
Dwelling with the Father,
   Endless in thy days,
Unto thee be glory,
   Honour, blessing, praise.

2 Faithful ones, communing
   Towards the close of day,
Desolate and weary,
   Met thee in the way:
So, when sun is setting,
   Come to us, and show
All the truth; and in us
   Make our hearts to glow.

3 In the upper chamber,
   Where the ten, in fear,
Gathered sad and troubled,
   There thou didst appear:
So, O Lord, this evening,
   Bid our sorrows cease;
Breathing on us, Saviour,
   Say: 'I give you peace'.

Patrick Miller Kirkland (1857–1943)

May also be sung to No. 507, PRAISE THE LORD OF HEAVEN

200
AT EASTERTIDE 8.8. (Refrain)

Traditional Melody
Arranged by June B. Tillman (1943–   ),
adapted Allen Percival (1925–   )

Unison

1 WHEN Eas – ter to the dark world came, Fair
flo – wers glowed like scar – let flame:

G D7 G D
Em Am G D

Refrain

At Eas – ter – tide, at Eas – ter – tide, O

E7 Am A7 D

(Vv. 1–5) glad was the world at Eas – ter – tide.
(v. 6) sing, all the world, for Eas – ter – tide.

G C D7 G

THE ETERNAL WORD

1 WHEN Easter to the dark world came,
  Fair flowers glowed like scarlet flame:
    At Eastertide, at Eastertide,
    O glad was the world at Eastertide.

2 When Mary in the garden walked,
  And with her risen Master talked:

3 When John and Peter in their gloom
  Met angels at the empty tomb:

4 When Thomas' heart with grief was black,
  Then Jesus like a king came back:

5 And friend to friend in wonder said:
  'The Lord is risen from the dead!'

6 This Eastertide with joyful voice
  We'll sing: 'The Lord is King! Rejoice!'
    At Eastertide, at Eastertide,
    O sing, all the world, for Eastertide.

W. H. Hamilton (1886–1958)

The Resurrection and the Ascension

201(i)

TRIUMPH 8.7.8.7.8.7.

Henry J. Gauntlett (1805–76)

201(ii)

REGENT SQUARE 8.7.8.7.8.7.

Henry Smart (1813–79)

THE ETERNAL WORD

For this tune in a higher key see No. 80

1 LOOK, ye saints, the sight is glorious;
   See the Man of Sorrows now
 From the fight returned victorious;
   Every knee to him shall bow:
     Crown him! Crown him!
   Crowns become the Victor's brow.

2 Crown the Saviour, angels, crown him;
   Rich the trophies Jesus brings;
 In the seat of power enthrone him,
   While the vault of heaven rings:
     Crown him! Crown him!
   Crown the Saviour, King of kings!

3 Sinners in derision crowned him,
   Mocking thus the Saviour's claim;
 Saints and angels throng around him, .
   Own his title, praise his name:
     Crown him! Crown him!
   Spread abroad the Victor's fame.

4 Hark, those bursts of acclamation;
   Hark, those loud triumphant chords;
 Jesus takes the highest station:
   O what joy the sight affords!
     Crown him! Crown him!
   King of kings, and Lord of lords!

Thomas Kelly (1769–1855)

The Resurrection and the Ascension

202
CHRIST AROSE 6.5.6.4. (Refrain)

R. Lowry (1826–99)

Refrain

1 LOW in the grave he lay,
   Jesus, my Saviour,
   Waiting the coming day,
   Jesus, my Lord:
   Up from the grave he arose,
   With a mighty triumph o'er his foes;
He arose a victor from the dark domain,
And he lives for ever with his saints to reign:
   He arose! He arose!
   Alleluia! Christ arose!

2 Vainly they watch his bed,
   Jesus, my Saviour;
   Vainly they seal the dead,
   Jesus, my Lord:

3 Death cannot keep his prey,
   Jesus, my Saviour;
   He tore the bars away,
   Jesus, my Lord:

Robert Lowry (1826–99)

The Resurrection and the Ascension

203
CHRISTCHURCH   6.6.6.6.8.8.   Charles Steggall (1826–1905)

1   NOW is eternal life,
    If risen with Christ we stand,
In him to life reborn,
    And holden in his hand;
No more we fear death's ancient dread,
In Christ arisen from the dead.

2   Man long in bondage lay,
    Brooding o'er life's brief span;
Was it, O God, for nought,
    For nought, thou madest man?
Thou art our hope, our vital breath;
Shall hope undying end in death?

3   And God, the living God,
    Stooped down to man's estate;
By death destroying death,
    Christ opened wide life's gate.
He lives, who died; he reigns on high;
Who lives in him shall never die.

4   Unfathomed love divine,
    Reign thou within my heart;
From thee nor depth nor height,
    Nor life nor death can part;
My life is hid in God with thee,
Now and through all eternity.

George Wallace Briggs (1875–1959)

May also be sung to No. 78, EASTVIEW

THE ETERNAL WORD

204

NOEL NOUVELET 11 11.10 11.

French melody
Arranged Geoffrey Laycock (1927–86)

1 NOW the green blade rises from the buried grain,
Wheat that in the dark earth many days has lain;
Love lives again, that with the dead has been:
Love is come again, like wheat that springs up green.

2 In the grave they laid him, Love whom men had slain,
Thinking that he never would awake again,
Laid in the earth like grain that sleeps unseen:

3 Forth he came at Easter, like the risen grain,
He that for the three days in the grave had lain,
Quick from the dead my risen Lord is seen:

4 When our hearts are wintry, grieving, or in pain,
Then your touch can call us back to life again,
Fields of our hearts that dead and bare have been:

J. M. C. Crum (1872–1958) alt.

The Resurrection and the Ascension

205

O FILII ET FILIAE 8.8.8. (Alleluias)

Melody from *Airs sur les hymnes sacrez* (Paris, 1623)
Harmonised by
Elizabeth Poston (1905–)

*Opening Alleluias to precede verse 1 only.

THE ETERNAL WORD

Alleluia! Alleluia! Alleluia!

1 O SONS and daughters, let us sing!
   The King of heav'n, the glorious King,
   O'er death today rose triumphing.
         Alleluia!

2 That night the apostles met in fear;
   Amidst them came their Lord most dear,
   And said: 'My peace be on all here.'
         Alleluia!

3 When Thomas first the tidings heard,
   That they had seen the risen Lord,
   He doubted the disciples' word.
         Alleluia!

4 'My piercèd side, O Thomas, see;
   Behold my hands, my feet,' said he;
   'Not faithless, but believing be.'
         Alleluia!

5 No longer Thomas then denied;
   He saw the feet, the hands, the side:
   'You are my Lord and God!' he cried:
         Alleluia!

6 How blest are they who have not seen,
   And yet whose faith has constant been,
   For they eternal life shall win:
         Alleluia!

Jean Tisserand (d. 1494)
tr. *John Mason Neale* (1818–66) and others
based on John 20:19–29

206

HERMANN L.M. (Alleluias)

N. Hermann (c.1485–1561)
Simplified harmonisation
based on J. S. Bach

THE ETERNAL WORD

1 OUR Lord is risen from the dead!
   Our Jesus is gone up on high!
   The powers of hell are captive led,
   Dragged to the portals of the sky:
   Alleluia!

2 There his triumphal chariot waits,
   And angels chant the solemn lay:
   Lift up your heads, ye heavenly gates;
   Ye everlasting doors, give way:
   Alleluia!

3 Loose all your bars of massy light,
   And wide unfold the ethereal scene:
   He claims these mansions as his right;
   Receive the King of Glory in!
   Alleluia!

4 Who is this King of Glory, who?
   The Lord, that all his foes o'ercame,
   The world, sin, death, and hell o'erthrew;
   And Jesus is the conqueror's name:
   Alleluia!

5 Lo! His triumphal chariot waits,
   And angels chant the solemn lay:
   Lift up your heads, ye heavenly gates;
   Ye everlasting doors, give way!
   Alleluia!

6 Who is this King of Glory, who?
   The Lord, of glorious power possessed;
   The King of saints, and angels too,
   God over all, for ever blest!
   Alleluia!

Charles Wesley (1707–88)
based on Psalm 24:7–10

The Resurrection and the Ascension

207

REJOICE AND BE GLAD Irregular John Jenkins Husband (1760–1825)

Refrain

THE ETERNAL WORD

1 REJOICE and be glad! The Redeemer hath come:
  Go, look on his cradle, his cross, and his tomb:
  Sound his praises, tell the story of him who was slain;
  Sound his praises, tell with gladness he liveth again.

2 Rejoice and be glad! For the Lamb that was slain,
  O'er death is triumphant, and liveth again:

3 Rejoice and be glad! Now the pardon is free;
  The just for the unjust hath died on the tree:

4 Rejoice and be glad! For our King is on high;
  He pleadeth for us on his throne in the sky:

5 Rejoice and be glad! For he cometh again;
  He cometh in glory, the Lamb that was slain:

Horatius Bonar (1808–89)

208

ELLACOMBE 7.6.7.6.D.

18th–century German melody,
as adapted and set in the
St. Gall *Gesangbuch* (1863)

THE ETERNAL WORD

1 THE day of resurrection,
   Earth, tell it out abroad!
The passover of gladness,
   The passover of God!
From death to life eternal,
   From earth unto the sky,
Our Christ has brought us over
   With hymns of victory.

2 Our hearts be pure from evil,
   That we may see aright
The Lord in rays eternal
   Of resurrection light;
And, listening to his accents,
   May hear, so calm and plain,
His own 'All hail!' and, hearing,
   May raise the victor strain.

3 Now let the heavens be joyful,
   Let earth her song begin,
The round world keep high triumph,
   And all that is therein;
Let all things seen and unseen
   Their notes of gladness blend,
For Christ the Lord is risen,
   Our joy that has no end.

John of Damascus (-*c.* 750)
tr. *John Mason Neale* (1818–66)

209

ST MAGNUS C.M.

Melody and bass
(slightly altered), probably by
Jeremiah Clarke (*c.* 1673–1707)

For this tune in a higher key see No. 2

DESCANT VERSION FOR VERSE 6　　　Arranged by John Wilson

Sopranos (other voices sing unison melody)

Organ (with breadth)

6 The cross he bore is life and health, Though

shame and death to him; His peo-ple's hope, his

cresc.

THE ETERNAL WORD

peo - ple's wealth, Their ev - er - last - ing theme.

1 THE head that once was crowned with thorns
   Is crowned with glory now;
A royal diadem adorns
   The mighty Victor's brow.

2 The highest place that heaven affords
   Is his, is his by right,
The King of kings and Lord of lords,
   And heaven's eternal light,

3 The joy of all who dwell above,
   The joy of all below
To whom he manifests his love
   And grants his name to know.

4 To them the cross, with all its shame,
   With all its grace, is given,
Their name an everlasting name,
   Their joy the joy of heaven.

5 They suffer with their Lord below,
   They reign with him above,
Their profit and their joy to know
   The mystery of his love.

6 The cross he bore is life and health,
   Though shame and death to him;
His people's hope, his people's wealth,
   Their everlasting theme.

Thomas Kelly (1769–1855)

Johann Gottfried Schicht (1753–1823)
Allgemeines Choralbuch (Leipzig, 1819)

THE ETERNAL WORD

1 THE Lord ascendeth up on high,
    The Lord hath triumphed gloriously,
        In power and might excelling;
    The grave and hell are captive led,
    Lo! He returns, our glorious Head,
        To his eternal dwelling.

2 The heavens with joy receive their Lord,
    By saints, by angel hosts adored;
        O day of exultation!
    O earth, adore thy glorious King!
    His rising, his ascension sing
        With grateful adoration!

3 Our great High Priest hath gone before,
    Now on his church his grace to pour,
        And still his love he giveth.
    O may our hearts to him ascend;
    May all within us upward tend
        To him who ever liveth!

Arthur Tozer Russell (1806–74)

211
GONFALON ROYAL   L.M.

P. C. Buck (1871–1947)

Unison. With movement.

A - - - - men.

THE ETERNAL WORD

1 THE Saviour, when to heaven he rose,
   In splendid triumph o'er his foes,
      Scattered his gifts on us below,
      And wide his royal bounties flow.

2 Hence sprung the apostles' honoured name,
   Sacred beyond heroic fame;
      In lowlier forms, to bless our eyes,
      Pastors from hence, and teachers rise.

3 From Christ their varied gifts derive,
   And, fed by Christ, their graces live;
      While, guarded by his mighty hand,
      Midst all the rage of hell they stand.

4 So shall the bright succession run
   Through the last courses of the sun;
      While unborn churches by their care
      Shall rise and flourish large and fair.

5 Jesus our Lord their hearts shall know—
   The Spring whence all these blessings flow;
      Pastors and people shout his praise
      Through all the round of endless days. Amen.

Philip Doddridge (1702–51) alt.
based on Ephesians 4:7–12

212

MACCABAEUS   10.11.11.11. (Refrain)

G. F. Handel (1685–1759)
Edited by John Wilson✻

Refrain (Unison ad lib.)

(Org.)

✻ From the differing versions given by Handel.

THE ETERNAL WORD

1 THINE be the glory, risen, conquering Son,
  Endless is the victory thou o'er death hast won;
    Angels in bright raiment rolled the stone away,
    Kept the folded grave-clothes where thy body lay.
      Thine be the glory, risen, conquering Son,
      Endless is the victory thou o'er death hast won.

2 Lo, Jesus meets us, risen from the tomb;
  Lovingly he greets us, scatters fear and gloom;
  Let the church with gladness hymns of triumph sing,
  For her Lord now liveth, death hath lost its sting:

3 No more we doubt thee, glorious Prince of Life;
  Life is nought without thee: aid us in our strife;
  Make us more than conquerors through thy deathless love;
  Bring us safe through Jordan to thy home above:

                    Edmond L. Budry (1854–1932)
                 tr. *Richard B. Hoyle* (1875–1939)

DESCANT VERSION FOR FINAL REFRAIN

Sopranos. (Other voices sing unison melody)   Arranged by J.W.

The Resurrection and the Ascension

6.7.6.7. (Refrain)

Dutch Melody, 17th century

Refrain (Unison)

Come, share our Eas - ter

joy That death could not im - pri - son, Nor a - ny power des-

- troy, Our Christ, who is a - ris - en, a - ris - en, a -

THE ETERNAL WORD

-ris - en, a - ris - - - - en!

1 THIS joyful Eastertide,
   What need is there for grieving?
Cast all your cares aside
   And be not unbelieving:
      Come, share our Easter joy
         That death could not imprison,
      Nor any power destroy,
         Our Christ, who is arisen!

2 No work for him is vain,
   No faith in him mistaken,
For Easter makes it plain
   His kingdom is not shaken:

3 Then put your trust in Christ,
   In waking and in sleeping.
His grace on earth sufficed;
   He'll never quit his keeping:

F. Pratt Green (1903–)

For permission to reproduce see p. xiii.

The Resurrection and the Ascension

214

VICTORY 8 8 8.4.

Adapted by W. H. Monk (1823–89) from a
Magnificat by Palestrina (1591)

Al - le - lu - ia!

1 THE strife is o'er, the battle done;
  Now is the Victor's triumph won;
  O let the song of praise be sung:
    Alleluia!

2 The powers of death have done their worst,
  But Christ their legions has dispersed;
  Let shouts of praise and joy outburst:
    Alleluia!

3 On the third morn he rose again,
  Glorious in majesty to reign;
  O let us swell the joyful strain:
    Alleluia!

4 He broke the age-bound chains of hell;
  The bars from heaven's high portals fell;
  Let hymns of praise his triumph tell:
    Alleluia!

5 Lord, by the stripes which wounded thee,
  From death's dread sting thy servants free,
  That we may live, and sing to thee:
    Alleluia!

17th Century
tr. *Francis Pott* (1832–1909)

215

AMAZING GRACE C.M.

Early American melody

1 AMAZING grace (how sweet the sound)
   That saved a wretch like me!
I once was lost, but now am found,
   Was blind, but now I see.

2 Through many dangers, toils and snares
   I have already come;
God's grace has brought me safe thus far,
   And he will lead me home.

3 The Lord has promised good to me,
   His word my hope secures;
He will my shield and portion be
   As long as life endures.

4 And, when this heart and flesh shall fail
   And mortal life shall cease,
I shall possess within the veil
   A life of joy and peace.

John Newton (1725–1807) alt.

Christ's Work of Salvation

216(i)

SAGINA 88.88.88.

Published by Thomas Campbell
in his *Bouquet* (1825)

(Repeat lines 5 and 6)

THE ETERNAL WORD

1 AND can it be that I should gain
   An interest in the Saviour's blood?
Died he for me, who caused his pain?
   For me, who him to death pursued?
Amazing love! How can it be
That thou, my God, shouldst die for me?

2 'Tis mystery all: the Immortal dies!
   Who can explore his strange design?
In vain the first-born seraph tries
   To sound the depths of love divine.
'Tis mercy all! Let earth adore,
Let angel minds enquire no more.

3 He left his Father's throne above—
   So free, so infinite his grace—
Emptied himself of all but love,
   And bled for Adam's helpless race.
'Tis mercy all, immense and free;
For, O my God, it found out me!

4 Long my imprisoned spirit lay
   Fast bound in sin and nature's night;
Thine eye diffused a quickening ray—
   I woke, the dungeon flamed with light,
My chains fell off, my heart was free,
I rose, went forth, and followed thee.

5 No condemnation now I dread;
   Jesus, and all in him, is mine!
Alive in him, my living Head,
   And clothed in righteousness divine,
Bold I approach the eternal throne,
And claim the crown, through Christ, my own.

Charles Wesley (1707–88)

Christ's Work of Salvation

216(ii)

DIDSBURY   88.88.88.

Cyril V. Taylor (1907–   )

THE ETERNAL WORD

1 AND can it be that I should gain
    An interest in the Saviour's blood?
Died he for me, who caused his pain?
    For me, who him to death pursued?
Amazing love! How can it be
That thou, my God, shouldst die for me?

2 'Tis mystery all: the Immortal dies!
    Who can explore his strange design?
In vain the first-born seraph tries
    To sound the depths of love divine.
'Tis mercy all! Let earth adore,
Let angel minds enquire no more.

3 He left his Father's throne above—
    So free, so infinite his grace—
Emptied himself of all but love,
    And bled for Adam's helpless race.
'Tis mercy all, immense and free;
For, O my God, it found out me!

4 Long my imprisoned spirit lay
    Fast bound in sin and nature's night;
Thine eye diffused a quickening ray—
    I woke, the dungeon flamed with light,
My chains fell off, my heart was free,
I rose, went forth, and followed thee.

5 No condemnation now I dread;
    Jesus, and all in him, is mine!
Alive in him, my living Head,
    And clothed in righteousness divine,
Bold I approach the eternal throne,
And claim the crown, through Christ, my own.

Charles Wesley (1707–88)

217

ST JOHN (ADORATION) 66.66.88.

From *The Parish Choir* (1851)
(with altered rhythms)

1 ARISE, my soul, arise,
      Shake off thy guilty fears;
   The bleeding sacrifice
      In my behalf appears:
   Before the throne my surety stands;
   My name is written on his hands.

2 He ever lives above,
      For me to intercede,
   His all-redeeming love,
      His precious blood, to plead;
   His blood atoned for all our race,
   And sprinkles now the throne of grace.

3 Five bleeding wounds he bears,
      Received on Calvary;
   They pour effectual prayers,
      They strongly speak for me:
   'Forgive him, O forgive!' they cry,
   'Nor let that ransomed sinner die!'

4 The Father hears him pray,
      His dear anointed one;
   He cannot turn away
      The presence of his Son:
   His Spirit answers to the blood,
   And tells me I am born of God.

5 He owns me for his child,
      His pardoning voice I hear;
   In Jesus reconciled
      I can no longer fear.
   With confidence I now draw nigh,
   And 'Father, Abba, Father!' cry.

Charles Wesley (1707–88) alt.

THE ETERNAL WORD

218

CAITHNESS C.M.

Melody from the *Scottish Psalter* (1635)
(as harmonised in *The English Hymnal*, 1906)

For this tune in a lower key see No. 131(ii)

1 FATHER of peace, and God of love,
   We own your power to save—
That power by which our Shepherd rose
   Victorious o'er the grave.

2 Him from the dead you brought again,
   When, by his sacred blood,
Confirmed and sealed for evermore
   The eternal covenant stood.

3 O may your Spirit seal our souls,
   And mould them to your will,
That our weak hearts no more may stray,
   But keep your precepts still;

4 That to perfection's sacred height
   We nearer still may rise,
And all we think, and all we do,
   Be pleasing in your eyes.

Scottish Paraphrases (1781) alt.
based on Hebrews 13: 20, 21.

May also be sung to No. 340, ST PAUL (ABERDEEN)

Christ's Work of Salvation

THE ETERNAL WORD

1 CHRIST is the world's Redeemer,
  The lover of the pure,
The fount of heavenly wisdom,
  Our trust and hope secure;
The armour of his soldiers,
  The Lord of earth and sky;
Our health while we are living,
  Our life when we shall die.

2 Christ has our host surrounded
  With clouds of martyrs bright,
Who wave their palms in triumph,
  And fire us for the fight.
For Christ the cross ascended
  To save a world undone,
And, suffering for the sinful,
  Our full redemption won.

3 Down in the realm of darkness
  He lay a captive bound,
But at the hour appointed
  He rose, a victor crowned;
And now, to heaven ascended,
  He sits upon the throne,
In glorious dominion,
  His Father's and his own.

4 Glory to God the Father,
  The unbegotten One;
All honour be to Jesus,
  His sole-begotten Son;
And to the Holy Spirit—
  The perfect Trinity.
Let all the worlds give answer:
  'Amen—so let it be!'

Ascribed to *Columba* (521–97)
tr. *Duncan MacGregor* (1854–1923)

May also be sung to No. 704(i), WOLVERCOTE

Christ's Work of Salvation

220

THEODORIC   6 6 6.6 6. and Refrain

Melody from *Piae Cantiones*, 1582
Harmony by G. H. Knight (1908–1979)

Sing a-loud, loud, loud!

Sing a-loud, loud, loud! God is good!

THE ETERNAL WORD

God is truth! God is beau-ty! Praise him!

Last verse only.

1 GOD is love: his the care,
Tending each, everywhere.
God is love—all is there!
Jesus came to show him,
That we all might know him:
    Sing aloud, loud, loud!
    Sing aloud, loud, loud!
        God is good!
        God is truth!
    God is beauty! Praise him!

2 None can see God above;
Neighbours here we can love;
Thus may we Godward move,
Finding him in others,
Sisters all, and brothers:

3 Jesus lived here for men,
Strove and died, rose again,
Rules our hearts, now as then;
For he came to save us
By the truth he gave us:

4 To our Lord praise we sing—
Light and life, friend and king,
Coming down love to bring,
Pattern for our duty,
Showing God in beauty:

Percy Dearmer (1867–1936) alt.

221

KESTON 8 8 8 7.

A. E. Floyd (1877–1974)

THE ETERNAL WORD

1 I AM not skilled to understand
   What God has willed, what God has planned;
   I only know at his right hand
      Stands one who is my Saviour.

2 I take God at his word and deed:
   Christ died to save me, this I read;
   And in my heart I find a need
      Of him to be my Saviour.

3 And was there then no other way
   For God to take? I cannot say;
   I only bless him, day by day,
      Who saved me through my Saviour.

4 That he should leave his place on high
   And come for sinners once to die,
   You count it strange? So do not I,
      Since I have known my Saviour.

5 And O that he fulfilled may see
   The travail of his soul in me,
   And with his work contented be,
      As I with my dear Saviour!

6 Yea, living, dying, let me bring
   My strength, my solace, from this spring,
   That he who lives to be my King
      Once died to be my Saviour.

Dora Greenwell (1821–82)

Christ's Work of Salvation

1 HAIL, thou once despisèd Jesus,
    Hail, thou Galilean King!
Thou didst suffer to release us,
    Thou didst free salvation bring.
Hail, thou agonizing Saviour,
    Bearer of our sin and shame;
By thy merits we find favour;
    Life is given through thy name!

2 Paschal Lamb by God appointed,
    All our sins on thee were laid;
By almighty love anointed,
    Thou hast full atonement made:
All thy people are forgiven
    Through the virtue of thy blood;
Opened is the gate of heaven;
    Peace is made 'twixt man and God.

3 Jesus, hail! enthroned in glory,
    There for ever to abide;
All the heavenly host adore thee,
    Seated at thy Father's side:
There for sinners thou art pleading,
    There thou dost our place prepare,
Ever for us interceding,
    Till in glory we appear.

4 Worship, honour, power, and blessing,
    Thou art worthy to receive;
Loudest praises without ceasing,
    Meet it is for us to give.
Help, ye bright angelic spirits,
    Bring your sweetest, noblest lays;
Help to sing our Saviour's merits,
    Help to chant Immanuel's praise!

John Bakewell (1721–1819) and others

May also be sung to No. 653, BETHANY

223
CALON LÂN 8.7.8.7. (Refrain)

John Hughes (Glandŵr) (1872–1914)

Refrain

1 I WILL sing the wondrous story
    Of the Christ who died for me,
  How he left the realms of glory
    For the cross on Calvary:
      Yes, I'll sing the wondrous story
        Of the Christ who died for me,
      Sing it with his saints in glory,
        Gathered by the crystal sea.

2 I was lost; but Jesus found me,
    Found the sheep that went astray,
  Raised me up, and gently led me
    Back into the narrow way:

3 Faint was I, and fears possessed me,
    Bruised was I from many a fall;
  Hope was gone, and shame distressed me;
    But his love has pardoned all:

4 Days of darkness still come o'er me;
    Sorrow's paths I often tread;
  But the Saviour still is with me,
    By his hand I'm safely led:

5 He will keep me till the river
    Rolls its waters at my feet;
  Then he'll bear me safely over,
    Where the loved ones I shall meet:

Francis Harold Rowley (1854–1952)

May also be sung to No. 272, HYFRYDOL

Christ's Work of Salvation

1 IT is a thing most wonderful,
   Almost too wonderful to be,
That God's own Son should come from heaven,
   And die to save a child like me.

2 And yet I know that it is true;
   He chose a poor and humble lot,
And wept and toiled and mourned and died,
   For love of those who loved him not.

3 It is most wonderful to know
   His love for me so free and sure;
But 'tis more wonderful to see
   My love for him so faint and poor.

4 And yet I want to love thee, Lord;
   O light the flame within my heart,
And I will love thee more and more,
   Until I see thee as thou art.
                    William Walsham How (1823–97)

THE ETERNAL WORD

ANTWERP L.M.

William Smallwood (1831–97)

For this tune in a higher key see No. 148

1 JESUS, thy blood and righteousness
   My beauty are, my glorious dress;
      Midst flaming worlds, in these arrayed,
      With joy shall I lift up my head.

2 Bold shall I stand in thy great day;
   For to my charge who aught shall lay?
      Fully absolved through these I am,
      From sin and fear, from guilt and shame.

3 That holy, meek, unspotted Lamb,
   Who from the Father's bosom came,
      Who died for me, e'en me, to atone,
      Now for my Lord and God I own.

4 Lord, I believe thy precious blood,
   Which at the mercy-seat of God
      For ever doth for sinners plead,
      For me, e'en for my soul, was shed.

5 When from the dust of death I rise
   To claim my mansion in the skies,
      E'en then this shall be all my plea—
      Jesus hath lived, hath died for me!

Nicolaus Ludwig von Zinzendorf (1700–60)
    tr. *John Wesley* (1703–91)

Christ's Work of Salvation

226

MILLENNIUM 6.6.6.6.88.

THE ETERNAL WORD

1 LET earth and heaven agree,
    Angels and men be joined,
To celebrate with me
    The Saviour of mankind;
To adore the all-atoning Lamb,
And bless the sound of Jesu's name.

2 Jesus, transporting sound!
    The joy of earth and heaven;
No other help is found,
    No other name is given,
By which we can salvation have;
But Jesus came the world to save.

3 Jesus, harmonious name!
    It charms the hosts above;
They evermore proclaim
    And wonder at his love;
'Tis all their happiness to gaze,
'Tis heaven to see our Jesu's face.

4 His name the sinner hears,
    And is from sin set free;
'Tis music in his ears,
    'Tis life and victory;
New songs do now his lips employ,
And dances his glad heart for joy.

5 Stung by the scorpion sin,
    My poor expiring soul
The healing sound drinks in,
    And is at once made whole:
See there my Lord upon the tree!
I hear, I feel, he died for me.

6 O unexampled love,
    O all-redeeming grace!
How swiftly didst thou move
    To save a fallen race!
What shall I do to make it known
What thou for all mankind hast done?

7 O for a trumpet voice
    On all the world to call,
To bid their hearts rejoice
    In him who died for all!
For all my Lord was crucified,
For all, for all my Saviour died.

Charles Wesley (1707–88)

Christ's Work of Salvation

227

CRUCIS VICTORIA   C.M.

M. B. Foster (1851–1922)

DESCANT

From *Hymns for Church and School* (1964)

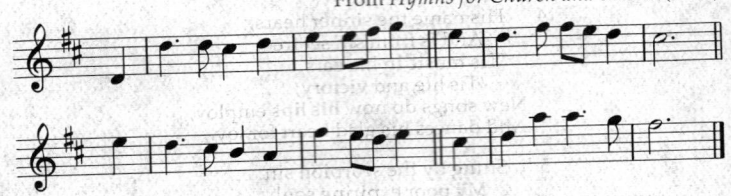

1 LIFT up your heads, ye gates of brass;
     Ye bars of iron, yield;
   And let the King of Glory pass;
     The cross is in the field.

2 A holy war his servants wage,
     Mysteriously at strife;
   The powers of heaven and hell engage
     For more than death or life.

3 Ye armies of the living God,
     His sacramental host,
   Where hallowed footstep never trod
     Take your appointed post.

4 Though few and small and weak your bands,
     Strong in your Captain's strength,
   Go to the conquest of all lands:
     All must be his at length.

THE ETERNAL WORD

5 Then fear not, faint not, halt not now;
   In Jesus' name be strong;
To him shall all the nations bow,
   And sing the triumph-song:

6 'Uplifted are the gates of brass;
   The bars of iron yield;
Behold the King of Glory pass:
   The cross has won the field!'

James Montgomery (1771–1854) alt.

228
GETHSEMANE   7 7 7.8.   Philipp Bliss (1838–76)

1 MAN of Sorrows! What a name
   For the Son of God, who came
   Ruined sinners to reclaim!
      Alleluia! What a Saviour!

2 Bearing shame and scoffing rude,
   In my place condemned he stood;
   Sealed my pardon with his blood:
      Alleluia! What a Saviour!

3 Guilty, vile, and helpless we;
   Spotless Lamb of God was he:
   Full atonement—can it be?
      Alleluia! What a Saviour!

4 Lifted up was he to die;
   'It is finished!' was his cry;
   Now in heaven exalted high:
      Alleluia! What a Saviour!

5 When he comes, our glorious King,
   All his ransomed home to bring,
   Then anew this song we'll sing:
      Alleluia! What a Saviour!

Philipp Bliss (1838–76)

Christ's Work of Salvation

229

PRO NOBIS L.M.

T. Kenneth Blackwell (1915–)

1 O LOVE, how deep, how broad, how high!
   It fills the heart with ecstasy,
      That God, the Son of God, should take
      Our mortal form, for mortals' sake.

2 For us he was baptized, and bore
   His holy fast, and hungered sore;
      For us temptation sharp he knew,
      For us the tempter overthrew.

3 For us he prayed, for us he taught,
   For us his daily works he wrought:
      By words and signs and actions thus
      Still seeking, not himself, but us.

4 For us to wicked men betrayed,
   Scourged, mocked, in purple robe arrayed,
      He bore the shameful cross and death,
      For us at length gave up his breath.

5 For us he rose from death again;
   For us he went on high to reign;
      For us he sent his Spirit here
      To guide, to strengthen, and to cheer.

6 To him whose boundless love has won
   Salvation for us through his Son,
      To God the Father, glory be,
      Both now and through eternity.

c. 15th Century
tr. *Benjamin Webb* (1819–85)

THE ETERNAL WORD

230

CROSS OF JESUS 8.7.8.7.

John Stainer (1840–1901)

For this tune in a higher key see No. 81(ii)

1 THERE'S a wideness in God's mercy
  Like the wideness of the sea;
  There's a kindness in his justice
  Which is more than liberty.

2 There is plentiful redemption
  In the blood that has been shed;
  There is joy for all the members
  In the sorrows of the Head.

3 There is grace enough for thousands
  Of new worlds as great as this;
  There is room for fresh creations
  In that upper home of bliss.

4 For the love of God is broader
  Than the measures of man's mind;
  And the heart of the Eternal
  Is most wonderfully kind.

5 But we make his love too narrow
  By false limits of our own;
  And we magnify his strictness
  With a zeal he will not own.

6 If our love were but more simple
  We should take him at his word;
  And our lives would be illumined
  By the presence of our Lord.

Frederick William Faber (1814–63) alt.

Christ's Work of Salvation

231(i)

GERONTIUS C.M.

J. B. Dykes (1823–76)

*The small notes are to be used with the Descant.

DESCANT

Verse 7

V. S. H. Russell (1900–56)

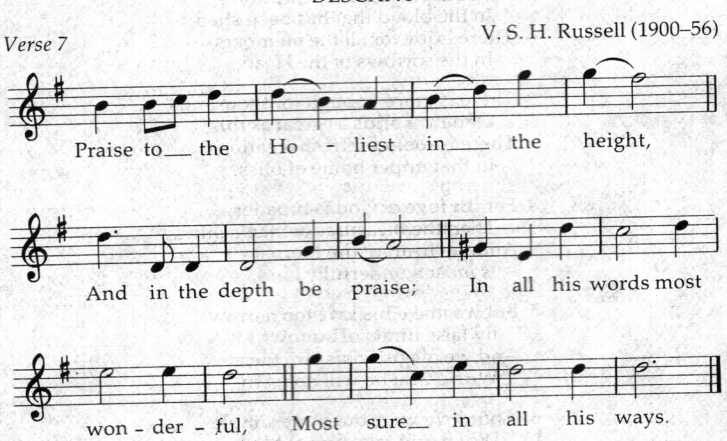

Praise to— the Ho - liest in— the height,

And in the depth be praise; In all his words most

won - der - ful, Most sure— in all his ways.

THE ETERNAL WORD

231(ii)

BILLING C.M.

R. R. Terry (1865–1938)

1 PRAISE to the Holiest in the height,
  And in the depth be praise;
In all his words most wonderful,
  Most sure in all his ways.

2 O loving wisdom of our God!
  When all was sin and shame,
A second Adam to the fight
  And to the rescue came.

3 O wisest love! that flesh and blood,
  Which did in Adam fail,
Should strive afresh against the foe,
  Should strive and should prevail;

4 And that a higher gift than grace
  Should flesh and blood refine,
God's presence and his very self,
  And essence all-divine.

5 O generous love! that he, who smote
  In man for man the foe,
The double agony in man
  For man should undergo;

6 And in the garden secretly,
  And on the cross on high,
Should teach his brethren, and inspire
  To suffer and to die.

7 Praise to the Holiest in the height,
  And in the depth be praise;
In all his words most wonderful,
  Most sure in all his ways.

John Henry Newman (1801–90)

May also be sung to No. 147, CHORUS ANGELORUM

Christ's Work of Salvation

232

TELL ME   7.6.7.6.D. (Refrain)

W. H. Doane (1832–1915)

THE ETERNAL WORD

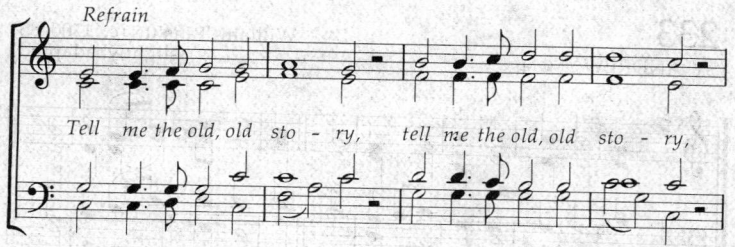

Refrain

Tell me the old, old sto - ry, tell me the old, old sto - ry,

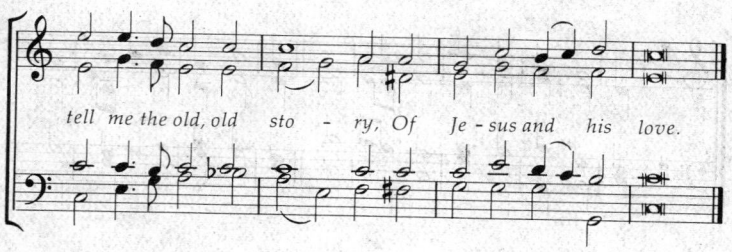

tell me the old, old sto - ry, Of Je - sus and his love.

1 TELL me the old, old story
   Of unseen things above,
   Of Jesus and his glory,
   Of Jesus and his love.
   Tell me the story simply,
   As to a little child;
   For I am weak, and weary,
   And helpless, and defiled:
   Tell me the old, old story,
   Of Jesus and his love.

2 Tell me the story slowly,
   That I may take it in—
   That wonderful redemption,
   God's remedy for sin.
   Tell me the story often,
   For I forget so soon;
   The early dew of morning
   Has passed away at noon:

3 Tell me the story softly,
   With earnest tones and grave;
   Remember, I'm the sinner
   Whom Jesus came to save.
   Tell me the story always,
   If you would really be
   In any time of trouble
   A comforter to me:

4 Tell me the same old story
   When you have cause to fear
   That this world's empty glory
   Is costing me too dear.
   And when that next world's glory
   Is dawning on my soul,
   Tell me the old, old story—
   Christ Jesus makes thee whole!

   Katherine Hankey (1834–1911)

Christ's Work of Salvation

233

ST ANDREW C.M.

William Tans'ur (*c.* 1700–83)
(slightly adapted)

1 THE Saviour died, but rose again
   Triumphant from the grave;
   And pleads our cause at God's right hand,
   Omnipotent to save.

2 Who then can e'er divide us more
   From Jesus and his love,
   Or break the sacred chain that binds
   The earth to heaven above?

3 Let troubles rise, and terrors frown,
   And days of darkness fall;
   Through him all dangers we'll defy,
   And more than conquer all.

4 Nor death nor life, nor earth nor hell,
   Nor time's destroying sway,
   Can e'er efface us from his heart,
   Or make his love decay.

5 Each future period he will bless,
   As he has blessed the past;
   He loved us from the first of time,
   He loves us to the last.

Scottish Paraphrases (1781)
based on Romans 8: 34–39

THE ETERNAL WORD

234

1 THOU art the Way: to thee alone
  From sin and death we flee;
  And they who would the Father seek
  Must seek him, Lord, by thee.

2 Thou art the Truth: thy word alone
  True wisdom can impart;
  Thou only canst inform the mind,
  And purify the heart.

3 Thou art the Life: the rending tomb
  Proclaims thy conquering arm;
  And those who put their trust in thee
  Nor death nor hell shall harm.

4 Thou art the Way, the Truth, the Life:
  Grant us that Way to know,
  That Truth to keep, that Life to win,
  Whose joys eternal flow.

George W. Doane (1799–1859)
based on John 14:6

Christ's Work of Salvation

235

SALZBURG C.M.

Melody adapted from
Johann Michael Haydn (1737–1806)

DESCANT VERSION FOR LAST VERSE

Arranged by John Wilson

Sopranos (other voices sing unison melody)

6 Then let our hum - ble faith ad - dress

Organ

His mer - cy and his power; We shall ob - tain de-

THE ETERNAL WORD

-liv-ering grace In each dis-tress-ing hour.

1 WITH joy we meditate the grace
   Of our High Priest above;
 His heart is made of tenderness,
   And overflows with love.

2 Touched with a sympathy within,
   He knows our feeble frame;
 He knows what sore temptations mean,
   For he has felt the same.

3 But spotless, innocent, and pure
   The great Redeemer stood,
 While Satan's fiery darts he bore,
   And did resist to blood.

4 He, in the days of feeble flesh,
   Poured out his cries and tears;
 And in his measure feels afresh
   What every member bears.

5 He'll never quench the smoking flax,
   But raise it to a flame;
 The bruisèd reed he never breaks,
   Nor scorns the meanest name.

6 Then let our humble faith address
   His mercy and his power;
 We shall obtain delivering grace
   In each distressing hour.

Isaac Watts (1674–1748)
based on Hebrews 4:14–16
and Isaiah 42:3

Christ's Work of Salvation

R. R. Terry (1865–1938)

THE ETERNAL WORD

1 HARK what a sound, and too divine for hearing,
   Stirs on the earth and trembles in the air!
Is it the thunder of the Lord's appearing?
   Is it the music of his people's prayer?

2 Surely he cometh, and a thousand voices
   Shout to the saints, and to the deaf are dumb;
Surely he cometh, and the earth rejoices,
   Glad in his coming who hath sworn: I come!

3 This hath he done, and shall we not adore him?
   This shall he do, and can we still despair?
Come, let us quickly fling ourselves before him,
   Cast at his feet the burden of our care.

4 Through life and death, through sorrow and through
      sinning,
   He shall suffice me, for he hath sufficed:
Christ is the end, for Christ was the beginning,
   Christ the beginning, for the end is Christ.

Frederic W. H. Myers (1843–1901)

Christ's Coming in Glory

237

LITTLE CORNARD 6.6.6.6.88.

Martin Shaw (1875–1958)

(Small notes Organ only)

THE ETERNAL WORD

1 HILLS of the north, rejoice,
    River and mountain-spring,
  Hark to the advent voice;
    Valley and lowland, sing.
Christ comes in righteousness and love,
He brings salvation from above.

2 Isles of the southern seas,
    Sing to the listening earth;
  Carry on every breeze
    Hope of a world's new birth:
In Christ shall all be made anew;
His word is sure, his promise true.

3 Lands of the east, arise!
    He is your brightest morn;
  Greet him with joyous eyes,
    Let praise his path adorn:
Your seers have longed to know their Lord;
To you he comes, the final Word.

4 Shores of the utmost west,
    Lands of the setting sun,
  Welcome the heavenly guest
    In whom the dawn has come:
He brings a never-ending light,
Who triumphed o'er our darkest night.

5 Shout, as you journey on;
    Songs be in every mouth!
  Lo, from the north they come,
    From east and west and south:
In Jesus all shall find their rest,
In him the universe be blest.

Charles E. Oakley (1832–65)
and editors of *English Praise* (1975) alt.

Christ's Coming in Glory

Irish traditional melody
Arranged by
John Barnard (1948–   )

THE ETERNAL WORD

1 I CANNOT tell why he, whom angels worship,
   Should set his love upon the sons of men,
 Or why, as Shepherd, he should seek the wanderers,
   To bring them back, they know not how or when.
 But this I know, that he was born of Mary
   When Bethlem's manger was his only home,
 And that he lived at Nazareth and laboured,
   And so the Saviour, Saviour of the world, is come.

2 I cannot tell how silently he suffered,
   As with his peace he graced this place of tears,
 Or how his heart upon the cross was broken,
   The crown of pain to three-and-thirty years.
 But this I know, he heals the broken-hearted,
   And stays our sin, and calms our lurking fear,
 And lifts the burden from the heavy-laden,
   For yet the Saviour, Saviour of the world, is here.

3 I cannot tell how he will win the nations,
   How he will claim his earthly heritage,
 How satisfy the needs and aspirations
   Of east and west, of sinner and of sage.
 But this I know, all flesh shall see his glory,
   And he shall reap the harvest he has sown,
 And some glad day his sun shall shine in splendour,
   When he the Saviour, Saviour of the world, is known.

4 I cannot tell how all the lands shall worship,
   When at his bidding every storm is stilled,
 Or who can say how great the jubilation
   When all the hearts of men with love are filled.
 But this I know, the skies will thrill with rapture,
   And myriad, myriad human voices sing,
 And earth to heav'n, and heav'n to earth, will answer:
   'At last the Saviour, Saviour of the world, is King!'

William Young Fullerton (1857–1932)

Christ's Coming in Glory

239(i)

GALILEE L.M.

P. Armes (1836–1908)

For this tune in a lower key see No. 338(ii)

239(ii)

RIMINGTON L.M.

F. Duckworth (1862–1941)

THE ETERNAL WORD

1 JESUS shall reign where'er the sun
  Doth his successive journeys run;
    His kingdom stretch from shore to shore,
    Till moons shall wax and wane no more.

2 For him shall endless prayer be made,
  And praises throng to crown his head;
    His name like sweet perfume shall rise
    With every morning sacrifice;

3 People and realms of every tongue
  Dwell on his love with sweetest song;
    And infant voices shall proclaim
    Their early blessings on his name.

4 Blessings abound where'er he reigns;
  The prisoner leaps to lose his chains;
    The weary find eternal rest,
    And all the sons of want are blest.

5 Let every creature rise and bring
  Peculiar honours to our King;
    Angels descend with songs again,
    And earth repeat the loud amen.

Isaac Watts (1674–1748)
based on Psalm 72: 5–19

Christ's Coming in Glory

240

TRURO L.M.   Melody from T. Williams's *Psalmodia Evangelica* (1789)

1 LIFT up your heads, you mighty gates,
  Behold, the King of Glory waits,
    The King of kings is drawing near,
    The Saviour of the world is here.

2 O blest the land, the city blest
  Where Christ the ruler is confessed!
    O happy hearts and happy homes
    To whom this King in triumph comes!

3 Fling wide the portals of your heart,
  Make it a temple set apart
    From earthly use for heaven's employ,
    Adorned with prayer and love and joy.

4 Come, Saviour, come, with us abide;
  Our hearts to thee we open wide:
    Thy Holy Spirit guide us on,
    Until our glorious goal is won.

Georg Weissel (1590–1635)
tr. *Catherine Winkworth* (1827–78)

Christ's Coming in Glory

241

HELMSLEY 8.7.8.7.4.7. (Ext.)

Later form of a melody in J. Wesley's *Select Hymns with Tunes Annext* (1765)

(Small notes organ only)

THE ETERNAL WORD

1 LO, he comes with clouds descending,
    Once for favoured sinners slain;
Thousand thousand saints attending
    Swell the triumph of his train:
        Alleluia!
    God appears on earth to reign.

2 Every eye shall now behold him
    Robed in dreadful majesty;
Those who set at nought and sold him,
    Pierced and nailed him to the tree,
        Deeply wailing,
    Shall the true Messiah see.

3 Those dear tokens of his passion
    Still his dazzling body bears;
Cause of endless exultation
    To his ransomed worshippers:
        With what rapture
    Gaze we on those glorious scars.

4 Yea, amen, let all adore thee,
    High on thine eternal throne;
Saviour, take the power and glory,
    Claim the kingdom for thine own:
        Come, Lord Jesus!
    Everlasting God, come down!

Charles Wesley (1707–88)

(See also following page)

Christ's Coming in Glory

241 (cont.)

Choir (S.A.T.B.) and Organ

f Yea, a - men, let all a - dore thee,

High on thine e - ter - nal throne; Sa - viour,

take the power and glo - ry, Claim the

king - dom for thine own: *mp* Come, Lord

THE ETERNAL WORD

Je - sus! Come, Lord Je - sus! *mf* Come, ___ Lord Je - sus!

(Small notes organ only)

Ped.

Sopranos

f Ev — — er - last — ing God, ___ come down!

A.T.B. in Unison

f Ev — — er - last — ing God, come down!

Organ (with breadth)

f

This arrangement may also be used:
(i) as an Organ accompaniment, with all voices singing the unison
melody;
(ii) as a Descant Version for Sopranos and Organ, with all other voices
singing the unison melody.

Christ's Coming in Glory

242

BATTLE-HYMN   Irreg.

Unison

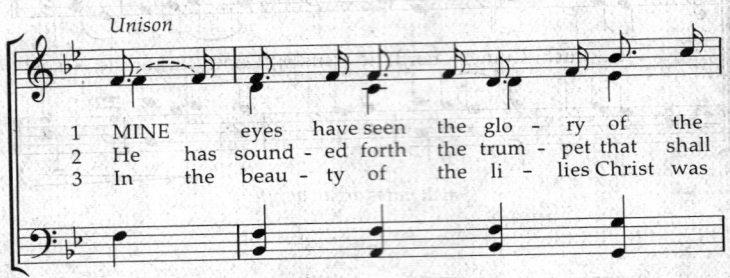

1 MINE   eyes have seen   the glo - ry of   the
2 He   has sound - ed forth   the trum - pet that   shall
3 In   the beau - ty of   the li – lies Christ was

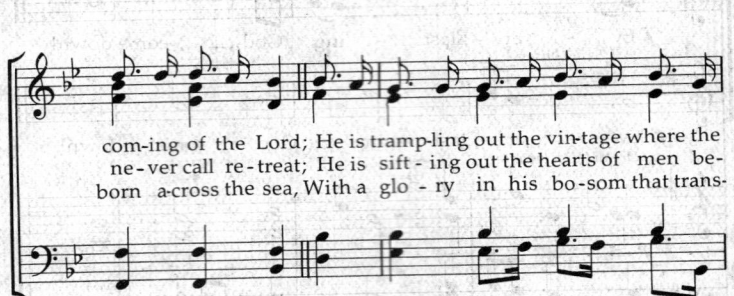

com-ing of the Lord; He is tramp-ling out the vin-tage where the
ne - ver call re - treat; He is sift - ing out the hearts of men be-
born a-cross the sea, With a glo - ry in his bo-som that trans-

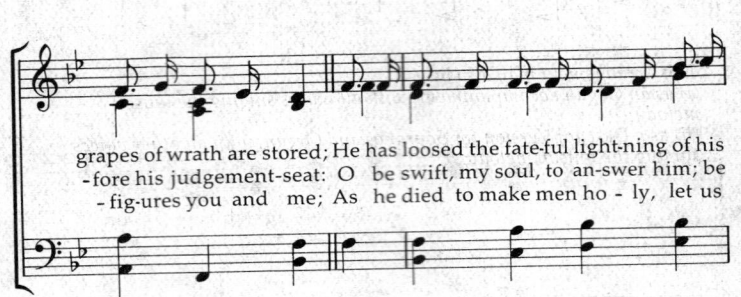

grapes of wrath are stored; He has loosed the fate-ful light-ning of his
-fore his judgement-seat: O be swift, my soul, to an-swer him; be
-fig-ures you and me; As he died to make men ho - ly, let us

THE ETERNAL WORD

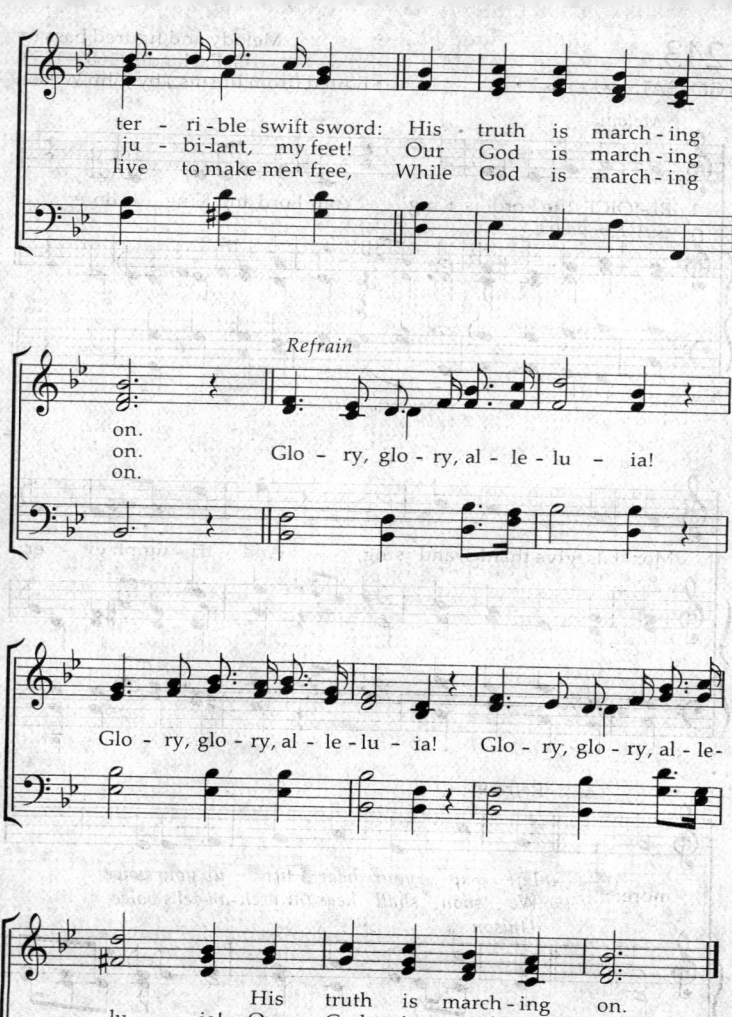

ter - ri - ble swift sword: His truth is march - ing
ju - bi - lant, my feet! Our God is march - ing
live to make men free, While God is march - ing

Refrain

on.
on. Glo - ry, glo - ry, al - le - lu - ia!
on.

Glo - ry, glo - ry, al - le - lu - ia! Glo - ry, glo - ry, al - le -

- lu - ia! His truth is march - ing on.
Our God is march - ing on.
While God is march - ing on.

Julia Ward Howe (1819–1910)

Christ's Coming in Glory

Melody and figured bass by
G. F. Handel (1685–1759)
Edited (from the ms.) by John Wilson

1 RE-JOICE, the Lord is King! Your Lord and King a-dore;

Mor-tals, give thanks, and sing, And tri-umph ev-er-

(Vv. 1—4) Lift up your heart, lift up your voice;

(v. 5) We soon shall hear the arch-an-gel's voice;

THE ETERNAL WORD

Re - joice! A - gain I __ say: Re - joice!
The trump of God shall sound: Re - joice!

1 REJOICE, the Lord is King!
   Your Lord and King adore;
   Mortals, give thanks, and sing,
   And triumph evermore:
      Lift up your heart, lift up your voice;
      Rejoice! Again I say: Rejoice!

2 Jesus the Saviour reigns,
   The God of truth and love;
   When he had purged our stains,
   He took his seat above:

3 His kingdom cannot fail,
   He rules o'er earth and heaven;
   The keys of death and hell
   Are to our Jesus given:

4 He sits at God's right hand
   Till all his foes submit,
   And bow to his command,
   And fall beneath his feet:

5 Rejoice in glorious hope;
   Jesus the Judge shall come,
   And take his servants up
   To their eternal home:

      We soon shall hear the archangel's voice;
      The trump of God shall sound: Rejoice!

            Charles Wesley (1707–88)

      (See also following page)

Christ's Coming in Glory

243 (cont.)

THE ETERNAL WORD

(Sopranos and Altos) Re – joice! Re – joice!

We soon shall hear Re – joice! The trump____ of

poco rit.

God shall sound, shall sound,_____ Re-joice!

A tempo

Christ's Coming in Glory

244

THE GLORY SONG   10.10.10.10. (Refrain)   C. H. Gabriel (1856–1932)

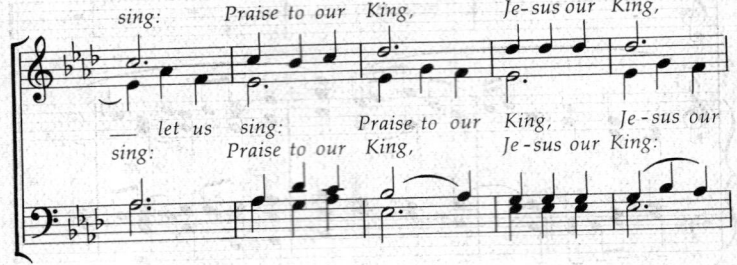

THE ETERNAL WORD

1 SING we the King who is coming to reign;
   Glory to Jesus, the Lamb that was slain!
     Life and salvation his empire shall bring,
     Joy to the nations when Jesus is King:
       Come let us sing: Praise to our King,
       Jesus our King, Jesus our King:
       This is our song, who to Jesus belong:
       Glory to Jesus, to Jesus our King.

2 All shall be well in his kingdom of peace;
   Freedom shall flourish and wisdom increase;
     Justice and truth from his sceptre shall spring;
     Wrong shall be ended when Jesus is King:

3 Souls shall be saved from the burden of sin;
   Doubt shall not darken his witness within;
     Hell has no terrors, and death has no sting;
     Love is victorious when Jesus is King:

4 Kingdom of Christ, for thy coming we pray;
   Hasten, O Father, the dawn of the day
     When this new song thy creation shall sing:
     Satan is vanquished, and Jesus is King:

Charles Silvester Horne (1865–1914)

Christ's Coming in Glory

For this tune in a lower key see No. 666

THE ETERNAL WORD

1 THE Lord will come, and not be slow;
   His footsteps cannot err;
  Before him righteousness shall go,
   His royal harbinger.

2 Truth from the earth, like to a flower,
   Shall bud and blossom then;
  And justice, from her heavenly bower,
   Look down on mortal men.

3 Surely to such as do him fear
   Salvation is at hand;
  And glory shall ere long appear
   To dwell within our land.

4 Rise, Lord, judge thou the earth in might,
   This wicked earth redress;
  For thou art he who shall by right
   The nations all possess.

5 The nations all whom thou hast made
   Shall come, and all shall frame
  To bow them low before thee, Lord,
   And glorify thy name.

6 For great thou art, and wonders great
   By thy strong hand are done:
  Thou in thine everlasting seat
   Remainest God alone.

John Milton (1608–74)
based on Psalms 82, 85 and 86

Christ's Coming in Glory

THERE'S A LIGHT UPON THE MOUNTAINS 15 15.15 15.

M. L. Wostenholm (1887–1959)

THE ETERNAL WORD

1 THERE'S a light upon the mountains, and the day is at the spring,
   When our eyes shall see the beauty and the glory of the King;
   Weary was our heart with waiting, and the night-watch seemed so long;
   But his triumph-day is breaking, and we hail it with a song.

2 There's a hush of expectation, and a quiet in the air;
   And the breath of God is moving in the fervent breath of prayer:
   For the suffering, dying Jesus is the Christ upon the throne,
   And the travail of our spirit is the travail of his own.

3 He is breaking down the barriers, he is casting up the way;
   He is calling for his angels to build up the gates of day:
   But his angels here are human, not the shining hosts above;
   For the drum-beats of his army are the heart-beats of our love.

4 Hark! We hear a distant music, and it comes with fuller swell;
   'Tis the triumph-song of Jesus, of our King, Immanuel:
   Zion, go ye forth to meet him; and, my soul, be swift to bring
   All thy finest and thy noblest for the triumph of our King!

Henry Burton (1840–1930)

Christ's Coming in Glory

1   THOU Judge of quick and dead,
        Before whose bar severe
With holy joy, or guilty dread,
        We all shall soon appear:
    Our cautioned souls prepare
        For that tremendous day,
And fill us now with watchful care,
        And stir us up to pray—

2   To pray, and wait the hour,
        That aweful hour unknown,
When, robed in majesty and power,
        Thou shalt from heaven come down,
    The immortal Son of Man,
        To judge the human race,
With all thy Father's dazzling train,
        With all thy glorious grace.

3   O may we thus be found
        Obedient to his word,
Attentive to the trumpet's sound,
        And looking for our Lord!
    O may we thus ensure
        Our lot among the blest;
And watch a moment to secure
        An everlasting rest!

Charles Wesley (1707–88)

THE ETERNAL WORD

248

NARENZA S.M.

Adapted by W. H. Havergal (1793–1870) from *Ave, Maria Klare* in Töpler's *Alte Choral-Melodien* (1832)

1 YE servants of the Lord,
    Each in his office wait,
Observant of his heavenly word,
    And watchful at his gate.

2 Let all your lamps be bright,
    And trim the golden flame;
Gird up your loins, as in his sight,
    For aweful is his name.

3 Watch: 'tis your Lord's command;
    And while we speak he's near;
Mark the first signal of his hand,
    And ready all appear.

4 O happy servant he,
    In such employment found!
He shall his Lord with rapture see,
    And be with honour crowned.

5 Christ shall the banquet spread
    With his own royal hand,
And raise that favoured servant's head
    Amid the angelic band.

Philip Doddridge (1702–51)

Christ's Coming in Glory

Melody by P. Nicolai (1556–1608)
Adapted and harmonised by
J. S. Bach (1685–1750)

THE ETERNAL WORD

1 WAKE, O wake! With tidings thrilling
The watchmen all the air are filling,
    Arise, Jerusalem, arise!
Midnight strikes! No more delaying,
'The hour has come!' we hear them saying,
    'Where are ye all, ye virgins wise?
        The Bridegroom comes in sight,
        Raise high your torches bright!'
            Alleluia!
        The wedding song
        Swells loud and strong:
    Go forth and join the festal throng.

2 Zion hears the watchmen shouting,
Her heart leaps up with joy undoubting,
    She stands and waits with eager eyes;
See her Friend from heaven descending,
Adorned with truth and grace unending!
    Her light burns clear, her star doth rise.
        Now come, thou precious Crown,
        Lord Jesus, God's own Son!
            Alleluia!
        Let us prepare
        To follow there,
    Where in thy supper we may share.

3 Every soul in thee rejoices;
From earth and from angelic voices
    Be glory given to thee alone!
Now the gates of pearl receive us,
Thy presence never more shall leave us,
    We stand with angels round thy throne.
        Earth cannot give below
        The bliss thou dost bestow.
            Alleluia!
        Grant us to raise,
        To length of days,
    The triumph-chorus of thy praise.

Philipp Nicolai (1556–1608)
tr. F. C. Burkitt (1864–1935)
based on Matthew 25: 1–13
and Revelation 19: 6–9

Christ's Coming in Glory

250

Don Fishel (1928–)

ALLELUIA, ALLELUIA   Irreg.   Arranged by Norman Warren (1934–)

Refrain. Unison

Al-le - lu-ia, al-le - lu - ia, give thanks to the risen Lord, Al-le-

Fine

- lu - ia, al - le - lu - ia, give praise to his name.

Verses

1 JE - SUS is Lord of all the earth;

He is the King of cre - a - - tion. Al-le-

THE ETERNAL WORD

DESCANT
Refrain

Angela Reith (1952–)

Al-le-lu – ia, al-le-lu – ia, thanks to the ris-en Lord,

Al-le-lu – ia, al-le-lu – ia, praise to his name.

Alleluia, alleluia, give thanks to the risen Lord,
Alleluia, alleluia, give praise to his name.

1 JESUS is Lord of all the earth;
He is the King of creation:

2 Spread the good news o'er all the earth:
Jesus has died and has risen:

3 We have been crucified with Christ;
Now we shall live for ever:

4 God has proclaimed the just reward:
New life for all! Alleluia!

5 Come, let us praise the living God,
Joyfully sing to our Saviour:

Don Fishel (1928–)

The Praises of Jesus

251

ALL FOR JESUS 8.7.8.7.

J. Stainer (1840–1901)

(It may be desirable to sing this tune a semitone lower.)

THE ETERNAL WORD

1 ALL for Jesus—all for Jesus,
    This our song shall ever be:
For we have no hope, nor Saviour,
    If we have not hope in thee.

2 All for Jesus—thou wilt give us
    Strength to serve thee, hour by hour;
None can move us from thy presence,
    While we trust thy love and power.

3 All for Jesus—thou hast loved us;
    All for Jesus—thou hast died;
All for Jesus—thou art with us;
    All for Jesus crucified.

4 All for Jesus—all for Jesus—
    This the church's song must be;
Till, at last, we all are gathered
    One in love and one in thee.

W. J. Sparrow-Simpson (1859–1952)

The Praises of Jesus

252(i)
MILES LANE C.M. (Ext.)

Later form of melody by W. Shrubsole
(*c.* 1759–1806)

And crown him, crown him, crown him, crown him Lord of all.

252(ii)
DIADEM C.M. (Ext.)

J. Ellor (1819–99)

crown

crown him, crown him,

THE ETERNAL WORD

him,

crown him, crown him

crown him, crown

crown him, and crown him Lord of all.

1 ALL hail the power of Jesu's name!
    Let angels prostrate fall;
    Bring forth the royal diadem,
    And crown him Lord of all.

2 Crown him, ye martyrs of your God,
    Who from his altar call;
    Extol the Stem-of-Jesse's Rod,
    And crown him Lord of all.

3 Ye seed of Israel's chosen race,
    Ye ransomed of the fall,
    Hail him who saves you by his grace,
    And crown him Lord of all.

4 Hail him, the heir of David's line
    Whom David Lord did call,
    The God incarnate, Man divine,
    And crown him Lord of all.

5 Sinners, whose love can ne'er forget
    The wormwood and the gall,
    Go, spread your trophies at his feet,
    And crown him Lord of all.

6 Let every kindred, every tribe
    On this terrestrial ball,
    To him all majesty ascribe,
    And crown him Lord of all.

7 O that with yonder sacred throng
    We at his feet may fall,
    Join in the everlasting song,
    And crown him Lord of all!

Edward Perronet (1726–92)
alt. *John Rippon* (1751–1836)

The Praises of Jesus

253

LALEHAM 10 10 10.4.

John Wilson (1905–)

Al – le – lu – ia, Al – le – lu – ia!

The opening of vv. 2–4 may be accompanied thus:

THE ETERNAL WORD

1 ALL praise to thee, for thou, O King divine,
  Didst yield the glory that of right was thine,
  That in our darkened hearts thy grace might shine:
      Alleluia!

2 Thou cam'st to us in lowliness of thought;
  By thee the outcast and the poor were sought,
  And by thy death was God's salvation wrought:
      Alleluia!

3 Let this mind be in us which was in thee,
  Who wast a servant that we might be free,
  Humbling thyself to death on Calvary:
      Alleluia!

4 Wherefore, by God's eternal purpose, thou
  Art high exalted o'er all creatures now,
  And given the name to which all knees shall bow:
      Alleluia!

5 Let every tongue confess with one accord
  In heaven and earth that Jesus Christ is Lord;
  And God the Father be by all adored:
      Alleluia!

F. Bland Tucker **(1895-1984)**
based on Philippians 2: 5–11

(See following page for Optional Harmony Version)

The Praises of Jesus

253 (cont.)

OPTIONAL HARMONY VERSION FOR VERSES 2 & 3

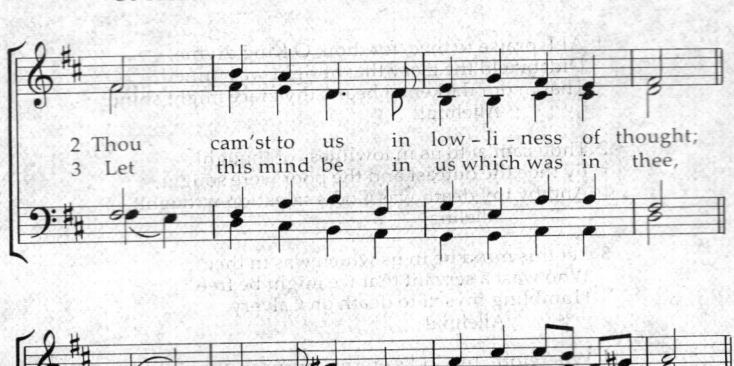

2 Thou cam'st to us in low - li - ness of thought;
3 Let this mind be in us which was in thee,

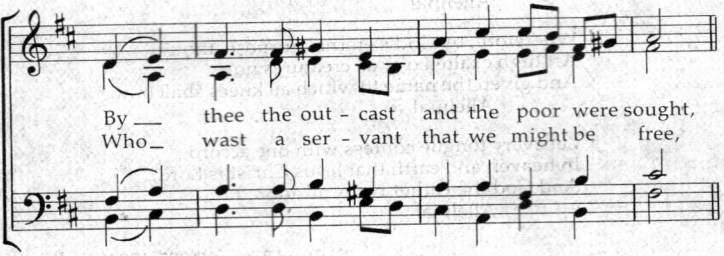

By __ thee the out - cast and the poor were sought,
Who __ wast a ser - vant that we might be free,

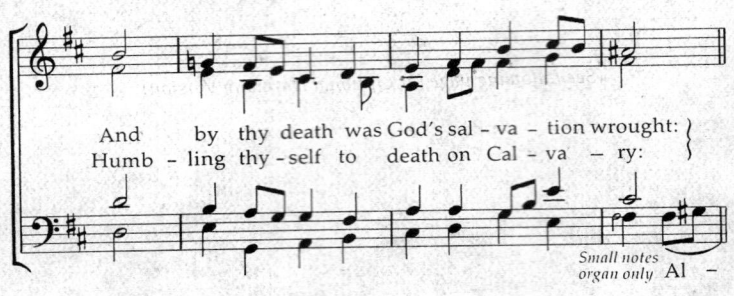

And by thy death was God's sal - va - tion wrought:)
Humb - ling thy - self to death on Cal - va - ry:)

Small notes organ only Al -

THE ETERNAL WORD

Al – le – lu – ia, Al – le – lu – ia!

(Ten.) Al – le – lu – ia, Al – le – lu – ia!

– le – lu – ia, Al – le – lu – ia!

Turn back for Verse 4.

In Verse 5 this Tenor part of the 'Alleluias' may be sung as a Descant by Sopranos and Tenors.

The Praises of Jesus

254

COME, MY WAY   7.7.7.7.

Alexander Brent Smith (1889–1950)

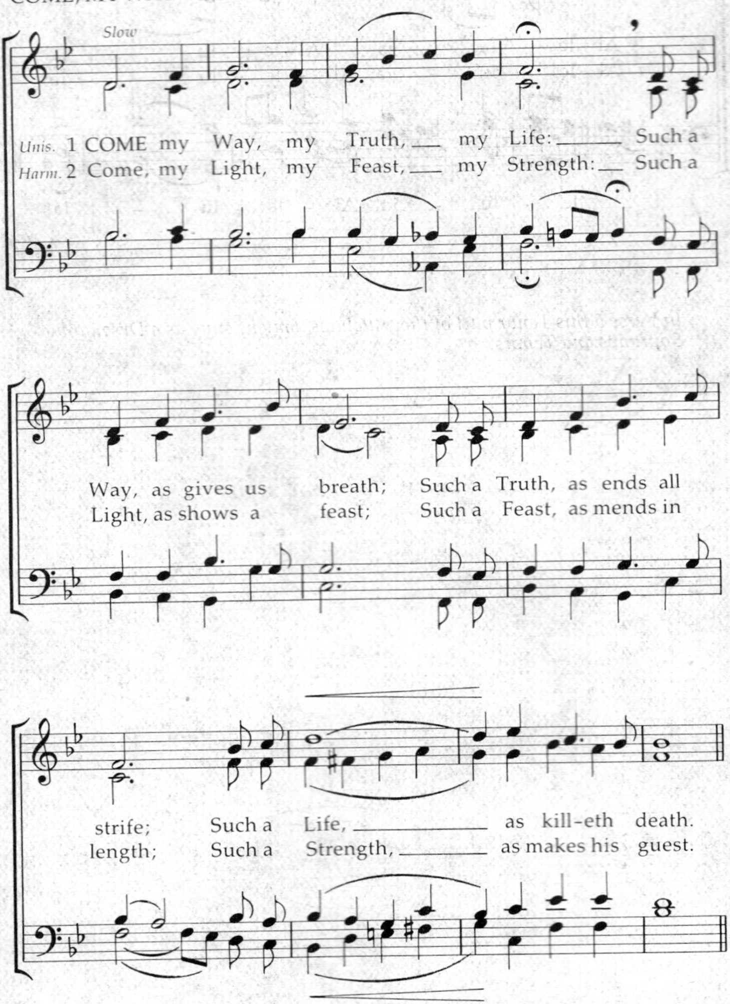

Slow

Unis. 1 COME my Way, my Truth, __ my Life: ___ Such a
Harm. 2 Come, my Light, my Feast, __ my Strength: __ Such a

Way, as gives us breath; Such a Truth, as ends all
Light, as shows a feast; Such a Feast, as mends in

strife; Such a Life, _____ as kill-eth death.
length; Such a Strength, _____ as makes his guest.

THE ETERNAL WORD

3 Come, my Joy, my Love,___ my Heart: Such a

Such a

Such a

Joy, as none can move; Such a Love, as none can

Joy,___ Such a Love,___

Joy, as none can move; Such a Love, as none can

part; Such a Heart,___ as joys in love.

part; Such a Heart,___ as joys in love.

(Small notes organ)

George Herbert (1593–1633)

The Praises of Jesus

255

DIADEMATA D.S.M

G. J. Elvey (1816–1893)

THE ETERNAL WORD

1 CROWN him with many crowns,
    The Lamb upon his throne;
Hark! How the heavenly anthem drowns
    All music but its own.
    Awake, my soul, and sing
    Of him who died for thee,
And hail him as thy matchless King
    Through all eternity.

2 Crown him the Son of God,
    Before the worlds began;
And ye, who tread where he has trod,
    Crown him the Son of Man,
    Who every grief has known
    That wrings the human breast,
And takes and bears them for his own,
    That all in him may rest.

3 Crown him the Lord of life,
    Who triumphed o'er the grave,
And rose victorious in the strife
    For those he came to save.
    His glories now we sing,
    Who died, and rose on high;
Who died, eternal life to bring,
    And lives, that death may die.

4 Crown him the Lord of peace,
    Whose power a sceptre sways
From pole to pole, that wars may cease,
    Absorbed in prayer and praise.
    His reign shall know no end,
    And round his piercèd feet
Fair flowers of paradise extend
    Their fragrance ever sweet.

5 Crown him the Lord of love;
    Behold his hands and side—
Rich wounds, yet visible above,
    In beauty glorified.
    All hail, Redeemer, hail!
    For thou hast died for me;
Thy praise and glory shall not fail
    Throughout eternity.

Matthew Bridges (1800–94)
and *Godfrey Thring* (1823–1903)

The Praises of Jesus

1   HE is Lord, he is Lord;
        He is risen from the dead, and he is Lord;
        Every knee shall bow, every tongue confess
            That Jesus Christ is Lord.

2   He is King, he is King;
        He will draw all nations to him, he is King;
        And the time shall be when the world shall sing
            That Jesus Christ is King.

3   He is love, he is love;
        He has shown us by his life that he is love;
        All his people sing with one voice of joy
            That Jesus Christ is love.

4   He is life, he is life;
        He has died to set us free and he is life;
        And he calls us all to live evermore,
            For Jesus Christ is life.

Anonymous

THE ETERNAL WORD

257

ST PETER C.M.

A. R. Reinagle (1799–1877)

1 HOW sweet the name of Jesus sounds
   In a believer's ear!
   It soothes his sorrows, heals his wounds,
   And drives away his fear.

2 It makes the wounded spirit whole,
   And calms the troubled breast;
   'Tis manna to the hungry soul,
   And to the weary, rest.

3 Dear name—the rock on which I build,
   My shield and hiding-place,
   My never-failing treasury, filled
   With boundless stores of grace!

4 Jesus! My Shepherd, Brother, Friend,
   My Prophet, Priest, and King,
   My Lord, my Life, my Way, my End,
   Accept the praise I bring.

5 Weak is the effort of my heart,
   And cold my warmest thought;
   But when I see thee as thou art,
   I'll praise thee as I ought.

6 Till then I would thy love proclaim
   With every fleeting breath;
   And may the music of thy name
   Refresh my soul in death.

John Newton (1725–1807)

The Praises of Jesus

258

WAREHAM L.M.

Melody by W. Knapp (1698–1768)

For this tune in a higher key see No. 549

1 JESU, thou joy of loving hearts,
   Thou fount of life, thou light of men,
From the best bliss that earth imparts
   We turn unfilled to thee again.

2 Thy truth unchanged hath ever stood;
   Thou savest those that on thee call;
To them that seek thee thou art good,
   To them that find thee, all in all.

3 We taste thee, O thou living bread,
   And long to feast upon thee still;
We drink of thee, the fountain head,
   And thirst our souls from thee to fill.

4 Our restless spirits yearn for thee,
   Where'er our changeful lot is cast;
Glad when thy gracious smile we see,
   Blest when our faith can hold thee fast.

5 O Jesus, ever with us stay;
   Make all our moments calm and bright;
Chase the dark night of sin away;
   Shed o'er the world thy holy light.

12th Century
tr. *Ray Palmer* (1808–87)

THE ETERNAL WORD

259

JESU, MEINE FREUDE   66.5.66.5.7.86.

Melody from J. Crüger's *Praxis Pietatis Melica* (1653),
as arranged by
J. S. Bach (1685–1750)

1 JESU, priceless treasure,
  Source of purest pleasure,
    Truest friend to me;
Ah! How long I've panted,
And my heart hath fainted,
    Thirsting, Lord, for thee!
Thine I am, O spotless Lamb,
I will suffer nought to hide thee,
    Nought I ask beside thee.

2 In thine arm I rest me;
  Foes who would molest me
    Cannot reach me here;
Though the earth be shaking,
Every heart be quaking,
    Jesus calms my fear;
Sin and hell in conflict fell
With their bitter storms assail me;
    Jesus will not fail me.

3 Hence, all fears and sadness!
  For the Lord of gladness,
    Jesus, enters in;
Those who love the Father,
Though the storms may gather,
    Still have peace within;
Yea, whate'er I here must bear,
Still in thee lies purest pleasure,
    Jesu, priceless treasure!

Johann Franck (1618–77)
tr. *Catherine Winkworth* (1827–78)

The Praises of Jesus

260

JESUS IS LORD   11.12.11.12 (Refrain)

David Mansell

THE ETERNAL WORD

1 JESUS is Lord! Creation's voice proclaims it,
   For by his power each tree and flower was planned and
       made.
   Jesus is Lord! The universe declares it;
   Sun, moon and stars in heaven cry: Jesus is Lord!
       Jesus is Lord! Jesus is Lord!
       Praise him with alleluias, for Jesus is Lord!

2 Jesus is Lord! Yet from his throne eternal
   In flesh he came to die in pain on Calvary's tree.
   Jesus is Lord! From him all life proceeding—
   Yet gave his life a ransom, thus setting us free:

3 Jesus is Lord! O'er sin the mighty conqueror,
   From death he rose; and all his foes shall own his name.
   Jesus is Lord! God sends his Holy Spirit
   To show by works of power that Jesus is Lord:

                                    David J. Mansell

The Praises of Jesus

261

COLDREY 7.6.7.6.7 7.

Henry Smart (1813–79)

THE ETERNAL WORD

1 JESUS, sun and shield art thou,
    Sun and shield for ever!
  Never canst thou cease to shine,
    Cease to guard us, never.
  Cheer our steps as on we go,
  Come between us and the foe.

2 Jesus, peace and joy art thou,
    Joy and peace for ever!
  Joy that fades not, changes not,
    Peace that leaves us never.
  Joy and peace we have in thee,
  Now and through eternity.

3 Jesus, song and strength art thou,
    Strength and song for ever!
  Strength that never can decay,
    Song that ceaseth never.
  Still to us this strength and song
  Through eternal days prolong.

4 Jesus, bread and wine art thou,
    Wine and bread for ever!
  Never canst thou cease to feed,
    Or refresh us, never.
  Feed we still on bread divine,
  Drink we still of heavenly wine.

Horatius Bonar (1808–89)

THE ETERNAL WORD

1   JESUS, the Conqueror, reigns,
        In glorious strength arrayed,
    His kingdom over all maintains,
        And bids the earth be glad.
        Ye peoples all, rejoice
        In Jesus' mighty love;
    Lift up your heart, lift up your voice,
        To him who rules above.

2   Extol his kingly power,
        Kiss the exalted Son,
    Who died; and lives, to die no more,
        High on his Father's throne:
        Our Advocate with God,
        He undertakes our cause,
    And spreads through all the earth abroad
        The vict'ry of his cross.

3   'Courage!' your Captain cries,
        Who all your toil foreknew;
    'Toil ye shall have; yet all despise,
        I have o'ercome for you.'
        This is the victory!
        Before our faith they fall;
    Jesus has died for you and me;
        Believe, and conquer all!

Charles Wesley (1707–88) alt.

263

GETHSEMANE (DYKES) 77.77.77.

J. B. Dykes (1823–76)

1 JESUS the good Shepherd is,
    Jesus died the sheep to save;
  He is mine and I am his,
    All I want in him I have:
  Life, and health, and rest, and food,
  All the plenitude of God.

2 Jesus loves and guards his own;
    Me in verdant pastures feeds,
  Makes me quietly lie down,
    By the streams of comfort leads:
  Following him where'er he goes,
  Silent joy my heart o'erflows.

3 He in sickness makes me whole,
    Guides into the paths of peace;
  He revives my fainting soul,
    Stablishes in righteousness;
  Who for me vouchsafed to die,
  Loves me still—I know not why!

4 Love divine shall still embrace,
    Love shall keep me to the end;
  Surely all my happy days
    I shall in thy temple spend,
  Till I to thy house remove,
  Thy eternal house above!

Charles Wesley (1707–88)
based on Psalm 23

THE ETERNAL WORD

264

LYDIA   C.M. (Ext.)

T. Phillips (1735–1807)

1 JESUS—the name high over all,
   In hell, or earth, or sky!
Angels and men before it fall,
   And devils fear and fly.

2 Jesus—the name to sinners dear,
   The name to sinners given!
It scatters all their guilty fear,
   It turns their hell to heaven.

3 Jesus—the prisoner's fetters breaks,
      And bruises Satan's head;
   Power into strengthless souls it speaks,
      And life into the dead.

4 O that the world might taste and see
      The riches of his grace!
   The arms of love that compass me
      Would all mankind embrace.

5 His only righteousness I show,
   His saving grace proclaim;
'Tis all my business here below
   To cry: 'Behold the Lamb!'

6 Happy if with my latest breath
   I might but gasp his name;
Preach him to all, and cry in death:
   'Behold, behold the Lamb!'

Charles Wesley (1707–88)

May also be sung to No. 821, NATIVITY

The Praises of Jesus

265(i)
METZLER'S REDHEAD C.M.

R. Redhead (1820–1901)

265(ii)
LAND OF REST C.M.

American Folk Hymn Tune
Harmonised by John Wilson

THE ETERNAL WORD

For this tune in a lower key see No. 621(i)

1 JESUS, the very thought of thee
    With sweetness fills the breast;
  But sweeter far thy face to see,
    And in thy presence rest.

2 Nor voice can sing, nor heart can frame,
    Nor can the memory find
  A sweeter sound than thy blest name,
    O Saviour of mankind!

3 O hope of every contrite heart,
    O joy of all the meek,
  To those who fall how kind thou art,
    How good to those who seek!

4 But what to those who find? Ah, this
    Nor tongue nor pen can show:
  The love of Jesus, what it is
    None but his lovers know.

5 Jesus, thy mercies are untold
    Through each returning day;
  Thy love exceeds a thousandfold
    Whatever we can say.

6 Jesus, our only joy be thou,
    As thou our prize wilt be;
  Jesus, be thou our glory now,
    And through eternity.

12th Century
tr. *Edward Caswall* (1814–78)

The Praises of Jesus

French Carol Melody, as harmonised in
The English Hymnal (1906)

THE ETERNAL WORD

1 LET all mortal flesh keep silence, and with fear and
   trembling stand;
 Ponder nothing earthly-minded, for with blessing in his
   hand
 Christ our God to earth descendeth, our full homage to
   demand.

2 King of kings, yet born of Mary, as of old on earth he
   stood,
 Lord of lords, in human vesture—in the body and the
   blood—
 He will give to all the faithful his own self for heav'nly
   food.

3 Rank on rank the host of heaven spreads its vanguard
   on the way,
 As the Light of light descendeth from the realms of
   endless day,
 That the powers of hell may vanish as the darkness
   clears away.

4 At his feet the six-winged seraph; cherubim with
   sleepless eye
 Veil their faces to the Presence, as with ceaseless voice
   they cry—
 Alleluia, alleluia, alleluia, Lord most high!

From the *Liturgy of St. James*
tr. G. Moultrie (1829–85)

The Praises of Jesus

267(i)

BLAENWERN   8.7.8.7.D.

W. P. Rowlands (1860–1937)

THE ETERNAL WORD

267(ii)

LOVE DIVINE 8.7.8.7.

John Stainer (1840–1901)

1 LOVE divine, all loves excelling,
  Joy of heaven to earth come down,
Fix in us thy humble dwelling,
  All thy faithful mercies crown.
Jesu, thou art all compassion,
  Pure, unbounded love thou art;
Visit us with thy salvation,
  Enter every trembling heart.

2 Come, almighty to deliver,
  Let us all thy life receive;
Suddenly return, and never,
  Never more thy temples leave.
Thee we would be always blessing,
  Serve thee as thy hosts above,
Pray, and praise thee, without ceasing,
  Glory in thy perfect love.

3 Finish then thy new creation,
  Pure and spotless let us be;
Let us see thy great salvation,
  Perfectly restored in thee:
Changed from glory into glory,
  Till in heaven we take our place,
Till we cast our crowns before thee,
  Lost in wonder, love, and praise!

Charles Wesley (1707–88)

May also be sung to No. 272, HYFRYDOL

The Praises of Jesus

267(iii)

WESTMINSTER
(SACRED HARMONY) 8 7.8 7.D

Melody and bass from
John Wesley's *Sacred Harmony* (1780)
based on Purcell's song, *Fairest Isle*

1 LOVE divine, all loves excelling,
Fix in us thy humble dwelling,
Joy of heaven to earth come down,
All thy faithful mercies crown.
Jesu, thou art all compassion,
Pure, unbounded love thou art;

THE ETERNAL WORD

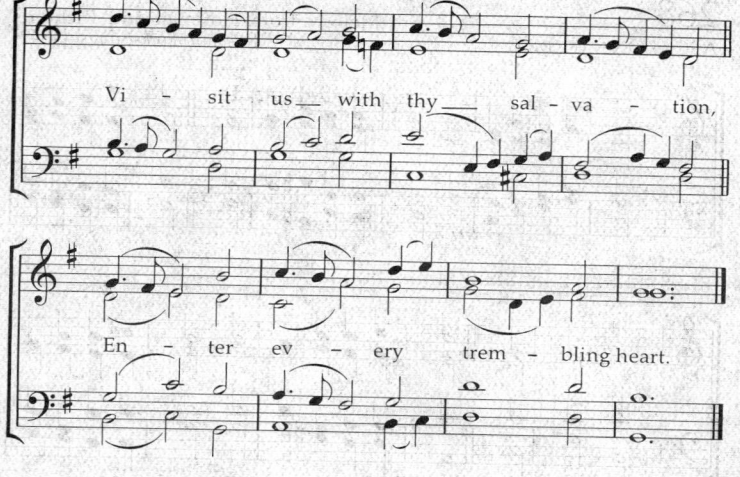

Vi - sit us with thy sal - va - tion,

En - ter ev - ery trem - bling heart.

1 LOVE divine, all loves excelling,
   Joy of heaven to earth come down,
   Fix in us thy humble dwelling,
   All thy faithful mercies crown.
   Jesu, thou art all compassion,
   Pure, unbounded love thou art;
   Visit us with thy salvation,
   Enter every trembling heart.

2 Come, almighty to deliver,
   Let us all thy life receive;
   Suddenly return, and never,
   Never more thy temples leave.
   Thee we would be always blessing,
   Serve thee as thy hosts above,
   Pray, and praise thee, without ceasing,
   Glory in thy perfect love.

3 Finish then thy new creation,
   Pure and spotless let us be;
   Let us see thy great salvation,
   Perfectly restored in thee:
   Changed from glory into glory,
   Till in heaven we take our place,
   Till we cast our crowns before thee,
   Lost in wonder, love, and praise!

Charles Wesley (1707–88)

May also be sung to No. 272, HYFRYDOL

The Praises of Jesus

ASCALON 66.8.D.

Melody from Hoffman and Richter's
Silesian Folk-Songs (1842)

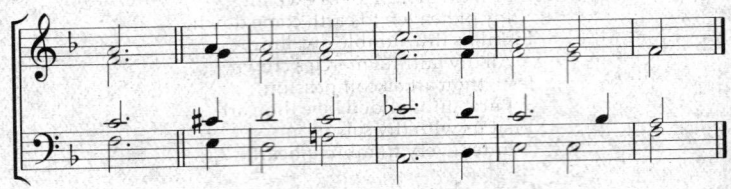

ANOTHER VERSION

Melody from Hoffman and Richter's
Silesian Folk-Songs (1842)

ASCALON 66.8.D.

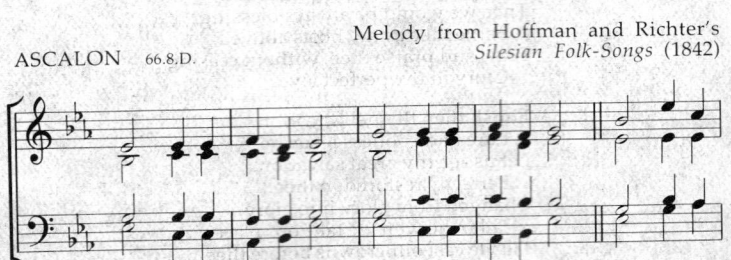

THE ETERNAL WORD

1   MY heart and voice I raise,
        To spread Messiah's praise;
Messiah's praise let all repeat:
    The universal Lord,
    By whose almighty word
Creation rose in form complete.

2   A servant's form he wore,
    And in his body bore
Our dreadful curse on Calvary:
    He like a victim stood,
    And poured his sacred blood,
To set the guilty captives free.

3   But soon the Victor rose
    Triumphant o'er his foes,
And led the vanquished host in chains:
    He threw their empire down,
    His foes compelled to own
O'er all the great Messiah reigns.

4   With mercy's mildest grace,
    He governs all our race
In wisdom, righteousness, and love:
    Who to Messiah fly
    Shall find redemption nigh,
And all his great salvation prove.

5   Hail, Saviour, Prince of Peace!
    Thy kingdom shall increase,
Till all the world thy glory see,
    And righteousness abound
    As the great deep profound,
And fill the earth with purity.

Benjamin Rhodes (1743–1815)

The Praises of Jesus

269(i)
LAND OF REST C.M.

American Folk Hymn Tune
Harmonised by John Wilson

For this tune in a lower key see No. 621(i)

269(ii)
METZLER'S REDHEAD C.M.

R. Redhead (1820–1901)

THE ETERNAL WORD

1 O JESUS, King most wonderful;
   Thou Conqueror renowned,
Thou sweetness most ineffable,
   In whom all joys are found!

2 When once thou visitest the heart,
   Then truth begins to shine,
Then earthly vanities depart,
   Then kindles love divine.

3 O Jesus, light of all below!
   Thou fount of living fire,
Surpassing all the joys we know,
   And all we can desire:

4 Jesus, may all confess thy name,
   Thy wondrous love adore;
And, seeking thee, themselves inflame
   To seek thee more and more.

5 Thee may our tongues for ever bless,
   Thee may we love alone,
And ever in our lives express
   The image of thine own.

6 Abide with us, and let thy light
   Shine, Lord, on every heart;
Dispel the darkness of our night,
   And joy to all impart.

7 Jesus, our love and joy, to thee,
   The Father's only Son,
All might, and praise, and glory be,
   While endless ages run.

12th Century
tr. *Edward Caswall* (1814–78)

The Praises of Jesus

270

Composer and author unknown

CANTICLE OF THE GIFT Irreg. Arranged by Betty Pulkingham (1928–)

Unison
Refrain

O what a gift! What a won-der-ful gift! Who can

Capo 2 (Am) Bm (Am)   A(G)   Bm(Am)

tell the won-ders of the Lord? Let us op - en our eyes, our

Em(Dm)   Bm(Am)   A(G)

ears, and our hearts; It is Christ the Lord, it is he!

Bm(Am)   A(G)   Bm(Am)

Fine

1 IN the still-ness of the night, when the
2 On the night be-fore he died it was
3 On the hill of Cal-va-ry the
4 Ear-ly on that morn-ing, when the
5 Some-day with the saints we will

Bm(Am)

THE ETERNAL WORD

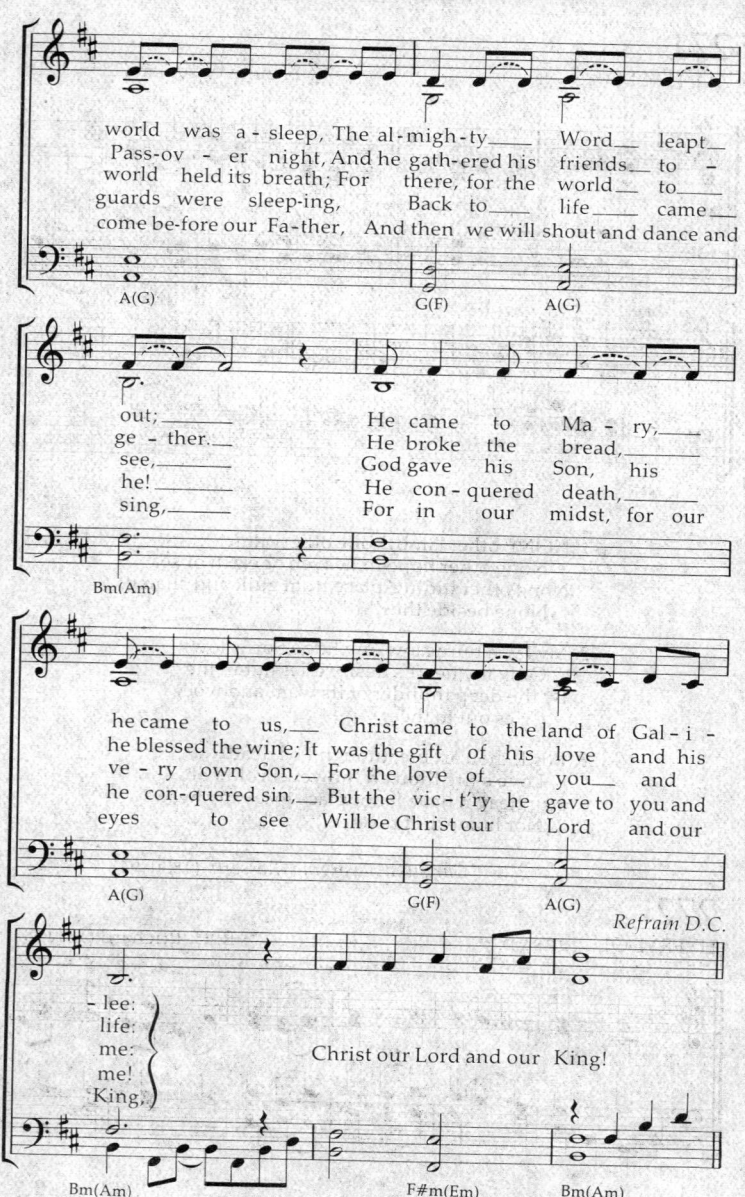

The Praises of Jesus

271

ALL HALLOWS 8.10.10.4. F. Luke Wiseman (1858–1944)

1 NONE other lamb, none other name,
    None other hope in heaven or earth or sea,
  None other hiding-place from guilt and shame,
    None beside thee!

2 My faith burns low, my hope burns low;
    Only my heart's desire cries out in me,
  By the deep thunder of its want and woe,
    Cries out to thee.

3 Lord, thou art life, though I be dead;
    Love's fire thou art, however cold I be:
  Nor heav'n have I, nor place to lay my head,
    Nor home, but thee.

Christina Georgina Rossetti (1830–94)

272

HYFRYDOL 8.7.8.7.D. R. H. Prichard (1811–87)

THE ETERNAL WORD

1 RIDE on, Jesus, all-victorious,
    Bear thy sword upon thy side;
  None on earth can e'er withstand thee,
    Nor yet hell, for all its pride:
  At thy mighty name tremendous
    Every foe is forced to yield;
  Hushed in awe, creation trembles:
    Come then, Jesus, take the field.

2 Rescue now our souls from bondage,
    In thy morn of victory,
  Batter down the doors of Babel,
    Break the bars and set us free:
  Let thy rescued hosts, exulting,
    Troop to freedom, wave on wave,
  Like the surge of mighty waters:
    O come quickly, come and save!

3 Hark! I hear already, faintly,
    Songs of vict'ry from afar,
  Where the heirs of thy redemption
    Hail thy triumph in the war.
  Clad in robes of shining glory,
    Palms of conquest in each hand,
  Joyful hosts, to freedom marching,
    Enter now the promised land.

William Williams (1717–91)
tr. G. O. Williams (1913–)

The Praises of Jesus

273

R. Redhead (1820–1901)
Church Hymn Tunes (1853)

THE ETERNAL WORD

1 ROCK of Ages, cleft for me,
   Let me hide myself in thee;
   Let the water and the blood,
   From thy riven side which flowed,
   Be of sin the double cure,
   Cleanse me from its guilt and power.

2 Not the labours of my hands
   Can fulfil thy law's demands;
   Could my zeal no respite know,
   Could my tears for ever flow,
   All for sin could not atone:
   Thou must save, and thou alone.

3 Nothing in my hand I bring,
   Simply to thy cross I cling;
   Naked, come to thee for dress;
   Helpless, look to thee for grace;
   Foul, I to the fountain fly;
   Wash me, Saviour, or I die.

4 While I draw this fleeting breath,
   When mine eyes shall close in death,
   When I soar through tracts unknown,
   See thee on thy judgement throne,
   Rock of Ages, cleft for me,
   Let me hide myself in thee.

Augustus Montague Toplady (1740–78)

274

NORFOLK PARK   6.5.6.5.D.   H. Coward (1849–1944)

THE ETERNAL WORD

1 SAVIOUR, blessèd Saviour,
  Listen while we sing;
Hearts and voices raising
  Praises to our King:
All we have we offer,
  All we hope to be,
Body, soul, and spirit,
  All we yield to thee.

2 Nearer, ever nearer,
  Christ, we draw to thee,
Deep in adoration,
  Bending low the knee.
Thou, for our redemption,
  Cam'st on earth to die;
Thou, that we might follow,
  Hast gone up on high.

3 Clearer still, and clearer,
  Dawns the light from heaven,
In our sadness bringing
  News of sin forgiven;
Life has lost its shadows,
  Pure the light within;
Thou hast shed thy radiance
  On a world of sin.

4 Onward, ever onward,
  Journeying o'er the road
Worn by saints before us,
  Journeying on to God;
Leaving all behind us,
  May we hasten on,
Backward never looking
  Till the prize is won.

Godfrey Thring (1823–1903)

275(i)
COLCHESTER   88.88.88.

S. S. Wesley (1810–76)

275(ii)
ST CHRYSOSTOM   88.88.88.

J. Barnby (1838–96)

THE ETERNAL WORD

1 THOU hidden source of calm repose,
    Thou all-sufficient love divine,
My help and refuge from my foes,
    Secure I am, if thou art mine:
And lo, from sin, and grief, and shame,
I hide me, Jesus, in thy name.

2 Thy mighty name salvation is,
    And keeps my happy soul above;
Comfort it brings, and power, and peace,
    And joy, and everlasting love:
To me, with thy dear name, are given
Pardon, and holiness, and heaven.

3 Jesus, my all in all thou art:
    My rest in toil, my ease in pain,
The med'cine of my broken heart,
    In war my peace, in loss my gain,
My smile beneath the tyrant's frown,
In shame my glory and my crown;

4 In want my plentiful supply,
    In weakness my almighty power,
In bonds my perfect liberty,
    My light in Satan's darkest hour,
In grief my joy unspeakable,
My life in death, my heaven in hell.

Charles Wesley (1707–88)

The Praises of Jesus

276(i)
LAUDES DOMINI 66.6.D.

J. Barnby (1838–96)

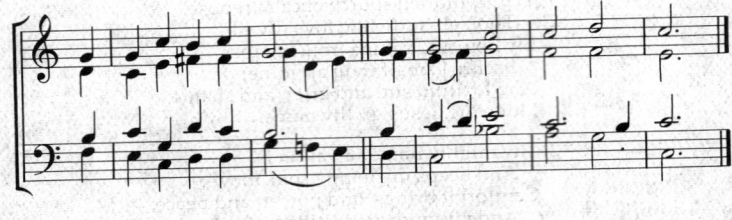

276(ii)
LUDGATE 66.6.D.

J. Dykes Bower (1905–81)

THE ETERNAL WORD

1 WHEN morning gilds the skies,
  My heart awaking cries:
      'May Jesus Christ be praised!'
  Alike at work and prayer
  To Jesus I repair:
      'May Jesus Christ be praised!'

2 Does sadness fill my mind?
  A solace here I find:
      'May Jesus Christ be praised!'
  When evil thoughts molest,
  With this I shield my breast:
      'May Jesus Christ be praised!'

3 To God, the Word, on high
  The hosts of angels cry:
      'May Jesus Christ be praised!'
  Let mortals, too, upraise
  Their voice in hymns of praise:
      'May Jesus Christ be praised!'

4 Let earth's wide circle round
  In joyful notes resound:
      'May Jesus Christ be praised!'
  Let air, and sea, and sky,
  From depth to height, reply:
      'May Jesus Christ be praised!'

5 Be this while life is mine
  My canticle divine:
      'May Jesus Christ be praised!'
  Be this the eternal song,
  Through all the ages long:
      'May Jesus Christ be praised!'

Anonymous
tr. *Edward Caswall* (1814–78)

The Praises of Jesus

277(i)
CELESTE   88.88. (Anapaestic)   *Lancashire Sunday School Songs, 1857*

277(ii)
LEURA   88.88. (Anapaestic)   Lawrence Bartlett (1933–   )

THE ETERNAL WORD

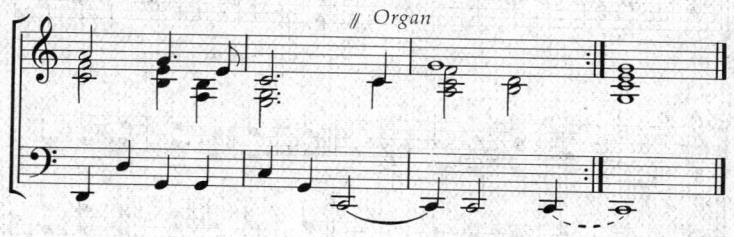

1 THIS, this is the God we adore,
 Our faithful, unchangeable friend,
 Whose love is as great as his power,
 And neither knows measure nor end:

2 'Tis Jesus, the first and the last,
 Whose Spirit shall guide us safe home;
 We'll praise him for all that is past,
 And trust him for all that's to come.

Joseph Hart (1712–68)

The Praises of Jesus

278(i)
LAUDATE DOMINUM (GAUNTLETT).

H. J. Gauntlett (1805–76)
(harmony slightly altered)

10 10.11 11.

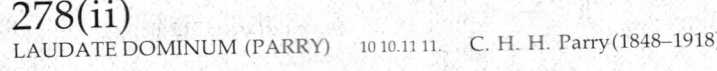

278(ii)
LAUDATE DOMINUM (PARRY)   10 10.11 11.   C. H. H. Parry (1848–1918)

THE ETERNAL WORD

1 YE servants of God, your Master proclaim,
   And publish abroad his wonderful name;
      The name all-victorious of Jesus extol;
      His kingdom is glorious, and rules over all.

2 God ruleth on high, almighty to save;
   And still he is nigh, his presence we have;
      The great congregation his triumph shall sing,
      Ascribing salvation to Jesus our King.

3 'Salvation to God who sits on the throne!'
   Let all cry aloud, and honour the Son;
      The praises of Jesus the angels proclaim,
      Fall down on their faces, and worship the Lamb.

4 Then let us adore, and give him his right:
   All glory and power, all wisdom and might,
      All honour and blessing, with angels above,
      And thanks never-ceasing, and infinite love.

Charles Wesley (1707–88)

(See also following page)

ALTERNATIVE HARMONISATION FOR VERSE 4

With great breadth

(C. H. H. Parry)

Unison

f 4 Then let us a - dore, and give him his

Organ

f

right: All glo - ry and power, all wis-dom and

might, All hon - our and bless-ing, with an - gels a -

mf

cresc.

THE ETERNAL WORD

-bove, And thanks ne - ver - ceas-ing, and in - fi - nite love.

A - men, A - men.

(Small notes Organ only)

279

CHURCH TRIUMPHANT L.M.

J. W. Elliott (1833–1915)

For this tune in a lower key see No. 58(i)

1 BORN by the Holy Spirit's breath,
Loosed from the law of sin and death,
Now cleared in Christ from every claim,
No judgement stands against our name.

2 In us the Spirit makes his home,
That we in him may overcome;
Christ's risen life, in all its powers,
Its all-prevailing strength, is ours.

3 Children and heirs of God most high,
We by his Spirit 'Father' cry;
That Spirit with our spirit shares
To frame and breathe our wordless prayers.

4 One is his love, his purpose one:
To form the likeness of his Son
In all who, called and justified,
Shall reign in glory at his side.

5 Nor death, nor life, nor powers unseen,
Nor height, nor depth, can come between;
We know through peril, pain and sword,
The love of God in Christ our Lord.

Timothy Dudley-Smith (1926–)
based on Romans 8

THE ETERNAL SPIRIT/The Giver of Life

280(i)

DOMINICA S.M.

H. S. Oakeley (1830–1903)

280(ii)

ST GEORGE S.M.

Henry J. Gauntlett (1805–76)

For this tune in a higher key see No. 768

1 BREATHE on me, Breath of God;
   Fill me with life anew,
That I may love what thou dost love,
   And do what thou wouldst do.

2 Breathe on me, Breath of God,
   Until my heart is pure,
Until with thee I will one will,
   To do and to endure.

3 Breathe on me, Breath of God,
   Till I am wholly thine,
Until this earthly part of me
   Glows with thy fire divine.

4 Breathe on me, Breath of God;
   So shall I never die,
But live with thee the perfect life
   Of thine eternity.

Edwin Hatch (1835–89)

The Giver of Life

281

DOWN AMPNEY 66.11.D.

Ralph Vaughan Williams (1872–1958)

THE ETERNAL SPIRIT

1 COME down, O Love divine,
   Seek thou this soul of mine,
 And visit it with thine own ardour glowing;
   O Comforter, draw near,
   Within my heart appear,
 And kindle it, thy holy flame bestowing.

2 O let it freely burn,
   Till earthly passions turn
 To dust and ashes, in its heat consuming;
   And let thy glorious light
   Shine ever on my sight,
 And clothe me round, the while my path illuming.

3 Let holy charity
   Mine outward vesture be,
 And lowliness become mine inner clothing;
   True lowliness of heart,
   Which takes the humbler part,
 And o'er its own shortcomings weeps with loathing.

4 And so the yearning strong,
   With which the soul will long,
 Shall far outpass the power of human telling;
   For none can guess its grace,
   Till he become the place
 Wherein the Holy Spirit makes his dwelling.

Bianco da Siena (d. 1434)
tr. *R. F. Littledale* (1833–90)

The Giver of Life

282

AD ASTRA 88.88.88.

Henry G. Ley (1887–1962)

THE ETERNAL SPIRIT

1 COME, Holy Ghost, all-quickening fire,
   Come, and in me delight to rest;
Drawn by the lure of strong desire,
   O come and consecrate my breast!
The temple of my soul prepare,
And fix thy sacred presence there!

2 If now thy influence I feel,
   If now in thee begin to live,
Still to my heart thyself reveal;
   Give me thyself, for ever give:
A grain my world, a drop my store,
Eager I ask, I pant for more.

3 Eager for thee I ask and pant:
   So strong, the principle divine
Carries me out with sweet constraint
   Till all my hallowed soul is thine,
Plunged in the Godhead's deepest sea,
And lost in thine immensity.

4 My peace, my life, my comfort thou,
   My treasure and my all thou art;
True witness of my sonship, now
   Engraving pardon on my heart,
Seal of my sins in Christ forgiven,
Earnest of love, and pledge of heaven.

5 Come then, my God, mark out thine heir,
   Of heaven a larger earnest give;
With clearer light thy witness bear,
   More sensibly within me live;
Let all my powers thine entrance feel,
And deeper stamp thyself the seal.

Charles Wesley (1707–88)

The Giver of Life

283

VENI CREATOR L.M.

Simplified version (Mechlin, 1848)
of proper plainsong melody

Unison

CONCLUSION OF VERSE 4

Unison

Praise— to thy— e - ter - nal me-rit, Fa - ther,

Organ

THE ETERNAL SPIRIT

Son,— and Ho — ly Spi-rit. A — -men.'

1 COME, Holy Ghost, our souls inspire,
  And lighten with celestial fire;
    Thou the anointing Spirit art,
    Who dost thy sevenfold gifts impart:

2 Thy blessèd unction from above
  Is comfort, life, and fire of love;
    Enable with perpetual light
    The dullness of our blinded sight:

3 Anoint and cheer our soilèd face
  With the abundance of thy grace;
    Keep far our foes, give peace at home;
    Where thou art guide no ill can come.

4 Teach us to know the Father, Son,
  And thee, of both, to be but One;
    That through the ages all along
    This may be our endless song:

    'Praise to thy eternal merit,
    Father, Son, and Holy Spirit. Amen.'

9th Century
tr. *John Cosin* (1594–1672)

The Giver of Life

Melody by S. Webbe the elder (1740–1816)
Harmonised by
W. H. Monk (1823–89)

THE ETERNAL SPIRIT

1 COME, thou Holy Spirit, come,
　And from thy celestial home
　　Thine unclouded light impart;
　Come, thou father of the poor;
　All good gifts are from thy store;
　　Come, illumine every heart.

2 Thou of comforters the best,
　Thou the soul's most welcome guest,
　　Sweet refreshment here below;
　Who in toil art rest complete,
　Tempered coolness in the heat,
　　Solace in the midst of woe,

3 O most blessèd light divine,
　Shine within these hearts of thine,
　　And our inmost being fill;
　Where thou art not, we have nought,
　Nothing good in deed or thought,
　　Nothing free from taint of ill.

4 Heal our wounds; our strength renew;
　On our dryness pour thy dew;
　　Wash the taint of guilt away:
　Bend the stubborn heart and will;
　Melt the frozen, warm the chill;
　　Guide the steps that go astray.

5 On the faithful, who adore
　And confess thee, evermore
　　In thy sevenfold gifts descend;
　Give them virtue's sure reward,
　Give them thy salvation, Lord,
　　Give them joys that never end.

13th Century
tr. *Edward Caswall* (1814–78)
and others

The Giver of Life

285
ATTWOOD (VENI CREATOR) 88.88.88

From an anthem by
Thomas Attwood (1765–1838)

THE ETERNAL SPIRIT

1 CREATOR Spirit, by whose aid
   The world's foundations first were laid,
   Come, visit every waiting mind;
   Come, pour thy joys on humankind;
   From sin and sorrow set us free,
   And make thy temples worthy thee.

2 O source of uncreated heat,
   The Father's promised Paraclete!
   Thrice holy fount, thrice holy fire,
   Our hearts with heavenly love inspire;
   Come, and thy sacred unction bring
   To sanctify us while we sing.

3 Plenteous of grace, descend from high,
   Rich in thy sevenfold energy;
   Make us eternal truths receive,
   And practise all that we believe;
   Give us thyself, that we may see
   The Father and the Son by thee.

4 Immortal honour, endless fame,
   Attend the almighty Father's name:
   The Saviour Son be glorified,
   Who for lost man's redemption died:
   And equal adoration be,
   Eternal Paraclete, to thee.

9th Century
tr. John Dryden (1631–1700) alt.

The Giver of Life

286

WELLSPRING 77.77.77.

Melody by D. S. Bortnianski (1752–1825)
Harmonised by J. F. Bridge (1844–1924)

THE ETERNAL SPIRIT

1 GRACIOUS Spirit, dwell with me;
  I myself would gracious be,
  And with words that help and heal
  Would thy life in mine reveal,
  And with actions bold and meek
  Would for Christ my Saviour speak.

2 Truthful Spirit, dwell with me;
  I myself would truthful be,
  And with wisdom kind and clear
  Let thy life in mine appear,
  And with actions neighbourly
  Speak my Lord's sincerity.

3 Silent Spirit, dwell with me;
  I myself would quiet be,
  Quiet as the growing blade
  Which through earth its way has made;
  Silently, like morning light,
  Putting mists and chills to flight.

4 Mighty Spirit, dwell with me;
  I myself would mighty be,
  Mighty so as to prevail
  Where unaided I must fail;
  Ever by a mighty hope
  Pressing on and bearing up.

5 Holy Spirit, dwell with me;
  I myself would holy be;
  Separate from sin, I would
  Choose and cherish all things good,
  And, whatever I can be,
  Give to him who gave me thee.

Thomas Toke Lynch (1818–71)

The Giver of Life

287

1 GRANTED is the Saviour's prayer,
  Sent the gracious Comforter;
  Promise of our parting Lord,
  Jesus now to heaven restored:

2 Christ who, now gone up on high,
  Captive leads captivity;
  While his foes from him receive
  Grace that God with man may live.

3 God, the everlasting God,
  Makes with mortals his abode;
  Whom the heav'ns cannot contain,
  He vouchsafes to dwell in man.

4 Never will he thence depart,
  Inmate of a humble heart;
  Carrying on his work within,
  Striving till he casts out sin.

5 Come, divine and peaceful Guest,
  Enter our devoted breast;
  Holy Ghost, our hearts inspire,
  Kindle there the Gospel-fire.

6 Now descend, and shake the earth;
  Wake us into second birth;
  Life divine in us renew,
  Thou the gift and giver too!

Charles Wesley (1707–88)

THE ETERNAL SPIRIT

288

DRAKE'S BROUGHTON 8.7.8.7.

Edward Elgar (1857–1934)

1 HOLY Spirit, come, confirm us
    In the truth that Christ makes known;
  We have faith and understanding
    Through your helping gifts alone.

2 Holy Spirit, come, console us,
    Come as Advocate to plead;
  Loving Spirit from the Father,
    Grant in Christ the help we need.

3 Holy Spirit, come, renew us,
    Come yourself to make us live:
  Holy through your loving presence,
    Holy through the gifts you give.

4 Holy Spirit, come, possess us,
    You the love of Three in One,
  Holy Spirit of the Father,
    Holy Spirit of the Son.

Brian Foley (1919–   )

May also be sung to No. 251, ALL FOR JESUS

The Giver of Life

289(i)

HARTS 7.7.7.7.

Melody and most of the harmony by
Benjamin Milgrove (1731–1810)

289(ii)

REBECCA 7.7.7.7.

Francis B. Westbrook (1903–1975)

1 HOLY Spirit, truth divine,
  Dawn upon this soul of mine;
  Word of God, and inward light,
  Wake my spirit, clear my sight.

2 Holy Spirit, love divine,
  Glow within this heart of mine,
  Kindle every high desire,
  Perish self in thy pure fire.

3 Holy Spirit, power divine,
  Fill and nerve this will of mine;
  By thee may I strongly live,
  Bravely bear, and nobly strive.

4 Holy Spirit, right divine,
  King within my conscience reign;
  Be my law, and I shall be
  Firmly bound, for ever free.

THE ETERNAL SPIRIT

5 Holy Spirit, peace divine,
  Still this restless heart of mine,
  Speak to calm this tossing sea,
  Stayed in thy tranquillity.

6 Holy Spirit, joy divine,
  Gladden thou this heart of mine;
  In the desert ways I sing:
  'Spring, O Well, for ever spring!'

Samuel Longfellow (1819–92)

290

BEWELEY 6.6.6.6.

Cyril V. Taylor (1907–)

1 INTO a world of dark,
  Waste and disordered space,
He came, a wind that moved
  Across the waters' face.

2 The Spirit in the wild
  Breathed, and a world began;
From shapelessness came form,
  From nothingness, a plan.

3 Light in the darkness grew;
  Land in the water stood;
And space and time became
  A beauty that was good.

4 Into a world of doubt,
  Through doors we closed, he came,
The Breath of God in power
  Like wind and roaring flame.

5 From empty wastes of death,
  On love's disordered grief
Light in the darkness blazed,
  And kindled new belief.

6 Still, with creative power,
  God's Spirit gives to men
A pattern of new life—
  And worlds begin again.

Ann Phillips (1930–) alt.

The Giver of Life

291

BICKLEY 88.88.88.

W. H. Monk (1823–89)

THE ETERNAL SPIRIT

1 I WANT the Spir't of power within,
    Of love, and of a healthful mind:
Of power, to conquer inbred sin;
    Of love, to thee and all mankind;
Of health, that pain and death defies,
Most vigorous when the body dies.

2 When shall I hear the inward voice
    Which only faithful souls can hear?
Pardon, and peace, and heavenly joys
    Attend the promised Comforter:
O come, and righteousness divine,
And Christ, and all with Christ, are mine!

3 O that the Comforter would come,
    Nor visit as a transient guest,
But fix in me his constant home,
    And take possession of my breast,
And fix in me his loved abode,
The temple of indwelling God!

4 Come, Holy Ghost, my heart inspire,
    Attest that I am born again!
Come, and baptize me now with fire,
    Nor let thy former gifts be vain;
I cannot rest in sins forgiven—
Where is the earnest of my heaven?

5 Where the indubitable seal
    That ascertains the kingdom mine,
The powerful stamp I long to feel,
    The signature of love divine?
O shed it in my heart abroad—
Fullness of love, of heaven, of God!

Charles Wesley (1707–88)

292

WHITSUN CANTICLE Irreg.

Erik Routley (1917–82)

ANTIPHON

I will pour out my Spi-rit on all flesh, Your sons and your daugh-ters shall pro-phe-sy, Your old men shall dream dreams, And your young men shall see vi - sions.

Fine

1 I WILL   pray the
2 The   Counsel -
3 And   suddenly a
4 Likewise the

THE ETERNAL SPIRIT

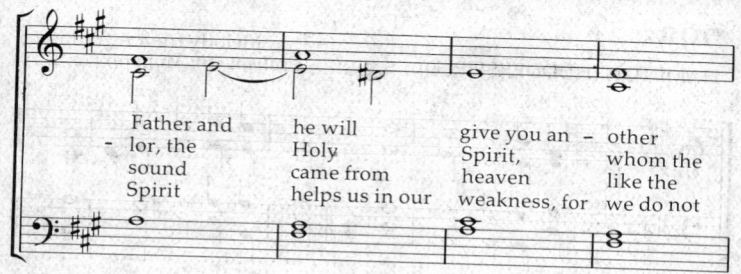

Father and | he will | give you an - other
- lor, the | Holy | Spirit, whom the
sound | came from | heaven | like the
Spirit | helps us in our | weakness, for | we do not

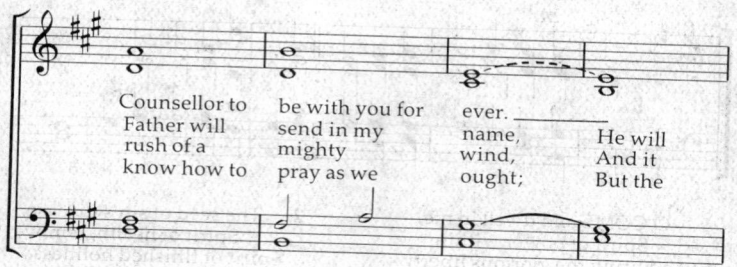

Counsellor to | be with you for | ever.
Father will | send in my | name, | He will
rush of a | mighty | wind, | And it
know how to | pray as we | ought; | But the

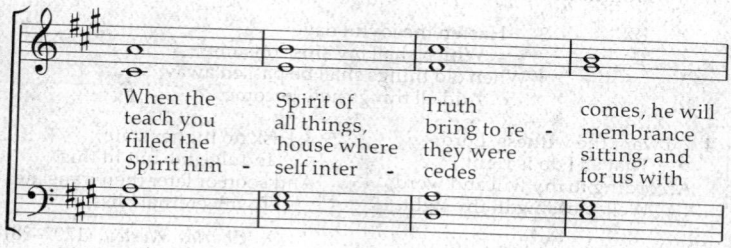

When the | Spirit of | Truth | comes, he will
teach you | all things, | bring to re - | membrance
filled the | house where | they were | sitting, and
Spirit him - self inter - | cedes | for us with

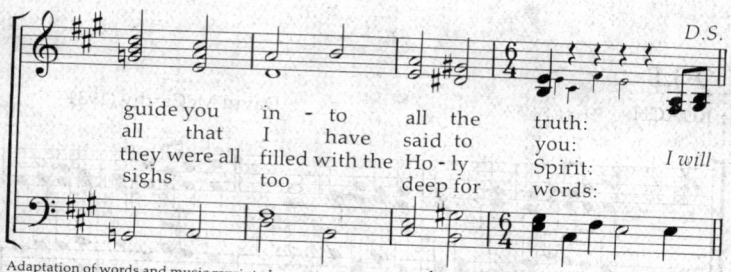

D.S.

guide you | in - to | all the | truth:
all that | I have | said to | you:
they were all | filled with the Ho - ly | Spirit:
sighs | too | deep for | words:

I will

adapted by *Alan Luff* (1928–)
from the Revised Standard Version of Joel 3:1;
John 14:16,26; 16:13;
Acts 2:2–4; Romans 8:26.

The Giver of Life

293

HAMPTON (HUDDERSFIELD) S.M.

Melody from A. Williams'
Psalmody in Miniature (c. 1770)

1 O COME and dwell in me,
　　Spirit of power within,
And bring the glorious liberty
　　From sorrow, fear, and sin.

2 The seed of sin's disease,
　　Spirit of health, remove,
Spirit of finished holiness,
　　Spirit of perfect love.

3 Hasten the joyful day
　　Which shall my sins consume,
When old things shall be passed away,
　　And all things new become.

4 I want the witness, Lord,
　　That all I do is right,
According to thy will and word,
　　Well-pleasing in thy sight.

5 I ask no higher state;
　　Indulge me but in this,
And soon or later then translate
　　To my eternal bliss.

Charles Wesley (1707–88)

294

RUACH 7.6.8.6.8.6.8.6.

David McCarthy (1931–   )

THE ETERNAL SPIRIT

1 SPIRIT of God within me,
　　Possess my human frame;
　Fan the dull embers of my heart,
　　Stir up the living flame.
　Strive till that image Adam lost,
　　New minted and restored,
　In shining splendour brightly bears
　　The likeness of the Lord.

2 Spirit of truth within me,
　　Possess my thought and mind;
　Lighten anew the inward eye
　　By Satan rendered blind;
　Shine on the words that wisdom speaks,
　　And grant me power to see
　The truth made known to all in Christ,
　　And in that truth be free.

3 Spirit of love within me,
　　Possess my hands and heart;
　Break through the bonds of self-concern
　　That seeks to stand apart;
　Grant me the love that suffers long,
　　That hopes, believes and bears,
　The love fulfilled in sacrifice
　　That cares as Jesus cares.

4 Spirit of life within me,
　　Possess this life of mine;
　Come as the wind of heaven's breath,
　　Come as the fire divine!
　Spirit of Christ, the living Lord,
　　Reign in this house of clay,
　Till from its dust with Christ I rise
　　To everlasting day.

Music reprinted
by permission of
Stainer & Bell Ltd.
For permission to
reproduce see p. xiii.

Timothy Dudley-Smith (1926–)

The Giver of Life

295
SPIRIT OF THE LIVING GOD

Unknown
7.5.7.5.44.7.5. Arranged by W. G. Hathaway

SPIRIT of the living God,
Fall afresh on me.
Spirit of the living God,
Fall afresh on me.
Break me, melt me,
Mould me, fill me.
Spirit of the living God,
Fall afresh on me.

Daniel Iverson

THE ETERNAL SPIRIT/The Giver of Life

296

ARDWICK 55.5 11

Henry J. Gauntlett (1805–76)

1. AWAY with our fears,
   Our troubles and tears:
   The Spirit is come,
   The witness of Jesus returned to his home.

2. The pledge of our Lord
   To his heaven restored
   Is sent from the sky,
   And tells us our Head is exalted on high.

3. Our Advocate there
   By his blood and his prayer
   The gift has obtained,
   For us he has prayed, and the Comforter gained.

4. Our glorified Head
   His Spirit has shed,
   With his people to stay,
   And never again will he take him away.

5. Our heavenly Guide
   With us shall abide,
   His comforts impart,
   And set up his kingdom of love in the heart.

6. The heart that believes
   His kingdom receives,
   His power and his peace,
   His life, and his joy's everlasting increase.

Charles Wesley (1707–88)

In the Church

297(i)

MANCHESTER C.M.

Robert Wainwright (1748–82)

297(ii)

ST ENODOC C.M.

C. S. Lang (1891–1971)

THE ETERNAL SPIRIT

1 COME, Holy Spirit, heavenly Dove,
    With all thy quickening powers;
  Kindle a flame of sacred love
    In these cold hearts of ours.

2 In vain we tune our formal songs,
    In vain we strive to rise;
  Hosannas languish on our tongues,
    And our devotion dies.

3 And shall we then for ever live
    At this poor dying rate?
  Our love so faint, so cold to thee,
    And thine to us so great!

4 Come, Holy Spirit, heavenly Dove,
    With all thy quickening powers;
  Come, shed abroad the Saviour's love,
    And that shall kindle ours.

Isaac Watts (1674–1748)

298(i)
STAPLEGROVE 8.7.8.7.   Martin Ellis (1943–)

298(ii)
CROSS OF JESUS 87.87.   John Stainer (1840–1901)

For this tune in a higher key see No. 81(ii)

1 COME, thou everlasting Spirit,
   Bring to every thankful mind
All the Saviour's dying merit,
   All his sufferings for mankind:

2 True recorder of his passion,
   Now the living faith impart,
Now reveal his great salvation,
   Preach his gospel to our heart.

3 Come, thou witness of his dying;
   Come, remembrancer divine,
Let us feel thy power, applying
   Christ to every soul, and mine.

May also be sung
to No. 189(ii).
SICILIAN MARINERS

Charles Wesley (1707–88)

THE ETERNAL SPIRIT

299

ILLSLEY L.M.

Melody and most of the harmony by
J. Bishop (1665–1737)

1 FATHER, if justly still we claim
    To us and ours the promise made,
To us be graciously the same,
    And crown with living fire our head.

2 Our claim admit, and from above
    Of holiness the Spirit shower,
Of wise discernment, humble love,
    And zeal, and unity, and power.

3 The Spirit of convincing speech,
    Of power demonstrative, impart,
Such as may every conscience reach,
    And sound the unbelieving heart;

4 The Spirit of refining fire,
    Searching the inmost of the mind,
To purge all fierce and foul desire,
    And kindle life more pure and kind;

5 The Spir't of faith, in this thy day,
    To break the power of cancelled sin,
Tread down its strength, o'erturn its sway,
    And still the conquest more than win.

6 The Spirit breathe of inward life,
    Which in our hearts thy laws may write;
Then grief expires, and pain, and strife:
    'Tis nature all, and all delight.

Henry More (1614–87)
alt. *John Wesley* (1703–91)

In the Church

300

STAMFORD 8 8.8.D.

Samuel Reay (1822–1905)

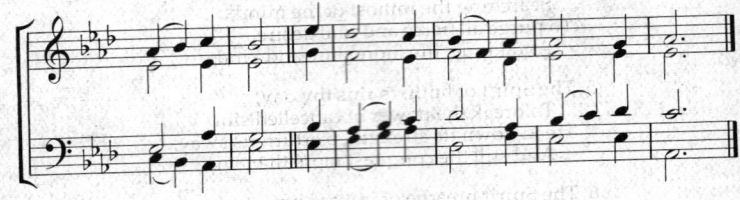

THE ETERNAL SPIRIT

1 FATHER of everlasting grace,
   Thy goodness and thy truth we praise,
      Thy goodness and thy truth we prove;
   Thou hast, in honour of thy Son,
   The gift unspeakable sent down,
      The Spir't of life, and power, and love.

2 Send us the Spirit of thy Son,
   To make the depths of Godhead known,
      To make us share the life divine;
   Send him the sprinkled blood to apply,
   Send him our souls to sanctify,
      And show and seal us ever thine.

3 So shall we pray, and never cease,
   So shall we thankfully confess
      Thy wisdom, truth, and power, and love,
   With joy unspeakable adore,
   And bless and praise thee evermore,
      And serve thee as thy hosts above:

4 Till, added to that heavenly choir,
   We raise our songs of triumph higher,
      And praise thee in a bolder strain,
   Out-soar the first-born seraph's flight,
   And sing, with all our friends in light,
      Thy everlasting love to man.

Charles Wesley (1707–88)

301(i)

CHARITY 7 7 7.5.

John Stainer (1840–1901)

(Small notes organ only)

301(ii)

CAPETOWN 7 7 7.5.

F. Filitz (1804–76)

THE ETERNAL SPIRIT

1 GRACIOUS Spirit, Holy Ghost,
   Taught by thee, we covet most,
   Of thy gifts at Pentecost,
      Holy, heavenly love.

2 Faith that mountains could remove,
   Tongues of earth or heaven above,
   Knowledge, all things, empty prove
      Without heavenly love.

3 Prophecy will fade away,
   Melting in the light of day;
   Love will ever with us stay:
      Therefore give us love.

4 Love is kind, and suffers long,
   Love is meek, and thinks no wrong,
   Love than death itself more strong:
      Therefore give us love.

5 Faith, and hope, and love we see,
   Joining hand in hand, agree;
   But the greatest of the three,
      And the best, is love.

Christopher Wordsworth (1807–85)
based on I Corinthians 13

302

SALVE FESTA DIES Irreg.

Ralph Vaughan Williams (1872–1958)

Unison. With vigour.

REFRAIN

Hail thee, Fes - ti - val Day! Blest day that art hal-lowed for

ev - er — Day where-in God from heav'n Shone on the

Fine VERSES 1 & 3

world with his grace. 1 LO! in the like - ness of
3 Hark! in a hun - dred —

fire, On them that a-wait his ap - pear - ing,
tongues Christ's own, his — cho - sen a - pos - tles,

THE ETERNAL SPIRIT

He whom the Lord fore-told Sud-den-ly, swift-ly, de-
Preach to a hun-dred tribes Christ and his won-der-ful

Repeat Refrain   VERSES 2 & 4

-scends: 2 Forth from the Fa-ther he comes With his sev'n-fold
works: 4 Praise to the Spi-rit of life, All praise to the

mys - ti-cal dow-ry, Pour-ing on hu - man
Fount of our be - ing, Light that dost light - en

Repeat Refrain

souls In - fi-nite ri - ches of God:
all, Life that in all dost a - bide:

c. 14th Century
tr. *Gabriel Gillett* (1873–1948)

In the Church

303

EVERTON 8.7.8.7.D.

Henry Smart (1813–79)

THE ETERNAL SPIRIT

1 HOLY Spirit, ever dwelling
    In the glorious realms of light;
Holy Spirit, ever brooding
    O'er a world of gloom and night;
Holy Spirit, ever giving
    Earthly children thrones on high;
Living, life-imparting Spirit,
    Thee we praise and magnify.

2 Holy Spirit, ever living
    As the church's very life;
Holy Spirit, ever striving
    Through her in a ceaseless strife;
Holy Spirit, ever forming
    In the church the mind of Christ;
Thee we praise with endless worship
    For thy fruit and gifts unpriced.

3 Holy Spirit, ever working
    Through the church's ministry;
Quick'ning, strength'ning, and absolving,
    Setting captive sinners free;
Holy Spirit, ever binding
    Age to age, and soul to soul,
In a fellowship unending—
    Thee we worship and extol.

Timothy Rees (1874–1939)

304(i)

GLENFINLAS 6.5.6.5.

K. G. Finlay (1882–1974)

304(ii)

DARWEN 6.5.6.5.

Philip Jones (1949–)

(c♯ *in last verse*)

THE ETERNAL SPIRIT

1 HOLY Spirit, hear us;
    Help us while we sing;
Breathe into the music
    Of the praise we bring.

2 Holy Spirit, prompt us
    When we kneel to pray;
Nearer come, and teach us
    What we ought to say.

3 Holy Spirit, shine thou
    On the book we read;
Gild its holy pages
    With the light we need.

4 Holy Spirit, give us
    Each a lowly mind;
Make us more like Jesus,
    Gentle, pure, and kind.

5 Holy Spirit, help us
    Daily by thy might,
What is wrong to conquer,
    And to choose the right.

W. H. Parker (1845–1929)

305

LUDGATE 66.6.D.

J. Dykes Bower (1905–81)

THE ETERNAL SPIRIT

1 LET every Christian pray,
This day, and every day,
   Come, Holy Spirit, come!
Was not the Church we love
Commissioned from above?
   Come, Holy Spirit, come!

2 The Spirit brought to birth
The Church of Christ on earth
   To seek and save the lost:
Never has he withdrawn,
Since that tremendous dawn,
   His gifts at Pentecost.

3 Age after age, he strove
To teach her how to love:
   Come, Holy Spirit, come!
Age after age, anew,
She proved the gospel true:
   Come, Holy Spirit, come!

4 Only the Spirit's power
Can fit us for this hour:
   Come, Holy Spirit, come!
Instruct, inspire, unite;
And make us see the light:
   Come, Holy Spirit, come!

F. Pratt Green (1903–   )

Words reprinted by permission of
Stainer & Bell Ltd.
For permission to reproduce see p. xiii.

In the Church

306(i)
WATCHMAN S.M.

James Leach (1762–98)
(adapted)

306(ii)
DONCASTER S.M.

Melody and bass by
Samuel Wesley (1766–1837)

THE ETERNAL SPIRIT

1   LORD God the Holy Ghost,
       In this accepted hour,
   As on the day of Pentecost,
       Descend in all thy power.

2   We meet with one accord
       In our appointed place,
   And wait the promise of our Lord,
       The Spirit of all grace.

3   Like mighty rushing wind
       Upon the waves beneath,
   Move with one impulse every mind,
       One soul, one feeling breathe.

4   The young, the old, inspire
       With wisdom from above;
   And give us hearts and tongues of fire,
       To pray and praise and love.

5   Spirit of light, explore
       And chase our gloom away,
   With lustre shining more and more
       Unto the perfect day.

6   Spirit of truth, be thou
       In life and death our guide;
   O Spirit of adoption, now
       May we be sanctified.

James Montgomery (1771–1854)

307

WINCHESTER NEW   L.M.

Adapted from a melody in
Musicalisches Hand-Buch
(Hamburg, 1690)

THE ETERNAL SPIRIT

1 LORD, we believe to us and ours
 The apostolic promise given;
We wait the pentecostal powers,
 The Holy Ghost sent down from heaven.

2 To every one whom God shall call
 The promise is securely made;
To you far off—he calls you all;
 Believe the word which Christ hath said:

3 'The Holy Ghost, if I depart,
 The Comforter, shall surely come,
Shall make the contrite sinner's heart
 His loved, his everlasting home.'

4 Assembled here with one accord,
 Calmly we wait the promised grace,
The purchase of our dying Lord:
 Come, Holy Ghost, and fill the place.

5 If every one that asks may find,
 If still thou dost on sinners fall,
Come as a mighty rushing wind;
 Great grace be now upon us all.

6 Behold, to thee our souls aspire,
 And languish thy descent to meet:
Kindle in each thy living fire,
 And fix in every heart thy seat.

Charles Wesley (1707–88)

308(i)

ABENDS L.M.

Herbert Oakeley (1830–1903)

org.ped.

308(ii)

CALM L.M.

J. B. Dykes (1823–76)

THE ETERNAL SPIRIT

1 O BREATH of God, breathe on us now,
   And move within us while we pray;
   The spring of our new life art thou,
   The very light of our new day.

2 O strangely art thou with us, Lord,
   Neither in height nor depth to seek:
   In nearness shall thy voice be heard;
   Spirit to spirit thou dost speak.

3 Christ is our Advocate on high;
   Thou art our Advocate within:
   O plead the truth, and make reply
   To every argument of sin.

4 But ah, this faithless heart of mine!
   The way I know, I know my guide;
   Forgive me, O my friend divine,
   That I so often turn aside.

5 Be with me when no other friend
   The mystery of my heart can share;
   And be thou known, when fears transcend,
   By thy best name of Comforter.

Alfred Henry Vine (1845–1917)

309

TAUNTON SCHOOL 8.7.4.48.7 Martin Ellis (1943–)

1 O GOD, O Spirit known to us
  Through wonders of creation,
    Help us to see,
    Help us to care,
  Help us to find you everywhere
  And voice our adoration.

2 O God, O Spirit known to us
  Through Christ's victorious living,
    Help us to love,
    Help us to dare,
  Help us to serve you everywhere
  Through sacrificial giving.

3 O God, O Spirit known to us
  Through lives of dedication,
    Help us to pray,
    Help us to share,
  Help us to praise you everywhere;
  And be our inspiration.

T. A. Dewing (1896–)

THE ETERNAL SPIRIT

310

TALLIS' ORDINAL C.M.   Thomas Tallis (c. 1505–85)

For this tune in a higher key see No. 586

1 O HOLY Spirit, Lord of grace,
    Eternal fount of love,
  Inflame, we pray, our inmost hearts
    With fire from heaven above.

2 As thou in bond of love dost join
    The Father and the Son,
  So fill us all with mutual love,
    And knit our hearts in one.

3 All glory to the Father be,
    All glory to the Son,
  All glory, Holy Ghost, to thee,
    While endless ages run.

                Charles Coffin (1676–1749)
    tr. *John Chandler* (1806–76) and others

311(i)

TEMPLE 6.6.8.4.

Walford Davies (1869–1941)

311(ii)

AMEN COURT 6.6.8.4.

J. Dykes Bower (1905–81)

1   O KING enthroned on high,
     Thou Comforter divine,
Blest Spirit of all truth, be nigh
     And make us thine.

2   Thou art the source of life,
     Thou art our treasure-store;
Give us thy peace, and end our strife
     For evermore.

3   Descend, O heavenly Dove,
     Abide with us alway;
And in the fullness of thy love
     Cleanse us, we pray.

c. 8th Century
tr. *J. Brownlie* (1857–1925)

THE ETERNAL SPIRIT

312

ST CUTHBERT 8.6.8.4.

J. B. Dykes (1823–76)

1 OUR blest Redeemer, ere he breathed
His tender, last farewell,
A Guide, a Comforter bequeathed,
With us to dwell.

2 He came in tongues of living flame,
To teach, convince, subdue;
All-powerful as the wind he came,
As viewless too.

3 He comes sweet influence to impart,
A gracious, willing guest,
While he can find one humble heart
Wherein to rest.

4 And his that gentle voice we hear,
Soft as the breath of even,
That checks each fault, that calms each fear,
And speaks of heaven.

5 And every virtue we possess,
And every victory won,
And every thought of holiness,
Are his alone.

6 Spirit of purity and grace,
Our weakness, pitying, see;
O make our hearts thy dwelling-place,
And worthier thee.

Henriette Auber (1773–1862)

In the Church

313

SHELDONIAN 10.10.10.10.

Cyril V. Taylor (1907–   )

THE ETERNAL SPIRIT

1 SPIRIT of God, descend upon my heart;
   Wean it from earth; through all its pulses move;
   Stoop to my weakness, mighty as thou art,
   And make me love thee as I ought to love.

2 I ask no dream, no prophet-ecstasies,
   No sudden rending of the veil of clay,
   No angel-visitant, no opening skies;
   But take the dimness of my soul away.

3 Hast thou not bid me love thee, God and King—
   All, all thine own, soul, heart, and strength, and mind?
   I see thy cross—there teach my heart to cling:
   O let me seek thee, and O let me find!

4 Teach me to feel that thou art always nigh;
   Teach me the struggles of the soul to bear,
   To check the rising doubt, the rebel sigh;
   Teach me the patience of unanswered prayer.

5 Teach me to love thee as thine angels love,
   One holy passion filling all my frame—
   The baptism of the heaven-descended Dove,
   My heart an altar, and thy love the flame.

George Croly (1780–1860)

314

CHILSWELL 10 10.10 10.
In moderate time. Unison

Gustav Holst (1874–1934)

OPTIONAL HARMONY VERSION

THE ETERNAL SPIRIT

1 FILLED with the Spirit's power, with one accord
The infant church confessed its risen Lord;
    O Holy Spirit, in the church today
    No less your power of fellowship display.

2 Now with the mind of Christ set us on fire,
That unity may be our great desire;
    Give joy and peace; give faith to hear your call,
    And readiness in each to work for all.

3 Widen our love, good Spirit, to embrace
With your compassion all the human race;
    Like wind and fire with life among us move,
    Till we are known as Christ's, and Christians prove.

                    J. R. Peacey (1896–1971) alt.

May also be sung to No. 313, SHELDONIAN

For the World

GO TELL EVERYONE   88.85 (Refrain)

Hubert Richards
Adapted by
Betty Pulkingham (1928–)

Freely

1 GOD'S Spi-rit is in my heart; He has called me and set me a-part.____ This is what I have to do____ What I have to do:____

Brightly   *Refrain*

He sent me to

THE ETERNAL SPIRIT

give the good news to the poor, Tell pri - soners

that they are pri - soners no more, Tell blind peo - ple

that they can see, _____ And set the down-trod-den

free, _____ And go tell ev - 'ry-

- one The news that the king-dom of God has come; And

For the World

go   tell   ev - 'ry - one   The

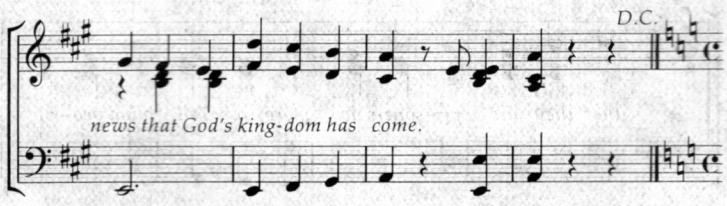

news that God's king-dom has come.

1 GOD'S spirit is in my heart;
He has called me and set me apart.
This is what I have to do—
What I have to do:
He sent me to give the good news to the poor,
Tell prisoners that they are prisoners no more,
Tell blind people that they can see,
And set the down-trodden free,
And go tell everyone
The news that the kingdom of God has come;
And go tell everyone
The news that God's kingdom has come.

2 Just as the Father sent me,
So I'm sending you out to be
My witness throughout the world—
The whole of the world:

3 Don't carry a load in your pack;
You don't need two shirts on your back;
A workman can earn his own keep—
Can earn his own keep:

4 Don't worry what you have to say;
Don't worry, because on that day
God's Spirit will speak in your heart—
Will speak in your heart:

Alan T. Dale (1902–79)
based on Luke 4:18
and Matthew 10:9, 10, 19, 20

THE ETERNAL SPIRIT

316

FULDA L.M.   Melody from Gardiner's *Sacred Melodies* (1815)

1 HEAD of thy church, whose Spirit fills
   And flows through every faithful soul,
 Unites in mystic love, and seals
   Them one, and sanctifies the whole:

2 'Come, Lord!' thy glorious Spirit cries;
   And souls beneath the altar groan;
 'Come, Lord,' the bride on earth replies,
   'And perfect all our souls in one!'

3 Pour out the promised gift on all,
   Answer the universal 'Come!'
 The fullness of the Gentiles call,
   And take thine ancient people home.

4 To thee let all the nations flow,
   Let all obey the gospel word;
 Let all their suffering Saviour know,
   Filled with the glory of the Lord.

5 O for thy truth and mercy's sake
   The purchase of thy passion claim;
 Thine heritage, the nations, take,
   And cause the world to know thy name!

Charles Wesley (1707–88)

For the World

THE SPAIN 8.7.77.8.9. Cyril V. Taylor (1907–)

Unison

1 IN the power of God's own Spi-rit Je-sus en-tered Ga - li - lee; With a fire di - vine a - flame, Un - to Na-za-reth he came; Bade his peo-ple hear the scripture: 'God's a-noint-ing Spi - - - rit

THE ETERNAL SPIRIT

is __ on __ me'. __

After Verse 4

1　IN the power of God's own Spirit
　　　Jesus entered Galilee;
　　　With a fire divine aflame,
　　　Unto Nazareth he came;
　　Bade his people hear the scripture:
　'God's anointing Spirit is on me'.

2　'God has sent me', said the prophet,
　　　'With good news the poor to cheer,
　　　News that captives will be free,
　　　News that eyes now blind will see,
　　Health for hearts all bruised and broken;
　God's own year of favour now is here'.

3　'True this very day', said Jesus,
　　　'This the task I must fulfil'.
　　　Forth he went, and through the land
　　　Moved with liberating hand.
　　Even though men crucified him,
　God's unconquered love shone through him still.

4　Lord, you tell us by your Spirit,
　　　We all need this news today.
　　　May our faith and service show
　　　All the gifts that you bestow—
　　Joy and health and freedom giving,
　Lord, from you, the Life, the Truth, the Way.

Albert F. Bayly (1901-84)
based on Luke 4: 14–21

For the World

318
ALDERSGATE STREET 88.88.88.

E. F. Horner (1864–1928)

THE ETERNAL SPIRIT

1 JESUS, the gift divine I know,
    The gift divine I ask of thee;
That living water now bestow—
    Thy Spirit and thyself, on me;
Thou, Lord, of life the fountain art;
Now let me find thee in my heart.

2 Thee let me drink, and thirst no more
    For drops of finite happiness;
Spring up, O Well, in heavenly power,
    In streams of pure perennial peace,
In joy that none can take away,
In life which shall for ever stay.

3 Father, on me the grace bestow,
    Unblamable before thy sight,
Whence all the streams of mercy flow;
    Mercy, thine own supreme delight,
To me, for Jesus' sake, impart,
And plant thy nature in my heart.

4 Thy mind throughout my life be shown,
    While, listening to the sufferer's cry,
The widow's and the orphan's groan,
    On mercy's wings I swiftly fly,
The poor and helpless to relieve,
My life, my all, for them to give.

5 Thus may I show thy Spir't within,
    Which purges me from every stain;
Unspotted from the world and sin,
    My faith's integrity maintain;
The truth of my religion prove
By perfect purity and love.

Charles Wesley (1707–88)

May also be sung to No. 275(i), COLCHESTER

319

LORD, GIVE US YOUR SPIRIT   Irreg.

Sandy Hardyman

Slow and sustained
Refrain

Lord, _____ give us your Spi - rit, _____ your

Spi - rit _____ that is love. _____

Lord, _____ fill us with your life, _____ free - ly

giv - en _____ for the world. _____

Fine

THE ETERNAL SPIRIT

1 WHERE_____ child-ren cry,_____ let us
2 Where_____ there is pain,_____ let us
3 Where_____ peo-ple hate,_____ let us

wipe their tears a - way;_____ And
be your heal - ing hands;_____ And
dwell a - mong them with love;_____ And

where_____ child-ren fall,_____ let us
where_____ there is grief,_____ let us
where_____ peo-ple fight,_____ let us

D.C.

raise them to their feet:
com - fort with your love:
bind their deep - est wounds:

For the World

320

RIPPONDEN 8 8 8. 4.

Norman Cocker (1889–1953)

1 OF all the Spirit's gifts to me,
   I pray that I may never cease
To take and treasure most these three:
   Love, joy, and peace.

2 He shows me love is at the root
   Of every gift sent from above,
Of every flower, of every fruit,
   That God is love.

3 He shows me that if I possess
   A love no evil can destroy,
However great is my distress,
   Then this is joy.

4 Though what's ahead is mystery,
   And life itself is ours on lease,
Each day the Spirit says to me:
   'Go forth in peace!'

5 We go in peace—but made aware
   That, in a needy world like this,
Our clearest purpose is to share
   Love, joy, and peace.

F. Pratt Green (1903–)

THE ETERNAL SPIRIT

321

SIMEON L.M.

Samuel Stanley (1767–1822)

1 ON all the earth thy Spirit shower;
   The earth in righteousness renew;
 Thy kingdom come, and hell's o'erpower,
   And to thy sceptre all subdue.

2 Like mighty winds, or torrents fierce,
   Let it opposers all o'errun;
 And every law of sin reverse,
   That faith and love may make all one.

3 Yea, let thy Spir't in every place
   Its richer energy declare;
 While lovely tempers, fruits of grace,
   The kingdom of thy Christ prepare.

4 Grant this, O holy God and true!
   The ancient seers thou didst inspire;
 To us perform the promise due;
   Descend, and crown us now with fire!

Henry More (1614–87)
alt. *John Wesley* (1703–91)

For the World

322(i)
MAINZER L.M.

Melody by Joseph Mainzer (1801–51)

For this tune in a higher key see No. 662.

322(ii)
ST BARTHOLOMEW L.M. (from W. Riley's *Parochial Harmony*, 1762)

Henry Duncalf (d. 1762)

THE ETERNAL SPIRIT

1 O SPIRIT of the living God,
   In all thy plenitude of grace,
Where'er the human foot has trod,
   Descend on our rebellious race.

2 Give tongues of fire and hearts of love
   To preach the reconciling word;
Give thine anointing from above,
   Whene'er the joyful sound is heard.

3 Be darkness, at thy coming, light;
   Confusion, order in thy path;
Souls without strength inspire with might;
   Bid mercy triumph over wrath.

4 O Spirit of the Lord, prepare
   The whole round world her God to meet;
Breathe thou abroad like morning air,
   Till hearts of stone begin to beat.

5 Baptize the nations; far and nigh
   The triumphs of the cross record;
The name of Jesus glorify,
   Till all the earth shall call him Lord.

6 God from eternity has willed
   All flesh shall his salvation see;
So be the Father's love fulfilled,
   The Saviour's sufferings crowned through thee.

James Montgomery (1771–1854) alt.

323

NAPHILL 7 7. 7 7. D. Iambic and Trochaic

Harold Darke (1888–1976)

THE ETERNAL SPIRIT

1 OUR Lord, his passion ended,
  Has gloriously ascended,
  Yet though from him divided,
  He leaves us not unguided;
      All his benefits to crown
      He has sent his Spirit down,
      Burning like a flame of fire,
      His disciples to inspire.

2 God's Spirit is directing;
  No more they sit expecting,
  But forth to all the nation
  They go with exultation;
      That which God in them has wrought
      Fills their life and soul and thought;
      So their witness now can do
      Work as great in others too.

3 The centuries go gliding,
  But still we have abiding
  With us that Spirit holy,
  To make us brave and lowly—
      Lowly, for we feel our need,
      God alone is strong indeed;
      Brave, for with the Spirit's aid
      We can venture unafraid.

F. C. Burkitt (1864–1935)

324

FINNIAN 8.7.8.7.8.7.

Christopher Dearnley (1930–)

THE ETERNAL SPIRIT

1 SING to him in whom creation
    Found its shape and origin;
Spirit, moving on the waters
    Troubled by the God within;
Source of breath to all things breathing,
    Life in whom all lives begin.

2 Sing to God, the close companion
    Of our inmost thoughts and ways;
Who, in showing us his wonders,
    Is himself the power to gaze,
And his will, to those who listen,
    By a still small voice conveys.

3 Holy men, both priest and prophet,
    Caught his accents, spoke his word;
His the truth behind the wisdoms
    Which as yet know not our Lord;
He the love of God eternal,
    Which in Christ was seen and heard.

4 Tell of how the ascended Jesus
    Armed a people for his own;
How a hundred men and women
    Turned the known world upside down,
To its dark and farthest corners
    By the wind of Whitsun blown.

5 Pray we, then, O Lord the Spirit,
    On our lives descend in might;
Let thy flame break out within us,
    Fire our hearts and clear our sight,
Till, white-hot in thy possession,
    We, too, set the world alight.

6 Praise, O praise the Holy Spirit,
    Praise the Father, praise the Word,
Source, and Truth, and Inspiration,
    Trinity in deep accord;
Through thy Voice which speaks within us
    We thy creatures own thee Lord.

Michael Hewlett (1916–)

325

ICH HALTE TREULICH STILL D.S.M.

Melody from
Schemelli's *Gesang-Buch* (1736)
Perhaps by J. S. Bach

*If sung in unison the accompaniment at No. 680 may be used.

THE ETERNAL SPIRIT

1   SPIRIT of faith, come down,
      Reveal the things of God;
  And make to us the Godhead known,
      And witness with the blood:
    'Tis thine the blood to apply,
      And give us eyes to see,
 Who did for every sinner die,
     Hath surely died for me.

2   No man can truly say
      That Jesus is the Lord,
 Unless thou take the veil away,
      And breathe the living word;
   Then, only then, we feel
      Our interest in his blood,
 And cry, with joy unspeakable:
     'Thou art my Lord, my God!'

3   O that the world might know
      The all-atoning Lamb!
 Spirit of faith, descend, and show
      The virtue of his name;
   The grace which all may find,
      The saving power, impart,
 And testify to all mankind,
     And speak in every heart.

4   Inspire the living faith,
      Which whosoe'er receives,
 The witness in himself he hath,
      And consciously believes;
   The faith that conquers all,
      And doth the mountain move,
 And saves whoe'er on Jesus call,
     And perfects them in love.

Charles Wesley (1707–88)

326

LAUDS 77.77

John Wilson (1905–   )

Flowing easily

(small notes
organ only)

(The key of F sharp may be preferred)

OPTIONAL DESCANT FOR VERSES 4 AND 7

Sopranos (other voices sing unison melody)

Praise___ the love!___   Praise___ the

love!_____   Al -   -   le - lu - ia!

Al -   -   -   le - lu - ia! ___

THE ETERNAL SPIRIT

1 THERE'S a spirit in the air,
   Telling Christians everywhere:
   Praise the love that Christ revealed,
   Living, working, in our world.

2 Lose your shyness, find your tongue;
   Tell the world what God has done:
   God in Christ has come to stay;
   We can see his power today.

3 When believers break the bread,
   When a hungry child is fed,
   Praise the love that Christ revealed,
   Living, working, in our world.

4 Still his Spirit leads the fight,
   Seeing wrong and setting right:
   God in Christ has come to stay;
   We can see his power today.

5 When a stranger's not alone,
   Where the homeless find a home,
   Praise the love that Christ revealed,
   Living, working, in our world.

6 May his Spirit fill our praise,
   Guide our thoughts and change our ways:
   God in Christ has come to stay;
   We can see his power today.

7 There's a Spirit in the air,
   Calling people everywhere:
   Praise the love that Christ revealed,
   Living, working, in our world.

Brian A. Wren (1936–)

327(i)

ST AGNES C.M.

J. B. Dykes (1823–76)

327(ii)

ETHERINGTON C.M.

Walford Davies (1869–1941)

(Small notes Organ Ped. ad. lib.)

THE ETERNAL SPIRIT

1 SPIRIT divine, attend our prayers
  And make this house your home;
  Descend with all your gracious powers:
  O come, great Spirit, come!

2 Come as the light: to us reveal
  Our emptiness and woe,
  And lead us in those paths of life
  Where all the righteous go.

3 Come as the fire; and purge our hearts
  Like sacrificial flame;
  Let our whole life an offering be
  To our Redeemer's name.

4 Come as the dove; and spread your wings,
  The wings of peaceful love;
  And let your church on earth become
  Blest as the church above.

5 Come as the wind, with rushing sound
  And pentecostal grace,
  That all of woman born may see
  The glory of your face.

6 Spirit divine, attend our prayers;
  Make this lost world your home;
  Descend with all your gracious powers;
  O come, great Spirit, come!

Andrew Reed (1787–1862)

May also be sung to No. 231(i), GERONTIUS

For the World

328(i)
GLASGOW C.M.

Melody from Moore's
Psalm-Singer's Pocket Companion (1756)

For this tune in a higher key see No. 50

328(ii)
KING'S LANGLEY C.M.

Traditional May-Day carol melody,
collected by Lucy Broadwood (1858–1929)
and harmonised
by Ralph Vaughan Williams (1872–1958)

THE ETERNAL SPIRIT

1 UPON the day of Pentecost
   The Holy Spirit came—
Like powerful, rushing, mighty wind
   And leaping, living flame.

2 The friends of Jesus till that hour
   Were fearful folk and weak;
But now the Holy Spirit made
   Them wise and bold to speak.

3 With joy and confidence they went
   To all whom they could reach,
In God the Holy Spirit's power
   To praise and heal and teach.

4 God's Holy Spirit still is here
   To guide our world today,
And helps the friends of Jesus Christ
   In what they do and say.

Patricia Hunt (1921–)

Words reprinted by permission of Stainer & Bell
Ltd and the Methodist Church Division of Education
and Youth. For permission to reproduce see p. xiii.

For the World

II

GOD'S WORLD

329

ST FRANCIS
(LASST UNS ERFREUEN) L.M. and Alleluias

Melody from *Geistliche Kirchengesang*,
Cologne, 1623. Arranged by
Ralph Vaughan Williams (1872–1958)

O__ praise him, O__ praise him, Al-le-lu-ia, al-le-lu-ia, al-le-lu-ia!

For this tune in a higher key see No. 489

THE NATURAL WORLD

1 ALL creatures of our God and King,
Lift up your voice and with us sing,
     Alleluia, alleluia!
Thou burning sun with golden beam,
Thou silver moon with softer gleam:
     O praise him, O praise him,
     Alleluia, alleluia, alleluia!

2 Thou rushing wind that art so strong,
Ye clouds that sail in heaven along,
     O praise him, alleluia!
Thou rising morn, in praise rejoice;
Ye lights of evening, find a voice:

3 Thou flowing water, pure and clear,
Make music for thy Lord to hear,
     Alleluia, alleluia!
Thou fire, so masterful and bright,
That givest us both warmth and light:

4 Dear mother earth, who day by day
Unfoldest blessings on our way,
     O praise him, alleluia!
The flowers and fruits that in thee grow,
Let them his glory also show:

5 All ye that are of tender heart,
Forgiving others, take your part,
     O sing ye, alleluia!
Ye who long pain and sorrow bear,
Praise God, and on him cast your care:

6 And thou, most kind and gentle death,
Waiting to hush our latest breath,
     O praise him, alleluia!
Thou leadest home the child of God,
And Christ our Lord the way has trod:

7 Let all things their creator bless,
And worship him in humbleness;
     O praise him, alleluia!
Praise, praise the Father, praise the Son,
And praise the Spirit, Three in One:

William Henry Draper (1855–1933) alt.
based on *Francis of Assisi* (1182–1226)

Delight in Creation

330(i)
ALL THINGS BRIGHT AND BEAUTIFUL

W. H. Monk (1823–1889)

7.6.7.6. (Refrain)

Fine

D.C.

(org.)

330(ii)
ROYAL OAK 7.6.7.6. (Refrain)
Unison

English traditional melody
Arranged by Martin Shaw (1875–1958)

THE NATURAL WORLD

All things bright and beautiful,
All creatures great and small,
All things wise and wonderful,
The Lord God made them all.

1 EACH little flower that opens,
Each little bird that sings,
He made their glowing colours,
He made their tiny wings:

2 The purple-headed mountain,
The river running by,
The sunset, and the morning
That brightens up the sky:

3 The cold wind in the winter,
The pleasant summer sun,
The ripe fruits in the garden,
He made them every one:

4 He gave us eyes to see them,
And lips that we might tell
How great is God Almighty,
Who has made all things well:

Cecil Frances Alexander (1818–95)

Delight in Creation

331

TE LAUDANT OMNIA 77.77.77.

James Frederick Swift (1847–1931)
(Slightly altered)

THE NATURAL WORLD

1 ALL things praise thee, Lord most high;
   Heaven and earth and sea and sky,
   All were for thy glory made,
   That thy greatness thus displayed
   Should all worship bring to thee;
   All things praise thee: Lord, may we.

2 All things praise thee; night to night
   Sings in silent hymns of light;
   All things praise thee; day to day
   Chants thy power, in burning ray;
   Time and space are praising thee;
   All things praise thee: Lord, may we.

3 All things praise thee; round her zones
   Earth, with her ten thousand tones,
   Rolls a ceaseless choral strain;
   Roaring wind and deep-voiced main,
   Rustling leaf and humming bee,
   All things praise thee: Lord, may we.

4 All things praise thee; high and low,
   Rain and dew and seven-hued bow,
   Crimson sunset, fleecy cloud,
   Rippling stream and tempest loud,
   Summer, winter, all to thee
   Glory render: Lord, may we.

5 All things praise thee; gracious Lord,
   Great Creator, powerful Word,
   Omnipresent Spirit, now
   At thy feet we humbly bow,
   Lift our hearts in praise to thee;
   All things praise thee: Lord, may we.

George William Conder (1821–74)

Delight in Creation

332

COSMIC PRAISE   10.10.10.9. and refrain   Richard Connolly (1927–   )

Refrain* Unison

Sing a new song, sing a new song, And wait up-on the pro-mise of the

Lord._____ Sing a new Lord. Lord. 1 Cre-

- a-tion sings a new song to the Lord; The u-ni-ver-sal e-nergies re-

-joice; Through all the magnitudes of space and time

*The Refrain may be sung first by a soloist or small group and then repeated by the
congregation. The verses may be sung either by the group or by the congregation.

THE NATURAL WORLD

Crea-tures pro-claim the gran-deur of Christ: Sing a new

Sing a new song, sing a new song,
And wait upon the promise of the Lord.
Sing a new song, sing a new song,
And wait upon the promise of the Lord:

1 CREATION sings a new song to the Lord;
  The universal energies rejoice;
    Through all the magnitudes of space and time
      Creatures proclaim the grandeur of Christ:

2 The mountains and the valleys and the plains,
  The cattle and the wild beasts and the birds,
    The shadows and the clouds, the rain and snow,
      Praise and reflect the bounty of Christ:

3 The ocean deeps, the currents and the tides,
  The diatoms, the fishes, and the whale,
    The storm, the reef, the waterspout, the calm,
      Praise and reflect the wonder of Christ:

4 The fruit-trees in their seasons and the vine,
  The sycamore, the cedar, and the palm,
    The lotus and the orchid and the rose,
      Praise and reflect the beauty of Christ:

5 The human eye, the shaping hand, the mind,
  With number and with symbol and design,
    In work and play and artistry and prayer,
      Praise and reflect the wisdom of Christ:

6 The love of man and woman clear as dawn,
  The will for truth and justice broad as day,
    The wisdom of the heart profound as night,
      Praise and reflect the glory of Christ:

J. P. McAuley (1917–76)

Delight in Creation

333(i)

LUCERNA LAUDONIAE 77.77.77.   David Evans (1874–1948)

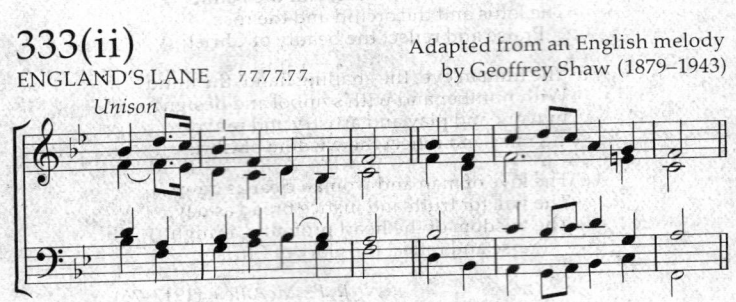

Gra-cious God, to thee we raise This our sac-ri - fice of praise.

333(ii)

ENGLAND'S LANE 7.7.7.7.7.7.   Adapted from an English melody
                                         by Geoffrey Shaw (1879–1943)

Unison

THE NATURAL WORLD

Gra-cious God, to thee we raise This our sac-ri-fice of praise.

1 FOR the beauty of the earth,
   For the beauty of the skies,
 For the love which from our birth
   Over and around us lies:
   Gracious God, to thee we raise
   This our sacrifice of praise.

2 For the beauty of each hour
   Of the day and of the night,
 Hill and vale, and tree and flower,
   Sun and moon and stars of light:

3 For the joy of ear and eye,
   For the heart and mind's delight,
 For the mystic harmony
   Linking sense to sound and sight:

4 For the joy of human love,
   Brother, sister, parent, child,
 Friends on earth, and friends above,
   Pleasures pure and undefiled:

5 For each perfect gift of thine
   To our race so freely given,
 Graces human and divine,
   Flowers of earth and buds of heaven:

F. S. Pierpoint (1835–1917) alt.
May also be sung to No. 791, NORICUM

Delight in Creation

334(i)

MONTROSE C.M.

Melody from Gilmour's
Psalm-singer's Assistant, Glasgow (1793)

334(ii)

ST SAVIOUR C.M.

F. G. Baker (1840–1919)

THE NATURAL WORLD

1 I SING the almighty power of God,
   That made the mountains rise,
That spread the flowing seas abroad,
   And built the lofty skies.

2 I sing the wisdom that ordained
   The sun to rule the day;
The moon shines full at his command,
   And all the stars obey.

3 I sing the goodness of the Lord,
   That filled the earth with food;
He formed the creatures with his word,
   And then pronounced them good.

4 Lord, how thy wonders are displayed
   Where'er I turn mine eye,
If I survey the ground I tread,
   Or gaze upon the sky!

5 God's hand is my perpetual guard,
   He guides me with his eye;
Why should I then forget the Lord,
   Whose love is ever nigh?

Isaac Watts (1674–1748)

Delight in Creation

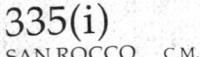

335(i)
SAN ROCCO   C.M.

Derek Williams (1945–)

335(ii)
LONDON NEW   C.M.

Melody from *Scottish Psalter* (1635)
as adapted in J. Playford's *Psalms
and Hymns in Solemn Musick* (1671)

THE NATURAL WORLD

1 LORD of the boundless curves of space
      And time's deep mystery,
  To your creative might we trace
      All nature's energy.

2 Your mind conceived the galaxy,
      Each atom's secret planned,
  And every age of history
      Your purpose, Lord, has spanned.

3 Your Spirit gave the living cell
      Its hidden, vital force:
  The instincts which all life impel
      Derive from you, their source.

4 You gave the growing consciousness
      That flowered at last in man,
  With all his longing to progress,
      Discover, shape and plan.

5 In Christ the living power of grace
      To liberate and lead
  Lights up the future of our race
      With mercy's crowning deed.

6 Lead us, whom love has made and sought,
      To find, when planets fall,
  That Omega of life and thought
      Where Christ is all in all.

Albert F. Bayly (1901-84)
and *Brian A. Wren* (1936–)

Delight in Creation

336

POLWHELE　　88.6.D.

Hubert Julian (1923–　　)

1 HOW wonderful this world of thine,
    A fragment of a fiery sun,
      How lovely and how small!
  Where all things serve thy great design,
    Where life's adventure is begun
      In God, the life of all.

2 The smallest seed in secret grows,
    And thrusting upward answers soon
      The bidding of the light;
  The bud unfurls into a rose;
    The wings within the white cocoon
      Are perfected for flight.

3 The migrant bird, in winter fled,
    Shall come again with spring, and build
      In this same shady tree;
  By secret wisdom surely led,
    Homeward across the clover-field
      Hurries the honey-bee.

4 O thou, whose greater gifts are ours—
    A conscious will, a thinking mind,
      A heart to worship thee—
  O take these strange unfolding powers,
    And teach us through thy Son to find
      The life more full and free.

F. Pratt Green (1903–   )

Words reprinted by permission of
Stainer & Bell Ltd.
For permission to reproduce see p. xiii.

Delight in Creation

337(i)
ALMSGIVING   888.4.   J. B. Dykes (1823–76)

337(ii)
PORTLAND   888.4.   Cyril V. Taylor (1907–   )

THE NATURAL WORLD

1 O LORD of heaven and earth and sea,
   To thee all praise and glory be;
   How shall we show our love to thee,
       Who givest all?

2 The golden sunshine, vernal air,
   Sweet flowers and fruits thy love declare;
   Where harvests ripen, thou art there,
       Who givest all.

3 For peaceful homes and healthful days,
   For all the blessings earth displays,
   We owe thee thankfulness and praise,
       Who givest all.

4 Thou didst not spare thine only Son,
   But gav'st him for a world undone,
   And freely with that blessèd One
       Thou givest all.

5 Thou giv'st the Spirit's blessèd dower,
   Spirit of life, and love, and power,
   And dost his sevenfold graces shower
       Upon us all.

6 For souls redeemed, for sins forgiven,
   For means of grace and hopes of heaven,
   Father, all praise to thee be given,
       Who givest all.

Christopher Wordsworth (1807–85)

Delight in Creation

338(i)

JUSTIFICATION L.M. (Extended)

Melody by
J. Eagleton (1785–1832)

338(ii)

GALILEE L.M.

P. Armes (1836–1908)

THE NATURAL WORLD

For this tune in a higher key see No. 239(i)

1 PRAISE ye the Lord! 'Tis good to raise
Our hearts and voices in his praise;
His nature and his works invite
To make this duty our delight.

2 He formed the stars, those heavenly flames,
He counts their numbers, calls their names;
His wisdom's vast, and knows no bound,
A deep where all our thoughts are drowned.

3 Sing to the Lord! Exalt him high,
Who spreads his clouds along the sky;
There he prepares the fruitful rain,
Nor lets the drops descend in vain.

4 He makes the grass the hills adorn,
And clothes the smiling fields with corn;
The beasts with food his hands supply,
And the young ravens when they cry.

5 What is the creature's skill or force?
The sprightly man, or warlike horse?
The piercing wit, the active limb?
All are too mean delights for him.

6 But saints are lovely in his sight,
He views his children with delight;
He sees their hope, he knows their fear,
And looks, and loves his image there.

Isaac Watts (1674–1748)
based on Psalm 147

Delight in Creation

THE NATURAL WORLD

(Small notes for Organ only)

1 THE spacious firmament on high,
  With all the blue ethereal sky,
    And spangled heavens, a shining frame,
    Their great Original proclaim.
  The unwearied sun, from day to day,
  Does his Creator's power display;
    And publishes to every land
    The work of an almighty hand.

2 Soon as the evening shades prevail,
  The moon takes up the wondrous tale,
    And nightly to the listening earth
    Repeats the story of her birth:
  While all the stars that round her burn,
  And all the planets in their turn,
    Confirm the tidings as they roll,
    And spread the truth from pole to pole.

3 What though in solemn silence all
  Move round this dark terrestrial ball;
    What though no real voice nor sound
    Amid their radiant orbs be found:
  In reason's ear they all rejoice,
  And utter forth a glorious voice,
    For ever singing as they shine:
    'The hand that made us is divine!'

Joseph Addison (1672–1719)

Delight in Creation

FIRMAMENT D.L.M.

Walford Davies (1869–1941)

A - men.

1 THE spacious firmament on high,
   With all the blue ethereal sky,
     And spangled heavens, a shining frame,
     Their great Original proclaim.
   The unwearied sun, from day to day,
   Does his Creator's power display;
     And publishes to every land
     The work of an almighty hand.

2 Soon as the evening shades prevail,
   The moon takes up the wondrous tale,
     And nightly to the listening earth
     Repeats the story of her birth:
   While all the stars that round her burn,
   And all the planets in their turn,
     Confirm the tidings as they roll,
     And spread the truth from pole to pole.

3 What though in solemn silence all
   Move round this dark terrestrial ball;
     What though no real voice nor sound
     Amid their radiant orbs be found:
   In reason's ear they all rejoice,
   And utter forth a glorious voice,
     For ever singing as they shine:
     'The hand that made us is divine!' (Amen)

Joseph Addison (1672–1719)

Delight in Creation

340

ST PAUL (ABERDEEN)   C.M.

Melody from *Chalmers' Collection*
(Aberdeen, c. 1749)

THE NATURAL WORLD

1 THERE is a book (who runs may read)
      Which heavenly truth imparts,
   And all the lore its scholars need,
      Pure eyes and Christian hearts.

2 The works of God above, below,
      Within us and around,
   Are pages in that book, to show
      How God himself is found.

3 The glorious sky, embracing all,
      Is like the Maker's love,
   Wherewith encompassed, great and small
      In peace and order move.

4 One name, above all glorious names,
      With its ten thousand tongues
   The everlasting sea proclaims,
      Echoing angelic songs.

5 The raging fire, the roaring wind,
      Thy boundless power display;
   And in the gentler breeze we find
      Thy Spirit's viewless way.

6 Two worlds are ours: 'tis only sin
      Forbids us to descry
   The mystic heaven and earth within,
      Plain as the sea and sky.

7 Thou who hast given me eyes to see
      And love this sight so fair,
   Give me a heart to find out thee,
      And read thee everywhere.

John Keble (1792–1866)

Delight in Creation

341

CHARING 888.7.

S. Leslie Russell (1901–78)

ALTERNATIVE HARMONY VERSION

THE NATURAL WORLD

1 FATHER, who on man dost shower
Gifts of plenty from thy dower,
To thy people give the power
All thy gifts to use aright.

2 Give pure happiness in leisure,
Temperance in every pleasure,
Wholesome use of earthly treasure,
Bodies clear and spirits bright.

3 Lift from this and every nation
All that brings us degradation;
Quell the forces of temptation;
Put thine enemies to flight.

4 Be with us, thy strength supplying,
That, with energy undying,
Every foe of man defying,
We may rally to the fight.

5 Thou who art our captain ever,
Lead us on to great endeavour;
May thy church the world deliver:
Give us wisdom, courage, might.

6 Father, who hast sought and found us,
Son of God, whose love has bound us,
Holy Spirit, in us, round us—
Hear us, Godhead infinite.

Percy Dearmer (1867–1936)

Living Faithfully in God's World

342(i)
EAST ACKLAM 84.84.888.4.

Francis Jackson (1917–)

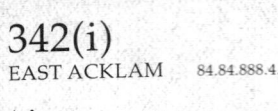

342(ii)
AR HYD Y NOS 84.84.888.4.

Welsh Traditional Melody

THE NATURAL WORLD

1 FOR the fruits of his creation,
   Thanks be to God;
   For his gifts to every nation,
   Thanks be to God;
   For the ploughing, sowing, reaping,
   Silent growth while we are sleeping,
   Future needs in earth's safe-keeping,
   Thanks be to God.

2 In the just reward of labour,
   God's will is done;
   In the help we give our neighbour,
   God's will is done;
   In our world-wide task of caring
   For the hungry and despairing,
   In the harvests we are sharing,
   God's will is done.

3 For the harvests of his Spirit,
   Thanks be to God;
   For the good we all inherit,
   Thanks be to God;
   For the wonders that astound us,
   For the truths that still confound us,
   Most of all, that love has found us,
   Thanks be to God.

F. Pratt Green (1903–   )

Living Faithfully in God's World

343(i)
STEWARDSHIP 11.10.11.10. Valerie Ruddle (1932–)

343(ii)
QUEDLINBURG 11.10.11.10.

From a melody in
Kittel's *Choralbuch* (1790)
Arranged by John Wilson

THE NATURAL WORLD

1 GOD, in his love for us lent us this planet,
   Gave it a purpose in time and in space:
   Small as a spark from the fire of creation,
   Cradle of life and the home of our race.

2 Thanks be to God for its bounty and beauty,
   Life that sustains us in body and mind:
   Plenty for all, if we learn how to share it,
   Riches undreamed-of to fathom and find.

3 Long have our human wars ruined its harvest;
   Long has earth bowed to the terror of force;
   Long have we wasted what others have need of,
   Poisoned the fountain of life at its source.

4 Earth is the Lord's: it is ours to enjoy it,
   Ours, as his stewards, to farm and defend.
   From its pollution, misuse, and destruction,
   Good Lord, deliver us, world without end!

F. Pratt Green (1903–   )

Words reprinted by permission of
Stainer & Bell Ltd on behalf of the Hymn Society
of America. For permission to reproduce see p. xiii.

Living Faithfully in God's World

English Traditional Melody
Collected by Lucy Broadwood (1858–1929)
Harmonised and arranged by
R. Vaughan Williams (1872–1958)

1 GOD, whose farm is all creation,
    Take the gratitude we give;
  Take the finest of our harvest,
    Crops we grow that all may live.

2 Take our ploughing, seeding, reaping,
    Hopes and fears of sun and rain,
  All our thinking, planning, waiting,
    Ripened in this fruit and grain.

3 All our labour, all our watching,
    All our calendar of care,
  In these crops of your creation,
    Take, O God: they are our prayer.

John Arlott (1914–)

THE NATURAL WORLD

345

BANGOR C.M.

Melody from
William Tans'ur's *Compleat Melody* (1735)

1 GOD, you have given us power to sound
  Depths hitherto unknown;
To probe earth's hidden mysteries,
  And make their might our own.

2 Great are your gifts; yet greater far
  This gift, O God, bestow,
That as to knowledge we attain
  We may in wisdom grow.

3 Let wisdom's godly fear dispel
  All fears that hate impart;
Give understanding to the mind,
  And with new mind new heart.

4 So for your glory and our good
  May we your gifts employ,
Lest, maddened by the lust of power,
  We should ourselves destroy.

George Wallace Briggs (1875–1959) alt.

Living Faithfully in God's World

346

THE NATURAL WORLD

1 HEAR us, O Lord, from heaven, thy dwelling-place:
     Like them of old, in vain we toil all night,
     Unless with us thou go, who art the light;
Come then, O Lord, that we may see thy face.

2 Thou, Lord, dost rule the raging of the sea,
     When loud the storm and furious is the gale;
     Strong is thine arm; our little barques are frail:
Send us thy help; remember Galilee.

*3 Our wives and children we commend to thee:
     For them we plough the land and plough the deep,
     For them by day the golden corn we reap,
By night the silver harvest of the sea.

4 We thank thee, Lord, for sunshine, dew, and rain,
     Broadcast from heaven by thine almighty hand—
     Source of all life, unnumbered as the sand—
Bird, beast, and fish, herb, fruit, and golden grain.

5 O Bread of Life, thou in thy word hast said:
     'Who feeds in faith on me shall never die'.
     In mercy hear thy hungry children's cry:
'Father, give us this day our daily bread!'

6 Sow in our hearts the seeds of thy dear love,
     That we may reap contentment, joy, and peace;
     And when at last our earthly labours cease,
Grant us to join thy harvest home above.

William Henry Gill (1839–1923)

V. 3 could appropriately be sung by men only.

Living Faithfully in God's World

347(i)
NEW EARTH 6.6.6.6.88.

Bernard S. Massey (1927–)

347(ii)
CREATION 6.6.6.6.88.

John Hastings (1927–)

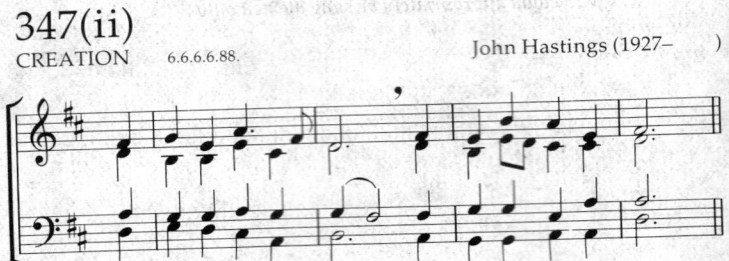

THE NATURAL WORLD

1. LORD, bring the day to pass
When forest, rock and hill,
The beasts, the birds, the grass,
Will know your finished will:
When we attain our destiny,
And nature its lost unity.

2. Forgive our careless use
Of water, ore and soil—
The plenty we abuse
Supplied by others' toil:
Save us from making self our creed;
Turn us towards our neighbour's need.

3. Give us, when we release
Creation's secret powers,
To harness them for peace—
Our children's peace and ours:
Teach us the art of mastering,
Which makes life rich, and draws death's sting.

4. Creation groans, travails,
Estranged its present plight,
Bound—till the hour it hails
The children of the light
Who enter on their true estate.
Come, Lord: new heavens and earth create.

Words reprinted by permission of
Stainer & Bell Ltd.
For permission to reproduce see p. xiii.

Ian Fraser (1917–)

Living Faithfully in God's World

348

HARVEST 9.8.9.8. (Anapaestic) Geoffrey Laycock (1927–86)

1 NOW join we, to praise the cre - a - tor, Our voi - ces in wor-ship and song; We stand to re - call with thanks-giv - ing That to him all sea - sons be - long.

ALTERNATIVE VERSION
(for selected Verses)

Solo (or Group of Voices)

S.A.T.B. (humming or vocalising)

THE NATURAL WORLD

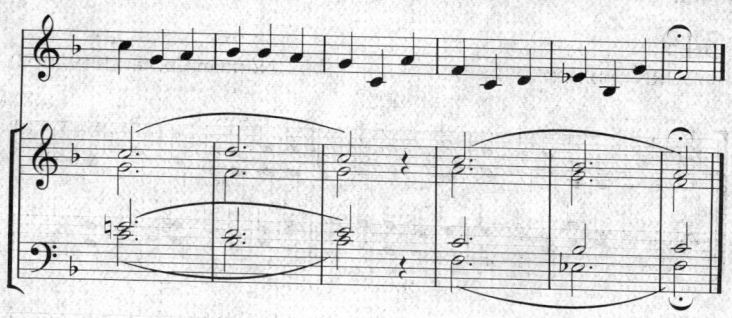

1 NOW join we, to praise the creator,
   Our voices in worship and song;
We stand to recall with thanksgiving
   That to him all seasons belong.

2 We thank you, O God, for your goodness,
   For the joy and abundance of crops,
For food that is stored in our larders,
   For all we can buy in the shops.

3 But also of need and starvation
   We sing with concern and despair—
Of skills that are used for destruction,
   Of land that is burnt and laid bare.

4 We cry for the plight of the hungry
   While harvests are left on the field,
For orchards neglected and wasting,
   For produce from markets withheld.

5 The song grows in depth and in wideness:
   The earth and its people are one.
There can be no thanks without giving,
   No words without deeds that are done.

6 Then teach us, O Lord of the harvest,
   To be humble in all that we claim,
To share what we have with the nations,
   To care for the world in your name.

Fred Kaan (1929–)

Words reprinted by permission of
Stainer & Bell Ltd.
For permission to reproduce see p. xiii.

Living Faithfully in God's World

349

Norman Cocker (1889–1953)

1 O FATHER, whose creating hand
  Brings harvest from the fruitful land,
  Your providence we gladly own,
  And bring our hymns before your throne,
  To praise you for the living bread
  On which our lives are daily fed.

2 Lord, who did in the desert feed
  The hungry thousands in their need,
  Where want and famine still abound
  Let your relieving love be found;
  And in your name may we supply
  Your hungry children when they cry.

3 O Spirit, your revealing light
  Has led our questing souls aright;
  Source of our science, you have taught
  The marvels human minds have wrought,
  So that the barren deserts yield
  The bounty by your love revealed.

Donald Hughes (1911–67)

THE NATURAL WORLD

350

BUNESSAN   5.5.5.4.D.   Gaelic Melody, arranged by John Wilson

For another harmonisation see No. 635

1 PRAISE and thanksgiving,
   Father, we offer,
For all things living
      You have made good;
Harvest of sown fields,
   Fruits of the orchard,
Hay from the mown fields,
      Blossom and wood.

2 Lord, bless the labour
   We bring to serve you,
That with our neighbour
      We may be fed.
Sowing or tilling,
   We would work with you;
Harvesting, milling,
      For daily bread.

3 Father, providing
      Food for your children,
Your wisdom guiding
      Teaches us share
One with another,
   So that, rejoicing
With us, our brother
      May know your care.

4 Then will your blessing
   Reach every people;
Each one confessing
      Your gracious hand.
When you are reigning
   No one will hunger:
Your love sustaining
      Fruitful the land.

Albert F. Bayly (1901-84) alt.

Living Faithfully in God's World

351

MINIVER 11.11.11.11.

Cyril V. Taylor (1907–   )

1 PRAISE God for the harvest of farm and of field,
   Praise God for the people who gather their yield,
   The long hours of labour, the skills of a team,
   The patience of science, the power of machine.

2 Praise God for the harvest that's sent from afar,
   From market and harbour, from tropical shore;
   Foods packed and transported, and planted and grown
   By God-given neighbours, unseen and unknown.

3 Praise God for the harvest that comes from the ground,
   By drill or by mineshaft, by opencast mound;
   For oil and for iron, for copper and coal,
   Praise God, who in love has provided them all.

4 Praise God for the harvest of science and skill,
   The urge to discover, create and fulfil;
   For all new inventions that promise to gain
   A future more hopeful, a world more humane.

5 Praise God for the harvest of conflict and love,
   For leaders and peoples who struggle and serve
   To conquer oppression, earth's plenty increase,
   And gather God's harvest of justice and peace.

Brian A. Wren (1936–   )

Living Faithfully in God's World

Melody by J. A. P. Schulz (1747–1800), as arranged by
J. B. Dykes in *Hymns A & M* (1868)
(harmony slightly revised)

Refrain

All good gifts a - round us

THE NATURAL WORLD

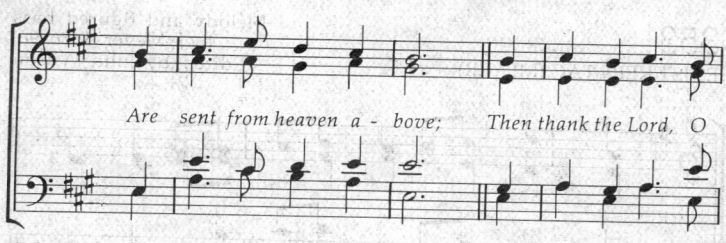

Are sent from heaven a-bove; Then thank the Lord, O

thank the Lord, For all his love.

1 WE plough the fields, and scatter
   The good seed on the land,
But it is fed and watered
   By God's almighty hand;
He sends the snow in winter,
   The warmth to swell the grain,
The breezes and the sunshine,
   And soft refreshing rain:
    All good gifts around us
      Are sent from heaven above;
    Then thank the Lord, O thank the Lord,
    For all his love.

2 He only is the maker
   Of all things near and far;
He paints the wayside flower,
   He lights the evening star;
The winds and waves obey him,
   By him the birds are fed;
Much more to us, his children,
   He gives our daily bread:

3 We thank thee then, O Father,
   For all things bright and good:
The seed-time and the harvest,
   Our life, our health, our food.
Accept the gifts we offer
   For all thy love imparts,
And, what thou most desirest,
   Our humble, thankful hearts:

M. Claudius (1740–1815)
tr. J. M. Campbell (1817–78)

Living Faithfully in God's World

ES IST KEIN TAG (MEYER) 8.8.8.4.

Melody and figured bass
by J. Meyer (1636–96)
Edited by John Wilson

(V. 5. glo - ry___ Of your name.)

THE NATURAL WORLD

1 WITH wonder, Lord, we see your works,
   We see your glory there displayed,
   Below, above, in all that is
   In beauty made.

2 With wonder, Lord, we see your works,
   And childlike in our joy we sing
   To praise you, bless you, Maker, Lord
   Of everything.

3 The stars that fill the skies above,
   The sun and moon which give our light,
   Are your designing for our use
   And our delight.

4 We praise your works, yet we ourselves
   Are works of wonder made by you,
   Not far from you in all we are
   And all we do.

5 All you have made is ours to rule,
   The birds and beasts at will to tame,
   All things to order for the glory
   Of your name.

Brian Foley (1919–   )
based on Psalm 8

Living Faithfully in God's World

354

DERBY   5 5. 5 11.

Melody from
J. Wesley's *Sacred Harmony* (1780)

THE NATURAL WORLD

1. COME, let us anew
   Our journey pursue,
   Roll round with the year,
   And never stand still till the Master appear.

2. His adorable will
   Let us gladly fulfil,
   And our talents improve,
   By the patience of hope and the labour of love.

3. Our life is a dream,
   Our time as a stream
   Glides swiftly away,
   And the fugitive moment refuses to stay.

4. The arrow is flown,
   The moment is gone;
   The millennial year
   Rushes on to our view, and eternity's here.

5. O that each in the day
   Of his coming may say:
   'I have fought my way through,
   I have finished the work thou didst give me to do!'

6. O that each from his Lord
   May receive the glad word:
   'Well and faithfully done;
   Enter into my joy, and sit down on my throne!'

Charles Wesley (1707–88)

The Seasons

355
ST GEORGE'S, WINDSOR   77.77.D.   George J. Elvey (1816–93)

For this tune in a lower key see No. 781

1 COME, ye thankful people, come,
Raise the song of harvest-home!
All is safely gathered in,
Ere the winter storms begin;
God, our maker, doth provide
For our wants to be supplied;
Come to God's own temple, come,
Raise the song of harvest-home!

2 All the world is God's own field,
Fruit unto his praise to yield;
Wheat and tares together sown,
Unto joy or sorrow grown;
First the blade, and then the ear,
Then the full corn shall appear;
Lord of harvest, grant that we
Wholesome grain and pure may be.

3 For the Lord our God shall come,
And shall take his harvest home;
From his field shall in that day
All offences purge away;
Give his angels charge at last
In the fire the tares to cast,
But the fruitful ears to store
In his garner evermore.

4 Even so, Lord, quickly come;
Bring thy final harvest home;
Gather thou thy people in,
Free from sorrow, free from sin,
There for ever purified,
In thy garner to abide:
Come, with all thine angels come,
Raise the glorious harvest-home!

Henry Alford (1810–71)

THE NATURAL WORLD

356

WAREHAM L.M.

Melody by W. Knapp (1698–1768)

For this tune in a higher key see No. 549

1 GREAT God, we sing that mighty hand
By which supported still we stand;
    The opening year thy mercy shows,
    And mercy crowns it till it close.

2 By day, by night, at home, abroad,
Still are we guarded by our God;
    By his incessant bounty fed,
    By his unerring counsel led.

3 With grateful hearts the past we own;
The future, all to us unknown,
    We to thy guardian care commit,
    And peaceful leave before thy feet.

4 In scenes exalted or depressed
Thou art our joy, and thou our rest;
    Thy goodness all our hopes shall raise,
    Adored throughout our changing days.

5 When death shall interrupt these songs,
And seal in silence mortal tongues,
    Our helper God, in whom we trust,
    In better worlds shall be our boast.

Philip Doddridge (1702–51)

The Seasons

357

SOLOTHURN L.M.

Swiss traditional melody
Harmonised by John Wilson

*In selected verses A.T.B. may hum the accompaniment.

THE NATURAL WORLD

1 LORD, hear our prayer for this new year (*day*):
    Despite our longing for release
 From all that fosters fear and strife,
    We have not walked your way of peace.

2 May we sow love where hate is found,
    Forgiveness though we suffer smart,
 In place of discord, unity,
    And faith to heal the doubting heart:

3 Replace despair with lively hope,
    Darkness dispel with dawning light,
 And where the night of sorrow reigns
    May we bring joy, the day-star bright.

4 Teach us anew each passing year (*day*)
    More readily to heed and share
 The gladness of rejoicing hearts,
    The burden of another's care.

5 As in our giving we receive,
    In pard'ning we shall be forgiven,
 And, rising to new life in Christ,
    Attain at last the joys of heaven.

Freda Head (1914–)

358

ST ANNE C.M.

Modern form of tune
(See 2nd version below)

FIRST VERSION

Verse 7

DESCANT

John Wilson

O God, our help in a-ges past, Our hope for years to come,

Be thou our guard while life shall last, And our e-ter-nal home.

SECOND VERSION
(with original rhythm)

ST ANNE C.M.

Melody and bass from
A Supplement to the New Version (1708)
Probably by William Croft (1678–1727)

THE NATURAL WORLD

Verse 7

John Wilson

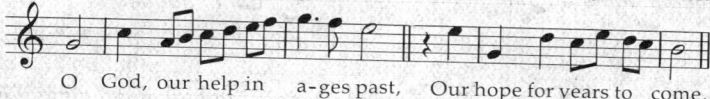

O God, our help in a-ges past, Our hope for years to come,

Be thou our guard while life shall last, And our e-ter-nal home.

1 O GOD, our help in ages past,
    Our hope for years to come,
  Our shelter from the stormy blast,
    And our eternal home;

2 Under the shadow of thy throne
    Thy saints have dwelt secure;
  Sufficient is thine arm alone,
    And our defence is sure.

3 Before the hills in order stood
    Or earth received her frame,
  From everlasting thou art God,
    To endless years the same.

4 A thousand ages in thy sight
    Are like an evening gone,
  Short as the watch that ends the night
    Before the rising sun.

5 The busy tribes of flesh and blood,
    With all their cares and fears,
  Are carried downward by the flood,
    And lost in following years.

6 Time, like an ever-rolling stream,
    Bears all its sons away;
  They fly forgotten, as a dream
    Dies at the opening day.

7 O God, our help in ages past,
    Our hope for years to come,
  Be thou our guard while life shall last,
    And our eternal home.

Isaac Watts (1674–1748)
based on Psalm 90:1–5.

The Seasons

Arranged by J. Wilkes (1861)
from a tune composed or adapted
by John Antes (1740–1811)

For this tune in a higher key see Nos. 27(i) and 508(i)

1 PRAISE, O praise our God and King!
   Hymns of adoration sing:
   For his mercies still endure,
   Ever faithful, ever sure.

2 Praise him that he gave the rain
   To mature the swelling grain:

3 And has bid the fruitful field
   Crops of precious increase yield:

4 Praise him for our harvest store;
   He has filled the garner floor:

5 And for richer food than this,
   Pledge of everlasting bliss:

6 Glory to our bounteous King!
   Glory let creation sing:
   Glory to the Father, Son,
   And blest Spirit, Three in One.

   Henry Williams Baker (1821–77)

THE NATURAL WORLD

360

NORTHROP C.M. (ext.)

Abraham Northrop (1863–1938)

1 SING to the great Jehovah's praise;
   All praise to him belongs;
Who kindly lengthens out our days
   Demands our choicest songs.

2 His providence has brought us through
   Another various year;
We all with vows and anthems new
   Before our God appear.

3 Father, thy mercies past we own,
   Thy still continued care;
To thee presenting, through thy Son,
   Whate'er we have or are.

4 Our lips and lives shall gladly show
   The wonders of thy love,
While on in Jesus' steps we go
   To see thy face above.

5 Our residue of days or hours
   Thine, wholly thine, shall be,
And all our consecrated powers
   A sacrifice to thee.

Charles Wesley (1707–88)

The Seasons

361

RUTH 6.5.6.5.D.

Samuel Smith (1821–1917)

THE NATURAL WORLD

1 SUMMER suns are glowing
    Over land and sea,
  Happy light is flowing
    Bountiful and free;
  Everything rejoices
    In the mellow rays,
  All earth's thousand voices
    Swell the psalm of praise.

2 God's free mercy streameth
    Over all the world,
  And his banner gleameth
    Everywhere unfurled.
  Broad and deep and glorious
    As the heaven above,
  Shines in might victorious
    His eternal love.

3 Lord, upon our blindness
    Thy pure radiance pour;
  For thy loving-kindness
    Make us love thee more;
  And when clouds are drifting
    Dark across our sky,
  Then, the veil uplifting,
    Father, be thou nigh.

4 We will never doubt thee,
    Though thou veil thy light;
  Life is dark without thee,
    Death with thee is bright.
  Light of light, shine o'er us
    On our pilgrim way;
  Go thou still before us
    To the endless day.

William Walsham How (1823–97)

362

BISHOPGARTH   8.7.8.7.D. (Iamb.)

Arthur Sullivan (1842–1900)

THE NATURAL WORLD

1 TO thee, O Lord, our hearts we raise
    In hymns of adoration,
  To thee bring sacrifice of praise
    With shouts of exultation;
  Bright robes of gold the fields adorn,
    The hills with joy are ringing,
  The valleys stand so thick with corn
    That even they are singing.

2 And now, on this our festal day,
    Thy bounteous hand confessing,
  Before thee thankfully we lay
    The first-fruits of thy blessing.
  By thee thy children's souls are fed
    With gifts of grace supernal;
  Thou who dost give us earthly bread,
    Give us the bread eternal.

3 We bear the burden of the day,
    And often toil seems dreary;
  But labour ends with sunset ray,
    And rest comes for the weary:
  May we, the angel-reaping o'er,
    Stand at the last accepted,
  Christ's golden sheaves for evermore
    To garners bright elected.

4 O blessèd is that land of God
    Where saints abide for ever,
  Where golden fields spread far and broad,
    Where flows the crystal river.
  The strains of all its holy throng
    With ours today are blending;
  Thrice blessèd is that harvest song
    Which never has an ending.

  William Chatterton Dix (1837–98) alt.

363 (i)
FESTUS L.M.

Adapted from a melody in
Freylinghausen's *Geistreiches Gesangbuch* (1704)

363(ii)
WILLIAMS L.M.

Templi Carmina (1829)

THE NATURAL WORLD

1 YES, God is good—in earth and sky,
    From ocean-depths and spreading wood,
  Ten thousand voices seem to cry:
    'God made us all, and God is good'.

2 The sun that keeps his trackless way
    And downward pours his golden flood,
  Night's sparkling hosts, all seem to say
    In accents clear that God is good.

3 The merry birds prolong the strain,
    Their song with every spring renewed;
  And balmy air and falling rain,
    Each softly whispers: 'God is good'.

4 We hear it in the rushing breeze;
    The hills that have for ages stood,
  The echoing sky and roaring seas,
    All swell the chorus: 'God is good'.

5 For all thy gifts we bless thee, Lord,
    But chiefly for our heavenly food,
  Thy pardoning grace, thy quickening word,
    These prompt our song, that God is good.

John Hampden Gurney (1802–62)

364

SUSSEX CAROL   88.88.88.

English traditional melody harmonised by
Ralph Vaughan Williams (1872–1958)

Reprinted by permission of Stainer & Bell Ltd
acting as agents for Ralph Vaughan Williams
Ltd. For permission to reproduce see p. xiii.

THE SOCIAL ORDER

1 AS man and woman we were made,
  That love be found and life begun;
So praise the Lord who made us two,
  And praise the Lord when two are one:
Praise for the love that comes to life
Through child or parent, man or wife.

2 Now Jesus lived and gave his love
  To make our life and loving new;
So celebrate with him today,
  And drink the joy he offers you
That makes the simple moment shine
And changes water into wine.

3 And Jesus died to live again;
  So praise the love that, come what may,
Can bring the dawn and clear the skies,
  And waits to wipe all tears away;
And let us hope for what shall be,
Believing where we cannot see.

4 Then spread the table, clear the hall,
  And celebrate till day is done;
Let peace go deep between us all,
  And joy be shared by everyone:
Laugh and make merry with your friends,
And praise the love that never ends!

Brian A. Wren (1936–)

365(i)
SEELENBRÄUTIGAM 5 5. 8 8. 5 5.

Melody attributed to
A. Drese (1620–1701)

365(ii)
WESTRON WYNDE 5 5. 8 8. 5 5.

William Llewellyn (1925–)

THE SOCIAL ORDER

1 JESUS, Lord, we pray,
    Be our guest today;
  Gospel story has recorded
  How your glory was afforded
    To a wedding day;
    Be our guest, we pray.

2 Lord of love and life,
    Blessing man and wife,
  As they stand, their need confessing,
  May your hand take theirs in blessing;
    You will share their life;
    Bless this man and wife.

3 Lord of hope and faith,
    Faithful unto death,
  Let the ring serve as a token
  Of a love sincere, unbroken,
    Love more strong than death,
    Lord of hope and faith.

Basil E. Bridge (1927–)

Marriage and Family Life

366

STRENGTH AND STAY 11.10.11.10.

J. B. Dykes (1823–76)

THE SOCIAL ORDER

1 HAPPY the home that welcomes you, Lord Jesus,
   Truest of friends, most honoured guest of all,
 Where hearts and eyes are bright with joy to greet you,
   Your lightest wishes eager to fulfil.

2 Happy the home where man and wife together
   Are of one mind believing in your love;
 Through love and pain, prosperity and hardship,
   Through good and evil days your care they prove.

3 Happy the home, O loving friend of children,
   Where they are giv'n to you with hands of prayer,
 Where at your feet they early learn to listen
   To your own words, and thank you for your care.

4 Happy the home where work is done to please you,
   In tasks both great and small, that you may see
 Your servants doing all as you would wish them
   As members of your household, glad and free.

5 Happy the home that knows your healing comfort,
   Where, unforgotten, every joy you share,
 Until they all, their work on earth completed,
   Come to your Father's house to meet you there.

Karl Johann Philipp Spitta (1801–59)
tr. *Honor Mary Thwaites* (1914–)

367

VERMONT L.M.

A. E. Floyd (1877–1974)

1 LORD of the home, your only Son
    Received a mother's tender love,
And from an earthly father won
    His vision of your home above.

2 Help us, O Lord, our homes to make
    Your Holy Spirit's dwelling-place;
Our hands and hearts' devotion take
    To be the servants of your grace.

3 Teach us to keep our homes so fair
    That, were our Lord a child once more,
He might be glad our hearth to share,
    And find a welcome at our door.

4 Lord, may your Spirit sanctify
    Each household duty we fulfil;
May we our Master glorify
    In glad obedience to your will.

Albert F. Bayly (1901-84)

THE SOCIAL ORDER

368

John Wilson (1905–   )

Unison*

Harmony (ad lib)

* *Bars 1–4, in selected verses, may be sung by*
men or women only, or by a soloist.

1   LORD, you give to us
       The precious gift of life,
    A stewardship for every husband, every wife.

2   Lord, you give to us
       Not only flesh and blood,
    But mind and heart and soul to know that they are good.

3   Lord, you offer us
       The water, bread and wine;
    By faith we reach to find your love within the sign.

4   Lord, you offer us
       New life that never ends;
    You suffer, serve, and die, and live to call us friends.

5   Lord, you ask of us
       A death to what we knew;
    Then, rising in your name, we'll put our trust in you.

6   Lord, you share with us
       Our hope for what will be;
    With us prepare each child by love, your love to see.

Stephen Orchard (1942–   ) and others

Marriage and Family Life

369

WYCH CROSS 88.88.88.

Erik Routley (1917–82)

1 O GOD in heaven, whose loving plan
   Ordained for us our parents' care,
And, from the time our life began,
   The shelter of a home to share:
     Our Father, on the homes we love
     Send down thy blessing from above.

2 May young and old together find
   In Christ the Lord of every day,
That fellowship our homes may bind
   In joy and sorrow, work and play:

3 The sins that mar our homes forgive;
   From all self-seeking set us free;
Parents and children, may we live
   In glad obedience, Lord, to thee:

Hugh Martin (1890–1964)

THE SOCIAL ORDER

370

O PERFECT LOVE 11.10.11.10.

J. Barnby (1838–96)

1 O PERFECT Love, all human thought transcending,
   Lowly we kneel in prayer before your throne,
 That theirs may be the love which knows no ending
   Who in your love for evermore are one.

2 O perfect Life, be now their full assurance
   Of tender charity and steadfast faith,
 Of patient hope, and quiet brave endurance,
   With childlike trust that fears not pain or death.

3 Grant them the joy which brightens earthly sorrow,
   Grant them the peace which calms all earthly strife;
 And to life's day the glorious unknown morrow
   That dawns upon eternal love and life.

Dorothy Frances Gurney (1858–1932) alt.

Marriage and Family Life

371

RHOSYMEDRE 6.6.6.6.888.

John David Edwards (1805–85)
Original Sacred Music (c. 1840)

1. OUR Father, by whose name
   All parenthood is known,
   Who in your love proclaim
   Each family your own,
   Direct all parents, guarding well,
   With constant love as sentinel,
   The homes in which your people dwell.

2. Lord Christ, yourself a child
   Within an earthly home,
   With heart still undefiled
   You did to manhood come;
   Our children bless in every place,
   That they may all behold your face,
   And, knowing you, may grow in grace.

3. Blest Spirit, who can bind
   Our hearts in unity,
   And teach us so to find
   The love from self set free,
   In all our hearts such love increase
   That every home, by this release,
   May be the dwelling-place of peace.

F. Bland Tucker (1895–1984)

THE SOCIAL ORDER

372

CONTEMPLATION C.M.

F. A. G. Ouseley (1825–89)

1 OUR Father, whose creative love
    The gift of life bestows,
Each child of earthly union born
    Thy heavenly likeness shows.

2 Grant those entrusted with the care
    Of precious life from thee,
Thy grace, that worthy of the gift
    And faithful they may be.

3 Teach them to meet the growing needs
    Of infant, child, and youth;
To build the body, train the mind
    To know and love the truth;

4 And, highest task, to feed the soul
    With Christ, the living bread;
That each unfolding life may grow
    Strong in thy paths to tread.

5 These parents need thy wisdom's light,
    Thy love within their heart;
Bless thou their home, and for their task
    Thy Spirit's grace impart.

Albert F. Bayly (1901-84)

Marriage and Family Life

373

LOVE UNKNOWN 6.6.6.6.88.

John Ireland (1879–1962)

Joint heirs of the grace of life

1 THE grace of life is theirs
    Who on this wedding-day
Delight to make their vows,
    And for each other pray.
May they, O Lord, together prove
The lasting joy of Christian love.

2 Where love is, God abides;
    And God shall surely bless
A home where trust and care
    Give birth to happiness.
May they, O Lord, together prove
The lasting joy of such a love.

3 How slow to take offence
    Love is! How quick to heal!
How ready in distress
    To know how others feel!
May they, O Lord, together prove
The lasting joy of such a love.

4 And when time lays its hand
    On all we hold most dear,
And life, by life consumed,
    Fulfils its purpose here,
May we, O Lord, together prove
The lasting joy of Christian love.

F. Pratt Green (1903–)
based on I Peter 3:7

THE SOCIAL ORDER

374

ST GODRIC 6.6.6.6.88.

J. B. Dykes (1823–1876)

1 THOU God of truth and love,
   We seek thy perfect way,
   Ready thy choice to approve,
   Thy providence to obey;
Enter into thy wise design,
And sweetly lose our will in thine.

2 Why hast thou cast our lot
   In the same age and place,
   And why together brought
   To see each other's face,
To join with loving sympathy,
And mix our friendly souls in thee?

3 Didst thou not make us one,
   That we might one remain,
   Together travel on,
   And share our joy and pain,
Till all thy utmost goodness prove,
And rise renewed in perfect love?

4 Then let us ever bear
   The blessèd end in view,
   And join, with mutual care,
   To fight our passage through;
And kindly help each other on,
Till all receive the starry crown.

5 O may thy Spirit seal
   Our souls unto that day,
   With all thy fullness fill,
   And then transport away:
Away to our eternal rest,
Away to our Redeemer's breast.

Charles Wesley (1707–88)

Marriage and Family Life

375(i)
HOLBORN   10 10 10 10.   Eric H. Thiman (1900–75)

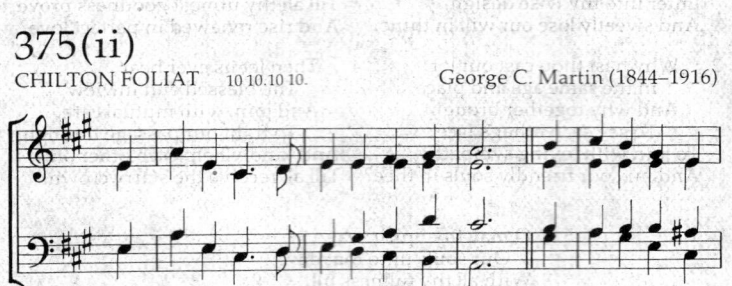

375(ii)
CHILTON FOLIAT   10 10 10 10.   George C. Martin (1844–1916)

THE SOCIAL ORDER

1 ALMIGHTY Father of all things that be,
   Our life, our work, we consecrate to thee,
      Whose heavens declare thy glory from above,
      Whose earth below is witness to thy love.

2 Thou dost the strength to worker's arms impart;
   From thee the skilled musician's subtle art;
      The grace of poet's pen or painter's hand
      Portrays the loveliness of sea and land.

3 For well we know this weary, fallen earth
   Is yet thine own by right of its new birth,
      Since that great cross upreared on Calvary
      And Easter's power redeemed it, Lord, for thee.

4 Then grant us, Lord, to spend ourselves in praise,
   To serve our Saviour's purpose all our days,
      To speak and think, and work and live and move,
      Reflecting thine own nature, suffering love;

5 That so, redeemed by Christ from sin and shame,
   And purified by thine own Spirit's flame,
      Ourselves, our work, and all our powers may be
      A sacrifice acceptable to thee.

Ernest Edward Dugmore (1843–1925) alt.

Life and Work

376

Adapted from an anthem
probably by John Hilton (d. 1608)

1 BEHOLD us, Lord, a little space
   From daily tasks set free,
And met within this holy place
   To rest awhile with thee.

2 Yet these are not the only walls
   Wherein thou may'st be sought;
On homeliest work thy blessing falls,
   In truth and patience wrought.

3 Thine is the loom, the forge, the mart,
   The wealth of land and sea,
The worlds of science and of art,
   Revealed and ruled by thee.

4 Then let us prove our heavenly birth
   In all we do and know,
And claim the kingdom of the earth
   For thee, and not thy foe.

5 Work shall be prayer, if all be wrought
   As thou wouldst have it done,
And prayer, by thee inspired and taught,
   Itself with work be one.

John Ellerton (1826–93)

THE SOCIAL ORDER

377

ANGEL VOICES 8.5.8.5.8.4.3.

E. G. Monk (1819–1900)

1 COME to us, creative Spirit,
   In our Father's house,
Every natural talent foster,
   Hidden skills arouse,
That within your earthly temple
   Wise and simple
     May rejoice.

2 Poet, painter, music-maker,
   All your treasures bring;
Craftsman, actor, graceful dancer,
   Make your offering;
Join your hands in celebration!
   Let creation
     Shout and sing!

3 Word from God eternal springing,
   Fill our minds, we pray,
And in all artistic vision
   Give integrity.
May the flame, within us burning,
   Kindle yearning
     Day by day.

4 In all places and for ever
   Glory be expressed
To the Son, with God the Father,
   And the Spirit blest.
In our worship and our living,
   Keep us striving
     Towards the best.

David Mowbray (1938–   )

Words reprinted by permission of Stainer & Bell
Ltd and the Methodist Church Division of Education
and Youth. For permission to reproduce see p. xiii.

Life and Work

SLANE 10 11.11 11.

Irish Traditional Melody
Harmonised by Erik Routley (1917–82)

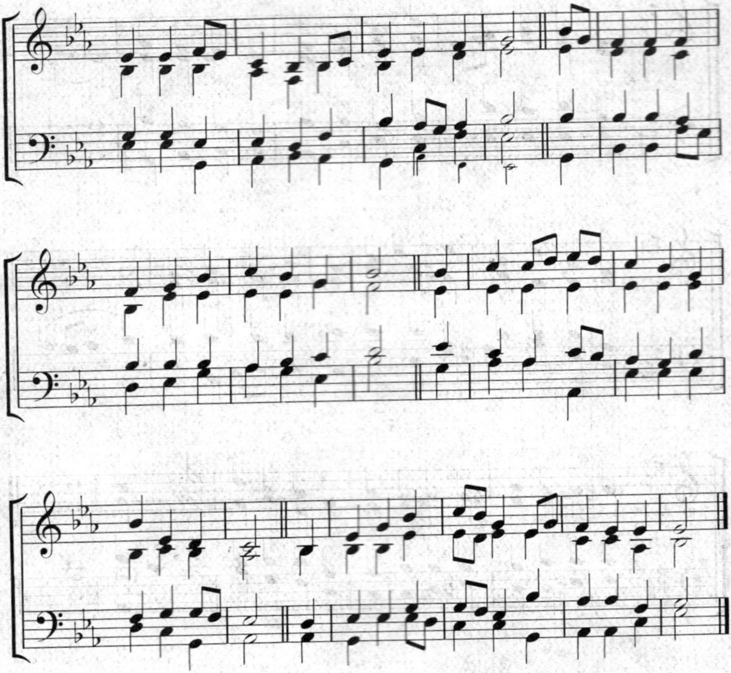

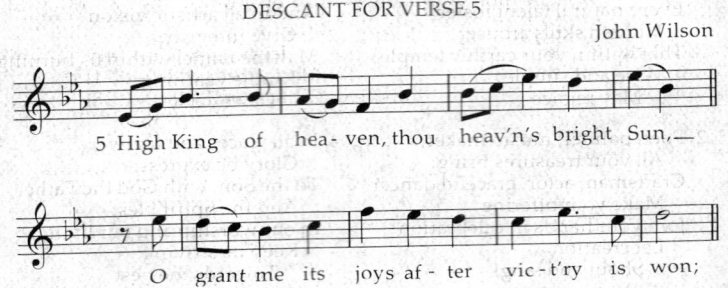

DESCANT FOR VERSE 5

John Wilson

5 High King of hea- ven, thou heav'n's bright Sun,—
O grant me its joys af - ter vic - t'ry is won;

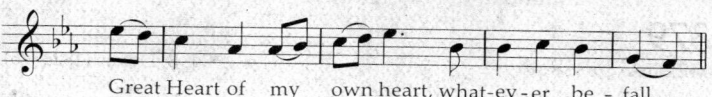

Great Heart of my own heart, what-ev-er be - fall, __

Still be thou my vi - sion, O Ru - ler of all.

1 BE thou my vision, O Lord of my heart,
  Be all else but naught to me, save that thou art;
    Be thou my best thought in the day and the night,
    Both waking and sleeping, thy presence my light.

2 Be thou my wisdom, be thou my true word,
  Be thou ever with me, and I with thee, Lord;
    Be thou my great Father, and I thy true son;
    Be thou in me dwelling, and I with thee one.

3 Be thou my breastplate, my sword for the fight;
  Be thou my whole armour, be thou my true might;
    Be thou my soul's shelter, be thou my strong tower:
    O raise thou me heavenward, great Power of my
        power.

4 Riches I heed not, nor man's empty praise:
  Be thou mine inheritance now and always;
    Be thou and thou only the first in my heart:
    O Sovereign of heaven, my treasure thou art.

5 High King of heaven, thou heaven's bright Sun,
  O grant me its joys after vict'ry is won;
    Great Heart of my own heart, whatever befall,
    Still be thou my vision, O Ruler of all.

Irish, *c.* 8th century
Tr. *Mary Byrne* (1880–1931)
Versified, *Eleanor Hull* (1860–1935)

379

MELITA 8 8.8 8.8 8.

J. B. Dykes (1823–76)

1 ETERNAL Father, strong to save,
  Whose arm doth bind the restless wave,
  Who bidd'st the mighty ocean deep
  Its own appointed limits keep:
    O hear us when we cry to thee
    For those in peril on the sea.

2 O Saviour, whose almighty word
  The winds and waves submissive heard,
  Who walkedst on the foaming deep,
  And calm amid its rage didst sleep:

3 O sacred Spirit, who didst brood
  Upon the chaos dark and rude,
  Who bad'st its angry tumult cease,
  And gavest light and life and peace:

4 O Trinity of love and power,
  Our brethren shield in danger's hour;
  From rock and tempest, fire and foe,
  Protect them wheresoe'er they go:
    And ever let there rise to thee
    Glad hymns of praise from land and sea.

William Whiting (1825–78)

THE SOCIAL ORDER

380

WATCHMAN S.M.

James Leach (1762–98)
(adapted)

1 COME, workers for the Lord,
   And lift up heart and hand;
Praise God, all skill at bench and board,
   Praise, all that brain has planned.

2 When Christ to manhood came,
   A craftsman was he made,
And served his glad apprentice-time
   Bound to the joiner's trade.

3 When Christ on Calvary
   Drank down his cruel draught,
The men who made the fatal tree
   Were men of his own craft.

4 So, God, our labour take,
   From spite and greed set free;
May nothing that we do or make
   Bring ill to man or thee.

5 All workers for the Lord,
   Come, sing with voice and heart;
In strength of hands be God adored,
   And praised in power of art.

Norman Nicholson (1914–) alt.

Life and Work

381

SONG 34 (ANGELS' SONG) L.M.

Melody and bass by
Orlando Gibbons (1583–1625)

Not too fast

DESCANT FOR VERSE 5

John Wilson

5 For thee de-light-ful-ly em - ploy ___ What-e'er thy boun - teous grace has given,

And run my course with e - ven joy, ___ And close-ly walk with thee to heaven.

THE SOCIAL ORDER

1 FORTH in thy name, O Lord, I go,
   My daily labour to pursue,
Thee, only thee, resolved to know
   In all I think, or speak, or do.

2 The task thy wisdom has assigned
   O let me cheerfully fulfil,
In all my works thy presence find,
   And prove thy good and perfect will.

3 Thee may I set at my right hand,
   Whose eyes my inmost substance see,
And labour on at thy command,
   And offer all my works to thee.

4 Give me to bear thy easy yoke,
   And every moment watch and pray,
And still to things eternal look,
   And hasten to thy glorious day;

5 For thee delightfully employ
   Whate'er thy bounteous grace has given,
And run my course with even joy,
   And closely walk with thee to heaven.

Charles Wesley (1707–88)

May also be sung to No. 148, ANTWERP

382

CHARTERHOUSE 7.7.7.7.7.7.

A. S. Cooper (1835–1900)

THE SOCIAL ORDER

1 LIFE and light and joy are found
    In the presence of the Lord:
Life with richest blessing crowned,
    Light from many fountains poured—
Life and light and holy joy,
None can darken or destroy.

2 Bring to him life's brightest hours,
    He will make them still more bright;
Give to him your noblest powers,
    He will hallow all your might;
Come to him with eager quest,
You shall hear his high behest.

3 All your questions large and deep,
    All the open thoughts of youth,
Bring to him, and you shall reap
    All the harvest of his truth;
You shall find in that great store
Largest love and wisest lore.

4 Then when comes life's wider sphere
    And its busier enterprise,
You shall find him ever near,
    Looking, with approving eyes,
On all honest work and true
His dear servants' hands can do.

Charles Edward Mudie (1818–90)

383

ST LEONARD (SMART) C.M.

Henry Smart (1813–79)

For this tune in a lower key see No. 422

1 SERVANT of all, to toil for man
  Thou didst not, Lord, refuse;
Thy majesty did not disdain
  To be employed for us.

2 Son of the carpenter, receive
  This humble work of mine;
Worth to my meanest labour give,
  By joining it to thine.

3 End of my every action thou,
  In all things thee I see;
Accept my hallowed labour now,
  I do it unto thee.

4 Whate'er the Father views as thine,
  He views with gracious eyes;
Jesus, this mean oblation join
  To thy great sacrifice.

Charles Wesley (1707–88)

384

HAREWOOD 6.6.6.6.88.

S. S. Wesley (1810–76)

THE SOCIAL ORDER

1. LORD God, in whom all worlds,
   All life, all work, began;
   Give us the faith to know
   We serve your master plan.
   How happy they who thus have found
   Contentment in the daily round.

2. But when good work receives
   No adequate reward;
   When meaningless routines
   Leave willing workers bored;
   When time is spent in needless strife:
   Make us ashamed, O Lord of life.

3. And if, in leaner years,
   What we had gained is lost;
   If progress must be bought
   At someone else's cost:
   Make us, one nation, swift to share
   The hardships others have to bear.

4. So, for tomorrow's sake,
   Teach us new skills today,
   To do your perfect will
   In our imperfect way,
   And live as those whom you have called
   To be your work-force in the world.

F. Pratt Green (1903–)

385(i)

PEMBROKE   88.6.D.   Melody by James Foster (1807–85)

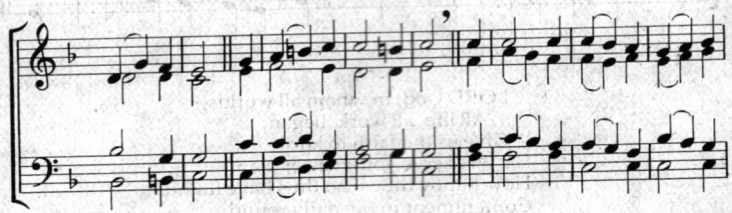

1 SPIRIT of wisdom, turn our eyes
  From earth and earthly vanities
    To heavenly truth and love;
  Spirit of understanding true,
  Our souls with heavenly light endue
    To seek the things above.

2 Spirit of counsel, be our guide;
  Teach us, by earthly struggles tried,
    Our heavenly crown to win;
  Spirit of fortitude, thy power
  Be with us in temptation's hour,
    To keep us pure from sin.

3 Spirit of knowledge, lead our feet
  In thine own paths, so safe and sweet,
    By angel footsteps trod;
  Where thou our guardian true shalt be,
  Spirit of gentle piety,
    To keep us close to God.

4 Through all our life be ever near,
  Spirit of God's most holy fear,
    In our heart's inmost shrine;
  Our souls with aweful reverence fill,
  To worship his most holy will,
    All-righteous and divine.

5 So lead us, Lord, through peace or strife,
  Onward to everlasting life,
    To win our high reward:
  So may we fight our lifelong fight,
  Strong in thine own unearthly might,
    And reign with Christ our Lord.

                              Anonymous

385(ii)

CHAPEL ROYAL   8 8.6.D.   William Boyce (1710–79)

THE SOCIAL ORDER

1 SPIRIT of wisdom, turn our eyes
  From earth and earthly vanities
    To heavenly truth and love;
  Spirit of understanding true,
  Our souls with heavenly light endue
    To seek the things above.

2 Spirit of counsel, be our guide;
  Teach us, by earthly struggles tried,
    Our heavenly crown to win;
  Spirit of fortitude, thy power
  Be with us in temptation's hour,
    To keep us pure from sin.

3 Spirit of knowledge, lead our feet
  In thine own paths, so safe and sweet,
    By angel footsteps trod;
  Where thou our guardian true shalt be,
  Spirit of gentle piety,
    To keep us close to God.

4 Through all our life be ever near,
  Spirit of God's most holy fear,
    In our heart's inmost shrine;
  Our souls with aweful reverence fill,
  To worship his most holy will,
    All-righteous and divine.

5 So lead us, Lord, through peace or strife,
  Onward to everlasting life,
    To win our high reward:
  So may we fight our lifelong fight,
  Strong in thine own unearthly might,
    And reign with Christ our Lord.

Anonymous

386

ST JOHN (ADORATION) 6.6.6.6.88.

From *The Parish Choir* (1851)
(with altered rhythms)

THE SOCIAL ORDER

1   THOU who dost rule on high,
      Our Father and our friend,
   All those who ride the sky
      We now to thee commend;
For though among the stars they move,
They cannot pass beyond thy love.

2   Alone in boundless space,
      May they remain with thee;
   The glory of thy face
      Among the heavens see;
For thou, by land and sea and air,
Art with thy children everywhere.

3   When tempests loose their power
      And dangers gather round,
   In thee, in that dread hour,
      May their defence be found;
O may that peace possess their mind
Which all thy trusting children find;

4   And soon from pole to pole
      Thy kingdom, Lord, arise;
   And peace alone control
      The commerce of the skies;
Till all the gifts thou givest men,
We to thy glory give again.

R. Wesley Littlewood (1908–76)

C. E. Willing (1830–1904)

1 YOUR light, O God, was given to earth,
   The light of truth, your wisdom's flame;
  From age to age it grew more clear,
   And glorious shone when Jesus came.

2 The Light of all the world was he;
   But men loved darkness more than light;
  With evil deeds of pride and hate
   They scorned God's love and chose the night.

3 But light unconquered shone again;
   No cross, no tomb its power could bind;
  In glory, Love and Life arose
   To shine for ever on mankind.

4 Forgive us, Lord, if we have spurned
   Your truth, your light, your wisdom's way;
  And lead our hearts through Christ to find
   In love the road to perfect day.

Albert F. Bayly (1901-84)

388

ENGELBERG 10 10 10.4.

Charles Villiers Stanford (1852–1924)

1 WHEN, in our mu-sic, God is glo-ri-fied, ___ And a-do-ra-tion leaves no room for pride, ___ It is as though the whole cre-a-tion cried: ___

vv. 1–4

THE SOCIAL ORDER

Al - le - lu - ia! sing al - ways:

Al - le - lu - ia! A — men.

Congregation

Choir (harmony)

A — men.

1 WHEN, in our music, God is glorified,
And adoration leaves no room for pride,
It is as though the whole creation cried:
Alleluia!

2 How often, making music, we have found
A new dimension in the world of sound,
As worship moved us to a more profound
Alleluia!

3 So has the Church, in liturgy and song,
In faith and love, through centuries of wrong,
Borne witness to the truth in every tongue:
Alleluia!

4 And did not Jesus sing a psalm that night
When utmost evil strove against the Light?
Then let us sing, for whom he won the fight:
Alleluia!

5 Let every instrument be tuned for praise!
Let all rejoice who have a voice to raise!
And may God give us faith to sing always:
Alleluia! Amen.

Words reprinted by permission of
Stainer & Bell Ltd.
For permission to reproduce see p. xiii.

F. Pratt Green (1903–)

(See also
following pages)

Life and Work

388 (cont.)

ALTERNATIVE VERSION FOR A VERSE BY THE CHOIR ALONE

Al — le — lu — ia!

1 WHEN, in our music, God is glorified,
  And adoration leaves no room for pride,
  It is as though the whole creation cried:
      Alleluia!

2 How often, making music, we have found
  A new dimension in the world of sound,
  As worship moved us to a more profound
      Alleluia!

3 So has the Church, in liturgy and song,
  In faith and love, through centuries of wrong,
  Borne witness to the truth in every tongue:
      Alleluia!

4 And did not Jesus sing a psalm that night
  When utmost evil strove against the Light?
  Then let us sing, for whom he won the fight:
      Alleluia!

5 Let every instrument be tuned for praise!
  Let all rejoice who have a voice to raise!
  And may God give us faith to sing always:
      Alleluia! Amen.

F. Pratt Green (1903–)

Words reprinted by permission of
Stainer & Bell Ltd.
For permission to reproduce see p. xiii.

THE SOCIAL ORDER

DESCANT FOR VERSE 5

John Wilson

Let all be tuned for praise! ____

All ____ re‑joice a___ voice to raise! ____

And may God give us faith to sing:_ Al ‑

‑ ‑ le ‑ lu ‑ ia! A ‑ ‑ men.

389
CREDITON   C.M.

Melody from Thomas Clark's
2nd Set of Psalm Tunes
[for] Country Choirs (c. 1807)

1 FROM thee all skill and science flow,
   All pity, care and love,
 All calm and courage, faith and hope;
   O pour them from above!

2 And part them, Lord, to each and all,
   As each and all shall need,
 To rise like incense, each to thee,
   In noble thought and deed.

3 And hasten, Lord, that perfect day
   When pain and death shall cease;
 And thy just rule shall fill the earth
   With health and light and peace;

4 When ever blue the sky shall gleam,
   And ever green the sod;
 And man's rude work deface no more
   The paradise of God.

Charles Kingsley (1819–75)

May also be sung to No. 397, ST MATTHEW

THE SOCIAL ORDER/Healing

390

KENWYN C.M.

E. J. Hopkins (1818–1901)

1 HEAL us, Immanuel! Hear our prayer;
   We wait to feel thy touch;
Deep-wounded souls to thee repair,
   And, Saviour, we are such.

2 Our faith is feeble, we confess;
   We faintly trust thy word;
But wilt thou pity us the less?
   Be that far from thee, Lord!

3 Remember him who once applied
   With trembling for relief:
'Lord, I believe!' with tears he cried,
   'O help my unbelief!'

4 She, too, who touched thee in the press,
   And healing virtue stole,
Was answered: 'Daughter, go in peace,
   Thy faith has made thee whole.'

5 Concealed amid the gathering throng,
   She would have shunned thy view;
And if her faith was firm and strong,
   Had strong misgivings too.

6 Like her, with hopes and fears we come
   To touch thee, if we may;
O send us not despairing home,
   Send none unhealed away!

William Cowper (1731–1800)

Healing

391

Melody, and most of the bass,
by Henry Lawes (1596–1662)

THE SOCIAL ORDER

1 I GREET thee, who my sure Redeemer art,
My only trust and Saviour of my heart,
    Who pain didst undergo for my poor sake;
    I pray thee from us anxious cares to take.

2 Thou art the King of mercy and of grace,
Reigning omnipotent in every place;
    So come, O King, and our whole being sway;
    Shine on us with the light of thy pure day.

3 Thou art the Life, by which alone we live,
And all our substance and our strength receive;
    Sustain us by thy faith and by thy power,
    And give us strength in every trying hour.

4 Thou hast the true and perfect gentleness,
No harshness hast thou and no bitterness:
    O grant to us the grace we find in thee,
    That we may dwell in perfect unity.

5 Our hope is in no other save in thee;
Our faith is built upon thy promise free;
    Lord, give us peace, and make us calm and sure,
    That in thy strength we evermore endure.

Attributed to *John Calvin* (1509–64)
tr. *Elizabeth Lee Smith* (1817–98) alt.

Healing

392(i)

HARESFIELD C.M.

J. Dykes Bower (1905–81)

392(ii)

STRACATHRO C.M.

Melody by
C. Hutcheson (1792–1860)

THE SOCIAL ORDER

1 IMMORTAL Love, forever full,
   Forever flowing free,
  Forever shared, forever whole,
   A never-ebbing sea!

2 Our outward lips confess the name
   All other names above;
  Love only knoweth whence it came,
   And comprehendeth love.

3 We may not climb the heavenly steeps
   To bring the Lord Christ down;
  In vain we search the lowest deeps,
   For him no depths can drown.

4 And not for signs in heaven above
   Or earth below they look,
  Who know with John his smile of love,
   With Peter his rebuke.

5 But warm, sweet, tender, even yet
   A present help is he;
  And faith has still its Olivet,
   And love its Galilee.

6 Through him the first fond prayers are said
   Our lips of childhood frame;
  The last low whispers of our dead
   Are burdened with his name.

7 Alone, O Love ineffable,
   Thy saving name is given!
  To turn aside from thee is hell,
   To walk with thee is heaven!

John Greenleaf Whittier (1807–92)

393

Unison

1 JESUS' hands were kind hands, doing good to all,
  Healing pain and sickness, blessing children small,
  Washing tired feet and saving those who fall;
  Jesus' hands were kind hands, doing good to all.

2 Take my hands, Lord Jesus, let them work for you;
  Make them strong and gentle, kind in all I do;
  Let me watch you, Jesus, till I'm gentle too,
  Till my hands are kind hands, quick to work for you.

Margaret Cropper (1886–1980)

THE SOCIAL ORDER

394

ETON L.M.

C. H. H. Parry (1848–1918)

1 LORD Christ, who on thy heart didst bear
   The burden of our shame and sin,
   And now on high dost stoop to share
   The fight without, the fear within;

2 Thy patience cannot know defeat,
   Thy pity will not be denied,
   Thy loving-kindness still is great,
   Thy tender mercies still abide.

3 So in our present need we pray
   To thee, our living, healing Lord,
   That we thy people, day by day,
   May follow thee and keep thy word;

4 That we may care, as thou hast cared,
   For sick and lame, for deaf and blind,
   And freely share, as thou hast shared,
   In all the sorrows of mankind;

5 That ours may be the holy task
   To help and bless, to heal and save;
   This is the privilege we ask,
   And this the happiness we crave.

6 So in thy mercy make us wise,
   And lead us in the ways of love,
   Until, at last, our wondering eyes
   Look on thy glorious face above.

Arnold Thomas (1848–1924) alt.

Healing

395

INVITATION L.M.

Later form of a tune
by J. F. Lampe (1703–51) mostly as in
The Temple Church Choral Service Book, 1880

For this tune in a lower key see No. 34

1 O CHRIST, the Healer, we have come
    To pray for health, to plead for friends.
  How can we fail to be restored,
    When reached by love that never ends?

2 From every ailment flesh endures
    Our bodies clamour to be freed;
  Yet in our hearts we would confess
    That wholeness is our deepest need.

3 How strong, O Lord, are our desires,
    How weak our knowledge of ourselves!
  Release in us those healing truths
    Unconscious pride resists or shelves.

4 In conflicts that destroy our health
    We diagnose the world's disease;
  Our common life declares our ills:
    Is there no cure, O Christ, for these?

5 Grant that we all, made one in faith,
    In your community may find
  The wholeness that, enriching us,
    Shall reach and shall enrich mankind.

F. Pratt Green (1903–   )

Words reprinted by permission of
Stainer & Bell Ltd.
For permission to reproduce see p. xiii.

THE SOCIAL ORDER

396

ST MATTHIAS 8 8.8 8.8 8.

W. H. Monk (1823–89)

1 O GOD, by whose almighty plan
  First order out of chaos stirred,
  And life, progressive at your word,
Matured through nature up to man;
  Grant us in light and love to grow,
  Your sovereign truth to seek and know.

2 O Christ, whose touch unveiled the blind,
  Whose presence warmed the lonely soul;
  Your love made broken sinners whole,
Your power cast devils from the mind.
  Grant us to bring your love, your care,
  Your health, to sufferers everywhere.

3 O Holy Spirit, by whose grace
  Our skills abide, our wisdom grows,
  In every healing work disclose
New paths to probe, new thoughts to trace.
  Grant us your wisest way to go
  In all we think, or speak, or do.

H. C. A. Gaunt (1902–83) alt.

Healing

397

Later form of a tune in
A Supplement to the New Version (1708)
Probably by William Croft (1678–1727)

ST MATTHEW   D.C.M.

1 THINE arm, O Lord, in days of old,
    Was strong to heal and save;
It triumphed o'er disease and death,
    O'er darkness and the grave.
To thee they went—the blind, the dumb,
    The palsied, and the lame,
The leper with his tainted life,
    The sick with fevered frame.

2 And, lo, thy touch brought life and health,
    Gave speech, and strength, and sight;
And youth renewed and frenzy calmed
    Owned thee, the Lord of light:
And now, O Lord, be near to bless,
    Almighty as of yore,
In crowded street, by restless couch,
    As by Gennesaret's shore.

3 Be thou our great deliverer still,
    Thou Lord of life and death;
Restore and quicken, soothe and bless,
    With thine almighty breath;
To hands that work and eyes that see
    Give wisdom's heavenly lore,
That whole and sick, and weak and strong,
    May praise thee evermore.

E. H. Plumptre (1821–91)

Healing

398

CURBAR EDGE 8.7.8.7. (Iambic)   Brian R. Hoare (1935–   )

1 YOUR will for us and others, Lord,
      Is perfect health and wholeness,
   And we must seek for nothing less
      Than life in all its fullness.

2 As Jesus dealt with human ills,
      Your purposes revealing,
   So may your servants in this day
      Be channels of your healing.

3 For suffering bodies, minds and souls
      That long for restoration,
   Accept our prayers of faith and love,
      And grant us all salvation;

4 So we would claim your promised grace,
      Your presence and protection;
   And, tasting now eternal life,
      Press on toward perfection.

Freda Head (1914–   )

THE SOCIAL ORDER/Healing

399

VERMONT L.M.

A. E. Floyd (1877–1974)

1 ALMIGHTY Father, who dost give
   The gift of life to all who live,
     Look down on all earth's sin and strife,
     And lift us to a nobler life.

2 Lift up our hearts, O King of kings,
   To brighter hopes and kindlier things,
     To visions of a larger good,
     And holier dreams of brotherhood.

3 Thy world is weary of its pain,
   Of selfish greed and fruitless gain,
     Of tarnished honour, falsely strong,
     And all its ancient deeds of wrong.

4 Hear thou the prayer thy servants pray,
   Uprising from all lands today,
     And o'er the vanquished powers of sin
     O bring thy great salvation in.

J. H. B. Masterman (1867–1933)

Justice and Peace

400

ST CYPRIAN 88.88.D. (Anapaestic)

J. Goss (1800–80)

1 ALL glory to God in the sky,
    And peace upon earth be restored!
O Jesus, exalted on high,
    Appear our omnipotent Lord!
Who, meanly in Bethlehem born,
    Didst stoop to redeem a lost race,
Once more to thy creatures return,
    And reign in thy kingdom of grace.

2 When thou in our flesh didst appear,
    All nature acknowledged thy birth;
Arose the acceptable year,
    And heaven was opened on earth;
Receiving its Lord from above,
    The world was united to bless
The giver of concord and love,
    The prince and the author of peace.

3 O wouldst thou again be made known!
    Again in thy Spirit descend,
And set up in each of thine own
    A kingdom that never shall end.
Thou only art able to bless,
    And make the glad nations obey,
And bid the dire enmity cease,
    And bow the whole world to thy sway.

4 Come then to thy servants again,
    Who long thy appearing to know;
Thy quiet and peaceable reign
    In mercy establish below;
All sorrow before thee shall fly,
    And anger and hatred be o'er,
And envy and malice shall die,
    And discord afflict us no more.

Charles Wesley (1707–88)

Justice and Peace

401

NETHERLANDS (WILHELMUS)

12 12. 12 12. .

(small notes organ only)

THE SOCIAL ORDER

1 ALMIGHTY Father, who for us thy Son didst give,
That men and women through his precious death might live,
In mercy guard us, lest by sloth and selfish pride
We cause to stumble those for whom the Saviour died.

2 We are thy stewards; thine our talents, wisdom, skill;
Our only glory that we will thy trust fulfil;
That we thy pleasure in our neighbours' good pursue,
If thou but workest in us both to will and do.

3 On just and unjust thou thy care dost freely shower;
Make us, thy children, free from greed and lust for power,
Lest human justice, yoked with man's unequal laws,
Oppress the needy and neglect the humble cause.

4 Let not our worship blind us to the claims of love;
But let thy manna lead us to the feast above,
To seek the country which by faith we now possess,
Where Christ, our treasure, reigns in peace and righteousness.

G. B. Caird (1917-84)

402

GRAFTON 8.7.8.7.8.7.

Melody from *Chants Ordinaires de l'Office Divin* (Paris, 1881)

THE SOCIAL ORDER

1 FOR the healing of the nations,
   Lord, we pray with one accord;
For a just and equal sharing
   Of the things that earth affords.
To a life of love in action
   Help us rise and pledge our word.

2 Lead us, Father, into freedom;
   From despair your world release,
That, redeemed from war and hatred,
   All may come and go in peace.
Show us how through care and goodness
   Fear will die and hope increase.

3 All that kills abundant living,
   Let it from the earth be banned;
Pride of status, race, or schooling,
   Dogmas that obscure your plan.
In our common quest for justice
   May we hallow life's brief span.

4 You, Creator-God, have written
   Your great name on humankind;
For our growing in your likeness
   Bring the life of Christ to mind;
That by our response and service
   Earth its destiny may find.

Fred Kaan (1929–   )

May also be sung to No. 409, RHUDDLAN

Words reprinted by permission of
Stainer & Bell Ltd.
For permission to reproduce see p. xiii.

403

CAROLYN 8.5.8.5.88.85.

Herbert Murrill (1909–52)

THE SOCIAL ORDER

1 GOD of love and truth and beauty,
   Hallowed be thy name;
Fount of order, law, and duty,
   Hallowed be thy name;
As in heaven thy hosts adore thee,
And their faces veil before thee,
So on earth, Lord, we implore thee,
   Hallowed be thy name.

2 Lord, remove our guilty blindness,
   Hallowed be thy name;
Show thy heart of loving-kindness,
   Hallowed be thy name;
By our hearts' deep-felt contrition,
By our minds' enlightened vision,
By our wills' complete submission,
   Hallowed be thy name.

3 In our worship, Lord most holy,
   Hallowed be thy name;
In our work, however lowly,
   Hallowed be thy name;
In each heart's imagination,
In the church's adoration,
In the conscience of the nation,
   Hallowed be thy name.

Timothy Rees (1874–1939)

VISION 15.15.15.7.

Walford Davies (1869–1941)
Arranged by John Wilson

Unison

1 IT is God who holds the na-tions in the hol-low of his hand;

Organ

It is God whose light is shi-ning in the dark-ness of the land;

It is God who builds his Ci-ty on the Rock and not on sand:

THE SOCIAL ORDER

May the liv-ing God be praised!

Choir ad lib.

May the liv-ing God be praised! God be praised!

Organ

v. 4

1 IT is God who holds the nations in the hollow of his hand;
It is God whose light is shining in the darkness of the land;
It is God who builds his City on the Rock and not on sand:
    May the living God be praised!

2 It is God whose purpose summons us to use the present hour;
Who recalls us to our senses when a nation's life turns sour;
In the discipline of freedom we shall know his saving power:
    May the living God be praised!

3 When a thankful nation, looking back, has cause to celebrate
Those who win our admiration by their service to the state;
When self-giving is a measure of the greatness of the great:
    May the living God be praised!

4 He reminds us every sunrise that the world is ours on lease:
For the sake of life tomorrow may our love for it increase;
May all races live together, share its riches, be at peace:
    May the living God be praised!

F. Pratt Green (1903–)

Words reprinted by permission of
Stainer & Bell Ltd.
For permission to reproduce see p. xiii.

Justice and Peace

Walter Greatorex (1877–1949)

THE SOCIAL ORDER

1 'LIFT up your hearts!' We lift them, Lord, to thee;
    Here at thy feet none other may we see;
        'Lift up your hearts!' E'en so, with one accord,
        We lift them up, we lift them to the Lord.

2 Above the swamps of subterfuge and shame,
    The deeds, the thoughts that honour may not name,
        The halting tongue that dares not tell the whole,
        O Lord of truth, lift every Christian soul!

3 Lift every gift that thou thyself hast given;
    Low lies the best till lifted up to heaven;
        Low lie the bounding heart, the teeming brain,
        Till, sent from God, they mount to God again.

4 And when the trumpet-call in after years—
    'Lift up your hearts!'—rings pealing in our ears,
        Still shall those hearts respond with full accord:
        'We lift them up, we lift them to the Lord!'

H. Montagu Butler (1833–1918)

406

TALBOT HOUSE (TOC H)   88.88.88.   Martin Shaw (1875–1958)

Small notes
organ only

THE SOCIAL ORDER

1 O CHRIST the Lord, O Christ the King,
   Who wide the gates of death didst fling,
   Whose place upon creation's throne
   By Easter triumph was made known,
   Rule now on earth from realms above,
   Subdue the nations by thy love.

2 Lord, vindicate against our greed
   The weak, whose tears thy justice plead;
   Thy pity, Lord, on those who lie
   Oppressed by war and tyranny;
   Show them the cross which thou didst bear,
   Give them the power that conquered there.

3 Let those whose pride usurps thy throne
   Acknowledge thou art Lord alone;
   Cause those whose lust wracks humankind
   Thy wrath to know, thy mercy find;
   Make all the rebel world proclaim
   The almighty power of thy blest name.

4 So shall creation's bondage cease,
   Its pangs of woe give birth to peace;
   And all the earth, redeemed by thee,
   Shall know a glorious liberty:
   O haste the time, make short the days,
   Till all our cries dissolve in praise!

R. T. Brooks (1918–85)

407

LOVE IS THE FULFILLING   11 10.11 10. (Refrain)   Richard Connolly (1927–)

Refrain* Unison

The law of Christ a-lone can make us free, And

love is the ful-fil-ling of the law, The law of

1st time, for repeating refrain

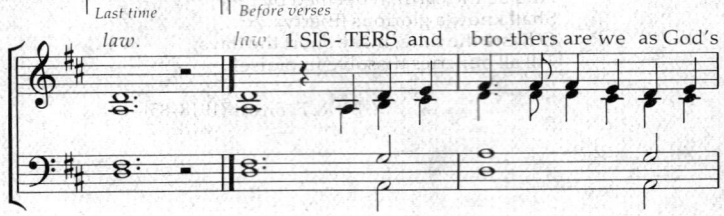

Last time | *Before verses*

law. law. 1 SIS-TERS and bro-thers are we as God's

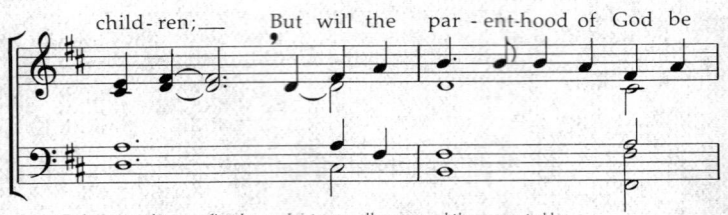

child-ren;__ But will the par-ent-hood of God be

* *The Refrain may be sung first by a soloist or small group and then repeated by the congregation. The verses may be sung either by the group or by the congregation.*

THE SOCIAL ORDER

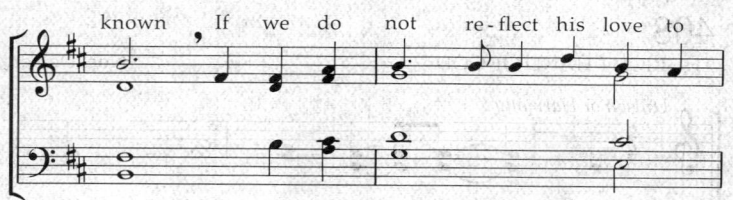

known, If we do not re-flect his love to

o-thers? In cha-ri - ty and jus-tice God is shown: *The law of*

Refrain

The law of Christ alone can make us free,
And love is the fulfilling of the law.
The law of Christ alone can make us free,
And love is the fulfilling of the law.

1 SISTERS and brothers are we as God's children;
   But will the parenthood of God be known
If we do not reflect his love to others?
   In charity and justice God is shown:

2 Millions believe the law of life is cunning
   Within a world of cruelty and greed;
How can they know God's charity and justice
   If helping hands have never reached their need?

3 Christ is at work through us who are his body:
   He chooses us to witness and to teach,
To heal and raise and liberate and strengthen,
   To be his hands and eyes, his heart and speech:

4 There is no promise that we shall not suffer,
   No promise that we shall not need to fight;
Only the word that love is our redemption,
   And freedom comes by turning to the light:

J. P. McAuley (1917–76) alt.

408

THE RIGHT HAND OF GOD   Irreg.   Noel Dexter

Unison or Harmony

1 THE right hand of God is writ-ing in our land, Writ - ing with pow - er and with love;
2 The right hand of God is point-ing in our land, Point - ing the way we must go;
3 The right hand of God is strik-ing in our land, Strik - ing out at en - vy, hate and greed;
4 The right hand of God is lift-ing in our land, Lift - ing the fal - len one by one;
5 The right hand of God is heal-ing in our land, Heal - ing broken bod - ies, minds and souls;
6 The right hand of God is plant-ing in our land, Plant - ing seeds of free - dom, hope and love;

THE SOCIAL ORDER

Our con-flicts and_ our fears, Our_
So cloud-ed is_ the way, So_
Our sel-fish-ness_ and lust, Our_
Each one is known by name, And_
So won-drous is_ its touch, With_
In these ma-ny-peo-pled lands, Let his

tri-umphs and_ our tears, Are re-
eas-i-ly_ we stray, But we're
pride and deeds un just, Are des-
lift-ed now_ from shame, By the
love that means so much, When we're
chil-dren all_ join hands, And be

-cord-ed by_ the right hand of God.
guid-ed by_ the right hand of God.
-troyed by_ the right hand of God.
lift-ing of_ the right hand of God.
healed by_ the right hand of God.
one_ with_ the right hand of God.

Patrick Prescod

Justice and Peace

409

RHUDDLAN 8.7.8.7.8.7.

Welsh Traditional Melody (as harmonised in *The English Hymnal*, 1906)

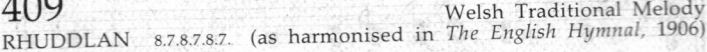

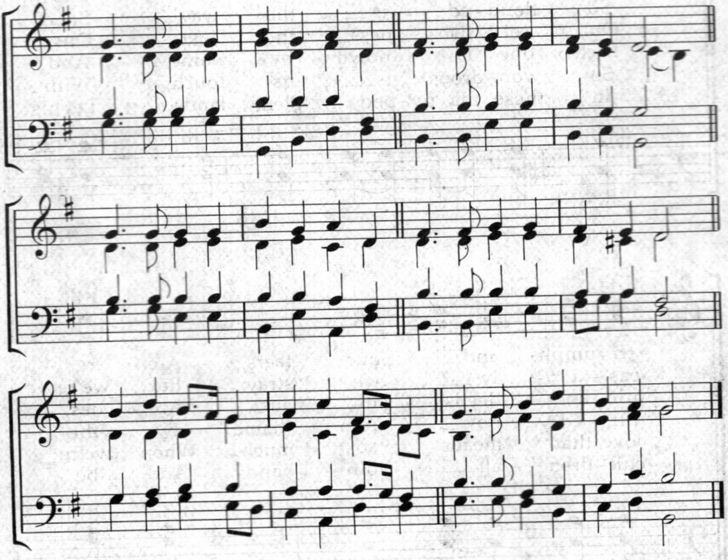

1 JUDGE eternal, throned in splendour,
   Lord of lords and King of kings,
With thy living fire of judgement
   Purge this realm of bitter things;
Solace all its wide dominion
   With the healing of thy wings.

2 Still the weary folk are pining
   For the hour that brings release;
And the city's crowded clangour
   Cries aloud for sin to cease;
And the homesteads and the woodlands
   Plead in silence for their peace.

3 Crown, O God, thine own endeavour;
   Cleave our darkness with thy sword;
Feed the faithless and the hungry
   With the richness of thy word;
Cleanse the body of this nation
   Through the glory of the Lord.

Henry Scott Holland (1847–1918) alt.

May also be sung to No. 712(ii), LINGWOOD

410

REDEMPTOR S.M.

John Wilson (1905–)

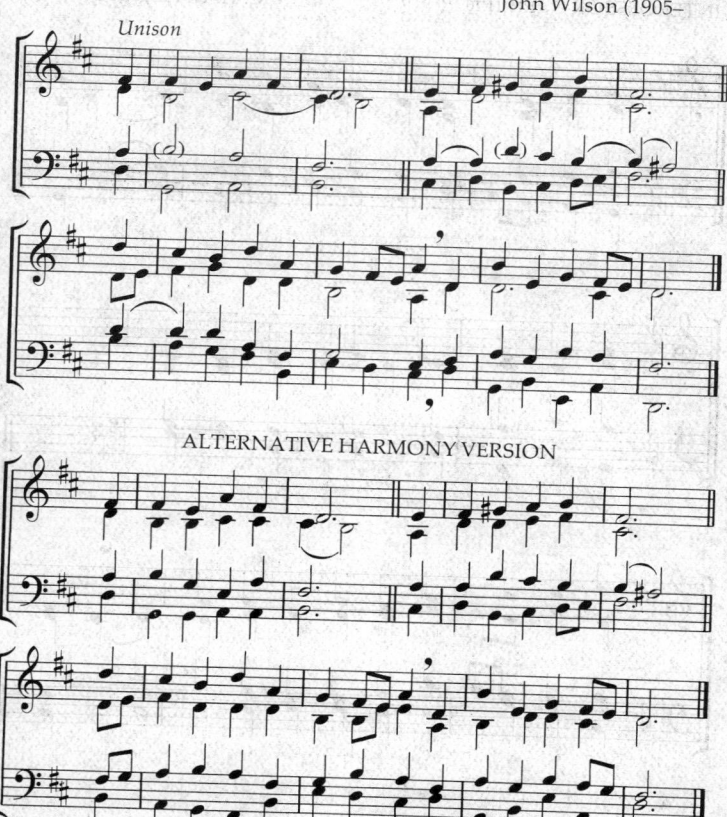

ALTERNATIVE HARMONY VERSION

1 THE Saviour's precious blood
    Has made all nations one.
  United let us praise this deed
    The Father's love has done.

2 In this vast world of men,
    A world so full of sin,
  No other theme can be our prayer
    Than this: your kingdom come!

3 In this sad world of war
    Can peace be ever found?
  Unless the love of Christ prevail,
    True peace will not abound.

4 The Master's new command
    Was: love each other well!
  O brothers, let us all unite
    To do his holy will.

Tai Jun Park (1900–   )
tr. *William Scott* and *Yung Oon Kim*

Justice and Peace

411
INTERCESSOR   11.10.11.10.

C. H. H. Parry (1848–1918)

THE SOCIAL ORDER

1 THY love, O God, has all mankind created,
   And led thy people to this present hour;
 In Christ we see love's glory consummated;
   Thy Spirit manifests his living power.

2 We bring thee, Lord, in fervent intercession
   The children of thy world-wide family;
 With contrite hearts we offer our confession,
   For we have sinned against thy charity.

3 From out the darkness of our hope's frustration,
   From all the broken idols of our pride,
 We turn to seek thy truth's illumination,
   And find thy mercy waiting at our side.

4 In pity look upon thy children's striving
   For life and freedom, peace and brotherhood;
 Till, at the fullness of thy truth arriving,
   We find in Christ the crown of every good.

5 Inspire thy church, mid earth's discordant voices,
   To preach the gospel of her Lord above;
 Until the day this warring world rejoices
   To hear the mighty harmonies of love—

6 Until the tidings earth has long awaited,
   From north to south, from east to west shall ring;
 And all the world, by Jesus liberated,
   Proclaims in jubilation: Christ is King!

Albert F. Bayly (1901-84)

412

INTERCESSOR 11.10.11.10.   C. H. H. Parry (1848–1918)

THE SOCIAL ORDER

1 WE turn to you, O God of every nation,
    Giver of life and origin of good;
  Your love is at the heart of all creation,
    Your hurt is people's broken brotherhood.

2 We turn to you, that we may be forgiven
    For crucifying Christ on earth again;
  We know that we have never wholly striven,
    Forgetting self, to love the other man.

3 Free every heart from pride and self-reliance;
    Our ways of thought inspire with simple grace;
  Break down among us barriers of defiance;
    Speak to the soul of all the human race.

4 On men who fight on earth for right relations
    We pray the light of love from hour to hour.
  Grant wisdom to the leaders of the nations,
    The gift of carefulness to those in power.

5 Teach us, good Lord, to serve the need of others;
    Help us to give and not to count the cost;
  Unite us all, for we are born as brothers;
    Defeat our Babel with your Pentecost.

Fred Kaan (1929–)

413

HERSTMONCEUX 46.6.6.6.8.

Ebenezer Prout (1835–1909),
Adapted by Eric Thiman (1900–75)

THE SOCIAL ORDER

1 WE pray for peace,
  But not the easy peace
  Built on complacency
  And not the truth of God;
  We pray for real peace,
  The peace God's love alone can seal.

2 We pray for peace,
  But not the cruel peace
  Leaving God's poor bereft
  And dying in distress;
  We pray for real peace,
  Enriching all humanity.

3 We pray for peace,
  And not the evil peace
  Defending unjust laws
  And nursing prejudice,
  But for the real peace
  Of justice, truth and brotherhood.

4 We pray for peace:
  Holy communion
  With Christ our risen Lord
  And all humanity;
  God's will fulfilled on earth,
  And all his creatures reconciled.

5 We pray for peace,
  And, for the sake of peace,
  Look to the risen Christ,
  Who gives the grace we need
  To serve the cause of peace
  And make our own self-sacrifice.

6 God, give us peace;
  If you withdraw your love
  There is no peace for us,
  Nor any hope of it.
  With you to lead us on,
  Through death or tumult, peace will come.

Alan Gaunt (1935–)

Justice and Peace

414

SHARPTHORNE   6.6.6.6.336.

Erik Routley (1917–82)

(Organ)

(Organ)

vv. 1—4

Last verse.

THE SOCIAL ORDER

1 WHAT does the Lord require
    For praise and offering?
What sacrifice desire,
    Or tribute bid you bring?
        Do justly;
        Love mercy;
Walk humbly with your God.

2 Rulers of earth, give ear!
    Should you not justice know?
Will God your pleading hear,
    While crime and cruelty grow?
        Do justly;
        Love mercy;
Walk humbly with your God.

3 All who gain wealth by trade,
    For whom the worker toils,
Think not to win God's aid,
    If greed your commerce soils:
        Do justly;
        Love mercy;
Walk humbly with your God.

4 Still down the ages ring
    The prophet's stern commands:
To merchant, worker, king,
    He brings God's high demands:
        Do justly;
        Love mercy;
Walk humbly with your God.

5 How shall our life fulfil
    God's law so hard and high?
Let Christ endue our will
    With grace to fortify;
        Then justly,
        In mercy,
We'll humbly walk with God.

Albert F. Bayly (1901-84)
based on Micah 6:6-8

415

ST SEPULCHRE L.M.

G. Cooper (1820–76)

1 AND art thou come with us to dwell,
   Our prince, our guide, our love, our Lord,
And is thy name Immanuel,
   God present with his world restored?

2 Thou bringest all again; with thee
   Is light, is space, is breadth, and room
For each thing fair, beloved, and free,
   To have its hour of life and bloom.

3 Each heart's deep instinct unconfessed;
   Each lowly wish, each daring claim;
All, all that life has long repressed
   Unfolds, undreading blight or blame.

4 Thy reign eternal will not cease;
   Thy years are sure, and glad, and slow;
Within thy mighty world of peace
   The humblest flower has leave to blow.

5 The world is glad for thee! The heart
   Is glad for thee! And all is well,
And fixed, and sure, because thou art,
   Whose name is called Immanuel.

Dora Greenwell (1821–82)

THE HUMAN CONDITION

416

MARTYRDOM C.M.

Melody by Hugh Wilson (1766–1824)

1 AS pants the hart for cooling streams
   When heated in the chase,
   So longs my soul, O God, for thee,
   And thy refreshing grace.

2 For thee, my God, the living God,
   My thirsty soul doth pine;
   O when shall I behold thy face,
   Thou Majesty divine?

3 God of my strength, how long shall I,
   Like one forgotten, mourn—
   Forlorn, forsaken, and exposed
   To my oppressor's scorn?

4 Why restless, why cast down, my soul?
   Hope still, and thou shalt sing
   The praise of him who is thy God,
   Thy health's eternal spring.

5 To Father, Son, and Holy Ghost,
   The God whom we adore,
   Be glory, as it was, is now,
   And shall be evermore.

Nahum Tate (1652–1715) and
Nicholas Brady (1659–1726)
based on Psalm 42

THE HUMAN CONDITION

1 CAN I forget bright Eden's grace,
  My beauteous crown and princely place,
    All lost, all lost to me?
  Long as I live I'll praise and sing
  My wondrous all-restoring King,
    Victor of Calvary.

2 Lo! Faith, behold the place, the tree
  Whereon the Prince of Heaven, for me,
    All innocent, was nailed;
  One here has crushed the dragon's might;
  Two fell, but One has won the fight;
    Christ Jesus has prevailed.

*William Williams (1717–91)
tr. H. A. Hodges (1905–76)*

THE HUMAN CONDITION

418

WARWICK C.M.
Samuel Stanley (1767–1822)
Harmonisation by David Evans (1874–1948)

1 COME, O thou all-victorious Lord,
   Thy power to us make known;
   Strike with the hammer of thy word,
   And break these hearts of stone.

2 Give us ourselves and thee to know,
   In this our gracious day;
   Repentance unto life bestow,
   And take our sins away.

3 Conclude us first in unbelief,
   And freely then release;
   Fill every soul with sacred grief,
   And then with sacred peace.

4 Impoverish, Lord, and then relieve,
   And then enrich the poor;
   The knowledge of our sickness give,
   The knowledge of our cure.

5 That blessèd sense of guilt impart,
   And then remove the load;
   Trouble, and wash the troubled heart
   In the atoning blood.

6 Our desperate state through sin declare,
   And speak our sins forgiven;
   By perfect holiness prepare,
   And take us up to heaven.

Charles Wesley (1707–88)

THE HUMAN CONDITION

419

PLAISTOW L.M.

Melody from *Magdalen Hymns* (*c.*1760)

With great breadth

1 CREATOR of the earth and skies,
　　To whom all truth and power belong,
Grant us your truth to make us wise;
　　Grant us your power to make us strong.

2 We have not known you: to the skies
　　Our monuments of folly soar;
And all our self-wrought miseries
　　Have made us trust ourselves the more.

3 We have not loved you: far and wide
　　The wreckage of our hatred spreads;
And evils wrought by human pride
　　Recoil on unrepentant heads.

4 We long to end this worldwide strife:
　　How shall we follow in your way?
Speak to us all your words of life,
　　Until our darkness turn to day.

Donald Hughes (1911–67) alt.

May also be sung to No. 425, BRESLAU

THE HUMAN CONDITION

420(i)

ST MARY C.M.

Melody from E. Prys's *Llyfr y Psalmau* (1621)
Harmony based on setting in Playford's *Psalms* (1677)

For this tune in another version and a higher key see No. 446

1 IN Adam we have all been one,
   One in rebellious man;
  We all have fled that evening voice
   That sought us as we ran.

2 We fled thee and, in losing thee,
   We lost our brother too;
  Each singly sought and claimed his own,
   Each man his brother slew.

3 But thy strong love, it sought us still,
   And sent thine only Son
  That we might hear his Shepherd's voice
   And, hearing him, be one.

4 O thou who, when we loved thee not,
   Didst love and save us all,
  Thou great Good Shepherd of mankind,
   O hear us when we call.

5 Send us thy Spirit, teach us truth;
   Thou Son, O set us free
  From fancied wisdom, self-sought ways,
   To make us one in thee.

6 Then shall our song united rise
   To thine eternal throne,
  Where with the Father evermore
   And Spirit thou art one.

Martin Franzmann (1907–76) alt. *(See also following page)*

THE HUMAN CONDITION

420(i) (cont.)

DESCANT VERSION FOR VERSE 6

Arranged by John Wilson

Our song shall rise, to thine e-ter-nal throne, Where with the Fa-ther ev-er-more, And Spi-rit thou art one.

THE HUMAN CONDITION

420(ii)

ST NICHOLAS C.M.

Later form of a melody from
Holdroyd's *Spiritual Man's Companion* (1753)

1 IN Adam we have all been one,
  One in rebellious man;
We all have fled that evening voice
  That sought us as we ran.

2 We fled thee and, in losing thee,
  We lost our brother too;
Each singly sought and claimed his own,
  Each man his brother slew.

3 But thy strong love, it sought us still,
  And sent thine only Son
That we might hear his Shepherd's voice
  And, hearing him, be one.

4 O thou who, when we loved thee not,
  Didst love and save us all,
Thou great Good Shepherd of mankind,
  O hear us when we call.

5 Send us thy Spirit, teach us truth;
  Thou Son, O set us free
From fancied wisdom, self-sought ways,
  To make us one in thee.

6 Then shall our song united rise
  To thine eternal throne,
Where with the Father evermore
  And Spirit thou art one.

Martin Franzmann (1907–76) alt.

THE HUMAN CONDITION

BROADMEAD (DAVID'S HARP) L.M.   Melody by J. Daniell (d. 1866)

1 HOW blest is life if lived for thee,
    My loving Saviour and my Lord!
  No pleasures that the world can give
    Such perfect gladness can afford —

2 To know I am thy ransomed child,
    Bought by thine own most precious blood;
  And from thy loving hand to take
    With grateful heart each gift of good;

3 All day to walk beneath thy smile,
    Watching thine eye to guide me still;
  To rest at night beneath thy care,
    Guarded by thee from every ill;

4 To feel that though I journey on
    By stony paths and rugged ways,
  Thy blessèd feet have gone before,
    And strength is given for weary days.

5 Such love shall ever make me glad,
    Strong in thy strength to work or rest,
  Until I see thee face to face,
    And in thy light am fully blest.

Anonymous

THE HUMAN CONDITION

422

ST LEONARD (SMART) C.M.

Henry Smart (1813–79)

For this tune in a higher key see No. 383

1 I WANT a principle within
    Of jealous, godly fear,
A sensibility of sin,
    A pain to feel it near.

2 I want the first approach to feel
    Of pride or fond desire,
To catch the wandering of my will,
    And quench the kindling fire.

3 That I from thee no more may part,
    No more thy goodness grieve,
The filial awe, the fleshly heart,
    The tender conscience, give.

4 Quick as the apple of an eye,
    O God, my conscience make;
Awake my soul when sin is nigh,
    And keep it still awake.

5 O may the least omission pain
    My well-instructed soul,
And drive me to the blood again
    Which makes the wounded whole.

Charles Wesley (1707–88)

THE HUMAN CONDITION

423

ELY L.M.

Melody by T. Turton (1780–1864)

THE HUMAN CONDITION

1 LORD, I was blind! I could not see
    In thy marred visage any grace;
    But now the beauty of thy face
In radiant vision dawns on me.

2 Lord, I was deaf! I could not hear
    The thrilling music of thy voice;
    But now I hear thee and rejoice,
And all thine uttered words are dear.

3 Lord, I was dumb! I could not speak
    The grace and glory of thy name;
    But now, as touched with living flame,
My lips thine eager praises wake.

4 Lord, I was dead! I could not stir
    My lifeless soul to come to thee;
    But now, since thou hast quickened me,
I rise from sin's dark sepulchre.

5 For thou hast made the blind to see,
    The deaf to hear, the dumb to speak,
    The dead to live; and lo, I break
The chains of my captivity!

William Tidd Matson (1833–99)

Welsh Hymn Melody
Harmonised by
David Evans (1874–1948)

THE HUMAN CONDITION

1 O CRUCIFIED Redeemer,
    Whose life-blood we have spilt,
  To you we raise our guilty hands,
    And humbly own our guilt;
  Today we see your passion
    Spread open to our gaze;
  The crowded street, the country road,
    Its Calvary displays.

2 We hear your cry of anguish,
    We see your life outpoured,
  Where battlefields run red with blood,
    Our neighbours' blood, O Lord;
  And in that other battle,
    The fight for daily bread,
  Where might is right and self is king,
    We see your thorn-crowned head.

3 The groaning of creation,
    Wrung out by pain and care,
  The anguish of a million hearts
    That break in dumb despair;
  O crucified Redeemer,
    These are your cries of pain;
  O may they break our selfish hearts,
    And love come in to reign.

Timothy Rees (1874–1939)

THE HUMAN CONDITION

German Traditional Melody
As harmonised by
Mendelssohn in *St. Paul* (1836)

For this tune in a lower key, with a Descant Version, see No. 775

THE HUMAN CONDITION

1 LORD, save thy world; in bitter need
   Thy children lift their cry to thee;
We wait thy liberating deed
   To signal hope and set us free.

2 Lord, save thy world; our souls are bound
   In iron chains of fear and pride;
High walls of ignorance around
   Our faces from each other hide.

3 Lord, save thy world; we strive in vain
   To save ourselves without thine aid;
What skill and science slowly gain
   Is soon to evil ends betrayed.

4 Lord, save thy world; but thou hast sent
   The Saviour whom we sorely need;
For us his tears and blood were spent,
   That from our bonds we might be freed.

5 Then save us now, by Jesus' power,
   And use the lives thy love sets free,
To bring at last the glorious hour
   When all will find thy liberty.

Albert F. Bayly (1901-84)

THE HUMAN CONDITION

1 O GOD of earth and altar,
   Bow down and hear our cry;
Our earthly rulers falter,
   Our people drift and die;
The walls of gold entomb us,
   The swords of scorn divide;
Take not thy thunder from us,
   But take away our pride.

2 From all that terror teaches,
   From lies of tongue and pen,
From all the easy speeches
   That comfort cruel men,
From sale and profanation
   Of honour and the sword,
From sleep and from damnation,
   Deliver us, good Lord!

3 Tie in a living tether
   The prince and priest and thrall;
Bind all our lives together;
   Smite us and save us all;
In ire and exultation,
   Aflame with faith, and free,
Lift up a living nation,
   A single sword to thee.

G. K. Chesterton (1874–1936)

May also be sung to No. 176, PASSION CHORALE

427(i)
OXFORD NEW   C.M.

By 'Mr Coombes' in *Twenty Psalm Tunes* (c. 1775);
probably George Coombes of Bristol (d. 1769)
(melody slightly simplified)

427(ii)
WEST BURN   C.M.

K. G. Finlay (1882–1974)

THE HUMAN CONDITION

1 O LIFT us up, strong Son of God;
   Restore our fallen race;
  We who have marred your image shall
   Regain it through your grace.

2 The subtle serpent of our sin
   Ensnares our helpless feet;
  The lifted serpent of your health
   Can make our souls complete.

3 And you, who came into the world
   To take our human frame,
  Did not condemn our fallen state,
   But took away our shame.

4 Your law is holy, just and good;
   But still we fail to do
  All that your gracious words require
   To keep us close to you.

5 So lift us up, strong Son of God,
   Restore your fallen race;
  We who have lost your image shall
   Regain it through your grace.

Cyril G. Hambly (1931–   )

E. J. Hopkins (1818–1901)

1 THERE is no moment of my life,
   No place where I may go,
No action which God does not see,
   No thought he does not know.

2 Before I speak, my words are known,
   And all that I decide,
To come or go: God knows my choice,
   And makes himself my guide.

3 If I should close my eyes to him,
   He comes to give me sight;
If I should go where all is dark,
   He makes my darkness light.

4 He knew my days before all days,
   Before I came to be;
He keeps me, loves me, in my ways—
   No lover such as he.

Brian Foley (1919–)
based on Psalm 139

THE HUMAN CONDITION

429

ST MARTIN   8.6.8.6.88.7.

J. H. Sheppard (1835–79)

THE HUMAN CONDITION

1 OUT of the depths I cry to thee,
    Lord God! O hear my prayer!
Incline a gracious ear to me,
    And bid me not despair:
If thou rememberest each misdeed,
If each should have its rightful meed,
    Lord, who shall stand before thee?

2 'Tis through thy love alone we gain
    The pardon of our sin;
The strictest life is but in vain,
    Our works can nothing win;
That none should boast himself of aught,
But own in fear thy grace hath wrought
    What in him seemeth righteous.

3 Wherefore my hope is in the Lord,
    My works I count but dust;
I build not there, but on his word,
    And in his goodness trust.
Up to his care myself I yield,
He is my tower, my rock, my shield,
    And for his help I tarry.

4 And though it linger till the night,
    And round again till morn,
My heart shall ne'er mistrust thy might,
    Nor count itself forlorn.
Do thus, O ye of Israel's seed,
Ye of the Spirit born indeed,
    Wait for your God's appearing.

5 Though great our sins and sore our wounds,
    And deep and dark our fall,
His helping mercy hath no bounds,
    His love surpasseth all:
Our trusty loving Shepherd, he
Who shall at last set Israel free
    From all their sin and sorrow.

Martin Luther (1483–1546)
tr. *Catherine Winkworth* (1827–78)
based on Psalm 130

1 WHAT Adam's disobedience cost,
   Let holy scripture say:
 Mankind estranged, an Eden lost,
   And then a judgement day:
   Each day a judgement day.

2 An Ark of Mercy rode the flood;
   But man, where waters swirled,
 Rebuilt, impatient of the good,
   Another fallen world:
   An unrepentant world.

3 And now a Child is Adam's heir,
   Is Adam's hope, and Lord.
 Sing joyful carols everywhere
   That Eden is restored:
   In Jesus is restored.

4 Regained is Adam's blessedness;
   The angels sheathe their swords;
 In joyful carols all confess
   The kingdom is the Lord's:
   The glory is the Lord's!

F. Pratt Green (1903–   )

Words reprinted by permission of
Stainer & Bell Ltd.
For permission to reproduce see p. xiii.

THE HUMAN CONDITION

431

FULDA L.M.

Melody from Gardiner's *Sacred Melodies* (1815)

1 WHERE cross the crowded ways of life,
   Where sound the cries of race and clan,
Above the noise of selfish strife,
   We hear thy voice, O Son of Man.

2 In haunts of wretchedness and need,
   On shadowed thresholds dark with fears,
From paths where hide the lures of greed,
   We catch the vision of thy tears.

3 The cup of water given for thee
   Still holds the freshness of thy grace;
Yet long these multitudes to see
   The strong compassion of thy face.

4 O Master, from the mountain-side
   Make haste to heal these hearts of pain;
Among these restless throngs abide,
   O tread the city's streets again:

5 Till sons of men shall learn thy love,
   And follow where thy feet have trod;
Till glorious from thy heaven above
   Shall come the city of our God.

Frank Mason North (1850–1935)

May also be sung to No. 12, ST BARTHOLOMEW

THE HUMAN CONDITION

432

CLINTON C.M.

C. H. H. Parry (1848–1918)

1 WHO fathoms the eternal thought?
　　Who talks of scheme and plan?
　The Lord is God! He needeth not
　　The poor device of man.

2 I see the wrong that round me lies,
　　I feel the guilt within;
　I hear, with groan and travail-cries,
　　The world confess its sin.

3 Yet, in the maddening maze of things,
　　And tossed by storm and flood,
　To one fixed stake my spirit clings;
　　I know that God is good!

4 And if my heart and flesh are weak
　　To bear an untried pain,
　The bruisèd reed he will not break,
　　But strengthen and sustain.

5 I know not what the future hath
　　Of marvel or surprise,
　Assured alone that life and death
　　His mercy underlies.

John Greenleaf Whittier (1807–92)

THE HUMAN CONDITION

III

GOD'S PEOPLE

433(i)

TRURO L.M. Melody from T. Williams's *Psalmodia Evangelica* (1789)

DESCANT FOR VERSE 5

John Wilson

Soprano (and optional Alto)

5 Where pure es-sen-tial joy__ is found, The

Lord's re-deemed their heads shall raise, With ev-er-last-ing

glad-ness crowned, And filled with love, and lost in praise.

A PILGRIM PEOPLE

433(ii)
DEUS TUORUM MILITUM (GRENOBLE) L.M.

Melody from *Grenoble Antiphoner* (1753)

1 ARM of the Lord, awake, awake!
   Thine own immortal strength put on;
   With terror clothed, hell's kingdom shake,
   And cast thy foes with fury down.

2 As in the ancient days appear;
   The sacred annals speak thy fame:
   Be now omnipotently near,
   To endless ages still the same.

3 Thy arm, Lord, is not shortened now,
   It wants not now the power to save;
   Still present with thy people, thou
   Bear'st them through life's disparted wave.

4 By death and hell pursued in vain,
   To thee the ransomed seed shall come;
   Shouting, their heavenly Zion gain,
   And pass through death triumphant home.

5 Where pure essential joy is found,
   The Lord's redeemed their heads shall raise,
   With everlasting gladness crowned,
   And filled with love, and lost in praise.

Charles Wesley (1707–88)

Covenant and Deliverance

434(i)
WRESTLING JACOB 88.88.88. S. S. Wesley (1810–76)

1 COME, O thou Traveller unknown,
  Whom still I hold, but cannot see!
My company before is gone,
  And I am left alone with thee;
With thee all night I mean to stay,
And wrestle till the break of day.

2 I need not tell thee who I am,
  My misery and sin declare;
Thyself hast called me by my name;
  Look on thy hands, and read it there:
But who, I ask thee, who art thou?
Tell me thy name, and tell me now.

3 In vain thou strugglest to get free;
  I never will unloose my hold!
Art thou the Man that died for me?
  The secret of thy love unfold:
Wrestling, I will not let thee go,
Till I thy name, thy nature know.

4 Wilt thou not yet to me reveal
  Thy new, unutterable name?
Tell me, I still beseech thee, tell;
  To know it now resolved I am:
Wrestling, I will not let thee go,
Till I thy name, thy nature know.

A PILGRIM PEOPLE

5 What though my shrinking flesh complain,
    And murmur to contend so long?
I rise superior to my pain,
    When I am weak, then I am strong;
And when my all of strength shall fail,
I shall with the God-Man prevail.

6 Yield to me now; for I am weak,
    But confident in self-despair;
Speak to my heart, in blessings speak,
    Be conquered by my instant prayer;
Speak, or thou never hence shalt move,
And tell me if thy name is Love.

7 'Tis Love! 'Tis Love! Thou diedst for me!
    I hear thy whisper in my heart;
The morning breaks, the shadows flee,
    Pure, universal love thou art;
To me, to all, thy mercies move:
Thy nature and thy name is Love.

8 My prayer has power with God; the grace
    Unspeakable I now receive;
Through faith I see thee face to face,
    I see thee face to face, and live!
In vain I have not wept and strove:
Thy nature and thy name is Love.

9 I know thee, Saviour, who thou art,
    Jesus, the feeble sinner's friend;
Nor wilt thou with the night depart,
    But stay and love me to the end;
Thy mercies never shall remove:
Thy nature and thy name is Love.

10 The Sun of Righteousness on me
    Has risen with healing in his wings;
Withered my nature's strength, from thee
    My soul its life and succour brings;
My help is all laid up above:
Thy nature and thy name is Love.

11 Contented now upon my thigh
    I halt, till life's short journey end;
All helplessness, all weakness, I
    On thee alone for strength depend;
Nor have I power from thee to move:
Thy nature and thy name is Love.

12 Lame as I am, I take the prey,
    Hell, earth, and sin with ease o'ercome;
I leap for joy, pursue my way,
    And as a bounding hart fly home,
Through all eternity to prove
Thy nature and thy name is Love.

Charles Wesley (1707–88)
based on Genesis 32:26–32

Covenant and Deliverance

434(ii)

DAVID'S HARP   88.88.88.

Melody and bass by
Robert King (1676–1713)
Mean parts by John Wilson

1 COME, O thou Traveller unknown,
    Whom still I hold, but cannot see!
My company before is gone,
    And I am left alone with thee;
With thee all night I mean to stay,
And wrestle till the break of day.

2 I need not tell thee who I am,
    My misery and sin declare;
Thyself hast called me by my name;
    Look on thy hands, and read it there:
But who, I ask thee, who art thou?
Tell me thy name, and tell me now.

3 In vain thou strugglest to get free;
    I never will unloose my hold!
Art thou the Man that died for me?
    The secret of thy love unfold:
Wrestling, I will not let thee go,
Till I thy name, thy nature know.

4 Wilt thou not yet to me reveal
    Thy new, unutterable name?
Tell me, I still beseech thee, tell;
    To know it now resolved I am:
Wrestling, I will not let thee go,
Till I thy name, thy nature know.

A PILGRIM PEOPLE

5 What though my shrinking flesh complain,
       And murmur to contend so long?
   I rise superior to my pain,
       When I am weak, then I am strong;
   And when my all of strength shall fail,
   I shall with the God-Man prevail.

6 Yield to me now; for I am weak,
       But confident in self-despair;
   Speak to my heart, in blessings speak,
       Be conquered by my instant prayer;
   Speak, or thou never hence shalt move,
   And tell me if thy name is Love.

7 'Tis Love! 'Tis Love! Thou diedst for me!
       I hear thy whisper in my heart;
   The morning breaks, the shadows flee,
       Pure, universal love thou art;
   To me, to all, thy mercies move:
   Thy nature and thy name is Love.

8 My prayer has power with God; the grace
       Unspeakable I now receive;
   Through faith I see thee face to face,
       I see thee face to face, and live!
   In vain I have not wept and strove:
   Thy nature and thy name is Love.

9 I know thee, Saviour, who thou art,
       Jesus, the feeble sinner's friend;
   Nor wilt thou with the night depart,
       But stay and love me to the end;
   Thy mercies never shall remove:
   Thy nature and thy name is Love.

10 The Sun of Righteousness on me
       Has risen with healing in his wings;
   Withered my nature's strength, from thee
       My soul its life and succour brings;
   My help is all laid up above:
   Thy nature and thy name is Love.

11 Contented now upon my thigh
       I halt, till life's short journey end;
   All helplessness, all weakness, I
       On thee alone for strength depend;
   Nor have I power from thee to move:
   Thy nature and thy name is Love.

12 Lame as I am, I take the prey,
       Hell, earth, and sin with ease o'ercome;
   I leap for joy, pursue my way,
       And as a bounding hart fly home,
   Through all eternity to prove
   Thy nature and thy name is Love.

Charles Wesley (1707–88)
based on Genesis 32:26–32

Covenant and Deliverance

435(i)

MOUNTAIN CHRISTIANS Irregular

Attributed to John Mannin (1802–65) in the
Fellowship Hymn Book (1909)

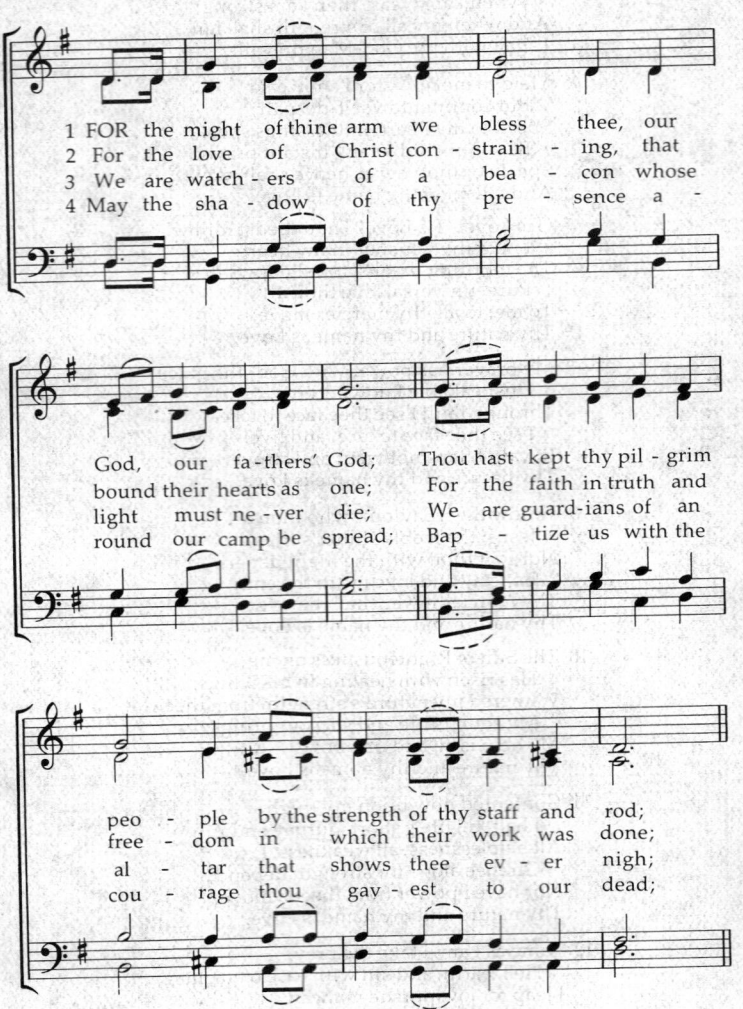

1 FOR the might of thine arm we bless thee, our
2 For the love of Christ con - strain - ing, that
3 We are watch - ers of a bea - con whose
4 May the sha - dow of thy pre - sence a -

God, our fa - thers' God; Thou hast kept thy pil - grim
bound their hearts as one; For the faith in truth and
light must ne - ver die; We are guard - ians of an
round our camp be spread; Bap - tize us with the

peo - ple by the strength of thy staff and rod;
free - dom in which their work was done;
al - tar that shows thee ev - er nigh;
cou - rage thou gav - est to our dead;

A PILGRIM PEOPLE

Thou hast called us to the jour - ney which
For the peace of God's e - van - gel where -
We are child - ren of thy free - men who
O _____ keep us in the path - way their

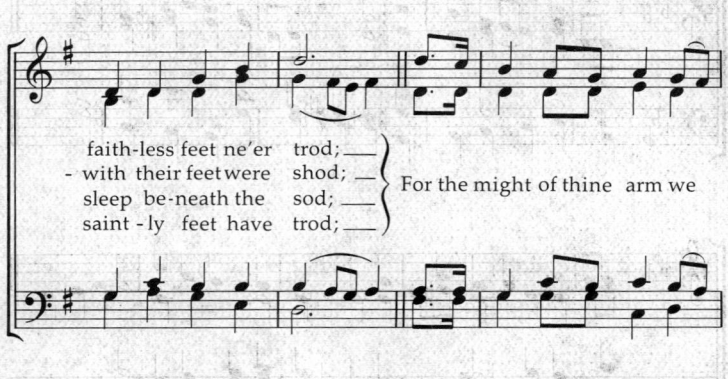

faith-less feet ne'er trod; ___
- with their feet were shod; ___
sleep be-neath the sod; ___
saint - ly feet have trod; ___

For the might of thine arm we

bless thee, our God, our _ fa - thers' God.

Charles Silvester Horne (1865–1914)

Covenant and Deliverance

435(ii)

TANWORTH Irreg.

Cyril V. Taylor (1907–   )

A PILGRIM PEOPLE

1 FOR the might of thine arm we bless thee, our God, our
    fathers' God;
Thou hast kept thy pilgrim people by the strength of thy
    staff and rod;
Thou hast called us to the journey which faithless feet
    ne'er trod;
For the might of thine arm we bless thee, our God, our
    fathers' God.

2 For the love of Christ constraining, that bound their
    hearts as one;
For the faith in truth and freedom in which their work
    was done;
For the peace of God's evangel wherewith their feet
    were shod;
For the might of thine arm we bless thee, our God, our
    fathers' God.

3 We are watchers of a beacon whose light must never
    die;
We are guardians of an altar that shows thee ever nigh;
We are children of thy freemen who sleep beneath the
    sod;
For the might of thine arm we bless thee, our God, our
    fathers' God.

4 May the shadow of thy presence around our camp be
    spread;
Baptize us with the courage thou gavest to our dead;
O keep us in the pathway their saintly feet have trod;
For the might of thine arm we bless thee, our God, our
    fathers' God.

Charles Silvester Horne (1865–1914)

436(i)

GOTT WILL'S MACHEN   8.7.8.7.   Melody by J. Steiner (1668–1761)

436(ii)

SUSSEX   8.7.8.7.   Adapted from an English Traditional Melody by Ralph Vaughan Williams (1872–1958)

A PILGRIM PEOPLE

1 FATHER, hear the prayer we offer:
   Not for ease that prayer shall be,
But for strength that we may ever
   Live our lives courageously.

2 Not for ever in green pastures
   Do we ask our way to be;
But the steep and rugged pathway
   May we tread rejoicingly.

3 Not for ever by still waters
   Would we idly rest and stay;
But would smite the living fountains
   From the rocks along our way.

4 Be our strength in hours of weakness,
   In our wanderings be our guide;
Through endeavour, failure, danger,
   Father, be thou at our side.

Love Maria Willis (1824–1908) and others

Covenant and Deliverance

437

CWM RHONDDA 8.7.8.7.4.7. John Hughes (1873–1932)

A PILGRIM PEOPLE

1 GUIDE me, O thou great Jehovah,
    Pilgrim through this barren land;
  I am weak, but thou art mighty;
    Hold me with thy powerful hand:
      Bread of heaven,
      Feed me now and evermore.

2 Open thou the crystal fountain,
    Whence the healing stream shall flow;
  Let the fiery, cloudy pillar
    Lead me all my journey through:
      Strong Deliverer,
      Be thou still my strength and shield.

3 When I tread the verge of Jordan,
    Bid my anxious fears subside;
  Death of death, and hell's destruction,
    Land me safe on Canaan's side:
      Songs of praises
      I will ever give to thee.

William Williams (1717–91)
tr. *Peter Williams* (1722–96) and others

Covenant and Deliverance

438

JOSIAH 7.6. 7.6. 7.6. 7.7. 7.6.

William Arnold (1768–1832)
(slightly adapted)

A PILGRIM PEOPLE

1 GREAT is our redeeming Lord
   In power, and truth, and grace;
Him, by highest heaven adored,
   His church on earth doth praise.
In the city of our God,
   In his holy mount below,
Publish, spread his name abroad,
   And all his greatness show.

2 For thy loving-kindness, Lord,
   We in thy temple stay;
Here thy faithful love record,
   Thy saving power display.
With thy name thy praise is known,
   Glorious thy perfections shine;
Earth's remotest bounds shall own
   Thy works are all divine.

3 See the gospel church secure,
   And founded on a rock;
All her promises are sure;
   Her bulwarks who can shock?
Count her every precious shrine;
   Tell, to after-ages tell:
Fortified by power divine,
   The church can never fail.

4 Zion's God is all our own,
   Who on his love rely;
We his pardoning love have known,
   And live to Christ, and die.
To the new Jerusalem
   He our faithful guide shall be:
Him we claim, and rest in him,
   Through all eternity.

Charles Wesley (1707–88)
based on Psalm 48

Covenant and Deliverance

439(i)

MONMOUTH   88.8.D.

Moving freely

Melody and bass by Gabriel Davis (d. 1824)

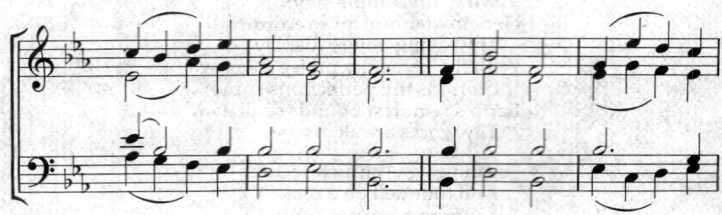

A PILGRIM PEOPLE

1 I'LL praise my Maker while I've breath;
   And when my voice is lost in death,
      Praise shall employ my nobler powers:
   My days of praise shall ne'er be past,
   While life and thought and being last,
      Or immortality endures.

2 Happy are they whose hopes rely
   On Israel's God! He made the sky,
      And earth and sea, with all their train:
   His truth for ever stands secure;
   He saves the oppressed, he feeds the poor,
      And none shall find his promise vain.

3 The Lord pours eyesight on the blind;
   The Lord supports the fainting mind;
      He sends the labouring conscience peace;
   He helps the stranger in distress,
   The widow and the fatherless,
      And grants the prisoner sweet release.

4 I'll praise him while he lends me breath;
   And when my voice is lost in death,
      Praise shall employ my nobler powers:
   My days of praise shall ne'er be past,
   While life and thought and being last,
      Or immortality endures.

Isaac Watts (1674–1748)
based on Psalm 146

Covenant and Deliverance

439(ii)

DRESDEN (LUCERNE) 88.8.D   Melody by J. Schmidlin (1722–72)

A PILGRIM PEOPLE

1 I'LL praise my Maker while I've breath;
  And when my voice is lost in death,
    Praise shall employ my nobler powers:
  My days of praise shall ne'er be past,
  While life and thought and being last,
    Or immortality endures.

2 Happy are they whose hopes rely
  On Israel's God! He made the sky,
    And earth and sea, with all their train:
  His truth for ever stands secure;
  He saves the oppressed, he feeds the poor,
    And none shall find his promise vain.

3 The Lord pours eyesight on the blind;
  The Lord supports the fainting mind;
    He sends the labouring conscience peace;
  He helps the stranger in distress,
  The widow and the fatherless,
    And grants the prisoner sweet release.

4 I'll praise him while he lends me breath;
  And when my voice is lost in death,
    Praise shall employ my nobler powers:
  My days of praise shall ne'er be past,
  While life and thought and being last,
    Or immortality endures.

Isaac Watts (1674–1748)
based on Psalm 146

Covenant and Deliverance

440(i)

HOSANNA IN EXCELSIS   7.7.4 4.7.D.   Sydney H. Nicholson (1875–1947)

A PILGRIM PEOPLE

1 OMNIPOTENT Redeemer,
   Our ransomed souls adore thee;
    Whate'er is done
    Thy work we own,
   And give thee all the glory;
With thankfulness acknowledge
   Our time of visitation;
    Thine hand confess,
    And gladly bless
   The God of our salvation.

2 Thou hast employed thy servants,
   And blessed their weak endeavours,
    And lo, in thee
    We myriads see
   Of practical believers;
The church of pardoned sinners,
   Exulting in their Saviour,
    Sing all day long
    The gospel song,
   And triumph in thy favour.

3 Thy wonders wrought already
   Require our ceaseless praises;
    But show thy power,
    And myriads more
   Endue with heavenly graces.
But fill our earth with glory,
   And, known by every nation,
    God of all grace,
    Receive the praise
   Of all thy new creation.

Charles Wesley (1707–88)

Covenant and Deliverance

440(ii)

WORSHIP 7.7.44.7.D.

Melody adapted from
Johann Michael Haydn (1737–1806)

A PILGRIM PEOPLE

1 OMNIPOTENT Redeemer,
    Our ransomed souls adore thee;
      Whate'er is done
      Thy work we own,
    And give thee all the glory;
With thankfulness acknowledge
    Our time of visitation;
      Thine hand confess,
      And gladly bless
    The God of our salvation.

2 Thou hast employed thy servants,
    And blessed their weak endeavours,
      And lo, in thee
      We myriads see
    Of practical believers;
The church of pardoned sinners,
    Exulting in their Saviour,
      Sing all day long
      The gospel song,
    And triumph in thy favour.

3 Thy wonders wrought already
    Require our ceaseless praises;
      But show thy power,
      And myriads more
    Endue with heavenly graces.
But fill our earth with glory,
    And, known by every nation,
      God of all grace,
      Receive the praise
    Of all thy new creation.

Charles Wesley (1707–88)

Covenant and Deliverance

441(i)
MARCHING 8.7.8.7.

Martin Shaw (1875–1958)

441(ii)
EBENEZER 8.7.8.7.D.

T. J. Williams (1869–1944)

A PILGRIM PEOPLE

1 THROUGH the night of doubt and sorrow,
   Onward goes the pilgrim band,
Singing songs of expectation,
   Marching to the promised land.

2 One the object of our journey,
   One the faith which never tires,
One the earnest looking forward,
   One the hope our God inspires;

3 One the strain that lips of thousands
   Lift as from the heart of one;
One the conflict, one the peril,
   One the march in God begun;

4 One the light of God's own presence,
   O'er his ransomed people shed,
Chasing far the gloom and terror,
   Brightening all the path we tread;

5 One the gladness of rejoicing
   On the far eternal shore,
Where the one almighty Father
Reigns in love for evermore.

6 Soon shall come the great awaking,
   Soon the rending of the tomb;
Then the scattering of all shadows,
   And the end of toil and gloom.

May also be sung to No. 75,
PILGRIM BROTHERS

Bernhardt Severin Ingemann (1789–1862)
tr. Sabine Baring-Gould (1834–1924)

Covenant and Deliverance

1 O GOD of Bethel, by whose hand
   Thy people still are fed;
   Who through this earthly pilgrimage
   Hast all our fathers led:

2 Our vows, our prayers, we now present
   Before thy throne of grace:
   God of our fathers, be the God
   Of their succeeding race.

3 Through each perplexing path of life
   Our wandering footsteps guide;
   Give us each day our daily bread,
   And raiment fit provide.

4 O spread thy covering wings around,
   Till all our wanderings cease,
   And at our Father's loved abode
   Our souls arrive in peace.

5 To thee as to our Covenant-God
   We'll our whole selves resign;
   And this not as a tithe alone,
   For all we have is thine.

Philip Doddridge (1702–51)
John Logan (1748–88) and others

May also be sung to No. 340, ST PAUL (ABERDEEN)

A PILGRIM PEOPLE

443

CHURCH TRIUMPHANT L.M. James William Elliott (1833–1915)

For this tune in a higher key see No. 279

1 WE praise, we worship thee, O God,
  Thy sovereign power we sound abroad;
    All nations bow before thy throne,
    And thee the eternal Father own.

2 Loud alleluias to thy name
  Angels and seraphim proclaim;
    The heavens and all the powers on high
    With rapture constantly do cry:

3 'O holy, holy, holy Lord,
  Thou God of hosts, by all adored,
    Earth and the heavens are full of thee,
    Thy light, thy power, thy majesty.'

4 Apostles join the glorious throng,
  And swell the loud immortal song;
    Prophets enraptured hear the sound,
    And spread the alleluia round.

5 Victorious martyrs join their lays,
  And shout the omnipotence of grace;
    While all thy church through all the earth
    Acknowledge and extol thy worth.

Philip Gell's Psalms and Hymns (1815)
based on *Te Deum Laudamus*

May also be sung to No. 322(i), MAINZER

Covenant and Deliverance

A PILGRIM PEOPLE

And has raised up a lad – der of mer – cy for me!

And has raised up a lad – der of mer – cy for me!

1 AS Jacob with travel was weary one day,
   At night on a stone for a pillow he lay;
   He saw in a vision a ladder so high
   That its foot was on earth and its top in the sky:
   Alleluia to Jesus, who died on the tree,
   And has raised up a ladder of mercy for me!

2 This ladder is long, it is strong and well made,
   Has stood hundreds of years and is not yet decayed;
   Many millions have climbed it and reached Zion's hill,
   And thousands by faith are climbing it still:

3 Come, let us ascend! All may climb it who will,
   For the angels of Jacob are guarding it still;
   And remember, each step that by faith we pass o'er,
   Some prophet or martyr has trod it before:

4 And when we arrive at the haven of rest
   We shall hear the glad words: 'Come up hither, ye blest,
   Here are regions of light, here are mansions of bliss.'
   O who would not climb such a ladder as this?

                                   Anonymous (18th Century)

Patriarchs and Prophets

445
LAUS DEO (REDHEAD 46) 8.7.8.7.

Richard Redhead (1820–1901)
from *Church Hymn Tunes* (1853)

For this tune in a lower key see No. 15(ii)

1 BRIGHT the vision that delighted
  Once the sight of Judah's seer;
Sweet the countless tongues united
  To entrance the prophet's ear.

2 Round the Lord in glory seated
  Cherubim and seraphim
Filled his temple, and repeated
  Each to each the alternate hymn:

3 'Lord, thy glory fills the heaven;
  Earth is with its fullness stored;
Unto thee be glory given,
  Holy, holy, holy Lord!'

4 Heaven is still with glory ringing,
  Earth takes up the angels' cry,
'Holy, holy, holy,' singing,
  'Lord of hosts, the Lord most high.'

5 With his seraph train before him,
  With his holy church below,
Thus unite we to adore him,
  Bid we thus our anthem flow:

6 'Lord, thy glory fills the heaven;
  Earth is with its fullness stored;
Unto thee be glory given,
  Holy, holy, holy Lord!'

Richard Mant (1776–1848)
based on Isaiah 6:1–3

A PILGRIM PEOPLE

446

ST MARY C.M.

Melody from E. Prys's *Llyfr y Psalmau* (1621)
Harmonised by S. S. Wesley (1810–1876)

For this tune in another version and a lower key see No. 420 (i)

1 HAST thou not known, hast thou not heard,
    That firm remains on high
  The everlasting throne of him
    Who formed the earth and sky?

2 Art thou afraid his power shall fail
    When comes thy evil day?
  And can an all-creating arm
    Grow weary or decay?

3 Supreme in wisdom as in power
    The Rock of Ages stands;
  Though him thou canst not see, nor trace
    The working of his hands.

4 He gives the conquest to the weak,
    Supports the fainting heart;
  And courage in the evil hour
    His heavenly aids impart.

5 Mere human power shall fast decay,
    And youthful vigour cease;
  But they who wait upon the Lord
    In strength shall still increase.

May also be sung
to No. 46(i),
ABRIDGE

Isaac Watts (1674–1748) and
William Cameron (1751–1811)
as in Scottish Paraphrases (1781)
based on Isaiah 40:28–31

Patriarchs and Prophets

447
NORTHOVER D.C.M.

Peter Cutts (1937–)

1 DEEP in the shadows of the past, Far out from set-tled lands, Some no-mads tra-velled with their God A-cross the de-sert sands. The dawn of hope for hu-man-kind Was glimpsed by them a-lone— A

A PILGRIM PEOPLE

pro-mise call-ing them a-head, A fu-ture yet un - known.

1 DEEP in the shadows of the past,
  Far out from settled lands,
Some nomads travelled with their God
  Across the desert sands.
The dawn of hope for humankind
  Was glimpsed by them alone—
A promise calling them ahead,
  A future yet unknown.

2 While others bowed to changeless gods,
  They met a mystery:
God with an uncompleted name,
  'I am what I will be';
And by their tents, around their fires,
  In story, song and law,
They praised, remembered, handed on
  A past that promised more.

3 From Abraham to Nazareth
  The promise changed and grew,
While some, remembering the past,
  Recorded what they knew,
And some, in letters or laments,
  In prophecy and praise,
Recovered, held, and re-expressed
  New hope for changing days.

4 For all the writings that survived,
  For leaders, long ago,
Who sifted, chose, and then preserved
  The Bible that we know,
Give thanks, and find its promise yet
  Our comfort, strength, and call,
The working model for our faith,
  Alive with hope for all.

Brian A. Wren (1936–)

Patriarchs and Prophets

A PILGRIM PEOPLE

1 HOW glorious Zion's courts appear,
  The city of our God!
His throne he has established here,
  Here fixed his loved abode.

2 Its walls, defended by his grace,
  No power shall e'er o'erthrow;
Salvation is its bulwark sure
  Against the assailing foe.

3 Lift up the everlasting gates,
  The doors wide open fling;
Enter, ye nations, who obey
  The statutes of our King.

4 Here those whose minds are stayed on thee
  Are kept in perfect peace:
They who have known Jehovah's name
  And trusted in his grace.

5 Trust in the Lord, for ever trust,
  And banish all your fears;
Strength in the Lord Jehovah dwells
  Eternal as his years.

Scottish Paraphrases (1781) alt.
based on Isaiah 26:1–4

449(i)
VENICE S.M.   William Amps (1824–1910)

449(ii)
DAY OF PRAISE S.M.   Charles Steggall (1826–1905)

A PILGRIM PEOPLE

1 HOW gracious are their feet
   Who stand on Zion's hill,
Who bring salvation on their tongues,
   And words of peace reveal!

2 How cheering is their voice,
   How sweet their tidings are:
'Zion, behold thy Saviour-King!
   He reigns and triumphs here.'

3 How happy are our ears
   That hear this joyful sound,
Which kings and prophets waited for,
   And sought, but never found!

4 How blessèd are our eyes
   That see this heavenly light!
Prophets and kings desired it long,
   But died without the sight.

5 The watchmen join their voice,
   And tuneful notes employ;
Jerusalem breaks forth in songs,
   And deserts learn the joy.

6 The Lord makes bare his arm
   Through all the earth abroad;
Let all the nations now behold
   Their Saviour and their God.

Isaac Watts (1674–1748) alt.

Patriarchs and Prophets

450

Unison

1 'MO-SES, I know you're the man,' The Lord said. 'You're going to work out my plan,' The Lord said, 'Lead all the Is-rael-ites out of sla-ver-y, And I shall make them a wan-der-ing race Called the Peo-ple of God.'

Refrain

So ev-ery day, We're on our way, For we're a

A PILGRIM PEOPLE

tra-vel-ling, wan-der - ing race, We're the Peo-ple of God.

E7   A   D   G   D

1 'MOSES, I know you're the man,'
   The Lord said.
   'You're going to work out my plan,'
   The Lord said.
   'Lead all the Israelites out of slavery,
   And I shall make them a wandering race
   Called the People of God.'
       So every day,
       We're on our way,
       For we're a travelling, wandering race,
       We're the People of God.

2 'Don't get too set in your ways,'
   The Lord said.
   'Each step is only a phase,'
   The Lord said.
   'I'll go before you and I shall be a sign
   To guide my travelling, wandering race;
   You're the People of God.'

3 'No matter what you may do,'
   The Lord said,
   'I shall be faithful and true,'
   The Lord said.
   'My love will strengthen you as you go along,
   For you're my travelling, wandering race,
   You're the People of God.'

4 'Look at the birds in the air,'
   The Lord said,
   'They fly unhampered by care,'
   The Lord said.
   'You will move easier if you're travelling light,
   For you're a wandering, vagabond race,
   You're the People of God.'

5 'Foxes have places to go,'
   The Lord said,
   'But I've no home here below,'
   The Lord said.
   'So if you want to be with me all your days,
   Keep up the moving and travelling on,
   You're the People of God.'

Estelle White (1925–   )

Words and music reprinted by permission of
Mayhew-McCrimmon Ltd and Stainer & Bell Ltd.
For permission to reproduce see p. xiii.

Patriarchs and Prophets

451(i)

WILMINGTON 6.4.6.4. 664.

Erik Routley (1917–82)

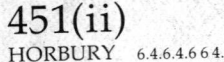

Unison   *Harmony*

451(ii)

HORBURY 6.4.6.4.6 6 4.

J. B. Dykes (1823–76)

A PILGRIM PEOPLE

1 NEARER, my God, to thee,
   Nearer to thee!
E'en though it be a cross
   That raiseth me,
Still all my song shall be:
'Nearer, my God, to thee,
   Nearer to thee!'

2 Though, like the wanderer,
   The sun gone down,
Darkness be over me,
   My rest a stone,
Yet in my dreams I'd be
Nearer, my God, to thee,
   Nearer to thee!

3 There let the way appear
   Steps unto heaven—
All that thou sendest me
   In mercy given—
Angels to beckon me
Nearer, my God, to thee,
   Nearer to thee!

4 Then, with my waking thoughts
   Bright with thy praise,
Out of my stony griefs
   Bethel I'll raise;
So by my woes to be
Nearer, my God, to thee,
   Nearer to thee!

5 Or if on joyful wing
   Cleaving the sky,
Sun, moon, and stars forgot,
   Upwards I fly,
Still all my song shall be:
'Nearer, my God, to thee,
   Nearer to thee!'

Sarah Flower Adams (1805–48)

Patriarchs and Prophets

1 THE God of Abraham praise,
   Who reigns enthroned above,
 Ancient of everlasting days,
   And God of love.
  Jehovah! Great I AM!
   By earth and heaven confessed;
 I bow and bless the sacred name
   For ever blessed.

2 He by himself has sworn,
   I on his oath depend:
 I shall, on eagles' wings upborne,
   To heaven ascend;
  I shall behold his face,
   I shall his power adore,
 And sing the wonders of his grace
   For evermore.

3 The God who reigns on high
   The great archangels sing;
 And 'Holy, holy, holy,' cry,
   'Almighty King.'
  Who was and is the same,
   And evermore shall be;
 Jehovah, Father, great I AM,
   We worship thee.

4 Before the Saviour's face
   The ransomed nations bow;
 O'erwhelmed at his almighty grace,
   For ever new:
  He shows his prints of love,
   They kindle to a flame,
 And sound through all the worlds above
   The slaughtered Lamb.

5 The whole triumphant host
   Give thanks to God on high;
 'Hail, Father, Son, and Holy Ghost!'
   They ever cry.
  Hail, Abraham's God, and mine!
   I join the heavenly lays;
 All might and majesty are thine,
   And endless praise.

Thomas Olivers (1725–99)

453

LUTHER 8.7.8.7.8 8.7.

1 WE come unto our fathers' God;
   Their Rock is our salvation;
The eternal arms, their dear abode,
   We make our habitation;
We bring thee, Lord, the praise they brought;
We seek thee as thy saints have sought
   In every generation.

2 The fire divine their steps that led
   Still goeth bright before us;
The heavenly shield around them spread
   Is still high holden o'er us;
The grace those sinners that subdued,
The strength those weaklings that renewed,
   Doth vanquish, doth restore us.

3 The cleaving sins that brought them low
   Are still our souls oppressing;
The tears that from their eyes did flow
   Fall fast, our shame confessing;
As with thee, Lord, prevailed their cry,
So our strong prayer ascends on high
   And bringeth down thy blessing.

4 Their joy unto their Lord we bring;
   Their song to us descendeth;
The Spirit who in them did sing
   To us his music lendeth;
His song in them, in us, is one;
We raise it high, we send it on,
   The song that never endeth.

5 Ye saints to come, take up the strain,
   The same sweet theme endeavour;
Unbroken be the golden chain;
   Keep on the song for ever;
Safe in the same dear dwelling-place,
Rich with the same eternal grace,
   Bless the same boundless giver.

Thomas Hornblower Gill (1819–1906)

Patriarchs and Prophets

A PILGRIM PEOPLE

1 THE God who sent the prophets
  Inspired them for our good,
To help us face the menace
  Of evils they withstood.
How faithfully they warn us,
  From Israel's stormy past,
That those who sow injustice
  Will reap the holocaust!

2 They say the Judge of nations
  Is making all things new;
That when the many fail him
  He saves us by the few.
In this prophetic promise
  Our anxious spirits rest:
In them, his chosen Remnant,
  The future shall be blessed.

3 Yet not by being righteous
  May we secure our place,
Or think to serve the future
  Save in the strength of grace.
For there is but one Saviour,
  The One we crucified,
The lonely Suffering Servant,
  Who calls us to his side.

F. Pratt Green (1903–)

May also be sung to No. 125, CRÜGER (HERRNHUT)

Words reprinted by permission of
Stainer & Bell Ltd.
For permission to reproduce see p. xiii.

Patriarchs and Prophets

455
CHRISTE SANCTORUM 10 11 11.6.

Melody from
Paris Antiphoner (1681)
(Arr. J.W.)

A PILGRIM PEOPLE

1 CHRIST is the world's Light, he and none other;
  Born in our darkness, he became our Brother.
  If we have seen him, we have seen the Father:
    Glory to God on high.

2 Christ is the world's Peace, he and none other;
  No one can serve him and despise his brother.
  Who else unites us, one in God the Father?
    Glory to God on high.

3 Christ is the world's Life, he and none other;
  Sold once for silver, murdered here, our Brother—
  He, who redeems us, reigns with God the Father:
    Glory to God on high.

4 Give God the glory, God and none other;
  Give God the glory, Spirit, Son, and Father;
  Give God the glory, God in Man my brother:
    Glory to God on high.

F. Pratt Green (1903–)

Words reprinted by permission of
Stainer & Bell Ltd.
For permission to reproduce see p. xiii.

People of the Light

456

RINKART 6.7.6.7.6.6.6.6.
(KOMMT SEELEN)

Melody and figured bass by
J. S. Bach (1685–1750)

Unison. Moving freely

1 CHRIST is the world's true Light,
The day-star shin-ing bright
Its cap-tain of sal-
To ev-ery man and

-va- tion, New life, new hope a-wakes,
na- tion;

Where'er men own his sway: Free-dom her bondage

breaks, _____ And night is turned to day. _____

(small notes
ad lib.)

1 CHRIST is the world's true Light,
   Its captain of salvation,
The day-star shining bright
   To every man and nation;
New life, new hope awakes,
   Where'er men own his sway:
Freedom her bondage breaks,
   And night is turned to day.

2 In Christ all races meet,
   Their ancient feuds forgetting,
The whole round world complete,
   From sunrise to its setting:
When Christ is throned as Lord,
   All shall forsake their fear,
To ploughshare beat the sword,
   To pruning-hook the spear.

3 One Lord, in one great name
   Unite us all who own thee;
Cast out our pride and shame
   That hinder to enthrone thee;
The world has waited long,
   Has travailed long in pain;
To heal its ancient wrong,
   Come, Prince of Peace, and reign.

George Wallace Briggs (1875–1959)

People of the Ligh

457(i)
HEATHLANDS 77.77.77.

Henry Smart (1813–79)

For this tune in a lower key see No. 630(i)

457(ii)
RATISBON 77.77.77.

Melody from
Werner's *Choralbuch* (Leipzig, 1815)
Harmony mostly by
W. H. Havergal (1793–1870)

1 CHRIST, whose glory fills the skies,
   Christ, the true, the only Light,
Sun of Righteousness, arise,
   Triumph o'er the shades of night;
Day-spring from on high, be near;
Day-star, in my heart appear.

2 Dark and cheerless is the morn
   Unaccompanied by thee:
Joyless is the day's return,
   Till thy mercy's beams I see,
Till they inward light impart,
Glad my eyes, and warm my heart.

3 Visit then this soul of mine;
   Pierce the gloom of sin and grief;
Fill me, radiancy divine;
   Scatter all my unbelief;
More and more thyself display,
Shining to the perfect day.

Charles Wesley (1707–88)

458(i)

CHALFONT PARK   8.6.88.6.

Erik Routley (1917–82)

458(ii)

NEWCASTLE   8.6.88.6.

H. L. Morley (c.1830–1916)

A PILGRIM PEOPLE

1 ETERNAL Light! Eternal Light!
   How pure the soul must be,
When, placed within thy searching sight,
It shrinks not, but with calm delight
   Can live and look on thee.

2 The spirits that surround thy throne
   May bear the burning bliss;
But that is surely theirs alone,
Since they have never, never known
   A fallen world like this.

3 O how shall I, whose native sphere
   Is dark, whose mind is dim,
Before the Ineffable appear,
And on my naked spirit bear
   The uncreated beam?

4 There is a way for man to rise
   To that sublime abode:
An offering and a sacrifice,
A Holy Spirit's energies,
   An Advocate with God.

5 These, these prepare us for the sight
   Of holiness above;
The sons of ignorance and night
May dwell in the eternal light
   Through the eternal Love!

Thomas Binney (1798–1874)

People of the Ligh

459

DIEU, NOUS AVONS VU 12.12. (and Refrain) Jean Langlais (1907–   )

God, your glory we have seen in your Son, Full of truth, full of heavenly grace; In Christ make us live, his love shine on our face, And the nations will see in us the triumph you have won.

(pauses last time only)

A PILGRIM PEOPLE

back to Refrain

God, your glory we have seen in your Son,
Full of truth, full of heavenly grace;
In Christ make us live, his love shine on our face,
And the nations will see in us the triumph you have won.

1 IN the fields of this world his good news he has sown,
And sends us out to reap till the harvest is done:

2 In his love like a fire that consumes he passed by;
The flame has touched our lips; let us shout: 'Here am I!':

3 He was broken for us, God-forsaken his cry,
And still the bread he breaks; to ourselves we must die:

4 He has trampled the grapes of new life on his cross;
Now drink the cup and live; he has filled it for us:

5 He has founded a kingdom that none shall destroy;
The corner-stone is laid; go to work, build with joy!

Didier Rimaud (1922–)
tr. *Ronald Johnson* (1913–)
and *Brian A. Wren* (1936–)

People of the Light

460

FULDA L.M.   Melody from Gardiner's *Sacred Melodies* (1815)

1 COME, sinners, to the gospel feast,
Let every soul be Jesu's guest;
    You need not one be left behind,
    For God has bidden all mankind.

2 Sent by my Lord, on you I call,
The invitation is to all;
    Come, all the world; come, sinner, thou!
    All things in Christ are ready now.

3 Come, all ye souls by sin oppressed,
Ye restless wanderers after rest,
    Ye poor, and maimed, and halt, and blind,
    In Christ a hearty welcome find.

4 His love is mighty to compel;
His conquering love consent to feel;
    Yield to his love's resistless power,
    And fight against your God no more.

5 See him set forth before your eyes;
Behold the bleeding sacrifice!
    His offered benefits embrace,
    And freely now be saved by grace.

6 This is the time; no more delay!
This is the Lord's accepted day;
    Come in, this moment, at his call,
    And live for him who died for all.

Charles Wesley (1707–88)

A PILGRIM PEOPLE

461

WINCHESTER NEW L.M.

Adapted from a tune in
Musikalisches Handbuch (Hamburg, 1690)

1 O SPLENDOUR of God's glory bright,
  Who bringest forth the light from Light;
      O Light, of light the fountain-spring;
      O Day, our days illumining;

2 Come, very Sun of truth and love,
  Come in thy radiance from above,
      And shed the Holy Spirit's ray
      On all we think or do today.

3 Teach us to work with all our might;
  Put Satan's fierce assaults to flight;
      Turn all to good that seems most ill;
      Help us our calling to fulfil.

4 O joyful be the livelong day,
  Our thoughts as pure as morning ray,
      Our faith like noonday's glowing height,
      Our souls undimmed by shades of night.

5 O Christ, with each returning morn
  Thine image to our hearts is borne;
      O may we ever clearly see
      Our Saviour and our God in thee!

Ambrose (c. 340–c. 397)
tr. *John Chandler* (1806–76) and others

People of the Light

462(i)

DURA 88.88.88.   Henry J. Gauntlett (1805–76)

462(ii)

BICKLEY 88.88.88.   W. H. Monk (1823–89)

1 STUPENDOUS height of heavenly love,
   Of pitying tenderness divine;
It brought the Saviour from above,
   It caused the springing day to shine;
The Sun of Righteousness to appear,
And gild our gloomy hemisphere.

2 God did in Christ himself reveal,
   To chase our darkness by his light,
Our sin and ignorance dispel,
   Direct our wandering feet aright;
And bring our souls, with pardon blest,
To realms of everlasting rest.

3 Come then, O Lord, thy light impart,
   The faith that bids our terrors cease;
Into thy love direct my heart,
   Into thy way of perfect peace;
And cheer my soul, of death afraid,
And guide me through the dreadful shade.

4 Answer thy mercy's whole design,
   My God incarnated for me;
My spirit make thy radiant shrine,
   My light and full salvation be;
And through the darkened vale unknown
Conduct me to thy dazzling throne.

Charles Wesley (1707–88) alt.

People of the Light

463

TO GOD BE THE GLORY 11 11.11 11.
(anapaestic and refrain)

W. H. Doane (1832–1915)

Refrain

Praise the Lord! Praise the Lord! Let the earth hear his voice!

Praise the Lord! Praise the Lord! Let the peo‑ple re‑joice!

A PILGRIM PEOPLE

O come_ to the Fa-ther, through Je-sus the Son;

And give him the glo—ry—great things he has done!

1 TO God be the glory, great things he has done!
   So loved he the world that he gave us his Son,
   Who yielded his life in atonement for sin,
   And opened the life-gate that all may go in:
   Praise the Lord! Praise the Lord!
   Let the earth hear his voice!
   Praise the Lord! Praise the Lord!
   Let the people rejoice!
   O come to the Father, through Jesus the Son;
   And give him the glory—great things he has done!

2 O perfect redemption, the purchase of blood,
   To every believer the promise of God!
   And every offender who truly believes,
   That moment from Jesus a pardon receives:

3 Great things he has taught us, great things he has done,
   And great our rejoicing through Jesus the Son;
   But purer, and higher, and greater will be
   Our wonder, our rapture, when Jesus we see:

Frances Jane van Alstyne (1820–1915) alt.

464

TILTEY ABBEY C.M.

A. H. Brown (1830–1926)

1 WALK in the light: so shalt thou know
   That fellowship of love
His Spirit only can bestow,
   Who reigns in light above.

2 Walk in the light: and thou shalt find
   Thy heart made truly his
Who dwells in cloudless light enshrined,
   In whom no darkness is.

3 Walk in the light: and thou shalt own
   Thy darkness passed away,
Because that Light has on thee shone
   In which is perfect day.

4 Walk in the light: and e'en the tomb
   No fearful shade shall wear;
Glory shall chase away its gloom,
   For Christ has conquered there.

5 Walk in the light: and thine shall be
   No thornless path, but bright;
For God, by grace, shall dwell in thee,
   And God himself is Light.

Bernard Barton (1784–1849)

People of the Light

465

FULDA L.M.

Melody from Gardiner's *Sacred Melodies* (1815)

1 WE have a gospel to proclaim,
    Good news for all throughout the earth;
  The gospel of a Saviour's name:
    We sing his glory, tell his worth.

2 Tell of his birth at Bethlehem—
    Not in a royal house or hall,
  But in a stable dark and dim,
    The Word made flesh, a light for all.

3 Tell of his death at Calvary:
    Hated by those he came to save,
  In lonely suffering on the cross,
    For all he loved his life he gave.

4 Tell of that glorious Easter morn:
    Empty the tomb, for he was free.
  He broke the power of death and hell
    That we might share his victory.

5 Tell of his reign at God's right hand,
    By all creation glorified.
  He sends his Spirit on his church
    To live for him, the Lamb who died.

6 Now we rejoice to name him King:
    Jesus is Lord of all the earth.
  This gospel-message we proclaim:
    We sing his glory, tell his worth.

Edward J. Burns (1938–)

A PILGRIM PEOPLE / People of the Light

466

CLIFTON C.M.

J. C. Clifton (1781–1841)
(altered)

1 ALMIGHTY God, thy word is cast
  Like seed into the ground;
Now let the sun and rain be given,
  And righteous fruits abound.

2 Let not the universal foe
  This holy seed remove,
But give it root in every heart
  To bring forth fruits of love.

3 Let not the world's deceitful cares
  The rising plant destroy,
But let it yield a hundredfold
  The fruits of peace and joy.

4 Oft as the precious seed is sown,
  Thy quickening grace bestow,
That all whose lives thy truth receive
  Thy saving power may know.

John Cawood (1775–1852) and others
based on Mark 4:3–9

May also be sung to No. 6, DUNFERMLINE

The Holy Scriptures

467

Rosalind F. Stainer (1884–1966)

1 BREAK thou the bread of life,
   O Lord, to me,
As thou didst break the loaves
   Beside the sea.
Beyond the sacred page
   I seek thee, Lord;
My spirit longs for thee,
   O living Word!

2 Thou art the Bread of Life,
   O Lord, to me,
Thy holy word the truth
   That saveth me;
Give me to eat and live
   With thee above;
Teach me to love thy truth,
   For thou art love.

3 O send thy Spirit, Lord,
   Now unto me,
That he may touch my eyes,
   And make me see;
Show me the truth concealed
   Within thy word,
And in thy book revealed
   I see the Lord.

v. 1 *Mary Artemisia Lathbury* (1841–1913)
vv. 2 and 3 *Alexander Groves* (1842–1909)

A PILGRIM PEOPLE

468

SPANISH CHANT 77.77.77.

From *Burgoyne's Collection* (1827)

1 COME, divine Interpreter,
 Bring us eyes thy book to read,
Ears the mystic words to hear,
 Words which did from thee proceed,
Words that endless bliss impart,
Kept in an obedient heart.

2 All who read, or hear, are blessed,
 If thy plain commands we do;
Of thy kingdom here possessed,
 Thee we shall in glory view—
When thou com'st on earth to abide,
Reign triumphant at thy side.

Charles Wesley (1707–88)

The Holy Scriptures

469(i)
NUN DANKET ALL (GRÄFENBERG)   C.M.

Melody from J. Crüger's
Praxis Pietatis Melica
(1647 edition)

469(ii)
ST COLUMBA   C.M.

Irish traditional melody

A PILGRIM PEOPLE

1 COME, Holy Ghost, our hearts inspire,
  Let us thine influence prove;
Source of the old prophetic fire,
  Fountain of life and love.

2 Come, Holy Ghost (for moved by thee
  The prophets wrote and spoke),
Unlock the truth, thyself the key,
  Unseal the sacred book.

3 Expand thy wings, celestial Dove,
  Brood o'er our nature's night;
On our disordered spirits move,
  And let there now be light.

4 God through himself we then shall know,
  If thou within us shine;
And sound, with all thy saints below,
  The depths of love divine.

Charles Wesley (1707–88)

May also be sung to No. 33, KILMARNOCK

470(i)

VENI, DOMINE   76.76.(Trochaic)

Late 17th-century German melody,
adapted by John Wilson

470(ii)

MELLING   76.76. (Trochaic)

Melody by J. Fawcett (1789–1867)
(shortened form)

1 COME, Lord, to our souls come down,
    Through the gospel speaking;
Let your words, your cross and crown,
    Lighten all our seeking.

2 Drive out darkness from the heart,
    Banish pride and blindness;
Plant in every inward part
    Truthfulness and kindness.

3 Eyes be open, spirits stirred,
    Minds new truth receiving;
Stir us, Lord, by your own word;
    Deepen our believing.

H. C. A. Gaunt (1902–83) alt.

A PILGRIM PEOPLE

471

BRUSHNORTH   8.7.8.7.77.   Michael Currah (1931–)

1 FOR your holy book we thank you,
    And for all who served you well,
Writing, guarding and translating,
    That its pages might forth tell
All your love and tender care
For your people everywhere.

2 For your holy book we thank you,
    And for those who work today
That all peoples hear its witness,
    Heed, and follow in your way,
Learn your love and tender care
For your people everywhere.

3 For your holy book we thank you;
    May its message be our guide;
May we understand its wisdom,
    And the laws it can provide
In your love and tender care
For your people everywhere.

4 For your holy book we thank you;
    May its message in our hearts
Lead us now to see in Jesus
    All the grace your word imparts—
Steadfast love and tender care
For your people everywhere.

Ruth Carter (1900-82) alt.

The Holy Scriptures

472

CAUSA DIVINA 14.14.4 7.8.

Frederick R. C. Clarke (1931–)

Unison

1 FOR who we are, we thank you; For who, how, know we thank you:
For all things great or small, Maker, you make, be our guide,
All we have and are we offer, In your care and keeping,
For your love, we praise, here.

2 For what may, hope we, thank you,
And for those still with us today,
That I put our fears to wiles;
Hear, and follow in your way,
Hear, your love, and render now,
For your helping, even where.

3 For your holy book, Lord, we thank you;
My the treasures in our words,
Treasure, it is us, to our sage,
A the power, your word, employs,
Shed the vow, and understand,
For your people even which.

A PILGRIM PEOPLE

1 GOD, who hast caused to be written thy word for our learning,
  Grant us that, hearing, our hearts may be inwardly burning.
        Give to us grace,
        That in thy Son we embrace
    Life, all its glory discerning.

2 Now may our God give us joy, and his peace in believing
  All things were written in truth for our thankful receiving.
        As Christ did preach,
        Love to our neighbour must reach;
    Grant us each day love's achieving.

3 Lord, should the powers of the earth and the heavens be shaken,
  Grant us to see thee in all things; our vision awaken.
        Help us to see,
        Though all the earth cease to be,
    Thy truth shall never be shaken.

T. Herbert O'Driscoll (1928–)

The Holy Scriptures

473

SALTASH 8.7.8.7.D.

Melody from *Plymouth Collection* (USA, 1855)
Arranged by Ralph Vaughan Williams (1872–1958)

A PILGRIM PEOPLE

1 HEAVENLY Father, may your blessing
   Rest upon your children now,
When in praise your name we hallow,
   When in prayer to you we bow;
In the wondrous story reading
   Of the Lord of truth and grace,
May we see your love reflected
   In the light of his dear face.

2 May we learn from this great story
   All the arts of friendliness;
Truthful speech and honest action,
   Courage, patience, steadfastness;
How to master self and temper,
   How to make our conduct fair;
When to speak and when be silent,
   When to do and when forbear.

3 May your Spirit wise and holy
   With his gifts our spirits bless,
Make us loving, joyous, peaceful,
   Rich in goodness, gentleness,
Strong in self-control, and faithful,
   Kind in thought and deed; for he
Teaches, 'What you do for others
   You are doing unto me.'

William Charter Piggott (1872–1943) alt.

474

SANDYS S.M.

Melody from W. Sandys' *Christmas Carols* (1833)
(as harmonised in *The English Hymnal*, 1906)

1 HELP us, O Lord, to learn
   The truths your word imparts,
To study that your laws may be
   Inscribed upon our hearts.

2 Help us, O Lord, to live
   That faith which we proclaim,
That all our thoughts and words and deeds
   May glorify your name.

3 Help us, O Lord, to teach
   The beauty of your ways,
That all who seek may find the Christ,
   And make a life of praise.

William Watkins Reid (1923–) alt.

A PILGRIM PEOPLE

475

SOUTHWELL (IRONS) C.M.

H. S. Irons (1834–1905)

1 LORD, I have made thy word my choice,
   My lasting heritage;
There shall my noblest powers rejoice,
   My warmest thoughts engage.

2 I'll read the histories of thy love,
   And keep thy laws in sight;
While through thy promises I rove,
   With ever fresh delight.

3 In this broad land of wealth unknown,
   Where springs of life arise,
Seeds of immortal bliss are sown,
   And hidden glory lies.

4 The best relief that mourners have,
   It makes our sorrows blest;
Our fairest hope beyond the grave,
   And our eternal rest.

Isaac Watts (1674–1748)

May also be sung to No. 490, WETHERBY

The Holy Scriptures

Adapted by W. H. Monk (1823–89) from a melody in
M. Weisse's *Gesangbuchlein* (1531)
(harmony slightly altered)

1 LORD, thy word abideth,
  And our footsteps guideth;
  Who its truth believeth
  Light and joy receiveth.

2 When our foes are near us,
  Then thy word doth cheer us,
  Word of consolation,
  Message of salvation.

3 When the storms are o'er us
  And dark clouds before us,
  Then its light directeth,
  And our way protecteth.

4 Who can tell the pleasure,
  Who recount the treasure,
  By thy word imparted
  To the simple-hearted?

5 Word of mercy, giving
  Succour to the living;
  Word of life, supplying
  Comfort to the dying!

6 O that we, discerning
  Its most holy learning,
  Lord, may love and fear thee,
  Evermore be near thee.

Henry Williams Baker (1821–77)

The Holy Scriptures

477(i)
MANNA 88.6.88.6.

Melody, and most of the harmony,
by J. G. Schicht (1753–1823)

477(ii)
CORNWALL 8 8.6.88.6.

S. S. Wesley (1810–76)

1 NOT far beyond the sea nor high
   Above the heavens, but very nigh
      Thy voice, O God, is heard.
   For each new step of faith we take
   Thou hast more truth and light to break
      Forth from thy holy word.

2 The babes in Christ thy Scriptures feed
   With milk sufficient for their need,
      The nurture of the Lord.
   Beneath life's burden and its heat
   The fully grown find stronger meat
      In thy unfailing word.

3 Rooted and grounded in thy love,
   With saints on earth and saints above
      We join in full accord,
   To grasp the breadth, length, depth, and height,
   The crucified and risen might
      Of Christ, the incarnate Word.

4 Help us to press toward that mark,
   And, though our vision now is dark,
      To live by what we see;
   So, when we see thee face to face,
   Thy truth and light our dwelling-place
      For evermore shall be.

G. B. Caird (1917-84)

The Holy Scriptures

478(i)
BENTLEY 7.6.7.6.D.

John Pyke Hullah (1812–84)

The Key of D flat may be preferred

478(ii)
NYLAND 7.6.7.6.D.

Finnish Melody
harmonised by David Evans (1874–1948)

A PILGRIM PEOPLE

1 O WORD of God incarnate,
   O wisdom from on high,
O truth unchanged, unchanging,
   O light of our dark sky,
We praise thee for the radiance
   That from the hallowed page,
A lantern to our footsteps,
   Shines on from age to age.

2 The church from her dear Master
   Received the gift divine,
And still that light she lifteth,
   O'er all the earth to shine;
It is the precious treasury
   Where gems of truth are stored;
It is the heaven-drawn picture
   Of Christ, the living Word.

3 It floateth like a banner
   Before God's host unfurled;
It shineth like a beacon
   Above the shadowed world;
It is the chart and compass
   That, o'er life's surging sea,
'Mid mists, and rocks, and quicksands,
   Still guides, O Christ, to thee.

4 O make thy church, dear Saviour,
   A lamp of burnished gold,
To bear before the nations
   Thy true light, as of old;
O teach thy wandering pilgrims
   By this their path to trace,
Till, clouds and darkness ended,
   They see thee face to face.

May also be sung
to No. 515,
AURELIA

William Walsham How (1823–97)

The Holy Scriptures

479

LIEBSTER IMMANUEL   11.10.11.10.

Melody from
Himmels–Lust (Jena, 1679)
Harmony mostly from J. S. Bach

(♯ last verse only)

1 POWERFUL in making us wise to salvation,
   Witness to faith in Christ Jesus the Word;
   Breathed out to all by the life-giving Father—
   These are the Scriptures, and thus speaks the Lord.

2 Tool for employment and compass for travel,
   Map in the desert and lamp in the dark;
   Teaching, rebuking, correcting, and training—
   These are the Scriptures, and this is their work.

3 History, prophecy, song, and commandment,
   Gospel and letter and dream from on high;
   Written by men borne along by the Spirit—
   These are the Scriptures; on them we rely.

4 Gift for God's servants to fit them completely,
   Fully equipping to walk in his ways;
   Guide to good work and effective believing—
   These are the Scriptures; for these we give praise!

Christopher Idle (1938–)

A PILGRIM PEOPLE

480

JENA (DAS NEUGEBORNE KINDELEIN) 88.88.88.

Melody by M. Vulpius (c. 1560–1615)
Harmonised by
J. S. Bach

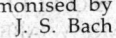

(♯ last verse only)

1 SPIRIT of truth, essential God,
   Who didst thine ancient saints inspire,
Shed in their hearts thy love abroad
   And touch their hallowed lips with fire;
Our God from all eternity,
World without end we worship thee.

2 Still we believe, almighty Lord,
   Whose presence fills both earth and heaven,
The meaning of the written word
   Is by thy inspiration given;
Thou only dost thyself explain
The secret mind of God to man.

3 Come then, divine Interpreter,
   The Scriptures to our hearts apply;
And, taught by thee, we God revere,
   Him in three Persons magnify,
In each the triune God adore,
Who was, and is, for evermore.

Charles Wesley (1707–88)

The Holy Scriptures

481(i)

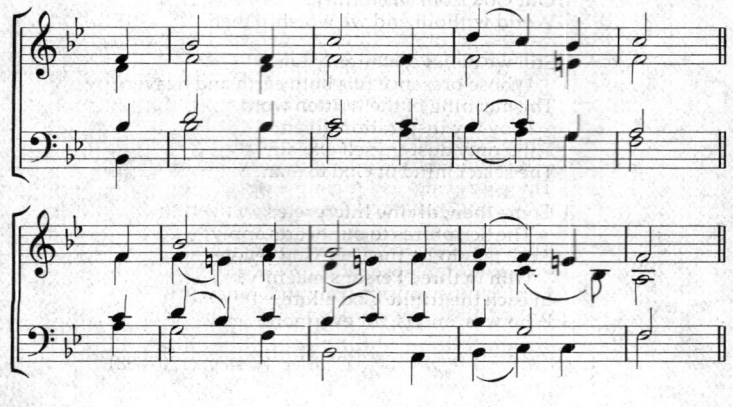

NEW SABBATH L.M. Thomas Phillips (1735–1807)

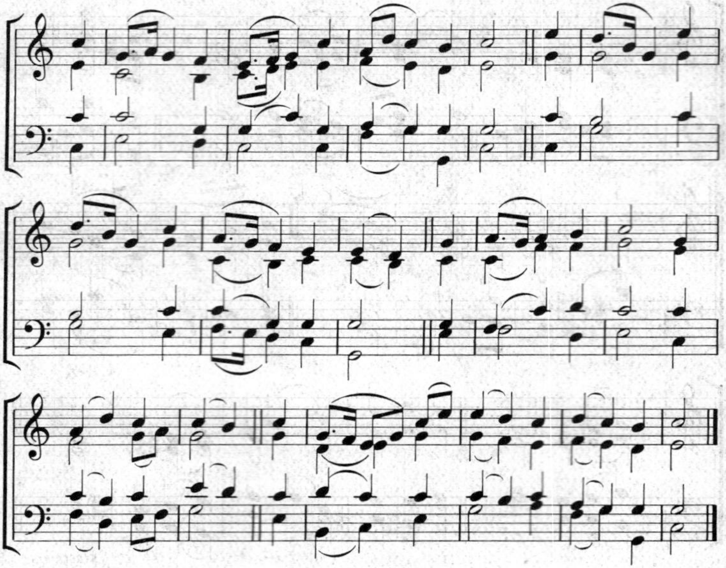

481(ii)

Henry Duncalf (d. 1762)

ST BARTHOLOMEW L.M. From W. Riley's *Parochial Harmony* (London, 1762)

1 THE heavens declare thy glory, Lord,
  In every star thy wisdom shines;
But when our eyes behold thy word,
  We read thy name in fairer lines.

2 The rolling sun, the changing light,
  And night and day, thy power confess;
But the blest volume thou hast writ
  Reveals thy justice and thy grace.

3 Sun, moon, and stars convey thy praise
  Round this whole earth, and never stand;
So when thy truth began its race,
  It touched and glanced on every land.

4 Nor shall thy spreading gospel rest
  Till through the world thy truth has run;
Till Christ has all the nations blest,
  That see the light or feel the sun.

5 Great Sun of Righteousness, arise,
  Bless our dark world with heavenly light:
Thy gospel makes the simple wise;
  Thy laws are pure, thy judgements right.

6 Thy noblest wonders here we view,
  In souls renewed, and sins forgiven;
Lord, cleanse my sins, my soul renew,
  And make thy word my guide to heaven.

Isaac Watts (1674–1748)

The Holy Scriptures

482

CAPEL   C.M.

English traditional melody
Harmony and arrangement by
Ralph Vaughan Williams (1872–1958)

1 YOUR words to me are life and health;
    They fortify my soul,
  Enable, guide, and teach my heart
    To reach its perfect goal.

2 Your words to me are light and truth;
    From day to day they show
  Their wisdom, passing earthly lore,
    As in their truth I grow.

3 Your words to me are full of joy,
    Of beauty, peace, and grace;
  From them I learn your blessèd will,
    Through them I see your face.

4 Your words are perfected in One,
    Yourself, the living Word;
  Within my heart your image print
    In clearest lines, O Lord.

George Currie Martin (1865–1937) alt.

The Holy Scriptures

483(i)
KINGLEY VALE 8.7.8.7.4.7. Hugh P. Allen (1869–1946)

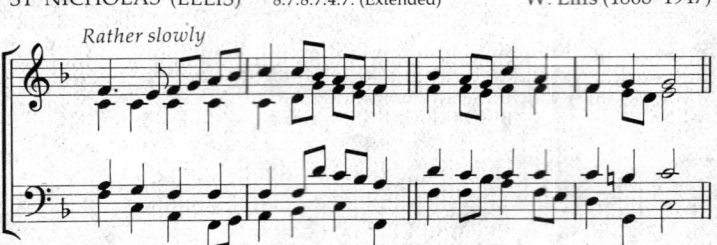

483(ii)
ST NICHOLAS (ELLIS) 8.7.8.7.4.7. (Extended) W. Ellis (1868–1947)

Rather slowly

1 THANKS to God whose Word was spoken
    In the deed that made the earth.
His the voice that called a nation,
    His the fires that tried her worth.
        God has spoken:
    Praise him for his open word.

2 Thanks to God whose Word incarnate
    Human flesh has glorified,
Who by life and death and rising
    Grace abundant has supplied.
        God has spoken:
    Praise him for his open word.

3 Thanks to God whose word was written
    In the Bible's sacred page,
Record of the revelation
    Showing God to every age.
        God has spoken:
    Praise him for his open word.

4 Thanks to God whose word is published
    In the tongues of every race.
See its glory undiminished
    By the change of time or place.
        God has spoken:
    Praise him for his open word.

5 Thanks to God whose word is answered
    By the Spirit's voice within.
Here we drink of joy unmeasured,
    Life redeemed from death and sin.
        God is speaking:
    Praise him for his open word.

R. T. Brooks (1918–85)

The Holy Scriptures

484(i)

ANGEL VOICES 8.5.8.5.8.4.3.

E. G. Monk (1819–1900)

484(ii)

ARTHOG 8.5.8.5.8.4.3.

G. Thalben-Ball (1896–   )

Unison

1 ANGEL voices, ever singing
   Round thy throne of light,
Angel harps, for ever ringing,
   Rest not day nor night;
Thousands only live to bless thee,
   And confess thee
      Lord of might.

2 Thou who art beyond the farthest
   Mortal eye can scan,
Can it be that thou regardest
   Songs of sinful man?
Can we know that thou art near us
   And wilt hear us?
      Yea, we can.

3 Lord, we know that thou rejoicest
   O'er each work of thine;
Thou didst ears and hands and voices
   For thy praise design;
Craftsman's art and music's measure
   For thy pleasure
      All combine.

4 In thy house, great God, we offer
   Of thine own to thee,
And for thine acceptance proffer,
   All unworthily,
Hearts and minds and hands and voices,
   In our choicest
      Psalmody.

5 Honour, glory, might, and merit
   Thine shall ever be,
Father, Son, and Holy Spirit,
   Blessèd Trinity;
Of the best that thou hast given
   Earth and heaven
      Render thee.

Francis Pott (1832–1909)

485

WESTMINSTER ABBEY   87.87.87.

Adapted from an anthem by
Henry Purcell (c.1659–95)

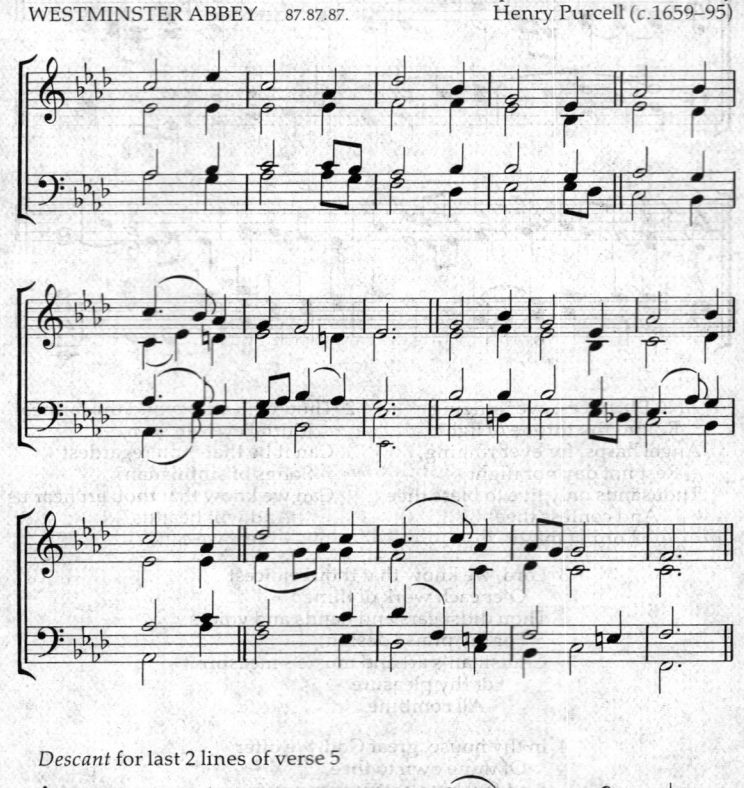

Descant for last 2 lines of verse 5

1 BLESSÈD city, heavenly Salem,
  Vision dear of peace and love,
Who of living stones art builded
  In the height of heaven above,
And by angel hosts encircled
  As a bride dost earthward move!

2 Christ is made the sure foundation,
  Christ the head and corner-stone,
Chosen of the Lord, and precious,
  Binding all the church in one,
Holy Zion's help for ever,
  And her confidence alone.

3 To this temple, where we call thee,
  Come, O Lord of Hosts, today;
With thy wonted loving-kindness
  Hear thy servants as they pray;
And thy fullest benediction
  Shed within its walls alway.

4 Here vouchsafe to all thy servants
  What they ask of thee to gain,
What they gain from thee for ever
  With the blessèd to retain,
And hereafter in thy glory
  Evermore with thee to reign.

5 Laud and honour to the Father,
  Laud and honour to the Son,
Laud and honour to the Spirit,
  Ever Three, and ever One,
Consubstantial, co-eternal,
  While unending ages run.

                    6th or 7th Century
tr. *John Mason Neale* (1818–66) alt.

THE WORSHIPPING PEOPLE

1 BORN in song!
God's people have always been singing.
Born in song!
Hearts and voices raised.
So today we worship together;
God alone is worthy to be praised.

2 Praise to God!
For he is the one who has made us.
Praise to God!
We his image bear.
Heav'n and earth are full of his glory;
Let creation praise him everywhere.

3 Christ is king!
He left all the glory of heaven.
Christ is king!
Born to share in our pain;
Crucified, for sinners atoning,
Risen, exalted, soon to come again.

4 Sing the song!
God's Spirit is poured out among us.
Sing the song!
He has made us anew.
Ev'ry member part of the Body;
Given his power, his will to seek and do.

5 Tell the world!
All power to Jesus is given.
Tell the world!
He is with us always.
Spread the word, that all may receive him;
Every tongue confess and sing his praise.

6 Then the end!
Christ Jesus shall reign in his glory.
Then the end
Of all earthly days.
Yet above the song will continue;
All his people still shall sing his praise.

Brian R. Hoare (1935–   )

487(i)
MOUNT EPHRAIM S.M.

Melody and almost all the bass
by Benjamin Milgrove (*c.* 1731–1810)

487(ii)
ASCENSION (GAUNTLETT) D.S.M.

Henry J. Gauntlett (1805–76)

Unison

Harmony

THE WORSHIPPING PEOPLE

1 COME, we that love the Lord,
   And let our joys be known;
Join in a song with sweet accord,
   And thus surround the throne.

2 The sorrows of the mind
   Be banished from the place;
Religion never was designed
   To make our pleasures less.

3 Let those refuse to sing
   That never knew our God;
But children of the heavenly King
   May speak their joys abroad.

4 The men of grace have found
   Glory begun below;
Celestial fruits on earthly ground
   From faith and hope may grow.

5 Then let our songs abound,
   And every tear be dry;
We're marching through Immanuel's ground
   To fairer worlds on high.

6 There we shall see his face,
   And never, never sin;
There, from the rivers of his grace,
   Drink endless pleasures in.

Isaac Watts (1674–1748)

Praise and Adoration

Melody and bass by
Jeremiah Clarke (c. 1673–1707)
Mean parts by John Wilson

THE WORSHIPPING PEOPLE

1 COMMAND thy blessing from above,
   O God, on all assembled here;
Behold us with a Father's love,
   While we look up with filial fear.

2 Command thy blessing, Jesus, Lord;
   May we thy true disciples be;
Speak to each heart the mighty word,
   Say to the weakest, 'Follow me'.

3 Command thy blessing in this hour,
   Spirit of truth, and fill this place
With humbling and exalting power,
   With quickening and confirming grace.

4 O thou, our Maker, Saviour, Guide,
   One true eternal God confessed:
Whom thou hast joined may none divide,
   Nor dare to curse whom thou hast blessed.

5 With thee and these for ever bound,
   May all who here in prayer unite,
With joyful songs thy throne surround,
   Rest in thy love, and reign in light.

James Montgomery (1771–1854)

May also be sung to No. 182(i), BOW BRICKHILL

ST FRANCIS   L.M. and Alleluias
(LASST UNS ERFREUEN)

Melody from
Geistliche Kirchengesang (Cologne, 1623)
Arranged by
Ralph Vaughan Williams (1872–1958)

Unison

Harmony

Al – le – lu – ia!   Al – le – lu – ia!

Unison

Harmony ad lib.

Al – le – lu – ia!   Al – le – lu – ia!   Al – le –

THE WORSHIPPING PEOPLE

lu – ia! Al-le -lu – ia! Al-le-lu – ia!

For this tune in a lower key see No. 329

1 FROM all that dwell below the skies
Let the Creator's praise arise:
Alleluia!
Let the Redeemer's name be sung,
Through every land, by every tongue:
Alleluia!

2 Eternal are thy mercies, Lord;
Eternal truth attends thy word:
Alleluia!
Thy praise shall sound from shore to shore,
Till suns shall rise and set no more:
Alleluia!

Isaac Watts (1674–1748)
based on Psalm 117

Praise and Adoration

490

WETHERBY C.M.

S. S. Wesley (1810–76)

1 GREAT Shepherd of thy people, hear;
   Thy presence now display;
   As thou hast given a place for prayer,
   So give us hearts to pray.

2 Within these walls let holy peace
   And love and concord dwell;
   Here give the troubled conscience ease,
   The wounded spirit heal.

3 May we in faith receive thy word,
   In faith present our prayers,
   And in the presence of our Lord
   Unburden all our cares.

4 The hearing ear, the seeing eye,
   The humble mind, bestow;
   And shine upon us from on high,
   That we in grace may grow.

John Newton (1725–1807) alt.

May also be sung to No. 46 (i), ABRIDGE

491

RENDEZ À DIEU 9.8.9.8.D.

Melody from *La Forme des Prières et Chants Ecclésiastiques* (Strasbourg 1545)
(2nd line as in *Genevan Psalter*, 1553)

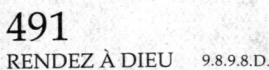

Psalm 98

1 NEW songs of celebration render
   To him who has great wonders done.
Awed by his power, his foes surrender
   And fall before the mighty One.
He has made known his great salvation
   Which all his friends with joy confess:
He has revealed to every nation
   His everlasting righteousness.

2 Joyfully, heartily resounding,
   Let every instrument and voice
Peal out the praise of grace abounding,
   Calling the whole world to rejoice.
Trumpets and organs, set in motion
   Such sounds as make the heavens ring;
All things that live in earth and ocean,
   Make music for your mighty King.

3 Rivers and seas and torrents roaring,
   Honour the Lord with wild acclaim;
Mountains and stones, look up adoring
   And find a voice to praise his name.
Righteous, commanding, ever glorious,
   Praises be his that never cease:
Just is our God, whose truth victorious
   Establishes the world in peace.

Erik Routley (1917–82)

Praise and Adoration

SING HOSANNA   10.8.10.9. (Refrain)   Traditional, arranged by compilers
of *New Church Praise* (1975)

1 GIVE me joy
2 Give me peace { in my heart, keep me { prais-ing,__
3 Give me love { lov – ing,__
{ serv- ing, _   Give me

Unison

joy
peace } in my heart, I pray;   Give me
love

joy
peace } in my heart, keep me { prais-ing,__
love { lov – ing__   Keep me
{ serv- ing__

THE WORSHIPPING PEOPLE

Refrain

{prais-ing / lov-ing / serv-ing} till the break of day: Sing ho-san-na!

Sing ho-san-na! Sing ho-san-na to the King of kings! Sing ho-san-na! Sing ho-san-na! Sing ho-san-na to the King!

Anonymous

Praise and Adoration

493

GLORY TO GOD   Irreg.   Christopher Walker (1947–   )

GLO-RY to God in the

high-est,____ And peace to his peo-ple on earth.____

Lord God, hea-ven-ly King,____ Al-migh-ty

THE WORSHIPPING PEOPLE

God and Fa - ther,___ We wor - ship you, we give_ you thanks, We praise you for your glo - ry___ Lord Je - sus Christ,___ on - ly Son of the Fa - ther,___ Lord God, Lamb of God, You take a-

-way the sin of the world: Have mer-cy on

us; You are seat-ed at the

right hand of the Fa-ther: Re - ceive our prayer.

A tempo For you a - lone are the

THE WORSHIPPING PEOPLE

Ho-ly One,___ You a - lone are the Lord,___

You a - lone are the Most High, Je-sus Christ, with the

Ho - ly Spi-rit,_____ In the glo-ry of God the

Fa - ther.___ A - men, A - men.

Gloria in Excelsis (ICET text)

Praise and Adoration

GRÖNINGEN (GOTT IST GEGENWÄRTIG)

Based on a melody by
Joachim Neander (1650–80)

6.6.8.6.6.8.33.6.6.

THE WORSHIPPING PEOPLE

1   GOD is in his temple,
      The Almighty Father;
    Round his footstool let us gather:
        Serve with adoration
        Him, the Lord most holy,
    Who has mercy on the lowly;
            Let us raise
            Hymns of praise,
        For his great salvation:
        God is in his temple.

2   Christ comes to his temple:
      We, his word receiving,
    Are made happy in believing,
        Now from sin delivered;
        He has turned our sadness,
    Our deep gloom, to light and gladness;
            Let us raise
            Hymns of praise,
        For our bonds are severed:
        Christ comes to his temple.

3   Come and claim your temple,
      Gracious Holy Spirit,
    In our hearts your home inherit;
        Make in us your dwelling,
        Your high work fulfilling,
    Into ours your will instilling;
            Till we raise
            Hymns of praise,
        Beyond mortal telling,
        In the eternal temple.

William Tidd Matson (1833–99)

495(i)

VERMONT L.M.

A. E. Floyd (1877–1974)

495(ii)

WHITEHALL L.M.

Melody by Henry Lawes (1596–1662)

THE WORSHIPPING PEOPLE

1 HE wants not friends that hath thy love,
 And may converse and walk with thee,
 And with thy saints here and above,
 With whom for ever I must be.

2 In the communion of thy saints
 Is wisdom, safety, and delight;
 And when my heart declines and faints,
 'Tis raisèd by their heat and light.

3 As for my friends, they are not lost;
 The several vessels of thy fleet,
 Though parted now, by tempests tossed,
 Shall safely in the haven meet.

4 Still are we centred all in thee,
 Members, though distant, of one Head;
 In the same family are we,
 By the same faith and Spirit led.

5 Before thy throne we daily meet
 As joint-petitioners to thee;
 In spirit we each other greet,
 And shall again each other see.

6 The heavenly hosts, world without end,
 Shall be my company above;
 And thou, my best and surest friend,
 Who shall divide me from thy love?

Richard Baxter (1615–91)

May also be sung to No. 299, ILLSLEY

496
DUNDEE C.M.

Melody from *Scottish Psalter* (1615)
Harmony from Ravenscroft's *Psalmes* (1621)

SECOND VERSION
(with later form of rhythm)

DUNDEE C.M.

THE WORSHIPPING PEOPLE

Psalm 121

1 I TO the hills will lift mine eyes;
　　From whence doth come mine aid?
　My safety cometh from the Lord,
　　Who heaven and earth hath made.

2 Thy foot he'll not let slide, nor will
　　He slumber that thee keeps;
　Behold, he that keeps Israel,
　　He slumbers not, nor sleeps.

3 The Lord thee keeps; the Lord thy shade
　　On thy right hand doth stay;
　The moon by night thee shall not smite,
　　Nor yet the sun by day.

4 The Lord shall keep thy soul; he shall
　　Preserve thee from all ill;
　Henceforth thy going out and in
　　God keep for ever will.

Scottish Psalter (1650)

497

ASCALON 6 6.8.D.

Melody from Hoffman and Richter's
Silesian Folk Songs, Leipzig (1842)

ANOTHER VERSION

ASCALON 66.8.D.

Melody from Hoffman and Richter's
Silesian Folk-Songs (1842)

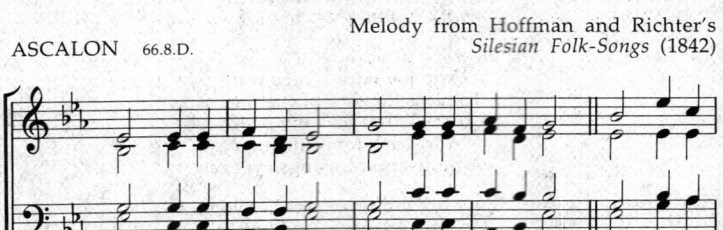

THE WORSHIPPING PEOPLE

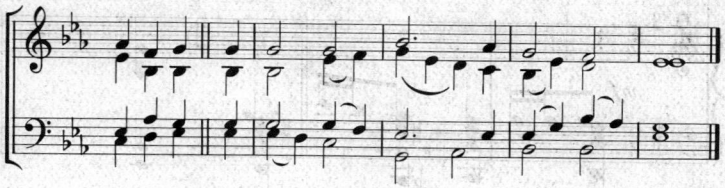

1   HOW pleased and blest was I
    To hear the people cry,
Come, let us seek our God today!
    Yes, with a cheerful zeal
    We haste to Zion's hill,
And there our vows and honours pay.

2   Zion, thrice happy place,
    Adorned with wondrous grace,
And walls of strength embrace thee round;
    In thee our tribes appear,
    To pray, and praise, and hear
The sacred gospel's joyful sound.

3   There David's greater Son
    Has fixed his royal throne,
He sits for grace and judgement there;
    He bids the saint be glad,
    He makes the sinner sad,
And humble souls rejoice with fear.

4   May peace attend thy gate,
    And joy within thee wait
To bless the soul of every guest;
    On all that seek thy peace
    And wish for thine increase
A thousand blessings ever rest.

5   My tongue repeats her vows,
    Peace to this sacred house!
For there my friends and kindred dwell;
    And since my glorious God
    Makes thee his blest abode,
My soul shall ever love thee well.

Isaac Watts (1674–1748) alt.
based on Psalm 122

Praise and Adoration

498

PSALM 121

Arthur Wills (1926–)

With quiet conviction (♩=56)

𝄋 *Antiphon (full)*

mf

I lift up mine eyes to the hills;___ From whence does my help come? My help comes from the Lord, Who made heaven and earth.

Fine

Verses

1 MAY he not suf-fer your foot__ to__ slip,_ He who
2 The_ Lord is your keep - er and shade; He de-
3 The_ Lord will_ keep you from all e-vil, He will
4 To the Fa - ther_ be__ the_ glo-ry, To the

keeps you not slum-ber!_ Be - hold, he__ who keeps
-fends your right; The sun__ shall not smite you by
keep your soul, He will keep your go-ing out and com-ing
Son, and to the Spi - rit,_ As it was, is now and e - ver

Repeat Antiphon (𝄋)

Is - ra - el Nei - ther slum-bers nor sleeps._
day,_____ Nor the moon by__ night._
in_____ From_ hence-forth for e - ver.
shall be, World with-out end._

Repeat Antiphon (𝄋)

Alan Luff (1928–)
based on Psalm 121

Praise and Adoration

499(i)

GWALCHMAI 7.4.7.4.D.

J. D. Jones (1827–70)

499(ii)

BEMERTON 7.4.7.4.D.

John Wilson (1905–)

THE WORSHIPPING PEOPLE

1 KING of Glory, King of Peace,
    I will love thee;
And that love may never cease
    I will move thee.
Thou hast granted my request,
    Thou hast heard me;
Thou didst note my working breast,
    Thou hast spared me.

2 Wherefore with my utmost art
    I will sing thee,
And the cream of all my heart
    I will bring thee.
Though my sins against me cried,
    Thou didst clear me;
And alone, when they replied,
    Thou didst hear me.

3 Seven whole days, not one in seven,
    I will praise thee;
In my heart, though not in heaven,
    I can raise thee.
Small it is, in this poor sort
    To enrol thee:
E'en eternity's too short
    To extol thee.

George Herbert (1593–1633)

Praise and Adoration

500

ABINGDON   8 8.8 8.8 8.

Erik Routley (1917–82)

THE WORSHIPPING PEOPLE

1 LORD God, your love has called us here
   As we, by love, for love were made;
Your living likeness still we bear,
   Though marred, dishonoured, disobeyed;
We come, with all our heart and mind,
Your call to hear, your love to find.

2 We come with self-inflicted pains
   Of broken trust and chosen wrong,
Half-free, half-bound by inner chains,
   By social forces swept along,
By powers and systems close confined,
Yet seeking hope for humankind.

3 Lord God, in Christ you call our name,
   And then receive us as your own,
Not through some merit, right or claim,
   But by your gracious love alone;
We strain to glimpse your mercy–seat,
And find you kneeling at our feet.

4 Then take the towel, and break the bread,
   And humble us, and call us friends;
Suffer and serve till all are fed,
   And show how grandly love intends
To work till all creation sings,
To fill all worlds, to crown all things.

5 Lord God, in Christ you set us free
   Your life to live, your joy to share;
Give us your Spirit's liberty
   To turn from guilt and dull despair
And offer all that faith can do,
While love is making all things new.

Brian A. Wren (1936–)

501

AMSTERDAM 7.6.7.6.7.7.7.6.

Melody as in John Wesley's *Sacred Harmony* (1780)

THE WORSHIPPING PEOPLE

1 MEET and right it is to sing,
    In every time and place,
Glory to our heavenly King,
    The God of truth and grace:
Join we then with sweet accord,
    All in one thanksgiving join;
Holy, holy, holy Lord,
    Eternal praise be thine.

2 Thee the first-born sons of light,
    In choral symphonies,
Praise by day, day without night,
    And never, never cease;
Angels and archangels all
    Praise the mystic Three in One,
Sing, and stop, and gaze, and fall
    O'erwhelmed before thy throne.

3 Vying with that happy choir,
    Who chant thy praise above,
We on eagles' wings aspire,
    The wings of faith and love:
Thee they sing with glory crowned,
    We extol the slaughtered Lamb;
Lower if our voices sound,
    Our subject is the same.

4 Father, God, thy love we praise,
    Which gave thy Son to die;
Jesus, full of truth and grace,
    Alike we glorify;
Spirit, Comforter dívine,
    Praise by all to thee be given;
Till we in full chorus join,
    And earth is turned to heaven.

Charles Wesley (1707–88)

502

O PRAISE GOD

Charles Villiers Stanford (1852–1924)

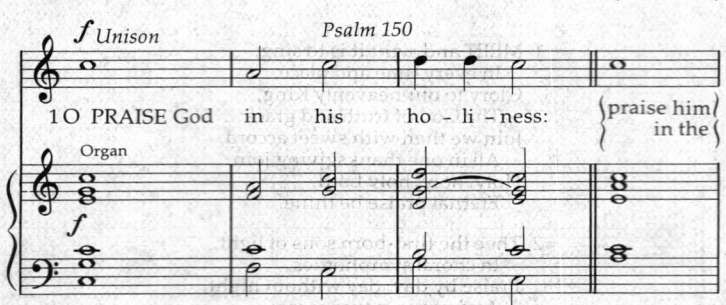

1 O PRAISE God in his ho-li-ness: {praise him/in the}

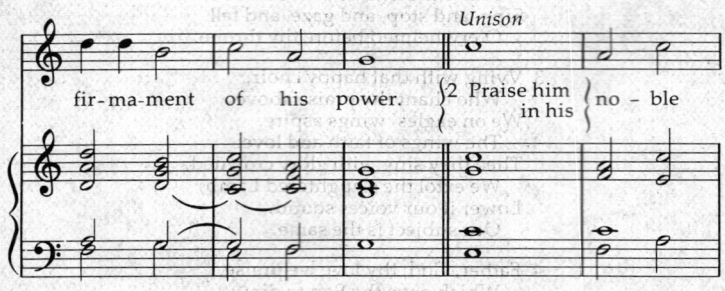

fir-ma-ment of his power. {2 Praise him/in his} no-ble

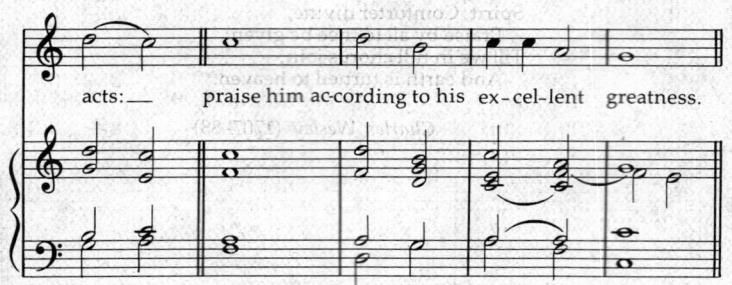

acts:___ praise him ac-cord-ing to his ex-cel-lent greatness.

THE WORSHIPPING PEOPLE

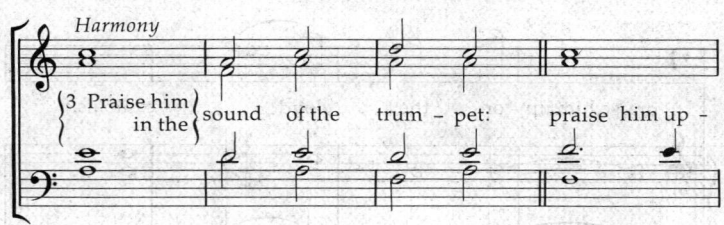

3 Praise him in the sound of the trum – pet: praise him up –

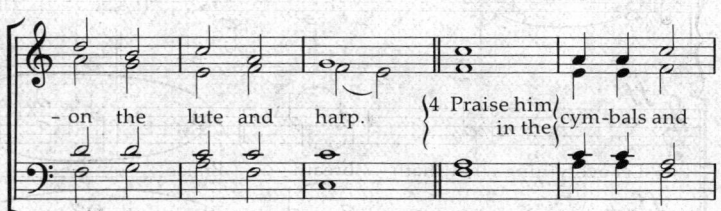

– on the lute and harp. 4 Praise him in the cym-bals and

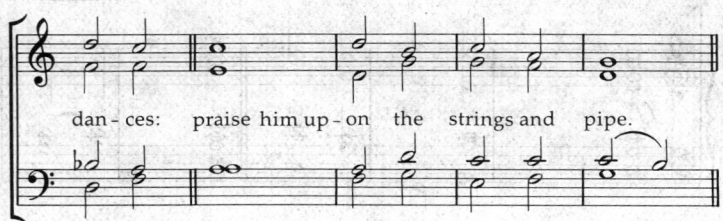

dan – ces: praise him up – on the strings and pipe.

ff *men's voices, unison*

5 Praise him upon the well – tuned cym – bals:

Praise and Adoration

praise him up-on   the   loud____ cymbals.

Full
ff
6 Let everything that hath breath_ Praise____

the   Lord!

GLORIA
Glory be to the Father, and   to   the

THE WORSHIPPING PEOPLE

Son,___ And to the Ho – ly Ghost;

As it was in the beginning, is now, and ev – er shall be, World without

end.___ A – – – – – men.

503

THE SONG OF CAEDMON   Irreg.   Donald Swann (1923–   )

1. O PRAISE him! O praise him! O praise____ him! O praise____ him! He made the heavens, he made our sky, The sun, the moon, the stars on high; He formed our world; his migh-ty hand Di-vi-ded sea____ and land; He moves in wind and

THE WORSHIPPING PEOPLE

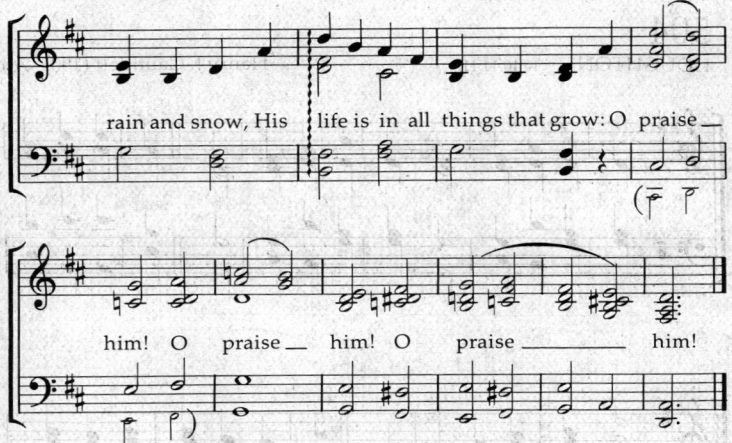

rain and snow, His | life is in all things that grow: O praise

him! O praise him! O praise him!

1 O PRAISE him! O praise him! O praise him!
O praise him! O praise him! O praise him!
   He made the heavens, he made our sky,
   The sun, the moon, the stars on high;
He formed our world; his mighty hand
Divided sea and land;
   He moves in wind and rain and snow,
   His life is in all things that grow:
O praise him! O praise him! O praise him!

2 O praise him! O praise him! O praise him!
O praise him! O praise him! O praise him!
   His joy is in the eagle's flight,
   The tiger's roar, the lion's might,
The lamb, the python and the whale,
The spider, ant and snail;
   All things that leap and swim and fly
   On land and sea and in the sky,
They praise him, they praise him, they praise him.

3 O praise him! O praise him! O praise him!
O praise him! O praise him! O praise him!
   He lives his life in love and joy,
   In man and woman, girl and boy;
His purpose is in me and you,
In what we are and do;
   His love is in us when we sing
   With every God-created thing,
And praise him, and praise him, and praise him.

Arthur Scholey (1932–)

Praise and Adoration

504

HOUGHTON 10 10.11 11.

Henry J. Gauntlett (1805–76)

505
WASHINGT S. 10.10.10

Melody from the *Fair-mada* MS, Gillington, 1769
as harmonized by
The *Episcopal Hymnal*, 1906

1 O HEAVENLY King, look down from above;
   Assist us to sing thy mercy and love:
      So sweetly o'erflowing, so plenteous the store,
      Thou still art bestowing, and giving us more.

2 O God of our life, we hallow thy name;
   Our business and strife is thee to proclaim.
      Accept our thanksgiving for creating grace;
      The living, the living shall show forth thy praise.

3 Our Father and Lord, almighty art thou;
   Preserved by thy word, we worship thee now;
      The bountiful donor of all we enjoy,
      Our tongues, to thine honour, and lives we employ.

4 But O above all thy kindness we praise,
   From sin and from thrall which saves the lost race;
      Thy Son thou hast given the world to redeem,
      And bring us to heaven whose trust is in him.

5 Wherefore of thy love we sing and rejoice,
   With angels above we lift up our voice;
      Thy love each believer shall gladly adore,
      For ever and ever, when time is no more.

Charles Wesley (1707–88)

505
WAS LEBET 13 10.13 10.

Melody from the 'Rheinhardt MS' (Üttingen, 1754)
As harmonised in
The English Hymnal (1906)

(Vv. 1 & 5)

(Vv. 1 & 5)

THE WORSHIPPING PEOPLE

1 O WORSHIP the Lord in the beauty of holiness,
    Bow down before him, his glory proclaim;
  With gold of obedience and incense of lowliness,
    Kneel and adore him: the Lord is his name.

2 Low at his feet lay thy burden of carefulness,
    High on his heart he will bear it for thee,
  Comfort thy sorrows, and answer thy prayerfulness,
    Guiding thy steps as may best for thee be.

3 Fear not to enter his courts in the slenderness
    Of the poor wealth thou wouldst reckon as thine;
  Truth in its beauty, and love in its tenderness,
    These are the offerings to lay on his shrine.

4 These, though we bring them in trembling and
        fearfulness,
    He will accept for the name that is dear;
  Mornings of joy give for evenings of tearfulness,
    Trust for our trembling, and hope for our fear.

5 O worship the Lord in the beauty of holiness,
    Bow down before him, his glory proclaim;
  With gold of obedience and incense of lowliness,
    Kneel and adore him: the Lord is his name.

John Samuel Bewley Monsell (1811–75)

506

PRAISE HIM IN THE MORNING

4.6.6.4.7.

Anon.
Arranged by
Douglas Coombes

1 PRAISE _____ him, praise _____ him,

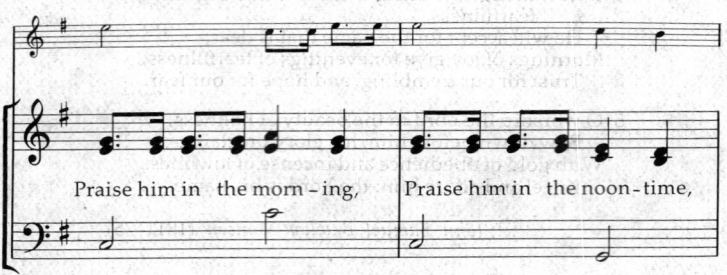

Praise him in the morn-ing, Praise him in the noon-time,

Praise _____ him, praise _____ him,

Praise him when the sun goes down.

1 PRAISE him, praise him,
Praise him in the morning,
Praise him in the noon-time,
Praise him, praise him,
Praise him when the sun goes down.

2 Trust him, trust him,
Trust him in the morning,
Trust him in the noon-time,
Trust him, trust him,
Trust him when the sun goes down.

3 Serve him, serve him,
Serve him in the morning,
Serve him in the noon-time,
Serve him, serve him,
Serve him when the sun goes down.

4 Praise him, praise him,
Praise him in the morning,
Praise him in the noon-time,
Praise him, praise him,
Praise him when the sun goes down.

Anonymous

Praise and Adoration

507
PRAISE THE LORD OF HEAVEN   6.5.6.5.D.

Norman L. Warren
(1934–)

Unison

1 PRAISE the Lord of hea-ven, Praise him in the height;

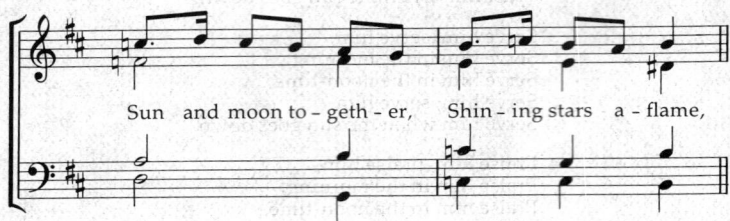

Praise him, all his an-gels, Praise him, hosts of light.

Sun and moon to-geth-er, Shin-ing stars a-flame,

Plan-ets in their cours-es, Mag-ni-fy his name!

THE WORSHIPPING PEOPLE

Psalm 148

1 PRAISE the Lord of heaven,
      Praise him in the height;
   Praise him, all his angels,
      Praise him, hosts of light.
   Sun and moon together,
      Shining stars aflame,
   Planets in their courses,
      Magnify his name!

2 Earth and ocean, praise him;
      Mountains, hills and trees;
   Fire and hail and tempest,
      Wind and storm and seas.
   Praise him, fields and forests,
      Birds on flashing wings,
   Praise him, beasts and cattle,
      All created things.

3 Now by prince and people
      Let his praise be told;
   Praise him, men and maidens,
      Praise him, young and old.
   He, the Lord of glory!
      We, his praise proclaim!
   High above all heavens
      Magnify his name!

Timothy Dudley-Smith (1926–   )

508(i)

MONKLAND 77.77.

Arranged by J. Wilkes (1861)
from a tune composed or adapted
by John Antes (1740–1811)

For this tune in a lower key see No. 359

1 PRAISE the Lord with joyful cry;
Let the mood of praise run high.
Praise him who with mighty deeds
Human greatness far exceeds.

2 Praise him with the sound that swings,
With percussion, brass and strings.
Let the world at every chance
Praise him with a song and dance.

3 Praise with life and voice the Lord,
Him who speaks in deed and word,
Who to life the world ordained:
Let our praise be unrestrained!

Fred Kaan (1929–)
based on Psalm 150

THE WORSHIPPING PEOPLE

Lawrence Bartlett (1933–   )

Unison. Boldly

1 PRAISE the Lord ___ with joy – ful cry; ___ Let the
2 Praise him with ___ the sound that swings, ___ With per –

mood of praise run high. Praise him who with migh-ty
–cus-sion, brass and strings. Let the world at ev–ery

deeds Hu – man great –ness far ___ ex – ceeds.
chance Praise him with a song ___ and ___ dance.

(See following page for v. 3)

Praise and Adoration

508(ii) (cont.)

Descant by John Wilson

Optional descant

Praise _____ the Lord, __

3 Praise with life ___ and voice the Lord, — Him who

in deed __ and word, __ Who__ to life or–

speaks in deed and word, Who to life ___ the world or–

– dained: our praise _____ un –re – strained!

– dained: Let our praise be un – re – strained!

Words reprinted by permission of
Stainer & Bell Ltd.
For permission to reproduce see p. xiii.

Fred Kaan (1929–   )
based on Psalm 150

THE WORSHIPPING PEOPLE

509

OLD 124th   10 10.10.10 10.   Melody from *Genevan Psalter* (1551)

1 PRAISE ye the Lord, ye servants of the Lord;
    Praise ye his name; his lordly honour sing:
    Thee we adore; to thee glad homage bring;
Thee we acknowledge; God to be adored
    For thy great glory, Sovereign, Lord, and King.

2 Father of Christ—of him whose work was done,
    When by his death he took our sins away—
    To thee belongeth worship, day by day,
Yea, holy Father, everlasting Son,
    And Holy Ghost, all praise be thine for aye!

Apostolic Constitutions (3rd Century)
tr. *George Ratcliffe Woodward* (1848–1934)
and others

Praise and Adoration

510

YORK C.M.

Melody from *Scottish Psalter* (1615). Harmony adapted from
J. Milton (senior) (*c.* 1563– 1647)
in Ravenscroft's *Psalmes* (1621)

1 PRAY that Jerusalem may have
    Peace and felicity:
  Let them that love thee and thy peace
    Have still prosperity.

2 Behold how good a thing it is,
    And how becoming well,
  Together such as kindred are
    In unity to dwell.

3 Therefore I wish that peace may still
    Within thy walls remain,
  And ever may thy palaces
    Prosperity retain.

4 Now, for my friends' and kindred's sake,
    Peace be in thee, I'll say;
  And for the house of God our Lord
    I'll seek thy good alway.

Scottish Psalter (1650)
based on Psalm 122: 6–9 and Psalm 133:1.

511

MIT FREUDEN ZART 8.7.8.7.88.7.

Later form of a melody in the
Bohemian Brethren's
Kirchengeseng (Berlin, 1566)

THE WORSHIPPING PEOPLE

1 SING praise to God who reigns above,
   The God of all creation,
The God of power, the God of love,
   The God of our salvation;
With healing balm my soul he fills,
And every faithless murmur stills:
   To God all praise and glory!

2 What God's almighty power has made
   That will he ever cherish,
And will, unfailing, soon and late,
   With loving-kindness nourish;
And where he rules in kingly might
There all is just and all is right:
   To God all praise and glory!

3 The Lord is never far away,
   But, through all grief distressing,
An ever-present help and stay,
   Our peace, and joy, and blessing;
As with a mother's tender hand,
He leads his own, his chosen band:
   To God all praise and glory!

4 O ye who name Christ's holy name,
   Give God all praise and glory:
All ye who own his power, proclaim
   Aloud the wondrous story.
Cast each false idol from his throne,
The Lord is God, and he alone:
   To God all praise and glory!

Johann Jakob Schütz (1640–90)
tr. *Frances Elizabeth Cox* (1812–97)
vv. 1, 3 and 4.
Honor Mary Thwaites (1914–) v. 2

512(i)

LAUDS 77.77.

John Wilson (1905–   )

Flowing easily

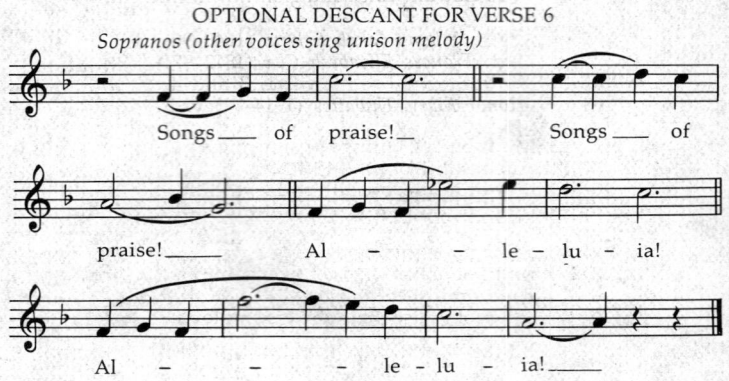

(small notes organ only)

(The key of F sharp may be preferred)

OPTIONAL DESCANT FOR VERSE 6

Sopranos (other voices sing unison melody)

Songs___ of praise!___ Songs___ of

praise!___ Al – – le – lu – ia!

Al – – – le – lu – ia!___

THE WORSHIPPING PEOPLE

512(ii)

NORTHAMPTON   77.77.

C. J. King (1859–1934)

1 SONGS of praise the angels sang,
  Heaven with alleluias rang,
  When Jehovah's work begun,
  When he spake, and it was done.

2 Songs of praise awoke the morn
  When the Prince of Peace was born;
  Songs of praise arose when he
  Captive led captivity.

3 Heaven and earth must pass away,
  Songs of praise shall crown that day;
  God will make new heavens, new earth,
  Songs of praise shall hail their birth.

4 And shall earth alone be dumb
  Till that glorious kingdom come?
  No! The church delights to raise
  Psalms and hymns and songs of praise.

5 Saints below, with heart and voice,
  Still in songs of praise rejoice,
  Learning here, by faith and love,
  Songs of praise to sing above.

6 Borne upon their latest breath,
  Songs of praise shall conquer death;
  Then, amidst eternal joy,
  Songs of praise their powers employ.

James Montgomery (1771–1854)

Praise and Adoration

513(i)
CARLISLE S.M.

Melody and most of the harmony
by C. Lockhart (1745–1815)

513(ii)
DONCASTER S.M.

Samuel Wesley (1766–1837)

1   STAND up, and bless the Lord,
     Ye people of his choice;
  Stand up, and bless the Lord your God
     With heart and soul and voice.

2   Though high above all praise,
     Above all blessing high,
  Who would not fear his holy name,
     And laud and magnify?

3   O for the living flame
     From his own altar brought,
  To touch our lips, our minds inspire,
     And wing to heaven our thought!

4   God is our strength and song,
     And his salvation ours;
  Then be his love in Christ proclaimed
     With all our ransomed powers.

5   Stand up, and bless the Lord,
     The Lord your God adore;
  Stand up. and bless his glorious name
     Henceforth for evermore.

James Montgomery (1771–1854)

514(i)
DEEP HARMONY L.M.

Handel Parker (1854–1928)

514(ii)
CARLISLE MEMORIAL L.M.

Charles Eyre (1927–)

1 SWEET is the work, my God, my King,
   To praise thy name, give thanks, and sing;
      To show thy love by morning light,
      And talk of all thy truth at night.

2 Sweet is the day of sacred rest,
   No mortal cares disturb my breast;
      O may my heart in tune be found
      Like David's harp of solemn sound!

3 My heart shall triumph in my Lord,
   And bless his works, and bless his word:
      Thy works of grace, how bright they shine!
      How deep thy counsels, how divine!

4 Then shall I bear a glorious part,
   When grace has well refined my heart,
      And fresh supplies of joy are shed,
      Like holy oil to cheer my head.

5 Then shall I see, and hear, and know
   All I desired or wished below;
      And every power find sweet employ
      In that eternal world of joy.

Isaac Watts (1674–1748)
based on Psalm 92

515

AURELIA 7.6.7.6.D.

S. S. Wesley (1810–76)

THE WORSHIPPING PEOPLE

1 THE church's one foundation
   Is Jesus Christ her Lord;
She is his new creation
   By water and the word;
From heaven he came and sought her
   To be his holy bride;
With his own blood he bought her,
   And for her life he died.

2 Elect from every nation,
   Yet one o'er all the earth,
Her charter of salvation
   One Lord, one faith, one birth;
One holy name she blesses,
   Partakes one holy food,
And to one hope she presses
   With every grace endued.

3 'Mid toil and tribulation,
   And tumult of her war,
She waits the consummation
   Of peace for evermore;
Till with the vision glorious
   Her longing eyes are blest,
And the great church victorious
   Shall be the church at rest.

4 Yet she on earth has union
   With God the Three in One,
And mystic sweet communion
   With those whose rest is won.
O happy ones and holy!
   Lord, give us grace that we,
Like them, the meek and lowly,
   On high may dwell with thee.

Samuel John Stone (1839–1900)

516

ST GEORGE'S, EDINBURGH   Andrew Mitchell Thomson (1778–1831)

D.C.M. and Alleluias

1 YE gates, lift up your heads on high; Ye
2 Ye gates, lift up your heads; ye doors, Doors

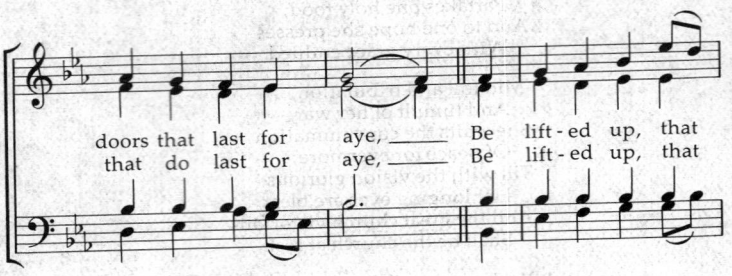

doors that last for aye,＿ Be lift-ed up, that
that do last for aye,＿ Be lift-ed up, that

so the King Of glo-ry en-ter may. → **A**
so the King Of glo-ry en-ter may. → **B**

(over)

→ **C**

Praise and Adoration

C

D.C. for V. 2

1 Ev'n that same Lord, that great in might And
2 The Lord of hosts, and none but he, The

1 strong in bat‑tle is. Ev'n that same Lord, that
2 King of glo‑ry is. The Lord of hosts, and

1 great in might And strong in bat‑tle is.
2 none but he, The King of glo‑ry is.

THE WORSHIPPING PEOPLE

CODA *(after verse 2)*

Al – le-lu – ia! Al – le-lu – ia!

Al – le-lu – ia! Al – le-lu – ia! Al-le-lu – ia!

With breadth

A – men, a – men, a – – men.

Scottish Psalter (1650)
based on Psalm 24:7–10

Praise and Adoration

517 (i)

NETTLETON 8.7.8.7.D.

American Folk Hymn Melody
Harmonised by John Wilson

517 (ii)

NORMANDY 8.7.8.7.D.

A. Bost (1790–1874)

THE WORSHIPPING PEOPLE

1 COME, thou fount of every blessing,
　　Tune my heart to sing thy grace;
Streams of mercy never ceasing
　　Call for songs of loudest praise.
Teach me some melodious measure
　　Sung by flaming tongues above;
O the vast, the boundless treasure
　　Of my Lord's unchanging love!

2 Here I find my greatest treasure:
　　'Hither by thy help I've come',
And I hope, by thy good pleasure,
　　Safely to arrive at home.
Jesus sought me when a stranger,
　　Wandering from the fold of God;
He, to rescue me from danger,
　　Interposed his precious blood.

3 O to grace how great a debtor
　　Daily I'm constrained to be!
Let that grace, Lord, like a fetter,
　　Bind my wandering heart to thee.
Prone to wander, Lord, I feel it,
　　Prone to leave the God I love;
Take my heart, O take and seal it,
　　Seal it from thy courts above!

Robert Robinson (1735–90) alt.

Confession and Supplication

518

LE P'ING 55.55.D.
('Joyous Peace')

Chinese Melody by Hu Te-ai (*c.* 1900–   )
Harmonised by Bliss Wiant (1895–1975)

THE WORSHIPPING PEOPLE

1 FATHER God in heaven,
   Hallowed be thy name;
Rule to thee be given,
   Power and all acclaim.
Thee may we obey
   As the hosts above;
Bread for us each day
   Broken by thy love.

2 Pardoned, as we share
   In thy pardoning power,
Kept from Satan's snare
   In temptation's hour:
So from sin set free,
   Lord, we seek thy face,
Sons of liberty,
   Heirs of saving grace.

3 Grace to all men shown,
   All that grace must know,
God, their Father, own,
   To their Father go.
Christ will come at last,
   Even now so near,
Night will soon be past
   And the dawn appear.

Daniel T. Niles (1908–70)
based on the Lord's Prayer

519

RIVAULX L.M.

J. B. Dykes (1823–76)

THE WORSHIPPING PEOPLE

1 FATHER of heaven, whose love profound
  A ransom for our souls has found,
    Before thy throne we sinners bend;
    To us thy pardoning love extend.

2 Almighty Son, incarnate Word,
  Our Prophet, Priest, Redeemer, Lord,
    Before thy throne we sinners bend;
    To us thy saving grace extend.

3 Eternal Spirit, by whose breath
  The soul is raised from sin and death,
    Before thy throne we sinners bend;
    To us thy quickening power extend.

4 Thrice holy—Father, Spirit, Son,
  Mysterious Godhead, Three in One,
    Before thy throne we sinners bend;
    Grace, pardon, life, to us extend.

Edward Cooper (1770–1833)

520

MELCOMBE L.M.

Melody and figured bass by
S. Webbe the elder (1740–1816)

ANOTHER HARMONISATION

MELCOMBE L.M.

Harmonised by W. H. Monk (1823–89)

THE WORSHIPPING PEOPLE

1 FATHER, whose everlasting love
   Thy only Son for sinners gave,
Whose grace to all did freely move,
   And sent him down the world to save:

2 Help us thy mercy to extol,
   Immense, unfathomed, unconfined;
To praise the Lamb who died for all,
   The general Saviour of mankind.

3 Thy undistinguishing regard
   Was cast on Adam's fallen race;
For all thou hast in Christ prepared
   Sufficient, sovereign, saving grace.

4 The world he suffered to redeem;
   For all he has the atonement made;
For those that will not come to him
   The ransom of his life was paid.

5 Arise, O God, maintain thy cause!
   The fullness of the nations call;
Lift up the standard of thy cross,
   And all shall own thou diedst for all.

Charles Wesley (1707–88)

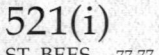

521(i)
ST BEES 77.77.

J. B. Dykes (1823–76)

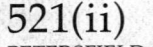

521(ii)
PETERSFIELD 77.77.

William H. Harris (1883–1973)

THE WORSHIPPING PEOPLE

1 HARK, my soul! It is the Lord;
   'Tis thy Saviour, hear his word;
   Jesus speaks, and speaks to thee:
   'Say, poor sinner, lov'st thou me?

2 'I delivered thee when bound,
   And, when bleeding, healed thy wound;
   Sought thee wandering, set thee right,
   Turned thy darkness into light.

3 'Can a woman's tender care
   Cease toward the child she bare?
   Yes, she may forgetful be,
   Yet will I remember thee.

4 'Mine is an unchanging love,
   Higher than the heights above,
   Deeper than the depths beneath,
   Free and faithful, strong as death.

5 'Thou shalt see my glory soon,
   When the work of grace is done;
   Partner of my throne shalt be;
   Say, poor sinner, lov'st thou me?'

6 Lord, it is my chief complaint
   That my love is weak and faint;
   Yet I love thee, and adore;
   O for grace to love thee more!

William Cowper (1731–1800)

May also be sung to No. 546 (ii), SAVANNAH

522

1 DEAR Master, in whose life I see
  All that I would, but fail to be,
    Let thy clear light for ever shine,
    To shame and guide this life of mine.

2 Though what I dream and what I do
  In my weak days are always two,
    Help me, oppressed by things undone,
    O thou, whose deeds and dreams were one!

John Hunter (1848–1917)

523

SAMUEL 6.6.6.6.88.

Arthur Sullivan (1842–1900)

THE WORSHIPPING PEOPLE

1   HUSHED was the evening hymn,
      The temple courts were dark,
    The lamp was burning dim
      Before the sacred ark,
When suddenly a voice divine
Rang through the silence of the shrine.

2   The old man, meek and mild,
      The priest of Israel, slept;
His watch the temple child,
      The little Levite, kept;
And what from Eli's sense was sealed
The Lord to Hannah's son revealed.

3   O give me Samuel's ear,
      The open ear, O Lord,
Alive and quick to hear
      Each whisper of thy word;
Like him to answer at thy call,
And to obey thee first of all.

4   O give me Samuel's heart,
      A lowly heart, that waits
Where in thy house thou art
      Or watches at thy gates
By day and night—a heart that still
Moves at the breathing of thy will.

5   O give me Samuel's mind,
      A sweet unmurmuring faith,
Obedient and resigned
      To thee in life and death,
That I may read with childlike eyes
Truths that are hidden from the wise.

James Drummond Burns (1823–64)

Confession and Supplication

524

I NEED THEE 6 4.6 4. (and refrain)

R. Lowry (1826–99)

Refrain

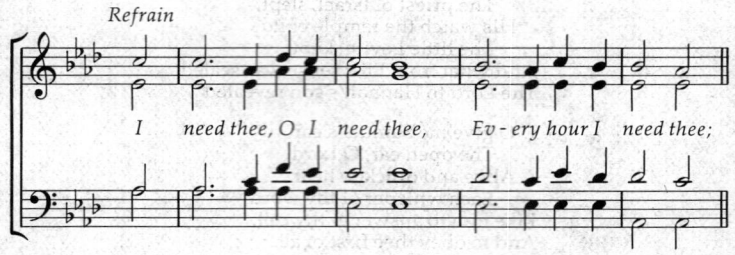

I need thee, O I need thee, Ev-ery hour I need thee;

O bless me now, my Sa-viour; I come to thee.

THE WORSHIPPING PEOPLE

1 I NEED thee every hour,
  Most gracious Lord;
No tender voice like thine
  Can peace afford:
    I need thee, O I need thee,
      Every hour I need thee;
    O bless me now, my Saviour;
      I come to thee.

2 I need thee every hour;
  Stay thou near by;
Temptations lose their power
  When thou art nigh:

3 I need thee every hour,
  In joy or pain;
Come quickly and abide,
  Or life is vain:

4 I need thee every hour;
  Teach me thy will,
And thy rich promises
  In me fulfil:

Annie Sherwood Hawks (1835–1918)

525

KUM BA YA   Irreg.

Traditional tune
Harmonised by compilers
of *New Church Praise* (1975)

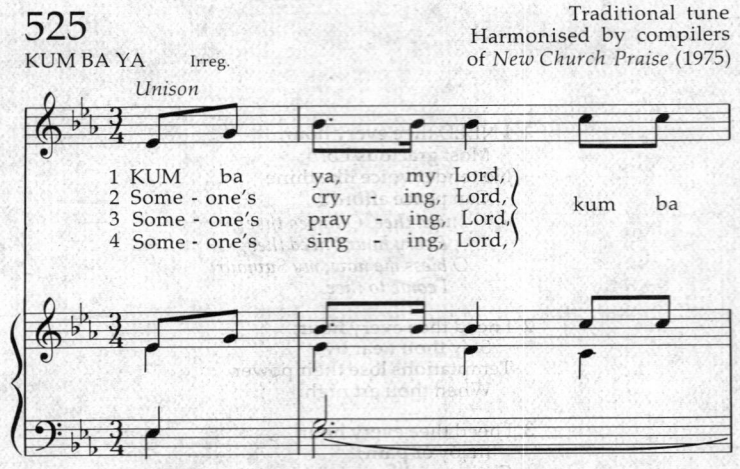

1 KUM ba ya, my Lord,
2 Some - one's cry - ing, Lord,
3 Some - one's pray - ing, Lord,
4 Some - one's sing - ing, Lord,   kum ba

ya!

Kum ba ya, my Lord,
Some-one's cry - ing, Lord,
Some-one's pray - ing, Lord,
Some-one's sing - ing, Lord,   kum ba

THE WORSHIPPING PEOPLE

Kum ba ya, my Lord,
Some-one's cry - ing, Lord,
Some-one's pray - ing, Lord,
Some-one's sing - ing, Lord,

kum ba ya! _____ O Lord, _ kum ba ya!

Anonymous

Confession and Supplication

526

IT PASSETH KNOWLEDGE 10 10.10 10.4.

I. D. Sankey (1840–1908)

1 IT passeth knowledge, that dear love of thine,
My Saviour, Jesus! Yet this soul of mine
Would of thy love, in all its breadth and length,
Its height and depth, and everlasting strength,
    Know more and more.

2 It passeth telling, that dear love of thine,
My Saviour, Jesus! Yet these lips of mine
Would fain proclaim to sinners far and near
A love which can remove all guilty fear,
    And love beget.

3 It passeth praises, that dear love of thine,
My Saviour, Jesus! Yet this heart of mine
Would sing that love, so full, so rich, so free,
Which brings a rebel sinner, such as me,
    Nigh unto God.

4 O fill me, Saviour Jesus, with thy love!
Lead, lead me to the living fount above;
Thither may I, in simple faith, draw nigh,
And never to another fountain fly,
    But unto thee.

5 And then, when Jesus face to face I see,
When at his lofty throne I bow the knee,
Then of his love, in all its breadth and length,
Its height and depth, its everlasting strength,
    My soul shall sing.

Mary Shekleton (1827–83)

Confession and Supplication

527

RESONET IN LAUDIBUS 777.6.

German Carol Melody (c. 1500)

(vv. 1, 2) Hear ____ us, ho – ly Je – sus.
(vv. 3–5) Save ____ us, ho – ly Je – sus.

1 JESUS, Saviour ever mild,
  Born for us a little child
  Of the Virgin undefiled:
    Hear us, holy Jesus.

2 Jesus, Son of God most high,
  Who didst in the manger lie,
  Who upon the cross didst die,
    Hear us, holy Jesus.

3 From all pride and vain conceit,
  From all spite and angry heat,
  From all lying and deceit,
    Save us, holy Jesus.

4 From refusing to obey,
  From the love of our own way,
  From forgetfulness to pray,
    Save us, holy Jesus.

5 By the name we bow before,
  Human name, which evermore
  All the hosts of heaven adore,
    Save us, holy Jesus.

Richard Frederick Littledale (1833–90)
and others

528(i)
ABERYSTWYTH 7.7.7.7.D.   Joseph Parry (1841–1903)

528(ii)
HOLLINGSIDE 7.7.7.7.D.   J. B. Dykes (1823–76)

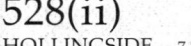

THE WORSHIPPING PEOPLE

1 JESUS, lover of my soul,
    Let me to thy bosom fly,
While the nearer waters roll,
    While the tempest still is high;
Hide me, O my Saviour, hide,
    Till the storm of life is past;
Safe into the haven guide,
    O receive my soul at last!

2 Other refuge have I none,
    Hangs my helpless soul on thee;
Leave, ah, leave me not alone,
    Still support and comfort me.
All my trust on thee is stayed,
    All my help from thee I bring;
Cover my defenceless head
    With the shadow of thy wing.

3 Thou, O Christ, art all I want;
    More than all in thee I find;
Raise the fallen, cheer the faint,
    Heal the sick, and lead the blind.
Just and holy is thy name,
    I am all unrighteousness;
False and full of sin I am,
    Thou art full of truth and grace.

4 Plenteous grace with thee is found,
    Grace to cover all my sin;
Let the healing streams abound,
    Make and keep me pure within.
Thou of life the fountain art;
    Freely let me take of thee;
Spring thou up within my heart,
    Rise to all eternity.

Charles Wesley (1707–88)

Confession and Supplication

Melody by Henry Carey (c. 1687–1743)
(slightly decorated)

1 JESUS, if still the same thou art,
　　If all thy promises are sure,
　Set up thy kingdom in my heart,
　　And make me rich, for I am poor;
　To me be all thy treasures given,
　The kingdom of an inward heaven.

2 Thou hast pronounced the mourners blest;
　　And lo, for thee I ever mourn:
　I cannot—no, I will not rest,
　　Till thou, my only rest, return;
　Till thou, the Prince of Peace, appear,
　And I receive the Comforter.

3 Where is the blessedness bestowed
　　On all that hunger after thee?
　I hunger now, I thirst for God;
　　See the poor fainting sinner, see,
　And satisfy with endless peace,
　And fill me with thy righteousness.

4 Shine on thy work, disperse the gloom,
　　Light in thy light I then shall see;
　Say to my soul: 'Thy light is come,
　　Glory divine is risen on thee,
　Thy warfare's past, thy mourning's o'er;
　Look up, for thou shalt weep no more!'

Charles Wesley (1707–88)

Confession and Supplication

530

CASWALL   6.5.6.5.   Melody by F. Filitz (1804–76)

1 JESUS, stand among us
   In thy risen power;
   Let this time of worship
   Be a hallowed hour.

2 Breathe the Holy Spirit
   Into every heart;
   Bid the fears and sorrows
   From each soul depart.

3 Thus with quickened footsteps
   We'll pursue our way,
   Watching for the dawning
   Of eternal day.

William Pennefather (1816–73)

531

VENI CITO   88.88.88.   J. B. Dykes (1823–76)
                                          (harmony slightly altered)

THE WORSHIPPING PEOPLE

1 LO, God is here, let us adore!
   How awe-inspiring is this place!
Let all within us feel his power,
   And silent bow before his face;
Who know his power, his grace who prove,
Serve him with fear, with reverence love.

2 Lo, God is here! Him day and night
   Th' united choirs of angels sing;
To him, enthroned above all height,
   Heaven's host their noblest praises bring;
Disdain not, Lord, our meaner song,
Who praise thee with a stammering tongue.

3 Gladly the things of earth we leave,
   Wealth, honour, fame, for thee alone;
To thee our will, soul, flesh, we give;
   O take, O seal them for thine own!
Thou art the God, thou art the Lord;
Be thou by all thy works adored.

4 Being of beings, may our praise
   Thy courts with grateful fragrance fill;
Still may we stand before thy face,
   Still hear and do thy sovereign will;
To thee may all our thoughts arise,
Ceaseless, accepted sacrifice.

Gerhard Tersteegen (1697–1769)
tr. John Wesley (1703–91)

May also be sung to No. 434 (ii), DAVID'S HARP

Confession and Supplication

532

ABINGDON 88.88.88.

Erik Routley (1917–82)

THE WORSHIPPING PEOPLE

1 LORD Christ, we praise your sacrifice,
   Your life in love so freely given;
For those who took your life away
   You prayed, that they might be forgiven;
And there, in helplessness arrayed,
God's power was perfectly displayed.

2 Once helpless in your mother's arms,
   Dependent on her mercy then,
You made yourself again, by choice,
   As helpless in the hands of men;
And, at their mercy crucified,
You claimed your victory and died.

3 Though helpless and rejected then,
   You reign as living Lord acclaimed;
For ever by your victory
   Is God's eternal love proclaimed—
The love which goes through death to find
New life and hope for humankind.

4 So, living Lord, prepare us now
   Your willing helplessness to share;
To give ourselves in sacrifice
   To overcome the world's despair;
In love to give our lives away
And claim your victory today.

                    Alan Gaunt (1935–   ) alt.

533

SOUTHWELL S.M.

Melody from
Damon's *The Psalmes of David* (1579)

1   LORD Jesus, think on me,
      And purge away my sin;
From earthborn passions set me free,
      And make me pure within.

2   Lord Jesus, think on me
      With care and woe oppressed;
Let me thy loving servant be,
      And taste thy promised rest.

3   Lord Jesus, think on me,
      Nor let me go astray;
Through darkness and perplexity
      Point thou the heavenly way.

4   Lord Jesus, think on me,
      That, when the flood is past,
I may the eternal brightness see,
      And share thy joy at last.

Synesius of Cyrene (5th Century)
tr. *A. W. Chatfield* (1808–96)

534

EDGWARE C. M.

Source unknown

1 NOW let us see thy beauty, Lord,
  As we have seen before;
  And by thy beauty quicken us
  To love thee and adore.

2 'Tis easy when with simple mind
  Thy loveliness we see,
  To consecrate ourselves afresh
  To duty and to thee.

3 Our every feverish mood is cooled,
  And gone is every load,
  When we can lose the love of self,
  And find the love of God.

4 Lord, it is coming to ourselves
  When thus we come to thee;
  The bondage of thy loveliness
  Is perfect liberty.

5 So now we come to ask again
  What thou hast often given,
  The vision of that loveliness
  Which is the life of heaven.

Benjamin Waugh (1839–1908)

Confession and Supplication

535(i)

OTTAWA   8.7.8.7.77.

Lowell Mason (1792–1872)

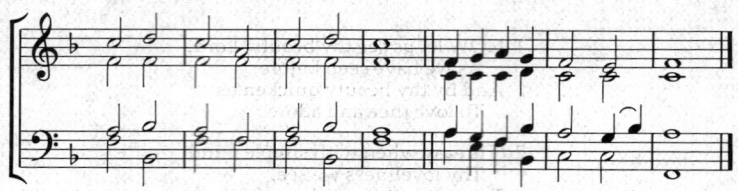

535(ii)

MORGEN, KINDER   8.7.8.7.77.

German Traditional Melody
Harmonised and arranged by
Anthony J. Hedges (1931–   )

THE WORSHIPPING PEOPLE

1 MASTER, speak! Thy servant heareth,
    Waiting for thy gracious word,
  Longing for thy voice that cheereth;
    Master, let it now be heard.
  I am listening, Lord, for thee;
  What hast thou to say to me?

2 Speak to me by name, O Master,
    Let me know it is to me;
  Speak, that I may follow faster,
    With a step more firm and free,
  Where the Shepherd leads the flock
  In the shadow of the rock.

3 Master, speak! Though least and lowest,
    Let me not unheard depart;
  Master, speak! For O thou knowest
    All the yearning of my heart,
  Knowest all its truest need;
  Speak, and make me blest indeed.

4 Master, speak: and make me ready,
    When thy voice is truly heard,
  With obedience glad and steady
    Still to follow every word.
  I am listening, Lord, for thee;
  Master, speak! O speak to me!

Frances Ridley Havergal (1836–79)

536(i)
STOCKTON C.M.

T. Wright (1763–1829)

536(ii)
ABRIDGE (ST STEPHEN) C.M.

Melody by Isaac Smith (1734–1805)
from *A Collection of Psalm Tunes* (c. 1780)

THE WORSHIPPING PEOPLE

1 O FOR a heart to praise my God,
   A heart from sin set free,
A heart that always feels thy blood
   So freely spilt for me;

2 A heart resigned, submissive, meek,
   My great Redeemer's throne,
Where only Christ is heard to speak,
   Where Jesus reigns alone;

3 A humble, lowly, contrite heart,
   Believing, true, and clean;
Which neither life nor death can part
   From him that dwells within;

4 A heart in every thought renewed,
   And full of love divine;
Perfect, and right, and pure, and good,
   A copy, Lord, of thine!

5 Thy nature, gracious Lord, impart;
   Come quickly from above,
Write thy new name upon my heart,
   Thy new, best name of love.

Charles Wesley (1707–88)

THE WORSHIPPING PEOPLE

1 O SEND thy light forth and thy truth;
    Let them be guides to me,
  And bring me to thy holy hill,
    E'en where thy dwellings be.

2 Then will I to God's altar go,
    To God my chiefest joy;
  Yea, God, my God, thy name to praise
    My harp I will employ.

3 Why art thou then cast down, my soul?
    What should discourage thee?
  And why with vexing thoughts art thou
    Disquieted in me?

4 Still trust in God; for him to praise
    Good cause I yet shall have;
  He of my count'nance is the health,
    My God that doth me save.

Scottish Psalter (1650)
based on Psalm 43:3–5

Confession and Supplication

538(i)
ALL OF THEE 8.7.8.8.7.

J. Mountain (1844–1933)

538(ii)
BOURNE 8.7.8.8.7.

Francis Westbrook (1903–75)

THE WORSHIPPING PEOPLE

1 O THE bitter shame and sorrow,
   That a time could ever be
 When I let the Saviour's pity
 Plead in vain, and proudly answered:
   All of self, and none of thee!

2 Yet he found me. I beheld him
   Bleeding on the accursèd tree,
 Heard him pray: Forgive them, Father!
 And my wistful heart said faintly:
   Some of self, and some of thee!

3 Day by day his tender mercy,
   Healing, helping, full and free,
 Sweet and strong, and, ah! so patient,
 Brought me lower, while I whispered:
   Less of self, and more of thee!

4 Higher than the highest heaven,
   Deeper than the deepest sea,
 Lord, thy love at last has conquered;
 Grant me now my supplication:
   None of self, and all of thee!

Theodore Monod (1836–1921)

Confession and Supplication

539(i)
FINGAL C.M.   James Smith Anderson (1853–1945)

539(ii)
AYRSHIRE C.M.   K. G. Finlay (1882–1974)

THE WORSHIPPING PEOPLE

1 ONE who is all unfit to count
    As scholar in thy school,
  Thou of thy love hast named a friend—
    O kindness wonderful!

2 So weak am I, O gracious Lord,
    So all unworthy thee,
  That e'en the dust upon thy feet
    Outweighs me utterly.

3 Thou dwellest in unshadowed light,
    All sin and shame above—
  That thou shouldst bear our sin and shame,
    How can I tell such love?

4 Ah, did not he the heavenly throne
    A little thing esteem,
  And not unworthy for my sake
    A mortal body deem?

5 When in his flesh they drove the nails,
    Did he not all endure?
  What name is there to fit a life
    So patient and so pure?

6 So, love itself in human form,
    For love of me he came;
  I cannot look upon his face
    For shame, for bitter shame.

7 If there is aught of worth in me,
    It comes from thee alone;
  Then keep me safe, for so, O Lord,
    Thou keepest but thine own.

Narayan Vaman Tilak (1862–1919)
tr. *Nicol MacNicol* (1870–1952)

Confession and Supplication

540

LEAMINGTON 7.6.7.6.7.7.7.6.

S. Arnold (1740–1802)

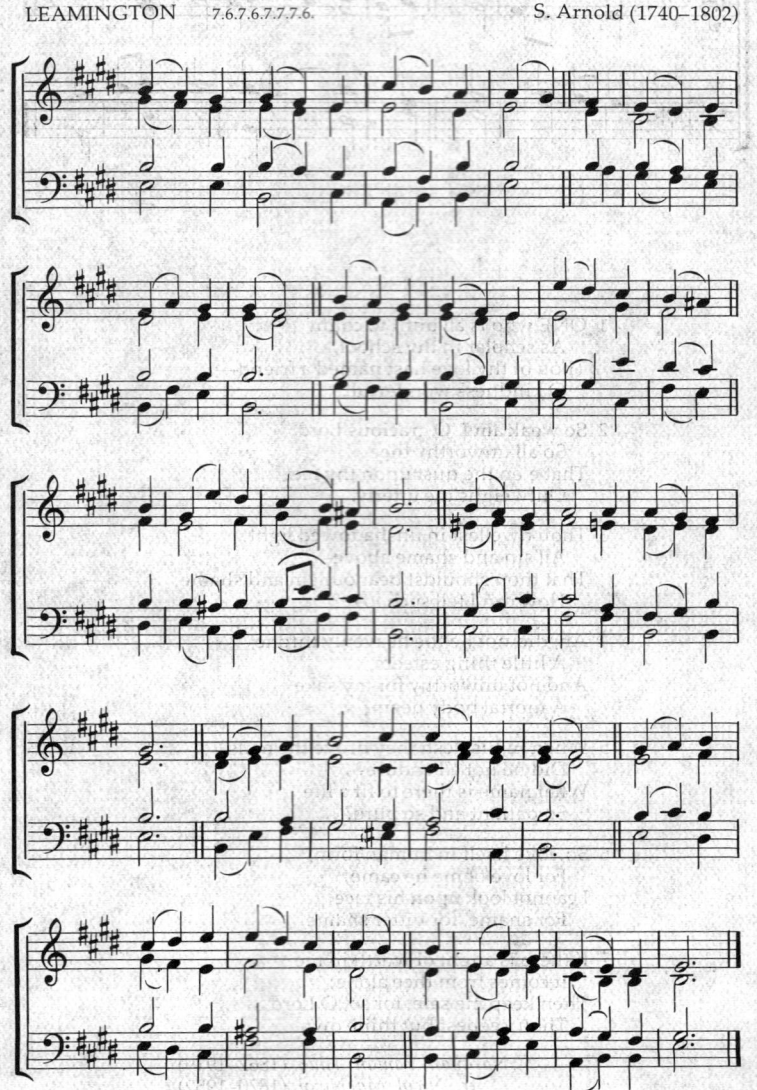

1 OPEN, Lord, my inward ear,
    And bid my heart rejoice;
Bid my quiet spirit hear
    Thy comfortable voice;
Never in the whirlwind found,
    Or where earthquakes rock the place,
Still and silent is the sound,
    The whisper of thy grace.

2 From the world of sin, and noise,
    And hurry I withdraw;
For the small and inward voice
    I wait with humble awe;
Silent am I now and still,
    Dare not in thy presence move;
To my waiting soul reveal
    The secret of thy love.

3 Thou didst undertake for me,
    For me to death wast sold;
Wisdom in a mystery
    Of bleeding love unfold;
Teach the lesson of thy cross:
    Let me die, with thee to reign;
All things let me count but loss,
    So I may thee regain.

4 Show me, as my soul can bear,
    The depth of inbred sin;
All the unbelief declare,
    The pride that lurks within;
Take me, whom thyself hast bought,
    Bring into captivity
Every high aspiring thought
    That would not stoop to thee.

5 Lord, my time is in thy hand,
    My soul to thee convert;
Thou canst make me understand,
    Though I am slow of heart;
Thine in whom I live and move,
    Thine the work, the praise is thine;
Thou art wisdom, power, and love,
    And all thou art is mine.

Charles Wesley (1707–88)

541(i)
DEVOTION 6 6.7.7.7.7. C. Garbutt (1827-1906)

541(ii)
DICH, JESU, LOBEN WIR (IRENE) 66.7.7.7.7.

Melody and almost all the harmony from Freylinghausen's *Geistreiches Gesangbuch* (1741 edition)

1   SAVIOUR, and can it be
      That thou shouldst dwell with me?
From thy high and lofty throne,
      Throne of everlasting bliss,
Will thy majesty stoop down
      To so mean a house as this?

2   I am not worthy, Lord,
      So foul, so self-abhorred,
Thee, my God, to entertain
      In this poor polluted heart:
I so frail and full of sin,
      All my nature cries: 'Depart!'

3   Yet come, thou heavenly guest,
      And purify my breast;
Come, thou great and glorious King,
      While before thy cross I bow;
With thyself salvation bring,
      Cleanse the house by entering now.

Charles Wesley (1707–88)

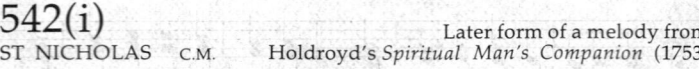

542(i)
ST NICHOLAS C.M.

Later form of a melody from
Holdroyd's *Spiritual Man's Companion* (1753)

542(ii)
TIVERTON C.M.

Melody by
Jacob Grigg (d. 1768) in John Rippon's
Selection of Psalm and Hymn Tunes (1796)

THE WORSHIPPING PEOPLE

1 TALK with us, Lord, thyself reveal,
    While here o'er earth we rove;
  Speak to our hearts, and let us feel
    The kindling of thy love.

2 With thee conversing, we forget
    All time, and toil, and care;
  Thy yoke is ease, thy burden light,
    And thou, my God, art here!

3 Here then, my God, vouchsafe to stay,
    And bid my heart rejoice;
  My bounding heart shall own thy sway,
    And echo to thy voice.

4 Thou callest me to seek thy face;
    'Tis all I wish to seek;
  To attend the whispers of thy grace,
    And hear thee inly speak.

5 Let this my every hour employ,
    Till I thy glory see,
  Enter into my Master's joy,
    And find my heaven in thee.

Charles Wesley (1707–88) alt.

543

SURSUM CORDA   10 10.10 10.   Alfred Morton Smith (1879–1971)

Unison or Harmony

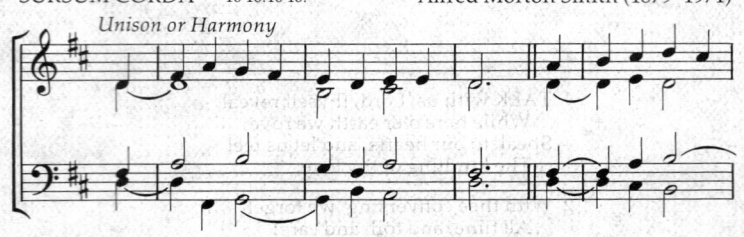

THE WORSHIPPING PEOPLE

1 THOU art before me, Lord, thou art behind,
   And thou above me hast spread out thy hand;
   Such knowledge is too wonderful for me,
   Too high to grasp, too great to understand.

2 Then whither from thy Spirit shall I go,
   And whither from thy presence shall I flee?
   If I ascend to heaven thou art there,
   And in the lowest depths I meet with thee.

3 If I should take my flight into the dawn,
   If I should dwell on ocean's farthest shore,
   Thy mighty hand would rest upon me still,
   And thy right hand would guard me evermore.

4 If I should say, 'Darkness will cover me,
   And I shall hide within the veil of night',
   Surely the darkness is not dark to thee,
   The night is as the day, the darkness light.

5 Search me, O God, search me and know my heart;
   Try me, O God, my mind and spirit try;
   Keep me from any path that gives thee pain,
   And lead me in the everlasting way.

Ian Pitt-Watson (1923–   )
based on Psalm 139

544

REST   88.88.88.

J. Stainer (1840–1901)

, Unison

Harmony

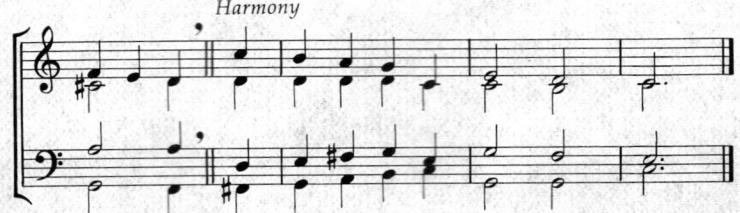

THE WORSHIPPING PEOPLE

1 THOU hidden love of God, whose height,
   Whose depth unfathomed, no-one knows,
I see from far thy beauteous light,
   Inly I sigh for thy repose;
My heart is pained, nor can it be
At rest, till it finds rest in thee.

2 Thy secret voice invites me still
   The sweetness of thy yoke to prove;
And fain I would, but though my will
   Seems fixed, yet wide my passions rove;
Yet hindrances strew all the way;
I aim at thee, yet from thee stray.

3 'Tis mercy all, that thou hast brought
   My mind to seek her peace in thee;
Yet, while I seek but find thee not,
   No peace my wandering soul shall see;
O when shall all my wanderings end,
And all my steps to thee-ward tend?

4 Each moment draw from earth away
   My heart, that lowly waits thy call;
Speak to my inmost soul, and say,
   'I am thy Love, thy God, thy All!'
To feel thy power, to hear thy voice,
To know thy love, be all my choice.

Gerhard Tersteegen (1697–1769)
tr. *John Wesley* (1703–91)

545

PRAYER CANTICLE   Irreg.

Music by Erik Routley (1917–82)

Andante piacevole

ORGAN
INTRODUCTION
(optional)

ANTIPHON *

We do not know how to pray as we ought,___

___ But the Spi-rit him-self in-ter-cedes for us___

* There should be a vocal contrast between Antiphon and Verses, with the Antiphon
in the style of a Refrain.

THE WORSHIPPING PEOPLE

With sighs too deep for words.

Fine

VERSES ($\textbf{o} = \textbf{.}$ of preceding)

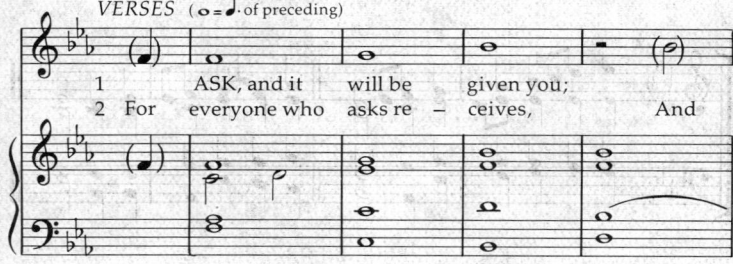

1. ASK, and it will be given you;
2. For everyone who asks re – ceives, And

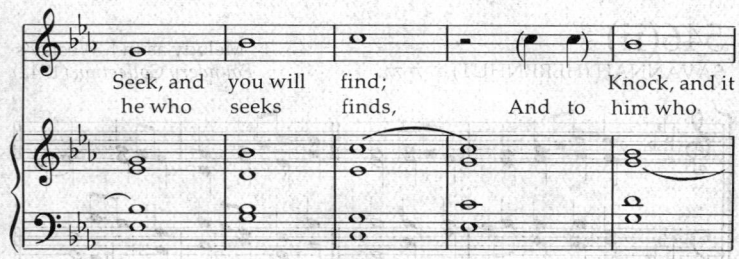

Seek, and you will find; Knock, and it
he who seeks finds, And to him who

Antiphon D.C.

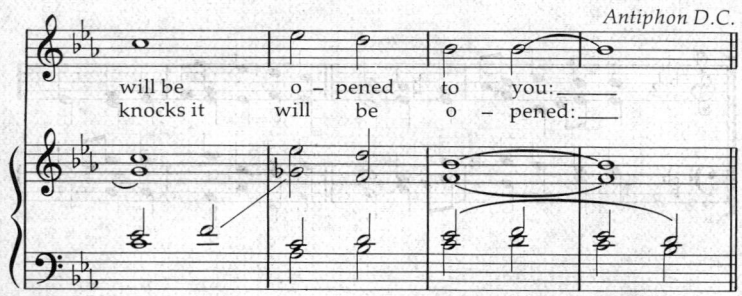

will be o – pened to you:
knocks it will be o – pened:

Adaptation of words and music reprinted by permission of Stainer & Bell Ltd. For permission to reproduce see p. xiii.

adapted by *Alan Luff* (1928–) using Romans 8:26 and Luke 11:9–10 in the Revised Standard Version

Petition and Intercession

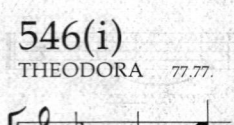

546(i)
THEODORA 77.77.

From an air in Handel's *Theodora* (1749)

546(ii)
SAVANNAH (HERRNHUT) 77.77.

Melody as in J. Wesley's
Foundery Collection (1742)

THE WORSHIPPING PEOPLE

1 COME, my soul, thy suit prepare,
  Jesus loves to answer prayer;
  He himself has bid thee pray,
  Therefore will not say thee nay.

2 Thou art coming to a King:
  Large petitions with thee bring;
  For his grace and power are such,
  None can ever ask too much.

3 With my burden I begin:
  Lord, remove this load of sin;
  Let thy blood, for sinners spilt,
  Set my conscience free from guilt.

4 Lord, I come to thee for rest;
  Take possession of my breast;
  There thy blood-bought right maintain,
  And without a rival reign.

5 While I am a pilgrim here,
  Let thy love my spirit cheer;
  As my guide, my guard, my friend,
  Lead me to my journey's end.

John Newton (1725–1807)

From an original hymn-tune by
J. S. Bach (1685–1750)
Adapted by John Wilson

For this tune in a lower key see No. 174(i)

THE WORSHIPPING PEOPLE

1 HEAD of the church, our risen Lord,
    Who by thy Spirit dost preside
O'er the whole body, by whose word
    We all are ruled and sanctified:

2 Our prayers and intercessions hear
    For all thy family at large,
That all in their appointed sphere
    Their proper service may discharge.

3 So, through the grace derived from thee,
    In whom all fullness dwells above,
May thy whole church united be,
    And edify itself in love.

Josiah Conder (1789–1855) alt.
based on *Gelasian Sacramentary* (5th Century)

May also be sung to No. 520, MELCOMBE

ALTERNATIVE HARMONY VERSION

THE WORSHIPPING PEOPLE

1 GIVE to me, Lord, a thankful heart
    And a discerning mind;
  Give, as I play the Christian's part,
  The strength to finish what I start
    And act on what I find.

2 When, in the rush of days, my will
    Is habit-bound and slow,
  Help me to keep in vision, still,
  What love and power and peace can fill
    A life that trusts in you.

3 By your divine and urgent claim,
    And by your human face,
  Kindle our sinking hearts to flame,
  And as you teach the world your name
    Let it become your place.

4 Jesus, with all your church I long
    To see your kingdom come:
  Show me your way of righting wrong
  And turning sorrow into song
    Until you bring me home.

Caryl Micklem (1925–)

549

WAREHAM L.M.

Melody by W. Knapp (1698–1768)

For this tune in a lower key see No. 258

1 JESUS, where'er thy people meet,
    There they behold thy mercy-seat;
        Where'er they seek thee, thou art found,
        And every place is hallowed ground.

2 For thou, within no walls confined,
    Inhabitest the humble mind;
        Such ever bring thee where they come,
        And going, take thee to their home.

3 Dear Shepherd of thy chosen few,
    Thy former mercies here renew;
        Here to our waiting hearts proclaim
        The sweetness of thy saving name.

4 Here may we prove the power of prayer,
    To strengthen faith and sweeten care,
        To teach our faint desires to rise,
        And bring all heaven before our eyes.

5 Lord, we are few, but thou art near;
    Nor short thine arm, nor deaf thine ear;
        O rend the heavens, come quickly down,
        And make a thousand hearts thine own!

William Cowper (1731–1800)

May also be sung to No. 22(i), WARRINGTON

550

ATONEMENT   7.6.7.6.7.8.7.6.   Adapted from a melody in the
Bohemian Brethren's *Kirchengeseng* (1566).
Harmonised by I.H.J.

O remember Cal-va-ry, And bid us go in peace.

1 LAMB of God, whose dying love
      We now recall to mind,
   Send the answer from above,
      And let us mercy find;
   Think on us, who think on thee;
   And every struggling soul release:
      O remember Calvary,
         And bid us go in peace!

2 By thine agonising pain
      And sweat of blood, we pray,
   By thy dying love to man,
      Take all our sins away;
   Burst our bonds, and set us free;
   From all iniquity release:
      O remember Calvary,
         And bid us go in peace!

3   Lord, we would not hence depart
         Till thou our wants relieve,
      Write forgiveness on our heart,
         And all thine image give.
      Still our souls shall cry to thee,
      Till perfected in holiness:
         O remember Calvary,
            And bid us go in peace!

Charles Wesley (1707–88)

THE WORSHIPPING PEOPLE

551

MAISEMORE   C.M.

J. Dykes Bower (1905–81)

1 LORD, teach us how to pray aright,
   With reverence and with fear;
   Though dust and ashes in thy sight,
   We may, we must draw near.

2 We perish if we cease from prayer;
   O grant us power to pray!
   And, when to meet thee we prepare,
   Lord, meet us by the way.

3 Give deep humility; the sense
   Of godly sorrow give;
   A strong desiring confidence
   To hear thy voice and live;

4 Faith in the only sacrifice
   That can for sin atone;
   To build our hopes, to fix our eyes,
   On Christ, on Christ alone;

5 Patience to watch, and wait, and weep,
   Though mercy long delay;
   Courage, our fainting souls to keep,
   And trust thee, though thou slay.

6 Give these, and then thy will be done:
   Thus strengthened with all might,
   We by thy Spirit and thy Son
   Shall pray, and pray aright.

James Montgomery (1771–1854)

May also be sung to No. 679 (i), ST HUGH

Petition and Intercession

552(i)

SLANE 10 11. 11 12

Irish Traditional Melody
Harmonised by Erik Routley (1917–82)

552(ii)

MINIVER 10 11.11 12.

Cyril V. Taylor (1907–   )

THE WORSHIPPING PEOPLE

1 LORD of all hopefulness, Lord of all joy,
   Whose trust, ever childlike, no cares could destroy,
     Be there at our waking, and give us, we pray,
       Your bliss in our hearts, Lord, at the break of the day.

2 Lord of all eagerness, Lord of all faith,
   Whose strong hands were skilled at the plane and the lathe,
     Be there at our labours, and give us, we pray,
       Your strength in our hearts, Lord, at the noon of the day.

3 Lord of all kindliness, Lord of all grace,
   Your hands swift to welcome, your arms to embrace,
     Be there at our homing, and give us, we pray,
       Your love in our hearts, Lord, at the eve of the day.

4 Lord of all gentleness, Lord of all calm,
   Whose voice is contentment, whose presence is balm,
     Be there at our sleeping, and give us, we pray,
       Your peace in our hearts, Lord, at the end of the day.

Jan Struther (1901–53)

Petition and Intercession

553

GALILEE L.M.

P. Armes (1836–1908)

For this tune in a higher key see No. 239(i)

1 LORD, speak to me, that I may speak
   In living echoes of thy tone;
As thou hast sought, so let me seek
   Thy erring children lost and lone.

2 O lead me, Lord, that I may lead
   The wandering and the wavering feet;
O feed me, Lord, that I may feed
   Thy hungering ones with manna sweet.

3 O strengthen me, that, while I stand
   Firm on the rock, and strong in thee,
I may stretch out a loving hand
   To wrestlers with the troubled sea.

4 O teach me, Lord, that I may teach
   The precious things thou dost impart;
And wing my words, that they may reach
   The hidden depths of many a heart.

5 O give thine own sweet rest to me,
   That I may speak with soothing power
A word in season, as from thee,
   To weary ones in needful hour.

6 O use me, Lord, use even me,
   Just as thou wilt, and when, and where,
Until thy blessèd face I see,
   Thy rest, thy joy, thy glory share.

Frances Ridley Havergal (1836–79)

554

DAVID'S HARP 88.88.88.

Melody and bass by
Robert King (1676–1713)
Mean parts by John Wilson

(v. 1) In whom thy

(v. 1) In whom ___ thy

smi-ling   In whom thou art

smi-ling   In whom ___ thou art

THE WORSHIPPING PEOPLE

1 O GOD of our forefathers, hear,
    And make thy faithful mercies known;
  To thee through Jesus we draw near,
    Thy suffering, well-belovèd Son,
  In whom thy smiling face we see,
  In whom thou art well pleased with me.

2 With solemn faith we offer up,
    And spread before thy glorious eyes,
  That only ground of all our hope,
    That precious, bleeding sacrifice,
  Which brings thy grace on sinners down,
  And perfects all our souls in one.

3 Acceptance through his only name,
    Forgiveness in his blood, we have;
  But more abundant life we claim
    Through him who died our souls to save,
  To sanctify us by his blood,
  And fill with all the life of God.

4 Father, behold thy dying Son,
    And hear the blood that speaks above;
  On us let all thy grace be shown,
    Peace, righteousness, and joy, and love—
  Thy kingdom—come to every heart,
  And all thou hast, and all thou art.

Charles Wesley (1707–88)

May also be sung to No. 434(i), WRESTLING JACOB

555

CHARMINSTER L.M.

Cyril V. Taylor (1907–)

THE WORSHIPPING PEOPLE

1 O THAT mine eyes might closèd be
To what concerns me not to see;

2 That deafness might possess mine ear
To what concerns me not to hear;

3 That truth my tongue might closely tie
From ever speaking foolishly;

4 That no vain thought might ever rest
Or be conceivèd in my breast!

5 Wash, Lord, and purify my heart,
And make it clean in every part;

6 And, when 'tis clean, Lord, keep it too;
For that is more than I can do.

Thomas Ellwood (1639–1713)

556

SONG 1 10 10.10 10.10 10.

Melody and bass by
Orlando Gibbons (1583–1625)

THE WORSHIPPING PEOPLE

1 PRAY for the Church, afflicted and oppressed,
    For all who suffer for the gospel's sake,
That Christ may show us how to serve them best
    In that one Kingdom Satan cannot shake.
But how much more than us they have to give,
Who by their dying show us how to live!

2 Pray for Christ's dissidents, who daily wait,
    As Jesus waited in the olive grove,
The unjust trial, the pre-determined fate,
    The world's contempt for reconciling love.
Shall all they won for us, at such a cost,
Be by our negligence or weakness lost?

3 Pray that if times of testing should lay bare
    What sort we are, who call ourselves his own,
We may be counted worthy then to wear,
    With quiet fortitude, Christ's only crown:
The crown that in his saints he wears again—
The crown of thorns that signifies his reign.

F. Pratt Green (1903–)

Words reprinted by permission of
Stainer & Bell Ltd.
For permission to reproduce see p. xiii.

Petition and Intercession

557(i)
NOX PRAECESSIT C.M.

J. B. Calkin (1827–1905)

557(ii)
WIGTOWN C.M.

Melody, and most of the harmony,
from *Scottish Psalter* (1635)

THE WORSHIPPING PEOPLE

1 PRAYER is the soul's sincere desire,
   Uttered or unexpressed,
   The motion of a hidden fire
   That trembles in the breast.

2 Prayer is the burden of a sigh,
   The falling of a tear,
   The upward glancing of an eye
   When none but God is near.

3 Prayer is the simplest form of speech
   That infant lips can try;
   Prayer the sublimest strains that reach
   The majesty on high.

4 Prayer is the contrite sinner's voice
   Returning from his ways,
   While angels in their songs rejoice,
   And cry: 'Behold, he prays!'

5 Prayer is the Christian's vital breath,
   The Christian's native air,
   Our watchword at the gates of death;
   We enter heaven with prayer.

6 O thou by whom we come to God,
   The Life, the Truth, the Way!
   The path of prayer thyself hast trod:
   Lord, teach us how to pray!

James Montgomery (1771–1854)

May also be sung to No. 539(ii), AYRSHIRE

Petition and Intercession

558(i)
ST ETHELDREDA C.M.   Thomas Turton (1780–1864)

558(ii)
SENNEN COVE C.M.   William H. Harris (1883–1973)

THE WORSHIPPING PEOPLE

1 SHEPHERD divine, our wants relieve
    In this our evil day,
  To all thy tempted followers give
    The power to watch and pray.

2 Long as our fiery trials last,
    Long as the cross we bear,
  O let our souls on thee be cast
    In never-ceasing prayer!

3 Thy Spirit's interceding grace
    Give us in faith to claim;
  To wrestle till we see thy face,
    And know thy hidden name.

4 Till thou thy perfect love impart,
    Till thou thyself bestow,
  Be this the cry of every heart:
    I will not let thee go—

5 I will not let thee go, unless
    Thou tell thy name to me,
  With all thy great salvation bless,
    And make me all like thee.

6 Then let me on the mountain-top
    Behold thine open face,
  Where faith in sight is swallowed up,
    And prayer in endless praise.

Charles Wesley (1707–88)
based on Genesis 32:24–30

559(i)
WHAT A FRIEND 8.7.8.7.D. C. C. Converse (1832–1918)

559(ii)
MANOR HOUSE 8.7.8.7.D. Frederick George Carter (1913–   )

THE WORSHIPPING PEOPLE

1 WHAT a friend we have in Jesus,
   All our sins and griefs to bear!
What a privilege to carry
   Everything to God in prayer!
O what peace we often forfeit,
   O what needless pain we bear,
All because we do not carry
   Everything to God in prayer!

2 Have we trials and temptations,
   Is there trouble anywhere?
We should never be discouraged:
   Take it to the Lord in prayer.
Can we find a friend so faithful
   Who will all our sorrows share?
Jesus knows our every weakness:
   Take it to the Lord in prayer.

3 Are we weak and heavy-laden,
   Cumbered with a load of care?
Precious Saviour, still our refuge—
   Take it to the Lord in prayer!
Do thy friends despise, forsake thee?
   Take it to the Lord in prayer;
In his arms he'll take and shield thee,
   Thou wilt find a solace there.

Joseph Medlicott Scriven (1819–86)

Petition and Intercession

560

SUPPLICATION   6.6.6.6. D.

G. F. Vincent (1855–1928)
Arranged by Charles Cleall (1927–)

1 SHINE thou upon us, Lord,
  The world's true light, today;
And through the written word
  Thy very self display;
That so, from hearts which burn
  With gazing on thy face,
The little ones may learn
  The wonders of thy grace.

2 Breathe thou upon us, Lord,
  Thy Spirit's living flame,
That so with one accord
  Our lips may tell thy name;
Speak thou for us, O Lord,
  In all we say of thee;
According to thy word
  Let all our teaching be.

3 Live thou within us, Lord;
  Thy mind and will be ours;
Be thou beloved, adored,
  And served, with all our powers;
That so our lives may teach
  Thy children what thou art,
And plead, by more than speech,
  For thee with every heart.

John Ellerton (1826–93) alt.

561

ALL KINDS OF LIGHT 5.8.85.5.

Caryl Micklem (1925–)

Not too slow

1 FA - THER, we thank you For the light that

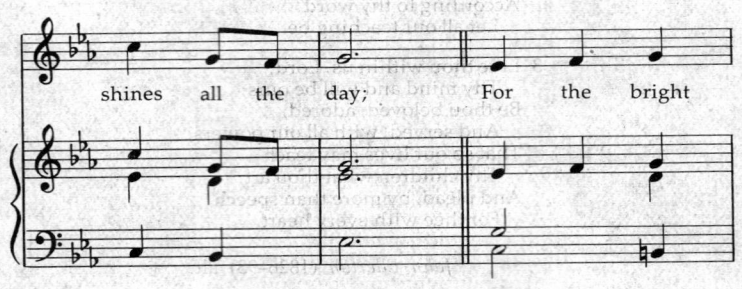

shines all the day; For the bright

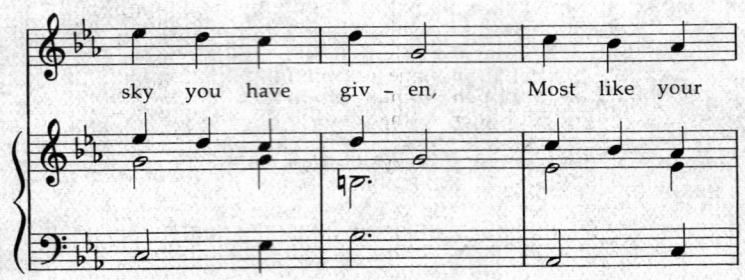

sky you have giv - en, Most like your

THE WORSHIPPING PEOPLE

hea – ven; Fa – ther, we thank you.

1　　FATHER, we thank you
　For the light that shines all the day;
　　For the bright sky you have given,
　　Most like your heaven;
　　　Father, we thank you.

2　　Father, we thank you
　For the lamps that lighten the way;
　　For human skill's exploration
　　Of your creation;
　　　Father, we thank you.

3　　Father, we thank you
　For the friends who brighten our play;
　　For your command to call others
　　Sisters and brothers;
　　　Father, we thank you.

4　　Father, we thank you
　For your love in Jesus today,
　　Giving us hope for tomorrow
　　Through joy and sorrow;
　　　Father, we thank you.

Caryl Micklem (1925–)

562

LASUS L.M.

A. H. Mann (1850–1929)

1 HOW do thy mercies close me round!
    For ever be thy name adored!
  I blush in all things to abound;
    The servant is above his Lord!

2 Inured to poverty and pain,
    A suffering life my Master led;
  The Son of God, the Son of Man,
    He had not where to lay his head.

3 But, lo, a place he has prepared
    For me, whom watchful angels keep;
  Yea, he himself becomes my guard,
    He smooths my bed, and gives me sleep.

4 Jesus protects; my fears, begone!
    What can the Rock of Ages move?
  Safe in thy arms I lay me down,
    Thy everlasting arms of love.

5 While thou art intimately nigh,
    Who, who shall violate my rest?
  Sin, earth, and hell I now defy;
    I lean upon my Saviour's breast.

6 I rest beneath the Almighty's shade,
    My griefs expire, my troubles cease;
  Thou, Lord, on whom my soul is stayed,
    Wilt keep me still in perfect peace.

7 Me for thine own thou lov'st to take,
    In time and in eternity;
  Thou never, never wilt forsake
    A helpless soul that trusts in thee.

Charles Wesley (1707–88)

563

HARWICH 5 5 11.D.

Melody and bass by
Benjamin Milgrove (1731–1810)

THE WORSHIPPING PEOPLE

1   MY God, I am thine;
      What a comfort divine,
  What a blessing to know that my Jesus is mine!
      In the heavenly Lamb
      Thrice happy I am,
  And my heart it doth dance at the sound of his name.

2   True pleasures abound
      In the rapturous sound;
  And whoever hath found it hath paradise found.
      My Jesus to know,
      As rejoicing I go
  To my life everlasting, 'tis heaven below.

3   Yet onward I haste
      To the heavenly feast:
  That, that is the fullness; but this is the taste;
      And this I shall prove,
      Till with joy I remove
  To the heaven of heavens in Jesus's love.

Charles Wesley (1707–88)

564

WENTWORTH   8.4.8.4.8.4.   Frederick Charles Maker (1844–1927)

THE WORSHIPPING PEOPLE

1 MY God, I thank thee, who hast made
    The earth so bright,
  So full of splendour and of joy,
    Beauty and light;
  So many glorious things are here,
    Noble and right.

2 I thank thee, Lord, that thou hast made
    Joy to abound,
  So many gentle thoughts and deeds
    Circling us round,
  That in the darkest spot of earth
    Some love is found.

3 I thank thee too that often joy
    Is touched with pain,
  That shadows fall on brightest hours,
    That thorns remain,
  So that earth's bliss may be our guide,
    And not our chain.

4 I thank thee, Lord, that thou hast kept
    The best in store;
  We have enough, yet not too much
    To long for more—
  A yearning for a deeper peace
    Not known before.

5 I thank thee, Lord, that here our lives,
    Though amply blest,
  Can never find, although they seek,
    A perfect rest,
  Nor ever shall, until we lean
    On Jesu's breast.

Adelaide Anne Procter (1825–64)

565

PRAISE HIM 10.6.10.6.

Melody arranged by Carey Bonner (1859–1938)
Harmonised by Eric Thiman (1900–75)

1 PRAISE him, praise him, all his children praise him!
    He is love, he is love.
  Praise him, praise him, all his children praise him!
    He is love, he is love.

2 Thank him, thank him, all his children thank him!
    He is love, he is love.
  Thank him, thank him, all his children thank him!
    He is love, he is love.

3 Love him, love him, all his children love him!
    He is love, he is love.
  Love him, love him, all his children love him!
    He is love, he is love.

4 Serve him, serve him, all his children serve him!
    He is love, he is love.
  Serve him, serve him, all his children serve him!
    He is love, he is love.

Percy Dearmer (1867–1936) vv. 1–3
Anonymous v. 4

566(i)
NUN DANKET   6.7.6.7.6.6.6.6.

Later form of a melody from
J. Crüger's *Praxis Pietatis
Melica* (1647)

566(ii)
FALMER   6.7.6.7.6.6.6.6.

I. A. Copley (1926–)

THE WORSHIPPING PEOPLE

1 NOW thank we all our God,
    With hearts and hands and voices,
Who wondrous things has done,
    In whom his world rejoices;
Who from our mothers' arms
    Has blessed us on our way
With countless gifts of love,
    And still is ours today.

2 O may this bounteous God
    Through all our life be near us,
With ever joyful hearts
    And blessèd peace to cheer us;
And keep us in his grace,
    And guide us when perplexed,
And free us from all ills
    In this world and the next.

3 All praise and thanks to God
    The Father now be given,
The Son, and him who reigns
    With them in highest heaven,
The one eternal God,
    Whom earth and heaven adore,
For thus it was, is now,
    And shall be evermore.

Martin Rinkart (1586–1649)
based on Ecclesiasticus 50:22–24
tr. *Catherine Winkworth* (1827–78)

Thanksgiving

566(iii)

GRACIAS 6.7.6.7.6.6.6.6.

Geoffrey Beaumont (1903–70)

Unison

1 NOW thank we all our God, With hearts and hands and
2   may this boun-teous God Through all our life be
3   praise and thanks to God The Fa - ther now be

voi - ces, Who won-drous things has done, In
near us, With ev - er joy - ful hearts And
gi - ven, The Son, and him who reigns With

whom his world re - joi - ces; Who from our
bless - èd peace to cheer us; And keep us
them in high-est hea - ven, The one e -

mo-thers' arms Has blessed us on our way With
in his grace, And guide us when per - plexed, And
- ter - nal God, Whom earth and heaven a - dore, For

count-less gifts of love, And still is ours to -
free us from all ills In this world and the
thus it was, is now, And shall be ev - er -

Vv. 1 & 2   *Last time*

- day.
next.   2 O
   3 All   - more.____

Thanksgiving

567

IRISH C.M. Melody from *Hymns and Sacred Poems* (Dublin, 1749)

1 O COME, and let us to the Lord
   In songs our voices raise,
With joyful noise let us the Rock
   Of our salvation praise.

2 Let us before his presence come
   With praise and thankful voice;
Let us sing psalms to him with grace,
   And make a joyful noise.

3 The Lord's a great God, and great King
   Above all gods he is;
Depths of the earth are in his hand,
   The strength of hills is his.

4 To him the spacious sea belongs,
   For he the same did make;
The dry land also from his hands
   Its form at first did take.

5 O come and let us worship him,
   Let us bow down withal,
And on our knees before the Lord
   Our Maker let us fall.

6 To Father, Son, and Holy Ghost,
   The God whom we adore,
Be glory, as it was, and is,
   And shall be evermore.

Irish Psalter (1880)
based on Psalm 95:1–6

EDEN   L.M.

Timothy Battle Mason (1801–61)

THE WORSHIPPING PEOPLE

1 O LORD, enlarge our scanty thought
   To know the wonders thou hast wrought;
      Unloose our stammering tongues, to tell
      Thy love immense, unsearchable.

2 What are our works but sin and death,
   Till thou thy quickening Spirit breathe?
      Thou giv'st the power thy grace to move:
      O wondrous grace! O boundless love!

3 How can it be, thou heavenly King,
   That thou shouldst us to glory bring;
      Make slaves the partners of thy throne,
      Decked with a never-fading crown?

4 Hence our hearts melt, our eyes o'erflow,
   Our words are lost; nor will we know,
      Nor will we think of aught beside,
      My Lord, my Love is crucified!

5 First-born of many brethren thou;
   To thee, lo! all our souls we bow;
      To thee our hearts and hands we give;
      Thine may we die, thine may we live!

Nicolaus Ludwig von Zinzendorf (1700–60) v. 1
Johann Nitschmann (1712–83) vv. 2–4
Anna Nitschmann (1715–60) v. 5
tr. *John Wesley* (1703–91)

Melody (and most of the bass)
from *A Supplement to the New Version* (1708)
Probably by Dr William Croft (1678–1727)

1 O WHAT shall I do my Saviour to praise,
   So faithful and true, so plenteous in grace,
      So strong to deliver, so good to redeem
      The weakest believer that hangs upon him!

2 How happy the man whose heart is set free,
   The people that can be joyful in thee;
      Their joy is to walk in the light of thy face,
      And still they are talking of Jesus's grace.

3 Their daily delight shall be in thy name;
   They shall as their right thy righteousness claim;
      Thy righteousness wearing, and cleansed by thy blood,
      Bold shall they appear in the presence of God.

4 For thou art their boast, their glory and power;
   And I also trust to see the glad hour,
      My soul's new creation, a life from the dead,
      The day of salvation, that lifts up my head.

Charles Wesley (1707–88)

570

ST CLAIR L.M.

Philip Jones (1949–)

1 THANKS be to God, whose Church on earth
  Has stood the tests of time and place,
  And everywhere proclaims new birth
  Through Christ whose love reveals God's face.

2 Thanks be to God, whose Spirit sent
  Apostles out upon his way;
  From east to west the message went;
  On Greek and Roman dawned the day.

3 Thanks be to God, whose later voice
  From west to east sent back the word
  Which, through the servants of his choice,
  At last in every tongue was heard.

4 Thanks be to God who now would reach
  His listeners in more global ways:
  Now each will send the news, and each
  Receive and answer it in praise.

5 Thanks be to God, in whom we share
  Today the mission of his Son:
  May all his Church that time prepare
  When, like the task, the world is one.

Caryl Micklem (1925–)

Thanksgiving

571(i)

JUBILATE 7.6.7.6.D.

C. H. H. Parry (1848–1918)

571(ii)

PETITION 7.6.7.6.D.

From the *Wesleyan Tune-Book* (1876)

THE WORSHIPPING PEOPLE

1 SOMETIMES a light surprises
   The Christian while he sings;
It is the Lord who rises
   With healing in his wings:
When comforts are declining,
   He grants the soul again
A season of clear shining,
   To cheer it after rain.

2 In holy contemplation,
   We sweetly then pursue
The theme of God's salvation,
   And find it ever new.
Set free from present sorrow,
   We cheerfully can say,
Now let the unknown morrow
   Bring with it what it may:

3 It can bring with it nothing
   But he will bear us through;
Who gives the lilies clothing
   Will clothe his people too:
Beneath the spreading heavens
   No creature but is fed;
And he who feeds the ravens
   Will give his children bread.

4 Though vine nor fig-tree neither
   Their wonted fruit should bear,
Though all the field should wither,
   Nor flocks nor herds be there,
Yet, God the same abiding,
   His praise shall tune my voice;
For, while in him confiding,
   I cannot but rejoice.

William Cowper (1731–1800)

Thanksgiving

572(i)

WE THANK YOU LORD 9.9.10.9 (Refrain)

Doreen Newport (1927–)
Arranged by
Peter Cutts (1937–)

Unison

1 THINK of a world with-out a-ny flow-ers,

Think of a wood with-out a-ny trees,

Think of a sky with-out a-ny sun-shine,

THE WORSHIPPING PEOPLE

Think of the air with-out a-ny breeze:____ We
thank you, Lord,__ for flowers and trees and sun-shine; We
thank you, Lord,__ and praise your ho-ly name.____

See following page for Coda

Thanksgiving

CODA

Hm ____ hm ____

pp

Words and music reprinted by permission of
Stainer & Bell Ltd.
For permission to reproduce see p. xiii

PART 1

1   THINK of a world without any flowers,
      Think of a wood without any trees,
    Think of a sky without any sunshine,
      Think of the air without any breeze:
   We thank you, Lord, for flowers and trees and sunshine;
   We thank you, Lord, and praise your holy name.

2   Think of a world without any animals,
      Think of a field without any herd,
    Think of a stream without any fishes,
      Think of a dawn without any bird:
   We thank you, Lord, for all your living creatures;
   We thank you, Lord, and praise your holy name.

PART 2

3   Think of a world without any paintings,
      Think of a room where all the walls are bare,
    Think of a rainbow without any colours,
      Think of the earth with darkness everywhere:
   We thank you, Lord, for paintings and for colours;
   We thank you, Lord, and praise your holy name.

4   Think of a world without any poetry,
      Think of a book without any words,
    Think of a song without any music,
      Think of a hymn without any verse:
   We thank you, Lord, for poetry and music;
   We thank you, Lord, and praise your holy name.

THE WORSHIPPING PEOPLE

5   Think of a world without any science,
        Think of a journey with nothing to explore,
    Think of a quest without any mystery,
        Nothing to seek and nothing left in store:
    We thank you, Lord, for miracles of science;
    We thank you, Lord, and praise your holy name.

6   Think of a world without any people,
        Think of a street with no-one living there,
    Think of a town without any houses,
        No-one to love and nobody to care:
    We thank you, Lord, for families and friendships;
    We thank you, Lord, and praise your holy name.

PART 3

7   Think of a world without any worship,
        Think of a God without his only Son,
    Think of a cross without a resurrection
        Only a grave and not a victory won:
    We thank you, Lord, for showing us our Saviour;
    We thank you, Lord, and praise your holy name.

8   Thanks to our Lord for being here among us,
        Thanks be to him for sharing all we do,
    Thanks for our church and all the love we find here,
        Thanks for this place and all its promise true:
    We thank you, Lord, for life in all its richness;
    We thank you, Lord, and praise your holy name.

                        Doreen Newport (1927–   )

572(ii)

GENESIS 9.9.10.9. (Refrain)

Smooth and flowing

Graham Westcott

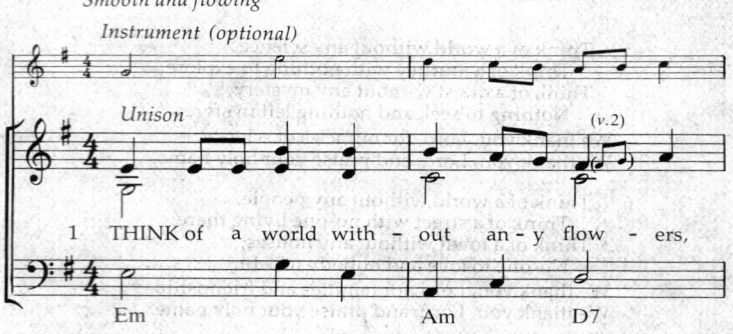

1 THINK of a world with-out an-y flow-ers,

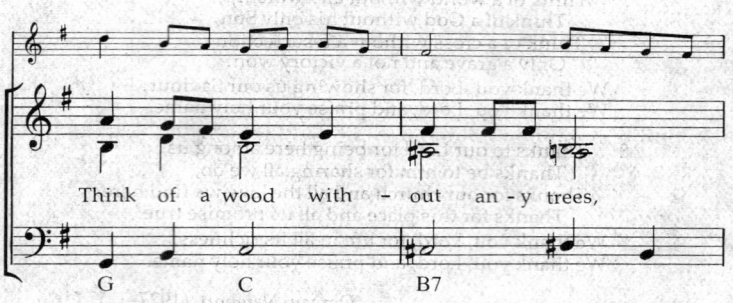

Think of a wood with-out an-y trees,

Think of a sky with-out an-y sun-shine,

THE WORSHIPPING PEOPLE

Think of the air with – out an-y breeze: We

G   C   B7

thank you, Lord,   for flowers and trees and sun- shine; We

G   Em   Am   D

thank you, Lord,   and praise your ho – ly   name.

B7   Em   Am   D7   G

(Turn back for later verses)

Thanksgiving

573(i)

CONTEMPLATION   C.M.

F. A. Gore Ouseley (1825–89)

573(ii)

HARINGTON (RETIREMENT)   C.M.

From a glee by Henry Harington
(1727–1816)

THE WORSHIPPING PEOPLE

1 WHEN all thy mercies, O my God,
   My rising soul surveys,
   Transported with the view, I'm lost
   In wonder, love, and praise.

2 Unnumbered comforts on my soul
   Thy tender care bestowed,
   Before my infant heart conceived
   From whom those comforts flowed.

3 Ten thousand thousand precious gifts
   My daily thanks employ,
   Nor is the least a cheerful heart
   That tastes those gifts with joy.

4 Through every period of my life
   Thy goodness I'll pursue,
   And after death, in distant worlds,
   The glorious theme renew.

5 Through all eternity to thee
   A joyful song I'll raise;
   For O eternity's too short
   To utter all thy praise!

Joseph Addison (1672–1719)

May also be sung to No. 740(ii), BELGRAVE

574(i)
DYING STEPHEN 7.7.4.4.7.D.

Melody and bass by J. F. Lampe (1703–51)
(edited John Wilson)

(with vigour)

574(ii)
DELIVERANCE 7.7.4.4.7.D.

Henry J. Gauntlett (1805–76)

THE WORSHIPPING PEOPLE

1 WORSHIP, and thanks, and blessing,
And strength ascribe to Jesus!
Jesus alone
Defends his own,
When earth and hell oppress us.
Jesus with joy we witness
Almighty to deliver;
Our seals set to,
That God is true,
And reigns a King for ever.

2 Omnipotent Redeemer,
Our ransomed souls adore thee:
Our Saviour thou,
We find it now,
And give thee all the glory.
We sing thine arm unshortened,
Brought through our sore temptation;
With heart and voice
In thee rejoice,
The God of our salvation.

3 Thine arm has safely brought us
A way no more expected,
Than when thy sheep
Passed through the deep,
By crystal walls protected.
Thy glory was our rearward,
Thine hand our lives did cover,
And we, ev'n we,
Have walked the sea,
And marched triumphant over.

4 The world and Satan's malice
Thou, Jesus, hast confounded;
And, by thy grace,
With songs of praise
Our happy souls resounded.
Accepting our deliverance,
We triumph in thy favour,
And for the love
Which now we prove
Shall praise thy name for ever.

Charles Wesley (1707–88)

Thanksgiving

575(i)

SUSSEX CAROL 88.88.88.

English traditional melody harmonised by
Ralph Vaughan Williams (1872–1958)

Unison

Reprinted by permission of Stainer & Bell Ltd
acting as agents for Ralph Vaughan Williams
Ltd. For permission to reproduce see p. xiii.

575(ii)

MADRID 88.88.88.

William Matthews (1759–1830)

THE WORSHIPPING PEOPLE

1 COME, let us with our Lord arise,
   Our Lord, who made both earth and skies:
   Who died to save the world he made,
   And rose triumphant from the dead;
   He rose, the Prince of life and peace,
   And stamped the day for ever his.

2 This is the day the Lord has made,
   That all may see his love displayed,
   May feel his resurrection's power,
   And rise again, to fall no more,
   In perfect righteousness renewed,
   And filled with all the life of God.

3 Then let us render him his own,
   With solemn prayer approach his throne,
   With meekness hear the gospel word,
   With thanks his dying love record,
   Our joyful hearts and voices raise,
   And fill his courts with songs of praise.

4 Honour and praise to Jesus pay
   Throughout his consecrated day;
   Be all in Jesus' praise employed,
   Nor leave a single moment void;
   With utmost care the time improve,
   And only breathe his praise and love.

Charles Wesley (1707–88)

The Lord's Day

576

GARELOCHSIDE S.M.

K. G. Finlay (1882–1974)

Unison

1 THE first day of the week,
   His own, in sad despair,
Could not believe for very joy
   The risen Lord was there.

2 Obedient to his word,
   They shared what Jesus gave,
And, one in him, in breaking bread
   Knew what it cost to save.

3 Each day throughout the week,
   As on the Lord's own day,
They walked in newfound liberty
   His true and living way.

4 So on this joyful day,
   From needless burdens freed,
We keep the feast he made for us
   To fit our inmost need.

5 How soon we forge again
   The fetters of our past!
As long as Jesus lives in us,
   So long our freedoms last.

6 Today his people meet,
   Today his word is sown;
Lord Jesus, show us how to use
   This day we call your own.

F. Pratt Green (1903–)

Words reprinted by permission of
Stainer & Bell Ltd.
For permission to reproduce see p. xiii.

May also be sung to No. 449(ii), DAY OF PRAISE,
or No. 708, ST THOMAS

THE WORSHIPPING PEOPLE

577

BROOMSGROVE C.M. (extended)

Adapted from a psalm-setting by
Thomas Collins (c. 1789)

1 THIS is the day the Lord has made,
   He calls the hours his own;
Let heaven rejoice, let earth be glad,
   And praise surround his throne.

2 Today he rose and left the dead,
   And Satan's empire fell;
Today the saints his triumphs spread,
   And all his wonders tell.

3 Hosanna to the anointed King,
   To David's holy Son!
Make haste to help us, Lord, and bring
   Salvation from thy throne.

4 Blest be the Lord, who comes to men
   With messages of grace;
Who comes, in God his Father's name,
   To save our sinful race.

5 Hosanna in the highest strains
   The church on earth can raise;
The highest heavens in which he reigns
   Shall give him nobler praise.

Isaac Watts (1674–1748)

The Lord's Day

THE WORSHIPPING PEOPLE

1 THIS is the day,
  This is the day that the Lord has made,
  That the Lord has made;
  We will rejoice,
  We will rejoice and be glad in it,
  And be glad in it.
  This is the day that the Lord has made;
  We will rejoice and be glad in it.
  This is the day that the Lord has made.

2 This is the day,
  This is the day when he rose again,
  When he rose again;
  We will rejoice,
  We will rejoice and be glad in it,
  And be glad in it.
  This is the day when he rose again;
  We will rejoice and be glad in it.
  This is the day when he rose again.

3 This is the day,
  This is the day when the Spirit came,
  When the Spirit came;
  We will rejoice,
  We will rejoice and be glad in it,
  And be glad in it.
  This is the day when the Spirit came;
  We will rejoice and be glad in it.
  This is the day when the Spirit came.

Anonymous

The Lord's Day

579

ST MAGNUS   C.M.

Melody and bass (slightly altered) probably by Jeremiah Clarke (*c.* 1673–1707)

For this tune in a higher key see No. 2

1 A MIGHTY mystery we set forth,
   A wondrous sign and seal;
  Lord, give our hearts to know its worth,
   And all its truth to feel.

2 Death to the world we thus avow,
   Death to each sinful lust;
  The risen life is our life now,
   The risen Christ our trust.

3 Baptized into the Father's name,
   We're children of our God;
  Baptized into the Son, we claim
   The ransom of his blood;

4 Baptized into the Holy Ghost,
   In this accepted hour,
  Give us to own the Pentecost,
   And the descending power.

George Rawson (1807–89)

580

ANTWERP   L.M.

William Smallwood (1831–97)

THE WORSHIPPING PEOPLE/ Baptism

1 COME, Father, Son, and Holy Ghost,
    Honour the means ordained by thee;
Make good our apostolic boast,
    And own thy glorious ministry.

2 We now thy promised presence claim;
    Sent to disciple all mankind,
Sent to baptize into thy name,
    We now thy promised presence find.

3 Father, in these reveal thy Son;
    In these, for whom we seek thy face,
The hidden mystery make known,
    The inward, pure, baptizing grace.

4 Jesus, with us thou always art;
    Effectual make the sacred sign,
The gift unspeakable impart,
    And bless the ordinance divine.

5 Eternal Spir't, descend from high,
    Baptizer of our spirits thou!
The sacramental seal apply,
    And witness with the water now.

6 O that the souls baptized therein
    May now thy truth and mercy feel;
May rise and wash away their sin!
    Come, Holy Ghost, their pardon seal!

Charles Wesley (1707–88)

Baptism

581

ST CECILIA 6.6.6.6. L. G. Hayne (1836–83)

SECOND VERSION
(with original form of rhythm)

ST CECILIA 6.6.6.6. L. G. Hayne (1836–83)

1 GLORY and praise to God
   Who loves the human race;
His all-creating word
   Provides each child a place.

2 Glory and praise to Christ
   Who from the Father came,
The Saviour of the world,
   Who calls *this* child by name. (*each*)

3 O Holy Spirit, come,
      Your gifts of grace instil,
   All the good will of God
      In *this new life* fulfil. (*these new lives*)

Bryn Rees (1911–83)

THE WORSHIPPING PEOPLE

582

WYCHBOLD 8.7.8.7.

W. G. Whinfield (1865–1919)

1 PRAISE to God, almighty maker
   Of all worlds, below, above;
 For his might is in redemption
   Manifest as holy love.

2 Praise the Son who thus revealed him,
   Love incarnate shown to us,
 Living, suffering, dying, risen,
   Love through death victorious.

3 Here, redemption's wondrous story
   We set forth in mystic rite:
 See him die, the grave receive him;
   See him rise, by God's great might.

4 Here, within the font we meet him;
   Here with him we buried lie;
 Here we plead his matchless merit;
   Here with him to sin we die.

5 Then, victorious through his passion,
   From the grave with him we rise,
 Born again to do him service
   In the strength his grace supplies.

6 Praise the Spirit, who is promised
   Here to be the gift divine,
 Making in our hearts his temple,
   Love, joy, peace, his holy sign.

William Robinson (1888–1963)

Baptism

583

ST BRIDE S.M.

Samuel Howard (1710–82)
(harmony altered in first line)

1 JESUS, we follow thee,
   In all thy footsteps tread,
   And seek for full conformity
   To our exalted Head.

2 We would, we would partake
   Thy every state below,
   And suffer all things for thy sake,
   And to thy glory go.

3 We in thy birth are born,
   Sustain thy grief and loss,
   Share in thy want, and shame, and scorn,
   And die upon thy cross.

4 Baptized into thy death,
   We sink into thy grave,
   Till thou the quickening Spirit breathe,
   And to the utmost save.

5 Thou saidst, 'Where'er I am,
   There shall my servants be.'
   Master, thy welcome word we claim,
   And die to live with thee.

6 To us who share thy pain,
   Thy joy shall soon be given,
   And we shall in thy glory reign,
   For thou art now in heaven.

Charles Wesley (1707–88) alt.

THE WORSHIPPING PEOPLE

584

ALSTONE L.M.

C. E. Willing (1830–1904)

1 LORD, here *is one* to be baptized, (*are some*)
  Not knowing how or when or where—
  Too young on earth to be surprised
  By all your wealth of silent care.

2 Jesus, you shared by Jordan's ford
  John's urgent call to be remade;
  Baptized, you heard God's gracious word
  And saw the Spirit's sign displayed.

3 Our deadness and our sin we mourn,
  But claim your Spirit's fresh rebirth;
  The church is here, by water born,
  To serve all families on earth.

4 Now at our font transcend this place;
  Display the sign of life made new;
  Make known the all-renewing grace
  That seals the youngest *one* for you. (*ones*)

5 High our surprise at what you do,
  Reclaiming us from sin's embrace;
  Lord, here is faith and water too—
  Receive *this* child to grow in grace. (*each*)

Richard G. Jones (1926–   )
based on *David Head* (1922–   )

Baptism

585

FRANCONIA S.M.

W. H. Havergal (1793–1870), adapted from a tune in
König's *Harmonischer Liederschatz* (1738)
(harmony slightly altered)

1 LORD Jesus, once a child,
    Saviour of young and old,
Receive *this little child* of ours (*these little ones*)
    Into your flock and fold.

2 You drank the cup of life,
    Its bitterness and bliss,
And loved us to the uttermost
    For *such a child as this. (children such as these)*

3 So help us, Lord, to trust,
    Through this baptismal rite,
Not in our own imperfect love,
    But in your saving might.

4 Lord Jesus, for *his* sake, (*her, their*)
    Lend us your constant aid,
That *he*, when older, may rejoice (*she, they*)
    We kept the vows we made.

F. Pratt Green (1903–   )

THE WORSHIPPING PEOPLE

586

TALLIS' ORDINAL   C.M.   Thomas Tallis (*c.* 1505–85)

For this tune in a lower key see No. 310

1 LORD, look upon *this* helpless child (*each*)
  Before *he knows* you're there; (*she knows, they know*)
Surround *him* with protective love, (*her, them*)
  Enfold *him* in your care. (*her, them*)

2 Your church on earth, O Lord, affirms
  By clear baptismal sign
What you from heaven made manifest
  By merciful design.

3 By merciful design and love
  Through Saviour Jesus' birth,
You succour every one that's born
  To serve you here on earth.

4 These joyful parents strengthen, Lord,
  And help them to provide
A Christian home, where faithfulness
  And patient love abide.

5 Thus may all children brought to you
  Be nurtured in your way,
And so in goodness and in truth
  Your Spirit's fruit display.

Derek R. Farrow (1925–   )

Baptism

FARRANT C.M.

Adapted from an anthem
probably by John Hilton (d. 1608)

1 LORD, let your grace descend on those
  Who, hoping in your word,
This day do publicly declare
  That Jesus is their Lord.

2 With cheerful feet may they advance,
  And run the Christian race;
And through the troubles of the way
  Find all-sufficient grace.

James Newton (1732–90)

THE WORSHIPPING PEOPLE

588

DUBLIN (HOWARD) C.M. — Melody from Wilson's *Psalm Tunes* (Edinburgh, 1825)

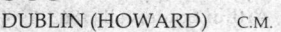

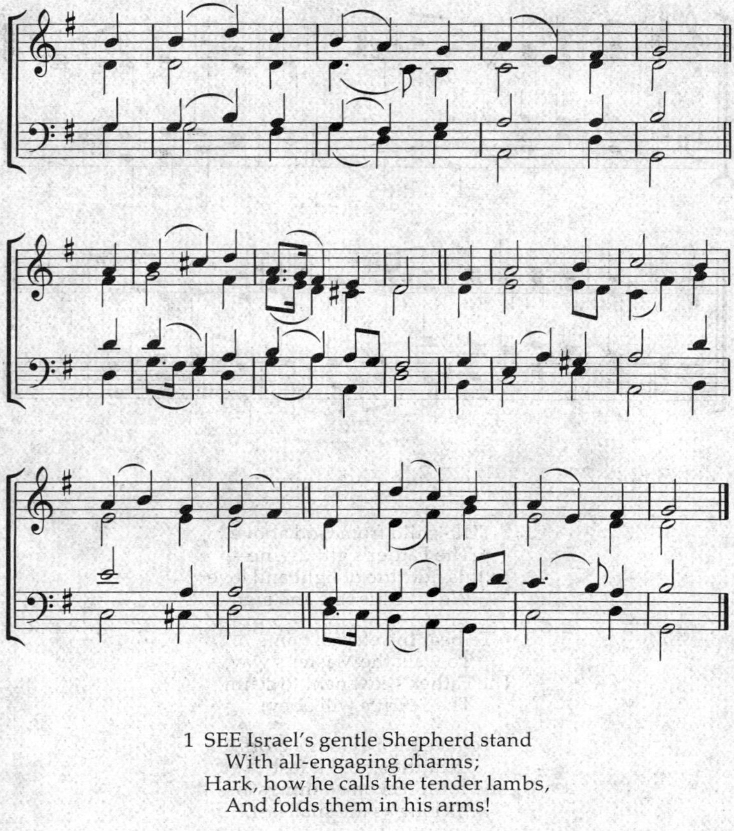

1 SEE Israel's gentle Shepherd stand
With all-engaging charms;
Hark, how he calls the tender lambs,
And folds them in his arms!

2 'Permit them to approach,' he cries,
'Nor scorn their humble name;
For 'twas to bless such souls as these
The Lord of angels came.'

3 We bring them, Lord, in thankful hands,
And yield them up to thee,
Joyful that we ourselves are thine;
Thine let our children be.

Philip Doddridge (1702–51)

589

WINDERMERE S.M.   Arthur Somervell (1863–1937)

1   THIS child from God above,
      The Father's gift divine—
To this new life of light and love
      We give his seal and sign;

2   To bear the eternal name,
      To walk the Master's way,
The Father's covenant to claim,
      The Spirit's will obey;

3   To take the Saviour's cross,
      In faith to hold it fast;
And for it reckon all things loss
      As long as life shall last;

4   To tell his truth abroad,
      To tread the path he trod,
With all who love and serve the Lord—
      The family of God.

Timothy Dudley-Smith (1926–)

THE WORSHIPPING PEOPLE

590

HERONGATE L.M.

English traditional melody
arranged by
Ralph Vaughan Williams (1872–1958)

1 NOW in the name of him who sent
To preach by word and sacrament,
Upon this new-born child we pray
The strength of God in doubtful day.

2 Our names are written in his hand;
He leads us to the promised land.
We rise in wonder from the flood
And love becomes our livelihood.

3 With Noah through disaster borne,
With Moses from the river drawn,
With Jonah from the sea released,
We celebrate this rising feast.

4 The water is a seal and sign
Of costly love that makes us clean;
This love we see in Christ portrayed,
Who rose triumphant from the dead.

5 We sing our thanks that old and young
So to the church of Christ belong.
This is the covenant of grace;
We look salvation in the face.

Fred Kaan (1929–)

Baptism

591

ST MICHAEL S.M.

From melody of 'Psalm 101'
in the *Genevan Psalter* (1551),
as adapted by William Crotch (1775–1847)

THE WORSHIPPING PEOPLE

1   STAND, soldier of the cross,
       Thy high allegiance claim,
   And vow to hold the world but loss
       For thy Redeemer's name.

2   Arise, and be baptized,
       And wash thy sins away;
   Thy league with God be solemnized,
       Thy faith avouched today.

3   No more thine own, but Christ's—
       With all the saints of old,
   Apostles, seers, evangelists,
       And martyr throngs enrolled,

4   In God's whole armour strong,
       Front hell's embattled powers;
   The warfare may be sharp and long,
       The vict'ry must be ours.

5   O bright the conqueror's crown,
       The song of triumph sweet,
   When faith casts every trophy down
       At our great Captain's feet!

E. H. Bickersteth (1825–1906)

592

HYFRYDOL   8.7.8.7.D.

R. H. Prichard (1811–87)

THE WORSHIPPING PEOPLE

1 ALLELUIA! Sing to Jesus,
    His the sceptre, his the throne;
  Alleluia! His the triumph,
    His the victory alone:
  Hark! The songs of peaceful Zion
    Thunder like a mighty flood;
  Jesus, out of every nation,
    Has redeemed us by his blood.

2 Alleluia! Not as orphans
    Are we left in sorrow now;
  Alleluia! He is near us,
    Faith believes, nor questions how;
  Though the cloud from sight received him
    When the forty days were o'er,
  Shall our hearts forget his promise,
    'I am with you evermore'?

3 Alleluia! Bread of angels,
    Thou on earth our food, our stay;
  Alleluia! Here the sinful
    Flee to thee from day to day:
  Intercessor, friend of sinners,
    Earth's Redeemer, plead for me,
  Where the songs of all the sinless
    Sweep across the crystal sea.

4 Alleluia! King eternal,
    Thee the Lord of lords we own;
  Alleluia! Born of Mary,
    Earth thy footstool, heaven thy throne:
  Thou within the veil hast entered,
    Robed in flesh, our great High Priest;
  Thou on earth both priest and victim
    In the eucharistic feast.

William Chatterton Dix (1837–98)

The Lord's Supper

593(i)
UNDE ET MEMORES 10.10. 10.10.10 10.   W. H. Monk (1823–89)

593(ii)
RAVENDALE 10.10. 10.10.10 10.   John Wilson (1905–   )

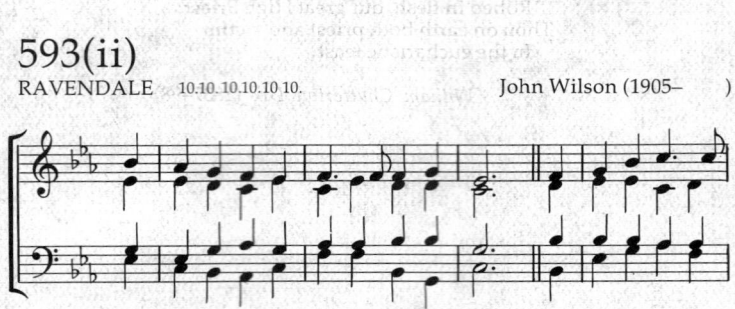

THE WORSHIPPING PEOPLE

(Organ small notes ad lib.)

1 AND now, O Father, mindful of the love
    That bought us, once for all, on Calvary's tree,
And having with us him that pleads above,
    We here present, we here spread forth to thee
That only offering perfect in thine eyes,
The one true, pure, immortal sacrifice.

2 Look, Father, look on his anointed face,
    And only look on us as found in him;
Look not on our misusings of thy grace,
    Our prayer so languid, and our faith so dim:
For lo! Between our sins and their reward
We set the passion of thy Son our Lord.

3 And so we come: O draw us to thy feet,
    Most patient Saviour, who canst love us still;
And by this food, so aweful and so sweet,
    Deliver us from every touch of ill:
In thine own service make us glad and free,
And grant us never more to part with thee.

William Bright (1824–1901)

The Lord's Supper

594

FOLKSONG 9.8.9.8.

English Traditional Melody
Arranged by John Wilson

Organ
Introduction
to Verse 1*

Voices in Unison

* This may be repeated before v.4, or before v.3 if the hymn has been so divided.
If any of vv.1–3 are sung by the choir alone, a soloist (or group) may sing the melody,
with other voices humming or vocalising the harmony.

1 AN Upper Room did our Lord prepare
   For those he loved until the end;
   And his disciples still gather there
   To celebrate their Risen Friend.

2 A lasting gift Jesus gave his own—
   To share his bread, his loving cup;
   Whatever burdens may bow us down,
   He by his cross shall lift us up.

3 And after supper he washed their feet,
   For service, too, is sacrament;
   In him our joy shall be made complete—
   Sent out to serve, as he was sent.

4 No end there is! We depart in peace;
   He loves beyond the uttermost;
   In every room in our Father's house
   He will be there, as Lord and Host.

F. Pratt Green (1903–)

Words reprinted by permission of
Stainer & Bell Ltd.
For permission to reproduce see p. xiii.

THE WORSHIPPING PEOPLE

595

Unison

1 AS your family, Lord, see us here,
   As your family, Lord, see us here,
   As your family, Lord, see us here,
     O Lord, see us here.

2 At your table, Lord, we are fed;
   At your table, Lord, we are fed;
   At your table, Lord, we are fed;
     O Lord, feed us here.

3 Fill our spirits, Lord, with your love,
   Fill our spirits, Lord, with your love,
   Fill our spirits, Lord, with your love,
     O Lord, give your love.

4 Make us faithful, Lord, to your will,
   Make us faithful, Lord, to your will,
   Make us faithful, Lord, to your will,
     O Lord, to your will.

5 As your family, Lord, see us here,
   As your family, Lord, see us here,
   As your family, Lord, see us here,
     O Lord, see us here.

Anonymous

The Lord's Supper

596

1   AUTHOR of life divine,
      Who hast a table spread,
    Furnished with mystic wine
      And everlasting bread,
    Preserve the life thyself hast given,
    And feed and train us up for heaven.

2   Our needy souls sustain
      With fresh supplies of love,
    Till all thy life we gain,
      And all thy fullness prove,
    And, strengthened by thy perfect grace,
    Behold without a veil thy face.

Charles Wesley (1707–88)

THE WORSHIPPING PEOPLE

1 BE known to us in breaking bread,
     But do not then depart;
   Saviour, abide with us, and spread
     Thy table in our heart.

2 There sup with us in love divine;
     Thy body and thy blood,
   That living bread, that heavenly wine,
     Be our immortal food.

James Montgomery (1771–1854)

The Lord's Supper

598

PADERBORN 5.5.5.5.6.5.6.5.

German folk melody, adapted in
Paderborn Gesangbuch (1765)

THE WORSHIPPING PEOPLE

1 BECAUSE thou hast said:
    'Do this for my sake',
The mystical bread
    We gladly partake;
We thirst for the Spirit
    That flows from above,
And long to inherit
    Thy fullness of love.

2 'Tis here we look up
    And grasp at thy mind;
'Tis here that we hope
    Thine image to find;
The means of bestowing
    Thy gifts we embrace;
But all things are owing
    To Jesus's grace.

Charles Wesley (1707–88) alt.

599

RENDEZ À DIEU 9.8.9.8.D.

Melody from *La Forme des Prieres et Chants Ecclesiastiques* (Strasbourg, 1545)
(2nd line as in *Genevan Psalter* of 1551)

BREAD of the world, in mer - cy bro - ken;

Wine of the soul, in mer - cy shed;

By whom the words of life were spo - ken,

And in whose death our sins are dead:

THE WORSHIPPING PEOPLE

Look on the heart by sor- row bro - ken,

Look on the tears by sin - ners shed;

And be thy feast to us the to - ken

That by thy grace our souls are fed.

Reginald Heber (1783–1826)

The Lord's Supper

600

RIPPONDEN 8 8 8.4.

Norman Cocker (1889–1953)

1 BY Christ redeemed, in Christ restored,
   We keep the memory adored,
   And show the death of our dear Lord
      Until he come.

2 His body, broken in our stead,
   Is here in this memorial bread,
   And so our feeble love is fed
      Until he come.

3 The drops of his dread agony,
   His life-blood shed for us, we see;
   The wine shall tell the mystery
      Until he come.

4 And thus that dark betrayal night
   With the last advent we unite,
   By one blest chain of loving rite,
      Until he come.

5 O blessèd hope! With this elate,
   Let not our hearts be desolate,
   But, strong in faith, in patience wait
      Until he come.

George Rawson (1807–89)

THE WORSHIPPING PEOPLE

601

AVE VIRGO VIRGINUM   7.6.7.6.D. (Troch.)

Melody from
Horn's *Gesangbuch* (1544)

1 CHRISTIAN people, raise your song,
   Chase away all grieving;
Sing your joy, and be made strong,
   Our Lord's life receiving;
Nature's gifts of wheat and vine
   Now are set before us:
As we offer bread and wine
   Christ comes to restore us.

2 Come to welcome Christ today,
   God's great revelation;
He has pioneered the way
   Of the new creation.
Greet him, Christ our risen King
   Gladly recognizing,
As with joy men greet the spring
   Out of winter rising.

Colin P. Thompson (1945–)

The Lord's Supper

602

ABRIDGE (ST STEPHEN) C.M.

Melody by Isaac Smith, (1734– 1805)
from his *Psalm Tunes*

For this tune in a higher key see No. 536 (ii)

1 COME, Holy Ghost, thine influence shed,
   And realize the sign;
   Thy life infuse into the bread,
   Thy power into the wine.

2 Effectual let the tokens prove
   And made, by heavenly art,
   Fit channels to convey thy love
   To every faithful heart.

Charles Wesley (1707–88)

603

LES COMMANDEMENS 9.8.9.8.

Melody from *La Forme des Prieres et Chants Ecclesiastiques* (Strasbourg, 1545)

1 FATHER, we give you thanks, who planted
    Your holy name within our hearts.
Knowledge and faith and life immortal
    Jesus your Son to us imparts.

2 Lord, you have made all for your pleasure,
    And given us food for all our days,
Giving in Christ the bread eternal;
    Yours is the power, be yours the praise.

3 Watch o'er your church, O Lord, in mercy,
    Save it from evil, guard it still,
And in your love unite, perfect it,
    Cleanse and conform it to your will.

4 As grain, once scattered on the hillsides,
    Was in the broken bread made one,
So may your world-wide church be gathered
    Into your kingdom by your Son.

F. Bland Tucker (1895-1984) and others,
based on the *Didache* (1st or 2nd Century)

The Lord's Supper

604(i)
CURBAR EDGE   8.7.8.7. (Iamb.)   Brian R. Hoare (1935–   )

604(ii)
DOMINUS REGIT ME   8.7.8.7.(Iambic)   J. B. Dykes (1823–76)

THE WORSHIPPING PEOPLE

1 HERE, Lord, we take the broken bread
   And drink the wine, believing
That by your life our souls are fed,
   Your parting gifts receiving.

2 As you have giv'n, so we would give
   Ourselves for others' healing;
As you have lived, so we would live,
   The Father's love revealing.

Charles Venn Pilcher (1879–1961)

The Lord's Supper

605(i)
STONER HILL 10.10.10.10.   William H. Harris (1883–1973)

605(ii)
BOROUGH 10.10.10.10.   Cyril V. Taylor (1907–)

THE WORSHIPPING PEOPLE

1 COME, risen Lord, and deign to be our guest;
   Nay, let us be thy guests; the feast is thine;
Thyself at thine own board make manifest,
   In thine own sacrament of bread and wine.

2 We meet, as in that upper room they met;
   Thou at the table, blessing, yet dost stand:
'This is my body': so thou givest yet:
   Faith still receives the cup as from thy hand.

3 One body we, one body who partake,
   One church united in communion blest;
One name we bear, one bread of life we break,
   With all thy saints on earth and saints at rest;

4 One with each other, Lord, for one in thee,
   Who art one Saviour and one living Head;
Then open thou our eyes, that we may see;
   Be known to us in breaking of the bread.

George Wallace Briggs (1875–1959)

The Lord's Supper

606

SCHMÜCKE DICH   88 88.D.   Melody from J. Crüger (1598–1662)

1 DECK thyself, my soul, with gladness,
  Leave the gloomy haunts of sadness,
  Come into the daylight's splendour,
  There with joy thy praises render
  Unto him whose grace unbounded
  Hath this wondrous banquet founded;
  High o'er all the heavens he reigneth,
  Yet to dwell with thee he deigneth.

2 Sun, who all my life dost brighten;
  Light, who dost my soul enlighten;
  Joy, the sweetest e'er one knoweth;
  Fount, whence all my being floweth:
  At thy feet I cry, my Maker,
  Let me be a fit partaker
  Of this blessèd food from heaven,
  For our good, thy glory, given.

THE WORSHIPPING PEOPLE

3 Jesus, Bread of Life, I pray thee,
  Let me gladly here obey thee;
  Never to my hurt invited,
  Be thy love with love requited:
  From this banquet let me measure,
  Lord, how vast and deep its treasure;
  Through the gifts thou here dost give me,
  As thy guest in heaven receive me.

Johann Franck (1618–77)
tr. *Catherine Winkworth (1827–78)*

607

QUEM PASTORES LAUDAVERE   888.7.

Melody adapted from
a German MS of 1410

1 FATHER, who in Jesus found us,
  God, whose love is all around us,
  Who to freedom new unbound us,
    Keep our hearts with joy aflame.

2 For the sacramental breaking,
  For the honour of partaking,
  For your life our lives remaking,
    Young and old, we praise your name.

3 From the service of this table
  Lead us to a life more stable;
  For our witness make us able,
    Blessing on our work we claim.

4 Through our calling closely knitted,
  Daily to your praise committed,
  For a life of service fitted,
    Let us now your love proclaim.

Fred Kaan (1929–)

The Lord's Supper

608(i)

ST AGNES   10 10. 10 10.   James Langran (1835–1909)

608(ii)

ANIMA CHRISTI   10 10. 10 10.   William Maher (1823–77)

THE WORSHIPPING PEOPLE

1 HERE, O my Lord, I see thee face to face;
    Here would I touch and handle things unseen,
Here grasp with firmer hand the eternal grace,
    And all my weariness upon thee lean.

2 Here would I feed upon the bread of God,
    Here drink with thee the royal wine of heaven;
Here would I lay aside each earthly load,
    Here taste afresh the calm of sin forgiven.

3 Mine is the sin, but thine the righteousness;
    Mine is the guilt, but thine the cleansing blood;
Here is my robe, my refuge, and my peace—
    Thy blood, thy righteousness, O Lord, my God.

****

4 Too soon we rise; the symbols disappear;
    The feast, though not the love, is past and gone;
The bread and wine remove, but thou art here,
    Nearer than ever, still our shield and sun.

5 Feast after feast thus comes and passes by,
    Yet, passing, points to the glad feast above,
Giving sweet foretaste of the festal joy,
    The Lamb's great bridal feast of bliss and love.

Horatius Bonar (1808–89)

The Lord's Supper

1 HOW happy are thy servants, Lord,
   Who thus remember thee!
   What tongue can tell our sweet accord,
   Our perfect harmony?

2 Who thy mysterious supper share,
   Here at thy table fed,
   Many, and yet but one we are,
   One undivided bread.

3 One with the living bread divine
   Which now by faith we eat,
   Our hearts and minds and spirits join,
   And all in Jesus meet.

4 So dear the tie where souls agree
   In Jesus' dying love;
   Then only can it closer be
   When all are joined above.

Charles Wesley (1707–88)

610(i)
ST BOTOLPH   C.M.   Gordon Slater (1896–1979)

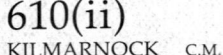

610(ii)
KILMARNOCK   C.M.   Melody by Neil Dougall (1776–1862)

THE WORSHIPPING PEOPLE

For this tune in a higher key see No. 758

1 I COME with joy to meet my Lord,
    Forgiven, loved, and free,
In awe and wonder to recall
    His life laid down for me.

2 I come with Christians far and near,
    To find, as all are fed,
The new community of love
    In Christ's communion bread.

3 As Christ breaks bread and bids us share,
    Each proud division ends;
The love that made us makes us one,
    And strangers now are friends.

4 And thus with joy we meet our Lord;
    His presence, always near,
Is in such friendship better known;
    We see and praise him here.

5 Together met, together bound,
    We'll go our different ways,
And as his people in the world
    We'll live and speak his praise.

Brian A. Wren (1936–)

The Lord's Supper

611

S. Suzanne Toolan

I AM THE BREAD OF LIFE Irreg. Arranged by Betty Pulkingham (1928–   )

Unison. Rich and full
Guitar Capo 3(G)

1 I AM the Bread of Life;_____ He who
(2) bread that__ I will give_____ Is my
(3) -less_____ you____ eat_____ Of the
4 I am the res - ur - rec - tion,_____
(5) Lord,_____ we be - lieve_____ That__

comes to me shall not hun - ger; He who be-
flesh for the life of the world;__ And he who
flesh of the Son of__ Man_____ And
I_____ am the__ life;__ He who be-
you_____ are the__ Christ,_____ The__

THE WORSHIPPING PEOPLE

The Lord's Supper

THE WORSHIPPING PEOPLE

raise ___ him up ___ On the

last ___ day.

Verses 1–4   final ending

2 The
3 Un- day.
5 Yes,

Anonymous

612

GALWAY S.M.

Melody, and most of the harmony,
by Edward Miller (1735–1807)

THE WORSHIPPING PEOPLE

1   JESUS invites his saints
       To meet around his board;
  Here pardoned sinners sit, and hold
       Communion with their Lord.

2   For food he gives his flesh,
       He bids us drink his blood;
  Amazing favour, matchless grace
       Of our descending God!

3   This holy bread and wine
       Maintains our fainting breath,
  By union with our living Lord,
       And interest in his death.

4   Our heavenly Father calls
       Christ and his members one;
  We the young children of his love,
       And he the first-born Son.

5   We are but several parts
       Of this same broken bread;
  Our body has its several limbs,
       But Jesus is the Head.

6   Let all our powers be joined
       His glorious name to raise;
  Pleasure and love fill every mind,
       And every voice be praise.

Isaac Watts (1674–1748)

May also be sung to No. 591, ST MICHAEL

The Lord's Supper

613(i)
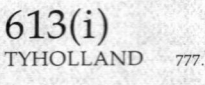
TYHOLLAND 777.

German Carol Melody, adapted by
D. F. R. Wilson (1871–1957)

613(ii)
LIVING BREAD 777.

Bernard S. Massey (1927–   )

1 JESUS, to your table led,
  Now let every heart be fed
  With the true and living Bread.

2 When we taste the mystic wine,
  Of your outpoured blood the sign,
  Fill our hearts with love divine.

3 From the bonds of sin release;
  Cold and wavering faith increase;
  Grant us, Lamb of God, your peace!

Robert Hall Baynes (1831–95)

THE WORSHIPPING PEOPLE

614

GILDAS S.M.
(ST AUGUSTINE, WEISSE)

Adapted from the chorale
Als der gütige Gott in J. S. Bach's
Vierstimmige Choralgesänge (1769)

1. JESUS, we thus obey
   Thy last and kindest word;
   Here, in thine own appointed way,
   We come to meet thee, Lord.

2. Our hearts we open wide
   To make the Saviour room;
   And lo! The Lamb, the Crucified,
   The sinners' friend, is come!

3. His presence makes the feast;
   And now our spirits feel
   The glory not to be expressed,
   The joy unspeakable.

4. With pure celestial bliss
   He doth our spirits cheer;
   His house of banqueting is this,
   And he hath brought us here.

5. He bids us drink and eat
   Imperishable food;
   He gives his flesh to be our meat,
   And bids us drink his blood.

6. Whate'er the Almighty can
   To pardoned sinners give,
   The fullness of our God made man
   We here with Christ receive.

Charles Wesley (1707–88)

The Lord's Supper

615

LET US BREAK BREAD 10 10 (Refrain)

Negro Spiritual, arranged by
Charles Cleall (1927–)

1 LET us break bread to-ge-ther with the Lord; Let us break bread to-ge-ther with the Lord:

Refrain When I fall on my knees, With my

THE WORSHIPPING PEOPLE

face to the ri-sing sun, O Lord, have mer-cy on me.

1 LET us break bread together with the Lord;
Let us break bread together with the Lord:
  When I fall on my knees,
  With my face to the rising sun,
  O Lord, have mercy on me.

2 Let us drink wine together with the Lord;
Let us drink wine together with the Lord:

3 Let us praise God together in the Lord;
Let us praise God together in the Lord:

(based on a Negro Spiritual)

The Lord's Supper

616(i)

ST HELEN 8.7.8.7.4.7. (Ext)

George C. Martin (1844–1916)

Unison

Harmony

Small notes organ only

616(ii)

BRYN CALFARIA 8.7.8.7.4.7. (Ext)

Melody by W. Owen (1813–96)

THE WORSHIPPING PEOPLE

1 LORD, enthroned in heavenly splendour,
      First-begotten from the dead,
Thou alone, our strong defender,
      Liftest up thy people's head.
            Alleluia!
      Jesus, true and living Bread.

2 Here our humblest homage pay we,
      Here in loving reverence bow;
Here for faith's discernment pray we,
      Lest we fail to know thee now.
            Alleluia!
      Thou art here, we ask not how.

3 Though the lowliest form doth veil thee
      As of old in Bethlehem,
Here as there thine angels hail thee
      Branch and Flower of Jesse's stem.
            Alleluia!
      We in worship join with them.

4 Paschal Lamb, thine offering, finished
      Once for all when thou wast slain,
In its fullness undiminished
      Shall for evermore remain,
            Alleluia!
      Cleansing souls from every stain.

5 Life-imparting, heavenly Manna,
      Stricken Rock with streaming side,
Heaven and earth with loud hosanna
      Worship thee, the Lamb who died,
            Alleluia!
      Risen, ascended, glorified!

G. H. Bourne (1840–1925)

The Lord's Supper

617

LIVING LORD 4.55.3.888.3.

Patrick Appleford (1925–)

Slow Beat Ballad

Harmony Version

1 LORD Je-sus Christ,___ You___ have come to us, You ___ are
2 Lord Je-sus Christ,___ Now___ and ev-ery day Teach___ us
3 Lord Je-sus Christ,___ You___ have come to us, Born___ as
4 Lord Je-sus Christ,___ We___would come to you, Live___ our

Unison Version

D   A   D   A   D   D7   G   Em7   F#m7   A7

one with us, Ma - ry's Son— Clean-sing our souls from
how to pray, Son of God. You have com-man - ded
one of us, Ma - ry's Son— Led out to die on
lives for you, Son of God; All your com-mands we

D   Bm   E7   Em7   A7   Em   A7

THE WORSHIPPING PEOPLE

all their sin, Pour-ing your love and good-ness in; Je-sus, our love for
us to do This, in re-mem-brance, Lord, of you; In - to our lives your
Cal-va-ry, Ris-en from death to set us free; Liv ing Lord Je-sus,
know are true; Your ma-ny gifts will make us new; In - to our lives your

D   Bm   Em   A7   Bm   B7   Em   Gm6

you we sing, Liv – ing Lord.
power breaks through, Liv - ing Lord.
help us see You are Lord.
power breaks through, Liv - ing Lord.

Vv. 1–3   V. 4

D   B7   Em7   A7   D   G6   A7   D

Patrick Appleford (1925–   )

The Lord's Supper

W. H. Havergal (1793–1870), adapted from a tune in
König's *Harmonischer Liederschatz* (1738)
(harmony slightly altered)

1   LORD of our highest love!
        Let now thy peace be given;
   Fix all our thoughts on things above,
        Our hearts on thee in heaven.

2   Then, dearest Lord, draw near,
        Whilst we thy table spread;
   And crown the feast with heavenly cheer,
        Thyself the living bread.

3   And when the loaf we break,
        Thine own rich blessing give;
   May all with loving hearts partake,
        And all new strength receive,

4   Thankful that whilst we view
        Thy body bruised and torn,
   Life, health, and healing still accrue
        From stripes which thou hast borne.

5   Dear Lord, what memories crowd
        Around the sacred cup:
   The upper room, Gethsemane,
        Thy foes, thy lifting up!

6   O scenes of suffering love,
        Enough our souls to win—
   Enough to melt our hearts, and prove
        The antidote to sin.

G. Y. Tickle (1819–88)

The Lord's Supper

619(i)
NIAGARA L.M.

Robert Jackson (1840–1914)

619(ii)
SOLOTHURN L.M.

Traditional Swiss Melody
Harmonised by John Wilson

*In selected verses A.T.B. may hum the accompaniment.

THE WORSHIPPING PEOPLE

1 NOW let us from this table rise
    Renewed in body, mind and soul;
With Christ we die and live again,
    His selfless love has made us whole.

2 With minds alert, upheld by grace,
    To spread the Word in speech and deed,
We follow in the steps of Christ,
    At one with all in hope and need.

3 To fill each human house with love,
    It is the sacrament of care;
The work that Christ began to do
    We humbly pledge ourselves to share.

4 Then give us courage, Father God,
    To choose again the pilgrim way,
And help us to accept with joy
    The challenge of tomorrow's day.

Fred Kaan (1929–)

Words reprinted by permission of
Stainer & Bell Ltd.
For permission to reproduce see p. xiii.

The Lord's Supper

SECOND VERSION
(for a verse by the choir alone)

PASSION CHORALE   7.6.7.6.D.

Melody by H. L. Hassler (1564–1612),
as set by J. S. Bach in the
St Matthew Passion (1727)

THE WORSHIPPING PEOPLE

1 O BREAD to pilgrims given,
   O food that angels eat,
O manna sent from heaven,
   For heav'n-born natures meet:
Give us, for thee long pining,
   To eat till richly filled;
Till, earth's delights resigning,
   Our every wish is stilled.

2 O water, life-bestowing,
   Forth from the Saviour's heart
A fountain purely flowing,
   A fount of love thou art:
O let us, freely tasting,
   Our burning thirst assuage;
Thy sweetness, never wasting,
   Avails from age to age.

3 Jesus, this feast receiving,
   We thee unseen adore;
Thy faithful word believing,
   We take, and doubt no more:
Give us, thou true and loving,
   On earth to live in thee;
Then, death the veil removing,
   Thy glorious face to see.

Maintzisch Gesangbuch (1661)
tr. *Ray Palmer* (1808–87) alt.

The Lord's Supper

621(i)
LAND OF REST C.M.

American Folk Hymn Tune
Harmonised by John Wilson

For this tune in a higher key see No. 269(i)

621(ii)
ST BOTOLPH C.M.

Gordon Slater (1896–1979)

THE WORSHIPPING PEOPLE

1 O THOU who this mysterious bread
   Didst in Emmaus break,
Return, herewith our souls to feed,
   And to thy followers speak.

2 Unseal the volume of thy grace,
   Apply the gospel word,
Open our eyes to see thy face,
   Our hearts to know the Lord.

3 Of thee communing still, we mourn
   Till thou the veil remove;
Talk with us, and our hearts shall burn
   With flames of fervent love.

4 Enkindle now the heavenly zeal,
   And make thy mercy known,
And give our pardoned souls to feel
   That God and love are one.

Charles Wesley (1707–88) alt.

622
CHRISTCHURCH   6.6.6.6.8.8.   C. Steggall (1826–1905)

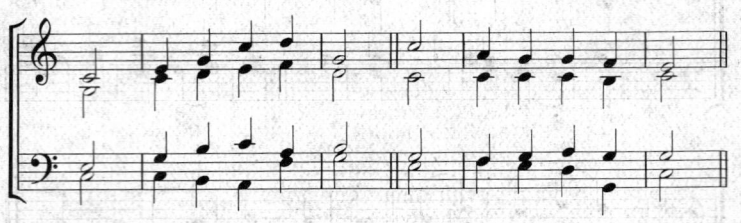

1 SEE where our great High Priest
    Before the Lord appears,
  And on his loving breast
    The tribes of Israel bears,
  Never without his people seen,
  The Head of all believing men!

2 With him the corner-stone
    The living stones conjoin;
  Christ and his church are one,
    One body and one vine;
  For us he uses all his powers,
  And all he has, or is, is ours.

3 The promptings of our Head
    The members all pursue,
  By his good Spirit led
    To act, and suffer too
  Whate'er he did on earth sustain,
  Till glorious all like him we reign.

Charles Wesley (1707–88)

623(i)

JUCUNDA LAUDATIO   10.7.10.7.4.6.6.6.   A. Gregory Murray (1905–   )

Bring bread, bring wine, Give glo-ry to the Lord;

Whose is the earth but God's,   Whose is the praise but   his?

THE WORSHIPPING PEOPLE

1 REAP me the earth as a harvest to God,
  Gather and bring it again,
  All that is his, to the Maker of all;
  Lift it and offer it high:
    Bring bread, bring wine,
    Give glory to the Lord;
    Whose is the earth but God's,
    Whose is the praise but his?

2 Go with your song and your music, with joy,
  Go to the altar of God;
  Carry your offerings, fruits of the earth,
  Work of your labouring hands:

3 Gladness and pity and passion and pain,
  All that is ours and must die—
  Lay all before him, return him his gift,
  God, to whom all shall go home:

Peter Icarus alt.

623(ii)

BAY HALL   10.7.10.7.4.6.6.6.

Michael Dawney (1942–   )

Refrain

All   (Choir Harmony ad lib.)

f Bring bread, bring wine, Give glo - ry to the Lord;

THE WORSHIPPING PEOPLE

Whose is the earth but God's, Whose is the praise but

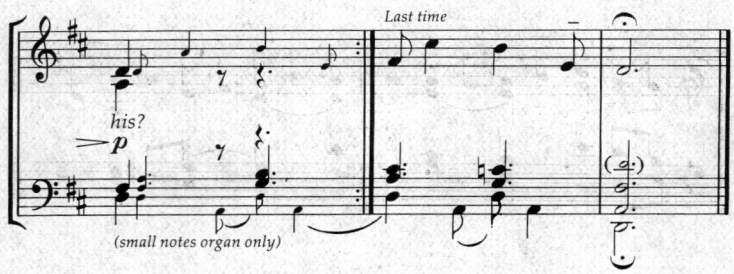

his?

(small notes organ only)

1 REAP me the earth as a harvest to God,
   Gather and bring it again,
   All that is his, to the Maker of all;
   Lift it and offer it high:
     Bring bread, bring wine,
     Give glory to the Lord;
     Whose is the earth but God's,
     Whose is the praise but his?

2 Go with your song and your music, with joy,
   Go to the altar of God;
   Carry your offerings, fruits of the earth,
   Work of your labouring hands:

3 Gladness and pity and passion and pain,
   All that is ours and must die—
   Lay all before him, return him his gift,
   God, to whom all shall go home:

                    Peter Icarus alt.

The Lord's Supper

624

PANGE LINGUA   87.87.87.   Plainsong Melody (Sarum form), Mode iii

A - men.

1 SING, my tongue, the Saviour's glory,
   Of his cross the mystery sing;
   Lift on high the wondrous trophy,
   Tell the triumph of the King:
   He, the world's Redeemer, conquers
   Death, through death now vanquishing.

2 Born for us, and for us given,
   Born a man like us below,
   He, as man with men abiding,
   Dwelt, the seeds of truth to sow;
   And at last faced death undaunted,
   Thus his greatest deed to show.

3 On the night of that last supper
   Seated with his chosen band,
   He, the paschal victim eating,
   First fulfils the law's command,
   Then as food to all his brethren
   Gives himself with his own hand.

4 Word made flesh! His word life-giving,
   Gives his flesh our meat to be;
   Bids us drink his blood, believing,
   Through his death, we life shall see:
   Blessèd they who thus receiving
   Are from death and sin set free.

5 Low in adoration bending,
   Now our hearts our God revere;
   Faith her aid to sight is lending,
   Though unseen the Lord is near;
   Ancient types and shadows ending,
   Christ our paschal Lamb is here.

6 Praise for ever, thanks and blessing,
   Thine, O gracious Father, be;
   Praise be thine, O Christ, who bringest
   Life and immortality;
   Praise be thine, thou quickening Spirit,
   Praise through all eternity.

Thomas Aquinas (*c*. 1225–74)
tr. *Edward Caswall* (1814–78) and others

The Lord's Supper

625

CULBACH 77.77.

German melody of 17th century or earlier,
adapted by W. H. Havergal (1793–1870)
(harmony slightly altered)

1 SPREAD the table of the Lord,
    Break the bread and pour the wine;
Gathered at the sacred board,
    We would taste the feast divine.

2 Saints and martyrs of the faith
    To the cross have turned their eyes,
Sharing, in their life and death,
    That eternal sacrifice.

3 Humbly now our place we claim
    In that glorious company,
Proud confessors of the name,
    Breaking bread, O Christ, with thee.

***** *****

4 By the memory of thy love,
    To the glory of the Lord,
Here we raise thy cross above;
    Gird us with thy Spirit's sword.

5 Guided by thy mighty hand,
    All thy mind we would fulfil,
Loyal to thy least command,
    Serving thee with steadfast will.

George Osborn Gregory (1881–1972)

THE WORSHIPPING PEOPLE

Melody from *Andachts Zymbeln*, Freiburg (1655)
Arranged by
J. S. Bach (1685–1750)

Rather slowly

1 STRENGTHEN for service, Lord, the hands
   That holy things have taken;
 Let ears that now have heard thy songs
   To clamour never waken.

2 Lord, may the tongues which 'Holy' sang
   Keep free from all deceiving;
 The eyes which saw thy love be bright,
   Thy blessèd hope perceiving.

3 The feet that tread thy hallowed courts
   From light do thou not banish;
 The bodies by thy body fed
   With thy new life replenish.

Liturgy of Malabar
tr. *C. W. Humphreys* (1840–1921)
and *Percy Dearmer* (1867–1936)

The Lord's Supper

627

MOUNT EPHRAIM S.M.

Melody and almost all the bass by
Benjamin Milgrove (1731–1810)

1 THE Son of God proclaim,
     The Lord of time and space;
   The God who bade the light break forth
     Now shines in Jesus' face.

2 He, God's creative Word,
     The church's Lord and Head,
   Here bids us gather as his friends
     And share his wine and bread.

3 Behold his outstretched hands;
     Though all was in his power,
   He took the towel and basin then,
     And serves us in this hour.

4 The Lord of life and death
     With wondering praise we sing;
   We break the bread at his command,
     And name him God and King.

5 We take this cup in hope;
     For he, who gladly bore
   The shameful cross, is risen again
     And reigns for evermore.

Basil E. Bridge (1927–)

THE WORSHIPPING PEOPLE

628

BROCKHAM L.M.

Melody and bass by
Jeremiah Clarke (c. 1673–1707)
Mean parts by John Wilson

1 UPON thy table, Lord, we place
    These symbols of our work and thine,
Life's food won only by thy grace,
    Who giv'st to all the bread and wine.

2 Within these simple things there lie
    The height and depth of human life,
Our inward thought, our tears and toil,
    Our hopes and fears, our joy and strife.

3 Accept them, Lord; from thee they come;
    We take them humbly at thy hand:
These gifts of thine for higher use
    We offer, as thou dost command.

4 All life is thine: O give us faith
    To know thee in the broken bread, ,
And drink with thee the wine of life,
    Thou Lord supreme of quick and dead.

5 To thee we come; refresh thou us
    With food from thy most holy board,
Until the kingdoms of this world
    Become the kingdom of the Lord.

M. F. C. Willson (1884–1944) alt.

The Lord's Supper

629(i)

CREDO 88.88.88.

John Stainer (1840–1901)

a little slower

(org.)

629(ii)

EUPHONY 88.88.88. (ext.)

H. Dennis (1818–87)

THE WORSHIPPING PEOPLE

1 VICTIM divine, thy grace we claim,
    While thus thy precious death we show;
Once offered up, a spotless Lamb,
    In thy great temple here below,
Thou didst for all mankind atone,
And standest now before the throne.

2 Thou standest in the holiest place,
    As now for guilty sinners slain;
Thy blood of sprinkling speaks, and prays,
    All-prevalent for helpless man;
Thy blood is still our ransom found,
And spreads salvation all around.

3 We need not now go up to heaven,
    To bring the long-sought Saviour down;
Thou art to all already given,
    Thou dost ev'n now thy banquet crown:
To every faithful soul appear,
And show thy real presence here!

Charles Wesley (1707–88)

May also be sung to No. 318, ALDERSGATE STREET

The Lord's Supper

630(i)
HEATHLANDS 7.7.7.7.7.7.

Henry Smart (1813–79)

For this tune in a higher key see No. 457(i)

630(ii)
RATISBON 7.7.7.7.7.7.

Melody from
Werner's *Choralbuch* (Leipzig, 1815)
Harmony mostly by
W. H. Havergal (1793–1870)

THE WORSHIPPING PEOPLE

1 AT thy feet, O Christ, we lay
Thine own gift of this new day;
Doubt of what it holds in store
Makes us crave thine aid the more;
Lest it prove a time of loss,
Mark it, Saviour, with thy cross.

2 If it flow on calm and bright,
Be thyself our chief delight;
If it bring unknown distress,
Good is all that thou canst bless;
Only, while its hours begin,
Pray we, keep them clear of sin.

3 Fain would we thy word embrace,
Live each moment in thy grace,
All our selves to thee consign,
Fold up all our wills in thine,
Think, and speak, and do, and be
Simply that which pleases thee.

4 Hear us, Lord, and that right soon;
Hear, and grant the choicest boon
That thy love can e'er impart,
Loyal singleness of heart;
So shall this and all our days,
Christ our God, show forth thy praise.

William Bright (1824–1901)

631

SHELTERED DALE 8.6.8.6.8.6. German Traditional Melody

1 AWAKE, awake to love and work,
  The lark is in the sky,
The fields are wet with diamond dew,
  The worlds awake to cry
Their blessings on the Lord of life,
  As he goes meekly by.

2 Come, let thy voice be one with theirs,
  Shout with their shout of praise;
See how the giant sun soars up,
  Great lord of years and days!
So let the love of Jesus come,
  And set thy soul ablaze—

3 To give and give and give again
  What God has given thee,
To spend thyself nor count the cost,
  To serve right gloriously
The God who gave all worlds that are,
  And all that are to be.

Geoffrey Anketell Studdert-Kennedy (1883–1929)

THE WORSHIPPING PEOPLE

632

MORNING HYMN L.M.

Melody and figured bass
by François H. Barthélémon (1741–1808)
(bass of 2nd bar altered)

1 AWAKE, my soul, and with the sun
   Thy daily stage of duty run;
      Shake off dull sloth, and joyful rise
      To pay thy morning sacrifice.

2 Redeem thy misspent moments past,
   And live this day as if thy last;
      Improve thy talent with due care;
      For the great day thyself prepare.

3 Let all thy converse be sincere,
   Thy conscience as the noonday clear;
      Think how all-seeing God thy ways
      And all thy secret thoughts surveys.

4 Wake, and lift up thyself, my heart,
   And with the angels bear thy part,
      Who all night long unwearied sing
      High praise to the eternal King.

5 Direct, control, suggest, this day,
   All I design, or do, or say,
      That all my powers, with all their might,
      In thy sole glory may unite.

6 Praise God, from whom all blessings flow;
   Praise him, all creatures here below;
      Praise him above, ye heavenly host;
      Praise Father, Son, and Holy Ghost.

Thomas Ken (1637–1711)

Morning

633

CHRISTE SANCTORUM   11.11.11.5.

Melody from *Paris Antiphoner* (1681)
Arranged J.W.

Unison or Harmony

1 FATHER, we praise thee, now the night is over;
     Active and watchful, stand we all before thee;
   Singing, we offer prayer and meditation:
        Thus we adore thee.

2 Monarch of all things, fit us for thy mansions;
     Banish our weakness, health and wholeness sending;
   Bring us to heaven, where thy saints united
        Joy without ending.

3 All-holy Father, Son, and equal Spirit,
     Trinity blessèd, send us thy salvation;
   Thine is the glory, gleaming and resounding
        Through all creation.

Attributed to *Gregory the Great* (545–604)
tr. *Percy Dearmer* (1867–1936)

THE WORSHIPPING PEOPLE

634

WHITEHALL L.M.

Melody and Bass by
Henry Lawes (1596–1662)

1 LORD, as I wake I turn to you,
   Yourself the first thought of my day;
My King, my God, whose help is sure,
   Yourself the help for which I pray.

2 There is no blessing, Lord, from you
   For those who make their will their way,
No praise for those who will not praise,
   No peace for those who will not pray.

3 Your loving gifts of grace to me,
   Those favours I could never earn,
Call for my thanks in praise and prayer,
   Call me to love you in return.

4 Lord, make my life a life of love,
   Keep me from sin in all I do;
Lord, make your law my only law,
   Your will my will, for love of you.

Brian Foley (1919–   )
based on Psalm 5

Morning

635

For another harmonisation see No. 350

1 MORNING has broken
   Like the first morning;
  Blackbird has spoken
   Like the first bird.
  Praise for the singing!
   Praise for the morning!
  Praise for them, springing
   Fresh from the Word!

2 Sweet the rain's new fall
   Sunlit from heaven,
  Like the first dewfall
   On the first grass.
  Praise for the sweetness
   Of the wet garden,
  Sprung in completeness
   Where his feet pass.

3 Mine is the sunlight!
   Mine is the morning
  Born of the one light
   Eden saw play!
  Praise with elation,
   Praise every morning,
  God's re-creation
   Of the new day!

Eleanor Farjeon (1881–1965)

THE WORSHIPPING PEOPLE

636

MELCOMBE L.M.

Melody and figured bass
by S. Webbe the elder (1740–1816)

For another harmonisation see No. 520

1 NEW every morning is the love
  Our wakening and uprising prove;
      Through sleep and darkness safely brought,
      Restored to life, and power, and thought.

2 New mercies each returning day
  Hover around us while we pray;
      New perils past, new sins forgiven,
      New thoughts of God, new hopes of heaven.

3 If on our daily course our mind
  Be set to hallow all we find,
      New treasures still, of countless price,
      God will provide for sacrifice.

4 Old friends, old scenes, will lovelier be,
  As more of heaven in each we see;
      Some softening gleam of love and prayer
      Shall dawn on every cross and care.

5 The trivial round, the common task,
  Will furnish all we ought to ask:
      Room to deny ourselves, a road
      To bring us daily nearer God.

6 Only, O Lord, in thy dear love
  Fit us for perfect rest above;
      And help us, this and every day,
      To live more nearly as we pray.

John Keble (1792–1866)

Morning

637

DORKING C.M.

English Traditional Melody
arranged by Martin Shaw (1875–1958)

THE WORSHIPPING PEOPLE

1 O LORD of life, thy quickening voice
    Awakes my morning song;
In gladsome words I would rejoice
    That I to thee belong.

2 I see thy light, I feel thy wind;
    Earth is thy uttered word;
Whatever wakes my heart and mind,
    Thy presence is, my Lord.

3 Therefore I choose my highest part,
    And turn my face to thee;
Therefore I stir my inmost heart
    To worship fervently.

4 Within my heart speak, Lord, speak on,
    My heart alive to keep,
Till comes the night, and, labour done,
    In thee I fall asleep.

George MacDonald (1824–1905) alt.

638(i)

THANET 8.33.6.

Joseph Jowett (1784–1856)

638(ii)
EVENSONG 8.33.6.

O. J. Stimpson (1835–1916)

THE WORSHIPPING PEOPLE

1 ERE I sleep, for every favour
    This day showed
        By my God,
    I will bless my Saviour.

2 O my Lord, what shall I render
    To thy name,
        Still the same,
    Gracious, good, and tender?

3 Thou hast ordered all my goings
    In thy way,
        Heard me pray,
    Sanctified my doings.

4 Visit me with thy salvation;
    Let thy care
        Now be near
    Round my habitation.

5 Leave me not, but ever love me;
    Let thy peace
        Be my bliss,
    Till thou hence remove me.

6 Thou my rock, my guard, my tower,
    Safely keep,
        While I sleep,
    Me, with all thy power.

7 So, whene'er in death I slumber,
    Let me rise
        With the wise,
    Counted in their number.

John Cennick (1718–55)

639

TE LUCIS L.M.

Plainsong Melody, Mode viii

1 TO you before the end of day,
Creator of the world, we pray:
    In love unfailing hear our prayer,
    Enfold us in your watchful care.

2 Keep all disturbing dreams away,
And hold the evil foe at bay;
    Repose untroubled let us find
    For soul and body, heart and mind.

3 Almighty Father, this accord
Through Jesus Christ, your Son, our Lord,
    Who reigns with you eternally
    In your blest Spirit's unity. Amen.

Anonymous (before 11th Century)
tr. *A. Canto*, St. Cecilia's Abbey

640

EVENING HYMN 88 .7.D.

William Jackson (1815–66)

THE WORSHIPPING PEOPLE

1 FATHER, in high heaven dwelling,
  May our evening song be telling
    Of thy mercy large and free;
  Through the day thy love has fed us,
  Through the day thy care has led us,
    With divinest charity.

2 This day's sins, O pardon, Saviour—
  Evil thoughts, perverse behaviour,
    Envy, pride, and vanity;
  From the world, the flesh, deliver,
  Save us now, and save us ever,
    O thou Lamb of Calvary!

3 From enticements of the devil,
  From the might of spirits evil,
    Be our shield and panoply;
  Let thy power this night defend us,
  And a heavenly peace attend us,
    And angelic company.

4 While the night-dews are distilling,
  Holy Ghost, each heart be filling
    With thine own serenity;
  Softly let our eyes be closing,
  Loving souls on thee reposing,
    Ever-blessèd Trinity.

George Rawson (1807–89)

641

AR HYD Y NOS   8.4.8.4.888.4.   Welsh Traditional Melody

1 GOD, that madest earth and heaven,
    Darkness and light,
Who the day for toil hast given,
    For rest the night,
May thine angel-guards defend us,
Slumber sweet thy mercy send us,
Holy dreams and hopes attend us,
    This livelong night.

2 Guard us waking, guard us sleeping;
    And, when we die,
May we in thy mighty keeping
    All peaceful lie.
When the last dread call shall wake us,
Do not thou, our Lord, forsake us,
But to reign in glory take us
    With thee on high.

Reginald Heber (1783–1826) and
Richard Whately (1787–1863)

May also be sung to No. 342(i), EAST ACKLAM

THE WORSHIPPING PEOPLE

642

TALLIS' CANON L.M.

Melody, and most of the harmony, by
Thomas Tallis (c. 1505–85). As shortened by
T. Ravenscroft (*Psalmes*, 1621)

1 GLORY to thee, my God, this night
  For all the blessings of the light;
    Keep me, O keep me, King of kings,
    Beneath thine own almighty wings.

2 Forgive me, Lord, for thy dear Son,
  The ill that I this day have done,
    That with the world, myself, and thee,
    I, ere I sleep, at peace may be

3 Teach me to live, that I may dread
  The grave as little as my bed;
    Teach me to die, that so I may
    Rise glorious at the judgement day.

4 O may my soul on thee repose,
  And may sweet sleep mine eyelids close—
    Sleep that shall me more vigorous make
    To serve my God when I awake.

5 When in the night I sleepless lie,
  My mind with heavenly thoughts supply;
    Let no ill dreams disturb my rest,
    No powers of darkness me molest.

6 Praise God, from whom all blessings flow;
  Praise him, all creatures here below;
    Praise him above, ye heavenly host;
    Praise Father, Son, and Holy Ghost.

Thomas Ken (1637–1711) alt.

Evening

643

ELLERS 10 10.10 10.

E. J. Hopkins (1818–1901)
arr. Arthur Sullivan (1842–1900)

THE WORSHIPPING PEOPLE

1 SAVIOUR, again to thy dear name we raise
  With one accord our parting hymn of praise;
    We stand to bless thee ere our worship cease,
    Then, lowly kneeling, wait thy word of peace.

2 Grant us thy peace upon our homeward way;
  With thee began, with thee shall end the day;
    Guard thou the lips from sin, the hearts from shame,
    That in this house have called upon thy name.

3 Grant us thy peace, Lord, through the coming night;
  Turn thou for us its darkness into light;
    From harm and danger keep thy children free,
    For dark and light are both alike to thee.

4 Grant us thy peace throughout our earthly life,
  Our balm in sorrow, and our stay in strife;
    Then, when thy voice shall bid our conflict cease,
    Call us, O Lord, to thine eternal peace.

John Ellerton (1826–93)

644

SEBASTE Irregular

John Stainer (1840–1901)

In free rhythm

1 HAIL, gladdening Light, of his pure glo - ry poured

Who is the immortal Fa - ther, heaven - ly, blest,

Ho - li - est of ho - lies, Je - sus Christ our Lord!

2 Now we are come to the sun's hour of rest;

The lights of eve - ning round us shine;

We hymn the Fa-ther, Son, and Ho-ly Spi – rit di-vine.

3 Worthiest art thou at all times to be sung

With un – de – fil – èd tongue, Son of our

God, giv – er of life, a – lone;

There-fore in all the world thy glo-ries, Lord, they own.

Anonymous (3rd Century)
tr. *John Keble* (1792–1866)

645

COMPANION 88.88.88.   R. S. Newman (1850–1927)

THE WORSHIPPING PEOPLE

1 LORD Jesus, in the days of old
   Two walked with thee in waning light;
And love's blind instinct made them bold
   To crave thy presence through the night.
As night descends, we too would pray:
O leave us not at close of day!

2 Did not their hearts within them burn?
   And, though their Lord they failed to know,
Did not their spirits inly yearn?
   They could not let the Stranger go.
Much more must we who know thee pray:
O leave us not at close of day!

3 Perchance we have not always wist
   Who has been with us by the way;
Amid day's uproar we have missed
   Some word that thou hast had to say.
In silent night, O Saviour dear,
We would not fail thy voice to hear.

4 Day is far spent, and night is nigh;
   Stay with us, Saviour, through the night;
Talk with us, touch us tenderly,
   Lead us to peace, to rest, to light;
Dispel our darkness with thy face,
Radiant with resurrection grace.

5 Nor this night only, blessèd Lord,
   We, every day and every hour,
Would walk with thee Emmaus-ward
   To hear thy voice of love and power;
And every night would by thy side
Look, listen, and be satisfied.

James Ashcroft Noble (1844–96)

May also be sung to No. 369, WYCH CROSS

646(i)
HURSLEY L.M.

Abridged from melody in
Katholisches Gesangbuch, Vienna (c. 1774)

646(ii)
ABENDS L.M.

Herbert Oakeley, (1830–1903)

org ped.

1 SUN of my soul, thou Saviour dear,
  It is not night if thou be near;
    O may no earth-born cloud arise
    To hide thee from thy servant's eyes!

2 When the soft dews of kindly sleep
  My wearied eyelids gently steep,
    Be my last thought: how sweet to rest
    For ever on my Saviour's breast!

3 Abide with me from morn till eve,
  For without thee I cannot live;
    Abide with me when night is nigh,
    For without thee I dare not die.

4 If some poor wandering child of thine
  Have spurned today the voice divine,
    Now, Lord, the gracious work begin;
    Let him no more lie down in sin.

5 Watch by the sick; enrich the poor
  With blessings from thy boundless store;
    Be every mourner's sleep tonight
    Like infant's slumbers, pure and light.

6 Come near and bless us when we wake,
  Ere through the world our way we take,
    Till in the ocean of thy love
    We lose ourselves in heaven above.

John Keble (1792–1866)

Evening

647

INNSBRUCK 7.7.6.7.7.8.

German Traditional Melody, as set by
J. S. Bach in the *St. Matthew Passion* (1727)

SECOND VERSION

INNSBRUCK 7.7.6.7.7.8.

Variant form of the melody,
with harmony chiefly based on J. S. Bach

THE WORSHIPPING PEOPLE

1 THE duteous day now closes,
  Each flower and tree reposes,
    Shade creeps o'er wild and wood:
  Let us, as night is falling,
  On God our maker calling,
    Give thanks to him, the giver good.

2 Now all the heavenly splendour
  Breaks forth in starlight tender
    From myriad worlds unknown;
  And we, the marvel seeing,
  Forget our selfish being,
    For joy of beauty not our own.

3 Awhile our mortal blindness
  May miss God's loving-kindness,
    And grope in faithless strife:
  But when life's day is over
  Shall death's fair night discover
    The fields of everlasting life.

  Robert Bridges (1844–1930) alt.
  based on *Paul Gerhardt* (1607–76)

Evening

648
ST CLEMENT 9.8.9.8.   C. C. Scholefield (1839–1904)

1 THE day thou gavest, Lord, is ended,
  The darkness falls at thy behest;
To thee our morning hymns ascended,
  Thy praise shall sanctify our rest.

2 We thank thee that thy church unsleeping,
  While earth rolls onward into light,
Through all the world her watch is keeping,
  And rests not now by day or night.

3 As o'er each continent and island
  The dawn leads on another day,
The voice of prayer is never silent,
  Nor dies the strain of praise away.

4 The sun that bids us rest is waking
  Our brethren 'neath the western sky,
And hour by hour fresh lips are making
  Thy wondrous doings heard on high.

5 So be it, Lord; thy throne shall never,
  Like earth's proud empires, pass away;
Thy kingdom stands, and grows for ever,
  Till all thy creatures own thy sway.

John Ellerton (1826–93)

THE WORSHIPPING PEOPLE

DESCANT VERSION FOR VERSE 5

Arranged by John Wilson

5 So be__ it, Lord; thy throne shall ne-ver, Like earth's proud em – pires, pass a – way; Thy king-dom stands, and grows for ev-er, Till all__ thy crea-tures own thy sway.

Evening

649

DUNDEE C.M.   Melody from *Scottish Psalter*, Edinburgh (1615)

For this tune in its original rhythm see No. 496

1 COME, let us use the grace divine,
    And all, with one accord,
  In a perpetual cov'nant join
    Ourselves to Christ the Lord:

2 Give up ourselves, through Jesu's power,
    His name to glorify;
  And promise, in this sacred hour,
    For God to live and die.

3 The cov'nant we this moment make
    Be ever kept in mind:
  We will no more our God forsake,
    Or cast his words behind.

4 We never will throw off his fear
    Who hears our solemn vow;
  And if thou art well pleased to hear,
    Come down, and meet us now.

5 To each the cov'nant blood apply,
    Which takes our sins away;
  And register our names on high,
    And keep us to that day.

Charles Wesley (1707–88)

650

COLLINGWOOD C.M.

H. A. Bate (1899–   )

1 FATHER, your church with thankfulness
   Receives as from your hand
   The different gifts of heart and mind
Which different lives possess.

2 Ours is the voice, but yours the grace
   That brings to these today
   The call to mark for us the way
By which to seek your face.

3 Give them again each day the love
   That brought them to this hour:
   Your peace their ministry empower,
Your hope their fears resolve.

4 Lord, may the team of faith each leads
   Be wise to do your will;
   To speak the word that strengthens still,
And seal its talk with deeds.

5 In heaven and earth your folk are one,
   Since all to you belong.
   We'll sing your church's thankful song,
And praise your living Son.

6 Your living Son the pattern gives:
   May we his pattern trace,
   And find for all the human race
The way of life that lives.

Caryl Micklem (1925–   )

651

RANDOLPH 9.88.9.   Ralph Vaughan Williams (1872–1958)

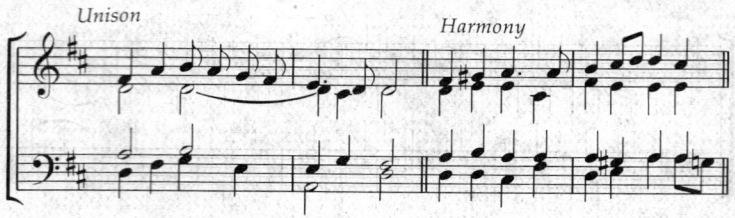

1 GOD be with you till we meet again;
   May he through the days direct you;
   May he in life's storms protect you;
God be with you till we meet again.

2 God be with you till we meet again;
   And when doubts and fears oppress you,
   May his holy peace possess you;
God be with you till we meet again.

3 God be with you till we meet again;
   In distress his grace sustain you;
   In success from pride restrain you;
God be with you till we meet again.

4 God be with you till we meet again;
   May he go through life beside you,
   And through death in safety guide you;
God be with you till we meet again.

Donald Hughes (1911–67)
based on *J. E. Rankin* (1828–1904)

THE WORSHIPPING PEOPLE

652

DISMISSAL   8.7.8.7.4.7.   William Letton Viner (1790–1867)

(Small notes organ only)

1 LORD, dismiss us with thy blessing,
    Fill our hearts with joy and peace;
Let us each, thy love possessing,
    Triumph in redeeming grace;
        O refresh us,
    Travelling through this wilderness.

2 Thanks we give, and adoration,
    For thy gospel's joyful sound;
May the fruits of thy salvation
    In our hearts and lives abound;
        May thy presence
    With us evermore be found.

John Fawcett (1740–1817)

653

BETHANY 8.7.8.7.D.

Henry Smart (1813–79)

For this tune in a higher key see No. 796

THE WORSHIPPING PEOPLE

1 GOD is here! As we his people
   Meet to offer praise and prayer,
 May we find in fuller measure
   What it is in Christ we share.
 Here, as in the world around us,
   All our varied skills and arts
 Wait the coming of his Spirit
   Into open minds and hearts.

2 Here are symbols to remind us
   Of our lifelong need of grace;
 Here are table, font, and pulpit;
   Here the cross has central place.
 Here in honesty of preaching,
   Here in silence, as in speech,
 Here, in newness and renewal,
   God the Spirit comes to each.

3 Here our children find a welcome
   In the Shepherd's flock and fold;
 Here as bread and wine are taken,
   Christ sustains us, as of old;
 Here the servants of the Servant
   Seek in worship to explore
 What it means in daily living
   To believe and to adore.

4 Lord of all, of Church and Kingdom,
   In an age of change and doubt,
 Keep us faithful to the gospel,
   Help us work your purpose out.
 Here, in this day's dedication,
   All we have to give, receive:
 We, who cannot live without you,
   We adore you! We believe!

F. Pratt Green (1903–   )

May also be sung to No. 267(i), BLAENWERN

Words reprinted by permission of
Stainer & Bell Ltd.
For permission to reproduce see p. xiii.

654

CHRISTE SANCTORUM 11.11.11.5.

Melody from *Paris Antiphoner* (1681)
arranged by J. W.

Unison or Harmony

1 LORD of the living, in your name assembled,
  We join to thank you for the life remembered.
  Father, have mercy, to your children giving
        Hope in believing.

2 Help us to treasure all that will remind us
  Of the enrichment in the days behind us.
  Your love has set us in the generations,
        God of creation.

3 May we, whenever tempted to dejection,
  Strongly recapture thoughts of resurrection.
  You gave us Jesus to defeat our sadness
        With Easter gladness.

4 Lord, you can lift us from the grave of sorrow
  Into the presence of your own tomorrow;
  Give to your people for the day's affliction
        Your benediction.

Fred Kaan (1929–   )

Words reprinted by permission of
Stainer & Bell Ltd.
For permission to reproduce see p. xiii.

655(i)

HALTON HOLGATE 8.7.8.7.

Later form of a tune by Dr William Boyce (c. 1710–1779)
as given in S. S. Wesley's
European Psalmist (1872)

655(ii)

ST OSWALD 8.7.8.7.

J. B. Dykes (1823–76)

THE WORSHIPPING PEOPLE

1 O HOW blest the hour, Lord Jesus,
    When we can to thee draw near,
  Promises so sweet and precious
    From thy gracious lips to hear.

2 Be with us this day to bless us,
    That we may not hear in vain;
  With the saving truths impress us
    Which the word of life contain.

3 Open thou our minds, and lead us
    Safely on our heavenward way;
  With the lamp of truth precede us,
    That we may not go astray.

4 Make us gentle, meek, and humble,
    And yet bold in doing right;
  Scatter darkness, lest we stumble:
    Safe our walking in the light.

5 Lord, endue thy word from heaven
    With such light, and love, and power,
  That in us its silent leaven
    May work on from hour to hour.

6 Give us grace to bear our witness
    To the truths we have embraced;
  And let others both their sweetness
    And their quickening virtue taste.

Karl Johann Philipp Spitta (1801–59)
tr. *Richard Massie* (1800–87)

656

THE WORSHIPPING PEOPLE

1 O THOU not made with hands,
    Not throned above the skies,
Nor walled with shining walls,
    Nor framed with stones of price,
More bright than gold or gem,
God's own Jerusalem!

2 Where'er the gentle heart
    Finds courage from above,
Where'er the heart forsook
    Warms with the breath of love,
Where faith bids fear depart,
City of God, thou art.

3 Thou art where'er the proud
    In humbleness melts down;
Where self itself yields up;
    Where martyrs win their crown;
Where faithful souls possess
Themselves in perfect peace.

4 Where in life's common ways
    With cheerful feet we go,
Where in his steps we tread
    Who trod the way of woe,
Where he is in the heart,
City of God, thou art.

5 Not throned above the skies,
    Nor golden-walled afar,
But where Christ's two or three
    In his name gathered are,
Lo, in the midst of them,
God's own Jerusalem!

Francis Turner Palgrave (1824–97)

657

NORTHUMBRIA   10 10.10 10.10 10.   Walter K. Stanton (1891–1978)

THE WORSHIPPING PEOPLE

1 REJOICE, O people, in the mounting years,
    Wherein God's mighty purposes unfold;
From age to age his righteous reign appears,
    From land to land the love of Christ is told.
Rejoice, O people, in your glorious Lord;
Lift up your hearts in jubilant accord.

2 Rejoice, O people, in the years of old,
    When prophets' glowing vision lit the way;
Till saint and martyr sped the venture bold,
    And eager hearts awoke to greet the day.
Rejoice in God's glad messengers of peace,
Who bore the Saviour's gospel of release.

3 Rejoice, O people, in this living hour:
    Low lies our pride and human wisdom dies;
But on the cross God's love reveals his power;
    And from his waiting church new hopes arise.
Rejoice that while our sinfulness divides,
One Christian fellowship of love abides.

4 Rejoice, O people, in the days to be,
    When o'er the strife of nations sounding clear,
Shall ring love's gracious song of victory,
    To east and west his kingdom bringing near.
Rejoice, rejoice, his church on earth is one,
And binds the ransomed nations 'neath the sun.

5 Rejoice, O people, in that final day
    When all the travail of creation ends;
Christ now attains his universal sway,
    O'er heaven and earth his royal Word extends:
That word proclaimed where saints and martyrs trod,
The glorious gospel of the blessèd God.

Albert F. Bayly (1901-84)

May also be sung to No. 556, SONG 1

658

ALDERSGATE STREET 88.88.88.

E. F. Horner (1864–1928)

THE WORSHIPPING PEOPLE

1 THAT mighty resurrected Word
    No fashioned timbers can restrain;
The fullness of our living Lord
    No stones, no bricks, no glass contain.
Yet to his glory here we raise
A place for prayer and joyful praise—

2 A place where love will come to dwell,
    And strangely warm each heart within;
Where faith and hope our fears dispel,
    Where peace and trust in God begin.
Rejoice! Our Lord reveals his name:
Christ Jesus, here your truth proclaim!

3 For you we work: we dedicate
    Our building and our zeal to you;
Lord, bless this church; in us create
    A people by your love made new;
May sacraments and preaching raise
Our souls to share your gifts of grace.

4 Come now, great Lord, with power and might:
    Our minds with lively vision fill;
Upon us shed your holy light:
    Help us to know and do your will:
That we who here acclaim you Lord
May then declare your name abroad.

Derek R. Farrow (1925–   )

659

WAREHAM L.M.

Melody by W. Knapp (1698–1768)

For this tune in a higher key see No. 549

1 THIS stone to thee in faith we lay;
   We build the temple, Lord, to thee:
Thine eye be open, night and day,
   To guard this house and sanctuary.

2 Here, when thy people seek thy face,
   And dying sinners pray to live,
Hear thou, in heaven thy dwelling-place,
   And when thou hearest, O forgive!

3 Here, when thy messengers proclaim
   The blessèd gospel of thy Son,
Still, by the power of his great name,
   Be mighty signs and wonders done.

4 But will the eternal Father deign
   Here to abide, no transient guest?
Will here the world's Redeemer reign,
   And here the Holy Spirit rest?

5 That glory never hence depart!
   Yet choose not, Lord, this house alone;
Thy kingdom come to every heart:
   In all the world be thine the throne.

James Montgomery (1771–1854) alt.
based on I Kings 8:27–30

THE WORSHIPPING PEOPLE

660

ST CATHERINE'S COURT   12.11.12.11.   R. Strutt (1848–1927)

1 IN our day of thanksgiving one psalm let us offer
    For the saints who before us have found their reward;
  When the shadow of death fell upon them, we sorrowed,
    But now we rejoice that they rest in the Lord.

2 In the morning of life, and at noon, and at even,
    He called them away from our worship below;
  But not till his love, at the font and the altar,
    Had girt them with grace for the way they should go.

3 These stones that have echoed their praises are holy,
    And dear is the ground where their feet have once trod;
  Yet here they confessed they were strangers and pilgrims,
    And still they were seeking the city of God.

4 Sing praise, then, for all who here sought and here found him,
    Whose journey is ended, whose perils are past:
  They believed in the Light; and its glory is round them,
    Where the clouds of earth's sorrow are lifted at last.

William Henry Draper (1855–1933)

661

EIN' FESTE BURG 8.7.8.7.66.66.7.

Later form of melody by
Martin Luther (1483–1546)

1 A SAFE stronghold our God is still,
    A trusty shield and weapon;
He'll help us clear from all the ill
    That hath us now o'ertaken.
      The ancient prince of hell
      Hath risen with purpose fell;
      Strong mail of craft and power
      He weareth in this hour;
On earth is not his fellow.

2 With force of arms we nothing can,
    Full soon were we down-ridden;
But for us fights the proper Man,
    Whom God himself hath bidden.
      Ask ye: Who is this same?
      Christ Jesus is his name,
      The Lord Sabaoth's Son;
      He, and no other one,
Shall conquer in the battle.

3 And were this world all devils o'er,
    And watching to devour us,
We lay it not to heart so sore;
    Not they can overpower us.
      And let the prince of ill
      Look grim as e'er he will,
      He harms us not a whit;
      For why? His doom is writ;
A word shall quickly slay him.

4 God's word, for all their craft and force,
    One moment will not linger,
But, spite of hell, shall have its course;
    'Tis written by his finger.
      And though before our eyes
      All that we dearly prize
      They seize beyond recall,
      Yet is their profit small:
God's kingdom ours remaineth.

Martin Luther (1483–1546)
tr. *Thomas Carlyle* (1795–1881)
v. 4 alt. *Rupert E. Davies* (1909–)

Faith and Confidence

662

MAINZER L.M.

Melody by Joseph Mainzer (1801–51)

For this tune in a lower key see No. 322(i).

1 AUTHOR of faith, eternal Word,
    Whose Spirit breathes the active flame;
  Faith, like its finisher and Lord,
    Today as yesterday the same:

2 To thee our humble hearts aspire,
    And ask the gift unspeakable;
  Increase in us the kindled fire,
    In us the work of faith fulfil.

3 By faith we know thee strong to save—
    Save us, a present Saviour thou!
  Whate'er we hope, by faith we have,
    Future and past subsisting now.

4 To him that in thy name believes
    Eternal life with thee is given;
  Into himself he all receives,
    Pardon, and holiness, and heaven.

5 The things unknown to feeble sense,
    Unseen by reason's glimmering ray,
  With strong, commanding evidence
    Their heav'nly origin display.

6 Faith lends its realizing light,
    The clouds disperse, the shadows fly;
  The Invisible appears in sight,
    And God is seen by mortal eye.

Charles Wesley (1707–88)

THE CHRISTIAN LIFE

663

SAMSON L.M.

Adapted from G. F. Handel (1685–1759)

1 AWAKE, our souls; away, our fears;
    Let every trembling thought be gone;
  Awake, and run the heavenly race,
    And put a cheerful courage on.

2 True, 'tis a strait and thorny road,
    And mortal spirits tire and faint;
  But they forget the mighty God
    Who feeds the strength of every saint—

3 Thee, mighty God, whose matchless power
    Is ever new and ever young,
  And firm endures, while endless years
    Their everlasting circles run!

4 From thee, the overflowing spring,
    Our souls shall drink a fresh supply,
  While such as trust their native strength
    Shall faint away, and droop, and die.

5 Swift as an eagle cuts the air,
    We'll mount aloft to thine abode:
  On wings of love our souls shall fly,
    Nor tire along the heavenly road.

Isaac Watts (1674–1748)
based on Isaiah 40:28–31

Faith and Confidence

664

MUFF FIELD   56.9.66.9.   Ivor H. Jones (1934–   )

THE CHRISTIAN LIFE

The Wesleys' Birthday Hymn

1 AWAY with our fears!
  The glad morning appears
When an heir of salvation was born!
  From Jehovah I came,
  For his glory I am,
And to him I with singing return.

2 I sing of thy grace,
  From my earliest days
Ever near to allure and defend;
  Hitherto thou hast been
  My preserver from sin,
And I trust thou wilt save to the end.

3 O the infinite cares,
  And temptations, and snares
Thy hand has conducted me through!
  O the blessings bestowed
  By a bountiful God,
And the mercies eternally new!

4 What a mercy is this,
  What a heaven of bliss,
How unspeakably happy am I;
  Gathered into the fold,
  With thy people enrolled,
With thy people to live and to die.

5 All honour and praise
  To the Father of grace,
To the Spirit, and Son, I return;
  The business pursue
  He has made me to do,
And rejoice that I ever was born.

6 In a rapture of joy
  My life I employ
The God of my life to proclaim;
  'Tis worth living for, this,
  To administer bliss
And salvation in Jesus's name.

7 My remnant of days
  I spend in his praise,
Who died the whole world to redeem:
  Be they many or few,
  My days are his due,
And they all are devoted to him.

Charles Wesley (1707–88)

Faith and Confidence

665

EVENTIDE   10 10.10 10.   W. H. Monk (1823–89)

1 ABIDE with me; fast falls the eventide;
The darkness deepens; Lord, with me abide;
    When other helpers fail, and comforts flee,
    Help of the helpless, O abide with me.

2 Swift to its close ebbs out life's little day;
Earth's joys grow dim, its glories pass away;
    Change and decay in all around I see;
    O thou who changest not, abide with me!

3 I need thy presence every passing hour;
What but thy grace can foil the tempter's power?
    Who like thyself my guide and stay can be?
    Through cloud and sunshine, O abide with me.

4 I fear no foe, with thee at hand to bless;
Ills have no weight, and tears no bitterness;
    Where is death's sting? Where, grave, thy victory?
    I triumph still, if thou abide with me.

5 Hold thou thy cross before my closing eyes;
Shine through the gloom, and point me to the skies;
    Heaven's morning breaks, and earth's vain shadows flee;
    In life, in death, O Lord, abide with me!

Henry Francis Lyte (1793–1847)

THE CHRISTIAN LIFE

Melody, and almost all the harmony,
by William Jones of Nayland (1726–1800)

For this tune in a higher key see No. 245.

1 BEHOLD the amazing gift of love
   The Father has bestowed
On us, the sinful sons of men,
   To call us sons of God!

2 Concealed as yet this honour lies,
   By this dark world unknown,
A world that knew not when he came,
   Ev'n God's eternal Son.

3 High is the rank we now possess;
   But higher we shall rise;
Though what we shall hereafter be
   Is hid from mortal eyes:

4 Our lives, we know, when he appears,
   Shall bear his image bright;
For all his glory, full disclosed,
   Shall open to our sight.

5 A hope so great and so divine
   May trials well endure;
And purify us all from sin,
   As Christ himself is pure.

Scottish Paraphrases (1781) alt.
based on I John 3:1–3

Faith and Confidence

667(i)

OLD 104th 10 10.11 11.

Melody (with 4th line adapted),
and most of the harmony, from
T. Ravenscroft's *Psalmes* (1621)

667(ii)

LAUDATE DOMINUM 10 10.11 11.

Henry J. Gauntlett
(1805–76)
(harmony slightly altered)

THE CHRISTIAN LIFE

1 BEGONE, unbelief;
  My Saviour is near,
And for my relief
  Will surely appear;
By prayer let me wrestle,
  And he will perform;
With Christ in the vessel,
  I smile at the storm.

2 Though dark be my way,
  Since he is my guide,
'Tis mine to obey,
  'Tis his to provide;
Though cisterns be broken
  And creatures all fail,
The word he has spoken
  Shall surely prevail.

3 His love in time past
  Forbids me to think
He'll leave me at last
  In trouble to sink;
While each Ebenezer
  I have in review
Confirms his good pleasure
  To help me quite through.

4 Why should I complain
  Of want or distress,
Temptation or pain?
  He told me no less;
The heirs of salvation,
  I know from his word,
Through much tribulation
  Must follow their Lord.

5 Since all that I meet
  Shall work for my good,
The bitter is sweet,
  The med'cine is food;
Though painful at present,
  'Twill cease before long;
And then, O how pleasant
  The conqueror's song!

John Newton (1725–1807)

Faith and Confidence

668

BLESSÈD ASSURANCE
9.10.99. and Refrain

Phoebe Palmer Knapp (1839–1908)

Refrain

This is my sto – ry, this is my

song, ___ Prais-ing my Sa – viour all the day long. ___

THE CHRISTIAN LIFE

This is my sto—ry, this is my song,____

Prais—ing my Sa—viour all the day long.____

1 BLESSÈD assurance, Jesus is mine:
   O what a foretaste of glory divine!
   Heir of salvation, purchase of God;
   Born of his Spirit, washed in his blood:
      This is my story, this is my song,
      Praising my Saviour all the day long.

2 Perfect submission, perfect delight,
   Visions of rapture burst on my sight;
   Angels descending bring from above
   Echoes of mercy, whispers of love:

3 Perfect submission, all is at rest,
   I in my Saviour am happy and blest—
   Watching and waiting, looking above,
   Filled with his goodness, lost in his love:

Frances Jane van Alstyne (1820–1915)

Faith and Confidence

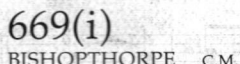

669(i)
BISHOPTHORPE C.M.

Melody and bass from
Select Portions of the Psalms
(published by H. Gardner, c. 1786)

669(ii)
SENNEN COVE C.M.

William H. Harris (1883–1973)

THE CHRISTIAN LIFE

1 BLEST be the everlasting God,
　　The Father of our Lord!
　Be his abounding mercy praised,
　　His majesty adored!

2 When from the dead he raised his Son,
　　And called him to the sky,
　He gave our souls a lively hope
　　That they should never die.

3 There's an inheritance divine
　　Reserved against that day;
　'Tis uncorrupted, undefiled,
　　And cannot fade away.

4 Saints by the power of God are kept,
　　Till that salvation come:
　We walk by faith as strangers here,
　　Till Christ shall call us home.

Isaac Watts (1674–1748)
based on 1 Peter 1:3–5

670(i)
MOUNT EPHRAIM S.M.

Melody and almost all the bass by
Benjamin Milgrove (1731–1810)

670(ii)
CAMBRIDGE S.M.

Melody by R. Harrison (1748–1810)

THE CHRISTIAN LIFE

For this tune in a lower key see No. 785(i)

1   BLEST are the saints, O God,
      That stay themselves on thee!
Who wait for thy salvation, Lord,
      Shall thy salvation see.

2   When we in darkness walk,
      Nor feel the heavenly flame,
Then is the time to trust our God,
      And rest upon his name.

3   Soon shall our doubts and fears
      Subside at his control;
His loving-kindness shall break through
      The midnight of the soul.

4   Wait till the shadows flee;
      Wait thy appointed hour;
Wait till the Bridegroom of thy soul
      Reveals his love with power.

Augustus Montague Toplady (1740–78) alt.

Faith and Confidence

671

DAY BY DAY *Irreg.*

D. Austin

Unison. Gently

DAY by day, dear Lord, Of thee three things I pray: To see thee more clear-ly, To love thee more dear-ly, To fol-low thee more near-ly, Day by day.

F Gm C7 F Dm G7 C7 F D7 G Gm7 C C7 F Bb6 F C7 F

Richard of Chichester (c. 1197–c. 1253)

THE CHRISTIAN LIFE

672

FOSTER S.M.

M. B. Foster (1851–1922)

PART 1

1   COMMIT thou all thy griefs
        And ways into his hands,
    To his sure truth and tender care,
        Who heaven and earth commands.

2   Who points the clouds their course,
        Whom winds and seas obey,
    He shall direct thy wandering feet,
        He shall prepare thy way.

3   Thou on the Lord rely,
        So safe shalt thou go on;
    Fix on his work thy steadfast eye,
        So shall thy work be done.

4   No profit canst thou gain
        By self-consuming care;
    To him commend thy cause; his ear
        Attends the softest prayer.

5   Thy everlasting truth,
        Father, thy ceaseless love,
    Sees all thy children's wants, and knows
        What best for each will prove.

6   Thou everywhere hast sway,
        And all things serve thy might;
    Thy every act pure blessing is,
        Thy path unsullied light.

Faith and Confidence

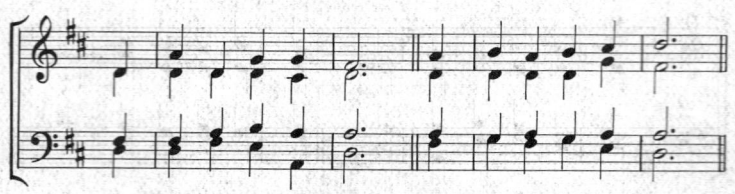

ALTERNATIVE HARMONISATION
(for selected verses in either Part)

Choir and Organ.
Congregation sing melody as above.

Version from
The Clarendon Hymn Book (1936)

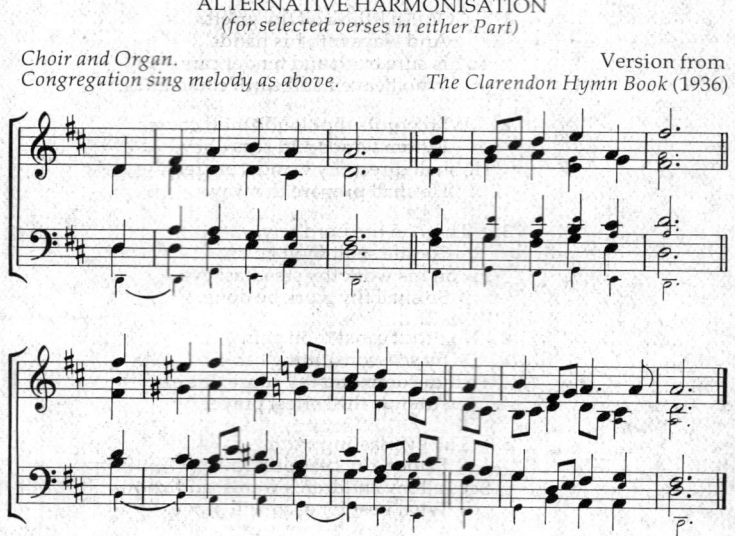

THE CHRISTIAN LIFE

7   Give to the winds thy fears;
      Hope, and be undismayed:
  God hears thy sighs, and counts thy tears,
      God shall lift up thy head.

8   Through waves, and clouds, and storms
      He gently clears thy way:
  Wait thou his time; so shall this night
      Soon end in joyous day.

9   Still heavy is thy heart?
      Still sink thy spirits down?
  Cast off the weight, let fear depart,
      Bid every care be gone.

10   What though thou rulest not?
      Yet heav'n, and earth, and hell
  Proclaim: God sitteth on the throne,
      And ruleth all things well!

11   Leave to his sovereign sway
      To choose and to command;
  So shalt thou wondering own his way
      How wise, how strong his hand.

12   Far, far above thy thought
      His counsel shall appear,
  When fully he the work hath wrought
      That caused thy needless fear.

13   Thou seest our weakness, Lord;
      Our hearts are known to thee:
  O lift thou up the sinking hand,
      Confirm the feeble knee!

14   Let us in life, in death,
      Thy steadfast truth declare,
  And publish with our latest breath
      Thy love and guardian care.

Paul Gerhardt (1607–76)
tr. *John Wesley* (1703–91)

Faith and Confidence

673(i)

REPTON 8.6.88.6.

C. H. H. Parry (1848–1918)
(from a song in his oratorio *Judith*)

Unison

673(ii)

MANSFIELD COLLEGE 8.6.88.6.

Bernard S. Massey (1927–)

THE CHRISTIAN LIFE

1 DEAR Lord and Father of mankind,
   Forgive our foolish ways;
Reclothe us in our rightful mind;
In purer lives thy service find,
   In deeper reverence, praise.

2 In simple trust like theirs who heard
   Beside the Syrian sea
The gracious calling of the Lord,
Let us, like them, without a word
   Rise up and follow thee.

3 O sabbath rest by Galilee!
   O calm of hills above,
Where Jesus knelt to share with thee
The silence of eternity,
   Interpreted by love!

4 With that deep hush subduing all
   Our words and works that drown
The tender whisper of thy call,
As noiseless let thy blessing fall
   As fell thy manna down.

5 Drop thy still dews of quietness,
   Till all our strivings cease;
Take from our souls the strain and stress,
And let our ordered lives confess
   The beauty of thy peace.

6 Breathe through the heats of our desire
   Thy coolness and thy balm;
Let sense be dumb, let flesh retire;
Speak through the earthquake, wind, and fire,
   O still small voice of calm!

John Greenleaf Whittier (1807–92)

Faith and Confidence

674(i)

ANTWERP L.M.

William Smallwood (1831–97)

For this tune in a higher key see No. 148

674(ii)

BLOCKLEY L.M.

John Blockley (1801–82)

THE CHRISTIAN LIFE

1 HAPPY the man that finds the grace,
   The blessing of God's chosen race,
      The wisdom coming from above,
      The faith that sweetly works by love.

2 Happy beyond description he
   Who knows 'The Saviour died for me',
      The gift unspeakable obtains,
      And heav'nly understanding gains.

3 Wisdom divine! Who tells the price
   Of wisdom's costly merchandise?
      Wisdom to silver we prefer,
      And gold is dross compared to her.

4 Her hands are filled with length of days,
   True riches, and immortal praise,
      Riches of Christ, on all bestowed,
      And honour that descends from God.

5 To purest joys she all invites,
   Chaste, holy, spiritual delights;
      Her ways are ways of pleasantness,
      And all her flowery paths are peace.

6 Happy the man who wisdom gains,
   Thrice happy who his guest retains;
      He owns, and shall for ever own,
      Wisdom, and Christ, and heaven are one.

Charles Wesley (1707–88)

Faith and Confidence

675

REDEMPTOR S.M.

John Wilson (1905–   )

ALTERNATIVE HARMONY VERSION

THE CHRISTIAN LIFE

1   HAVE faith in God, my heart,
      Trust and be unafraid;
God will fulfil in every part
      Each promise he has made.

2   Have faith in God, my mind,
      Though oft your light burns low;
God's mercy holds a wiser plan
      Than you can fully know.

3   Have faith in God, my soul;
      His cross for ever stands;
And neither life nor death can pluck
      His children from his hands.

4   Lord Jesus, make me whole;
      Grant me no resting place,
Until I rest, heart, mind, and soul,
      The captive of your grace.

Bryn Rees (1911–83)

May also be sung to No. 513(i), CARLISLE

Faith and Confidence

676(i)

SHEPHERD BOY'S SONG C.M.

J. H. Alden (1900–76)

1 HE that is down needs fear no fall,
He that is low, no pride;
He that is hum-ble ev-er shall Have God to be his guide.

2 I am con-tent with what I have,
Lit-tle be it or much;
And, Lord, con-tent-ment still I crave, Be-cause thou sa-vest such.

3 Full-ness to such a bur-den is That go on pil-grim-age;
Here lit-tle, and here-af-ter bliss, Is best from age to age.

THE CHRISTIAN LIFE

676(ii)

WIGTOWN C.M.

Melody, and most of the harmony,
from *Scottish Psalter* (1635)

1 HE that is down needs fear no fall,
   He that is low, no pride;
   He that is humble ever shall
   Have God to be his guide.

2 I am content with what I have,
   Little be it or much;
   And, Lord, contentment still I crave,
   Because thou savest such.

3 Fullness to such a burden is
   That go on pilgrimage;
   Here little, and hereafter bliss,
   Is best from age to age.

John Bunyan (1628–88)

Faith and Confidence

677

ARDEN C.M.

George Thalben-Ball (1896–   )

1 I'M not ashamed to own my Lord,
   Or to defend his cause,
   Maintain the honour of his word,
   The glory of his cross.

2 Jesus, my God, I know his name,
   His name is all my trust;
   Nor will he put my soul to shame,
   Nor let my hope be lost.

3 Firm as his throne his promise stands,
   And he can well secure
   What I've committed to his hands
   Till the decisive hour.

4 Then will he own my worthless name
   Before his Father's face,
   And in the new Jerusalem
   Appoint my soul a place.

Isaac Watts (1674–1748)
based on II Timothy 1:12

678

PENLAN 7.6.7.6.D.

David Jenkins (1848–1915)

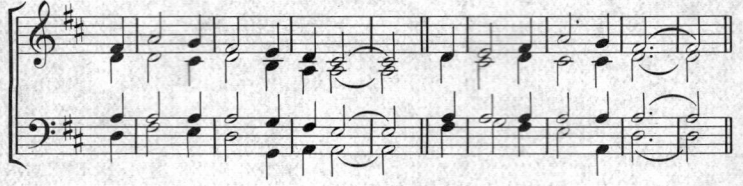

THE CHRISTIAN LIFE

1 IN heavenly love abiding,
   No change my heart shall fear;
And safe is such confiding,
   For nothing changes here:
The storm may roar without me,
   My heart may low be laid;
But God is round about me,
   And can I be dismayed?

2 Wherever he may guide me,
   No want shall turn me back;
My Shepherd is beside me,
   And nothing can I lack:
His wisdom ever waketh,
   His sight is never dim;
He knows the way he taketh,
   And I will walk with him.

3 Green pastures are before me,
   Which yet I have not seen;
Bright skies will soon be o'er me,
   Where darkest clouds have been;
My hope I cannot measure,
   My path to life is free;
My Saviour has my treasure,
   And he will walk with me.

Anna Laetitia Waring (1823–1910)

Faith and Confidence

679(i)
ST HUGH C.M.

E. J. Hopkins (1818–1901)

For this tune in a lower key see No. 717(ii)

679(ii)
ASHWELL C.M.

Edric Cundell (1893–1961)

THE CHRISTIAN LIFE

1 LORD, it belongs not to my care
    Whether I die or live;
To love and serve thee is my share,
    And this thy grace must give.

2 If life be long, I will be glad
    That I may long obey;
If short, yet why should I be sad
    To soar to endless day?

3 Christ leads me through no darker rooms
    Than he went through before;
He that into God's kingdom comes
    Must enter by this door.

4 Come, Lord, when grace has made me meet
    Thy blessèd face to see;
For if thy work on earth be sweet,
    What will thy glory be!

5 My knowledge of that life is small,
    The eye of faith is dim;
But 'tis enough that Christ knows all,
    And I shall be with him.

Richard Baxter (1615–91)

680

ICH HALTE TREULICH STILL   D.S.M.

Melody and figured bass from Schemelli's
Gesang-Buch (1736)
Perhaps by J. S. Bach

A version for singing in harmony is at No. 325

THE CHRISTIAN LIFE

1   JESUS, my strength, my hope,
      On thee I cast my care,
With humble confidence look up,
      And know thou hear'st my prayer.
   Give me on thee to wait,
      Till I can all things do,
   On thee, almighty to create,
      Almighty to renew.

2   I want a godly fear,
      A quick-discerning eye
That looks to thee when sin is near,
      And sees the tempter fly:
   A spirit still prepared,
      And armed with jealous care,
For ever standing on its guard
      And watching unto prayer.

3   I want a true regard,
      A single, steady aim,
Unmoved by threatening or reward,
      To thee and thy great name;
   A jealous, just concern
      For thine immortal praise;
A pure desire that all may learn
      And glorify thy grace.

4   I want with all my heart
      Thy pleasure to fulfil,
To know thyself, and what thou art,
      And what thy perfect will—
   This blessing over all,
      Always to pray, I want,
Out of the deep on thee to call,
      And never, never faint.

5   I rest upon thy word;
      The promise is for me;
My succour and salvation, Lord,
      Shall surely come from thee:
   But let me still abide,
      Nor from my hope remove,
Till thou my patient spirit guide
      Into thy perfect love.

Charles Wesley (1707–88) alt.

681(i)

HULL 88.6.D.

The American Musical Miscellany (1798)

681(ii)

ALLGÜTIGER, MEIN PREISGESANG 88.6.D.
(ERFURT)

Melody by
G. P. Weimar (1734–1800)

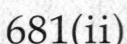

THE CHRISTIAN LIFE

1 LIGHT of the world, thy beams I bless;
On thee, bright Sun of Righteousness,
   My faith has fixed its eye;
Guided by thee, through all I go,
Nor fear the ruin spread below,
   For thou art always nigh.

2 Not all the powers of hell can fright
A soul that walks with Christ in light;
   He walks, and cannot fall:
Clearly he sees, and wins his way,
Shining unto the perfect day,
   And more than conquers all.

3 I rest in thine almighty power;
The name of Jesus is a tower
   That hides my life above;
Thou canst, thou wilt my helper be;
My confidence is all in thee,
   The faithful God of love.

4 Wherefore, in never-ceasing prayer,
My soul to thy continual care
   I faithfully commend;
Assured that thou through life shalt save,
And show thyself beyond the grave
   My everlasting friend.

Charles Wesley (1707–88)

Faith and Confidence

682

THE STAFF OF FAITH   8.6.8.6.888.6.   Traditional Swiss Melody

1 MY faith, it is an oaken staff,
   The traveller's well-loved aid;
My faith, it is a weapon stout,
   The soldier's trusty blade.
I'll travel on, and still be stirred
To action at my Master's word;
By all my perils undeterred,
   A soldier unafraid.

2 My faith, it is an oaken staff;
   O let me on it lean!
My faith, it is a sharpened sword;
   May falsehood find it keen.
Thy Spirit, Lord, to me impart,
O make me what thou ever art,
Of patient and courageous heart,
   As all true saints have been.

Thomas Toke Lynch (1818–71) alt.

THE CHRISTIAN LIFE

683

OLIVET (HARLAN) 66.4.666.4.

Lowell Mason (1792–1872)
Spiritual Songs for Social Worship (1831)

1 MY faith looks up to thee,
  Thou Lamb of Calvary,
    Saviour divine:
Now hear me while I pray;
Take all my guilt away;
O let me from this day
  Be wholly thine!

2 While life's dark maze I tread,
  And griefs around me spread,
    Be thou my guide;
Bid darkness turn to day,
Wipe sorrow's tears away,
Nor let me ever stray
  From thee aside.

3 May thy rich grace impart
  Strength to my fainting heart,
    My zeal inspire;
As thou hast died for me,
O may my love to thee
Pure, warm, and changeless be,
  A living fire.

Ray Palmer (1808–87)

Faith and Confidence

684(i)

MADRID 88.88.88.

William Matthews (1759–1830)

1 NOW I have found the ground wherein
　　Sure my soul's anchor may remain—
The wounds of Jesus, for my sin
　　Before the world's foundation slain;
Whose mercy shall unshaken stay,
When heav'n and earth are fled away.

2 Father, thine everlasting grace
　　Our scanty thought surpasses far,
Thy heart still melts with tenderness,
　　Thy arms of love still open are
Returning sinners to receive,
That mercy they may taste and live.

3 O Love, thou bottomless abyss,
　　My sins are swallowed up in thee!
Covered is my unrighteousness,
　　Nor spot of guilt remains on me,
While Jesu's blood through earth and skies
'Mercy, free, boundless mercy!' cries.

4 With faith I plunge me in this sea,
　　Here is my hope, my joy, my rest;
Hither, when hell assails, I flee,
　　I look into my Saviour's breast;
Away, sad doubt and anxious fear!
Mercy is all that's written there.

5 Though waves and storms go o'er my head,
　　Though strength, and health, and friends be gone,
Though joys be withered all and dead,
　　Though every comfort be withdrawn,
On this my steadfast soul relies—
Father, thy mercy never dies!

6 Fixed on this ground will I remain,
　　Though my heart fail and flesh decay;
This anchor shall my soul sustain,
　　When earth's foundations melt away;
Mercy's full power I then shall prove,
Loved with an everlasting love.

J. A. Rothe (1688–1758)
tr. *John Wesley* (1703–91)

684(ii)

ANCHOR 88.88.88.

Alfred Beer (1874–1963)

1 NOW I have found the ground wherein
    Sure my soul's anchor may remain—
The wounds of Jesus, for my sin
    Before the world's foundation slain;
Whose mercy shall unshaken stay,
When heav'n and earth are fled away.

2 Father, thine everlasting grace
    Our scanty thought surpasses far,
Thy heart still melts with tenderness,
    Thy arms of love still open are
Returning sinners to receive,
That mercy they may taste and live.

3 O Love, thou bottomless abyss,
    My sins are swallowed up in thee!
Covered is my unrighteousness,
    Nor spot of guilt remains on me,
While Jesu's blood through earth and skies
'Mercy, free, boundless mercy!' cries.

4 With faith I plunge me in this sea,
    Here is my hope, my joy, my rest;
Hither, when hell assails, I flee,
    I look into my Saviour's breast;
Away, sad doubt and anxious fear!
Mercy is all that's written there.

5 Though waves and storms go o'er my head,
    Though strength, and health, and friends be gone,
Though joys be withered all and dead,
    Though every comfort be withdrawn,
On this my steadfast soul relies—
Father, thy mercy never dies!

6 Fixed on this ground will I remain,
    Though my heart fail and flesh decay;
This anchor shall my soul sustain,
    When earth's foundations melt away;
Mercy's full power I then shall prove,
Loved with an everlasting love.

J. A. Rothe (1688–1758)
tr. *John Wesley* (1703–91)

Faith and Confidence

685

ST MARGARET 8 8.8 8 6.

A. L. Peace (1844–1912)

1 O LOVE that wilt not let me go,
   I rest my weary soul in thee:
 I give thee back the life I owe,
 That in thine ocean depths its flow
   May richer, fuller be.

2 O light that followest all my way,
   I yield my flickering torch to thee:
 My heart restores its borrowed ray,
 That in thy sunshine's blaze its day
   May brighter, fairer be.

3 O joy that seekest me through pain,
   I cannot close my heart to thee:
 I trace the rainbow through the rain,
 And feel the promise is not vain,
   That morn shall tearless be.

4 O cross that liftest up my head,
   I dare not ask to fly from thee:
 I lay in dust life's glory dead,
 And from the ground there blossoms red
   Life that shall endless be.

George Matheson (1842–1906)

THE CHRISTIAN LIFE

686

NEW MALDEN 8.7.8.7.8.7. David McCarthy (1931–)

1 WHEN our confidence is shaken
   In beliefs we thought secure;
When the spirit in its sickness
   Seeks but cannot find a cure:
God is active in the tensions
   Of a faith not yet mature.

2 Solar systems, void of meaning,
   Freeze the spirit into stone;
Always our researches lead us
   To the ultimate Unknown:
Faith must die, or come full circle
   To its source in God alone.

3 In the discipline of praying,
   When it's hardest to believe;
In the drudgery of caring,
   When it's not enough to grieve:
Faith, maturing, learns acceptance
   Of the insights we receive.

4 God is love; and he redeems us
   In the Christ we crucify:
This is God's eternal answer
   To the world's eternal why;
May we in this faith maturing
   Be content to live and die!

F. Pratt Green (1903–)

Words and music reprinted by permission of
Stainer & Bell Ltd.
For permission to reproduce see p. xiii

Faith and Confidence

687

TRUST AND OBEY   6 6.9.D (with refrain)   Daniel Brink Towner (1850–1919)

Refrain

Trust and o - bey, for there's no o - ther way

THE CHRISTIAN LIFE

To be hap-py in Je-sus, But to trust and o-bey.

1   WHEN we walk with the Lord
     In the light of his word,
   What a glory he sheds on our way!
     While we do his good will,
     He abides with us still,
   And with all who will trust and obey:
      Trust and obey, for there's no other way
       To be happy in Jesus,
       But to trust and obey.

2   Not a burden we bear,
     Not a sorrow we share,
   But our toil he doth richly repay;
     Not a grief nor a loss,
     Not a frown nor a cross,
   But is blest if we trust and obey:

3   But we never can prove
     The delights of his love
   Until all on the altar we lay;
     For the favour he shows,
     And the joy he bestows,
   Are for them who will trust and obey:

4   Then in fellowship sweet
     We will sit at his feet,
   Or we'll walk by his side in the way;
     What he says we will do,
     Where he sends we will go—
   Never fear, only trust and obey:

John Henry Sammis (1846–1919)

Faith and Confidence

688

Adapted from an
English Traditional Melody
Ralph Vaughan Williams (1872–1958)

THE CHRISTIAN LIFE

1 WHO would true valour see,
   Let him come hither;
One here will constant be,
   Come wind, come weather;
There's no discouragement
Shall make him once relent
His first avowed intent
   To be a pilgrim.

2 Whoso beset him round
   With dismal stories
Do but themselves confound;
   His strength the more is.
No lion can him fright;
He'll with a giant fight;
But he will have a right
   To be a pilgrim.

3 Hobgoblin nor foul fiend
   Can daunt his spirit;
He knows he at the end
   Shall life inherit.
Then fancies fly away,
He'll fear not what men say;
He'll labour night and day
   To be a pilgrim.

John Bunyan (1628–88)

689

WILL YOUR ANCHOR HOLD Irregular   W. J. Kirkpatrick (1838–1921)

Refrain

We have an an-chor that

keeps the soul   Stead - fast and sure while the bil - lows roll;

THE CHRISTIAN LIFE

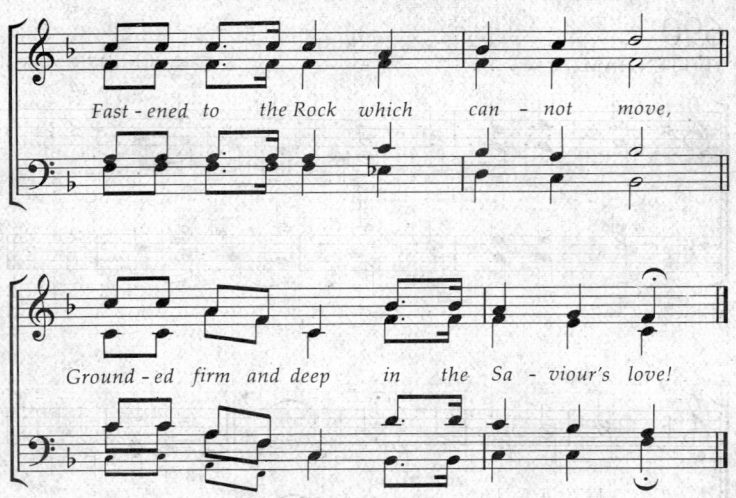

Fast-ened to the Rock which can-not move,

Ground-ed firm and deep in the Sa-viour's love!

1 WILL your anchor hold in the storms of life,
    When the clouds unfold their wings of strife?
    When the strong tides lift, and the cables strain,
    Will your anchor drift, or firm remain?
        We have an anchor that keeps the soul
        Steadfast and sure while the billows roll;
        Fastened to the Rock which cannot move,
        Grounded firm and deep in the Saviour's love!

2 Will your anchor hold in the straits of fear,
    When the breakers roar and the reef is near?
    While the surges rave, and the wild winds blow,
    Shall the angry waves then your barque o'erflow?

3 Will your anchor hold in the floods of death,
    When the waters cold chill your latest breath?
    On the rising tide you can never fail,
    While your anchor holds within the veil:

4 Will your eyes behold through the morning light
    The city of gold and the harbour bright?
    Will you anchor safe by the heavenly shore,
    When life's storms are past for evermore?

Priscilla Owens (1829–99)

Faith and Confidence

690

TOTTENHAM C.M.

T. Greatorex (1758–1831)

THE CHRISTIAN LIFE

1 BEING of beings, God of love,
    To thee our hearts we raise:
Thy all-sustaining power we prove,
    And gladly sing thy praise.

2 Thine, wholly thine, we long to be:
    Our sacrifice receive;
Made, and preserved, and saved by thee,
    To thee ourselves we give.

3 Heav'nward our every wish aspires;
    For all thy mercies' store,
The sole return thy love requires
    Is that we ask for more.

4 For more we ask; we open then
    Our hearts to embrace thy will;
Turn, and revive us, Lord, again,
    With all thy fullness fill.

5 Come, Holy Ghost, the Saviour's love
    Shed in our hearts abroad;
So shall we ever live, and move,
    And be with Christ in God.

Charles Wesley (1707–88)

May also be sung to No. 669(ii), SENNEN COVE

691

WONDERFUL LOVE   10.4.10.7.4.10.   F. Luke Wiseman (1858–1944)

THE CHRISTIAN LIFE

1 COME, let us sing of a wonderful love,
    Tender and true;
Out of the heart of the Father above,
    Streaming to me and to you:
        Wonderful love
Dwells in the heart of the Father above.

2 Jesus, the Saviour, this gospel to tell,
    Joyfully came;
Came with the helpless and hopeless to dwell,
    Sharing their sorrow and shame;
        Seeking the lost,
Saving, redeeming at measureless cost.

3 Jesus is seeking the wanderers yet;
    Why do they roam?
Love only waits to forgive and forget;
    Home, weary wanderer, home!
        Wonderful love
Dwells in the heart of the Father above.

4 Come to my heart, O thou wonderful love,
    Come and abide,
Lifting my life, till it rises above
    Envy and falsehood and pride,
        Seeking to be
Lowly and humble, a learner of thee.

Robert Walmsley (1831–1905)

692(i)
TILTEY ABBEY C.M.

A. H. Brown (1830–1926)

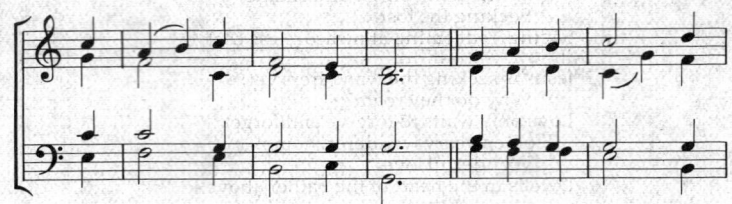

692(ii)
ST BOTOLPH C.M.

Gordon Slater (1896–1979)

THE CHRISTIAN LIFE

1 ENTHRONE thy God within thy heart,
   Thy being's inmost shrine;
He doth to thee the power impart
   To live the life divine.

2 Seek truth in him with Christlike mind;
   With faith his will discern;
Walk on life's way with him, and find
   Thy heart within thee burn.

3 With love that overflows thy soul
   Love him who first loved thee;
Is not his love thy life, thy goal,
   Thy soul's eternity?

4 Serve him in his sufficing strength:
   Heart, mind, and soul employ;
And he shall crown thy days at length
   With everlasting joy.

W. J. Penn (1875–1956)

Melody and bass (slightly altered)
probably by Jeremiah Clarke (c. 1673–1707)

For this tune in a higher key see No. 2

THE CHRISTIAN LIFE

1 FATHER of Jesus Christ—my Lord,
      My Saviour, and my Head—
   I trust in thee, whose powerful word
      Has raised him from the dead.

2 Thou know'st for my offence he died,
      And rose again for me,
   Fully and freely justified
      That I might live to thee.

3 Faith in thy power thou seest I have,
      For thou this faith hast wrought;
   Dead souls thou callest from their grave,
      And speakest worlds from nought.

4 In hope, against all human hope,
      Self-desperate, I believe;
   Thy quickening word shall raise me up,
      Thou shalt thy Spirit give.

5 Faith, mighty faith, the promise sees,
      And looks to that alone,
   Laughs at impossibilities,
      And cries: 'It shall be done!'

6 Obedient faith, that waits on thee,
      Thou never wilt reprove,
   But thou wilt form thy Son in me,
      And perfect me in love.

Charles Wesley (1707–88)

694

GOD BE IN MY HEAD Irreg.

Walford Davies (1869–1941)

GOD be in my head,

and in my un-der-stand-ing; God be in mine

eyes, and in my look-ing; God be in my

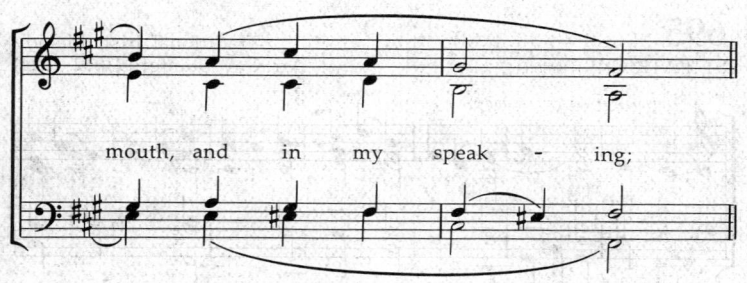

mouth, and in my speak - ing;

God be in my heart, and in my think - ing;

God be at mine end, and at my de - part - ing.

Book of Hours (1514)

Conversion and Commitment

695

ST PATRICK 8888.D

Traditional Irish Melody
Arr. C. V. Stanford (1852–1924)

Unison. For Verses 1–4, and 6.

V. 1 ends here

Turn facing page for Verse 5

THE CHRISTIAN LIFE

1 I BIND unto myself today
   The strong name of the Trinity,
By invocation of the same,
   The Three in One, and One in Three.

2 I bind this day to me for ever,
   By power of faith, Christ's incarnation;
His baptism in the Jordan river;
   His death on cross for my salvation;
His bursting from the spicèd tomb;
   His riding up the heavenly way;
His coming at the day of doom;
   I bind unto myself today.

3 I bind unto myself today
   The virtues of the star-lit heaven,
The glorious sun's life-giving ray,
   The whiteness of the moon at even,
The flashing of the lightning free,
   The whirling wind's tempestuous shocks,
The stable earth, the deep salt sea
   Around the old eternal rocks.

4 I bind unto myself today
   The power of God to hold and lead,
His eye to watch, his might to stay,
   His ear to hearken to my need,
The wisdom of my God to teach,
   His hand to guide, his shield to ward,
The word of God to give me speech,
   His heavenly host to be my guard.

5 Christ be with me, Christ within me,
   Christ behind me, Christ before me,
Christ beside me, Christ to win me,
   Christ to comfort and restore me,
Christ beneath me, Christ above me,
   Christ in quiet, Christ in danger,
Christ in hearts of all that love me,
   Christ in mouth of friend and stranger.

6 I bind unto myself the name,
   The strong name of the Trinity,
By invocation of the same,
   The Three in One, and One in Three,
Of whom all nature hath creation,
   Eternal Father, Spirit, Word.
Praise to the Lord of my salvation:
   Salvation is of Christ the Lord.   (Amen.)

Attributed to *Patrick* (*c*. 386–*c*. 460)
tr. *Cecil Frances Alexander* (1818–95)

Conversion and Commitment

695 (cont.)
DEIRDRE 88.88.
VERSE 5
(1st Tune)
Adapted from a
Traditional Irish Melody

5. Christ be with me, Christ with-in me, Christ be-hind me, Christ be-fore me, Christ be-side me, Christ to win me, Christ to com-fort and re-store me,

Christ be-neath me, Christ a-bove me, Christ in qui-et, Christ in dan-ger, Christ in hearts of all that love me, Christ in mouth of friend and stran-ger.

THE CHRISTIAN LIFE

CLONMACNOISE 8.8.8.8.D.

Ancient Irish Melody
Arr. R. R. Terry (1865–1938)

5. Christ be with me Christ with-in me, Christ be-hind me, Christ be-fore me, Christ be-side me, Christ to win me, Christ to com-fort and re-store me,

[continued

Conversion and Commitment

Christ be-neath me, Christ a-bove me, Christ in qui-et, Christ in dan-ger, Christ in hearts of all that love me, Christ in mouth of friend and stran-ger.

THE CHRISTIAN LIFE

Arr. C. V. Stanford (1852–1924)

A little slower
Unison Voices

6. I bind un - to__ my - self the name, The

Organ

strong name of __ the Tri - ni - ty, By

in - vo - ca - tion of the same, The

Conversion and Commitment

Three in One, and One in Three,___

Of whom all na - ture hath cre - a - tion, E -

-ter - nal Fa - ther, Spi - rit, Word. Praise to ___ the

THE CHRISTIAN LIFE

Lord of my sal-va-tion: Sal-va-tion is___ of Christ the Lord.___

A - - men.___

rall.

Conversion and Commitment

696

DAVID'S HARP 88.88.88

Melody and bass by
Robert King (1676–1713)
Mean parts by John Wilson

(v. 1) Thine wholly,

v. 1 Thine whol - ly,

thine   Be thou a-lone

thine   Be thou   a-lone

THE CHRISTIAN LIFE

1 JESUS, thy boundless love to me
   No thought can reach, no tongue declare;
O knit my thankful heart to thee,
   And reign without a rival there:
Thine wholly, thine alone, I am;
Be thou alone my constant flame.

2 From all eternity, with love
   Unchangeable thou hast me viewed;
Ere knew this beating heart to move,
   Thy tender mercies me pursued:
Ever with me thy love abide,
And close me in on every side.

3 O grant that nothing in my soul
   May dwell, but thy pure love alone;
O may thy love possess me whole,
   My joy, my treasure, and my crown:
Strange fires far from my heart remove;
My every act, word, thought, be love.

4 Still let thy love point out my way;
   How wondrous things thy love has wrought!
Still lead me, lest I go astray;
   Direct my word, inspire my thought;
And if I fall, soon may I hear
Thy voice, and know that love is near.

5 In suffering be thy love my peace,
   In weakness my almighty power;
And when the storms of life shall cease,
   Jesus, in that important hour,
In death as life be thou my guide,
And save me, who for me hast died.

Paul Gerhardt (1607–76)
tr. *John Wesley* (1703–91)

697(i)

MISERICORDIA   8 8 8.6.   Henry Smart (1813–79)

697(ii)

SAFFRON WALDEN   8 8 8.6.   A. H. Brown (1830–1926)

THE CHRISTIAN LIFE

1 JUST as I am, without one plea
But that thy blood was shed for me,
And that thou bidd'st me come to thee,
O Lamb of God, I come!

2 Just as I am, though tossed about
With many a conflict, many a doubt,
Fightings and fears within, without,
O Lamb of God, I come!

3 Just as I am, poor, wretched, blind;
Sight, riches, healing of the mind,
Yea, all I need, in thee to find,
O Lamb of God, I come!

4 Just as I am, thou wilt receive,
Wilt welcome, pardon, cleanse, relieve;
Because thy promise I believe,
O Lamb of God, I come!

5 Just as I am—thy love unknown
Has broken every barrier down—
Now to be thine, yea, thine alone,
O Lamb of God, I come!

6 Just as I am, of that free love
The breadth, length, depth, and height to prove,
Here for a season, then above,
O Lamb of God, I come!

Charlotte Elliott (1789–1871)

698

BYZANTIUM C.M.

Melody by Thomas Jackson (1715–1781)
Twelve Psalm Tunes, 1780 (simplified)

THE CHRISTIAN LIFE

1 LET him to whom we now belong
    His sovereign right assert,
  And take up every thankful song
    And every loving heart.

2 He justly claims us for his own,
    Who bought us with a price;
  The Christian lives to Christ alone,
    To Christ alone he dies.

3 Jesus, thine own at last receive,
    Fulfil our hearts' desire,
  And let us to thy glory live,
    And in thy cause expire.

4 Our souls and bodies we resign;
    With joy we render thee
  Our all, no longer ours, but thine
    To all eternity.

Charles Wesley (1707–88)

699(i)

SLANE 10.11.11.11. (Irreg.)

Irish Traditional Melody,
harmonised by Erik Routley (1917–82)

699(ii)

TARPORLEY 10.11.11.11. (Irreg.)

Martin Ellis (1943–   )

THE CHRISTIAN LIFE

1 LORD of creation, to you be all praise!
  Most mighty your working, most wondrous your ways!
    Your glory and might are beyond us to tell,
    And yet in the heart of the humble you dwell.

2 Lord of all power, I give you my will,
  In joyful obedience your tasks to fulfil.
    Your bondage is freedom; your service is song;
    And, held in your keeping, my weakness is strong.

3 Lord of all wisdom, I give you my mind,
  Rich truth that surpasses my knowledge to find;
    What eye has not seen and what ear has not heard
    Is taught by your Spirit and shines from your word.

4 Lord of all bounty, I give you my heart;
  I praise and adore you for all you impart,
    Your love to inspire me, your counsel to guide,
    Your presence to shield me, whatever betide.

5 Lord of all being, I give you my all;
  If e'er I disown you, I stumble and fall;
    But, led in your service your word to obey,
    I'll walk in your freedom to the end of the way.

Jack Winslow (1882–1974) alt.

700(i)

Melody from the *Reinhardt* MS (Üttingen, 1754),
as harmonised in
The English Hymnal (1906)

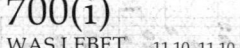

700(ii)

EPIPHANY HYMN   11 10. 11 10.   Joseph Francis Thrupp (1827–1867)

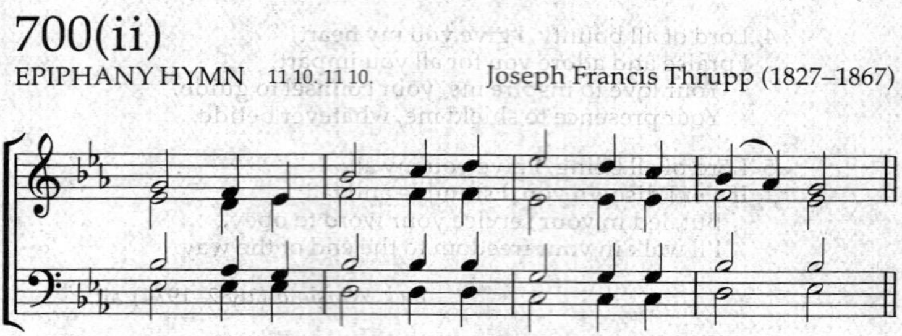

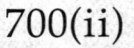

THE CHRISTIAN LIFE

1 LORD, we have come at your own invitation,
   Chosen by you, to be counted your friends;
Yours is the strength that sustains dedication,
   Ours a commitment we know never ends.

2 Here, at your table, confirm our intention,
   Give it your seal of forgiveness and grace;
Teach us to serve, without pride or pretension,
   Lord, in your kingdom, whatever our place.

3 When, at your table, each time of returning,
   Vows are renewed and our courage restored,
May we increasingly glory in learning
   All that it means to accept you as Lord.

4 So, in the world, where each duty assigned us
   Gives us the chance to create or destroy,
Help us to make those decisions that bind us,
   Lord, to yourself, in obedience and joy.

F. Pratt Green (1903–)

Words reprinted by permission of
Stainer & Bell Ltd.
For permission to reproduce see p. xiii.

Conversion and Commitment

701

ST PETER C.M.

A. R. Reinagle (1799–1877)

1 MY God, accept my heart this day,
   And make it always thine,
   That I from thee no more may stray,
   No more from thee decline.

2 Before the cross of him who died,
   Behold, I prostrate fall;
   Let every sin be crucified,
   And Christ be all in all.

3 Anoint me with thy heavenly grace,
   And seal me for thine own;
   That I may see thy glorious face,
   And worship near thy throne.

4 Let every thought and work and word
   To thee be ever given;
   Then life shall be thy service, Lord,
   And death the gate of heaven.

5 All glory to the Father be,
   All glory to the Son,
   All glory, Holy Ghost, to thee,
   While endless ages run.

Matthew Bridges (1800–94)

May also be sung to No. 740(ii), BELGRAVE

THE CHRISTIAN LIFE

702

FESTUS L.M.

Adapted from a melody in
Freylinghausen's *Geistreiches Gesangbuch* (1704)

1 O HAPPY day that fixed my choice
   On thee, my Saviour and my God!
Well may this glowing heart rejoice,
   And tell its raptures all abroad.

2 O happy bond that seals my vows
   To him who merits all my love!
Let cheerful anthems fill his house,
   While to that sacred shrine I move.

3 'Tis done, the great transaction's done!
   I am my Lord's, and he is mine;
He drew me, and I followed on,
   Charmed to confess the voice divine.

4 Now rest, my long-divided heart,
   Fixed on this blissful centre, rest;
Nor ever from thy Lord depart,
   With him of every good possessed.

5 High heaven, that heard the solemn vow,
   That vow renewed shall daily hear,
Till in life's latest hour I bow,
   And bless in death a bond so dear.

Philip Doddridge (1702–51)

Conversion and Commitment

703
EPWORTH C.M.

Adapted from a melody by
Charles Wesley the younger (1757–1834)
Harmony chiefly by Martin Shaw (1875–1958)

1 WHAT shall I render to my God
    For all his mercy's store?
I'll take the gifts he has bestowed,
    And humbly ask for more.

2 The sacred cup of saving grace
    I will with thanks receive,
And all his promises embrace,
    And to his glory live.

3 My vows I will to his great name
    Before his people pay,
And all I have, and all I am,
    Upon his altar lay.

4 Thy lawful servant, Lord, I owe
    To thee whate'er is mine,
Born in thy family below,
    And by redemption thine.

5 Thy hands created me, thy hands
    From sin have set me free;
The mercy that has loosed my bands
    Has bound me fast to thee.

6 The God of all-redeeming grace
    My God I will proclaim,
Offer the sacrifice of praise,
    And call upon his name.

7 Praise him, ye saints, the God of love,
    Who has my sins forgiven,
Till, gathered to the church above,
    We sing the songs of heaven.

Charles Wesley (1707–88)

Conversion and Commitment

704(i)

WOLVERCOTE 7.6.7.6.D.

W. H. Ferguson (1874–1950)

THE CHRISTIAN LIFE

1 O JESUS, I have promised
    To serve thee to the end;
Be thou for ever near me,
    My master and my friend;
I shall not fear the battle
    If thou art by my side,
Nor wander from the pathway
    If thou wilt be my guide.

2 O let me feel thee near me;
    The world is ever near;
I see the sights that dazzle,
    The tempting sounds I hear;
My foes are ever near me,
    Around me and within;
But, Jesus, draw thou nearer,
    And shield my soul from sin.

3 O let me hear thee speaking
    In accents clear and still,
Above the storms of passion,
    The murmurs of self-will;
O speak to reassure me,
    To hasten or control;
O speak, and make me listen,
    Thou guardian of my soul.

4 O Jesus, thou hast promised
    To all who follow thee,
That where thou art in glory
    There shall thy servant be;
And, Jesus, I have promised
    To serve thee to the end;
O give me grace to follow
    My master and my friend!

J. E. Bode (1816–74)

704(ii)

DAY OF REST 7.6.7.6.D.

James William Elliott (1833–1915)

Unison   Harmony

1 O JESUS, I have promised
    To serve thee to the end;
Be thou for ever near me,
    My master and my friend;
I shall not fear the battle
    If thou art by my side,
Nor wander from the pathway
    If thou wilt be my guide.

2 O let me feel thee near me;
    The world is ever near;
I see the sights that dazzle,
    The tempting sounds I hear;
My foes are ever near me,
    Around me and within;
But, Jesus, draw thou nearer,
    And shield my soul from sin.

3 O let me hear thee speaking
    In accents clear and still,
Above the storms of passion,
    The murmurs of self-will;
O speak to reassure me,
    To hasten or control;
O speak, and make me listen,
    Thou guardian of my soul.

4 O Jesus, thou hast promised
    To all who follow thee,
That where thou art in glory
    There shall thy servant be;
And, Jesus, I have promised
    To serve thee to the end;
O give me grace to follow
    My master and my friend!

J. E. Bode (1816–74)

705(i)

CONSECRATION 77.77.   W. H. Havergal (1793–1870)

705(ii)

EMMA 77.77.   Paul Wright (1951–   )

THE CHRISTIAN LIFE

1 TAKE my life, and let it be
   Consecrated, Lord, to thee;
   Take my moments and my days,
   Let them flow in ceaseless praise.

2 Take my hands, and let them move
   At the impulse of thy love;
   Take my feet, and let them be
   Swift and beautiful for thee.

3 Take my voice, and let me sing
   Always, only, for my King;
   Take my lips, and let them be
   Filled with messages from thee.

4 Take my silver and my gold,
   Not a mite would I withhold;
   Take my intellect, and use
   Every power as thou shalt choose.

5 Take my will, and make it thine;
   It shall be no longer mine;
   Take my heart—it is thine own;
   It shall be thy royal throne.

6 Take my love; my Lord, I pour
   At thy feet its treasure-store;
   Take myself, and I will be
   Ever, only, all for thee.

Frances Ridley Havergal (1836–79)

Conversion and Commitment

706(i)

CRUCIFIXION   8.8.8.8.8.8.   S. Akeroyd, in the *Divine Companion* (1701)

NOTE. – There is strong reason to believe that this is the tune sung by John Wesley on the night of his conversion, May 24, 1738. He subsequently inserted it in his 'Foundery' Collection of Tunes, for the hymn 'And Can It Be'.

THE CHRISTIAN LIFE

1 WHERE shall my wondering soul begin?
    How shall I all to heaven aspire?
A slave redeemed from death and sin,
    A brand plucked from eternal fire,
How shall I equal triumphs raise,
Or sing my great deliverer's praise?

2 O how shall I the goodness tell,
    Father, which thou to me hast showed?
That I, a child of wrath and hell,
    I should be called a child of God,
Should know, should feel my sins forgiven,
Blest with this antepast of heaven!

3 And shall I slight my Father's love?
    Or basely fear his gifts to own?
Unmindful of his favours prove?
    Shall I, the hallowed cross to shun,
Refuse his righteousness to impart
By hiding it within my heart?

4 Outcasts of men, to you I call,
    Harlots, and publicans, and thieves!
He spreads his arms to embrace you all;
    Sinners alone his grace receives:
No need of him the righteous have;
He came the lost to seek and save.

5 Come, O my guilty brethren, come,
    Groaning beneath your load of sin!
His bleeding heart shall make you room,
    His open side shall take you in;
He calls you now, invites you home:
Come, O my guilty brethren, come!

Charles Wesley (1707–88)

Conversion and Commitment

706(ii)

CAREY'S (SURREY) 88.88.88.

Later form of melody by
Henry Carey (*c.* 1687–1743)

THE CHRISTIAN LIFE

1. WHERE shall my wondering soul begin?
   How shall I all to heaven aspire?
A slave redeemed from death and sin,
   A brand plucked from eternal fire,
How shall I equal triumphs raise,
Or sing my great deliverer's praise?

2. O how shall I the goodness tell,
   Father, which thou to me hast showed?
That I, a child of wrath and hell,
   I should be called a child of God,
Should know, should feel my sins forgiven,
Blest with this antepast of heaven!

3. And shall I slight my Father's love?
   Or basely fear his gifts to own?
Unmindful of his favours prove?
   Shall I, the hallowed cross to shun,
Refuse his righteousness to impart
By hiding it within my heart?

4. Outcasts of men, to you I call,
   Harlots, and publicans, and thieves!
He spreads his arms to embrace you all;
   Sinners alone his grace receives:
No need of him the righteous have;
He came the lost to seek and save.

5. Come, O my guilty brethren, come,
   Groaning beneath your load of sin!
His bleeding heart shall make you room,
   His open side shall take you in;
He calls you now, invites you home:
Come, O my guilty brethren, come!

Charles Wesley (1707–88)

707

FALCON STREET S.M. (with Alleluias) Melody by Isaac Smith (1734–1805)

Doxology

Praise ye the Lord,_

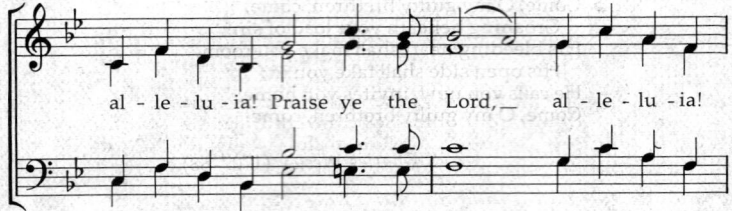

al - le - lu - ia! Praise ye the Lord,_ al - le - lu - ia!

THE CHRISTIAN LIFE

Al-le-lu-ia, al-le-lu-ia, al-le-lu-ia, Praise ye the Lord!

1. AND are we yet alive,
   And see each other's face?
   Glory and praise to Jesus give
   For his redeeming grace!

2. Preserved by power divine
   To full salvation here,
   Again in Jesu's praise we join,
   And in his sight appear.

3. What troubles have we seen,
   What conflicts have we passed,
   Fightings without, and fears within,
   Since we assembled last!

4. But out of all the Lord
   Hath brought us by his love;
   And still he doth his help afford,
   And hides our life above.

5. Then let us make our boast
   Of his redeeming power,
   Which saves us to the uttermost,
   Till we can sin no more:

6. Let us take up the cross,
   Till we the crown obtain;
   And gladly reckon all things loss,
   So we may Jesus gain.

   Praise ye the Lord, alleluia!
   Praise ye the Lord, alleluia!
   Alleluia, alleluia, alleluia,
   Praise ye the Lord!

Charles Wesley (1707–88)

Suffering and Conflict

708

1. BELIEVE not those who say
    The upward path is smooth,
Lest thou shouldst stumble in the way
    And faint before the truth.

2. It is the only road
    Unto the realms of joy;
But he who seeks that blest abode
    Must all his powers employ.

3. Arm, arm thee for the fight!
    Cast useless loads away;
Watch through the darkest hours of night;
    Toil through the hottest day.

4. To labour and to love,
    To pardon and endure,
To lift thy heart to God above,
    And keep thy conscience pure—

5. Be this thy constant aim,
    Thy hope, thy chief delight;
What matter who should whisper blame
    Or who should scorn or slight,

6. If but thy God approve,
    And if, within thy breast,
Thou feel the comfort of his love,
    The earnest of his rest?

Anne Brontë (1820–49)

THE CHRISTIAN LIFE

709

1 CHRIST be my leader by night as by day;
  Safe through the darkness, for he is the way.
    Gladly I follow, my future his care,
    Darkness is daylight when Jesus is there.

2 Christ be my teacher in age as in youth,
  Drifting or doubting, for he is the truth.
    Grant me to trust him; though shifting as sand,
    Doubt cannot daunt me; in Jesus I stand.

3 Christ be my Saviour in calm as in strife;
  Death cannot hold me, for he is the life.
    Nor darkness nor doubting nor sin and its stain
    Can touch my salvation; with Jesus I reign.

Timothy Dudley-Smith (1926–)

Suffering and Conflict

710(i)

DUKE STREET L.M.

Melody, and most of the bass, from H. Boyd's
Psalm and Hymn Tunes (1793)
Later attributed to J. Hatton (d. 1793)

For this tune in a higher key see No. 26

710(ii)

JOB L.M.

Melody by William Arnold (1768–1832)

THE CHRISTIAN LIFE

1 FIGHT the good fight with all thy might;
  Christ is thy strength, and Christ thy right;
    Lay hold on life, and it shall be
    Thy joy and crown eternally.

2 Run the straight race through God's good grace,
  Lift up thine eyes, and seek his face;
    Life with its way before thee lies;
    Christ is the path, and Christ the prize.

3 Cast care aside; upon thy guide
  Lean, and his mercy will provide;
    Lean, and the trusting soul shall prove
    Christ is its life, and Christ its love.

4 Faint not nor fear, his arm is near;
  He changes not, and thou art dear;
    Only believe, and thou shalt see
    That Christ is all in all to thee.

John Samuel Bewley Monsell (1811–75)

Suffering and Conflict

711

BINCHESTER C.M.

Melody and bass by William Croft (1678–1727)
(harmony slightly simplified)

THE CHRISTIAN LIFE

1 HAPPY are they, they that love God,
   Whose hearts have Christ confessed,
 Who by his cross have found their life,
   And 'neath his yoke their rest.

2 Glad is the praise, sweet are the songs,
   When they together sing;
 And strong the prayers that bow the ear
   Of heaven's eternal King.

3 Christ to their homes giveth his peace,
   And makes their loves his own:
 But ah, what tares the evil one
   Hath in his garden sown!

4 Sad were our lot, evil this earth,
   Did not its sorrows prove
 The path whereby the sheep may find
   The fold of Jesu's love.

5 Then shall they know, they that love him,
   How all their pain is good;
 And death itself cannot unbind
   Their happy brotherhood.

Robert Bridges (1844–1930)
based on *Charles Coffin* (1676–1749)

Suffering and Conflict

712(i)

RHUDDLAN 8.7.8.7.8.7.

Welsh Traditional Melody
(as harmonised in *The English Hymnal*, 1906)

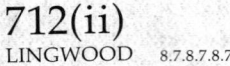

712(ii)

LINGWOOD 8.7.8.7.8.7.

C. Armstrong Gibbs (1889–1960)

THE CHRISTIAN LIFE

1 GOD of grace and God of glory,
   On thy people pour thy power;
Crown thine ancient church's story;
   Bring her bud to glorious flower.
      Grant us wisdom,
      Grant us courage,
   For the facing of this hour.

2 Heal thy children's warring madness;
   Bend our pride to thy control;
Shame our wanton, selfish gladness,
   Rich in things and poor in soul.
      Grant us wisdom,
      Grant us courage,
   Lest we miss thy kingdom's goal.

3 Lo, the hosts of evil round us
   Scorn thy Christ, assail his ways!
Fears and doubts too long have bound us;
   Free our hearts to work and praise.
      Grant us wisdom,
      Grant us courage,
   For the living of these days.

H. E. Fosdick (1878–1969)

Suffering and Conflict

713

NICHT DAS ICH'S SCHON
ERGRIFFEN 9.8.9.8.88.

Melody, and almost all the harmony,
by Johann Gottfried Schicht (1753–1823)

THE CHRISTIAN LIFE

1 IF thou but suffer God to guide thee,
  And hope in him through all thy ways,
He'll give thee strength, whate'er betide thee,
  And bear thee through the evil days;
Who trusts in God's unchanging love
Builds on the rock that nought can move.

2 Only be still, and wait his leisure
  In cheerful hope, with heart content
To take whate'er thy Father's pleasure
  And all-discerning love have sent;
Nor doubt our inmost wants are known
To him who chose us for his own.

3 Sing, pray, and keep his ways unswerving;
  So do thine own part faithfully,
And trust his word: though undeserving,
  Thou yet shalt find it true for thee;
God never yet forsook at need
The soul that trusted him indeed.

Georg Neumark (1621–81)
tr. *Catherine Winkworth* (1827–78)

714

Melody by
George Walter Martin (1828–81)

THE CHRISTIAN LIFE

1   MAKE me a captive, Lord,
     And then I shall be free;
Force me to render up my sword,
     And I shall conqueror be.
 I sink in life's alarms
     When by myself I stand;
Imprison me within thine arms,
     And strong shall be my hand.

2   My power is faint and low
     Till I have learned to serve;
It wants the needed fire to glow,
     It wants the breeze to nerve;
 It cannot freely move,
     Till thou hast wrought its chain;
Enslave it with thy matchless love,
     And deathless it shall reign.

3   My will is not my own
     Till thou hast made it thine;
If it would reach a monarch's throne
     It must its crown resign;
 It only stands unbent,
     Amid the clashing strife,
When on thy bosom it has leant
     And found in thee its life.

George Matheson (1842–1906)

May also be sung to No. 325, ICH HALTE TREULICH STILL

Suffering and Conflict

715

Henry Gauntlett (1805–76)

1 OFT in danger, oft in woe,
   Onward, Christians, onward go;
   Bear the toil, maintain the strife,
   Strengthened with the Bread of Life.

2 Onward, Christians, onward go,
   Join the war, and face the foe;
   Will ye flee in danger's hour?
   Know ye not your captain's power?

3 Let your drooping hearts be glad;
   March in heavenly armour clad;
   Fight, nor think the battle long,
   Vict'ry soon shall tune your song.

4 Let not sorrow dim your eye,
   Soon shall every tear be dry;
   Let not fears your course impede,
   Great your strength, if great your need.

5 Onward then in battle move;
   More than conquerors ye shall prove;
   Though opposed by many a foe,
   Christian soldiers, onward go!

Henry Kirke White (1785–1806)
F. S. Fuller-Maitland (1809–77)
and others

THE CHRISTIAN LIFE

716

C. Steggall (1826–1905)

1   MARCH on, my soul, with strength,
       March forward void of fear;
    He who has led will lead
       Through each succeeding year;
    And as you travel on your way,
    His hand shall hold you day by day.

2   March on, my soul, with strength;
       In ease you dare not dwell;
    High duty calls you forth;
       Then up, and serve him well!
    Take up your cross, take up your sword,
    And fight the battles of your Lord!

3   March on, my soul, with strength,
       With strength, but not your own;
    The conquest you will gain
       Through Christ your Lord alone;
    His grace shall nerve your feeble arm,
    His love preserve you safe from harm.

4   March on, my soul, with strength,
       From strength to strength march on;
    Warfare shall end at length,
       All foes be overthrown.
    And then, my soul, if faithful now,
    The crown of life awaits your brow.

William Wright (1859–1924) alt.

Suffering and Conflict

717(i)
ST SWITHUN C.M.

Sydney Watson (1903–   )

717(ii)
ST HUGH C.M.

E. J. Hopkins (1818–1901)

For this tune in a higher key see No. 679(i).

THE CHRISTIAN LIFE

1 O LORD and Master of us all,
   Whate'er our name or sign,
We own thy sway, we hear thy call,
   We test our lives by thine.

2 Our thoughts lie open to thy sight;
   And, naked to thy glance,
Our secret sins are in the light
   Of thy pure countenance.

3 Yet, weak and blinded though we be,
   Thou dost our service own;
We bring our varying gifts to thee,
   And thou rejectest none.

4 To thee our full humanity,
   Its joys and pains, belong;
The wrong of each to each on thee
   Inflicts a deeper wrong.

5 Who hates, hates thee; who loves, becomes
   Therein to thee allied;
All sweet accords of hearts and homes
   In thee are multiplied.

6 Apart from thee all gain is loss,
   All labour vainly done;
The solemn shadow of thy cross
   Is better than the sun.

7 Our friend, our brother, and our Lord,
   What may thy service be?
Nor name, nor form, nor ritual word,
   But simply following thee.

8 We faintly hear, we dimly see,
   In differing phrase we pray;
But, dim or clear, we own in thee
   The Light, the Truth, the Way.

John Greenleaf Whittier (1807–92)

718

ST GERTRUDE   6.5.6.5.D.

Arthur Sullivan (1842–1900)

Refrain

On - ward, Chris-tian   sol - diers,___

THE CHRISTIAN LIFE

March-ing as to war, With the cross of
war, With the cross of

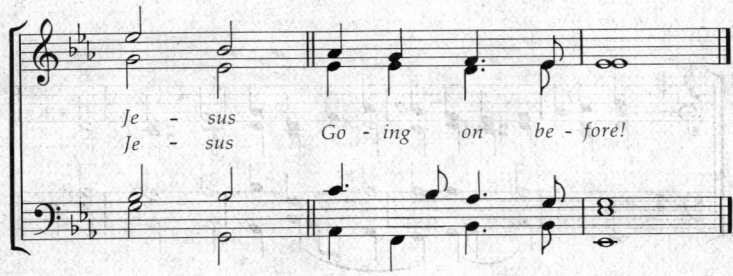

Je - sus Go - ing on be - fore!
Je - sus

1 ONWARD, Christian soldiers,
   Marching as to war,
   With the cross of Jesus
   Going on before!
   Christ, the royal master,
   Leads against the foe;
   Forward into battle,
   See! His banners go!
     Onward, Christian soldiers,
     Marching as to war,
     With the cross of Jesus
     Going on before!

2 At the sign of triumph
   Satan's host doth flee;
   On then, Christian soldiers,
   On to victory!
   Hell's foundations quiver
   At the shout of praise;
   Brothers, lift your voices;
   Loud your anthems raise:

3 Crowns and thrones may perish,
   Kingdoms rise and wane,
   But the church of Jesus
   Constant will remain;
   Gates of hell can never
   'Gainst that church prevail;
   We have Christ's own promise,
   And that cannot fail:

4 Onward, then, ye people!
   Join our happy throng;
   Blend with ours your voices
   In the triumph-song:
   Glory, laud, and honour
   Unto Christ the King!
   This through countless ages
   Men and angels sing:

Sabine Baring-Gould (1834–1924)

Suffering and Conflict

719(i)

FROM STRENGTH TO STRENGTH   D.S.M.   E. W. Naylor (1867–1934)

Unison. Alla marcia.

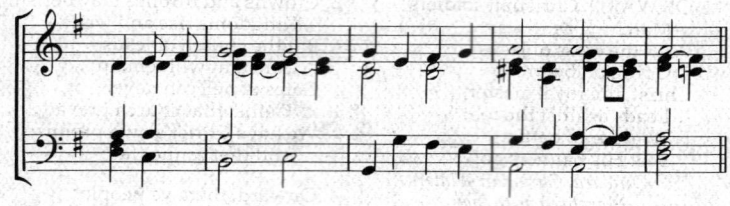

THE CHRISTIAN LIFE

719(ii)

ST ETHELWALD S.M.

W. H. Monk (1823–89)

PART 1

1 SOLDIERS of Christ, arise,
   And put your armour on,
Strong in the strength which God supplies
   Through his eternal Son;

   Strong in the Lord of hosts,
      And in his mighty power,
Who in the strength of Jesus trusts
      Is more than conqueror.

2 Stand then in his great might,
   With all his strength endued;
But take, to arm you for the fight,
   The panoply of God;

   That, having all things done,
      And all your conflicts passed,
Ye may o'ercome through Christ alone,
      And stand entire at last.

3 Leave no unguarded place,
   No weakness of the soul;
Take every virtue, every grace,
   And fortify the whole:

   Indissolubly joined,
      To battle all proceed;
But arm yourselves with all the mind
   That was in Christ, your Head.

4 From strength to strength go on,
   Wrestle, and fight, and pray,
Tread all the powers of darkness down,
   And win the well-fought day;

   Still let the Spirit cry
      In all his soldiers: come!
Till Christ the Lord descend from high,
   And take the conquerors home.

Suffering and Conflict

719(i)

FROM STRENGTH TO STRENGTH   D.S.M.   E. W. Naylor (1867–1934)

Unison. Alla marcia.

719(ii)

ST ETHELWALD S.M.

W. H. Monk (1823–89)

PART 2

5 Pray, without ceasing pray,
    Your captain gives the word;
His summons cheerfully obey,
    And call upon the Lord:

To God your every want
    In instant prayer display;
Pray always; pray, and never faint;
    Pray, without ceasing pray!

6 In fellowship, alone,
    To God with faith draw near,
Approach his courts, besiege his throne
    With all the powers of prayer:

Go to his temple, go,
    Nor from his altar move;
Let every house his worship know,
    And every heart his love.

7 Pour out your souls to God,
    And bow them with your knees,
And spread your hearts and hands abroad,
    And pray for Zion's peace;

Your guides and brethren bear
    For ever on your mind;
Extend the arms of mighty prayer,
    Ingrasping all mankind.

Charles Wesley (1707–88)

Suffering and Conflict

720

GERSAU 7.6.7.6.7.8.7.6.

L. M. White (1860–1950)

THE CHRISTIAN LIFE

1   SON of God, if thy free grace
         Again has raised me up,
     Called me still to seek thy face,
         And given me back my hope:
     Still thy timely help afford,
 And all thy loving-kindness show:
     Keep me, keep me, gracious Lord,
         And never let me go!

2   By me, O my Saviour, stand
         In sore temptation's hour;
     Save me with thine outstretched hand,
         And show forth all thy power;
     O be mindful of thy word,
 Thy all-sufficient grace bestow:
     Keep me, keep me, gracious Lord,
         And never let me go!

3   Give me, Lord, a holy fear,
         And fix it in my heart,
     That I may from evil near
         With timely care depart;
     Sin be more than hell abhorred;
 Till thou destroy the tyrant foe,
     Keep me, keep me, gracious Lord,
         And never let me go!

4   Never let me leave thy breast,
         From thee, my Saviour, stray;
     Thou art my support and rest,
         My true and living way;
     My exceeding great reward,
 In heav'n above and earth below:
     Keep me, keep me, gracious Lord,
         And never let me go!

Charles Wesley (1707–88)

May also be sung to No. 729, SHARROW VALE

721

From a song by
George James Webb (1803–87)

THE CHRISTIAN LIFE

1 STAND up! Stand up for Jesus,
   Ye soldiers of the cross!
Lift high his royal banner;
   It must not suffer loss.
From vict'ry unto vict'ry
   His army he shall lead,
Till every foe is vanquished,
   And Christ is Lord indeed.

2 Stand up! Stand up for Jesus!
   The trumpet-call obey;
Forth to the mighty conflict
   In this his glorious day!
Ye that are his, now serve him
   Against unnumbered foes;
Let courage rise with danger,
   And strength to strength oppose.

3 Stand up! Stand up for Jesus!
   Stand in his strength alone;
The arm of flesh will fail you;
   Ye dare not trust your own.
Put on the gospel armour,
   Each piece put on with prayer;
Where duty calls, or danger,
   Be never wanting there.

4 Stand up! Stand up for Jesus!
   The strife will not be long;
This day the noise of battle,
   The next the victor's song.
To him that overcometh
   A crown of life shall be;
He with the King of Glory
   Shall reign eternally.

George Duffield (1818–88)

Suffering and Conflict

722(i)

ARMAGEDDON 6.5. (12 lines)

German Melody
adapted by John Goss (1800–80)

THE CHRISTIAN LIFE

1 WHO is on the Lord's side?
   Who will serve the King?
Who will be his helpers
   Other lives to bring?
Who will leave the world's side?
   Who will face the foe?
Who is on the Lord's side?
   Who for him will go?
     By thy call of mercy,
      By thy grace divine,
     We are on the Lord's side;
     Saviour, we are thine.

2 Jesus, thou hast bought us,
   Not with gold or gem,
But with thine own life-blood,
   For thy diadem.
With thy blessing filling
   Each who comes to thee,
Thou hast made us willing,
   Thou hast made us free.
     By thy great redemption,
      By thy grace divine,
     We are on the Lord's side;
     Saviour, we are thine.

3 Fierce may be the conflict,
   Strong may be the foe;
But the King's own army
   None can overthrow.
Round his standard ranging,
   Victory is secure;
For his truth unchanging
   Makes the triumph sure.
     Joyfully enlisting,
      By thy grace divine,
     We are on the Lord's side;
     Saviour, we are thine.

4 Chosen to be soldiers
   In an alien land,
Chosen, called, and faithful,
   For our Captain's band,
In the service royal
   Let us not grow cold;
Let us be right loyal,
   Noble, true, and bold.
     Master, thou wilt keep us,
      By thy grace divine,
     Always on the Lord's side,
     Saviour, always thine.

Frances Ridley Havergal (1836–79)

Suffering and Conflict

722(ii)

RACHIE 6.5. (12 lines)

Caradog Roberts (1878–1935)

1 WHO is on the Lord's side?
   Who will serve the King?
Who will be his helpers
   Other lives to bring?
Who will leave the world's side?
   Who will face the foe?
Who is on the Lord's side?
   Who for him will go?
      By thy call of mercy,
         By thy grace divine,
      We are on the Lord's side;
         Saviour, we are thine.

2 Jesus, thou hast bought us,
   Not with gold or gem,
But with thine own life-blood,
   For thy diadem.
With thy blessing filling
   Each who comes to thee,
Thou hast made us willing,
   Thou hast made us free.
      By thy great redemption,
         By thy grace divine,
      We are on the Lord's side;
         Saviour, we are thine.

3 Fierce may be the conflict,
   Strong may be the foe;
But the King's own army
   None can overthrow.
Round his standard ranging,
   Victory is secure;
For his truth unchanging
   Makes the triumph sure.
      Joyfully enlisting,
         By thy grace divine,
      We are on the Lord's side;
         Saviour, we are thine.

4 Chosen to be soldiers
   In an alien land,
Chosen, called, and faithful,
   For our Captain's band,
In the service royal
   Let us not grow cold;
Let us be right loyal,
   Noble, true, and bold.
      Master, thou wilt keep us,
         By thy grace divine,
      Always on the Lord's side,
         Saviour, always thine.

Frances Ridley Havergal (1836–79)

Suffering and Conflict

723

COLCHESTER 88.88.88.

S. S. Wesley (1810–76)

1 ALL things are possible to them
   That can in Jesu's name believe:
 Lord, I no more thy truth blaspheme,
   Thy truth I lovingly receive;
 I can, I do believe in thee;
 All things are possible to me.

2 The most impossible of all
   Is that I e'er from sin should cease;
 Yet shall it be, I know it shall:
   Jesus, look to thy faithfulness!
 If nothing is too hard for thee,
 All things are possible to me.

3 Though earth and hell the word gainsay,
   The word of God can never fail;
 The Lamb shall take my sins away,
   'Tis certain, though impossible;
 The thing impossible shall be;
 All things are possible to me.

THE CHRISTIAN LIFE / Growth in Grace and Holiness

4 All things are possible to God,
  To Christ, the power of God in man,
To me, when I am all renewed,
  When I in Christ am formed again,
And witness, from all sin set free,
All things are possible to me.

Charles Wesley (1707–88)

724

FRANCONIA S.M.

W. H. Havergal (1793–1870), adapted from a tune in
König's *Harmonischer Liederschatz* (1738)
(harmony slightly altered)

1   BLEST are the pure in heart,
       For they shall see our God:
  The secret of the Lord is theirs;
       Their soul is Christ's abode.

2   The Lord, who left the heavens
       Our life and peace to bring,
  To dwell on earth in lowliness,
       Our pattern and our King—

3   Still to the lowly soul
          He doth himself impart,
    And for his dwelling and his throne
          Chooseth the pure in heart.

4   Lord, we thy presence seek;
          May ours this blessing be;
    Give us a pure and lowly heart,
          A temple meet for thee.

John Keble (1792–1866) vv. 1 and 3
Hall's Psalms and Hymns (1836) vv. 2 and 4

Growth in Grace and Holiness

725(i)

CROSS DEEP L.M.

Barry Rose (1934–)

725(ii)

ETON L.M.

C. H. H. Parry (1848–1918)

THE CHRISTIAN LIFE

1 COME, dearest Lord, descend and dwell
    By faith and love in every breast;
    Then shall we know and taste and feel
    The joys that cannot be expressed.

2 Come, fill our hearts with inward strength,
    Make our enlargèd souls possess
    And learn the height and breadth and length
    Of thine unmeasurable grace.

3 Now to the God whose power can do
    More than our thoughts or wishes know
    Be everlasting honours done
    By all the church, through Christ his Son.

Isaac Watts (1674–1748)
based on Ephesians 3:16–21

726

OMBERSLEY L.M.

W. H. Gladstone (1840–91)

1 GOD of all power, and truth, and grace,
   Which shall from age to age endure,
Whose word, when heaven and earth shall pass,
   Remains and stands for ever sure;

2 That I thy mercy may proclaim,
   That all mankind thy truth may see,
Hallow thy great and glorious name,
   And perfect holiness in me.

3 Thy sanctifying Spirit pour
   To quench my thirst and make me clean;
Now, Father, let the gracious shower
   Descend, and make me pure from sin.

4 Give me a new, a perfect heart,
   From doubt, and fear, and sorrow free;
The mind which was in Christ impart,
   And let my spirit cleave to thee.

5 O that I now, from sin released,
   Thy word may to the utmost prove,
Enter into the promised rest,
   The Canaan of thy perfect love!

6 Now let me gain perfection's height,
   Now let me into nothing fall,
Be less than nothing in thy sight,
   And feel that Christ is all in all.

Charles Wesley (1707–88)

THE CHRISTIAN LIFE

727

SALZBURG 7.7.7.7.D.

Melody by Jakob Hintze (1622–1702)
Harmonised by J. S. Bach

1 GOD of all-redeeming grace,
    By thy pardoning love compelled,
Up to thee our souls we raise,
    Up to thee our bodies yield:
Thou our sacrifice receive,
    Acceptable through thy Son,
While to thee alone we live,
    While we die to thee alone.

2 Meet it is, and just, and right,
    That we should be wholly thine,
In thine only will delight,
    In thy blessèd service join:
O that every work and word
    Might proclaim how good thou art,
'Holiness unto the Lord'
    Still be written on our heart!

Charles Wesley (1707–88)

Growth in Grace and Holiness

728

ST MICHAEL S.M.

From melody of 'Psalm 101'
in *Genevan Psalter* (1551),
as adapted by William Crotch (1775–1847)

THE CHRISTIAN LIFE

1 HOW can we sinners know
      Our sins on earth forgiven?
   How can our gracious Saviour show
      Our names inscribed in heaven?

2 We who in Christ believe
      That he for us hath died,
   We all his unknown peace receive,
      And feel his blood applied.

3 His love, surpassing far
      The love of all beneath,
   We find within our hearts, and dare
      The pointless darts of death.

4 Stronger than death and hell
      The mystic power we prove;
   And, conquerors of the world, we dwell
      In heaven, who dwell in love.

5 The meek and lowly heart
      That in our Saviour was,
   To us his Spirit doth impart,
      And signs us with his cross.

6 Our nature's turned, our mind
      Transformed in all its powers;
   And both the witnesses are joined,
      The Spir't of God with ours.

7 His glory our design,
      We live our God to please;
   And rise with filial fear divine,
      To perfect holiness.

Charles Wesley (1707–88)

729

SHARROW VALE 7.6.7.6.7.8.7.6. Ivor H. Jones (1934–)

Not too fast

THE CHRISTIAN LIFE

1 GOD of my salvation, hear,
     And help me to believe;
   Simply do I now draw near,
     Thy blessing to receive:
   Full of sin, alas! I am,
   But to thy wounds for refuge flee:
     Friend of sinners, spotless Lamb,
       Thy blood was shed for me.

2 Standing now as newly slain,
     To thee I lift mine eye;
   Balm of all my grief and pain,
     Thy grace is always nigh:
   Now as yesterday the same
   Thou art, and wilt for ever be:

3 Nothing have I, Lord, to pay,
     Nor can thy grace procure;
   Empty send me not away,
     For I, thou know'st, am poor:
   Dust and ashes is my name,
   My all is sin and misery:

4 No good word, or work, or thought
     Bring I to gain thy grace;
   Pardon I accept unbought,
     Thine offer I embrace,
   Coming, as at first I came,
   To take, and not bestow on thee:

5 Saviour, from thy wounded side
     I never will depart;
   Here will I my spirit hide
     When I am pure in heart:
   Till my place above I claim,
   This only shall be all my plea:

             Charles Wesley (1707–88)

730

IBSTONE 6.6.6.6.

Maria Tiddeman (*c.* 1837–1915)

1 I HUNGER and I thirst;
   Jesus, my manna be:
   Ye living waters, burst
   Out of the rock for me.

2 Thou bruised and broken Bread,
   My life-long wants supply;
   As living souls are fed,
   O feed me, or I die.

3 Thou true life-giving Vine,
   Let me thy sweetness prove;
   Renew my life with thine,
   Refresh my soul with love.

4 Rough paths my feet have trod
   Since first their course began;
   Feed me, thou Bread of God;
   Help me, thou Son of Man.

5 For still the desert lies
   My thirsting soul before;
   O living waters, rise
   Within me evermore.

John Samuel Bewley Monsell (1811–75)

THE CHRISTIAN LIFE

731

CREDITON C.M.

Melody from Thomas Clark's *2nd Set of Psalm Tunes [for] Country Choirs* (*c.* 1807)

1 I KNOW that my Redeemer lives,
   And ever prays for me;
A token of his love he gives,
   A pledge of liberty.

2 I find him lifting up my head,
   He brings salvation near,
His presence makes me free indeed,
   And he will soon appear.

3 He wills that I should holy be;
   What can withstand his will?
The counsel of his grace in me
   He surely shall fulfil.

4 Jesus, I hang upon thy word;
   I steadfastly believe
Thou wilt return and claim me, Lord,
   And to thyself receive.

5 Thy love I soon expect to find
   In all its depth and height,
To comprehend the eternal mind,
   And grasp the Infinite.

6 When God is mine, and I am his,
   Of paradise possessed,
I taste unutterable bliss
   And everlasting rest.

Charles Wesley (1707–88)

Growth in Grace and Holiness

732
QUEM PASTORES LAUDAVERE 888.7.

Melody adapted from
a German MS of 1410

1 JESUS, good above all other,
   Gentle child of gentle mother,
   In a stable born our brother,
      Give us grace to persevere.

2 Jesus, cradled in a manger,
   For us facing every danger,
   Living as a homeless stranger,
      Make we thee our King most dear.

3 Jesus, for thy people dying,
   Risen master, death defying,
   Lord in heaven, thy grace supplying,
      Keep us to thy presence near.

4 Jesus, who our sorrows bearest,
   All our thoughts and hopes thou sharest;
   Thou to man the truth declarest;
      Help us all thy truth to hear.

5 Lord, in all our doings guide us;
   Pride and hate shall ne'er divide us;
   We'll go on with thee beside us,
      And with joy we'll persevere!

Percy Dearmer (1867–1936)

THE CHRISTIAN LIFE

733

COLLINGWOOD C.M.

H. A. Bate (1899–   )

1 JESUS has died that I might live,
   Might live to God alone,
 In him eternal life receive,
   And be in spirit one.

2 Saviour, I thank thee for the grace,
   The gift unspeakable!
 And wait with arms of faith to embrace,
   And all thy love to feel.

3 My soul breaks out in strong desire
   The perfect bliss to prove;
 My longing heart is all on fire
   To be dissolved in love.

4 Give me thyself—from every boast,
   From every wish set free,
 Let all I am in thee be lost;
   But give thyself to me.

5 Thy gifts, alone, cannot suffice
   Unless thyself be given;
 Thy presence makes my paradise,
   And where thou art is heaven.

Charles Wesley (1707–88)

734
POTSDAM S.M.

Adapted from J. S. Bach (1685–1750)

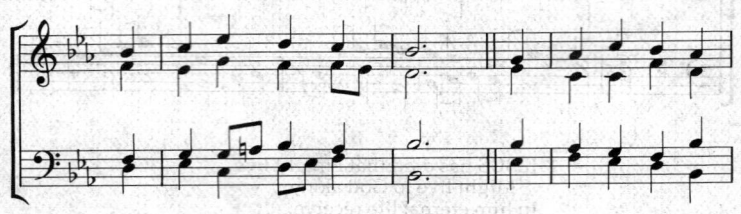

1   JESUS, my Truth, my Way,
     My sure, unerring Light,
On thee my feeble steps I stay,
     Which thou wilt lead aright.

2   My Wisdom and my Guide,
     My Counsellor, thou art;
O never let me leave thy side,
     Or from thy paths depart!

3   Teach me the happy art
     In all things to depend
On thee; O never, Lord, depart,
     But love me to the end!

4   Through fire and water bring
     Into the wealthy place;
And teach me the new song to sing,
     When perfected in grace.

5   O make me all like thee,
     Before I hence remove!
Settle, confirm, and stablish me,
     And build me up in love.

6   Let me thy witness live,
     When sin is all destroyed;
And then my spotless soul receive,
     And take me home to God.

Charles Wesley (1707–88)

735(i)
ST OLAVE 66.66.66.

J. Barnby (1838–96)

Slow

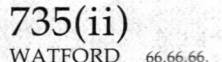

735(ii)
WATFORD 66.66.66.

Melody by A. T. Gosden (1897-1976) (rhythm alt.)
harmonised by Ivor H. Jones (1934–   )

THE CHRISTIAN LIFE

1 JESUS, the First and Last,
  On thee my soul is cast:
  Thou didst thy work begin
  By blotting out my sin;
  Thou wilt the root remove,
  And perfect me in love.

2 Yet when the work is done,
  The work is but begun:
  Partaker of thy grace,
  I long to see thy face;
  The first I prove below,
  The last I die to know.

  Charles Wesley (1707–88)

736

METZLER'S REDHEAD C.M.

Richard Redhead (1820–1901)

1 LORD, I believe a rest remains
   To all thy people known,
   A rest where pure enjoyment reigns,
   And thou art loved alone:

2 A rest, where all our soul's desire
   Is fixed on things above;
   Where fear, and sin, and grief expire,
   Cast out by perfect love.

3 O that I now the rest might know,
   Believe, and enter in!
   Now, Saviour, now the power bestow,
   And let me cease from sin.

4 Remove this hardness from my heart,
   This unbelief remove;
   To me the rest of faith impart,
   The sabbath of thy love.

5 Thy name to me, thy nature grant;
   This, only this be given:
   Nothing beside my God I want,
   Nothing in earth or heaven.

6 Come, Father, Son, and Holy Ghost,
   And seal me thine abode;
   Let all I am in thee be lost,
   Let all be lost in God.

Charles Wesley (1707–88)

THE CHRISTIAN LIFE

737

SIMPLICITY (SONG 13) 77.77.

Adapted from
Orlando Gibbons (1583–1625)
as in *Church Hymns* (SPCK 1874)

For another version of this tune see No. 183

1 LORD, that I may learn of thee,
   Give me true simplicity;
   Wean my soul, and keep it low,
   Willing thee alone to know.

2 Let me cast myself aside,
   All that feeds my knowing pride;
   Not to man, but God submit,
   Lay my reasonings at thy feet;

3 Of my boasted wisdom spoiled,
   Docile, helpless, as a child,
   Only seeing in thy light,
   Only walking in thy might.

4 Then infuse the teaching grace,
   Spir't of truth and righteousness;
   Knowledge, love divine, impart,
   Life eternal, to my heart.

Charles Wesley (1707–88)

738(i)
INNOCENTS 77.77.

Melody of uncertain origin
Arranged by W. H. Monk (1823–89)
in *The Parish Choir* (1850)

738(ii)
GENTLE JESUS 77.77

Martin Shaw (1875–1958)

THE CHRISTIAN LIFE

1 LOVING Jesus, gentle Lamb,
  In thy gracious hands I am;
  Make me, Saviour, what thou art;
  Live thyself within my heart.

2 Fain I would to thee be brought;
  Gracious Lord, forbid it not;
  In the kingdom of thy grace
  Give a little child a place.

3 Fain I would be as thou art;
  Give me thy obedient heart;
  Thou art pitiful and kind;
  Let me have thy loving mind.

4 Let me above all fulfil
  God my heavenly Father's will;
  Never his good Spirit grieve,
  Only to his glory live.

5 I shall then show forth thy praise,
  Serve thee all my happy days;
  Then the world shall always see
  Christ, the holy child, in me.

Charles Wesley (1707–88)

Growth in Grace and Holiness

739(i)

GRIFFIN'S BROOK   8.7.8.5.   John Wilson (1905–   )

739(ii)

ST LEONARD'S (GOULD)   Arthur Cyril Barham-Gould (1891–1953)
                8.7.8.5.

THE CHRISTIAN LIFE

1 MAY the mind of Christ my Saviour
  Live in me from day to day,
By his love and power controlling
  All I do or say.

2 May the word of God dwell richly
  In my heart from hour to hour,
So that all may see I triumph
  Only through his power.

3 May the peace of God my Father
  Rule my life in everything,
That I may be calm to comfort
  Sick and sorrowing.

4 May the love of Jesus fill me,
  As the waters fill the sea;
Him exalting, self abasing—
  This is victory.

5 May I run the race before me,
  Strong and brave to face the foe,
Looking only unto Jesus
  As I onward go.

Kate Barclay Wilkinson (1859–1928)

740(i)
WARWICK C.M.

Samuel Stanley (1767–1822)
Harmonisation by David Evans (1874–1948)

740(ii)
BELGRAVE C.M.

William Horsley (1774–1858)

THE CHRISTIAN LIFE

1 MY God! I know, I feel thee mine,
    And will not quit my claim,
Till all I have is lost in thine
    And all renewed I am.

2 I hold thee with a trembling hand,
    But will not let thee go,
Till steadfastly by faith I stand
    And all thy goodness know.

3 When shall I see the welcome hour
    That plants my God in me—
Spirit of health, and life, and power,
    And perfect liberty?

4 Jesus, thine all-victorious love
    Shed in my heart abroad;
Then shall my feet no longer rove,
    Rooted and fixed in God.

5 O that in me the sacred fire
    Might now begin to glow,
Burn up the dross of base desire,
    And make the mountains flow!

6 O that it now from heaven might fall,
    And all my sins consume!
Come, Holy Ghost, for thee I call,
    Spirit of burning, come!

7 Refining fire, go through my heart,
    Illuminate my soul;
Scatter thy life through every part,
    And sanctify the whole.

                    Charles Wesley (1707–88)

R. Harrison (1748–1810)
(Original harmony,
except in last 2 bars)

For this tune in a higher key see No. 22(i)

THE CHRISTIAN LIFE

1 MY gracious Lord, I own thy right
    To every service I can pay;
And call it my supreme delight
    To hear thy dictates and obey.

2 What is my being, but for thee,
    Its sure support, its noblest end,
Thy ever-smiling face to see,
    And serve the cause of such a friend?

3 I would not live for worldly joy,
    Or to increase my worldly good,
Nor future days or powers employ
    To spread a sounding name abroad:

4 'Tis to my Saviour I would live,
    To him who for my ransom died;
Nor could untainted Eden give
    Such bliss as blossoms at his side.

5 His work my hoary age shall bless,
    When youthful vigour is no more,
And my last hour of life confess
    His love has animating power.

Philip Doddridge (1702–51)

Growth in Grace and Holiness

THE CHRISTIAN LIFE

1 O JESUS Christ, grow thou in me,
   And all things else recede;
My heart be daily nearer thee,
   From sin be daily freed.

2 Each day let thy supporting might
   My weakness still embrace;
My darkness vanish in thy light,
   Thy life my death efface.

3 In thy bright beams which on me fall,
   Fade every evil thought;
That I am nothing, thou art all,
   I would be daily taught.

4 More of thy glory let me see,
   Thou holy, wise, and true!
I would thy living image be,
   In joy and sorrow too.

5 Fill me with gladness from above,
   Hold me by strength divine!
Lord, let the glow of thy great love
   Through my whole being shine.

6 Make this poor self grow less and less,
   Be thou my life and aim;
O make me daily, through thy grace,
   More meet to bear thy name!

Johann Caspar Lavater (1741–1801)
   tr. *Elizabeth Lee Smith* (1817–98)

Growth in Grace and Holiness

743

MONTGOMERY L.M.

Melody from
Magdalen Hospital Hymns (c. 1762)

THE CHRISTIAN LIFE

1 MY Saviour, how shall I proclaim,
   How pay the mighty debt I owe?
   Let all I have, and all I am,
   Ceaseless to all thy glory show.

2 Too much to thee I cannot give;
   Too much I cannot do for thee;
   Let all thy love, and all thy grief,
   Grav'n on my heart for ever be.

Paul Gerhardt (1607–76)
tr. *John Wesley* (1703–91)

744(i)

LYDIA C.M. (Ext.)

Thomas Phillips (1735–1807)

THE CHRISTIAN LIFE

1 O FOR a thousand tongues to sing
    My great Redeemer's praise,
  The glories of my God and King,
    The triumphs of his grace!

2 My gracious Master and my God,
    Assist me to proclaim,
  To spread through all the earth abroad
    The honours of thy name.

3 Jesus—the name that charms our fears,
    That bids our sorrows cease;
  'Tis music in the sinner's ears,
    'Tis life, and health, and peace.

4 He breaks the power of cancelled sin,
    He sets the prisoner free;
  His blood can make the foulest clean,
    His blood availed for me.

5 He speaks; and, listening to his voice,
    New life the dead receive;
  The mournful, broken hearts rejoice;
    The humble poor believe.

6 Hear him, ye deaf; his praise, ye dumb,
    Your loosened tongues employ;
  Ye blind, behold your Saviour come;
    And leap, ye lame, for joy!

7 See all your sins on Jesus laid:
    The Lamb of God was slain;
  His soul was once an offering made
    For every soul of man.

8 In Christ, our Head, you then shall know,
    Shall feel, your sins forgiven,
  Anticipate your heaven below,
    And own that love is heaven.

Charles Wesley (1707–88)

Melody by T. Haweis (1734–1820)
as adapted by S. Webbe
the younger (c. 1770–1843)

For this tune in a higher key (with slightly different harmony) see No. 809

Melody and most of the harmony from
John Randall's *Isola* and *Hymn Tunes* (1794)
Foundery Hymn Tunes Collection (1742–43)

1 O FOR a thousand tongues to sing
    My great Redeemer's praise,
The glories of my God and King,
    The triumphs of his grace!

2 My gracious Master and my God,
    Assist me to proclaim,
To spread through all the earth abroad
    The honours of thy name.

3 Jesus—the name that charms our fears,
    That bids our sorrows cease;
'Tis music in the sinner's ears,
    'Tis life, and health, and peace.

4 He breaks the power of cancelled sin,
    He sets the prisoner free;
His blood can make the foulest clean,
    His blood availed for me.

5 He speaks; and, listening to his voice,
    New life the dead receive;
The mournful, broken hearts rejoice;
    The humble poor believe.

6 Hear him, ye deaf; his praise, ye dumb,
    Your loosened tongues employ;
Ye blind, behold your Saviour come;
    And leap, ye lame, for joy!

7 See all your sins on Jesus laid:
    The Lamb of God was slain;
His soul was once an offering made
    For every soul of man.

8 In Christ, our Head, you then shall know,
    Shall feel, your sins forgiven,
Anticipate your heaven below,
    And own that love is heaven.

Charles Wesley (1707–88)

Growth in Grace and Holiness

744(iii)

UNIVERSITY C.M.

Melody and most of the harmony from
John Randall's *Psalm and Hymn Tunes* (1794)
Probably by Charles Collignon (1725–85)

For this tune in a higher key see No. 43

1 O FOR a thousand tongues to sing
    My great Redeemer's praise,
The glories of my God and King,
    The triumphs of his grace!

2 My gracious Master and my God,
    Assist me to proclaim,
To spread through all the earth abroad
    The honours of thy name.

3 Jesus—the name that charms our fears,
    That bids our sorrows cease;
'Tis music in the sinner's ears,
    'Tis life, and health, and peace.

4 He breaks the power of cancelled sin,
    He sets the prisoner free;
His blood can make the foulest clean,
    His blood availed for me.

5 He speaks; and, listening to his voice,
    New life the dead receive;
The mournful, broken hearts rejoice;
    The humble poor believe.

6 Hear him, ye deaf; his praise, ye dumb,
    Your loosened tongues employ;
Ye blind, behold your Saviour come;
    And leap, ye lame, for joy!

7 See all your sins on Jesus laid:
    The Lamb of God was slain;
His soul was once an offering made
    For every soul of man.

8 In Christ, our Head, you then shall know,
    Shall feel, your sins forgiven,
Anticipate your heaven below,
    And own that love is heaven.

Charles Wesley (1707–88)

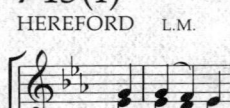

745(i)
HEREFORD L.M.

S. S. Wesley (1810–76)

745(ii)
WILTON L.M.

Samuel Stanley (1767–1822)

1 O THOU who camest from above
  The pure celestial fire to impart,
Kindle a flame of sacred love
  On the mean altar of my heart!

2 There let it for thy glory burn
  With inextinguishable blaze,
And trembling to its source return,
  In humble prayer and fervent praise.

3 Jesus, confirm my heart's desire
  To work, and speak, and think for thee;
Still let me guard the holy fire,
  And still stir up thy gift in me—

4 Ready for all thy perfect will,
  My acts of faith and love repeat,
Till death thy endless mercies seal,
  And make the sacrifice complete.

Charles Wesley (1707–88)

Growth in Grace and Holiness

SOUTHCOTE Irreg

Sydney Carter (1915–   )

And it's from the old I tra-vel to the new; Keep me tra-vel-ling a-long with you.

Words and music reprinted by permission of
Stainer & Bell Ltd.
For permission to reproduce see p. xiii

THE CHRISTIAN LIFE

1 ONE more step along the world I go,
  One more step along the world I go;
    From the old things to the new
    Keep me travelling along with you:
      And it's from the old I travel to the new;
      Keep me travelling along with you.

2 Round the corner of the world I turn,
  More and more about the world I learn;
    All the new things that I see
    You'll be looking at along with me:

3 As I travel through the bad and good,
  Keep me travelling the way I should;
    Where I see no way to go
    You'll be telling me the way, I know:

4 Give me courage when the world is rough,
  Keep me loving though the world is tough;
    Leap and sing in all I do,
    Keep me travelling along with you:

5 You are older than the world can be,
  You are younger than the life in me;
    Ever old and ever new,
    Keep me travelling along with you:

Sydney Carter (1915–)

747

ST CATHERINE (HEMY)   88.88.88.

Henri Friedrich Hemy (1818–88)
Adapted by
James George Walton (1821–1905)

THE CHRISTIAN LIFE

1 SAVIOUR from sin, I wait to prove
    That Jesus is thy healing name;
To lose, when perfected in love,
    Whate'er I have, or can, or am.
I stay me on thy faithful word:
The servant shall be as his Lord.

2 Answer that gracious end in me
    For which thy precious life was given;
Redeem from all iniquity,
    Restore, and make me meet for heaven:
Unless thou purge my every stain,
Thy suffering and my faith are vain.

3 Didst thou not die that I might live
    No longer to myself, but thee,
Might body, soul, and spirit give
    To him who gave himself for me?
Come then, my Master and my God,
Take the dear purchase of thy blood.

4 Thine own devoted servant claim
    For thine own truth and mercy's sake;
Hallow in me thy glorious name;
    Me for thine own this moment take,
And change, and throughly purify;
Thine only may I live and die.

Charles Wesley (1707–88)

748

SOLOTHURN L.M.

Swiss Traditional Melody
Harmonised by John Wilson

*In selected verses A.T.B. may hum the accompaniment

1 TEACH me, O Lord, thy holy way,
    And give me an obedient mind,
    That in thy service I may find
My soul's delight from day to day.

2 Guide me, O Saviour, with thy hand,
    And so control my thoughts and deeds,
    That I may tread the path which leads
Right onward to the blessèd land.

3 Help me, O Saviour, here to trace
    The sacred footsteps thou hast trod,
    And, meekly walking with my God,
To grow in goodness, truth, and grace.

4 Guard me, O Lord, that I may ne'er
    Forsake the right or do the wrong;
    Against temptation make me strong,
And round me spread thy sheltering care.

5 Bless me in every task, O Lord,
    Begun, continued, done for thee;
    Fulfil thy perfect work in me;
And thine abounding grace afford.

William Tidd Matson (1833–99)

THE CHRISTIAN LIFE

749

CREDITON C.M.

Melody from Thomas Clark's
2nd Set of Psalm Tunes
[for] Country Choirs (*c.* 1807)

1 WHAT is our calling's glorious hope
    But inward holiness?
  For this to Jesus I look up,
    I calmly wait for this.

2 I wait, till he shall touch me clean,
    Shall life and power impart,
  Give me the faith that casts out sin
    And purifies the heart.

3 This is the dear redeeming grace,
    For every sinner free;
  Surely it shall on me take place,
    The chief of sinners, me.

4 From all iniquity, from all,
    He shall my soul redeem;
  In Jesus I believe, and shall
    Believe myself to him.

5 When Jesus makes my heart his home,
    My sin shall all depart;
  And lo, he saith: 'I quickly come,
    To fill and rule thy heart.'

6 Be it according to thy word!
    Redeem me from all sin;
  My heart would now receive thee, Lord,
    Come in, my Lord, come in!

Charles Wesley (1707–88)

Growth in Grace and Holiness

750(i)

SHEPHERD 88.88.D. (Anapaestic)

Melody perhaps by John Kidd (19th Century)
Arranged by Martin Ellis (1943-   )

750(ii)

TREWEN 88.88.D. (Anapaestic)

D. Emlyn Evans (1843–1913)

THE CHRISTIAN LIFE

1 THOU Shepherd of Israel, and mine,
   The joy and desire of my heart,
For closer communion I pine,
   I long to reside where thou art;
The pasture I languish to find
   Where all, who their Shepherd obey,
Are fed, on thy bosom reclined,
   And screened from the heat of the day.

2 Ah, show me that happiest place,
   The place of thy people's abode,
Where saints in an ecstasy gaze,
   And hang on a crucified God;
Thy love for a sinner declare,
   Thy passion and death on the tree;
My spirit to Calvary bear,
   To suffer and triumph with thee.

3 'Tis there, with the lambs of thy flock,
   There only, I covet to rest,
To lie at the foot of the rock,
   Or rise to be hid in thy breast;
'Tis there I would always abide,
   And never a moment depart,
Concealed in the cleft of thy side,
   Eternally held in thy heart.

Charles Wesley (1707–88)

Growth in Grace and Holiness

751

FESTUS L.M.

Adapted from a melody in
Freylinghausen's *Geistreiches Gesangbuch* (1704)

1 YE faithful souls who Jesus know,
   If risen indeed with him ye are,
 Superior to the joys below,
   His resurrection's power declare.

2 Your faith by holy tempers prove,
   By actions show your sins forgiven,
 And seek the glorious things above,
   And follow Christ, your Head, to heaven.

3 There your exalted Saviour see,
   Seated at God's right hand again,
 In all his Father's majesty,
   In everlasting power to reign.

4 To him continually aspire,
   Contending for your native place;
 And emulate the angel choir,
   And only live to love and praise.

5 For who by faith your Lord receive,
   Ye nothing seek or want beside;
 Dead to the world and sin ye live,
   Your creature-love is crucified.

6 Your réal life, with Christ concealed,
   Deep in the Father's bosom lies;
 And, glorious as your Head revealed,
   Ye soon shall meet him in the skies.

Charles Wesley (1707–88)

THE CHRISTIAN LIFE/Growth in Grace and Holiness

752
TIVERTON C.M.

Melody by
Jacob Grigg (d. 1768) in John Rippon's
Selection of Psalm and Hymn Tunes (1796)

1 BLEST be the dear uniting love,
      That will not let us part;
   Our bodies may far off remove,
      We still are one in heart.

2 Joined in one spirit to our Head,
      Where he appoints we go;
   And still in Jesu's footsteps tread,
      And show his praise below.

3 O may we ever walk in him,
      And nothing know beside,
   Nothing desire, nothing esteem,
      But Jesus crucified!

4 Closer and closer let us cleave
      To his belov'd embrace;
   Expect his fullness to receive,
      And grace to answer grace.

5 Partakers of the Saviour's grace,
      The same in mind and heart,
   Nor joy, nor grief, nor time, nor place,
      Nor life, nor death can part.

Charles Wesley (1707–88)

Fellowship

753(i)
ST STEPHEN (NEWINGTON) C.M.

Melody, and almost all
the harmony, by William Jones
of Nayland (1726–1800)

For this tune in a higher key see No. 245.

753(ii)
LUCIUS C.M.

Attributed to
Templi Carmina (1829)

THE CHRISTIAN LIFE

1 ALL praise to our redeeming Lord,
  Who joins us by his grace,
And bids us, each to each restored,
  Together seek his face.

2 He bids us build each other up;
  And, gathered into one,
To our high calling's glorious hope
  We hand in hand go on.

3 The gift which he on one bestows,
  We all delight to prove;
The grace through every vessel flows,
  In purest streams of love.

4 Ev'n now we think and speak the same,
  And cordially agree;
Concentred all, through Jesu's name,
  In perfect harmony.

5 We all partake the joy of one,
  The common peace we feel,
A peace to sensual minds unknown,
  A joy unspeakable.

6 And if our fellowship below
  In Jesus be so sweet,
What heights of rapture shall we know
  When round his throne we meet!

Charles Wesley (1707–88)

754
FALCON STREET S.M.

Melody by Isaac Smith (1734–1805)

1 BLEST be the tie that binds
    Our hearts in Jesu's love;
The fellowship of Christian minds
    Is like to that above.

2 Before our Father's throne
    We pour our fervent prayers:
Our fears, our hopes, our aims are one,
    Our comforts and our cares.

3 When for a while we part,
    One thought shall not be vain,
That we shall still be joined in heart,
    Until we meet again.

4 One glorious hope revives
    Our courage by the way:
That each in expectation lives
    Of that tremendous day—

5 When from all toil and pain
    And sin we shall be free,
And perfect love and friendship reign
    Through all eternity.

John Fawcett (1740–1817) alt.

755

ATTERCLIFFE C.M.

W. Mather (1756–1808)

1 COME, let us, who in Christ believe,
  Our common Saviour praise,
To him with joyful voices give
  The glory of his grace.

2 He now stands knocking at the door
  Of every sinner's heart;
The worst need keep him out no more,
  Or force him to depart.

3 Through grace we hearken to thy voice,
  Yield to be saved from sin;
In sure and certain hope rejoice,
  That thou wilt enter in.

4 Come quickly in, thou heavenly guest,
  Nor ever hence remove;
But sup with us, and let the feast
  Be everlasting love.

Charles Wesley (1707–88)

Fellowship

756(i)
LOVE FEAST 77.77.D.

Later form of a melody
in the *Foundery Collection* (1742)

PART 1

1 COME, and let us sweetly join
  Christ to praise in hymns divine;
  Give we all with one accord
  Glory to our common Lord,

2 Hands and hearts and voices raise,
  Sing as in the ancient days,
  Antedate the joys above,
  Celebrate the feast of love.

3 Jesu, dear expected Guest,
  Thou art bidden to the feast;
  For thyself our hearts prepare,
  Come, and rest, and banquet there.

4 Sanctify us, Lord, and bless,
  Breathe thy Spirit, give thy peace;
  Thou thyself within us move,
  Make our feast a feast of love.

THE CHRISTIAN LIFE

5 LET us join—'tis God commands—
  Let us join our hearts and hands;
  Help to gain our calling's hope,
  Build we each the other up.

6 God his blessings shall dispense,
  God shall crown his ordinance,
  Here in his appointed ways
  Nourish us with social grace.

7 Plead we then for faith alone,
  Faith which by our works is shown:
  God it is who justifies;
  Only faith the grace applies—

8 Active faith that lives within,
  Conquers earth, and hell, and sin,
  Sanctifies and makes us whole,
  Forms the Saviour in the soul.

9 Let us for this faith contend;
  Sure salvation is its end:
  Heav'n already is begun,
  Everlasting life is won.

10 Only let us persevere,
   Till we see our Lord appear:
   Never from the Rock remove,
   Saved by faith, which works by love.

11 Hence may all our actions flow,
   Love the proof that Christ we know;
   Mutual love the token be,
   Lord, that we belong to thee.

12 Love, thine image, love impart!
   Stamp it on our face and heart!
   Only love to us be given!
   Lord, we ask no other heaven.

Charles Wesley (1707–88)

756(ii)

DA CHRISTUS GEBOREN WAR   77.77.D.

Melody and almost all the harmony from
J. F. Doles's *Choralbuch*
(Leipzig, 1785)

PART I

1 COME, and let us sweetly join
Christ to praise in hymns divine;
Give we all with one accord
Glory to our common Lord,

2 Hands and hearts and voices raise,
Sing as in the ancient days,
Antedate the joys above,
Celebrate the feast of love.

3 Jesu, dear expected Guest,
Thou art bidden to the feast;
For thyself our hearts prepare,
Come, and rest, and banquet there.

4 Sanctify us, Lord, and bless,
Breathe thy Spirit, give thy peace;
Thou thyself within us move,
Make our feast a feast of love.

5 LET us join—'tis God commands—
  Let us join our hearts and hands;
  Help to gain our calling's hope,
  Build we each the other up.

6 God his blessings shall dispense,
  God shall crown his ordinance,
  Here in his appointed ways
  Nourish us with social grace.

7 Plead we then for faith alone,
  Faith which by our works is shown:
  God it is who justifies;
  Only faith the grace applies—

8 Active faith that lives within,
  Conquers earth, and hell, and sin,
  Sanctifies and makes us whole,
  Forms the Saviour in the soul.

9 Let us for this faith contend;
  Sure salvation is its end:
  Heav'n already is begun,
  Everlasting life is won.

10 Only let us persevere,
   Till we see our Lord appear:
   Never from the Rock remove,
   Saved by faith, which works by love.

11 Hence may all our actions flow,
   Love the proof that Christ we know;
   Mutual love the token be,
   Lord, that we belong to thee.

12 Love, thine image, love impart!
   Stamp it on our face and heart!
   Only love to us be given!
   Lord, we ask no other heaven.

Charles Wesley (1707–88)

757

UBI CARITAS   13.12 12 12 12.   A. Gregory Murray (1905–   )

Refrain
Not too slowly

God is love, and where true love_ is,   God him-self is there.

Unison

Verses
(Choir Harmony ad lib.)

1 HERE in Christ we ga - ther,_ love of Christ our call - ing.

Christ, our love, is with_ us,_ glad-ness be his greet - ing.

THE CHRISTIAN LIFE

Let us all re - vere _ and _ love him, God e - ter - nal.

Refrain D.C.

Lov - ing him, let each _ love _ Christ in all his bro - thers:

God is love,
and where true love is,
God himself is there.

1 HERE in Christ we gather, love of Christ our calling.
   Christ, our love, is with us, gladness be his greeting.
   Let us all revere and love him, God eternal.
   Loving him, let each love Christ in all his brothers:

2 When we Christians gather, members of one Body,
   Let there be in us no discord, but one spirit.
   Banished now be anger, strife, and every quarrel.
   Christ, our God, be present always here among us:

3 Grant us love's fulfilment, joy with all the blessèd,
   When we see your face, O Saviour, in its glory.
   Shine on us, O purest light of all creation,
   Be our bliss while endless ages sing your praises:

James Quinn (1919–   ) alt.

Fellowship

758(i)
McKEE C.M.

Negro melody adapted by
Harry T. Burleigh (1866–1949)

With dignity

758(ii)
KILMARNOCK C.M.

Melody, and almost all the harmony,
by Neil Dougall (1776–1862)

THE CHRISTIAN LIFE

For this tune in a lower key see No. 33

1 IN Christ there is no east or west,
   In him no south or north,
   But one great fellowship of love
     Throughout the whole wide earth.

2 In him shall true hearts everywhere
     Their high communion find,
   His service is the golden cord
     Close-binding all mankind.

3 Join hands, then, brothers of the faith,
     Whate'er your race may be;
   Who serves my Father as a son
     Is surely kin to me.

4 In Christ now meet both east and west,
     In him meet south and north,
   All Christlike souls are one in him,
     Throughout the whole wide earth.

John Oxenham (1852–1941)

Fellowship

759

THEODORA 77.77.   From an air in Handel's *Theodora* (1749)

1 JESUS, Lord, we look to thee,
  Let us in thy name agree;
  Show thyself the Prince of Peace;
  Bid our jarring conflicts cease.

2 By thy reconciling love,
  Every stumbling-block remove;
  Each to each unite, endear;
  Come, and spread thy banner here.

3 Make us of one heart and mind,
  Courteous, pitiful, and kind,
  Lowly, meek in thought and word,
  Altogether like our Lord.

4 Let us for each other care,
  Each the other's burden bear,
  To thy church the pattern give,
  Show how true believers live.

5 Free from anger and from pride,
  Let us thus in God abide;
  All the depth of love express,
  All the height of holiness.

Charles Wesley (1707–88) alt.

THE CHRISTIAN LIFE

760

REUBEN S.M. S. Wakeley (1805–81)

Sopranos and Tenors

1 JESUS, we look to thee,
      Thy promised presence claim;
   Thou in the midst of us shalt be,
      Assembled in thy name.

2 Thy name salvation is,
      Which here we come to prove;
   Thy name is life and health and peace
      And everlasting love.

3 We meet, the grace to take
      Which thou hast freely given;
   We meet on earth for thy dear sake,
      That we may meet in heaven.

4 Present we know thou art,
      But O thyself reveal!
   Now, Lord, let every bounding heart
      The mighty comfort feel.

5 O may thy quickening voice
      The death of sin remove;
   And bid our inmost souls rejoice
      In hope of perfect love!

Charles Wesley (1707–88)

Fellowship

761

POLWHELE 88.6.D.

Hubert Julian (1923–   )

1 JESUS, thou soul of all our joys,
   For whom we now lift up our voice
      And all our strength exert,
   Vouchsafe the grace we humbly claim,
   Compose into a thankful frame,
      And tune thy people's heart.

2 The secret pride, the subtle sin,
   O let it never more steal in,
      To offend thy glorious eyes,
   To desecrate our hallowed strain,
   And make our solemn service vain,
      And mar our sacrifice.

3 Thee let us praise, our common Lord,
   And sweetly join with one accord
      Thy goodness to proclaim;
   Jesus, thyself in us reveal,
   And all our faculties shall feel
      Thy harmonizing name.

THE CHRISTIAN LIFE

4 With calmly reverential joy,
  O let us all our lives employ
    In setting forth thy love;
  And raise in death our triumph higher,
  And sing with all the heavenly choir
    That endless song above!

Charles Wesley (1707–88)

762
GOTT DES HIMMELS   8.7.8.7.

Adapted by C. Steggall (1826–1905)
from J. S. Bach's setting of a melody
by H. Albert (1604–51)

1 MAY the grace of Christ our Saviour,
    And the Father's boundless love,
  With the Holy Spirit's favour,
    Rest upon us from above.

2 Thus may we abide in union
    With each other and the Lord,
  And possess, in sweet communion,
    Joys which earth cannot afford.

John Newton (1725–1807)

Fellowship

763(i)
BISHOPTHORPE C.M.

Melody and bass from
Select Portions of the Psalms
(published by H. Gardner, *c.* 1786)

763(ii)
TWYFORD C.M.

Leonard Blake (1907–)

THE CHRISTIAN LIFE

1 SEE, Jesus, thy disciples see,
    The promised blessing give;
  Met in thy name, we look to thee,
    Expecting to receive.

2 Thee we expect, our faithful Lord,
    Who in thy name are joined;
  We wait, according to thy word,
    Thee in the midst to find.

3 With us thou art assembled here;
    But O thyself reveal!
  Son of the living God, appear!
    Let us thy presence feel.

4 Whom now we seek, O may we meet!
    Jesus the crucified,
  Show us thy bleeding hands and feet,
    Thou who for us hast died.

5 Cause us the record to receive,
    Speak, and the tokens show:
  'O be not faithless, but believe
    In me, who died for you!'

Charles Wesley (1707–88)

764

VIENNA 77.77.   Melody and bass by J. H. Knecht (1752–1817)

1 CHRIST, from whom all blessings flow,
   Perfecting the saints below,
   Hear us, who thy nature share,
   Who thy mystic body are.

2 Join us, in one spirit join,
   Let us still receive of thine;
   Still for more on thee we call,
   Thou who fillest all in all.

3 Closer knit to thee, our Head,
   Nourished, Lord, by thee, and fed,
   Let us daily growth receive,
   More in Jesus Christ believe,

4 Never from thy service move,
   Needful to each other prove,
   Use the grace on each bestowed,
   Tempered by the art of God.

5 Love, like death, has all destroyed,
   Rendered all distinctions void;
   Names, and sects, and parties fall:
   Thou, O Christ, art all in all.

Charles Wesley (1707–88) alt.

THE CALLING OF THE CHURCH / Mission and Unity

765

TALLIS' CANON L.M.

Melody, and most of the harmony, by
Thomas Tallis (*c.* 1505–85). As shortened by
T. Ravenscroft (*Psalmes*, 1621)

1 COME, all who look to Christ today,
    Stretch out your hands, enlarge your mind,
Together share his living way
    Where all who humbly seek will find.

2 Come, all who will from every race;
    Find here new powers of brotherhood,
Accept the Spirit's strong embrace
    Which binds us to the common good.

3 Come, young and old from every church,
    Bring all your treasuries of prayer,
Join the dynamic Spirit's search
    To press beyond the truths we share.

4 Bring your traditions' richest store,
    Your hymns and rites and cherished creeds;
Explore our visions, pray for more,
    Since God delights to meet fresh needs.

5 Come, trust in Christ and live in peace,
    Anticipate that final light
When strife and bigotry shall cease,
    And faith be lost in praise and sight.

Richard G. Jones (1926–)

Mission and Unity

766

ST PANCRAS L.M.

Melody and almost all the harmony
by Jonathan Battishill (1738–1801)

THE CALLING OF THE CHURCH

1 ETERNAL Son, eternal Love,
   Take to thyself thy mighty power;
Let all earth's sons thy mercy prove,
   Let all thy saving grace adore.

2 The triumphs of thy love display,
   In every heart reign thou alone,
Till all thy foes confess thy sway,
   And glory ends what grace began.

3 Spirit of grace, and health, and power,
   Fountain of light and love below,
Abroad thy healing influence shower,
   O'er all the nations let it flow.

4 Wisdom, and might, and love are thine;
   Prostrate before thy face we fall,
Confess thine attributes divine,
   And hail thee sovereign Lord of all.

5 Thee, sovereign Lord, let all confess
   That moves in earth, or air, or sky,
Revere thy power, thy goodness bless,
   Tremble before thy piercing eye.

6 Blessing and honour, praise and love,
   Co-equal, co-eternal Three,
In earth below, and heaven above,
   By all thy works be paid to thee!

John Wesley (1703–91)

767

MOUNT SION   8.8.8.8.8.8.

Adapted from
I. J. Pleyel (1757–1831)

THE CALLING OF THE CHURCH

1 GIVE me the faith which can remove
    And sink the mountain to a plain;
  Give me the childlike praying love,
    Which longs to build thy house again;
  Thy love, let it my heart o'erpower,
  And all my simple soul devour.

2 I would the precious time redeem,
    And longer live for this alone:
  To spend, and to be spent, for them
    Who have not yet my Saviour known;
  Fully on these my mission prove,
  And only breathe, to breathe thy love.

3 My talents, gifts, and graces, Lord,
    Into thy blessèd hands receive;
  And let me live to preach thy word,
    And let me to thy glory live;
  My every sacred moment spend
  In publishing the sinners' friend.

4 Enlarge, inflame, and fill my heart
    With boundless charity divine:
  So shall I all my strength exert,
    And love them with a zeal like thine;
  And lead them to thy open side,
  The sheep for whom their Shepherd died.

Charles Wesley (1707–88)

768

ST GEORGE S.M.

Henry J. Gauntlett (1805–76)

For this tune in a lower key see No. 280(ii)

1 JESUS, the word bestow,
      The true immortal seed;
   Thy gospel then shall greatly grow,
      And all our land o'erspread;

2 Through earth extended wide
      Shall mightily prevail,
   Destroy the works of self and pride,
      And shake the gates of hell.

3 Its energy exert
      In the believing soul;
   Diffuse thy grace through every part,
      And sanctify the whole;

4 Its utmost virtue show
      In pure consummate love,
   And fill with all thy life below,
      And give us thrones above.

Charles Wesley · (1707–88)

THE CALLING OF THE CHURCH

769

BENSON Irreg. Millicent D. Kingham (1866–1927)

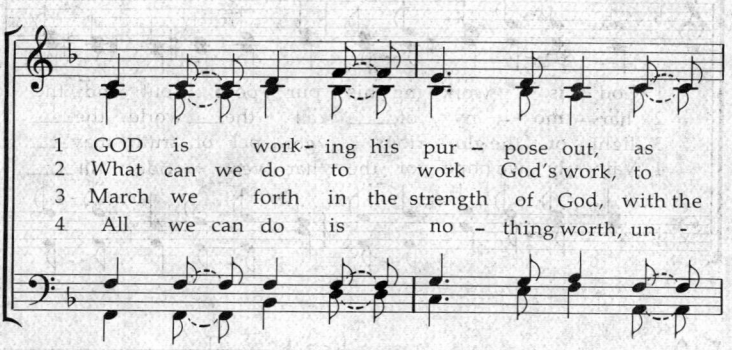

1 GOD is work-ing his pur — pose out, as
2 What can we do to work God's work, to
3 March we forth in the strength of God, with the
4 All we can do is no — thing worth, un -

1 year suc — ceeds to year;
2 pros — per and in — crease The
3 ban — ner of Christ un — furled, That the
4 less God bless — es the deed;

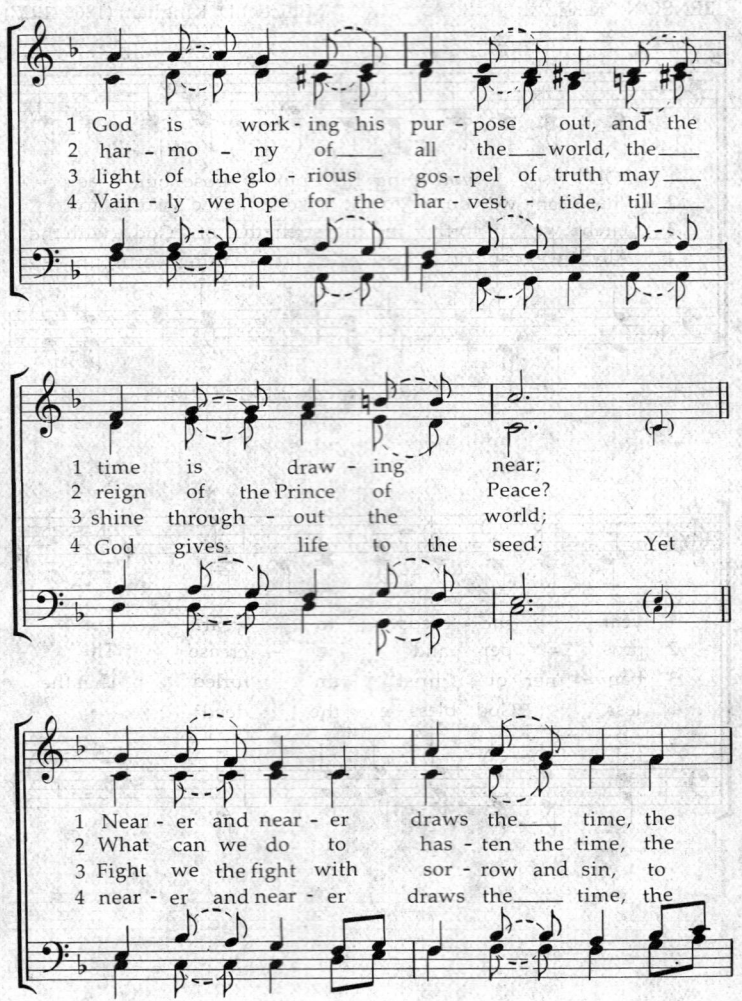

1 God is work-ing his pur-pose out, and the
2 har-mo-ny of___ all the___world, the___
3 light of the glo-rious gos-pel of truth may___
4 Vain-ly we hope for the har-vest - tide, till___

1 time is draw-ing near;
2 reign of the Prince of Peace?
3 shine through - out the world;
4 God gives life to the seed; Yet

1 Near - er and near - er draws the___ time, the
2 What can we do to has - ten the time, the
3 Fight we the fight with sor - row and sin, to
4 near - er and near - er draws the___ time, the

THE CALLING OF THE CHURCH

1 time that shall sure - ly be, When the
2 time that shall sure - ly be, When the
3 set their cap - tives free, That the
4 time that shall sure - ly be, When the

1 earth shall be filled with the glo - ry of God, as the
2 earth shall be filled with the glo - ry of God, as the
3 earth may be filled with the glo - ry of God, as the
4 earth shall be filled with the glo - ry of God, as the

1 wa - ters co - ver the sea.
2 wa - ters co - ver the sea?
3 wa - ters co - ver the sea.
4 wa - ters co - ver the sea.

Arthur Campbell Ainger (1841–1919)

Mission and Unity

770

Michael Baughen (1930–)
arr. Charles Cleall (1927–)

1 GO forth and tell! O church of God, awake!
  God's saving news to all the nations take.
    Proclaim Christ Jesus, Saviour, Lord, and King,
    That all the world his worthy praise may sing.

2 Go forth and tell! God's love embraces all:
  He will in grace respond to all who call.
    How shall they call if they have never heard
    The gracious invitation of his word?

3 Go forth and tell! Some still in darkness lie:
  In wealth or want, in sin they live and die.
    Give us, O Lord, concern of heart and mind,
    A love like yours which cares for all mankind.

4 Go forth and tell! The doors are open wide:
  Share God's good gifts with people long denied.
    Live out your life as Christ, your Lord, shall choose,
    Your ransomed powers for his sole glory use.

J. E. Seddon (1915–83)

THE CALLING OF THE CHURCH

771

MOUNT EPHRAIM S.M.

Melody and almost all the bass
by Benjamin Milgrove (1731–1810)

1   LORD, if at thy command
        The word of life we sow,
  Watered by thy almighty hand,
        The seed shall surely grow;

2   The virtue of thy grace
        A large increase shall give,
  And multiply the faithful race
        Who to thy glory live.

3   Now then the ceaseless shower
        Of gospel blessings send,
  And let the soul-converting power
        Thy ministers attend.

4   On multitudes confer
        The heart-renewing love,
  And by the joy of grace prepare
        For fuller joys above.

Charles Wesley (1707–88)

Mission and Unity

772(i)

ELIM (HESPERUS) L.M.

H. Baker (1835–1910)

772(ii)

HEREFORD L.M.

S. S. Wesley (1810–1876)

THE CALLING OF THE CHURCH

1 JESUS, thy wandering sheep behold!
   See, Lord, with tenderest pity see
The sheep that cannot find the fold,
   Till sought and gathered in by thee.

2 Lost are they now, and scattered wide,
   In pain, and weariness, and want;
With no kind shepherd near to guide
   The sick, and spiritless, and faint.

3 Thou, only thou, the kind and good
   And sheep-redeeming Shepherd art:
Collect thy flock, and give them food,
   And pastors after thine own heart.

4 Give the pure word of general grace,
   And great shall be the preachers' crowd;
Preachers, who all the sinful race
   Point to the all-atoning blood.

5 Open their mouth, and utterance give;
   Give them a trumpet-voice, to call
On all the world to turn and live,
   Through faith in him who died for all.

6 Thy only glory let them seek;
   O let their hearts with love o'erflow!
Let them believe, and therefore speak,
   And spread thy mercy's praise below.

7 Mercy for all be all their song,
   Mercy which every soul may claim,
Mercy which doth to all belong,
   Mercy for all in Jesu's name.

Charles Wesley (1707–88)

773(i)
ST BERNARD C.M.

Melody, and most of the bass, from
Easy Hymn-Tunes for Catholic Schools (1851)
(based on an 18th-century German melody)

773(ii)
LUNENBURG C.M.

From an air in Handel's *Siroe* (1728)

THE CALLING OF THE CHURCH

1 JESUS, united by thy grace
   And each to each endeared,
   With confidence we seek thy face,
   And know our prayer is heard.

2 Still let us own our common Lord,
   And bear thine easy yoke,
   A band of love, a threefold cord,
   Which never can be broke.

3 O make us of one spirit drink;
   Baptize into thy name;
   And let us always kindly think
   And sweetly speak the same.

4 Touched by the lodestone of thy love,
   Let all our hearts agree,
   And ever t'ward each other move,
   And ever move t'ward thee.

5 To thee, inseparably joined,
   Let all our spirits cleave;
   O may we all the loving mind
   That was in thee receive.

6 This is the bond of perfectness,
   Thy spotless charity;
   O let us (still we pray) possess
   The mind that was in thee.

Charles Wesley (1707–88)

774

ABBOT'S LEIGH   8.7.8.7.D.   Cyril V. Taylor (1907–)

THE CALLING OF THE CHURCH

For this tune in a higher key see No. 817(ii)

1 LORD, thy church on earth is seeking
   Thy renewal from above;
 Teach us all the art of speaking
   With the accent of thy love.
 We would heed thy great commission:
   Go ye into every place—
 Preach, baptize, fulfil my mission,
   Serve with love and share my grace.

2 Freedom give to those in bondage,
   Lift the burdens caused by sin.
 Give new hope, new strength and courage,
   Grant release from fears within:
 Light for darkness; joy for sorrow;
   Love for hatred; peace for strife.
 These and countless blessings follow
   As the Spirit gives new life.

3 In the streets of every city
   Where the bruised and lonely dwell,
 Let us show the Saviour's pity,
   Let us of his mercy tell.
 In all lands and with all races
   Let us serve, and seek to bring
 All the world to render praises,
   Christ, to thee, Redeemer, King.

                    Hugh Sherlock (1905–   ) alt.

775

German Traditional Melody,
as harmonised by Mendelssohn in his *St Paul* (1836)

Slowly

For this tune in a higher key see No. 425

1 LORD, we your church are deaf and dumb,
 Bewildered in a threatening world:
 Our ears are closed to hear your Son,
 Our tongues too tied to speak your word.

2 Though deaf because we will not hear,
 And dumb because we fear to speak,
 In healing power again draw near,
 And all that binds our spirits break.

3 Then speak, Lord, in our deafened ear;
 Release again the stifled voice,
 That we may make the good news clear,
 And all again in Christ rejoice.

Alan Luff (1928–)

THE CALLING OF THE CHURCH

DESCANT VERSION FOR VERSE 3

Arranged by John Wilson

Sopranos

3 Then speak, Lord, in our deaf - ened ear; ___ Re-lease a-gain the sti-fled voice, That we may make the good news clear, And all a - gain ___ in Christ re - joice.

Organ and unison voices

776

Sebastian Temple

CHANNEL OF PEACE Irreg. arranged by Betty Pulkingham (1928–)

MAKE me a chan-nel of your peace.____ Where there is ha-tred, let me bring your love;____ Where there is in-ju-ry, your par-don, Lord;____ And where there's doubt, true faith in you:____ O Mas-ter, grant that I may ne-ver seek____ So

THE CALLING OF THE CHURCH

much to be con-soled as to con-sole;_____ To be

A7   D   D7

un-der-stood as to un-der – stand;_____ To be

G   D

D.C. al Fine

loved, as to love with all my soul._____

E   E7   A

1 MAKE me a channel of your peace.
   Where there is hatred, let me bring your love;
   Where there is injury, your pardon, Lord;
   And where there's doubt, true faith in you:

      O Master, grant that I may never seek
      So much to be consoled as to console;
      To be understood as to understand;
      To be loved, as to love with all my soul.

2 Make me a channel of your peace.
   Where there's despair in life, let me bring hope;
   Where there is darkness, only light;
   And where there's sadness, ever joy:

      O Master, grant that I may never seek
      So much to be consoled as to console;
      To be understood as to understand;
      To be loved, as to love with all my soul.

3 Make me a channel of your peace.
   It is in pardoning that we are pardoned,
   In giving to all men that we receive,
   And in dying that we're born to eternal life.

based on a traditional prayer

Mission and Unity

777

ISLINGTON   9.8.9.8 (extended)

Partly based on a psalm-setting
by Andrew Roner (1721)
(edited by John Wilson)

(v.1) And   fit ____ your church, and   fit ____ your

THE CALLING OF THE CHURCH

church___ to meet___ this hour.

1 O BREATH of life, come sweeping through us,
    Revive your church with life and power;
  O Breath of life, come, cleanse, renew us,
    And fit your church to meet this hour.

2 O Wind of God, come, bend us, break us,
    Till humbly we confess our need;
  Then in your tenderness remake us,
    Revive, restore; for this we plead.

3 O Breath of love, come, breathe within us,
    Renewing thought and will and heart;
  Come, love of Christ, afresh to win us,
    Revive your church in every part.

Bessie Porter Head (1850–1936)

778

MORECAMBE   10 10. 10 10.   Frederic Cook Atkinson (1841–96)

THE CALLING OF THE CHURCH

1 O GOD our Father, who dost make us one,
   Heart bound to heart, in love of thy dear Son,
      Now as we part and go our several ways,
      Touch every lip, may every voice be praise—

2 Praise for the fellowship that here we find,
   The fellowship of heart and soul and mind,
      Praise for the bonds of love and brotherhood,
      Bonds wrought by thee, who makest all things good.

3 Lord, make us strong, for thou alone dost know
   How oft we turn our faces from the foe;
      How oft, when claimed by dark temptation's hour,
      We lose our hold on thee, and of thy power.

4 Go with us, Lord, from hence; we only ask
   That thou be sharer in our daily task;
      So, side by side with thee, shall each one know
      The blessedness of heaven begun below.

William Vaughan Jenkins (1868–1920)

779

Melody and bass by
Orlando Gibbons (1583–1625)

THE CALLING OF THE CHURCH

1 O THOU who at thy eucharist didst pray
   That all thy church might be for ever one,
Grant us at every eucharist to say
   With longing heart and soul: 'Thy will be done';
O may we all one bread, one body be,
One through this sacrament of unity.

2 For all thy church, O Lord, we intercede;
   Make thou our sad divisions soon to cease;
Draw us the nearer each to each, we plead,
   By drawing all to thee, O Prince of Peace;
Thus may we all one bread, one body be,
One through this sacrament of unity.

3 We pray thee too for wanderers from thy fold;
   O bring them back, Good Shepherd of the sheep,
Back to the faith which saints believed of old,
   Back to thy church which still one faith doth keep;
Soon may we all one bread, one body be,
One through this sacrament of unity.

4 So, Lord, at length when sacraments shall cease,
   May we be one with all thy church above,
One with thy saints in undivided peace,
   One with thy saints in one unbounded love;
More blessèd still, in peace and love to be
One with the Trinity in Unity.

W. H. Turton (1856–1938)

REVIVE THY WORK, O LORD   S.M. Refrain   W. H. Doane (1832–1915)

Refrain

Re – vive thy work, O   Lord,   While here to thee we bow; ___ De – scend, O   gra – cious

THE CALLING OF THE CHURCH

Lord, de - scend! O come and bless us now.

1   REVIVE thy work, O Lord;
        Thy mighty arm make bare;
  Speak with the voice that wakes the dead,
        And make thy people hear:
        Revive thy work, O Lord,
          While here to thee we bow;
        Descend, O gracious Lord, descend!
          O come and bless us now.

2   Revive thy work, O Lord;
        Now let us thirst for thee;
  And hungering for the bread of life
        May all our spirits be:

3   Revive thy work, O Lord;
        Exalt thy precious name;
  And, by the Holy Ghost, our love
        For thee and thine inflame:

4   Revive thy work, O Lord;
        Give power unto thy word;
  Grant that thy blessèd gospel may
        In living faith be heard:

5   Revive thy work, O Lord,
        And give refreshing showers;
  The glory shall be all thine own,
        The blessing, Lord, be ours:

Albert Midlane (1825–1909)

781

ST GEORGE'S, WINDSOR 77.77.D. George Job Elvey (1816–93)

For this tune in a higher key see No. 355

THE CALLING OF THE CHURCH

1 SEE how great a flame aspires,
   Kindled by a spark of grace!
Jesu's love the nations fires,
   Sets the kingdoms on a blaze.
To bring fire on earth he came;
   Kindled in some hearts it is:
O that all might catch the flame,
   All partake the glorious bliss!

2 When he first the work begun,
   Small and feeble was his day:
Now the word doth swiftly run,
   Now it wins its widening way;
More and more it spreads and grows
   Ever mighty to prevail;
Sin's strongholds it now o'erthrows,
   Shakes the trembling gates of hell.

3 Sons of God, your Saviour praise!
   He the door has opened wide;
He has given the word of grace,
   Jesu's word is glorified;
Jesus, mighty to redeem,
   He alone the work has wrought;
Worthy is the work of him,
   Him who spake a world from nought.

4 Saw ye not the cloud arise,
   Little as a human hand?
Now it spreads along the skies,
   Hangs o'er all the thirsty land:
Lo, the promise of a shower
   Drops already from above;
But the Lord will shortly pour
   All the Spirit of his love!

Charles Wesley (1707–88)

782

WILVERON   Irreg.   Graham Bishop (1953–)

1 SHOUT it in the street,   Tell it to your friend,

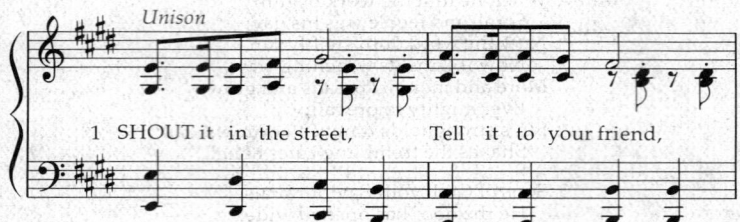

Spread it through the earth from end to   end,

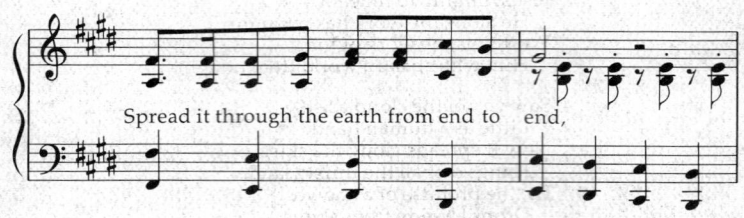

Go to ev-ery peo-ple,   Tell them all to come, For the

THE CALLING OF THE CHURCH

Spi-rit of God shall make us one.   still.

Words and music reprinted by permission of
Stainer & Bell Ltd.
For permission to reproduce see p. xiii

1   SHOUT it in the street,
      Tell it to your friend,
   Spread it through the earth from end to end,
      Go to every people,
      Tell them all to come,
   For the Spirit of God shall make us one.

2   Listen in the world,
      Listen in your room,
   Listen for his call come late or soon,
      Ready for adventure,
      Following his will,
   For the Spirit of God shall lead us still.

Edmund Banyard (1920–   )

783

ST CECILIA 66.66. L. G. Hayne (1836–83)

SECOND VERSION
(with original form of rhythm)

ST CECILIA 66.66. L. G. Hayne (1836–83)

THE CALLING OF THE CHURCH

See following page for Harmony version of Verse 2

1 THY hand, O God, has guided
    Thy flock, from age to age;
The wondrous tale is written,
    Full clear, on every page;
Our fathers owned thy goodness,
    And we their deeds record;
And both of this bear witness:
    One church, one faith, one Lord.

2 Thy heralds brought glad tidings
    To greatest, as to least;
They bade men rise, and hasten
    To share the great King's feast;
Their gospel of redemption,
    Sin pardoned, right restored,
Was all in this enfolded:
    One church, one faith, one Lord.

3 Thy mercy will not fail us,
    Nor leave thy work undone;
With thy right hand to help us,
    The vict'ry shall be won;
And then, by men and angels,
    Thy name shall be adored,
And this shall be their anthem:
    One church, one faith, one Lord!

E. H. Plumptre (1821–91)

784 (cont.)

VERSE 2, HARMONY.

2 Thy he-ralds brought glad ti - dings To great-est, as to

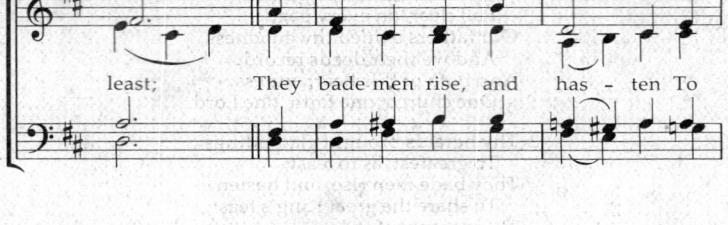

least; They bade men rise, and has - ten To

share the great King's feast; Their gos - pel of re -

- demp - tion, Sin par-doned, right re - stored,

THE CALLING OF THE CHURCH

One church, one
Was all in this en – fold – ed: One church, one

faith, one Lord.
faith, one Lord. one faith, one Lord.

Turn back for Verse 3

Mission and Unity

785(i)

CAMBRIDGE S.M. Melody by R. Harrison (1748–1810)

For this tune in a higher key see No. 670 (ii)

785(ii)

ST GEORGE S.M. Henry J. Gauntlett (1805–76)

For this tune in a higher key see No. 768

1 A CHARGE to keep I have:
    A God to glorify;
  A never-dying soul to save,
    And fit it for the sky;

2 To serve the present age,
    My calling to fulfil;—
  O may it all my powers engage
    To do my Master's will!

3 Arm me with jealous care,
    As in thy sight to live;
  And O thy servant, Lord, prepare
    A strict account to give!

4 Help me to watch and pray,
    And on thyself rely,
  So shall I not my trust betray,
    Nor love within me die.

Charles Wesley (1707–88) alt.

THE CALLING OF THE CHURCH/Witness and Service

786

1 BE it my only wisdom here
To serve the Lord with filial fear,
  With loving gratitude;
Superior sense may I display,
By shunning every evil way,
  And walking in the good.

2 O may I still from sin depart!
A wise and understanding heart,
  Jesus, to me be given;
And let me through thy Spirit know
To glorify my God below,
  And find my way to heaven.

Charles Wesley (1707–88)

Witness and Service

787

LADYWELL D.C.M.

W. H. Ferguson (1874–1950)

THE CALLING OF THE CHURCH

1 A GLORIOUS company we sing,
    The Master and his men:
He sent them forth to tell his love
    By voice and hand and pen;
Then with his Spirit's mighty flame
    He made their hearts to glow,
And bade them on a troubled world
    His grace and power bestow.

2 A faithful company we sing,
    The steadfast martyr band;
Against the rage of ruler proud
    They boldly made their stand;
And still when men defy Christ's name,
    The cross is raised on high,
And for his sake his hosts go forth
    To battle and to die.

3 A company of love we sing,
    Whom Jesus called to save
All sick and blind and hungry folk,
    The outcast and the slave;
And now when life of man or child
    Is hurt by sin and pain,
He calls for eager, willing hands
    To share his love again.

4 O we would join this company
    Of Jesus and his friends;
This church which now in every land
    The reign of Christ extends:
And may that Spirit which of old
    His servants did inspire
With love and joy and faith and power
    Set all our hearts afire.

Albert F. Bayly (1901-84)

THE CALLING OF THE CHURCH

1 BEHOLD the servant of the Lord!
   I wait thy guiding eye to feel,
To hear and keep thy every word,
   To prove and do thy perfect will,
Joyful from my own works to cease,
Glad to fulfil all righteousness.

2 Me if thy grace vouchsafe to use,
   Meanest of all thy creatures, me,
The deed, the time, the manner choose;
   Let all my fruit be found of thee;
Let all my works in thee be wrought,
By thee to full perfection brought.

3 My every weak though good design
   O'errule or change, as seems thee meet;
Jesus, let all my work be thine!
   Thy work, O Lord, is all complete,
And pleasing in thy Father's sight;
Thou only hast done all things right.

4 Here then to thee thine own I leave;
   Mould as thou wilt thy passive clay;
But let me all thy stamp receive,
   But let me all thy words obey,
Serve with a single heart and eye,
And to thy glory live and die.

Charles Wesley (1707–88)

788(ii)

AD ASTRA 88.88.88.

Henry G. Ley (1887–1962)

THE CALLING OF THE CHURCH

1 BEHOLD the servant of the Lord!
    I wait thy guiding eye to feel,
To hear and keep thy every word,
    To prove and do thy perfect will,
Joyful from my own works to cease,
Glad to fulfil all righteousness.

2 Me if thy grace vouchsafe to use,
    Meanest of all thy creatures, me,
The deed, the time, the manner choose;
    Let all my fruit be found of thee;
Let all my works in thee be wrought,
By thee to full perfection brought.

3 My every weak though good design
    O'errule or change, as seems thee meet;
Jesus, let all my work be thine!
    Thy work, O Lord, is all complete,
And pleasing in thy Father's sight;
Thou only hast done all things right.

4 Here then to thee thine own I leave;
    Mould as thou wilt thy passive clay;
But let me all thy stamp receive,
    But let me all thy words obey,
Serve with a single heart and eye,
And to thy glory live and die.

Charles Wesley (1707–88)

789

MILTON ABBAS   66.4.66 6.4.   Eric Thiman (1900–75)

1 CHRIST for the world, we sing!
  The world to Christ we bring
    With fervent prayer:
  The wayward and the lost,
  By restless passions tossed,
  Redeemed at countless cost
    From dark despair.

2 Christ for the world, we sing!
  The world to Christ we bring
    With one accord;
  With us the work to share,
  With us reproach to dare,
  With us the cross to bear,
    For Christ our Lord.

3 Christ for the world, we sing!
  The world to Christ we bring
    With joyful song:
  The new-born souls, whose days,
  Reclaimed from error's ways,
  Inspired with hope and praise,
    To Christ belong.

Samuel Wolcott (1813–86)

THE CALLING OF THE CHURCH

790

1 FATHER, lead me day by day
   Ever in thine own good way;
   Teach me to be pure and true,
   Show me what I ought to do.

2 When in danger, make me brave;
   Make me know that thou canst save;
   Keep me safe by thy dear side;
   Let me in thy love abide.

3 When I'm tempted to do wrong,
   Make me steadfast, wise, and strong;
   And, when all alone I stand,
   Shield me with thy mighty hand.

4 When my heart is full of glee,
   Help me to remember thee,
   Happy most of all to know
   That my Father loves me so.

5 When my work seems hard and dry,
   May I press on cheerily;
   Help me patiently to bear
   Pain and hardship, toil and care.

6 May I see the good and bright
   When they pass before my sight;
   May I hear the heavenly voice
   When the pure and wise rejoice.

John Page Hopps (1834–1911)

Witness and Service

791

NORICUM 77.77.77.

Frederic James (1858–1922)

THE CALLING OF THE CHURCH

1 FATHER, Son, and Holy Ghost,
   One in Three, and Three in One,
 As by the celestial host,
   Let thy will on earth be done;
 Praise by all to thee be given,
 Glorious Lord of earth and heaven.

2 If a sinner such as I
   May to thy great glory live,
 All my actions sanctify,
   All my words and thoughts receive;
 Claim me for thy service, claim
 All I have and all I am.

3 Take my soul and body's powers;
   Take my memory, mind, and will,
 All my goods, and all my hours,
   All I know, and all I feel,
 All I think, or speak, or do;
 Take my heart, but make it new.

4 Now, O God, thine own I am,
   Now I give thee back thine own;
 Freedom, friends, and health, and fame
   Consecrate to thee alone:
 Thine I live, thrice happy I;
 Happier still if thine I die.

5 Father, Son, and Holy Ghost,
   One in Three, and Three in One,
 As by the celestial host,
   Let thy will on earth be done;
 Praise by all to thee be given,
 Glorious Lord of earth and heaven.

Charles Wesley (1707–88) alt.

792(i)
ST FULBERT C.M.

Henry J. Gauntlett (1805–76)

For this tune in a higher key see No. 823

792(ii)
BEATITUDO C.M.

J. B. Dykes (1823–76)

THE CALLING OF THE CHURCH

1 FILL thou my life, O Lord my God,
    In every part with praise,
That my whole being may proclaim
    Thy being and thy ways.

2 Not for the lip of praise alone
    Nor e'en the praising heart
I ask, but for a life made up
    Of praise in every part:

3 Praise in the common things of life,
    Its goings out and in;
Praise in each duty and each deed,
    However small and mean.

4 Fill every part of me with praise;
    Let all my being speak
Of thee and of thy love, O Lord,
    Poor though I be and weak.

5 So shalt thou, gracious Lord, from me
    Receive the glory due;
And so shall I begin on earth
    The song for ever new.

6 So shall no part of day or night
    From sacredness be free;
But all my life, in every step,
    Be fellowship with thee.

Horatius Bonar (1808–89)

793(i)
SHERE S.M.

Eric Thiman (1900–75)

793(ii)
CARLISLE S.M.

Melody and most of the harmony
by C. Lockhart (1745–1815)

THE CALLING OF THE CHURCH

1 GOD of almighty love,
      By whose sufficient grace
   I lift my heart to things above,
      And humbly seek thy face:

2 Through Jesus Christ the just
      My faint desires receive,
   And let me in thy goodness trust,
      And to thy glory live.

3 Whate'er I say or do,
      Thy glory be my aim;
   My offerings all be offered through
      The ever-blessèd name.

4 Jesus, my single eye
      Be fixed on thee alone:
   Thy name be praised on earth, on high,
      Thy will by all be done.

5 Spirit of faith, inspire
      My consecrated heart;
   Fill me with pure, celestial fire,
      With all thou hast and art.

Charles Wesley (1707–88)

794

WILDERNESS L.M.

R. S. Thatcher (1888–1957)

Unison

Verses 1—3

Verse 4, last line

The mid-night cry, 'Be-hold, I come!'

THE CALLING OF THE CHURCH

1 JESUS, I fain would find
      Thy zeal for God in me,
   Thy yearning pity for mankind,
      Thy burning charity.

2 In me thy Spirit dwell;
      In me thy mercies move:
   So shall the fervour of my zeal
      Be thy pure flame of love.

Charles Wesley (1707–88)

796

BETHANY 8.7.8.7.D.

Henry Smart (1813–79)

For this tune in a lower key see No. 653

THE CALLING OF THE CHURCH

1 LORD of light, whose name shines brighter
  Than all stars and suns of space,
Deign to make us your co-workers
  In the kingdom of your grace;
Use us to fulfil your purpose
  In the gift of Christ your Son:
    Father, as in highest heaven,
    So on earth your will be done.

2 By the toil of lonely workers
  In some far-outlying field,
By the courage where the radiance
  Of the cross is still revealed,
By the victories of meekness
  Through reproach and suffering won:

3 Grant that knowledge, still increasing,
  At your feet may lowly kneel;
With your grace our triumphs hallow,
  With your charity our zeal;
Lift the nations from the shadows
  To the gladness of the sun:

4 By the prayers of faithful watchers,
  Never-ceasing day or night;
By the cross of Jesus, bringing
  Peace to all, and healing light;
By the love that passes knowledge,
  Making all your children one:

Howell Elvet Lewis (1860–1953) alt.

797

CLIFF TOWN 10 10.10 10.

Erik Routley (1917–82)

Unison or Harmony

1 LORD of all good, our gifts we bring to thee:
    Use them thy holy purpose to fulfil;
Tokens of love and pledges they shall be
    That our whole life is offered to thy will.

2 We give our mind to understand thy ways;
    Hands, eyes, and voice to serve thy great design;
Heart with the flame of thine own love ablaze,
    Till for thy glory all our powers combine.

3 Father, whose bounty all creation shows,
    Christ, by whose willing sacrifice we live,
Spirit, from whom all life in fullness flows,
    To thee with grateful hearts ourselves we give.

Albert F. Bayly (1901-84)

THE CALLING OF THE CHURCH

798

ZU MEINEM HERRN   11.10.11.10.   Johann Gottfried Schicht (1753–1823)

1 O LOVING Lord, who art for ever seeking
   Those of thy mind, intent to do thy will,
Strong in thy strength, thy power and grace bespeaking,
   Faithful to thee, through good report and ill—

2 To thee we come, and humbly make confession,
   Faithless so oft, in thought and word and deed,
Asking that we may have, in true possession,
   Thy free forgiveness in the hour of need.

3 In duties small be thou our inspiration,
   In large affairs endue us with thy might;
Through faithful service cometh full salvation;
   So may we serve, thy will our chief delight,

4 Not disobedient to the heavenly vision,
   Faithful in all things, seeking not reward;
Then, following thee, may we fulfil our mission,
   True to ourselves, our neighbours, and our Lord.

William Vaughan Jenkins (1868–1920)

Witness and Service

799(i)

WORSLEY 88.88.88

Melody by J. Howgate
in his *Sacred Music* (*c.* 1820)
Arranged by C. L. Fouvy (1928-)

THE CALLING OF THE CHURCH

1 MY heart is full of Christ, and longs
  Its glorious matter to declare!
Of him I make my loftier songs,
  I cannot from his praise forbear;
My ready tongue makes haste to sing
The glories of my heavenly King.

2 Fairer than all the earth-born race,
  Perfect in comeliness thou art;
Replenished are thy lips with grace,
  And full of love thy tender heart:
God ever blest! We bow the knee,
And own all fullness dwells in thee.

3 Gird on thy thigh the Spirit's sword,
  And take to thee thy power divine;
Stir up thy strength, almighty Lord,
  All power and majesty are thine:
Assert thy worship and renown;
O all-redeeming God, come down!

4 Come, and maintain thy righteous cause,
  And let thy glorious toil succeed;
Dispread the victory of thy cross,
  Ride on, and prosper in thy deed;
Through earth triumphantly ride on,
And reign in every heart alone.

Charles Wesley (1707–88)

799(ii)

TALBOT HOUSE (TOC H) 88.88.88. Martin Shaw (1875–1958)

Small notes organ only

THE CALLING OF THE CHURCH

1 MY heart is full of Christ, and longs
     Its glorious matter to declare!
  Of him I make my loftier songs,
     I cannot from his praise forbear;
  My ready tongue makes haste to sing
  The glories of my heavenly King.

2 Fairer than all the earth-born race,
     Perfect in comeliness thou art;
  Replenished are thy lips with grace,
     And full of love thy tender heart:
  God ever blest! We bow the knee,
  And own all fullness dwells in thee.

3 Gird on thy thigh the Spirit's sword,
     And take to thee thy power divine;
  Stir up thy strength, almighty Lord,
     All power and majesty are thine:
  Assert thy worship and renown;
  O all-redeeming God, come down!

4 Come, and maintain thy righteous cause,
     And let thy glorious toil succeed;
  Dispread the victory of thy cross,
     Ride on, and prosper in thy deed;
  Through earth triumphantly ride on,
  And reign in every heart alone.

Charles Wesley (1707–88)

800

ST MICHAEL   S.M.

From melody of 'Psalm 101'
in the *Genevan Psalter* (1551),
as adapted by William Crotch (1775-1847)

1 LORD, in the strength of grace,
  With a glad heart and free,
 Myself, my residue of days,
  I consecrate to thee.

2 Thy ransomed servant, I
  Restore to thee thine own;
 And, from this moment, live or die
  To serve my God alone.

Charles Wesley (1707–88)

801

PATER OMNIUM   88.88.88.   Henry J. E. Holmes (1852–1938)

THE CALLING OF THE CHURCH

1 O GOD, what offering shall I give
      To thee, the Lord of earth and skies?
   My spirit, soul, and flesh receive,
      A holy, living sacrifice:
   Small as it is, 'tis all my store;
   More shouldst thou have, if I had more.

2 Now, O my God, thou hast my soul,
      No longer mine, but thine I am;
   Guard thou thine own, possess it whole,
      Cheer it with hope, with love inflame;
   Thou hast my spirit, there display
   Thy glory to the perfect day.

3 Thou hast my flesh, thy hallowed shrine,
      Devoted solely to thy will;
   Here let thy light for ever shine,
      This house still let thy presence fill;
   O source of life, live, dwell, and move
   In me, till all my life be love!

4 Send down thy likeness from above,
      And let this my adorning be;
   Clothe me with wisdom, patience, love,
      With lowliness and purity,
   Than gold and pearls more precious far,
   And brighter than the morning star.

5 Lord, arm me with thy Spirit's might,
      Since I am called by thy great name;
   In thee let all my thoughts unite,
      Of all my works be thou the aim:
   Thy love attend me all my days,
   And my sole business be thy praise.

Joachim Lange (1670–1744)
tr. John Wesley (1703–91)

Witness and Service

802

LONDON (KETTERING) D.L.M.

Melody, and most of the harmony,
by John Sheeles (1688-1761)

THE CALLING OF THE CHURCH

(Small notes for Organ only)

1 O MASTER, let me walk with thee
  In lowly paths of service free;
    Teach me thy secret; help me bear
    The strain of toil, the fret of care;
  Help me the slow of heart to move
  By some clear winning word of love;
    Teach me the wayward feet to stay,
    And guide them in the homeward way.

2 Teach me thy patience; still with thee
  In closer, dearer company,
    In work that keeps faith sweet and strong,
    In trust that triumphs over wrong,
  In hope that sends a shining ray
  Far down the future's broadening way,
    In peace that only thou canst give,
    With thee, O Master, let me live!

Washington Gladden (1836–1918)

803

Melody from W. Sandys' *Christmas Carols* (1833)
(as harmonised in *The English Hymnal*, 1906)

1 TEACH me, my God and King,
     In all things thee to see,
And what I do in anything,
     To do it as for thee.

2 A man that looks on glass
     On it may stay his eye;
Or if he pleaseth, through it pass,
     And then the heaven espy.

3 All may of thee partake:
     Nothing can be so mean,
Which with this tincture, 'For thy sake',
     Will not grow bright and clean.

4 A servant with this clause
     Makes drudgery divine;
Who sweeps a room, as for thy laws,
     Makes that and the action fine.

5 This is the famous stone
     That turneth all to gold;
For that which God doth touch and own
     Cannot for less be told.

George Herbert (1593–1633)

THE CALLING OF THE CHURCH

804

HERONGATE L.M.

English traditional melody arranged by
Ralph Vaughan Williams (1872–1958)

1 THE Church of Christ, in every age
   Beset by change but Spirit-led,
Must claim and test its heritage
   And keep on rising from the dead.

2 Across the world, across the street,
   The victims of injustice cry
For shelter and for bread to eat,
   And never live until they die.

3 Then let the servant Church arise,
   A caring Church that longs to be
A partner in Christ's sacrifice,
   And clothed in Christ's humanity.

4 For he alone, whose blood was shed,
   Can cure the fever in our blood,
And teach us how to share our bread
   And feed the starving multitude.

5 We have no mission but to serve
   In full obedience to our Lord:
To care for all, without reserve,
   And spread his liberating Word.

Words reprinted by permission of
Stainer & Bell Ltd.
For permission to reproduce see p. xiii.   *F. Pratt Green* (1903–   )

May also be sung to No. 258, WAREHAM

Witness and Service

805

LAUDATE DOMINUM 10 10.11 11.

Henry J. Gauntlett (1805–76)
(harmony slightly altered)

1 THY faithfulness, Lord, each moment we find,
So true to thy word, so loving and kind;
  Thy mercy so tender to all the lost race,
  The vilest offender may turn and find grace.

2 O let me commend my Saviour to you,
I set to my seal that Jesus is true;
  You all may find favour who come at his call;
  O come to my Saviour! His grace is for all.

3 To save what was lost, from heaven he came;
Come, sinners, and trust in Jesus's name;
  He offers you pardon, he bids you be free:
  'If sin be your burden, O come unto me!'

4 Then let us submit his grace to receive,
Fall down at his feet and gladly believe;
  We all are forgiven for Jesus's sake;
  Our title to heaven his merits we take.

Charles Wesley (1707–88)

THE CALLING OF THE CHURCH

806

MOSCOW   66.4.666.4.   Melody by Felice de Giardini (1716–96)

1 WHAT shall our greeting be:
    Sign of our unity?
        'Jesus is Lord!'
    May we no more defend
    Barriers he died to end:
    Give me your hand, my friend—
        One Church, one Lord!

2 What is our mission here?
    He makes his purpose clear:
        One world, one Lord!
    Spirit of truth, descend;
    All our confusions end:
    Give me your hand, my friend—
        'Jesus is Lord!'

3 He comes to save us now:
    To serve him is to know
        Life's true reward.
    May he our lives amend,
    All our betrayals end:
    Give me your hand, my friend—
        'Jesus is Lord!'

F. Pratt Green (1903–)

Witness and Service

807

DUKE STREET L.M.

Melody, and most of the bass, from
H. Boyd's *Psalm and Hymn Tunes* (1793)
Later attributed to J. Hatton (d. 1793)

For this tune in a higher key see No. 26

THE CALLING OF THE CHURCH

1 WHAT shall we offer our good Lord,
    Poor nothings, for his boundless grace?
Fain would we his great name record
    And worthily set forth his praise.

2 Great object of our growing love,
    To whom our more than all we owe,
Open the fountain from above,
    And let it our full souls o'erflow.

3 Open a door which earth and hell
    May strive to shut, but strive in vain;
Let thy word richly in us dwell,
    And let our gracious fruit remain.

4 O multiply the sower's seed!
    And fruit we every hour shall bear,
Throughout the world thy gospel spread,
    Thy everlasting truth declare.

5 So shall our lives thy power proclaim,
    Thy grace for every sinner free;
Till all mankind shall learn thy name,
    Shall all stretch out their hands to thee.

August Gottlieb Spangenberg (1704–92)
            tr. *John Wesley* (1703–91)

808

DRESDEN (LUCERNE) 88.7.D. Melody by J. Schmidlin (1722-72)

THE CALLING OF THE CHURCH

1 BEHOLD the temple of the Lord!
  The work of God, by man abhorred,
    Appearing fair and splendid;
  Its walls are built in spite of foes,
  And though a hostile world oppose,
    The work will yet be ended.

2 A building this, not made with hands;
  On firm foundations, lo, it stands,
    For God himself has laid them;
  The workmanship of God alone,
  The rich materials all his own:
    'Twas he himself that made them.

3 He builds it for his glory's sake,
  Its solid frame no force can shake,
    Although the world despise it;
  And time, that other work destroys,
  'Gainst this in vain its power employs;
    The work of God defies it.

4 From age to age his work goes on,
  The stones collected one by one;
    Ere long it will be finished:
  And when he works his grand design,
  The temple will for ever shine
    With lustre undiminished.

Thomas Kelly (1769–1855)

809

RICHMOND C.M.

Melody by T. Haweis (1734–1820), as adapted by S. Webbe the younger (c. 1770–1843)

For this tune in a lower key (with slightly different harmony) see No. 744(ii)

DESCANT FOR VERSE 5

John Wilson

Sopranos

5 In vain the sur - ge's ang - ry__ shock,

THE CALLING OF THE CHURCH

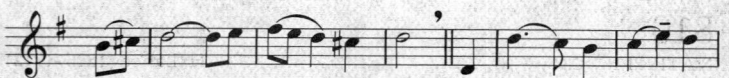

In_ vain_ the drift - ing sands: Un - harmed up - on_ th' e

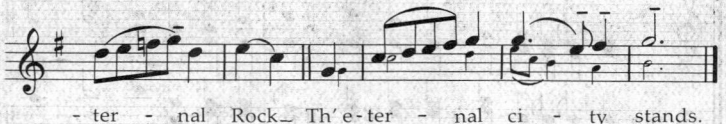

\- ter - nal Rock_ Th' e - ter - nal ci - ty stands.

(Small notes for altos, ad lib.)

1 CITY of God, how broad and far
    Outspread thy walls sublime!
The true thy chartered freemen are
    Of every age and clime—

2 One holy church, one army strong,
    One steadfast, high intent;
One working band, one harvest-song,
    One King omnipotent.

3 How purely has thy speech come down
    From man's primeval youth!
How grandly has thine empire grown,
    Of freedom, love, and truth!

4 How gleam thy watch-fires through the night
    With never-fainting ray!
How rise thy towers, serene and bright,
    To meet the dawning day!

5 In vain the surge's angry shock,
    In vain the drifting sands:
Unharmed upon the eternal Rock
    The eternal city stands.

Samuel Johnson (1822–82)

The Church Triumphant

810

H. Lahee (1826–1912)

1 COME, let us join our cheerful songs
  With angels round the throne;
Ten thousand thousand are their tongues,
  But all their joys are one.

2 'Worthy the Lamb that died,' they cry,
  'To be exalted thus!'
'Worthy the Lamb!' our lips reply,
  'For he was slain for us.'

3 Jesus is worthy to receive
  Honour and power divine;
And blessings, more than we can give,
  Be, Lord, for ever thine.

4 Let all creation join in one
  To bless the sacred name
Of him that sits upon the throne,
  And to adore the Lamb.

Isaac Watts (1674–1748)
based on Revelation 5:11–13

THE CALLING OF THE CHURCH

811

EPHRAIM 77.77. Henry Temple Leslie (*c.* 1825–76)

1 EARTH, rejoice, our Lord is King!
  Sons of men, his praises sing;
  Sing ye in triumphant strains,
  Jesus the Messiah reigns!

2 Power is all to Jesus given,
  Lord of hell, and earth, and heaven,
  Every knee to him shall bow;
  Satan, hear, and tremble now!

3 Angels and archangels join,
  All triumphantly combine,
  All in Jesu's praise agree,
  Carrying on his victory.

4 Though the sons of night blaspheme,
  More there are with us than them;
  God with us, we cannot fear;
  Fear, ye fiends, for Christ is here!

5 Lo, to faith's enlightened sight,
  All the mountain flames with light!
  Hell is nigh, but God is nigher,
  Circling us with hosts of fire.

6 Christ the Saviour is come down,
  Points us to the victor's crown,
  Bids us take our seats above,
  More than conquerors in his love.

Charles Wesley (1707–88)

The Church Triumphant

812

ST MATTHEW D.C.M.

Later form of a tune in
A Supplement to the New Version (1708)
Probably by William Croft (1678–1727)

THE CALLING OF THE CHURCH

1 COME, let us join our friends above
   That have obtained the prize,
And on the eagle wings of love
   To joys celestial rise:
Let all the saints terrestrial sing
   With those to glory gone;
For all the servants of our King,
   In earth and heaven, are one.

2 One family we dwell in him,
   One church, above, beneath,
Though now divided by the stream,
   The narrow stream of death:
One army of the living God,
   To his command we bow;
Part of his host have crossed the flood,
   And part are crossing now.

3 Ten thousand to their endless home
   This solemn moment fly;
And we are to the margin come,
   And we expect to die;
Ev'n now by faith we join our hands
   With those that went before,
And greet the blood-besprinkled bands
   On the eternal shore.

4 Our spirits too shall quickly join,
   Like theirs with glory crowned,
And shout to see our captain's sign,
   To hear his trumpet sound.
O that we now might grasp our guide!
   O that the word were given!
Come, Lord of hosts, the waves divide,
   And land us all in heaven.

Charles Wesley (1707–88)

The Church Triumphant

813
NEANDER 8.7.8.7.8.7.
Melody from
J. Neander's *Alpha und Omega* (1680)

THE CALLING OF THE CHURCH

1 COME, ye faithful, raise the anthem,
       Cleave the skies with shouts of praise;
    Sing to him who found the ransom,
       Ancient of eternal days,
    God of God, the Word incarnate,
       Whom the heaven of heaven obeys.

2 Ere he raised the lofty mountains,
       Formed the seas, or built the sky,
    Love eternal, free, and boundless,
       Moved the Lord of life to die,
    Fore-ordained the Prince of princes
       For the throne of Calvary.

3 There, for us and our redemption,
       See him all his life-blood pour!
    There he wins our full salvation,
       Dies that we may die no more;
    Then, arising, lives for ever,
       Reigning where he was before.

4 Yet this earth he still remembers,
       Still by him the flock are fed;
    Yea, he gives them food immortal,
       Gives himself, the living Bread;
    Leads them where the precious fountain
       From the smitten rock is shed.

5 Trust him, then, ye fearful pilgrims;
       Who shall pluck you from his hand?
    Pledged he stands for your salvation,
       Leads you to the promised land.
    O that we, with all the faithful,
       There around his throne may stand!

John Mason Neale (1818–66) and others
        based on *J. Hupton* (1762–1849)

814

SINE NOMINE   10 10 10.4.   Ralph Vaughan Williams (1872–1958)

Unison. Verses 1, 2, 3, 7 and 8.

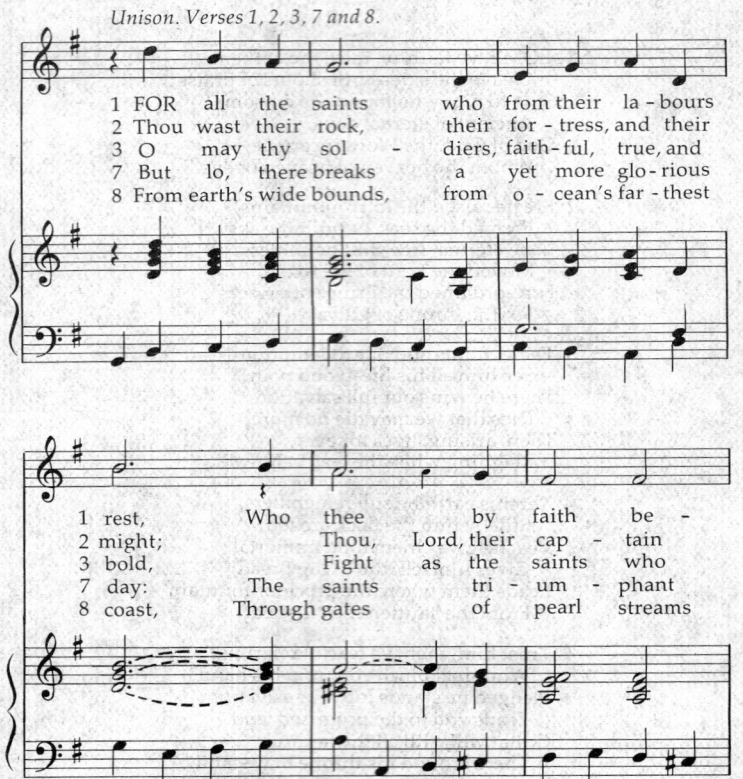

1 FOR all the saints who from their la-bours
2 Thou wast their rock, their for-tress, and their
3 O may thy sol - diers, faith-ful, true, and
7 But lo, there breaks a yet more glo-rious
8 From earth's wide bounds, from o - cean's far-thest

1 rest, Who thee by faith be -
2 might; Thou, Lord, their cap - tain
3 bold, Fight as the saints who
7 day: The saints tri - um - phant
8 coast, Through gates of pearl streams

THE CALLING OF THE CHURCH

1 -fore the world con - fessed, Thy name, O
2 in the well-fought fight; Thou in the
3 no - bly fought of old, And win, with
7 rise in bright ar - ray; The King of
8 in the count-less host, Sing - ing to

1 Je - sus, be for ev - er blest:
2 dark - ness still their one true light:
3 them, the vic-tor's crown of gold! Al -
7 Glo - ry pas - ses on his way!
8 Fa - ther, Son, and Ho - ly Ghost:

- le - lu - ia, al - le - lu - ia!

(Vv. 4-6 are overleaf)

William Walsham How (1823–97)

The Church Triumphant

Harmony. Verses 4, 5, and 6.

4 O blest com – mu – nion, fel – low-ship di – vine!
5 And when the strife is fierce, the war-fare long,
6 The gol – den eve – ning bright-ens in the west;

4 We feeb-ly strug – gle, they in glo – ry shine;
5 Steals on the ear the dis – tant tri – umph song,
6 Soon, soon to faith – ful war-riors comes their rest;

4 Yet all are one in thee, for all are thine:
5 And hearts are brave a – gain, and arms are strong; Al –
6 — Sweet is the calm of pa – ra – dise the blest:

– le-lu – ia, al – le – lu – ia!

(Turn back for vv. 7 and 8)

THE CALLING OF THE CHURCH

815(i)

Melody attributed to
J. G. Naumann (1741–1801)

1 GIVE me the wings of faith to rise
    Within the veil, and see
  The saints above, how great their joys,
    How bright their glories be.

2 Once they were mourners here below,
    And poured out sighs and tears;
  They wrestled hard, as we do now,
    With sins and doubts and fears.

3 I ask them whence their victory came;
    They, with united breath,
  Ascribe their conquest to the Lamb,
    Their triumph to his death.

4 They marked the footsteps that he trod,
    (His zeal inspired their breast)
  And, following their incarnate God,
    Possess the promised rest.

5 Our glorious Leader claims our praise
    For his own pattern given;
  While the long cloud of witnesses
    Show the same path to heaven.

Isaac Watts (1674–1748)

The Church Triumphant

815(ii)

SAN ROCCO C.M.

Derek Williams (1945–)

Unison

*Optional Interlude
between verses*

THE CALLING OF THE CHURCH

1 GIVE me the wings of faith to rise
    Within the veil, and see
  The saints above, how great their joys,
    How bright their glories be.

2 Once they were mourners here below,
    And poured out sighs and tears;
  They wrestled hard, as we do now,
    With sins and doubts and fears.

3 I ask them whence their victory came;
    They, with united breath,
  Ascribe their conquest to the Lamb,
    Their triumph to his death.

4 They marked the footsteps that he trod,
    (His zeal inspired their breast)
  And, following their incarnate God,
    Possess the promised rest.

5 Our glorious Leader claims our praise
    For his own pattern given;
  While the long cloud of witnesses
    Show the same path to heaven.

Isaac Watts (1674–1748)

The Church Triumphant

816

EATINGTON C.M.

Melody and bass by William Croft (1678–1727)
Mean parts by John Wilson

(Small notes organ only)

THE CALLING OF THE CHURCH

1 HAPPY the souls to Jesus joined,
    And saved by grace alone;
Walking in all thy ways, we find
    Our heaven on earth begun.

2 The church triumphant in thy love,
    Their mighty joys we know;
They sing the Lamb in hymns above,
    And we in hymns below.

3 Thee in thy glorious realm they praise,
    And bow before thy throne,
We in the kingdom of thy grace—
    The kingdoms are but one.

4 The holy to the holiest leads;
    From hence our spirits rise,
And whoso in thy statutes treads
    Shall meet thee in the skies.

Charles Wesley (1707–88)

May also be sung to No. 383, ST LEONARD (SMART)

The Church Triumphant

817(i)

AUSTRIA   8.7.8.7.D.

Franz Joseph Haydn (1732–1809)

THE CALLING OF THE CHURCH

1 GLORIOUS things of thee are spoken,
  Zion, city of our God;
He whose word cannot be broken
  Formed thee for his own abode.
On the Rock of Ages founded,
  What can shake thy sure repose?
With salvation's walls surrounded,
  Thou mayest smile at all thy foes.

2 See! The streams of living waters,
  Springing from eternal love,
Well supply thy sons and daughters,
  And all fear of want remove;
Who can faint, while such a river
  Ever flows their thirst to assuage—
Grace, which, like the Lord, the giver,
  Never fails from age to age?

3 Saviour, if of Zion's city
  I, through grace, a member am,
Let the world deride or pity,
  I will glory in thy name.
Fading is the worldling's pleasure,
  All his boasted pomp and show;
Solid joys and lasting treasure
  None but Zion's children know.

John Newton (1725–1807)

The Church Triumphant

817(ii)
ABBOT'S LEIGH 8.7.8.7.D.

Cyril V. Taylor (1907–   )

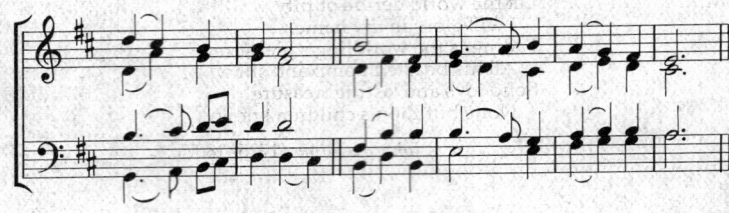

THE CALLING OF THE CHURCH

For this tune in a lower key see No. 774
(For a Descant Version of verse 3 see following page)

1 GLORIOUS things of thee are spoken,
   Zion, city of our God;
He whose word cannot be broken
   Formed thee for his own abode.
On the Rock of Ages founded,
   What can shake thy sure repose?
With salvation's walls surrounded,
   Thou mayest smile at all thy foes.

2 See! The streams of living waters,
   Springing from eternal love,
Well supply thy sons and daughters,
   And all fear of want remove;
Who can faint, while such a river
   Ever flows their thirst to assuage—
Grace, which, like the Lord, the giver,
   Never fails from age to age?

3 Saviour, if of Zion's city
   I, through grace, a member am,
Let the world deride or pity,
   I will glory in thy name.
Fading is the worldling's pleasure,
   All his boasted pomp and show;
Solid joys and lasting treasure
   None but Zion's children know.

John Newton (1725–1807)

The Church Triumphant

817(ii) (cont.)

DESCANT VERSION FOR VERSE 3

Arranged by John Wilson

3 Sa - viour, if of Zi - on's ci - ty I, — through grace, a mem - ber am, Let the world de ride or pi - ty, I will glo - ry in — thy name.

THE CALLING OF THE CHURCH

Fad - ing is___ the world - ling's plea-sure, All___ his boast - ed pomp and show; So - lid joys and last - ing trea-sure None but Zi - on's child-ren know.

The Church Triumphant

DYING STEPHEN 7.7.44.7.D.

Melody and bass by J. F. Lampe (1703–51)
(edited by John Wilson)

(with vigour)

THE CALLING OF THE CHURCH

1 HEAD of thy church triumphant,
    We joyfully adore thee;
        Till thou appear,
        Thy members here
    Shall sing like those in glory.
We lift our hearts and voices
    With blest anticipation,
        And cry aloud,
        And give to God
    The praise of our salvation.

2 The name we still acknowledge
    That burst our bonds in sunder,
        And loudly sing
        Our conquering King,
    In songs of joy and wonder.
In every day's deliverance
    Our Jesus we discover;
        'Tis he, 'tis he
        That smote the sea,
    And led us safely over!

3 While in affliction's furnace,
    And passing through the fire,
        Thy love we praise,
        Which knows our days
    And ever brings us nigher.
We clap our hands exulting
    In thine almighty favour;
        The love divine
        Which made us thine
    Shall keep us thine for ever.

4 By faith we see the glory
    To which thou shalt restore us;
        The cross despise
        For that high prize
    Which thou hast set before us.
And if thou count us worthy,
    We each, as dying Stephen,
        Shall see thee stand
        At God's right hand
    To take us up to heaven.

Charles Wesley (1707–88)

819

ABINGDON   8.8.8.8.8.8.   Erik Routley (1917–82)

THE CALLING OF THE CHURCH

1 LEADER of faithful souls, and guide
   Of all that travel to the sky,
 Come and with us, ev'n us, abide,
   Who would on thee alone rely,
 On thee alone our spirits stay,
 While held in life's uneven way.

2 We've no abiding city here,
   But seek a city out of sight;
 Thither our steady course we steer,
   Aspiring to the plains of light,
 Jerusalem, the saints' abode,
 Whose founder is the living God.

3 Through thee, who all our sins hast borne,
   Freely and graciously forgiven,
 With songs to Zion we return,
   Contending for our native heaven;
 That palace of our glorious King,
 We find it nearer while we sing.

4 Raised by the breath of love divine,
   We urge our way with strength renewed;
 The church of the first-born to join,
   We travel to the mount of God,
 With joy upon our heads arise,
 And meet our Captain in the skies.

Charles Wesley (1707–88)

May also be sung to No. 275(i), COLCHESTER

The Church Triumphant

820

1 LIFT up your hearts to things above,
   Ye followers of the Lamb,
   And join with us to praise his love
   And glorify his name.

2 To Jesu's name give thanks and sing,
   Whose mercies never end:
   Rejoice! Rejoice! The Lord is King;
   The King is now our friend!

3 Our life is hid with Christ in God;
   Our Life shall soon appear,
   And shed his glory all abroad
   In all his members here.

4 Our souls are in his mighty hand,
   And he shall keep them still;
   And you and I shall surely stand
   With him on Zion's hill.

5 Him face to face we there shall see,
   Illustrious we shall shine:
   O what a glorious company,
   When saints and angels join!

Charles Wesley (1707–88)

THE CALLING OF THE CHURCH

821

NATIVITY C.M.

H. Lahee (1826–1912)

1 SING we the song of those who stand
   Around the eternal throne,
Of every kindred, clime, and land,
   A multitude unknown.

2 Life's poor distinctions vanish here;
   Today the young, the old,
Our Saviour and his flock appear,
   One Shepherd and one fold.

3 Worthy the Lamb for sinners slain,
   Cry the redeemed above,
Blessing and honour to obtain,
   And everlasting love.

4 Worthy the Lamb, on earth we sing,
   Who died our souls to save;
Henceforth, O death, where is thy sting?
   Thy victory, O grave?

5 Then, alleluia! Power and praise
   To God in Christ be given!
May all who now this anthem raise
   Renew the strain in heaven.

James Montgomery (1771–1854)

The Church Triumphant

822(i)

MENDIP   C.M.

English Traditional Melody, collected and
adapted by Cecil Sharp (1859–1924)
Harmony by Ralph Vaughan Williams (1872–1958)

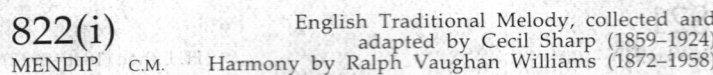

822(ii)

BEULAH   C.M.

G. M. Garrett (1834–97)

THE CALLING OF THE CHURCH

1 THERE is a land of pure delight,
   Where saints immortal reign;
Infinite day excludes the night,
   And pleasures banish pain.

2 There everlasting spring abides,
   And never-withering flowers;
Death, like a narrow sea, divides
   This heavenly land from ours.

3 Sweet fields beyond the swelling flood
   Stand dressed in living green;
So to the Jews old Canaan stood,
   While Jordan rolled between.

4 But timorous mortals start and shrink
   To cross this narrow sea,
And linger, shivering on the brink,
   And fear to launch away.

5 O could we make our doubts remove,
   Those gloomy thoughts that rise,
And see the Canaan that we love
   With unbeclouded eyes:

6 Could we but climb where Moses stood,
   And view the landscape o'er,
Not Jordan's stream, nor death's cold flood,
   Should fright us from the shore!

Isaac Watts (1674–1748)

The Church Triumphant

823

ST FULBERT C.M.

Henry J. Gauntlett (1805–1876)

After last verse

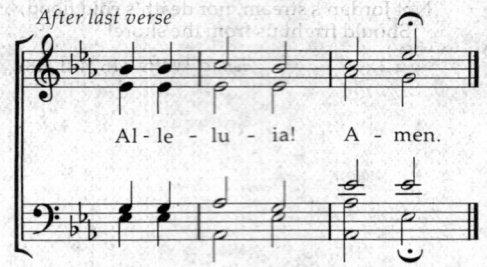

Al - le - lu - ia! A - men.

THE CALLING OF THE CHURCH

1 YE choirs of new Jerusalem,
   Your sweetest notes employ,
The paschal victory to hymn
   In strains of holy joy.

2 For Judah's lion burst his chains,
   And crushed the serpent's head;
And brought with him from death's domains
   The long-imprisoned dead.

3 From hell's devouring jaws the prey
   Alone our leader bore;
His ransomed hosts pursue their way
   Where he has gone before.

4 Triumphant in his glory now,
   To him all power is given;
To him in one communion bow
   All saints in earth and heaven.

5 While joyful thus his praise we sing,
   His mercy we implore,
Into his palace bright to bring
   And keep us evermore.

6 All glory to the Father be,
   All glory to the Son,
All glory, Holy Ghost, to thee,
   While endless ages run.
   Alleluia! Amen.

Fulbert of Chartres (d. 1028)
tr. *Robert Campbell* (1814–68) alt.

CANTICLES AND PSALMS 824—888

Canticles 824–833

:*THE ALTERNATIVE SERVICE BOOK 1980*
© The Central Board of Finance of the Church of England
© The Church of the Province of South Africa
© International Consultation on English Texts/SPCK
:827 adapted by Alan Luff from the *NEW ENGLISH BIBLE*
© Oxford University Press

Psalms 834–888

:*THE PSALMS: A NEW TRANSLATION FOR WORSHIP*
© English text 1976, 1977 David L. Frost, John A. Emerton, Andrew A. Macintosh
© Pointing 1976, 1977
Wm Collins Sons & Co. Ltd.

INTRODUCTION TO THE CANTICLES AND PSALMS

1. The canticles and psalms are set out for congregational reading. Some parts are set in bold type; these are for the congregation. Other parts are not in bold type; these are for the leader of worship. The leader should join in saying the final words with the congregation.

2. The Gloria (see below) may be said at the end of each psalm.

3. Asterisks indicate a pause; extra space between words indicates a 'mental comma'.

4. If the canticles and psalms are sung, the following indications may be noted.
    (i) The dot indicates how the syllables within a bar are to be divided when there are more than two.
    (ii) A change of chant is always indicated
    (iii) The words 'second part' indicate use of the second half of a double chant.

5. Psalm verses are numbered consecutively for ease of congregational use. They do not coincide with the biblical numeration of the psalm verses.

6. Some longer psalms are divided into sections (marked A, B or C) and may be used as independent units.

GLORIA

Glory to the Father and | to the | Son:
    and | to the | Holy | Spirit;
as it was in the be|ginning is | now:
    and shall be for | ever | A|men.

824

A SONG OF CREATION

T. A. Walmisley (1814–56)

J. L. Hopkins (1819–73)

W. Parratt (1841–1924)

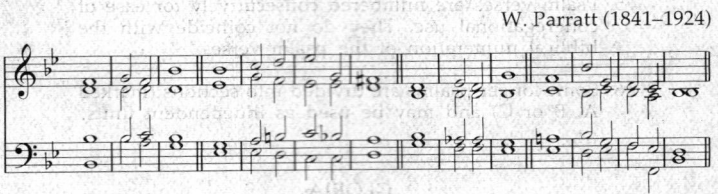

G. Thalben-Ball (1896–   )

vv. 4–17 may be omitted.

1 Bless the Lord all cre|ated | things:
   sing his | praise · and ex|alt him · for | ever.

2 **Bless the | Lord you | heavens:**
   sing his | praise · and ex|alt him · for | ever.

3 Bless the Lord you | angels · of the | Lord:
    bless the | Lord all | you his | hosts;

4 bless the Lord you waters a|bove the | heavens:
    sing his | praise · and ex|alt him · for | ever.

5 Bless the Lord | sun and | moon:
    bless the | Lord you | stars of | heaven;

6 bless the Lord all | rain and | dew:
    sing his | praise · and ex|alt him · for | ever.

7 Bless the Lord all | winds that | blow:
    bless the | Lord you |fire and | heat;

8 bless the Lord scorching wind and | bitter | cold:
    sing his | praise · and ex|alt him · for | ever.

9 Bless the Lord dews and | falling | snows:
    bless the | Lord you | nights and | days;

10 bless the Lord | light and | darkness:
    sing his | praise · and ex|alt him · for | ever.

11 Bless the Lord | frost and | cold:
    bless the | Lord you | ice and | snow;

12 bless the Lord | lightnings · and | clouds:
    sing his | praise · and ex|alt him · for | ever,

13 O let the earth | bless the | Lord:
    bless the | Lord you | mountains · and | hills;

14 bless the Lord all that | grows · in the | ground:
    sing his | praise · and ex|alt him · for | ever.

15 Bless the | Lord you | springs:
    bless the | Lord you | seas and | rivers;

16 bless the Lord you whales and all that | swim · in the | waters:
    sing his | praise · and ex|alt him · for | ever.

17 Bless the Lord all | birds · of the | air:
    bless the | Lord you | beasts and | cattle;

18 bless the Lord all | men · on the | earth:
    sing his | praise · and ex|alt him · for | ever.

19 O People of God | bless the | Lord:
    bless the | Lord you | priests · of the | Lord;

20 bless the Lord you | servants · of the | Lord:
    sing his | praise · and ex|alt him · for | ever.

21 Bless the Lord all men of | upright | spirit:
    bless the Lord you that are | holy · and | humble · in | heart.

Bless the Father the Son and the | Holy | Spirit:
    sing his | praise · and ex|alt him · for | ever.

BENEDICTUS
(The Song of Zechariah)

E. Cutler (1831–1916)

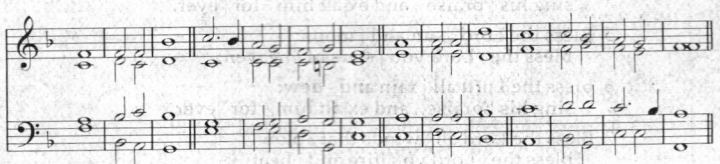

S. Elvey (1805–60)

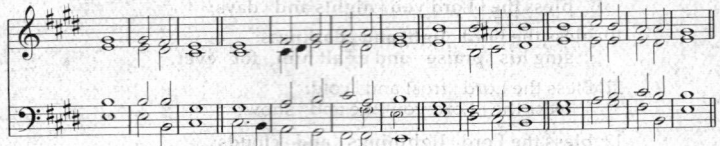

W. H. Havergal (1793–1870)

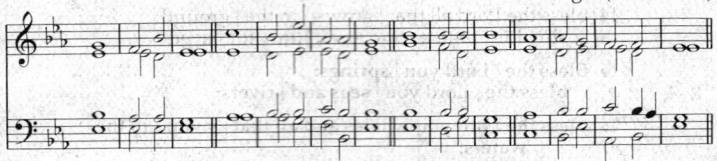

E. Day (1891–1983)

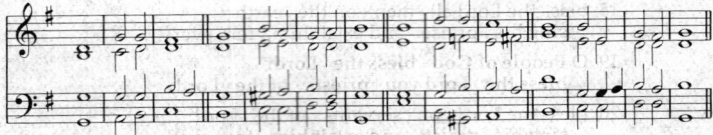

1 Blessèd be the Lord the | God of | Israel:
    for he has come to his | people · and | set them | free.

2 **He has raised up for us a | mighty | saviour:**
    born of the | house · of his | servant | David.

3 Through his holy prophets he | promised · of | old:
    that he would save us from our enemies
    from the | hands of | all that | hate us.

4 **He promised to show | mercy · to our | fathers:**
    and to re|member · his | holy | covenant.

5 This was the oath he swore to our | father | Abraham:
    to set us | free · from the | hands of · our | enemies,

6 **free to worship him with|out | fear;**
    holy and righteous in his sight | all the | days of · our | life.

7 You my child shall be called the prophet of the | Most | High:
    for you will go before the | Lord · to pre|pare his | way,

8 **to give his people knowledge | of sal|vation:**
    by the for|giveness · of | all their | sins.

9 In the tender compassion | of our | God:
    the dawn from on | high shall | break up|on us,

10 **to shine on those who dwell in darkness and the | shadow · of | death:**
    and to guide our feet | into · the | way of | peace.

Glory to the Father and | to the | Son:
    and | to the | Holy | Spirit;
as it was in the be|ginning · is | now:
    and shall be for | ever. | A|men.

MAGNIFICAT
(The Song of Mary)

J. Turle (1802–82)

W. Hawes (1785–1846)

J. Robinson (1682–1762)

G. Thalben-Ball (1896–)

1 My soul proclaims the | greatness · of the | Lord:
   my spirit re|joices · in | God my | saviour;

2 for he has looked with favour on his | lowly | servant:
   from this day all gener|ations · will | call me |
         blessèd;

3 **the Almighty has done | great things | for me:**
   and | holy | is his | name.

4 He has mercy on | those who | fear him:
   in | every | gener|ation.

5 **He has shown the | strength · of his | arm:**
   he has scattered the | proud in | their con|ceit.

6 He has cast down the mighty | from their | thrones:
   and has | lifted | up the | lowly.

7 **He has filled the hungry with | good | things:**
   and the rich he has | sent a|way | empty.

8 He has come to the help of his | servant | Israel:
   for he has re|membered · his | promise · of | mercy,

9 **the promise he | made · to our | fathers:**
   to Abraham | and his | children · for|ever.

  Glory to the Father and | to the | Son:
   and | to the | Holy | Spirit;
   as it was in the be|ginning · is | now;
   and shall be for | ever. | A|men.

A SONG OF THE INCARNATION

1 The grace of God has dawned upon the world
  with healing for all mankind.
  **The people who walked in darkness have seen a great
      light:**
  **Light has dawned upon us, dwellers in a land as dark as
      death.**
  For a boy has been born for us, a son given to us.

2 God is love; and his love was disclosed to us in this,
  that he sent his only Son into the world to bring us life.
  We know how generous our Lord Jesus Christ has been:
  he was rich, yet for our sake he became poor,
  so that through his poverty you might become rich.

3 God has spoken to us in the Son
  whom he has made heir to the whole universe.
  The Word became flesh; he came to dwell among us,
  **and we saw his glory, such glory as befits the Father's
      only Son,**
  full of grace and truth.

828

E. J. Hopkins (1818–1901)

T. Kelway (c.1695–1749)

Tonus Peregrinus

C. H. Lloyd (1849–1919)

1 Lord now you let your servant | go in | peace:
   your | word has | been ful|filled.

2 **My own eyes have | seen the sal | vation:**
   which you have prepared in the | sight of |
   every | people;

3 a light to re|veal you · to the | nations:
   and the | glory of your | people | Israel.

  Glory to the Father and | to the | Son:
   and | to the | Holy | Spirit;
  as it was in the be|ginning is | now:
   and shall be for | ever. | A|men.

SAVIOUR OF THE WORLD

C. H. H. Parry (1848–1918)

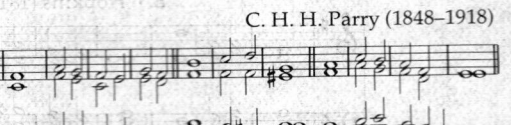

J. Goss (1800–80)

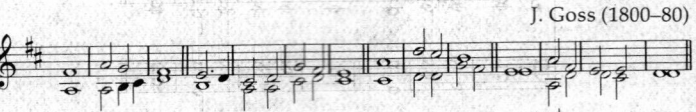

1 Jesus saviour of the world * come to us | in your | mercy:
   we look to | you to | save and | help us.

2 **By your cross and your life laid down
you set your | people | free:
we look to | you to | save and | help us.**

3 When they were ready to perish you |
saved · your dis|ciples:
   we look to | you to | come to · our | help.

4 In the greatness of your mercy loose us | from our | chains:
   forgive the | sins of | all your | people.

5 **Make yourself known as our saviour and | mighty
de|liverer:
save and | help us · that | we may | praise you.**

6 Come now and dwell with us | Lord Christ | Jesus:
   hear our | prayer · and be | with us | always.

Second part

7 **And when you | come in · your | glory:
make us to be one with you * and to | share the |
life of · your | kingdom.**

830

A SONG OF RESURRECTION

P. Humfrey (1647–74)

G. Thalben-Ball (1896–)

H. Ley (1887–1962)

G. Thalben-Ball (1896–)

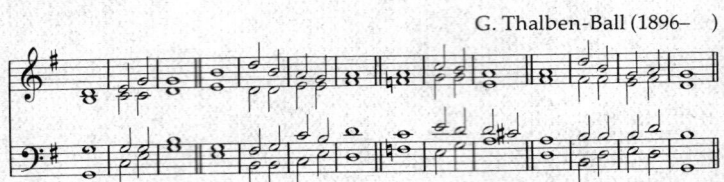

1 Christ our passover has been | sacri·ficed | for us:
  so let us | cele|brate the | feast,

2 **not with the old leaven of cor|ruption · and |
    wickedness:**
  **but with the unleavened | bread of · sin|cerity · and |
    truth.**

3 Christ once raised from the dead | dies no | more:
  death has no | more do|minion | over him.

4 **In dying he died to sin | once for | all:**
  In | living · he | lives to | God.

5 See yourselves therefore as | dead to | sin:
  and alive to God in | Jesus |Christ our | Lord.

6 **Christ has been | raised · from the | dead:**
  the | firstfruits · of | those who | sleep.

7 For as by | man came | death:
  by man has come also the resur|rection | of the | dead:

8 **for as in | Adam · all | die:**
  even so in Christ shall | all be | made a|live.

  Glory to the Father and | to the | Son:
  and | to the | Holy | Spirit;
  as it was in the be|ginning · is | now:
  and shall be for | ever | A|men.

A SONG OF CHRIST'S GLORY

1 Christ Jesus was in the form of God:
   but he did not cling to equality with God.

2 He emptied himself taking the form of a servant:
   and was born in the likeness of men.

3 Being found in human form he humbled himself:
   **and became obedient unto death even
   death on a cross.**

4 **Therefore God has highly exalted him:
   and bestowed on him the name above every name,**

5 that at the name of Jesus every knee should bow:
   in heaven and on earth and under the earth;

6 **and every tongue confess that Jesus Christ is Lord:
   to the glory of God the Father.**

   Glory to the Father and to the Son:
   and to the Holy Spirit;
   **as it was in the beginning is now:
   and shall be for ever. Amen.**

832

GREAT AND WONDERFUL

J. Harrison (1808–71)

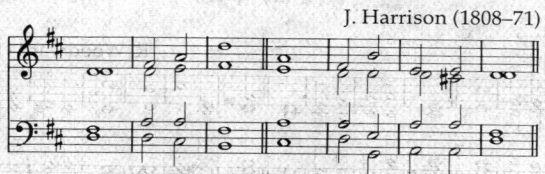

F. A. G. Ouseley (1825–89)

1 Great and wonderful are your deeds Lord |
  God · the Al|mighty:
  just and true are your | ways O | King · of the | nations.

2 Who shall not revere and praise your | name O | Lord?
  for | you a|lone are | holy.

3 **All nations shall come and worship | in your | presence:**
  for your just | dealings · have | been re|vealed.

4 **To him who sits on the throne | and · to the | Lamb:**
  be praise and honour glory and might
  for ever · and | ever | A|men.

833

TE DEUM
(1)

R. Woodward (1744–77)

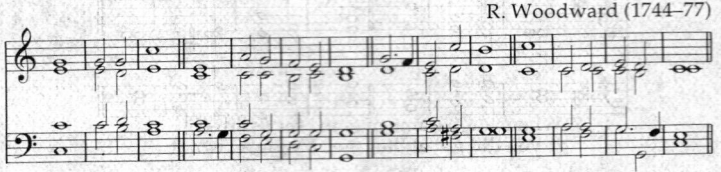

Verses 14–18 may be omitted

1 You are | God   and we | praise you:
  you are the | Lord and | we ac | claim you;

2 you are the e|ternal | Father:
  all cre|ation | worships | you.

3 To you all angels * all the | powers of | heaven:
  cherubim and seraphim | sing in | endless | praise,

4 **Holy holy holy Lord * God of | power and | might:
  heaven and | earth are | full of   your | glory.**

5 The glorious company of ap|ostles | praise you:
  the noble fellowship of prophets praise you,
  the white-robed | army · of | martyrs | praise you.

6 **Throughout the world the holy | Church ac|claims you:
  Father of | majes|ty un|bounded;**

Second part

7 **your true and only Son * worthy of | all | worship:
  and the Holy | Spirit | advocate   and | guide.**

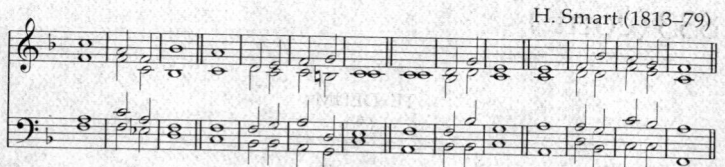

H. Smart (1813–79)

8 You Christ are the | King of | glory:
   the e|ternal | Son · of the | Father.

9 **When you became man to | set us | free:
   you did not ab|hor the | Virgin's | womb.**

10 You overcame the | sting of | death:
   and opened the kingdom of | heaven · to | all
   be|lievers.

11 **You are seated at God's right | hand in | glory:
    we believe that you will | come and | be our | judge.**

12 Come then Lord and | help your | people:
    bought with the | price of | your own | blood;

13 **and bring us | with your | saints:
    to | glory | ever|lasting.**

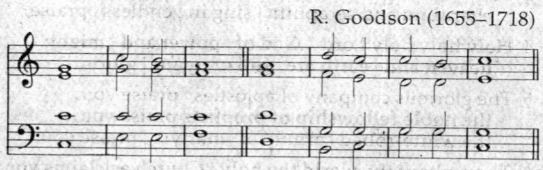

R. Goodson (1655–1718)

14 Save your people Lord and | bless · your in|heritance:
   govern and up|hold them | now and | always.

15 Day by | day we | bless you:
   we | praise your | name for | ever.

16 Keep us today Lord from | all | sin:
   have mercy | on us | Lord have | mercy.

17 Lord show us your | love and | mercy:
   for we | put our | trust in | you.

18 In you Lord | is our | hope:
   let us not be con|founded | at the | last.

TE DEUM
(2)

R. Cooke (1768–1814)

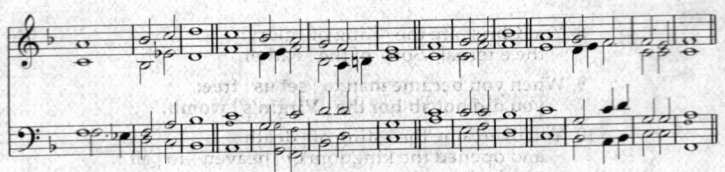

Verses 14–18 may be omitted

1 You are | God · and we | praise you:
  you are the | Lord and | we ac | claim you;

2 you are the e|ternal | Father:
  all cre|ation | worships | you.

3 To you all angels * all the | powers of | heaven:
  cherubim and seraphim | sing in | endless | praise,

4 **Holy holy holy Lord * God of | power and | might:**
  heaven and | earth are | full of · your | glory.

5 The glorious company of ap|ostles · praise you:
  the noble fellowship of prophets praise you,
  the white-robed | army · of | martyrs | praise you.

6 **Throughout the world the holy | Church ac|claims you:**
  Father of | majes|ty un|bounded;

Second part

7 **your true and only Son * worthy of | all | worship:**
  and the Holy | Spirit | advocate · and | guide.

H. Lawes (1596–1662)

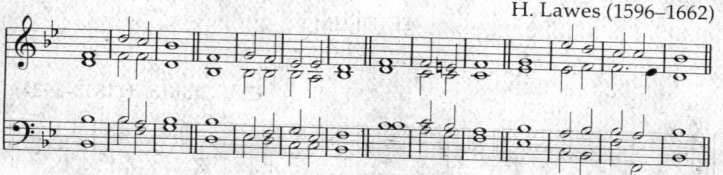

8 You Christ are the | King of | glory:
the e|ternal | Son · of the | Father.

9 **When you became man to | set us | free:**
you did not ab|hor the | Virgin's | womb.

10 You overcame the | sting of | death:
and opened the kingdom of | heaven · to | all
be|lievers.

11 **You are seated at God's right | hand in | glory:**
we believe that you will | come and | be our | judge.

12 Come then Lord and | help your | people:
bought with the | price of | your own | blood;

13 **and bring us | with your | saints:**
to | glory | ever|lasting.

H. Aldrich (1647–1710)

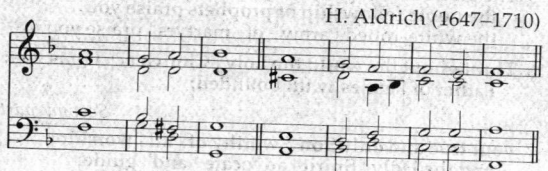

14 Save your people Lord and | bless · your in|heritance:
govern and up|hold them | now and | always.

15 Day by | day we | bless you:
we | praise your | name for | ever.

16 Keep us today Lord from | all | sin:
have mercy | on us | Lord have | mercy.

17 Lord show us your | love and | mercy:
for we | put our | trust in | you.

18 In you Lord | is our | hope:
let us not be con|founded | at the | last.

TE DEUM
(3)

C. V. Stanford (1852–1924)

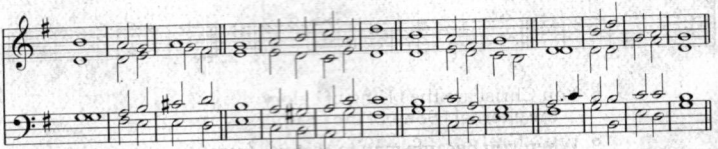

Verses 14–18 may be omitted

1 You are | God · and we | praise you:
   you are the | Lord and | we ac | claim you;

2 you are the e|ternal | Father:
   all cre|ation | worships | you.

3 To you all angels * all the | powers of | heaven:
   cherubim and seraphim | sing in | endless | praise,

4 **Holy holy holy Lord * God of | power and | might:**
   heaven and | earth are | full of · your | glory.

5 The glorious company of ap|ostles | praise you:
   the noble fellowship of prophets praise you,
   the white-robed | army · of | martyrs | praise you.

6 **Throughout the world the holy | Church ac|claims you:**
   Father of | majes|ty un|bounded;

Second part

7 **your true and only Son * worthy of | all | worship:**
   and the Holy | Spirit | advocate · and | guide.

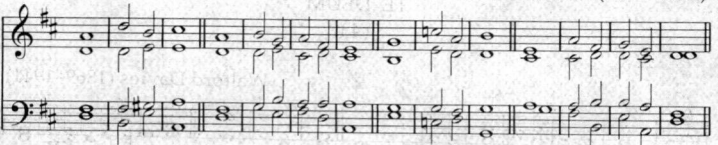

8 You Christ are the | King of | glory:
   the e|ternal | Son · of the | Father.

**9 When you became man to | set us | free:
   you did not ab|hor the | Virgin's | womb.**

10 You overcame the | sting of | death:
   and opened the kingdom of | heaven · to | all
         be|lievers.

**11 You are seated at God's right | hand in | glory:
   we believe that you will | come and | be our | judge.**

12 Come then Lord and | help your | people:
   bought with the | price of | your own | blood;

**13 and bring us | with your | saints:
   to | glory | ever|lasting.**

G. Woodward (1848–1934)

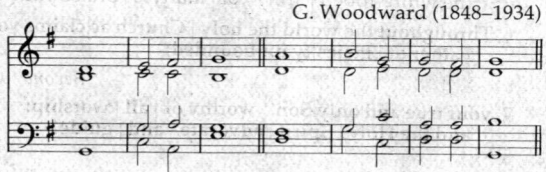

14 Save your people Lord and | bless · your in|heritance:
   govern and up|hold them | now and | always.

15 Day by | day we | bless you:
   we | praise your | name for | ever.

16 Keep us today Lord from | all | sin:
   have mercy | on us | Lord have | mercy.

17 Lord show us your | love and | mercy:
   for we | put our | trust in | you.

18 In you Lord | is our | hope:
   let us not be con|founded | at the | last.

833 (cont.)

TE DEUM
(4)

Walford Davies (1869–1941)

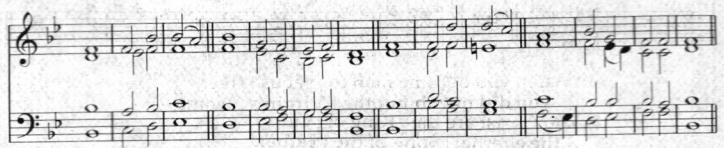

Verses 14–18 may be omitted

1 You are | God · and we | praise you:
  you are the | Lord and | we ac | claim you;

2 you are the e|ternal | Father:
  all cre|ation | worships | you.

3 To you all angels * all the | powers of | heaven:
  cherubim and seraphim | sing in | endless | praise,

4 **Holy holy holy Lord * God of | power and | might:**
  heaven and | earth are | full of · your | glory.

5 The glorious company of ap|ostles | praise you:
  the noble fellowship of prophets praise you,
  the white-robed | army · of | martyrs | praise you.

6 **Throughout the world the holy | Church ac|claims you:**
  Father of | majes|ty un|bounded;

Second part

7 **your true and only Son * worthy of | all | worship:**
  and the Holy | Spirit | advocate · and | guide.

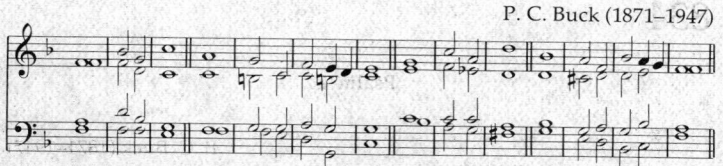

P. C. Buck (1871–1947)

8 You Christ are the | King of | glory:
   the e|ternal | Son · of the | Father.

9 **When you became man to | set us | free:**
   you did not ab|hor the | Virgin's | womb.

10 You overcame the | sting of | death:
   and·opened the kingdom of | heaven · to | all
   be|lievers.

11 **You are seated at God's right | hand in | glory:**
   we believe that you will | come and | be our | judge.

12 Come then Lord and | help your | people:
   bought with the | price of | your own | blood;

13 **and bring us | with your | saints:**
   to | glory | ever|lasting.

R. P. Stewart (1825–94)

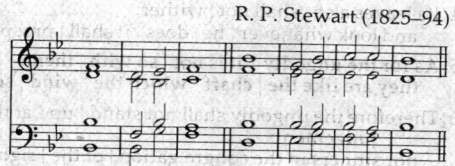

14 Save your people Lord and | bless · your in|heritance:
   govern and up|hold them | now and | always.

15 Day by | day we | bless you:
   we | praise your | name for | ever.

16 Keep us today Lord from | all | sin:
   have mercy | on us | Lord have | mercy.

17 Lord show us your | love and | mercy:
   for we | put our | trust in | you.

18 In you Lord | is our | hope:
   let us not be con|founded | at the | last.

834

Psalm 1

P. C. Buck (1871–1947)

1 Blessèd is the man
    who has not walked in the counsel | of the · un |
    godly:
  nor followed the way of sinners
    nor taken his | seat a|mongst the | scornful.

2 But his delight is in the | law · of the | Lord:
  and on that law will he | ponder | day and | night.

3 **He is like a tree planted beside | streams of | water:**
  that yields its | fruit in | due | season.

4 Its leaves also | shall not | wither:
  and look what|ever he | does · it shall | prosper.

5 **As for the ungodly * it is not | so with | them:**
  they are like the | chaff · which the | wind | scatters.

6 Therefore the ungodly shall not stand | up · at the |
    judgement:
  nor sinners in the congre|gation | of the | righteous.

  Second part

7 **For the Lord cares for the | way · of the | righteous:**
  but the | way of · the un|godly · shall | perish.

835

Psalm 4

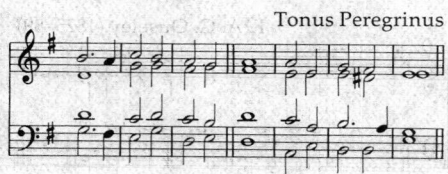

1 Answer me when I call O | God of · my | righteousness:
   when I was hard-pressed you set me free
   be gracious to me | now and | hear my | prayer.

2 Sons of men how long will you turn my | glory · to my |
   shame:
   how long will you love what is worthless
   and | seek | after | lies?

3 **Know that the Lord has shown me his | wonder ful |**
   kindness:
   when I call to the | Lord | he will | hear me.

4 Tremble and | do no | sin:
   commune with your own heart up|on your | bed · and
   be | still.

5 Offer the sacrifices | that are | right:
   and | put your | trust · in the | Lord.

6 **There are many who say 'Who will | show us · any |**
   good?:
   the light of your countenance O | Lord has | gone |
   from us.'

7 **Yet you have given my | heart more | gladness:**
   than they have when their corn | wine and | oil
   in|crease.

8 **In peace I will lie | down and | sleep:**
   for you alone Lord | make me | dwell in | safety.

See also No. 876 by J. Soaper

Psalm 8

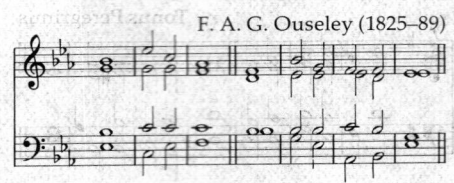

F. A. G. Ouseley (1825–89)

T. A. Walmisley (1814–56)

1 O | Lord our | Governor:
   how glorious is your | name in | all the | earth!

2 Your majesty above the heavens is | yet re|counted:
   by the | mouths of | babes and | sucklings.

Second part

3 **You have founded a strong defence**
   a|gainst your | adversaries:
   to quell the | ene·my | and · the a|venger.

4 When I consider your heavens the | work of · your |
   fingers:
   the moon and the stars which | you have | set in |
   order,

5 What is man that you should be | mindful | of him:
   or the son of | man that | you should | care for him?

6 Yet you have made him little | less · than a | god:
   and have | crowned him · with | glory · and |
   honour.

7 You have made him the | master · of your |
   handiwork:
   and have put all things in sub|jection · be|neath
   his | feet,

8 All | sheep and | oxen:
   and all the | creatures | of the | field,

9 **The birds of the air and the | fish · of the | sea:**
   and everything that moves
   in the pathways | of the | great | waters.

Second part

10 O | Lord our | Governor:
   how glorious is your | name in | all the | earth!

837

Psalm 15

T. Kelway (*c.*1695–1749)

J. Goss (1800–80)

1 Lord who may a|bide in · your | tabernacle:
   or who may dwell up|on your | holy | hill?

2 **He that leads an uncorrupt life**
      and does the | thing · which is | right:
   who speaks the truth from his heart
      and has not | slandered | with his | tongue;

3 **He that has done no evil | to his | fellow:**
   nor vented a|buse a|gainst his | neighbour;

4 In whose eyes the worthless | have no | honour:
   but he makes much of | those that | fear the | Lord;

5 **He that has | sworn · to his | neighbour:**
   and will | not go | back · on his | oath;

6 He that has not put his | money · to | usury:
   nor taken a | bribe a|gainst the | innocent.

Second part

7 **He that | does these | things:**
   shall | never · be | over|thrown.

838

Psalm 16

E. J. Hopkins (1818–1901)

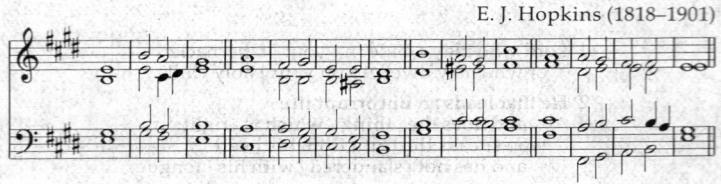

1 Preserve | me O | God:
   for in | you · have I | taken | refuge.

2 **I have said to the Lord | You are | my lord:**
   and all my | good de|pends on | you.

3 As for those who are held | holy · on the | earth:
   the other | gods · in whom | men de|light,

4 Though the idols are many that | men run | after:
   their offerings of blood I will not offer
      nor take their | name up|on my | lips.

5 **The Lord is my appointed portion | and my | cup:**
   you | hold my | lot · in your | hands.

6 The share that has fallen to me is in | pleasant |
      places:
   and a fair | land is | my pos|session.

7 **I will bless the Lord who has | given · me | counsel:**
   at night also | he · has in|structed · my | heart.

8 I have set the Lord | always · be|fore me:
   he is at my right | hand · and I | shall not | fall.

Second part

9 **Therefore my heart is glad and my | spirit · re|joices:**
   my flesh | also · shall | rest se|cure.

10 For you will not give me over to the | power of |
      death:
   nor suffer your | faithful one · to | see the | Pit.

11 **You will show me the | path of | life:**
   in your presence is the fulness of joy
      and from your right hand flow de|lights for |
      ever|more.

839

Psalm 18

R. Cooke (1768–1814)

A

1 I love you O | Lord my | strength:
   O Lord my crag my | fortress · and | my de|liverer,

2 My God · the rock to which I | come for | refuge:
   my shield my mighty saviour | and my | high
   de|fence.

Second part

3 I called to the Lord with | loud · lamen|tation:
   and I was | rescued | from my | enemies.

4 The waves of | death en|compassed me:
   and the floods of | chaos | over|whelmed me;

5 The cords of the grave | tightened · a|bout me:
   and the snares of | death lay | in my | path.

6 In my anguish I | called · to the | Lord:
   I cried for | help | to my | God.

7 From his temple he | heard my | voice:
   and my cry came | even | to his | ears.

8 He reached down from on | high and | took me:
   he drew me | out of · the | great | waters.

9 He delivered me from my | strongest | enemy:
   from my | foes · that were | mightier · than | I.

T. Hanforth (1867–1948)

B

10 He brought me out into a | place of | liberty:
and rescued me be|cause · I de|lighted · his | heart.

11 **With the faithful you | show your·self | faithful:**
with the | blameless · you | show your·self |
blameless;

12 With the | pure · you are | pure:
but with the | crooked · you | show yourself ·
per|verse.

13 **For you will save a | humble | people:**
but you bring down the | high looks | of the |
proud.

14 You light my lamp O | Lord my | God:
you make my | darkness | to be | bright.

15 **For with your help I can charge a | troop of | men:**
with the help of my God I can | leap a | city | wall.

If B and C are sung as one Psalm, Chant C by W. Parratt may be used for both sections.

W. Parratt (1841–1924)

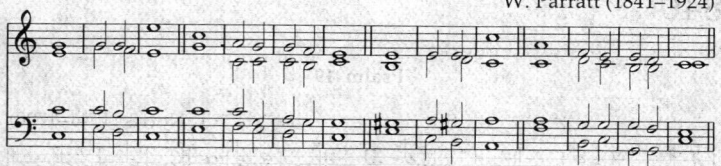

C

16 The way of our God is perfect
    the word of the Lord has been | tried · in the |
        fire:
    he is a shield to | all that | trust in | him.

17 For who is | God · but the | Lord:
    or who is our | rock | but our | God?

18 It is God that | girded me · with | strength:
    that | made my | way | perfect.

19 You gave me the shield of | your sal|vation:
    your right hand upheld me
    and your swift re|sponse has | made me | great.

Second part

20 The Lord lives   and blessèd | be my | rock:
    exalted be the | God of | my sal|vation.

Psalm 19

T. Norris (1741–1790)

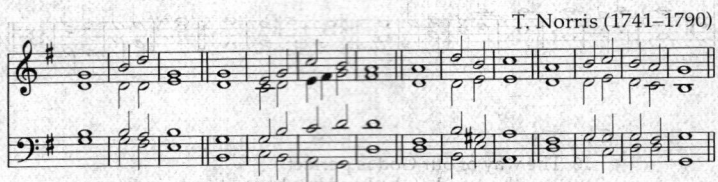

A

1 The heavens declare the | glory ⸱ of | God:
   and the | firmament ⸱ pro|claims his | handiwork;

2 One day | tells it ⸱ to an|other:
   and night to | night com|muni⸱cates | knowledge.

3 There is no | speech or ⸱ | language:
   nor | are their | voices | heard;

4 **Yet their sound has gone out through | all the | world:**
   and their | words ⸱ to the | ends ⸱ of the | earth.

5 There he has pitched a | tent ⸱ for the | sun:
   which comes out as a bridegroom from his chamber
      and rejoices like a | strong ⸱ man to | run his |
      course.

6 **Its rising is at one end of the heavens**
      and its circuit to their | farthest | bound:
   and nothing is | hidden | from its | heat.

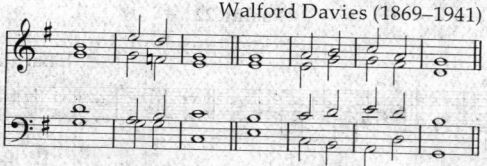

Walford Davies (1869–1941)

B

7 The law of the Lord is perfect re|viving · the | soul:
**the command of the Lord is true | and makes | wise
the | simple.**

8 The precepts of the Lord are right and re | joice the |
heart:
**the commandment of the Lord is pure | and gives |
light · to the | eyes.**

9 The fear of the Lord is clean and en|dures for | ever:
**the judgements of the Lord are unchanging
and | righteous | every | one.**

10 More to be desired are they than gold
even | much fine | gold:
**sweeter also than honey
than the | honey · that | drips · from the | comb.**

11 Moreover by them is your | servant | taught:
and in keeping them | there is | great re|ward.

12 Who can know his own un|witting | sins?:
O cleanse me | from my | secret | faults.

13 Keep your servant also from presumptuous sins
lest they get the | master·y | over me:
so I shall be clean and | innocent · of | great of|fence.

14 **May the words of my mouth and the meditation of my
heart
be acceptable | in your | sight:
O Lord my | strength and | my re|deemer.**

Psalm 22

J. Barnby (1838–96)

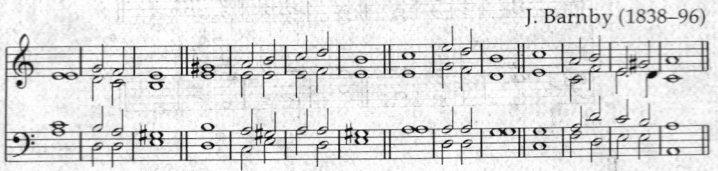

A

1 My God my God   why have | you for|saken me:
    why are you so far from helping me
      and from the | words | of my | groaning?

2 **My God I cry to you by day   but you | do not | answer:**
    and by night | also · I | take no | rest.

3 But you con|tinue | holy:
    you that | are the | praise of | Israel.

4 **In you our | fathers | trusted:**
    they | trusted · and | you de|livered them;

5 To you they cried and | they were | saved:
    they put their trust in you | and were | not
      con|founded.

6 **But as for me   I am a worm and | no | man:**
    the scorn of | men   and de|spised   by the | people.

7 All those that see me | laugh me · to | scorn:
    they shoot out their lips at me and | wag their |
      heads | saying,

8 'He trusted in the Lord | let him · de|liver him:
    let him de|liver him · if | he de|lights in him.'

Second part

9 **But you are he that took me | out of · the | womb:**
    that brought me to lie at | peace · on my | mother's |
      breast.

10 On you have I been cast | since my | birth:
    you are my God | even · from my | mother's | womb.

11 **O go not from me   for trouble is | hard at | hand:**
    and | there is | none to | help.

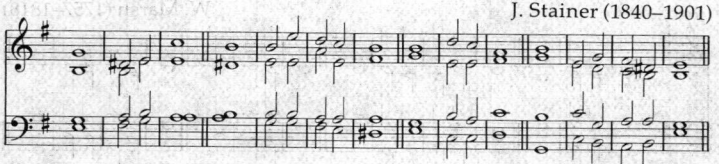

J. Stainer (1840–1901)

B

12 I am poured out like water
    and all my bones are | out of | joint:
    my heart within my | breast · is like | melting | wax.

13 **My mouth is dried | up · like a | potsherd:**
    and my | tongue | clings · to my | gums.

14 My hands and my | feet are | withered:
    and you | lay me · in the | dust of | death.

15 **For many dogs are | come a|bout me:**
    and a band of evil|doers | hem me | in.

16 I can count | all my | bones:
    they stand | staring · and | gazing up|on me.

17 **They part my | garments · a|mong them:**
    and cast | lots | for my | clothing.

18 O Lord do not | stand far | off:
    you are my helper · | hasten | to my | aid.

19 **Deliver my | body · from the | sword:**
    my | life · from the | power · of the | dogs;

20 O save me from the | lion's | mouth:
    and my afflicted soul from the | horns · of the | wild |
    oxen.

21 **I will tell of your | name · to my | brethren:**
    in the midst of the congre|gation | will I | praise you.

841 (cont.)

W. Marsh (1757–1818)

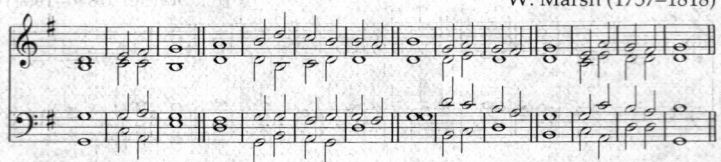

C

22 O praise the Lord all | you that | fear him:
   hold him in honour O seed of Jacob
      and let the seed of | Israel | stand in | awe of him.

23 For he has not despised nor abhorred the poor man | in
      his | misery:
   nor did he hide his face from him
      but | heard him | when he | cried.

24 From you springs my praise in the | great ·
      congre|gation:
   I will pay my vows in the | sight of | all that | fear
      you;

25 The meek shall eat of the sacrifice | and be | satisfied:
   and those who seek the Lord shall praise him
      may their | hearts re|joice for | ever!

26 Let all the ends of the earth remember and | turn · to
      the | Lord:
   and let all the families of the | nations | worship ·
      be|fore him.

27 **For the kingdom | is the | Lord's:**
   and he shall be | ruler | over · the | nations.

842

Psalm 23

T. A. Walmisley (1814–56)

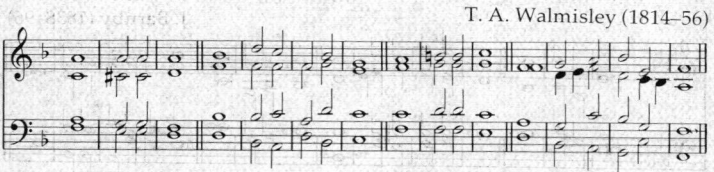

J. Goss (1800–80)

1 The Lord | is my | shepherd:
   therefore | can I | lack | nothing.

2 He will make me lie down in | green | pastures:
   and | lead me be|side still | waters.

3 He will re|fresh my | soul:
   and guide me in right pathways | for his | name's |
   sake.

4 Though I walk through the valley of the shadow of death
   I will | fear no | evil:
   for you are with me
   your | rod and your | staff | comfort me.

5 You spread a table before me
   in the face of | those who | trouble me:
   you have anointed my head with oil | and my | cup
   will be | full.

6 Surely your goodness and loving-kindness will follow
   me * all the | days of my | life:
   and I shall dwell in the | house of the | Lord for |
   ever.

843

Psalm 24

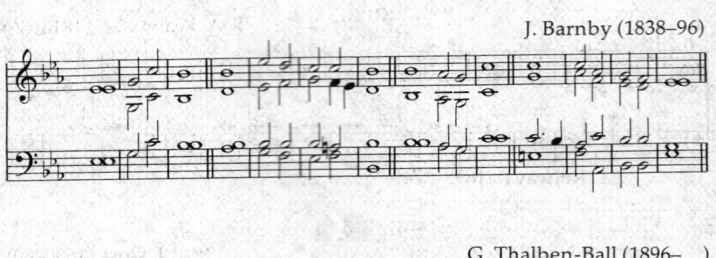

J. Barnby (1838–96)

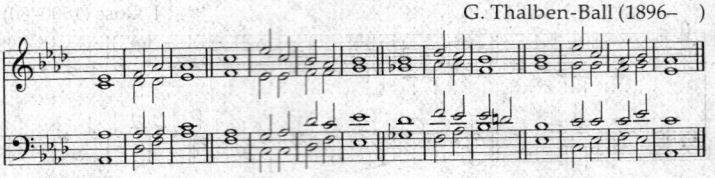

G. Thalben-Ball (1896–   )

vv. 7, 9

1 The earth is the Lord's and | all that is | in it:
   **the compass of the | world and | those who | dwell
      therein.**

2 For he has founded it up|on the | seas:
   and es|tablished it up|on the | waters.

3 Who shall ascend the | hill of the | Lord:
   or who shall | stand · in his | holy | place?

4 **He that has clean hands and a | pure | heart:
   who has not set his soul upon idols
      nor | sworn his | oath to a | lie.**

5 He shall receive | blessing from the.| Lord:
   and recompense from the | God of | his sal|vation.

6 Of such a kind as this are | those who | seek him:
   those who seek your | face O | God of | Jacob.

7 Lift up your heads O you gates
      and be lifted up you ever|lasting | doors:
   and the King of | glory | shall come | in.

8 Who is the | King of | glory?:
   **the Lord strong and mighty * the | Lord | mighty
      in | battle.**

9 Lift up your heads O you gates
      and be lifted up you ever|lasting | doors:
   and the King of | glory | shall come | in.

10 Who is the | King of | glory?:
   the Lord of hosts | he · is the | King of | glory.

Psalm 27

G. J. Elvey (1816–93)

A

1 The Lord is my light and my salvation
   whom then | shall I | fear?:
   the Lord is the stronghold of my life
   of whom | shall I | be a|fraid?

2 When the wicked even my enemies and my foes
   come upon me | to de|vour me:
   they shall | stumble | and | fall.

3 If an army encamp against me
   my heart shall | not   be a|fraid:
   and if war should rise a|gainst me | yet · will I |
   trust.

4 One thing I have asked from the Lord which I | will
   re|quire:
   that I may dwell in the house of the Lord | all the |
   days · of my | life,

Second part

5 **To see the fair | beauty · of the | Lord:**
   and to | seek his | will · in his | temple.

6 For he will hide me under his shelter in the | day of |
   trouble:
   and conceal me in the shadow of his tent
   and set me | high up|on a | rock.

7 And now he will lift | up my | head:
   above my | ene · mies | round a|bout me.

Second part

8 **And I will offer sacrifices in his sanctuary**
   with | exul|tation:
   I will sing I will sing | praises | to the | Lord.

E. J. Hopkins (1818–1901)

B

9 O Lord hear my | voice · when I | cry:
   have | mercy · up|on me · and | answer me.

10 **My heart has said of you | 'Seek his | face':**
    your | face Lord | I will | seek.

11 Do not | hide your | face from me:
    or thrust your | servant · a|side · in dis|pleasure;

12 For you have | been my | helper:
    do not cast me away or forsake me O | God of | my
    sal|vation.

13 Though my father and my | mother · for|sake me:
    the | Lord will | take me | up.

14 **Teach me your | way O | Lord:**
    and lead me in an even path | for they | lie in | wait
    for me.

                              Second part

15 Do not give me over to the | will of · my | enemies:
    for false witnesses have risen against me
    and | those who | breathe out | violence.

16 But I believe that I shall surely see the | goodness · of
    the | Lord:
    in the | land | of the | living.

17 **O wait for the Lord**
    stand firm and he will | strengthen · your |
    heart:
    and | wait I | say · for the | Lord.

845

Psalm 32

W. Russell (1777–1813)

1 Blessèd is he whose | sin · is for|given:
    whose in|iquity · is | put a|way.

**2 Blessèd is the man to whom the Lord im|putes no |
    blame:
    and in whose | spirit · there | is no | guile.**

3 For whilst I | held my | tongue:
    my bones wasted a|way · with my | daily ·
        com|plaining.

**4 Your hand was heavy upon me | day and | night:
    and my moisture was dried | up · like a | drought in |
    summer.**

5 Then I ack|nowledged · my | sin to you:
    and my in|iquity · I | did not | hide;

6 I said 'I will confess my trans|gressions · to the | Lord':
    and so you forgave the | wicked ness | of my | sin.

7 For this cause shall everyone that is faithful make his
        prayer to you * in the | day of | trouble:
    **and in the time of the great water-floods | they shall |
    not come | near him.**

8 You are a place to hide me in
        you will pre|serve me · from | trouble:
    **You will surround me with de|liverance · on|every |
    side.**

9 'I will instruct you
        and direct you in the way that | you should | go:
    I will fasten my eye up|on you · and | give you |
        counsel.

10 'Be not like horse or mule that have no |
        under|standing:
    whose forward course must be | curbed with | bit
        and | bridle.'

**11 Great tribulations remain | for the · un|godly:
    but whoever puts his trust in the Lord
        mercy em|braces him · on | every | side.**

**12 Rejoice in the Lord you righteous | and be | glad:
    and shout for joy all | you · that are | true of | heart.**

See also No. 876 by K. J. Pye

Psalm 33

G. Thalben-Ball (1896–)

1 Rejoice in the | Lord you | righteous:
   for it be|fits the | just to | praise him.

2 Give the Lord thanks up|on the | harp:
   and sing his praise to the | lute of | ten | strings.

3 O sing him a | new | song:
   make sweetest | melody · with | shouts of | praise.

4 For the word of the | Lord is | true:
   and | all his | works are | faithful.

5 He loves | righteousness · and | justice:
   **the earth is filled with the loving-|kindness | of the |
   Lord.**

6 By the word of the Lord were the | heavens | made:
   **and their numberless | stars · by the | breath of · his |
   mouth.**

7 He gathered the waters of the sea as | in a | water-skin:
   and laid up the | deep | in his | treasuries.

8 Let the whole earth | fear the | Lord:
   **and let all the inhabitants of the | world | stand in |
   awe of him.**

9 For he spoke and | it was | done:
   he commanded | and it | stood | fast.

10 The Lord frustrates the | counsels · of the | nations:
   he brings to nothing the de|vices | of the | peoples.

11 But the counsels of the Lord shall en|dure for | ever:
   **the purposes of his heart from gener|ation · to |
   gener|ation.**

12 **Blessèd is that nation whose | God · is the | Lord:**
   the people he chose to | be his | own pos|session.

See also No. 884 by R. Woodward

847

Psalm 34

F. A. G. Ouseley (1825–89)

A

1 I will bless the | Lord con|tinually:
  his praise shall be | always | in my | mouth.

2 Let my soul | boast · of the | Lord:
  the humble shall | hear it | and re|joice.

3 O praise the | Lord with | me:
  let us ex|alt his | name to|gether.

4 For I sought the Lord's | help · and he | answered:
  and he | freed me · from | all my | fears.

5 **Look towards him and be | bright with | joy:**
  your | faces shall | not · be a|shamed.

6 Here is a wretch who cried and the | Lord | heard him:
  and | saved him · from | all his | troubles.

7 **The angel of the Lord encamps round | those who | fear**
  him:
  and de|livers · them | in their | need.

8 O taste and see that the | Lord is | good:
  happy the | man who | hides in | him!

9 Fear the Lord all | you his | holy ones:
  for those who | fear him | never | lack.

10 Lions may suffer | want · and go | hungry:
  but those who seek the | Lord lack | nothing | good.

See also No. 879 by C. F. South

E. Higgins (d.1769)

B

11 Come my children | listen · to | me:
   and I will | teach you   the | fear · of the | Lord.

12 Which of you | relish·es | life:
   wants | time · to en|joy good | things?

13 Keep your | tongue from | evil:
   and your | lips from | telling | lies.

14 Turn from evil and | do | good:
   seek | peace | and pur|sue it.

15 **The eyes of God are | on the | righteous:**
   and his | ears to|wards their | cry.

16 **The Lord sets his face against | wrong|doers:**
   to root out their | memo ry | from the | earth.

17 **The righteous cry   the | Lord | hears it:**
   and | frees them   from | all   their af|flictions.

18 **The Lord is close to those who are | broken-|hearted:**
   and the | crushed in | spirit   he | saves.

Psalm 40

H. Aldrich (1647–1710)

A

1 I waited patiently | for the | Lord:
   and he in|clined to me · and | heard my | cry.

2 He brought me up from the pit of roaring waters
      out of the | mire and | clay:
   **and set my feet upon a | rock · and made | firm my
   | foothold.**

3 And he has put a new | song · in my | mouth:
   even a song of | thanks·giving | to our | God.

4 Many shall | see it · and | fear:
   and shall | put their | trust · in the | Lord.

5 Blessèd is the man who has made the | Lord his |
   hope:
   who has not turned to the proud
     or to those who | wander | in de|ceit.

6 **O Lord my God**
   **great are the wonderful things which you have
     done**
   **and your thoughts which | are to|wards us:
   there is none to | be com|pared with | you;**

7 Were I to de|clare them · and | speak of them:
   they are more than I am | able | to ex|press.

8 **Sacrifice and offering you do | not de|sire:
   but my | ears · you have | marked · for o|bedience;**

9 Burnt-offering and sin-offering you have | not
   re|quired:
   then | said I | Lo I | come.

10 **In the scroll of the book it is written of me
     that I should | do your | will:
   O my God I long to do it** * **your | law de|lights my |
   heart.**

11 I have declared your righteousness in the | great ·
     congre|gation:
   **I have not restrained my lips O | Lord and | that
   you | know.**

12 I have not hidden your righteousness | in my | heart:
    I have spoken of your faithfulness | and of | your
    sal|vation.

Second part

**13 I have not kept back your loving-kindness | and
    your | truth:
    from the | great | congre|gation.**

G. Thalben-Ball (1896–)

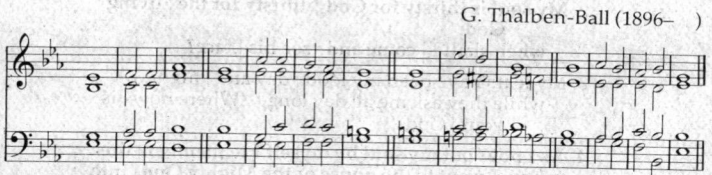

B

  14 O Lord do not withhold your | mercy | from me:
     let your loving-kindness and your | truth | ever ·
     pre|serve me.

  **15 For innumerable troubles have | come up|on me:
     my sins have overtaken me | and I | cannot | see.**

  16 They are more in number than the | hairs · of my |
     head:
     there|fore my | heart | fails me.

  **17 Be pleased O | Lord to de|liver me:
     O | Lord make | haste to | help me.**

  18 Let those who seek my life to | take it a|way:
     be put to shame and con|founded | alto|gether.

  **19 Let all who seek you be joyful and \ glad be\cause of
     you:
     let those who love your salvation say | always
     'The | Lord is | great.'**

  20 As for me I am | poor and | needy:
     but the | Lord will | care | for me.

  **21 You are my helper and | my de | liverer:
     make no long de|lay O | Lord my | God.**

849

Psalms 42 and 43

L. L. Dix (1861–1935)

A

1 As a deer longs for the | running | brooks:
    so longs my | soul for | you O | God.

2 **My soul is thirsty for God * thirsty for the | living |
    God:
    when shall I | come and | see his | face?**

3 My tears have been my food | day and | night:
    while they ask me all day long | 'Where now | is
    your | God?'

4 **As I pour out my soul by myself I re|member | this:
    how I went to the house of the Mighty One | into
    the | temple · of | God,**

Second part

5 **To the shouts and | songs of * thanks|giving:
    a multitude | keeping | high | festival.**

W. Crotch (1775–1847)

6 Why are you so full of | heaviness · my | soul:
    and | why · so un|quiet · with|in me?

7 **O put your | trust in | God:
    for I will *praise him yet*
        who is my de|liver · er | and my | God.**

L. L. Dix (1861–1935)

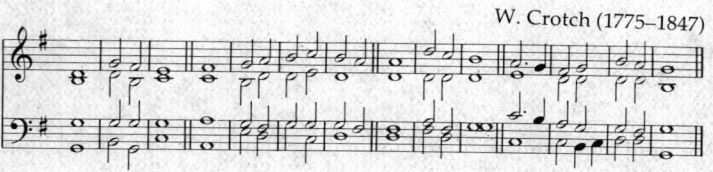

B

8 Give judgement for me O God
   take up my cause against an un|godly | people:
   deliver me from de|ceitful · and | wicked | men.

9 **For you are God my refuge | why have you | turned ·
   me a|way:
   why must I go like a mourner be|cause the | enemy ·
   op|presses me?**

10 O send out your light and your truth and | let them |
    lead me:
    **let them guide me to your holy | hill and | to your |
    dwelling.**

11 Then I shall go to the altar of God
    to God my joy and | my de | light:
    **and to the harp I shall sing your | praises · O | God
    my | God.**

W. Crotch (1775–1847)

12 Why are you so full of | heaviness · my | soul:
    and | why · so un|quiet · with|in me?

13 **O put your | trust in | God:
    for I will praise him yet
    who is my de|liver er | and my | God.**

850

Psalm 46

G. A. Macfarren (1813–87)

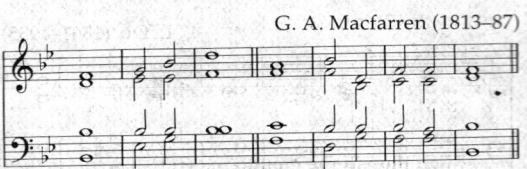

from M. Luther's *Ein' Feste Burg* (1529)

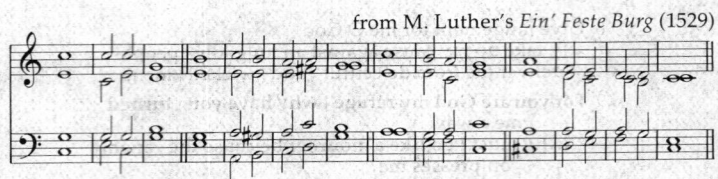

1 God is our | refuge · and | strength:
    a very | present | help in | trouble.

2 Therefore we will not fear though the | earth be |
      moved:
    and though the mountains are | shaken · in the |
      midst · of the | sea;

Second part

3 Though the waters | rage and | foam:
    and though the mountains quake at the | rising | of
    the | sea.

4 There is a river whose streams make glad the | city ·
      of | God:
    the holy dwelling-place | of the | Most | High.

5 **God is in the midst of her**
    therefore she shall | not be | moved:
    God will | help her · and at | break of | day.

6 The nations make uproar and the | kingdoms · are |
      shaken:
    but God has lifted his | voice · and the | earth shall
      | tremble.

7 **The Lord of | hosts is | with us:**
    the God of | Jacob | is our | stronghold.

8 Come then and see what the | Lord has | done:
    what destruction he has | brought up|on the |
      earth.

9 **He makes wars to cease in | all the | world:**
    he breaks the bow and shatters the spear
    and burns the | chari·ots | in the | fire.

10 'Be still and know that | I am | God:
    I will be exalted among the nations
    I will be ex|alted · up|on the | earth.'

11 **The Lord of | hosts is | with us:**
    the God of | Jacob | is our | stronghold.

851

Psalm 47

W. Russell (1777–1813)

1 O clap your hands | all you | peoples:
   and cry aloud to | God with | shouts of | joy.

2 **For the Lord Most High | is to · be | feared:**
   he is a great | King · over | all the | earth.

3 He cast down | peoples | under us:
   and the | nations · be|neath our | feet.

4 **He chose us a land for | our pos|session:**
   that was the pride of | Jacob | whom he | loved.

5 God has gone up with the | sound · of re|joicing:
   and the | Lord · to the | blast · of the | horn.

6 **O sing praises sing | praises · to | God:**
   O sing praises sing | praises | to our | King.

7 For God is the King of | all the | earth:
   O | praise him · in a | well-wrought | psalm.

8 **God has become the | King · of the | nations:**
   he has taken his seat up|on his | holy | throne.

9 The princes of the peoples are | gathered · to|gether:
   with the | people · of the | God of | Abraham.

10 **For the mighty ones of the earth are become the |**
   servants · of | God:
   and | he is | greatly · ex|alted.

852

Psalm 51

Walford Davies (1869–1941) from F. Schubert

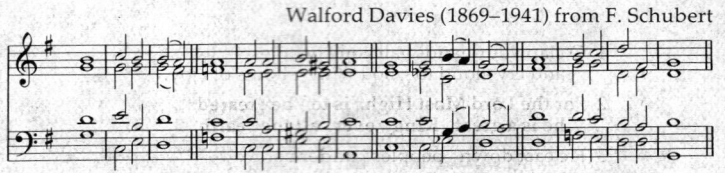

M. Camidge (1758–1844)

1 Have mercy on me O God in your en|during |
      goodness:
  according to the fulness of your compassion | blot
    out | my of|fences.

2 Wash me thoroughly | from my | wickedness:
  and | cleanse me | from my | sin.

3 For I acknowledge | my re|bellion:
  and my | sin is | ever · be|fore me.

4 Against you only have I sinned
      and done what is evil | in your | eyes:
  so you will be just in your sentence
    and | blameless | in your | judging.

5 Create in me a clean | heart O | God:
  and re|new a · right | spirit | with|in me.

6 Do not cast me | out · from your | presence:
  do not take your | holy | spirit | from me.

7 O give me the gladness of your | help a|gain:
  and sup|port me · with a | willing | spirit.

8 Then will I teach trans|gressors · your | ways:
  and sinners shall | turn to | you a|gain.

9 O Lord God of my salvation de|liver me · from |
      bloodshed:
  and my | tongue shall | sing of · your | righteousness.

10 O Lord | open · my | lips:
  and my | mouth · shall pro|claim your | praise.

11 You take no pleasure in sacrifice or | I would | give it:
  burnt-|offerings · you | do not | want.

12 The sacrifice of God is a | broken | spirit:
  a broken and contrite heart O God | you will | not
    de|spise.

853

Psalm 63

J. Battishill (1738–1801)

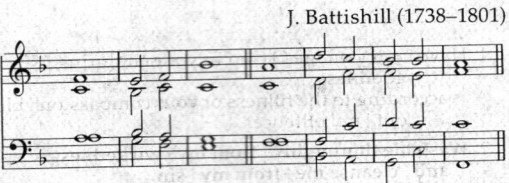

1 O God | you are · my | God:
    eagerly | will I | seek | you.

2 **My soul thirsts for you my | flesh | longs for you:**
    as a dry and thirsty | land · where no | water | is.

3 So it was when I beheld you | in the | sanctuary:
    and | saw your | power · and your | glory.

4 **For your unchanging goodness is | better · than | life:**
    there|fore my | lips shall | praise you.

5 And so I will bless you as | long as · I | live:
    and in your name will I | lift my | hands on | high.

6 **My longing shall be satisfied as with | marrow · and**
    | fatness:
    my mouth shall | praise you · with ex|ultant | lips.

7 When I remember you up|on my | bed:
    when I meditate up|on you · in the | night |
    watches,

8 How you have | been my | helper:
    then I sing for joy in the | shadow | of your | wings,

9 **Then my | soul | clings to you:**
    and | your right | hand up|holds me.

854

Psalm 65

C. V. Stanford (1852–1924)

1 You are to be praised O | God in | Zion:
   to you shall vows be paid | you that | answer | prayer.

2 **To you shall all flesh come to con|fess their | sins:**
   when our misdeeds prevail against us | you will |
   purge   them a|way.

Second   part

3 Blessèd is the man whom you choose
   and take to yourself to dwell with|in your |
   courts:
   we shall be filled with the good things of your
   house | of your | holy | temple.

4 You will answer us in your righteousness with
   terrible deeds O | God our | saviour:
   you that are the hope of all the ends of the earth
   and | of the | distant | seas;

5 Who by your strength made | fast the | mountains:
   you | that are | girded · with | power;

6 Who stilled the raging of the seas the | roaring · of
   the | waves:
   and the | tumult | of the | peoples.

7 **Those who dwell at the ends of the earth are a|fraid**
   at · your | wonders:
   the dawn and the | even·ing | sing your | praises.

8 You tend the | earth and | water it:
   you | make it · rich and | fertile.

9 **The river of God is | full of | water:**
   and so providing for the earth you pro|vide | grain
   for | men.

10 You drench its furrows · you level the | ridges ·
   be|tween:
   you soften it with showers and | bless its | early |
   growth.

11 **You crown the | year · with your | goodness:**
   and the tracks where you have | passed | drip
   with | fatness.

12 The pastures of the | wilderness · run | over:
   and the | hills are | girded · with | joy.

13 **The meadows are | clothed with | sheep:**
   and the valleys stand so thick with corn they |
   shout for | joy and | sing.

855

Psalm 67

S. Wesley (1766–1837)

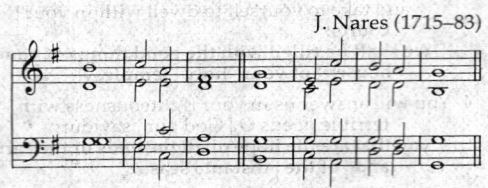

J. Nares (1715–83)

1 Let God be gracious to | us and | bless us:
  and make his | face | shine up|on us,

2 That your ways may be | known on | earth:
  your liberating | power a|mong all | nations.

3 Let the peoples | praise you O | God:
  let | all the | peoples | praise you.

4 Let the nations be | glad and | sing:
  for you judge the peoples with integrity
  and govern the | nations up|on | earth.

5 Let the peoples | praise you O | God:
  let | all the | peoples | praise you.

6 Then the earth will | yield its | fruitfulness:
  and | God our | God will | bless us.

Second part

7 God | shall | bless us:
  and all the | ends of the | earth will | fear him.

Psalm 69

L. Flintoft (1678–1727)

W. Morley (c.1680–1721)

1 Save | me O | God:
    for the waters have come up | even | to my | throat.

2 **I sink in the deep mire | where no | footing is:**
    I have come into deep waters | and the | flood
        sweeps | over me.

3 I am weary with crying out my | throat is | parched:
    my eyes fail with | watching · so | long · for my |
        God.

4 **Those that hate me without cause**
    are more in number than the | hairs · of my | head:
    those that would destroy me are many
      they oppose me wrongfully
      for I must restore | things · that I | never | took.

Second part

5 **O God you | know my | foolishness:**
    and my | sins · are not | hidden | from you.

6 Let not those who wait for you be shamed because of
    me
      O Lord | God of | hosts:
    let not those who seek you be disgraced on | my
      account · O | God of | Israel.

7 For your sake have I | suffered · re|proach:
    and | shame has | covered · my | face.

8 **I have become a stranger | to my | brothers:**
    an alien | to my · own | mother's | sons.

9 Zeal for your house has | eaten · me | up:
    and the taunts of those who taunt | you have | fallen
      on | me.

857

Psalm 72

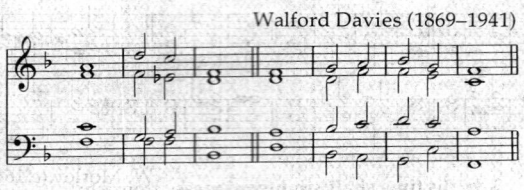

Walford Davies (1869–1941)

F. A. G. Ouseley (1825–89)

1 Give the king your | judgement · O | God:
   and your righteousness to the | son | of a | king.

2 May he come down like rain upon the | new-mown |
      fields:
   and as | showers · that | water · the | earth.

3 **In his time shall | righteous·ness | flourish:**
   and abundance of peace till the | moon shall | be
      no | more.

4 The kings of Tarshish and of the isles shall | bring |
      tribute:
   the kings of Sheba and | Seba · shall | offer | gifts.

5 **All kings shall fall | down be|fore him:**
   and all | nations | do him | service.

6 He will deliver the needy | when they | cry:
   and the | poor man · that | has no | helper.

7 **He will pity the helpless | and the | needy:**
   and | save the | lives · of the | poor.

8 He will redeem them from op|pression · and |
      violence:
   and their blood shall be | precious | in his | sight.

9 **Let his name | live for | ever:**
   and en|dure as | long · as the | sun.

10 Let all peoples use his | name in | blessing:
   and all | nations | call him | blessèd.

858

Psalm 77

J. Stainer (1840–1901)

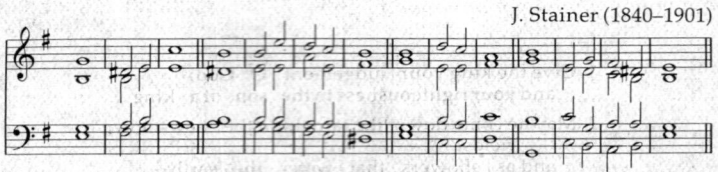

1 I call to my God I cry | out to|ward him:
    I call to my God and | surely | he will | answer.

2 In the day of my distress I seek the Lord
        I stretch out my hands to | him by | night:
    my soul is poured out without ceasing
        it re|fuses | all | comfort.

3 I think upon God and | groan a|loud:
    I | muse and my | spirit | faints.

4 And I say * 'Has the right hand of the Most High |
        lost its | strength:
    has the | arm of the | Lord | changed?'

5 'Is his mercy clean | gone for | ever:
    and his promise come to an | end for | all
        gener|ations?

6 **'Has God for|gotten to be | gracious:**
    has he shut up his | pity | in dis|pleasure?'

C. V. Stanford (1852–1924)

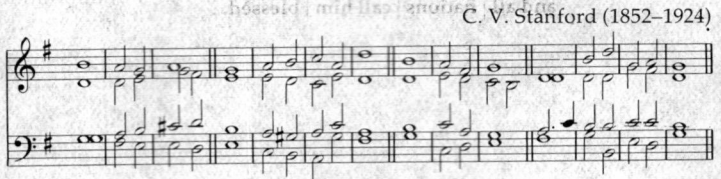

7 I will declare the mighty | acts · of the | Lord:
    I will call to | mind your | wonders · of | old.

8 I will think on all that | you have | done:
    and | meditate · up|on your | works.

9 Your way O | God is | holy:
    who is so | great a | god as | our God?

10 You are the God that | works | wonders:
    you made known your | power a|mong the | nations;

PSALMS

11 By your mighty arm you re|deemed your | people:
the | children · of | Jacob · and | Joseph.

12 The waters saw you O God
the waters saw you and | were a|fraid:
the | depths | also · were | troubled.

13 The clouds poured out water · the | heavens | spoke:
and your | arrows | darted | forth.

14 The voice of your thunder was | heard · in the |
whirlwind:
your lightnings lit the world
the | earth | shuddered · and | quaked.

15 Your way was in the sea * your path in the | great |
waters:
and your | footsteps | were not | seen.

16 **You led your | people · like | sheep:
by the | hand of | Moses · and | Aaron.**

859

Psalm 80

J. L. Hopkins (1819–73)

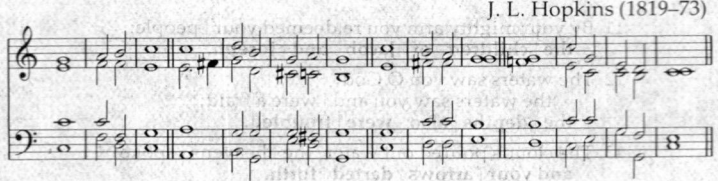

A

1 Hear O Shepherd of Israel
   you that led | Joseph · like a | flock:
   you that are enthroned upon the cherubim | shine |
   out in | glory;

2 Before Ephraim Benjamin | and Man|asseh:
   stir up your | power and | come to | save us.

Second part

3 **Restore us again O | Lord of | Hosts:**
   show us the light of your countenance | and we |
   shall be | saved.

4 O Lord | God of | hosts:
   how long will you be | angry · at your | people's |
   prayer?

5 You have fed them with the | bread of | tears:
   and given them tears to | drink in | good | measure.

6 **You have made us the victim | of our | neighbours:**
   and our | ene·mies | laugh us · to | scorn.

7 **Restore us again O | Lord of | hosts:**
   show us the light of your countenance | and we |
   shall be | saved.

See also No. 850 by M. Luther

G. Thalben-Ball (1896–   )

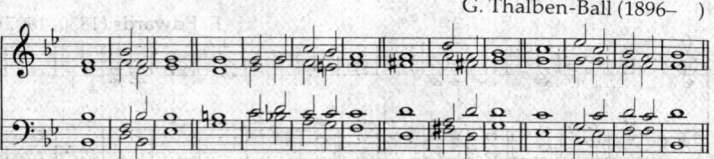

B

8 You brought a | vine · out of | Egypt:
　　you drove out the | nations · and | planted · it | in.

9 **You cleared the | ground be|fore it:**
　　and it struck | root and | filled the | land.

10 The hills were | covered · with its | shadow:
　　and its boughs were like the | boughs · of the |
　　　great | cedars.

11 **It stretched out its | branches · to the | sea:**
　　and its tender | shoots · to the | Great | River.

12 Why then have you broken | down its | walls:
　　so that every passer-|by can | pluck its | fruit?

13 **The wild boar out of the woods | roots it | up:**
　　and the locusts from the | wild | places · de|vour it.

14 Turn to us again O | Lord of | hosts:
　　look | down from | heaven · and | see.

15 **Bestow your care up|on this | vine:**
　　the stock which your | own right | hand has |
　　　planted.

16 As for those that burn it with fire and | cut it | down:
　　let them perish at the re|buke · of your |
　　　countenance.

17 **Let your power rest on the man at your | right | hand:**
　　on that son of man whom you | made so | strong ·
　　　for your|self.

18 And so we shall | not turn | back from you:
　　give us life · and we will | call up|on your | name.

19 **Restore us again O | Lord of | hosts:**
　　show us the light of your countenance | and we |
　　　shall be | saved.

Psalm 84

E. Edwards (1830–1907)

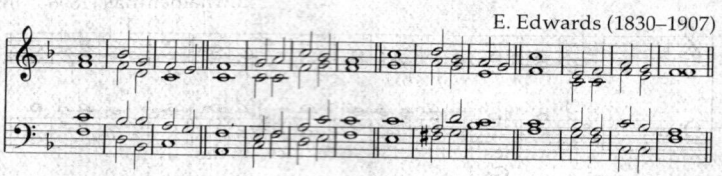

P. Henley (1728–64)

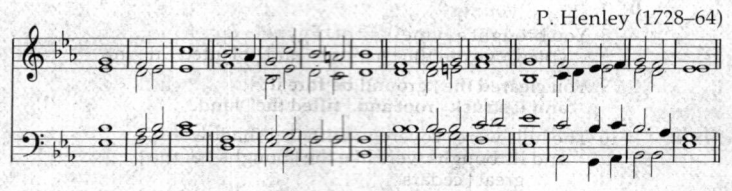

1 How lovely | is your | dwelling-place:
    O | Lord | God of | hosts!

2 **My soul has a desire and longing to enter the | courts**
    of the | Lord:
    my heart and my flesh re|joice · in the | living |
    God.

3 The sparrow has found her a home
    and the swallow a nest where she may | lay her |
    young:
    even your altar · O Lord of | hosts my | King · and
    my | God.

4 Blessèd are those who | dwell in · your | house:
    they will | always · be | praising | you.

5 Blessèd is the man whose | strength · is in | you:
    in whose | heart · are the | highways · to | Zion;

6 Who going through the valley of dryness
    finds there a spring from | which to | drink:
    till the autumn | rain shall | clothe it · with |
    blessings.

Second part

7 **They go from | strength to | strength:**
    they appear every one of them before the | God of |
    gods in | Zion.

8 O Lord God of hosts | hear my | prayer:
    give | ear O | God of | Jacob.

9 **Behold O God | him who · reigns | over us:**
    and look upon the | face of | your a|nointed.

10 One day in your courts is | better · than a | thousand:
    I would rather stand at the threshold of the house
    of my God
    than | dwell · in the | tents of · un|godliness.

11 For the Lord God is a rampart and a shield
    the Lord gives | favour · and | honour:
    and no good thing will he withhold from | those
    who | walk in | innocence.

Second part

12 **O Lord | God of | hosts:**
    blessèd is the man who | puts his | trust in | you.

Psalm 85

S. Wesley (1766–1837)

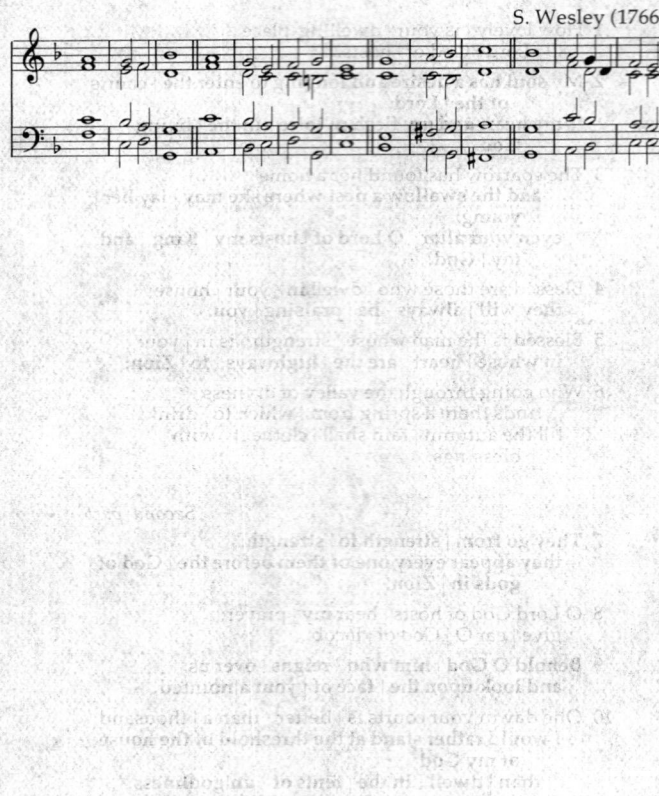

1 O Lord you were gracious | to your | land:
    you re|stored the | fortunes of | Jacob.

2 You forgave the iniquity | of your | people:
    and | covered | all their | sin.

3 Will you not give us | life a|gain:
    that your | people | may re|joice in you?

4 **Show us your | mercy O | Lord:**
    and | grant us | your sal|vation.

5 I will hear what the Lord | God will | speak:
    for he will speak peace to his people
        to his faithful ones whose | hearts are | turned to |
    him.

6 Truly his salvation is near to | those that | fear him:
    and his | glory shall | dwell in our | land.

7 Mercy and truth are | met to|gether:
    righteousness and | peace have | kissed each | other;

8 Truth shall flourish | out of the | earth:
    and righteousness | shall look | down from | heaven.

9 The Lord will also give us | all that is | good:
    and our | land shall | yield its | plenty.

10 **For righteousness shall | go be|fore him:**
    and tread the | path be|fore his | feet.

862

Psalm 86

J. Battishill (1738–1801)

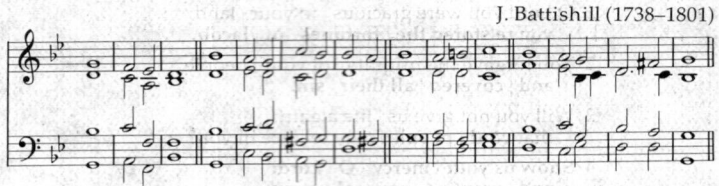

1 Incline your ear to me O | God and | answer me:
  for | I am | poor · and in | misery.

2 Preserve my life for | I am | faithful:
  my God save your servant who | puts his | trust in |
  you.

3 Be merciful to | me O | Lord:
  for I | call to · you | all the · day | long.

4 O make glad the | soul of · your | servant:
  for I put my | hope in | you O | Lord.

Second part

5 For you Lord are | good · and for|giving:
  of great and continuing kindness to | all who | call
  up|on you.

6 Hear my | prayer O | Lord:
  and give heed to the | voice · of my | suppli|cation.

7 In the day of my trouble I | call up|on you:
  for | you will | surely | answer.

J. Battishill (1738–1801)

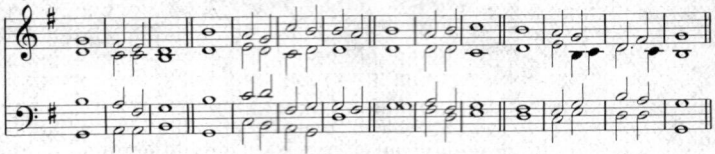

8 Among the gods there is none like | you O | Lord:
  nor are there | any | deeds like | yours.

9 All the nations you have made shall come and |
  worship · be|fore you:
  O Lord they shall | glori | fy your | name.

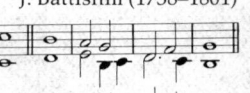
Second part

10 For you are great and do | marvel·lous | things:
  and | you a|lone are | God.

Psalm 90

J. Turle (1802–82)

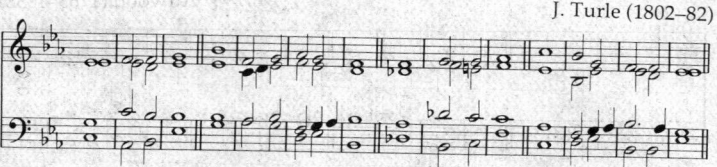

A

1 Lord you have | been our | refuge:
  from one gener|ation | to an|other.

2 **Before the mountains were born**
        or the earth and the world were | brought to |
        be:
  from eternity to e|terni·ty | you are | God.

3 You turn man | back · into | dust:
  saying 'Return to | dust you | sons of | Adam.'

4 **For a thousand years in your sight are like |**
        yester·day | passing:
  or | like one | watch · of the | night.

5 You cut them | short · like a | dream:
  like the fresh | grass | of the | morning;

6 **In the morning it is | green and | flourishes:**
  at evening it is | withered · and | dried | up.

7 And we are con|sumed · by your | anger:
  because of your indig|nation · we | cease to | be.

8 **You have brought our in|iquities · be|fore you:**
  and our secret | sins · to the | light of · your |
        countenance.

9 Our days decline be|neath your | wrath:
  and our years | pass a|way · like a | sigh.

10 The days of our life are three score years and ten
        or if we have | strength four | score:
  the pride of our labours is but toil and sorrow
        for it passes quickly a|way and | we are | gone.

11 Who can know the | power of · your | wrath:
  who can know your indig|nation · like | those that |
        fear you?

12 **Teach us so to | number · our | days:**
  that we may ap|ply our | hearts to | wisdom.

If A and B are sung as one Psalm, either Chant may be used for both sections.

863 (cont.)

T. Attwood (1765–1838)

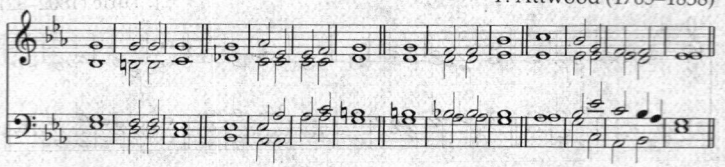

B

13 Relent O Lord * how long will | you be | angry?:
   take | pity | on your | servants.

14 O satisfy us early | with your | mercy:
   that all our days we | may re|joice and | sing.

15 Give us joy for all the days you | have af|flicted us:
   for the | years   we have | suffered   ad|versity.

16 Show your | servants   your | work:
   and let their | children | see your | glory.

Second part

17 May the gracious favour of the Lord our | God · be
   up|on us:
   prosper the work of our hands
      O | prosper · the | work · of our | hands!

864

Psalm 93

E. G. Monk (1819–1900)

1 The Lord is King * and has put on | robes of | glory:
   the Lord has put on his glory
      he has | girded · him|self with | strength.

2 He has made the | world so | firm:
   that it | cannot | be | moved.

3 **Your throne is es|tablished · from of | old:**
   you | are from | ever|lasting.

4 The floods have lifted up O Lord
      the floods have lifted | up their | voice:
   the | floods lift | up their | pounding.

5 But mightier than the sound of many waters
         than the mighty waters or the | breakers · of the |
      sea:
   the | Lord on | high is | mighty.

6 **Your decrees are | very | sure:**
   and holiness O Lord a|dorns your | house for | ever.

See also No. 868 by G. A. Macfarren

865

Psalm 95

G. Thalben-Ball (1896–   )

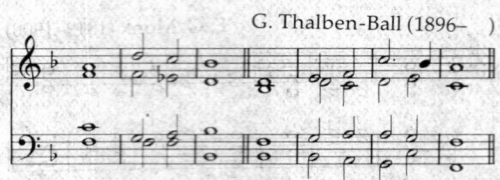

F. A. G. Ouseley (1825–89)

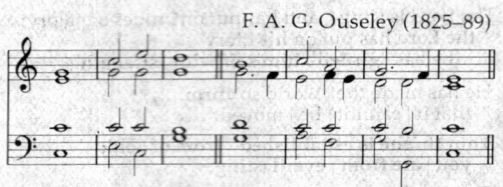

J. Battishill (1738–1801)

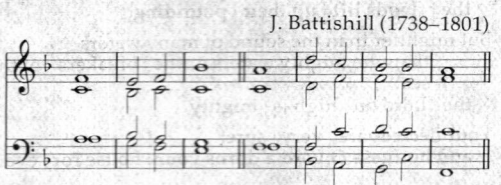

W. Russell (1777–1813)

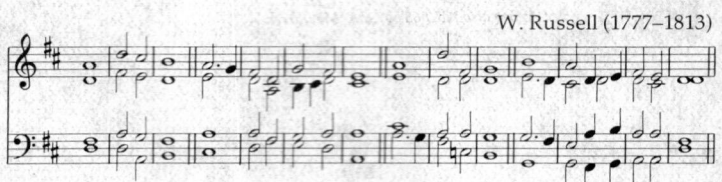

1 O come let us sing | out · to the | Lord:
   let us shout in triumph to the | rock of | our
      sal|vation.

2 Let us come before his | face with | thanksgiving:
   and cry | out to | him | joyfully · in | psalms.

3 For the Lord is a | great | God:
   and a great | king a·bove | all | gods.

4 In his hand are the | depths · of the | earth:
   and the peaks of the | mountains · are | his | also.

Second part

5 The sea is his and | he | made it:
   his hands | moulded | dry | land.

6 Come let us worship and | bow | down:
   and kneel be|fore the | Lord our | maker.

7 For he is the | Lord our | God:
   we are his | people · and the | sheep of · his |
      pasture.

866

Psalm 96

W. Parratt (1841–1924)

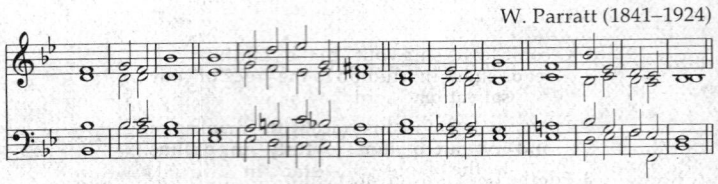

J. Robinson (1682–1762)

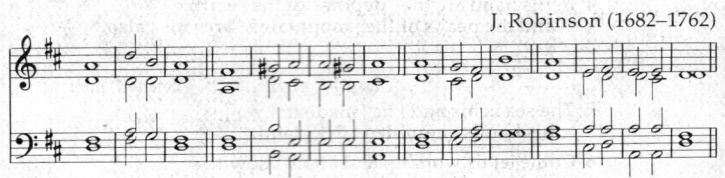

A

1 O sing to the Lord a | new | song:
   sing to the | Lord | all the | earth.

2 Sing to the Lord and bless his | holy | name:
   **proclaim the good news of his sal|vation · from |
   day to | day.**

3 Declare his glory a|mong the | nations:
   and his | wonders · a|mong all | peoples.

4 For great is the Lord and | greatly · to be | praised:
   he is more to be | feared than | all | gods.

5 As for all the gods of the nations | they are · mere |
   idols:
   it is the | Lord who | made the | heavens.

6 **Majesty and | glory · are be|fore him:**
   beauty and | power are | in his | sanctuary.

7 Render to the Lord you families | of the | nations:
   render to the | Lord | glory · and | might.

8 **Render to the Lord the honour | due · to his | name:**
   bring offerings and | come in|to his | courts.

9 O worship the Lord in the beauty | of his | holiness:
   let the whole earth | stand in | awe of | him.

10 Say among the nations that the | Lord is | king:
   he has made the world so firm that it can never be
      moved
     and he shall | judge the | peoples · with | equity.

11 **Let the heavens rejoice · and let the | earth be | glad:**
   let the sea | roar and | all that | fills it;

12 Let the fields rejoice and | every · thing | in them:
   then shall all the trees of the wood shout with | joy
   be|fore the | Lord;

Second part

13 **For he comes · he comes to | judge the | earth:**
   he shall judge the world with righteousness
    and the | peoples | with his | truth.

867

Psalm 98

H. G. Ley (1887–1962)

J. S. Smith (1750–1836)

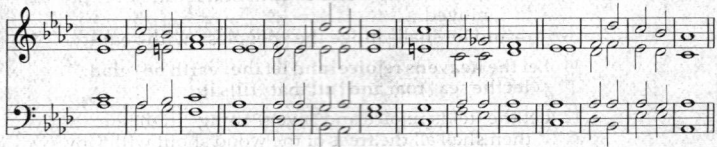

1 O sing to the Lord a | new | song:
   for he has | done | marvel·lous | things;

2 **His right hand and his | holy | arm:**
   they have | got | him the | victory.

3 The Lord has made | known · his sal|vation:
   he has revealed his just de|liverance · in the | sight
   of · the | nations.

4 He has remembered his mercy and faithfulness
   towards the | house of | Israel:
   and all the ends of the earth have seen the sal|vation |
   of our | God.

5 Shout with joy to the Lord | all the | earth:
   break into | singing · and | make | melody.

6 Make melody to the Lord up|on the | harp:
   upon the harp and | with the | sounds of | praise.

7 With trumpets | and with | horns:
   cry out in triumph be|fore the | Lord the | king.

8 Let the sea roar and | all that | fills it:
   the good earth and | those who | live up|on it.

9 Let the rivers | clap their | hands:
   and let the mountains ring out to|gether · be|fore
   the | Lord;

10 For he comes to | judge the | earth:
   he shall judge the world with righteousness
   and the | peoples | with | equity.

868

Psalm 100

Walford Davies (1869–1941)

G. A. Macfarren (1813–87)

G. J. Elvey (1816–93)

W. Parratt (1841–1924)

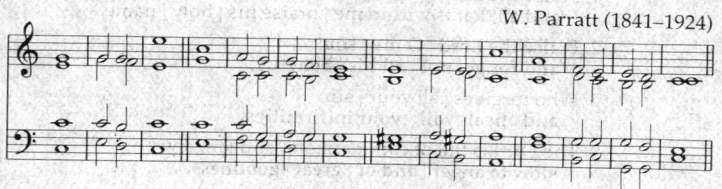

1 O shout to the Lord in triumph | all the | earth:
serve the Lord with gladness
and come before his | face with | songs of | joy.

2 **Know that the Lord | he is | God:**
it is he who has made us and we are his
we are his | people   and the | sheep of   his |
pasture.

3 Come into his gates with thanksgiving
and into his | courts with | praise:
give thanks to him and | bless his | holy | name.

4 **For the Lord is good * his loving mercy | is for | ever:**
his faithfulness through|out all | gener|ations.

869

Psalm 103

Walford Davies (1869–1941)

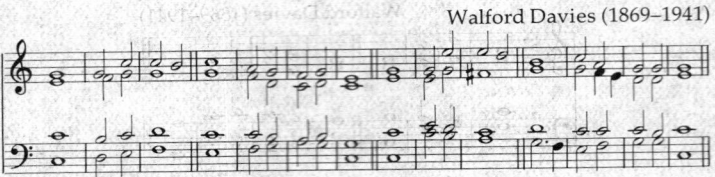

J. Lemon (1754–1814)

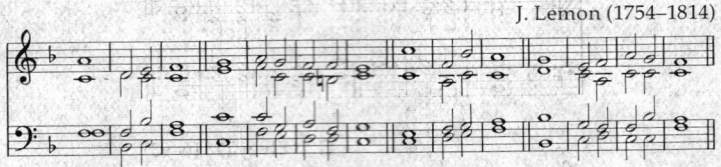

If the Chant by J. Lemon is chosen, it should be used throughout the Psalm.
If the Chants by Walford Davies are used, verses 9-12 may be allocated to the choir alone.

1 Praise the Lord | O my | soul:
  and all that is within me | praise his | holy | name.

2 **Praise the Lord | O my | soul:**
  and for|get not | all his | benefits,

3 Who forgives | all your | sin:
  and | heals | all · your in|firmities.

4 The Lord is full of com|passion · and | mercy:
  slow to anger | and of | great | goodness.

5 He will not | always · be | chiding:
  nor will he | keep his | anger · for | ever.

6 He has not dealt with us ac|cording · to our | sins:
  nor rewarded us ac|cording | to our | wickedness.

7 For as the heavens are high a|bove the | earth:
  so great is his | mercy · over | those that | fear him;

8 **As far as the east is | from the | west:**
  so far has he | set our | sins | from us.

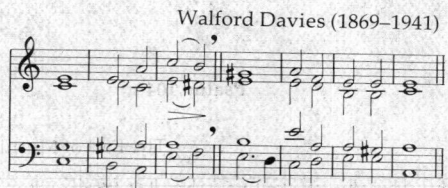

Walford Davies (1869–1941)

9 As a father is tender to|wards his | children:
    so is the Lord | tender · to | those that | fear him.

10 **For he knows of | what · we are | made:**
    he re|members · that we | are but | dust.

11 The days of man are | but as | grass:
    he flourishes | like a | flower · of the | field;

12 **When the wind goes over it | it is | gone:**
    and its | place will | know it · no | more.

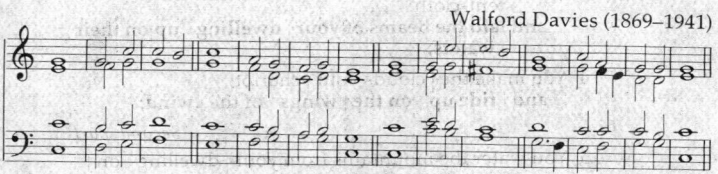

Walford Davies (1869–1941)

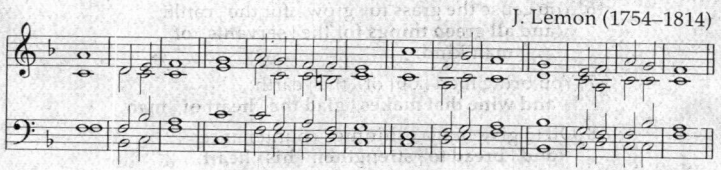

J. Lemon (1754–1814)

13 But the merciful goodness of the Lord
    endures for ever and ever toward | those that |
    fear him:
  **and his righteousness up|on their | children's |
  children;**

14 **Upon those who | keep his | covenant:**
    and | remember · his com|mandments · to | do them.

PSALMS

870

Psalm 104

The Earl of Mornington (1735–81)

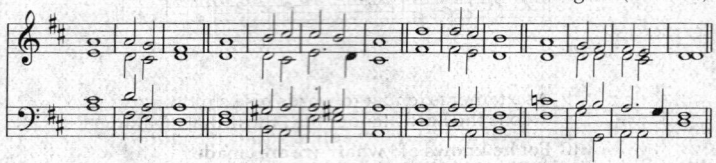

A

1 Bless the Lord | O my | soul:
  O Lord my | God how | great you | are!

2 Clothed with | majesty · and | honour:
  wrapped in | light as | in a | garment.

3 You have stretched out the | heavens · like a |
    tent-cloth:
  **and laid the beams of your | dwelling · up|on their
    | waters;**

4 You make the | clouds your | chariot:
  and | ride up · on the | wings · of the | wind;

Second part

5 You water the mountains from your | dwelling · on |
    high:
  **and the earth is | filled · by the | fruits of · your |
    work.**

6 You cause the grass to | grow · for the | cattle:
  **and all green things for the | servants | of
    man|kind.**

7 You bring food | out of · the | earth:
  and wine that makes | glad the | heart of | man,

8 Oil to give him a | shining | countenance:
  and | bread to | strengthen · his | heart.

9 You created the moon to | mark the | seasons:
  and the sun | knows the | hour · of its | setting.

10 You make darkness | and it · is | night:
  in which all the beasts of the | forest | move by |
    stealth.

11 **Man goes | out · to his | work:**
  and to his | labour · un|til the | evening.

T. A. Walmisley (1814–56)

10 He commanded the Red Sea and it | dried | up:
    and he led them through the | deep as | through a |
        desert.

11 He delivered them from the | hand · of their |
        adversary:
    and redeemed them | from the | power · of the |
        enemy.

12 He remembered his | coven·ant | with them:
    and relented according to the a|bundance · of his |
        loving-|kindness.

13 And he caused them | to be | pitied:
    even by | those that | held them | captive.

Second part

14 .Save us O Lord our God
        and gather us from a|mong the | nations:
    that we may give thanks to your holy name
        and | make our | boast · in your | praises.

872

Psalm 107

W. Parratt (1841–1924)

A

1 O give thanks to the Lord for | he is | good:
  for his loving | mercy | is for | ever.

2 Let the Lord's re|deemed | say so:
  whom he has redeemed from the | hand | of the |
  enemy,

Second part

3 **And gathered in from every land
  from the east and | from the | west:
  from the | north and | from the | south.**

4 Some went astray in the wilderness and | in the |
  desert:
  and found no | path to · an in|habit ed | city;

5 **They were | hungry · and | thirsty:
  and their | heart | fainted · with|in them.**

6 Then they cried to the Lord in | their dis|tress:
  and he | took them | out of · their | trouble.

7 **He led them by the | right | path:
  till they | came to · an in|habit ed | city.**

From M. Luther's *Ein' Feste Burg* (1529)

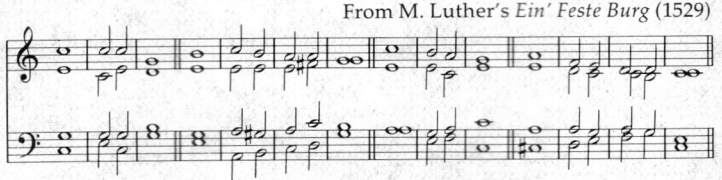

8 **Let them thank the | Lord · for his | goodness:
  and for the wonders that he | does · for the |
  children · of | men;**

9 **For he | satisfies · the | thirsty:
  and fills the | hungry · with | good | things.**

C. H. Stewart (1884–1932)

B

10 Those who go down to the | sea in | ships:
   and follow their | trade on | great | waters,

11 These men have seen the | works of | God:
   and his | wonders | in the | deep.

12 For he spoke and | raised the | storm-wind:
   and it lifted | high the | waves · of the | sea.

13 They go up to the sky · and down a|gain · to the | depths:
   their courage melts a|way · in the | face · of dis|aster.

14 They reel and stagger like | drunken | men:
   and are | at their | wits' | end.

15 Then they cried to the Lord in | their dis|tress:
   and he | took them | out of · their | trouble.

16 He calmed the | storm · to a | silence:
   and the | waves · of the | sea were | stilled.

17 Then they were glad be|cause · they were | quiet:
   and he | brought them · to the | haven · they | longed for.

From M. Luther's *Ein' Feste Burg* (1529)

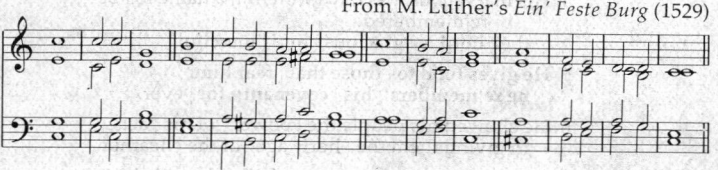

18 **Let them thank the | Lord · for his | goodness:**
   and for the wonders that he | does · for the | children · of | men;

19 **Let them exalt him in the as|sembly · of the | people:**
   and | praise him · in the | council · of | elders.

Psalm 111

M. J. Ellis (1943–)

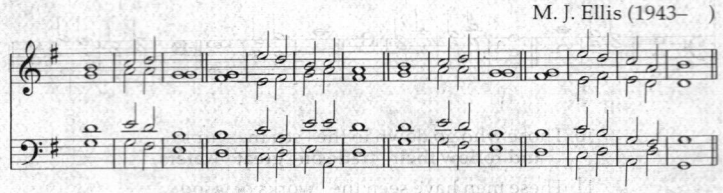

R. Cooke (1768–1814)

1 O praise the Lord
   I will praise the Lord with my | whole | heart:
   **in the company of the upright
   and a|mong the | congre|gation.**

2 The works of the | Lord are | great:
   and studied by | all who | take de|light in them.

3 **His deeds are ma|jestic · and | glorious:
   and his | righteous ness | stands for | ever.**

4 His marvellous acts have won him a name to | be
      re|membered:
   the | Lord is | gracious · and | merciful.

5 **He gives food to | those that | fear him:
   he re|members · his | covenant · for | ever.**

6 He showed his people the | power · of his | acts:
   in giving them the | herit age | of the | heathen.

7 **The words of his hands are | faithful · and | just:
   and | all · his com|mandments · are | sure;**

8 They stand firm for | ever · and | ever:
   they are done in | faithful ness | and in | truth.

9 **He sent redemption to his people
      he ordained his | covenant · for | ever:
   holy is his name and | worthy | to be | feared.**

10 The fear of the Lord is the beginning of wisdom
      and of good understanding are those that | keep
         his com|mandments:
   his | praise · shall en|dure for | ever.

874

Psalm 116

E. C. Bairstow (1874–1946)

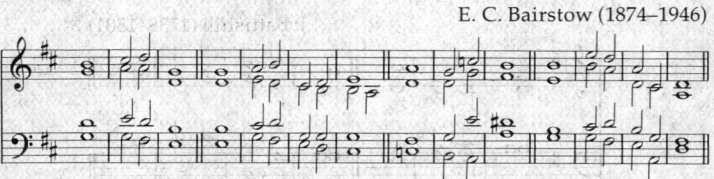

S. Elvey (1805–60)

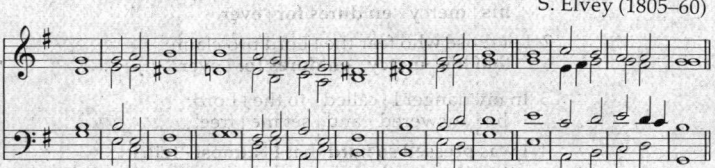

1 How shall I re|pay the | Lord:
　　for | all his | bene·fits | to me?

2 **I will take up the | cup of · sal|vation:**
　　and | call up·on the | name · of the | Lord.

3 I will pay my | vows · to the | Lord:
　　in the | presence · of | all his | people.

4 **Grievous in the | sight · of the | Lord:**
　　is the | death | of his | faithful ones.

5 O Lord I am your servant
　　your servant and the | son of · your | handmaid:
　　you | have un|loosed my | bonds.

6 **I will offer you a sacrifice of | thanks|giving:**
　　and | call up·on the | name · of the | Lord.

7 I will pay my | vows · to the | Lord:
　　in the | presence · of | all his | people,

8 **In the courts of the | house · of the | Lord:**
　　even in your midst O Jerusalem |
　　　　Praise | — the | Lord.

875

Psalm 118

J. Battishill (1738–1801)

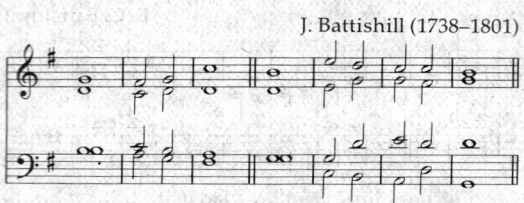

1 O give thanks to the Lord for | he is | good:
his | mercy · en|dures for | ever.

2 Let those who fear the | Lord pro|claim:
that his | mercy · en|dures for | ever.

3 In my danger I | called · to the | Lord:
he | answered · and | set me | free.

4 **I was pressed so hard that I | almost | fell:
but the | Lord | was my | helper.**

5 The Lord is my | strength · and my | song:
and has be|come | my sal|vation.

T. Attwood (1765–1838)

6 **The sounds of | joy · and del|iverance:
are | in the | tents · of the | righteous.**

7 The right hand of the Lord does | mighty | things:
the right hand of the | Lord | raises | up.

8 I shall not | die but | live:
and pro|claim the | works · of the | Lord.

9 **The Lord has | disciplined · me | hard:
but he has not | given · me | over · to | death.**

10 Open me the | gates of | righteousness:
and I will enter and give | thanks | to the | Lord.

11 This is the | gate · of the | Lord:
    the | righteous | shall | enter it.

12 I will praise you | for you | answered me:
    and have be|come | my sal|vation.

13 The stone that the | builders · re|jected:
    has be|come the | head · of the | corner.

14 This is the | Lord's | doing:
    and it is | marvel·lous | in our | eyes.

15 This is the day that the | Lord has | made:
    let us re|joice | and be | glad in it.

Second part

16 O give thanks to the Lord for | he is | good:
    and his | mercy · en|dures for | ever.

876

Psalm 119

H. G. Ley (1887–1962)

A

1 Blessèd are those whose | way is | blameless:
    who | walk · in the | law · of the | Lord.

2 Blessèd are those who | keep · his com|mands:
    and seek him | with their | whole | heart;

3 Those who | do no | wrong:
    but | walk · in the | ways of · our | God.

4 For you Lord | have com|manded us:
    to perse|vere in | all your | precepts.

5 If only my | ways · were un|erring:
    towards the | keeping | of your | statutes!

6 Then I should | not · be a|shamed:
    when I | looked on | all · your com|mandments.

7 I will praise you with sin|cerity · of | heart:
    as I | learn your | righteous | judgements.

8 I will | keep your | statutes:
    O for|sake me | not | utterly.

876(cont.)

W. H. Longhurst (1819–1904)

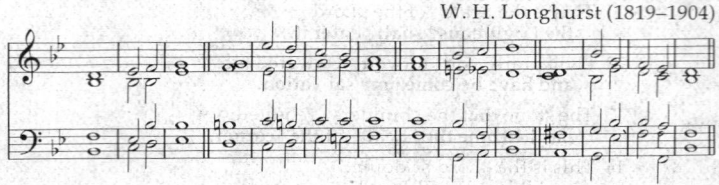

B

1 Lord your | word · is for | ever:
   it stands | firm | in the | heavens.

**2 Your faithfulness abides from one gener|ation · to
an|other:
firm as the | earth which | you have | made.**

3 As for your judgements they stand | fast this | day:
   for | all things | are your | servants.

**4 If your law had not been | my de|light:
I would have | perished · in | my af|fliction.**

5 I will never for|get your | precepts:
   for by | them · you have | given · me | life.

**6 I am | yours O | save me:
for | I have | sought your | precepts.**

7 The wicked have lain in wait for me | to de|stroy me:
   but I | think on | your com|mands.

**8 I have seen that all perfection | comes · to an | end:
only your com|mandment | has no | bounds.**

K. J. Pye (1812–1901)

C

1 Lord how I | love your | law:
   it is my medi|tation | all the · day | long.

**2 Your commandments have made me wiser | than my |
enemies:
for they re|main with | me for | ever.**

3 I have more understanding than | all my | teachers:
   for I | study | your com|mands.

4 I am wiser | than the | agèd:
  be|cause · I have | kept your | precepts.

5 I have held back my feet from every | evil | path:
  that | I might | keep your | word;

6 I have not turned a|side from · your | judgements:
  for | you your|self are · my | teacher.

7 How sweet are your | words · to my | tongue:
  sweeter than | honey | to my | mouth.

8 Through your precepts I get | under|standing:
  therefore I | hate all | lying | ways.

J. Soaper (1743–94)

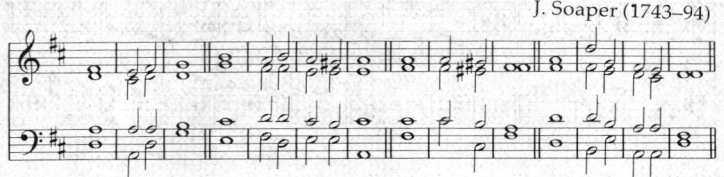

D

1 Consider my affliction | and de|liver me:
  for I do | not for|get your | law.

2 Plead my cause and | set me | free:
  O give me life ac|cording | to your | word.

3 Salvation is | far · from the | wicked:
  for they | do not | seek your | statutes.

4 Numberless O Lord are your | tender | mercies:
  according to your | judgements | give me | life.

5 Many there are that persecute | me and | trouble me:
  but I have not | swerved from | your com|mands.

6 I am cut to the heart when I | see the | faithless:
  for they | do not | keep your | word.

7 Consider O Lord how I | love your | precepts:
  and in your | mercy | give me | life.

8 The sum of your | word is | truth:
  and all your righteous | judgements | stand for | ever.

877

Psalm 121

Walford Davies (1869–1941)

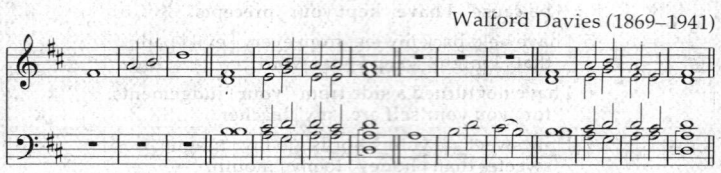

P. Henley (1728–64)

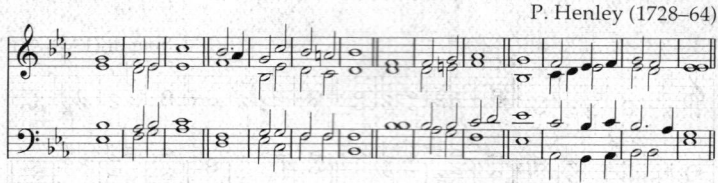

1 I lift up my | eyes · to the | hills:
  but | where · shall I | find | help?

2 **My help | comes · from the | Lord:**
  who has | made | heaven · and | earth.

3 He will not suffer your | foot to | stumble:
  and he who watches | over · you | will not | sleep.

4 **Be sure he who has | charge of | Israel:**
  will | neither | slumber · nor | sleep.

5 The Lord him|self is · your | keeper:
  the Lord is your defence up|on your | right | hand;

6 The sun shall not | strike you · by | day:
  nor | shall the | moon by | night.

7 The Lord will defend you from | all | evil:
  it is | he · who will | guard your | life.

8 **The Lord will defend your going out and your |**
  coming | in:
  from this time | forward · for | ever|more.

Psalm 122

J. Turle (1802–82)

C. H. Stewart (1884–1932)

1 I was glad when they | said to | me:
   'Let us | go to the | house · of the | Lord.'

2 **And now our | feet are | standing:**
   with|in your | gates O Je|rusalem;

Second part

3 Jerusalem which is | built · as a | city:
   where the | pilgrims | gather · in | unity.

4 **There the tribes go up the | tribes · of the | Lord:**
   as he commanded Israel
     to give | thanks · to the | name · of the | Lord.

5 There are set | thrones of | judgement:
   the | thrones · of the | house of | David.

6 O pray for the | peace · of Je|rusalem:
   may | those who | love you | prosper.

7 **Peace be with|in your | walls:**
   and pros|peri ty | in your | palaces.

8 For the sake of my brothers | and com|panions:
   I will | pray that | peace be | with you.

9 **For the sake of the house of the | Lord our | God:**
   I will | seek | for your | good.

879

Psalm 126

C. F. South (1850–1916)

1 When the Lord turned again the | fortunes · of | Zion:
   then were we like | men re|stored to | life.

2 **Then was our mouth | filled with | laughter:
   and | our | tongue with | singing.**

3 Then said they a|mong the | heathen:
   'The Lord has | done great | things for | them.

4 **Truly the Lord has done great | things for | us:
   and | therefore | we re|joiced.**

5 Turn again our | fortunes · O | Lord:
   as the streams re|turn · to the | dry | south.

6 **Those that | sow in | tears:
   shall | reap with | songs of | joy.**

Second part

7 **He who goes out weeping | bearing · the | seed:
   shall come again in gladness | bringing · his |
   sheaves | with him.**

See also No. 885 by W. Crotch

880

Psalm 127

J. Turle (1802–82)

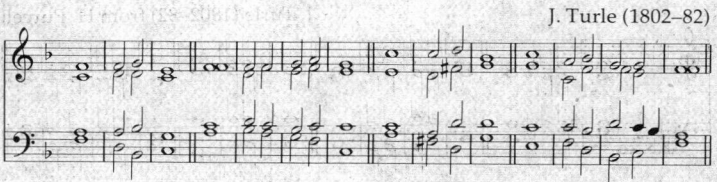

1 Unless the Lord | builds the | house:
   their labour | is but | lost that | build it.

2 **Unless the Lord | keeps the | city:**
   the | watchmen | watch in | vain.

3 It is in vain that you rise up early and go so late to rest
      eating the | bread of | toil:
   for the Lord bestows honour | and on | those · whom
     he | loves.

4 Behold children are a heritage | from the | Lord:
   and the | fruit · of the | womb is · his | gift.

5 Like arrows in the | hand · of a | warrior:
   are the | sons · of a | man's | youth.

6 **Happy the man who has his | quiver | full of them:**
   he will not be put to shame
     when he confronts his | enem ies | at the | gate.

Psalm 130

J. Turle (1802–82) from H. Purcell

Walford Davies (1869–1941)

1 Out of the depths have I called to | you O | Lord:
  Lord | hear | my | voice;

2 **O let your ears con|sider | well:**
  the | voice of my | suppli|cation.

3 If you Lord should note what | we do | wrong:
  who | then O | Lord could | stand?

4 **But there is for|giveness · with | you:**
  so that | you | shall be | feared.

5 I wait for the Lord * my | soul | waits for him:
  and | in his | word · is my | hope.

6 **My soul | looks · for the | Lord:**
  more than watchmen for the morning
  more I say than | watchmen | for the | morning.

7 O Israel trust in the Lord * for with the | Lord · there is |
  mercy:
  and with | him is | ample · re|demption.

8 **He will re|deem | Israel:**
  from the | multi·tude | of his | sins.

See also No. 828, Tonus Peregrinus

882

Psalm 133

J. Nares (1715–83)

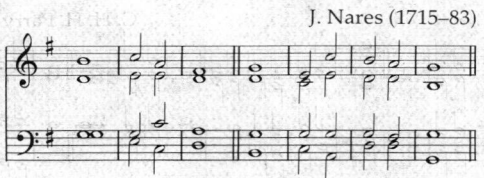

B. Cooke (1734–93)

1 Behold how good and how | lovely · it | is:
   when brothers | live to|gether · in | unity.

2 It is fragrant as oil upon the head
      that runs down | over · the | beard:
   **fragrant as oil upon the beard of Aaron
      that ran down over the | collar | of his | robe.**

3 It is like a | dew of | Hermon:
   like the dew that falls up|on the | hill of | Zion.

4 **For there the Lord has com|manded · his | blessing:
   which is | life for | ever|more.**

883

Psalm 139

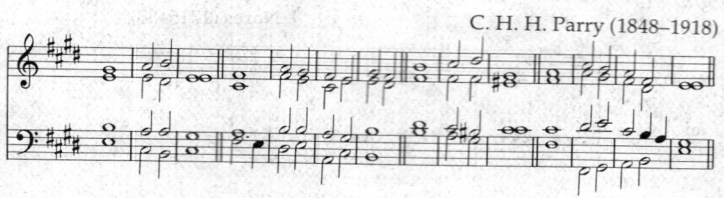

C. H. H. Parry (1848–1918)

A

1 O Lord you have searched me | out and | known me:
  you know when I sit or when I stand
      you comprehend my | thoughts | long be|fore.

2 **You discern my path and the places** | **where I** | **rest:**
  you are ac|quainted · with | all my | ways.

3 **For there is not a** | **word** · **on my** | **tongue:**
  but you Lord | **know it** | **alto**|**gether.**

4 You have encompassed me be|hind · and be|fore:
  and have | laid your | hand up|on me.

Second part

5 **Such knowledge is too** | **wonder ful** | **for me:**
  so | **high** · **that I** | **cannot · en**|**dure it.**

6 Where shall I | go · from your | spirit:
  or where shall I | **flee** | **from your** | **presence?**

7 If I ascend into heaven | you are | there:
  if I make my bed in the grave | **you are** | **there** |
      also.

8 If I spread out my wings to|wards the | morning:
  or dwell in the | utter most | parts · of the | sea,

9 Even there your | hand shall | lead me:
  and | your right | hand shall | hold me.

10 If I say 'Surely the | darkness · will | cover me:
  and the | night | will en|close me',

11 **The darkness is no darkness with you**
      but the night is as | **clear** · **as the** | **day:**
  the darkness and the | **light are** | **both a**|**like.**

B

12 You have created my | inward | parts:
you knit me together | in my | mother's | womb.

13 I will praise you for | you are · to be | feared:
**fearful are your | acts and | wonderful · your |
works.**

14 You knew my soul * and my bones were not | hidden |
from you:
**when I was formed in secret
and | woven · in the | depths · of the | earth**

15 Your eyes saw my limbs when they were | yet
im|perfect:
**and in your book were | all my | members |
written;**

Second part

16 Day by | day · they were | fashioned:
and not | one was | late in | growing.

17 How deep are your thoughts to | me O | God:
and how | great | is the | sum of them!

18 **Were I to count them
they are more in number | than the | sand:
were I to come to the | end · I would | still be | with
you.**

19 Search me out O God and | know my | heart:
put me to the | proof and | know my | thoughts.

20 **Look well lest there be any way of | wicked · ness | in
me:
and lead me in the | way · that is | ever|lasting.**

See also No. 876 by H. G. Ley

884

Psalm 145

T. Norris (1741–90)

A

1 I will exalt you O | God my | king:
  I will bless your | name for | ever · and | ever.

2 Every | day · will I | bless you:
  and praise your | name for | ever · and | ever.

3 Great is the Lord * and wonderfully | worthy · to be praised:
  his greatness is | past | searching | out.

4 One generation shall praise your | works · to an|other;
  and de|clare your | mighty | acts.

5 As for me * I will be talking of the glorious splendour | of your | majesty:
  I will tell the | story · of your | marvel·lous | works.

6 Men shall recount the power of your | terri·ble | deeds:
  and | I will · pro|claim your | greatness.

Second part

7 Their lips shall flow with the remembrance of your a|bundant | goodness:
  they shall | shout for | joy at · your | righteousness.

8 The Lord is | gracious · and com|passionate:
  slow to anger | and of | great | goodness.

9 The Lord is | loving · to | every man:
  and his mercy is | over | all his | works.

10 All creation | praises you · O | Lord:
  and your faithful | servants | bless your | name.

11 They speak of the glory | of your | kingdom:
  and | tell of · your | great | might,

Second part

12 **That all mankind may know your | mighty | acts:
  and the glorious | splendour | of your | kingdom.**

PSALMS

R. Woodward (1744–77)

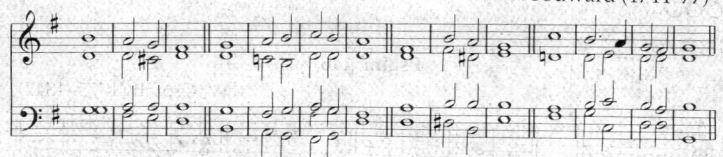

B

13 Your kingdom is an ever|lasting | kingdom:
   **and your dominion en|dures through | all ·
   gener|ations.**

14 The Lord upholds all | those who | stumble:
   and raises up | those   that are | bowed | down.

15 The eyes of all look to | you in | hope:
   and you give them their | food in | due | season;

16 You open | wide your | hand:
   **and fill all things | living   with your | bounte ous |
   gift.**

17 The Lord is just in | all his | ways:
   and | faithful   in | all his | dealings.

18 The Lord is near to all who | call up|on him:
   to all who | call up|on him   in | truth.

19 He will fulfil the desire of | those that | fear him:
   he will | hear their | cry and | save them.

20 The Lord preserves all | those that | love him:
   but the wicked | he will | utterly   de|stroy.

Second part

21 My mouth shall speak the | praises   of the | Lord:
   **and let all flesh bless his holy | name for | ever
   and | ever.**

885

Psalm 146

W. Crotch (1775–1847)

M. J. Ellis (1943–   )

1 Praise the Lord
    praise the Lord | O my | soul:
    while I | live · I will | praise the | Lord;

2 **While I | have · any | being:**
    I will sing | praises | to my | God.

3 Put not your | trust in | princes:
    nor in the sons of | men who | cannot | save.

4 **For when their breath goes from them**
    they return a | gain · to the | earth:
    and on that day | all their | thoughts | perish.

5 Blessèd is the man whose help is the | God of | Jacob:
    whose hope is | in the | Lord his | God,

6 The God who made | heaven · and | earth:
    the sea and | all | that is | in them,

7 Who keeps | faith for | ever:
    who deals justice to | those that | are op | pressed.

8 The Lord gives | food · to the | hungry:
    and | sets the | captives | free.

9 The Lord gives | sight · to the | blind:
    the Lord lifts up | those · that are | bowed | down.

10 The Lord | loves the | righteous:
    the Lord cares for the | stranger | in the | land.

11 He upholds the | widow · and the | fatherless:
    as for the way of the wicked he | turns it | upside
    down.

12 The Lord shall be | king for | ever:
    your God O Zion shall reign through all
    generations | Praise | — the | Lord.

886

Psalm 147

C. V. Stanford (1852–1924)

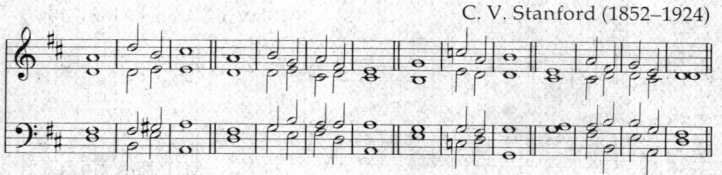

1 O praise the Lord
    for it is good to sing praises | to our | God:
    and to | praise him · is | joyful · and | right.

2 **The Lord is re|building · Je|rusalem:**
    he is gathering together the | scattered | outcasts ·
    of | Israel.

3 He heals the | broken · in | spirit:
    and | binds | up their | wounds.

4 **He counts the | number · of the | stars:**
    and | calls them | all by | name.

5 Great is our Lord and | great · is his | power:
    there is no | measuring · his | under|standing.

6 **The Lord re|stores the | humble:**
    but he brings down the | wicked | to the | dust.

7 O sing to the Lord a | song of | thanksgiving:
    sing praises to our | God up|on the | harp.

8 He covers the heavens with cloud
    and prepares | rain · for the | earth:
    and makes the grass to | sprout up|on the |
    mountains.

9 **He gives the | cattle · their | food:**
    and feeds the young | ravens · that | call | to him.

10 He takes no pleasure in the | strength · of a | horse:
    nor does he de|light in | any · man's | legs,

Second part

11 **But the Lord's delight is in | those that | fear him:**
    who | wait in | hope · for his | mercy.

See also No. 833 by R. Woodward

887

Psalm 148

W. G. Alcock (1861–1947)

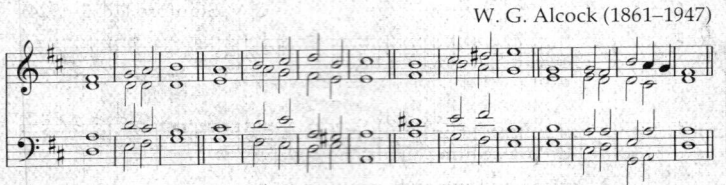

J. Turle (1802–82)

1 Praise the Lord
      praise the | Lord from | heaven:
   O | praise him | in the | heights.

2 Praise him | all his | angels:
   O | praise him | all his | host.

3 Praise him | sun and | moon:
   praise him | all you | stars of | light.

4 Praise him you | highest | heaven:
   and you waters that | are a|bove the | heavens.

5 Let them praise the | name · of the | Lord:
   for he com|manded · and | they were | made.

6 He established them for | ever · and | ever:
   he made an ordinance which | shall not | pass
   a|way.

7 O praise the | Lord · from the | earth:
   praise him you sea-|monsters · and | all | deeps;

8 Fire and hail | mist and | snow:
   and storm-wind ful|filling | his com|mand;

9 Mountains and | all | hills:
   fruiting | trees and | all | cedars;

10 Beasts of the wild and | all | cattle:
   creeping | things and | winged | birds;

11 Kings of the earth and | all | peoples:
   princes and all | rulers | of the | world;

12 Young | men and | maidens:
   old | men and | children · to|gether.

13 Let them praise the | name · of the | Lord:
   for | his · name a|lone · is ex|alted.

14 His glory is above | earth and | heaven:
   and he has lifted | high the | horn · of his | people.

Second part

15 Therefore he is the praise of | all his | servants:
   of the children of Israel · a people that is near him |
      Praise | — the | Lord.

888

Psalm 150

P. Humfrey (1647–74)

1 Praise the Lord
  O praise | God in his | sanctuary:
  praise him in the | firma ment | of his | power.

2 Praise him for his | mighty | acts:
  praise him according to | his a|bundant | goodness.

3 Praise him in the | blast of the | ram's horn:
  praise him up|on the | lute and | harp.

4 Praise him with the | timbrel and | dances:
  praise him up|on the | strings and | pipe.

5 Praise him on the | high- sounding | cymbals:
  praise him up|on the | loud | cymbals.

6 Let everything that has breath | praise the | Lord:
  O | praise | — the | Lord!

See also No. 865 by G. Thalben Ball

Note: *An alternative setting of Psalm 150 is to be found at Hymn No. 502.*

Acknowledgements

1. The publishers wish to thank the following who have given permission for copyright material to be included. Every effort has been made to trace all copyright owners, but if, through inadvertence, any surviving rights have been overlooked, the necessary correction will gladly be made in subsequent editions.

2. It is not permissible to reprint or copy any copyright material without the written consent of the copyright owner or controller. In general, music can only be reproduced under the terms of a Code of Fair Practice agreed in 1979 between representatives of composers, music users and music publishers. Churches are advised to make themselves aware of the arrangements as laid down in the Code, a copy of which can be obtained from the Music Publishers Association, 7th Floor, Kingsway House, 103, Kingsway, London WC2.

3. Those wishing to reproduce words or music text that are in copyright should apply in writing to the copyright controller as shown. A blank in the second column indicates that the author or composer also controls the copyright. The addresses of the major copyright controllers are to be found on page *xxx*. Where no address is given written requests should be sent to the Methodist Publishing House, Wellington Road, Wimbledon, London SW19 8EU, who will forward them on to the copyright controllers concerned.

MUSIC

No.	Composer or Arranger †denotes arrangement *denotes descant †Maquiso, E. G.	Permission granted by
3	†Fletcher, P.	
5	†Wilson, J.	Oxford University Press
8	†Wilson, J.	Oxford University Press
9	*Lang, C. S.	Novello & Co. Ltd
10(i)	Harwood, B.	Executors of the late Dr Basil Harwood
10(ii)	Routley, E.	Hinshaw Music Inc
12	*Wilson, J.	Oxford University Press
13(i)	*Blake, L.	
16	*Lang, C. S.	Novello & Co. Ltd
17(i)	Buck, P. C.	Oxford University Press and Mr G. Buck
18	†Wilson, J.	Oxford University Press
20	*Blake, L.	
21	*Wilson, J.	Oxford University Press
23	†Wilson, J.	Oxford University Press
25	†Fletcher, P.	
27(i)	*Wilson, J.	Oxford University Press

113(i)	†Williams, R. Vaughan	Oxford University Press (from the *English Hymnal*)
113(ii)	†Williams, R. Vaughan	Oxford University Press
115	†Williams, R. Vaughan	Stainer & Bell Ltd. Acting as agents for Ralph Vaughan Williams Ltd (for USA – Galaxy Music Corp)
116	†Dixon, N.	
118	Perry, M.	Jubilate Hymns Ltd
	†Ellis, M.	Banks Music Publications
119	†Blake, L.	
121	*Wilson, J.	Oxford University Press
122	*Wilson, J.	Oxford University Press
123(ii)	Thalben-Ball, G.	Oxford University Press (from the *BBC Hymn Book*)
124(i)	Dearnley, C.	Oxford University Press (from *English Praise*)
124(ii)	Ruddle, V.	
126(ii)	Williamson, M.	Josef Weinberger Ltd (from *Twelve New Hymn Tunes*)
127	†Shaw, G.	Oxford University Press (from the *Oxford Book of Carols*)
128(i)	Finlay, K.	Broomhill Church of Scotland, Glasgow
131(i)	Brockless, G. F.	Methodist Conference
133	Llewellyn, W.	Oxford University Press
134(ii)	Laycock, G.	Faber Music Ltd (from *New Catholic Hymnal*)
135	†How, Martin	Royal School of Church Music
137	†Westbrook, F. B.	Oxford University Press
138	Lafferty, K.	Maranatha! Music Publishing
	†Bradshaw, R.	
139	Barnes, G. L. (1935–)	
140	Shaw, M.	J. Curwen & Sons Ltd
145	†Colvin, T.	© 1969 Agape, Carol Stream, IL 60188, USA International Copyright Secured
146(i)	Shaw, M.	Oxford University Press
146(ii)	Naylor, C. L.	Methodist Church Division of Education and Youth
147	Somervell, Arthur	Abbot of Downside
151	Smith, Peter D.	Stainer & Bell Ltd and the Methodist Church Division of Education and Youth (for USA – Galaxy Music Corp)
153(i)	Challinor, F. A.	National Christian Education Council
153(ii)	†Thalben-Ball, G.	
155	Nicholson, S. H.	Hymns Ancient & Modern
157	Dearnley, C.	Oxford University Press (from *English Praise*)
161	†Williams, R. Vaughan	Oxford University Press (from the *English Hymnal*)
162	Reid, Eric	Stainer & Bell Ltd (for USA – Galaxy Music Corp)
167	Hunt, J. Eric	Exors of the late J. Eric Hunt
168	†Williams, R. Vaughan	Oxford University Press (from the *English Hymnal*)
170	Nicholson, S. H.	Hymns Ancient & Modern

173	Ireland, J.	The John Ireland Trust
174(i)	†Wilson, J.	Oxford University Press
174(ii)	†Thiman, E.	United Reformed Church
179	Buck, P. C.	Oxford University Press and Mr G. Buck
180	*Wilson, J.	Oxford University Press
181	†Westbrook, F. B.	Oxford University Press
182(i)	Nicholson, S. H.	Hymns Ancient & Modern
185(i)	Cocker, N.	Oxford University Press
185(ii)	Taylor, C. V.	Oxford University Press
186	Hoare, B. R.	Stainer & Bell Ltd (for USA – Galaxy Music Corp)
191	†Ley, H. G.	Oxford University Press (from *Enlarged Songs of Praise*)
192(ii)	†Williams, R. Vaughan	Oxford University Press (from the *English Hymnal*)
195	†Wilson, J.	Oxford University Press
199	Williams, R. Vaughan	Oxford University Press (from *Enlarged Songs of Praise*)
200	Percival, A.	Stainer & Bell Ltd (for USA – Galaxy Music Corp)
204	Laycock, G.	
205	Poston, E.	Cambridge University Press (from the *Cambridge Hymnal*)
209	†Wilson, J.	Oxford University Press
211	Buck, P. C.	Oxford University Press and Mr G. Buck
212	†Wilson, J.	Oxford University Press
216(ii)	Taylor, C. V.	Oxford University Press
219	†Kitson, C. H.	APCK
220	†Knight, G. H.	Royal School of Church Music
221	Floyd, A. E.	Methodist Church Division of Education and Youth
224	†Williams, R. Vaughan	Oxford University Press (from the *English Hymnal*)
229	Blackwell, T. K.	
231(i)	*Russell, V. S. H.	
231(ii)	Terry, R. R.	Search Press Ltd
235	†Wilson, J.	Oxford University Press
236	Terry, R. R.	Oxford University Press
237	Shaw, M.	J. Curwen & Sons Ltd
238	Barnard, John	Jubilate Hymns Ltd
239(ii)	Duckworth, F.	Mrs B. A. Duckworth
241	†Wilson, J.	Oxford University Press
242	Laycock, G.	Faber Music Ltd (from *New Catholic Hymnal*)
243	†Wilson, J.	Oxford University Press
246	Wostenholm, M. L.	Methodist Conference
250	Fishel, D.	The Word of God, PO Box 8617, Ann Arbor, MI 48107, USA
253	Wilson, J.	Oxford University Press
254	Brent-Smith, A.	Exors of A. Brent-Smith
256	Warren, N.	Jubilate Hymns Ltd
260	Mansell, D.	© Springtide 1980, 11 Wilmot Road, London N17 6LH

265(ii)	Buchanan, Annabel Morris	© 1938/66 J. Fischer & Bro. (a division of Belwin Mills Pub. Corp., New York). Reprinted by permission of Belwin Mills Music Ltd
	†Wilson, J.	Oxford University Press
267(i)	Rowlands, W. P.	G. A. Gabe
269(i)	Buchanan, Annabel Morris	© 1938/66 J. Fischer & Bro. (a division of Belwin Mills Pub. Corp., New York). Reprinted by permission of Belwin Mills Music Ltd
	†Wilson, J.	Oxford University Press
270	†Pulkingham, Betty	American Catholic Press
271	Wiseman, F. Luke	
274	Coward, H.	J. Curwen & Sons Ltd
276(ii)	Dykes Bower, J.	Royal School of Church Music
277(ii)	Bartlett, L. F.	
281	Williams, R. Vaughan	Oxford University Press (from the *English Hymnal*)
282	Ley, H. G.	SPCK
289(ii)	Westbrook, F. B.	Oxford University Press
290	Taylor, C. V.	Oxford University Press (from the *BBC Hymn Book*)
292	Routley, E.	Adaptation of music reprinted by permission of Stainer & Bell Ltd (for USA – Galaxy Music Corp)
294	McCarthy, D.	Stainer & Bell Ltd
297(ii)	Lang, C. S.	Novello & Co. Ltd
298(i)	Ellis, M.	Banks Music Publications
302	Williams, R. Vaughan	Oxford University Press (from the *English Hymnal*)
304(i)	Finlay, K. G.	Broomhill Church of Scotland, Glasgow
304(ii)	Jones, P.	
305	Dykes Bower, J.	Royal School of Church Music
309	Ellis, M.	A. P. Gardiner
311(i)	Davies, Walford	Oxford University Press
311(ii)	Dykes Bower, J.	Exors of the late Sir John Dykes Bower
313	Taylor, C. V.	Oxford University Press (from the *BBC Hymn Book*)
315	Richards, Hubert	Vanguard Music Corp., 1595 Broadway, New York, NY 10019, USA
	†Pulkingham, B.	
317	Taylor, C. V.	Oxford University Press
319	Hardyman, S	© Celebration Services (International) Ltd, c/ Thankyou Music Ltd, P.O. Box 75, Eastbourne, East Sussex BN23 6NW
320	Cocker, N.	Oxford University Press
323	Darke, H.	Hymns Ancient & Modern
324	Dearnley, C.	Oxford University Press (from *English Praise*)
326	Wilson, J.	Oxford University Press
327(ii)	Davies, Walford	Oxford University Press
328(ii)	†Williams, R. Vaughan	Oxford University Press (from the *English Hymnal*)

329	†Williams, R. Vaughan	Oxford University Press (from the *English Hymnal*)
330(ii)	†Shaw, M.	J. Curwen & Sons Ltd
332	Connolly, R.	
333(i)	†Evans, D.	Oxford University Press (from the *Revised Church Hymnary 1927*)
333(ii)	†Shaw, G.	Oxford University Press
335(i)	Williams, D.	
336	Julian, H.	
337(ii)	Taylor, C. V.	Oxford University Press (from the *BBC Hymn Book*)
339(ii)	Davies, Walford	Oxford University Press
341	Russell, S. L.	Oxford University Press (from *Enlarged Songs of Praise*)
342(i)	Jackson, F.	
343(i)	Ruddle, V.	Stainer & Bell Ltd (for USA – Galaxy Music Corp)
343(ii)	†Wilson, J.	Oxford University Press
344	†Williams, R. Vaughan	Oxford University Press (from the *English Hymnal*)
347(i)	Massey, B. S.	
347(ii)	Hastings, J.	
348	Laycock, G.	
349	Cocker, N.	Oxford University Press
350	†Wilson, J.	Oxford University Press
351	Taylor, C. V.	Oxford University Press (from the *BBC Hymn Book*)
353	†Wilson, J.	Oxford University Press
357	†Wilson, J.	Oxford University Press
358	*Wilson, J.	Oxford University Press
360	Northrop, A.	J. T. Park, The Cross Printing Works, Stainland, Halifax, Yorkshire
364	†Williams, R. Vaughan	Stainer & Bell Ltd acting as agents for Ralph Vaughan Williams, Ltd (for USA – Galaxy Music Corp)
365(ii)	Llewellyn, W.	Oxford University Press
367	Floyd, A. E.	J. Floyd
368	Wilson, J.	Oxford University Press
369	Routley, E.	Oxford University Press
373	Ireland, J.	The John Ireland Trust
375(i)	Thiman, E. H.	United Reformed Church
378	†Routley, E.	Oxford University Press
	*Wilson, J.	Oxford University Press
381	*Wilson, J.	Royal School of Church Music
388	*Wilson, J.	Oxford University Press
392(i)	Dykes Bower, J.	Exors of the late Sir John Dykes Bower
393	From *New Church Praise*	United Reformed Church
398	Hoare, B. R.	
399	Floyd, A. E.	J. Floyd
401	†Wilson, J.	Oxford University Press
403	Murrill, H.	Miss C. Evans
404	Davies, Walford	Oxford University Press
404	†Wilson, J.	Oxford University Press
405	Greatorex, W.	Oxford University Press

406	Shaw, M.	Oxford University Press
407	Connolly, R.	
408	Dexter, N.	© 1981 Caribbean Conference of Churches from *Sing A New Song No. 3* published by The Cedar Press
410	Wilson, J.	Oxford University Press
413	†Thiman, E.	United Reformed Church
414	Routley, E.	Oxford University Press
417	St. John (Welsh)	Baptist Union of Wales
418	†Evans, D.	Oxford University Press (from the *Revised Church Hymnary 1927*)
420(i)	*Wilson, J.	Oxford University Press
424	†Evans, D.	Oxford University Press (from the *Revised Church Hymnary 1927*)
426	†Williams, R. Vaughan	Oxford University Press (from the *English Hymnal*)
427(ii)	Finlay, K. G.	Broomhill Church of Scotland, Glasgow
433(i)	*Wilson, J.	Oxford University Press
434(ii)	†Wilson, J.	Oxford University Press
435(ii)	Taylor, C. V.	Oxford University Press
436(ii)	†Williams, R. Vaughan	Oxford University Press (from the *English Hymnal*)
440(i)	Nicholson, S. H.	Hymns Ancient & Modern
441(i)	Shaw, M.	J. Curwen & Sons Ltd
441(ii)	Williams, T. J.	Miss D. Evans and Mrs Crump
444	†Knight, G. H.	Exors of the late G. H. Knight
447	Cutts, Peter	Oxford University Press
450	White, E.	Mayhew McCrimmon Ltd and Stainer & Bell Ltd (for USA – Galaxy Music Corp)
451(i)	Routley, E.	Oxford University Press
454	†Williams, R. Vaughan	Oxford University Press (from the *English Hymnal*)
455	†Wilson, J.	Oxford University Press
458(i)	Routley, E.	© 1971 Carl Fischer, Inc., New York. International copyright secured. Reprinted by permission of Carl Fischer, Inc., New York
459	Langlais, J.	Secretariat des Editeurs de Fiches Musicales
467	Stainer, R. F.	Methodist Conference
470(i)	†Wilson, J.	Oxford University Press
471	Currah, M.	
472	Clarke, F. R. C.	
473	†Williams, R. Vaughan	Oxford University Press (from the *English Hymnal*)
478(ii)	†Evans, D.	Oxford University Press (from the *Revised Church Hymnary 1927*)
482	†Williams, R. Vaughan	Oxford University Press (from the *English Hymnal*)
483(i)	Allen, Hugh P.	Exors of the late Lady Edith Winifred Allen
483(ii)	Ellis, W.	Royal School of Church Music
484(ii)	Thalben-Ball, G.	Oxford University Press (from the *BBC Hymn Book*)
486	Hoare, B. R.	
488	†Wilson, J.	Oxford University Press
489	†Williams, R. Vaughan	Oxford University Press (from the *English Hymnal*)

492	†As set in *New Church Praise*	United Reformed Church
493	Walker, Christopher	
495(i)	A. E. Floyd	J. Floyd
498	Wills, A.	Royal School of Church Music
499(ii)	Wilson, J.	Oxford University Press
500	Routley, E.	Oxford University Press © 1977 by Agape, Carol Stream, IL 60188. All rights reserved. Used by permission.
503	Swann, D.	Stainer & Bell Ltd, administrators of the copyright (for USA – Galaxy Music Corp)
506	†Coombes, Douglas	
507	Warren, N.	Jubilate Hymns Ltd
508(ii)	Bartlett, L. F.	
	*Wilson, J.	Oxford University Press
512(i)	Wilson, J.	Oxford University Press
514(ii)	Eyre, C.	
517(i)	†Wilson, J.	Oxford University Press
518	Wiant, Bliss	
521(ii)	Harris, W. H.	Oxford University Press
522	†Williams, R. Vaughan	Oxford University Press (from the *English Hymnal*)
525	†As set in *New Church Praise*	United Reformed Church
532	Routley, E.	Oxford University Press © 1977 by Agape, Carol Stream, IL 60188. All rights reserved. Used by permission
535(ii)	†Hedges, A. J.	
538(ii)	Westbrook, F. B.	Oxford University Press
539(i)	Anderson, J. S.	Oxford University Press
539(ii)	Finlay, K. G.	Broomhill Church of Scotland, Glasgow
543	Smith, A. M.	Mrs D. W. Smith
545	Routley, E.	Adaptation of music reprinted by permission of Stainer & Bell Ltd (for USA – Galaxy Music Corp)
547	†Wilson, J.	Oxford University Press
548	Micklem, C.	
550	†Jones, I. H.	
551	Dykes Bower, J.	Exors of the late Sir John Dykes Bower
552(i)	†Routley, E.	Oxford University Press
552(ii)	Taylor, C. V.	Oxford University Press (from the *BBC Hymn Book*)
554	†Wilson, J.	Oxford University Press
555	Taylor, C. V.	Oxford University Press
558(ii)	Harris, W. H.	Oxford University Press
559(ii)	Carter, F. G.	
560	†Cleall, C.	
561	Micklem, C.	
565	Bonner, Carey	National Christian Education Council
	†Thiman, E.	United Reformed Church
566(ii)	Copley, I. A.	
566(iii)	Beaumont, G.	Paxton Music Ltd
570	Jones, P.	
572(i)	Newport, Doreen	
	Cutts, Peter	Stainer & Bell Ltd (for USA – Galaxy Music Corp)

572(ii)	Westcott, G.	Stainer & Bell Ltd (for USA – Galaxy Music Corp)
574(i)	†Wilson, J.	Oxford University Press
575(i)	†Williams, R. Vaughan	Stainer & Bell Ltd acting as agents for Ralph Vaughan Williams Ltd (for USA – Galaxy Music Corp)
576	Finlay, K. G.	Broomhill Church of Scotland, Glasgow
578	†Jones, I. H.	
589	Somervell, A.	Trustees of the late Sir Arthur Somervell
590	†Williams, R. Vaughan	Oxford University Press (from the *English Hymnal*)
593(ii)	Wilson, J.	Oxford University Press
594	†Wilson, J.	Oxford University Press
595	†How, Martin	Royal School of Church Music
600	Cocker, N.	Oxford University Press
604(i)	Hoare, B. R.	
605(i)	Harris, W. H.	Oxford University Press
605(ii)	Taylor, C. V.	Oxford University Press
609	Harris, W. H.	Oxford University Press
610(i)	Slater, G.	Oxford University Press
611	†Pulkingham, Betty	GIA Publications Inc., USA
613(i)	†Wilson, D. F. R.	Dean of St Patrick's Cathedral, Dublin
613(ii)	Massey, B. S.	
615	†Cleall, C.	
617	Appleford, P.	© 1960 Josef Weinberger Ltd from *Living Lord*
619(ii)	†Wilson, J.	Oxford University Press
621(i)	Buchanan, Annabel Morris	© 1938/66. J. Fischer & Bro (a division of Belwin Mills Pub. Corp., New York). Reprinted by permission of Belwin Mills Music Ltd
621(i)	†Wilson, J.	Oxford University Press
621(ii)	Slater, G.	Oxford University Press
623(i)	Murray, A. Gregory	
623(ii)	Dawney, M.	
628	†Wilson, J.	Oxford University Press
633	†Wilson, J.	Oxford University Press
635	†As set in *New Church Praise*	United Reformed Church
637	†Shaw, M.	Oxford University Press (from *Enlarged Songs of Praise*)
648	*Wilson, J.	Oxford University Press
650	Bate, H. A.	
651	Williams, R. Vaughan	Oxford University Press (from the *English Hymnal*)
654	†Wilson, J.	Oxford University Press
656	Taylor, C. V.	Oxford University Press (from the *BBC Hymn Book*)
657	Stanton, W. K.	Oxford University Press (from the *BBC Hymn Book*)
664	Jones, I. H.	
669(ii)	Harris, W. H.	Oxford University Press
671	Austin, D.	
673(ii)	Massey B. S.	
675	Wilson, J.	Oxford University Press

676(i)	Alden, J. H.	Oxford University Press
677	Thalben- Ball, G.	Oxford University Press (from the BBC Hymn Book)
679(ii)	Cundell, E.	Cambridge University Press (from The Cambridge Hymnal)
684(ii)	Beer, A.	Exors of the late A. Beer
686	McCarthy, D.	Stainer & Bell Ltd (for USA – Galaxy Music Corp)
688	†Williams, R. Vaughan	Oxford University Press (from the English Hymnal)
691	Wiseman, F. Luke	
692(ii)	Slater, G.	Oxford University Press
694	Davies, Walford	Oxford University Press
695	†Terry, R. R.	
696	†Wilson, J.	Oxford University Press
699(i)	†Routley, E.	Oxford University Press
699(ii)	Ellis, M.	A. P. Gardiner
703	†Shaw, M.	Oxford University Press (from Enlarged Songs of Praise)
704(i)	Ferguson, W. H.	Oxford University Press
705(ii)	Wright, Paul	
712(ii)	Gibbs, C. Armstrong	J. Curwen & Sons Ltd
717(i)	Watson, S.	
720	White, L. M.	Methodist Conference
722(ii)	Exors of C. Roberts	
725(i)	Rose, B.	
729	Jones, I. H.	
733	Bate, H. A.	
735(ii)	†Jones, I. H.	
738(ii)	Shaw, M.	J. Curwen & Sons Ltd
739(i)	Wilson, J.	Oxford University Press
739(ii)	Barham-Gould, A. C.	D. R. Gould
740(i)	†Evans, D.	Oxford University Press (from the Revised Church Hymnary 1927)
746	Carter, S.	Stainer & Bell Ltd (for USA – Galaxy Music Corp)
748	†Wilson, J.	Oxford University Press
750(i)	†Ellis, M.	Banks Music Publications
757	Murray, A. Gregory	
761	Julian, H.	
763(ii)	Blake, L.	Novello & Co. Ltd
770	Baughen, M.	Jubilate Hymns Ltd
	†Cleall, C.	
774	Taylor, C. V.	Oxford University Press (from the BBC Hymn Book)
775	*Wilson, J.	Oxford University Press
776	Temple, Sebastian	
	†Pulkingham, Betty	Francisan Communications, Los Angeles, CA 90015, USA
777	†Wilson, J.	Oxford University Press
782	Bishop, G.	Stainer & Bell Ltd (for USA – Galaxy Music Corp)
784	Harwood, B.	Exors of the late Dr Basil Harwood
787	Ferguson, W. H.	Royal School of Church Music
788(ii)	Ley, H. G.	SPCK
789	Thiman, E.	Royal Academy of Music

793(i)	Thiman, E.	Oxford University Press
794	Thatcher, R. S.	Oxford University Press (from the *Clarendon Hymn Book*)
795(i)	Somervell, A.	Trustees of the late Sir Arthur Somervell
797	Routley, E.	Oxford University Press © 1977 by Agape, Carol Stream, IL 60188. All rights reserved. Used by permission
799(i)	†Fouvy, C. L.	
799(ii)	Shaw, M.	Oxford University Press
804	†Williams, R. Vaughan	Oxford University Press (from the *English Hymnal*)
809	*Wilson, J.	Oxford University Press
814	Williams, R. Vaughan	Oxford University Press (from the *English Hymnal*)
815(ii)	Williams, D.	
816	†Wilson, J.	Oxford University Press
817(ii)	Taylor, C. V.	Oxford University Press (from the *BBC Hymn Book*)
	*Wilson, J.	Oxford University Press
818	†Wilson, J.	Oxford University Press
819	Routley, E.	Oxford University Press © 1977 by Agape, Carol Stream, IL 60188. All rights reserved. Used by permission

CHANTS

824	Thalben-Ball, G.	
825	Day, Edgar	Tree Russell & Co
826	Thalben-Ball, G.	
830	Thalben-Ball, G.	
830	Ley, H. G.	Oxford University Press
833	Buck, P. C.	Mr G. M. Buck
833	Davies, Walford	
834	Buck, P. C.	Mr G. M. Buck
839	Hanforth, T.	Banks Music Publications
840	Davies, Walford	Oxford University Press
843	Thalben-Ball, G.	
846	Thalben-Ball, G.	
848	Thalben-Ball, G.	
852	Davies, Walford	Oxford University Press
857	Davies, Walford	Oxford University Press
859	Thalben-Ball, G.	
865	Thalben-Ball, G.	
867	Ley, H. G.	Oxford University Press
868	Davies, Walford	Oxford University Press
869	Davies, Walford	Oxford University Press
870	Thalben-Ball, G.	
871	Ellis, M. J.	Banks Music Publications
873	Ellis, M. J.	Banks Music Publications
874	E. C. Bairstow	Mrs G. Brown
876	Ley, H. G.	Oxford University Press
877	Davies, Walford	Oxford University Press
881	Davies, Walford	Oxford University Press
885	Ellis, M. J.	Banks Music Publications
887	Alcock, W. G.	R. M. Alcock

WORDS

No. of Hymn	Author	Permission granted by
3	Niles, D. T.	Christian Conference of Asia
16	Davies, R. E.	
23	Routley, Erik	Oxford University Press
36	Rees, Timothy	A. R. Mowbray & Co. Ltd
44		The Grail Ltd
45	Niles, D. T.	Christian Conference of Asia
54	Davies, R. E.	
57	Dudley-Smith, Timothy	
60	Dudley-Smith, Timothy	
64	Briggs, G. W.	Hymn Society of America
66	Chisholm, T. O.	© 1923 Renewal 1951 extended by Hope Publishing Co., Carol Stream, IL 60188
71	Jarvis, Peter G.	
75	Jones, Ivor H.	
76	Cosnett, Elizabeth	
83	Green, F. P.	Stainer & Bell Ltd (for Canada & USA – Hope Publishing Inc.)
86	Dudley-Smith, Timothy	
88	Chisholm, Emily	Stainer & Bell Ltd (for USA – Galaxy Music Corp)
95	Ainger, G.	Stainer & Bell Ltd (for USA – Galaxy Music Corp)
97	Collison, V.	High-Fye Music Ltd
111	Dearmer, Percy	Oxford University Press (from the *Oxford Book of Carols*)
116	Jones, A. M.	
118	Perry, Michael	Jubilate Hymns Ltd
124	Dudley-Smith, Timothy	
127	Dearmer, Percy	Oxford University Press (from the *Oxford Book of Carols*)
128	East, J. T.	Methodist Conference
129	Tucker, F. Bland	© 1978 The Church Pension Fund
132	Green, F. P.	Stainer & Bell Ltd (for Canada and USA – Hope Publishing Inc)
134	Herklots, R. E.	Oxford University Press
135	Marshall-Taylor, G.	
137	Monahan, Dermott	Methodist Church Division of Education & Youth
138	Lafferty, K.	Maranatha! Music Publishing
139	Rees, Bryn	
140	Icarus, Peter	Mayhew-McCrimmon Ltd
143	McIlhagga, D.	
145	Colvin, T. S.	© 1969 by Agape, Carol Stream, IL 60188. International copyright secured. All rights reserved
151	Smith, Peter	Stainer & Bell Ltd and Methodist Church Division of Education & Youth (for USA – Galaxy Music Corp)
152	Briggs, G. W.	Oxford University Press
153	Fagg, Ruth	
155	Wren, Brian A.	Oxford University Press

157	Hewlett, M.	Stainer & Bell Ltd (for USA – Galaxy Music Corp)
161	Cropper, M.	Mrs A. Hopkinson
162	Reid, Eric	Stainer & Bell Ltd (for USA – Galaxy Music Corp)
169	Green, F. P.	Stainer & Bell Ltd (for Canada and USA – Hope Publishing Inc.) A full version of the text of 'Jesus in the olive grove' (*A Hymn for Holy Week*) is printed in *Partners in Praise* published jointly by Stainer & Bell and Chester House Publications
170	Newbolt, M. R.	Hymns Ancient & Modern
172	Andrew, Father (H. E. Hardy)	A. R. Mowbray & Co. Ltd
176	Davies, R. E.	
177	Dearmer, Percy	Oxford University Press (from the *English Hymnal*)
179	Davies, R. E.	
186	Green, F. P.	Stainer & Bell Ltd (for Canada and USA – Hope Publishing Inc)
187	Shillito, E.	Oxford University Press
190	Wren, Brian A.	Oxford University Press
191	Alington, C. A.	Hymns Ancient & Modern
195	Milner-Barry, Alda M.	The National Society
199	Kirkland, P. M.	
200	Hamilton, W. H.	Oxford University Press (from *Children Praising*)
203	Briggs, G. W.	Oxford University Press
204	Crum, J. M. C.	Oxford University Press (from the *Oxford Book of Carols*)
212	Hoyle, Richard B.	World Student Christian Federation
213	Green, F. P.	Stainer & Bell Ltd (for Canada and USA – Hope Publishing Inc)
220	Dearmer, Percy	Oxford University Press (from *Enlarged Songs of Praise*)
223	Rowley, F. H.	
237	Oakley, Charles E.	Oxford University Press (from *English Praise*)
249	Burkitt, F. C.	Oxford University Press (from the *English Hymnal*)
250	Fishel, Don	The Word of God, PO Box 8617, Ann Arbor, MI 48107, USA
251	Sparrow-Simpson, W. J.	Novello & Co. Ltd
253	Tucker, F. Bland	The Church Pension Fund (from *The Hymnal 1940*)
260	Mansell, D. J.	© Springtide 1981, 11 Wilmot Road, London N17 6LH
272	Williams, G. O.	
279	Dudley-Smith, Timothy	
288	Foley, Brian	Faber Music Ltd (from the *New Catholic Hymnal*)
290	Phillips, Ann	United Reformed Church
292	Luff, Alan	Stainer & Bell Ltd (for USA – Galaxy Music Corp)
294	Dudley-Smith, Timothy	

302	Gillett, G.	Oxford University Press (from the *English Hymnal*)
303	Rees, Timothy	Community of the Ressurection
305	Green, F. P.	Stainer & Bell Ltd (for Canada and USA – Hope Publishing Inc)
309	Dewing, T. A.	
314	Peacey, J. R.	Mrs M. E. Peacey
315	Dale, Alan	Oxford University Press
317	Bayly, Albert F.	Oxford University Press
319	Hardyman, S.	Celebration Services (International) Ltd, c/o Thankyou Music Ltd, P.O. Box 75, Eastbourne
320	Green, F. P.	Stainer & Bell Ltd (for Canada and USA – Hope Publishing Inc)
324	Hewlett, M.	Oxford University Press (from *English Praise*)
326	Wren, Brian A.	Oxford University Press
328	Hunt, P.	Stainer & Bell Ltd. (for USA – Galaxy Music Corp)
332	McAuley, J. P.	Mrs N. McAuley, C/o Curtis Brown (Aust) Pty Ltd, Sydney
335	Bayly, Albert F. Wren, Brian	Oxford University Press
336	Green, F. P.	Stainer & Bell Ltd (for Canada and USA – Hope Publishing Inc)
341	Dearmer, Percy	Oxford University Press (from the *English Hymnal*)
342	Green, F. P.	Stainer & Bell Ltd (for Canada and USA – Hope Publishing Inc)
343	Green, F. P.	Stainer & Bell Ltd (for Canada and USA – Hope Publishing Inc)
344	Arlott, John	
345	Briggs, G. W.	Oxford University Press
347	Fraser, Ian	Stainer & Bell Ltd (for USA – Galaxy Music Corp)
348	Kaan, F.	Stainer & Bell Ltd (for USA – Hope Publishing Inc.)
349	Hughes, Donald	Methodist Conference
350	Bayly, Albert, F.	Oxford University Press
351	Wren, Brian A.	Oxford University Press
353	Foley, Brian	Faber Music Ltd (from *New Catholic Hymnal*)
357	Head, Freda	
364	Wren, Brian A.	Oxford University Press
365	Bridge, Basil E.	
366	Thwaites, Honor Mary	
367	Bayly, Albert F.	Oxford University Press
368	Orchard, Stephen	
369	Martin, Hugh	Hymn Society of America
371	Tucker, F. Bland	The Church Pension Fund (from *The Hymnal 1940*)
372	Bayly, Albert F.	Oxford University Press
373	Green, F. P.	Stainer & Bell Ltd (for Canada and USA – Hope Publishing Inc)
377	Mowbray, David	Stainer & Bell Ltd (for USA – Galaxy Music Corp)

380	Nicholson, Norman	
384	Green, F. P.	Stainer & Bell Ltd (for Canada and USA – Hope Publishing Inc)
386	Littlewood, R. W.	Methodist Church Division of Education and Youth
387	Bayly, Albert, F.	Oxford University Press
388	Green, F. P.	Stainer & Bell Ltd (for Canada and USA – Hope Publishing Inc)
393	Cropper, M.	Mrs A Hopkinson
395	Green, F. P.	Stainer & Bell Ltd (for Canada and USA – Hope Publishing Inc)
396	Gaunt, H. C. A.	Oxford University Press
398	Head, Freda	
401	Caird, G. B.	
402	Kaan, F.	Stainer & Bell Ltd. An original version of Hymn No. 402 'For the healing of the nations' is printed in *Partners in Praise*, published jointly by Stainer & Bell and Chester House Publications (for USA – Hope Publishing Inc.)
403	Rees, Timothy	Community of the Ressurection
404	Green, F. P.	Stainer & Bell Ltd (for Canada and USA – Hope Publishing Inc)
406	Brooks, R. T.	© Agape, Carol Stream, IL 60188, USA
407	McAuley, J. P.	Mrs Norma McAuley, C/o Curtis Brown (Aust) Pty Ltd, Sydney
408	Prescod, P.	Caribbean Conference of Churches from *Sing A New Song No. 3* published by the Cedar Press
410	Scott, W.	World Student Christian Federation
411	Bayly, Albert F.	Oxford University Press
412	Kaan, F.	© 1967 B. Feldman & Co. Ltd (reproduced by permission of EMI Music Publishing Ltd)
413	Gaunt, Alan	John Paul, The Preacher's Press
414	Bayly, Albert F.	Oxford University Press
417	Hodges, H. A.	Mrs Vera Hodges
419	Hughes, Donald	Methodist Conference
420	Franzmann, M.	© 1969 Concordia Publishing House (from *Worship Supplement*)
424	Rees, Timothy	Community of the Resurrection
425	Bayly, Albert F.	Oxford University Press
426	Chesterton, G. K.	Oxford University Press
427	Hambly, C. G.	
428	Foley, Brian	Faber Music Ltd (from *New Catholic Hymnal*)
430	Green, F. P.	Stainer & Bell Ltd (for Canada and USA – Hope Publishing Inc)
447	Wren, Brian A.	Oxford University Press
450	White, Estelle	Mayhew-McCrimmon Ltd & Stainer & Bell Ltd (for USA – Galaxy Music Corp)
454	Green, F. P.	Stainer & Bell Ltd (for Canada and USA – Hope Publishing Inc)

455	Green, F. P.	Stainer & Bell Ltd (for Canada and USA – Hope Publishing Inc)
456	Briggs, G. W.	Oxford University Press
459	Johnson, R.	Oxford University Press
	Rimaud, D.	Secretariat des Editeurs de Fiches Musicales
	Wren, Brian A.	Oxford University Press
465	Burns, E. J.	
470	Gaunt, H. C. A.	Oxford University Press
471	Carter, Ruth	The Exors of Miss Ruth Carter
472	O'Driscoll, T. H.	
473	Piggott, W. C.	Oxford University Press
474	Reid, W. W.	Hymn Society of America
477	Caird, G. B.	
479	Idle, C.	Jubilate Hymns Ltd
482	Exors of G. C. Martin	
483	Brooks, R. T.	© 1954 Renewal 1982 by Agape, Carol Stream, IL 60188, USA
486	Hoare, Brian R.	
491	Routley, Erik	© 1974 by Agape, Carol Stream, IL 60188, USA. International Copyright secured
493	ICET Text	SPCK
498	Luff, Alan	Oxford University Press
500	Wren, Brian A.	Oxford University Press
503	Scholey, A.	Stainer & Bell Ltd (for USA – Galaxy Music Corp)
507	Dudley-Smith, Timothy	
508	Kaan, F.	Stainer & Bell Ltd (for USA – Hope Publishing Inc.)
511	Thwaites, Honor Mary	
518	Niles, D. T.	Christian Conference of Asia
532	Gaunt, Alan	John Paul, The Preacher's Press
539	Macnicol, N.	Trustees of the late Helen Margaret Macnicol
543	Pitt-Watson, Ian	
545	Luff, Alan	Stainer & Bell Ltd (for USA – Galaxy Music Corp)
548	Micklem, Caryl	
552	Struther, Jan	Oxford University Press (from *Enlarged Songs of Praise*)
556	Green, F. P.	Stainer & Bell Ltd (for Canada and USA – Hope Publishing Inc)
561	Micklem, Caryl	
565	Dearmer, Percy	Oxford University Press
570	Micklem, Caryl	
572	Newport, Doreen	Stainer & Bell Ltd (for USA – Galaxy Music Corp)
576	Green, F. P.	Stainer & Bell Ltd (for Canada and USA – Hope Publishing Inc)
581	Rees, Bryn	
582	Robinson, W.	
584	Jones, R. G.	
585	Green, F. P.	Stainer & Bell Ltd (for Canada and USA – Hope Publishing Inc)
586	Farrow, Derek R.	Methodist Conference
589	Dudley-Smith, Timothy	

590	Kaan, F.	Stainer & Bell Ltd (for USA – Hope Publishing Inc.)
594	Green, F. P.	Stainer & Bell Ltd (for Canada and USA – Hope Publishing Inc)
601	Thompson, Colin P.	
603	Tucker, F. Bland	The Church Pension Fund
604	Pilcher, Chas. Venn	F. E. Pilcher
605	Briggs, G. W.	Oxford University Press
607	Kaan, F.	Stainer & Bell Ltd (for USA – Hope Publishing Inc.)
610	Wren, Brian A.	Oxford University Press
617	Appleford, Patrick	Josef Weinberger Ltd
619	Kaan, F.	Stainer & Bell Ltd (for USA – Hope Publishing Inc.)
623	Icarus, Peter	Mayhew-McCrimmon Ltd
625	Exors of G. O. Gregory	
626	Dearmer, Percy	Oxford University Press (from *Enlarged Songs of Praise*)
627	Bridge, Basil E.	
628	Willson, M. F. C.	
633	Dearmer, Percy	Oxford University Press (from the *English Hymnal*)
634	Foley, Brian	Faber Music Ltd (from *New Catholic Hymnal*)
635	Farjeon, Eleanor	David Higham Associates Ltd
650	Micklem, Caryl	
651	Hughes, Donald	Methodist Conference
653	Green, F. P.	Stainer & Bell Ltd (for Canada and USA – Hope Publishing Inc)
654	Kaan, F.	Stainer & Bell Ltd (for USA – Hope Publishing Inc.)
657	Bayly, Albert F.	Oxford University Press
658	Farrow, Derek R.	Methodist Conference
661	Davies, R. E.	
675	Rees, Bryn	
686	Green, F. P.	Stainer & Bell Ltd (for Canada and USA – Hope Publishing Inc)
692	Penn, W. J.	E. J. Penn
699	Winslow, Jack	Mrs J. Tyrrell
700	Green, F. P.	Stainer & Bell Ltd (for Canada and USA – Hope Publishing Inc)
709	Dudley-Smith, Timothy	
712	Fosdick, H. E.	Mrs E. F. Downs
732	Dearmer, Percy	Oxford University Press (from the *English Hymnal*)
746	Carter, Sydney	Stainer & Bell Ltd (for USA – Galaxy Music Corp)
757	Quinn, J.	Geoffrey Chapman, a division of Cassells Ltd
758	Oxenham, John	Desmond Dunkerley
765	Jones, R. G.	
770	Seddon, J. E.	Jubilate Hymns Ltd
774	Sherlock, H.	
775	Luff, Alan	Oxford University Press

777	Head, Bessie P.	Africa Evangelical Fellowship
779	Turton, W. H.	Hymns Ancient & Modern
782	Banyard, Edmund	Stainer & Bell Ltd (for USA – Galaxy Music Corp)
787	Bayly, Albert F.	Oxford University Press
797	Bayly, Albert F.	Oxford University Press
804	Green, F. P.	Stainer & Bell Ltd (for Canada and USA – Hope Publishing Inc)
806	Green, F. P.	Stainer & Bell Ltd (for Canada and USA – Hope Publishing Inc)
824	Alternative Service Book 1980	Central Board of Finance of the Church of England
825	ICET	SPCK
826	ICET	SPCK
827	Luff, Alan	Oxford University Press
828	ICET	SPCK
831	ASB, 1980	Church of the Province of South Africa
832	Joint Liturgical Group	SPCK
833	ICET	SPCK
834–888	The Psalms	English Text: 1976, 1977 David L. Frost, John A. Emerton, Andrew A. Mackintosh Pointing: 1976, 1977 Wm Collins Sons & Co. Ltd

ADDRESSES

Cambridge University Press, The Edinburgh Building, Shaftesbury Road, Cambridge CB2 2RU.

Wm Collins Sons & Co. Ltd, 187 Piccadilly, London W1V 9DA.

J. Curwen & Sons, Ltd, Stockley Close, Stockley Road, West Drayton, Middlesex, UB7 9DE.

Hymns Ancient & Modern Ltd, St Mary's Works, St Mary's Plain, Norwich, Norfolk NR3 3BH.

Hymn Society of America, Texas Christian University, Fort Worth, Texas 76129 U.S.A.

Jubilate Hymns Ltd, 2 All Souls Place, London W1N 3DB.

Methodist Publishing House, Wellington Road, Wimbledon, London SW19 8EU.

Novello & Co. Ltd, Borough Green, Sevenoaks, Kent TN15 8DT.

Oxford University Press, Ely House, 37 Dover Street, London W1X 4AH.

Royal School of Church Music, Addington Palace, Croydon CR9 5AD.

Stainer & Bell Ltd, 82 High Road, London N2 9PW.

The United Reformed Church, 86 Tavistock Place, London WC1H 9RT.

Index of Biblical Texts

THIS index, while seeking to be exhaustive in the sense that no echo of scriptural words or themes has been omitted, normally contains only one reference to a phrase or theme in the Old Testament, one in the Gospels, or in the epistles. Thus an incident or parable is normally quoted from one Gospel only, as is a phrase found in more than one Psalm, etc.; but the use of biblical marginal references will enable parallel passages to be identified. (Gk) or (Heb.) implies that the hymnwriter is echoing the original language; (BCP) that he is echoing the Prayer Book version of the Psalms; (RV) the Revised Version of the Bible.

A fuller index, together with an index working from hymns to scriptures, is to be found in the separate *Subject, Textual and Lineal Index* to the hymn-book.

ch. v.	hymn	v.	ch. v.	hymn	v.	ch. v.	hymn	v.
GENESIS								
1	335		1 : 9–10	290	3		823	2
	384	1	14–19	353	3	23–4	417	1
1 : 1	21	1	16	334	2	24	430	4
	101	2	21	334	3	4 : 8	420	2
	152	1	25	778	2	5 : 22	678	2
	483	1	26	500	1	22, 24	392	7
	512	1	26–7	372	1		802	1
	582	1		581	1	24	381	5
	639	1		427	1, 5	6–8	430	2
	647	1		486	2	7–8	590	3
	654	2	26–8	420	1	8 : 22	66	2
	695	6	27–8	364	1		35	2
1–2	29	1	27, 31	338	6	9 : 13	685	3
	268	1	31	330		13–16	11	3
	290	1		334	3	10 : 10	108	2
1–3	23	1		363		11 : 1–7	430	2
1–4	641	1		484	3	11 : 4	419	2
1–8	419	1	2 : 7	280			412	4
1–27	396	1		294	4	12 : 1–4	447	1
2	29	3		308	1	3	237	5
	303	1		324	1	15 : 1	84	3
	324	1		58	3		452	1, 5
2–3	379	3	8	741	4		661	1
2–4	285	1	17	558	3		720	4
	327	2	21–4	364	1	16 : 13	632	3
3	29	1	23	101	4	17 : 2	442	5
	79	2	24	374	3	17	693	5
	627	1	3	427		18 : 25	390	2
3–4	290	3		430	1		454	2
5	635	1	3 : 6	420	1	27	49	3
6	79	2	8	420	1		551	1
6–8	290	3	15	264	3		729	3

Liturgical Index

9 before Christmas THE CREATION
7, 21, 24, 26, 28, 49, 54, 60, 61, 260, 276, 329, 330, 333, 334, 335, 338, 339, 340, 353, 503, 572, 635, 641.

8 before Christmas THE FALL
2, 24, 46, 185, 231, 239, 245, 399, 405, 409, 412, 418, 419, 420, 427, 429, 430, 458, 519, 533, 550, 742.

7 before Christmas THE ELECTION OF GOD'S PEOPLE: ABRAHAM
378, 435, 442, 452, 453, 447, 517, 567, 675, 693, 695.
cf. also 19th Sunday after Pentecost.

6 before Christmas THE PROMISE OF REDEMPTION: MOSES
26, 27, 62, 433, 436, 437, 441, 447, 450, 511, 566, 574, 616, 620, 730, 745, 780, 813, 822.

5 before Christmas THE REMNANT OF ISRAEL
53, 68, 73, 227, 358, 429, 441, 454, 511, 540, 549, 571, 656, 673, 677, 715, 721, 784.

Advent 1: 4 before Christmas THE ADVENT HOPE
57, 81, 85, 88, 147, 168, 207, 236, 237, 240, 241, 242, 243, 244, 245, 246, 247, 248, 249, 400, 415, 425, 449, 491, 600, 719, 769, 783.

Advent 2: 3 before Christmas THE WORD OF GOD IN THE OLD TESTAMENT
2, 23, 64, 75, 82, 239, 245, 252, 315, 317, 468, 469, 472, 476, 478, 479, 480, 483, 489, 630.

Advent 3: 2 before Christmas THE FORERUNNER
50, 84, 241, 243, 264, 315, 449, 455, 456, 492, 553, 613.

Advent 4: 1 before Christmas THE ANNUNCIATION
77, 79, 83, 85, 86, 87, 88, 89, 108, 240, 512, 724, 815.

Christmas Eve THE BIRTH OF CHRIST
79, 91, 92, 93, 95, 98, 99, 102, 108, 111, 112, 113, 115, 116, 117, 120.

Christmas Day
89, 90, 94, 95, 96, 97, 99, 101, 103, 104, 105, 106, 109, 110, 114, 117, 118, 124, 127, 512, 666.

1 after Christmas THE WISE MEN
77, 100, 107, 119, 121, 122, 123, 125, 128, 237, 456, 461, 464, 505.

2 after Christmas (1) THE PRESENTATION IN THE TEMPLE
80, 92, 99, 124, 126, 446, 527, 529, 532, 732, 738,
(2) THE VISIT TO JERUSALEM
1, 127, 143, 146, 152, 282, 371, 382, 446, 522, 552.

Epiphany
89, 121, 122, 123, 125, 464, 505.

1 after Epiphany THE BAPTISM OF CHRIST
80, 125, 129, 132, 203, 215, 229, 264, 303, 313, 437, 470, 758, 788.

2 after Epiphany THE FIRST DISCIPLES
68, 139, 141, 153, 211, 522, 523, 535, 539, 542, 549, 671, 673, 704, 705, 745, 748.

3 after Epiphany (1) THE WEDDING AT CANA
7, 148, 273, 455, 458, 596.
(2) THE NEW TEMPLE
63, 267, 448, 485, 494, 531, 549, 653, 656, 658, 724, 808, 817.

4 after Epiphany
33, 45, 46, 48, 429.
(1) THE FRIEND OF SINNERS
136, 146, 149, 217, 235, 526, 528, 546, 614, 713.
(2) LIFE FOR THE WORLD
226, 219, 230, 261, 290, 390, 559, 725, 729.

5 after Epiphany
cf. 23rd Sunday after Pentecost.

6 after Epiphany
cf. 22nd Sunday after Pentecost.

9 before Easter CHRIST THE TEACHER (Education Sunday)
12, 16, 23, 32, 39, 76, 133, 136, 137, 139, 140, 211, 232, 234, 313, 377, 466, 475, 482, 539, 634, 674, 679, 699, 709, 710, 724, 734, 737, 765, 768, 771.

8 before Easter CHRIST THE HEALER
29, 80, 140, 142, 148, 150, 151, 152, 263, 389, 390, 391, 392, 393, 395, 396, 397, 398, 415, 511, 528, 766.

Easter 1 (1) THE UPPER ROOM APPEARANCES
188, 194, 196, 198, 199, 200, 205, 208, 256, 530, 575, 577, 578, 601, 606, 669.

      (2) THE BREAD OF LIFE
137, 213, 258, 349, 359, 467, 599, 603, 611, 614, 616, 620, 697, 730.

Easter 2 (1) THE EMMAUS ROAD
52, 199, 224, 465, 542, 577, 578, 597, 605, 610, 621, 645, 692, 755.

      (2) THE GOOD SHEPHERD
43, 69, 70, 218, 230, 238, 263, 490, 535, 549, 645, 678, 750, 772, 821.

Easter 3 (1) THE LAKESIDE
192, 208, 213, 214, 315, 467, 530.

      (2) THE RESURRECTION AND THE LIFE
198, 202, 204, 467, 627, 673, 751, 764, 820.

Easter 4 (1) THE CHARGE TO PETER
80, 209, 223, 257, 499, 521, 553, 560, 612, 653, 704, 713, 755, 767, 772.

      (2) THE WAY, THE TRUTH AND THE LIFE
11, 198, 229, 234, 250, 254, 387, 419, 557, 717, 734.

Easter 5 GOING TO THE FATHER
9, 196, 217, 219, 220, 221, 222, 225, 233, 255, 262, 268, 279, 300, 401, 433, 463, 546, 551, 557, 558, 593, 731, 751, 763, 813.

Ascension Day THE ASCENSION OF CHRIST
197, 206, 210, 516
cf. also 6th Sunday after Easter.

Easter 6
189, 197, 201, 206, 210, 222, 243, 252, 255, 256, 260, 271, 502, 508, 592, 616, 736, 810, 811, 823.

Pentecost (Whitsunday) THE GIFT OF THE SPIRIT
280, 281, 282, 283, 284, 288, 296, 297, 298, 302, 305, 306, 307, 311, 312, 314, 323, 324, 327, 469, 602.

Pentecost 1 (Trinity)
4–8, 29.

      (1) THE RICHES OF GOD
71, 72, 266, 285, 300, 308, 331, 336, 443, 445, 504, 513, 519, 762, 791.

      (2) THE CHURCH'S MESSAGE
219, 322, 323, 324, 695, 761, 766, 770.

Liturgical Index of Psalms

Day	Morning	Evening
9 before Christmas	824 & 870 A & C	834 & 884
8 before Christmas	881	862 or 883A
7 before Christmas	865	834
6 before Christmas	858	871
5 before Christmas	831, 859A, 839A	859B, 860
Advent 1	867	864
Advent 2	840B	876A
Advent 3	853, 879	825
Advent 4	874, 836	826
Christmas Eve	827, 861	(Midnight) 840
Christmas Day	842, 840	839B & C, 867
1 after Christmas	827, 857	827, 855, 874
2 after Christmas	828, 865	828, 844
Epiphany	857	836, 866
1 after Epiphany	851	849 A & B
2 after Epiphany	844, 868	884
3 after Epiphany	831, 860	872A
4 after Epiphany	875	848A
5 after Epiphany	866, 874	870A & C or 874
6 after Epiphany	868	879, 873
9 before Easter	869 or 844	847B, 840
8 before Easter	886, 869	883
7 before Easter	850	873
Ash Wednesday	852	863A, 881
Lent 1	852, 876A	845 & 876B
Lent 2	839A	863
Lent 3	876C	853, 863B
Lent 4	847	839B
Lent 5	829, 841A, 881	829, 841B, 877
Palm Sunday	831, 843, 841A	856, 857
Maundy Thursday	874	
Good Friday	829, 841B	829, 848, 849A & B
Easter Day	830, 875	830, 883A
Easter 1	884A	847A, 888
Easter 2	873	842
Easter 3	838	867
Easter 4	844	858
Easter 5	854 & 860	853 & 837
Ascension Day	831 & 836	843 & 831
Easter 6	888 & 843	864 & 851
(Sunday after Ascension)		
Pentecost (Whitsunday)	878	870B & C
Trinity (Pentecost 1)	833 & 864	855
Pentecost 2	865	882
Pentecost 3	860	839B & 888
Pentecost 4	853	837 & 855

Pentecost 5	840	876B
Pentecost 6	848A & 845	844
Pentecost 7	876A	869
Pentecost 8	844A	887
Pentecost 9	839A	837
Pentecost 10	840B	835 & 863
Pentecost 11	877 & 884B	848A
Pentecost 12	866	846
Pentecost 13	829 & 859A	849 & 883
Pentecost 14	847A	847B
Pentecost 15	880	850
Pentecost 16	851 & 872A	873
Pentecost 17	842	844
Pentecost 18	884B	863B & 875
Pentecost 19	883A	854A & 869
Pentecost 20	832 & 878	837 & 885
Pentecost 21	877	855
Pentecost 22	849	839A
Pentecost 23	872	842

SPECIAL DAYS

Watchnight	829, 863
Aldersgate Sunday	881
Education Sunday	844
All Saints Day	868 & 884B
Remembrance Sunday	850
Christian Citizenship Sunday	826, 855, 857, 868, 878
Overseas Missions	827, 828, 850, 851, 855, 866, 868
Harvest Thanksgiving	824, 854, 855, 870
Church Anniversary	860, 878
Mothering Sunday	826, 860, 878
Marriage	855, 877, 880
Funeral	842, 844, 849A, 869, 877, 883A

Index of Chants

Where a chant has been transposed, the original key is shown in brackets.
† Denotes where a chant has been altered by the Editors
S Single
D Double

Metrical Index of Tunes

Alphabetical Index of Tunes

Index of Composers, Arrangers, and Sources of Tunes

* indicates arranged, edited or collected
† indicates descant or antiphon
? indicates some doubt about the source

AINGER, Geoffrey (1925–) 95
Airs sur les hymnes sacrez (Paris 1623) 205
Akeroyd, S. in the *Divine Companion* (1701) 706(i)
Albert, H. (1604–51) 762
Alden, J. H. (1900–76) 676(i)
Allen, Hugh P. (1869–1946) 483(i)
Allgemeines Choralbuch (Leipzig 1819) 210 (see Schicht, J. G.)
Alpha and Omega (1680) Neander 813*
Alte Choral-Melodien (1832) 248, 474
American folk hymns 181, 215, 265(ii), 269(i), 517(i), 621(i)
American Musical Miscellany (1798) 681(i)
Amps, William (1824–1910) 156, 449(i)
Andachts Zymbeln (Freiburg 1655) 626
Anderson, James Smith (1853–1945) 539(i)
Anonymous 226, 256, 270, 295, 506, 534, 738(i), 750(i)
Antes, John (1740–1811) 27(i), 359, 508(i)
Appleford, Patrick (1925–) 617
Armes, P. (1836–1908) 239(i), 338(ii), 553
Arnold, S. (1740–1802) 540
Arnold, William (1768–1832) 55(i), 438, 710(ii)
Atkinson, Frederic Cook (1841–96) 778
Attwood, Thomas (1765–1838) 285
Austin, D. 671

BACH, J. C. (1642–1703) 149(ii)
Bach, J. S. (1685–1750) 21*, 49*, 100*, 164*, 174(i), 176*, 206*, 249*, 259*, 352?, 456, 479*, 480*, 547, 614*, 620*, 626*, 647*, 680?, 727*, 734, 762*
Baker, F. G. (1840–1919) 334(ii)
Baker, H. (1835–1910) 772(i)
Barnard, John (1948–) 238*
Barnby, J. (1838–96) 275(ii), 276(i), 370, 735(i)
Barnes, Gerald L. (1935–) 139
Barthelemon, Francois H. (1741–1808) 632

Bartlett, Lawrence (1933–) 277(ii), 508(ii)
Basque carol melody 45(ii), 87
Bate, H. A. (1899–) 650, 733
Battishill, Jonathan (1738–1801) 766
Baughen, Michael A. (1930–) 770
BBC Hymnbook, The (1951) 633, 654
Beaumont, Geoffrey (1903–70) 566(iii)
Beer, Alfred (1874–1963) 684(ii)
Bishop, Graham (1953–) 782
Bishop, J. (1665–1737) 175, 299
Blackwell, T. Kenneth (1915–) 229
Blake, Leonard (1907–) 13(i)†, 20†, 119*†, 103, 763(ii)
Bliss, Philipp (1838–76) 228
Blockley, John (1801–82) 674(ii)
Bohemian, Brethren, *Kirchengeseng* (Berlin 1566) 511, 550
Bonner, Carey (1859–1938) 565*
Bortnianski, Dmitri Stepanovich (1752–1825) 286
Bost, A. (1790–1874) 517(ii)
Bouquet (1825), Campbell, T. 216(i)*
Bower, J. Dykes (1905–81) 276(ii), 305, 311(ii), 392, 551
Boyce, William (1710–79) 385(ii), 655(i)
Boyd, H., *Psalm and Hymn Tunes* (1793) 26, 710(i), 807
Bradshaw, Richard 138*
Bridge, John Frederick (1844–1924) 123(i), 286 (on 286 see Bortnianski, D. S.)
Brierley, Michael (1932–) 74(ii)
Broadwood, Lucy (1858–1929) 161*, 328(ii)*, 344*
Brockless, G. F. (1887–1957) 131(i)
Brown, A. H. (1830–1926) 464, 692(i), 697(ii)
Buck, Percy C. (1871–1947) 17(i), 179, 211
Burgoyne's Collection (1827) 468
Burleigh, Harry T. (1866–1949) 758(i)*

CALKIN, J. B. (1827–1905) 143, 557(i), 790
Cambridge Hymnal, The (1967) Poston 93*
Campbell, T. (1825) 216(i)

Index of Authors,
Translators and Sources

⊘ The authorship of these hymns is in dispute. They may be the work of John Wesley. The discussion regarding the authorship of the Wesley corpus is continuing and the present index should not be taken as a final word on the issue.

Index of First Lines